W9-BEQ-933

Also by Mark Bowden
Doctor Dealer

BRINGING THE HEAT

BRINGING THE HEAT

by

Mark Bowden

Alfred A. Knopf   New York   1994

THIS IS A BORZOI BOOK
PUBLISHED BY ALFRED A. KNOPF, INC.

Copyright © 1994 by Mark Bowden

All rights reserved under International and Pan-American Copyright
Conventions. Published in the United States by Alfred A. Knopf, Inc., New
York, and simultaneously in Canada by Random House of Canada Limited,
Toronto. Distributed by Random House, Inc., New York.

Library of Congress Cataloging-in-Publication Data
Bowden, Mark.
Bringing the heat / by Mark Bowden.—1st ed.
p.   cm.
ISBN 0-679-42841-0
1. Philadelphia Eagles (Football team).   I. Title.
GV956.P44B69   1994
796.332'64'0974811—dc20   94-7218
CIP

Manufactured in the United States of America
First Edition

For Gail

Contents

BRINGING THE HEAT

1

JEROME

A colossus, Jerome Brown strides the sun-soaked playing fields
of his youth beset by children.

Dozens of children, all ages, sizes, and colors, the bigger
and bolder ones shouldering in close, clutching, hollering "Me, J'rome!
Me, J'rome!" while the smaller and more timid hop at the fringes,
waving, begging.

"Please, J'rome. Me! Me!"

"Sit Down!" bellows the beleaguered big man.

He is weary, but patient. He knows exactly where these kids are
coming from. The millionaire star defensive lineman of the Philadelphia Eagles knows all about the *Gimme! Gimme!* instinct. He and the rest
of his teammates are enthusiastic adherents to the MEAT (Maximize
Earnings at All Times) principle. Asked what it meant to him the first
year he was elected to the NFL's Pro Bowl, the year he was first
acknowledged by his peers to be the very best at what he does, Jerome
didn't go all mushy. He rolled his eyes, flashed his trademark shit-
eating grin, and sang out, "Mo' money! Mo' money! Mo' money!"

Jerome is big and black and wide as an old cast-iron stove, only
instead of heat he gives off noise. "Even as a little boy, we always heard
him comin' before we seen him," says his father, Willie, a big, wide
man, though not as formidable as his son. Everything about Jerome
is wide. His head widens from the temples to the place where his neck
joins his shoulders. Inside this frame his deep-set brown eyes are set
wide over a broad, flat nose and even wider mouth, thick lips closing
over big white teeth, perfectly straight, even, amazing teeth, teeth that
jump out of that broad dark face like one of those blazing electric
marquees that line the Strip in Vegas. Wide chin, wide neck, wide
shoulders, wide chest, wide belly, wide butt, wide thighs, wide calves,
wide ankles—why, even Jerome's posture is wide; he stands with his
feet set on a line with the far reach of his shoulders to provide secure

undergirding for the bulwark above. You would expect someone so large to move slowly, but not Jerome. He's always bouncing on that wide-open stance, always on the move or ready to move, like a motor with its idle set too fast. Jerome is hardwired for fun and action, and there isn't a calculating neuron in his brain.

"I mean it!" he warns the children.

He's here in his hometown of sleepy Brooksville, Florida, to host the First Annual Jerome Brown Football Camp—you know, trying to *give something back.* It ain't easy. Jerome has had the idea now for several years. His teammates Keith Byars and Byron Evans do it, hold a weekend football clinic for kids from their hometowns. But he'd put it off. The details of staging Camp Jerome were daunting—reserving the field, advertising, coordinating the date with all his teammates' schedules—who has time for that shit?

"Pay attention!" he pleads.

To no avail. Cradled in Brown's massive arms are T-shirts, Eagles pins and pens, color team portraits, travel bags, all manner of goodies, icing on the cake for these kids after a morning of autographs and football drills led by real NFL football players—Jerome, Reggie White, Randall Cunningham, Seth Joyner, Wes Hopkins, Clyde Simmons, Andre Waters, Ron Heller, and others. But instead of setting up some kind of system for handing these things out, Jerome just scoops up armfuls and wades in, provoking this kiddie riot. It's like trying to line up a swarm of bees single file with a bucket of honey under one arm.

But hey, planning ahead has never been Jerome's way. Thinking things through, organizing, taking things one step at a time, heeding caution, slowing down for yellow lights—none of this is Jerome's way. Jerome's way is to feel the itch of impulse and *act,* throttle wide, cylinders afire, wind in his hair. Speed and daring are Jerome's friends. And don't knock it. Jerome's way, after all, has served him astonishingly well. Just a decade back Jerome was one of these shirtless, backcountry Florida homeboys, dusty and scraped from playing ball on these very fields. Now his barrel-ass methods have sped him to the dizzying pinnacle of American pro sports, made him a millionaire at age twenty-seven, awarded him with fame, his pick of beautiful women, the admiration of family, friends, and football fans everywhere—given him so much, in fact, that every once in a while it all becomes a strain.

Of course, off the football field, Jerome's way sometimes makes for trouble.

In just six weeks, it will make big, bad, lovable Jerome dead.

But there is no shadow on this day in early May, the day Jerome *gives something back.* It hadn't been as hard to arrange as he had feared. A couple of days before this weekend event, Jerome had roared his big black motorcycle up to his buddy Tim Jinkens's bar, the Red Mule, and sauntered into the cool with an empty yellow legal pad and a pen.

"Okay, Tim. What do we do?"

From behind the bar, his chubby old friend was brought up short. "Tell me it isn't true, G."

"What?"

"You haven't done anything yet?"

"There's time!" Jerome complained. "You're gonna help me, right, Tim?" with the big, soulful grin.

"Jerome! This all should have been done two months ago!"

"Mr. Worrywart," sneered the football star.

Of course, Tim knew what this meant. It meant he and his mother and brother, Jerome's support team, were going to be working their asses off day and night to make sure that this idea of Jerome's got off the ground. Jerome would get all the credit, of course. But that was okay. Tim understood. How was a big star like Jerome supposed to know how to get kid-sized T-shirts printed up? How to set up a Coke-and-hot-dog stand to serve a crowd like that? And how was Jerome going to keep that many kids moving through a long morning of activity without its degenerating into chaos?

Tim and his mom sort of adopted Jerome way back, when Tim coached him on the junior-high football team, and they're used to their big friend dropping by with tall orders on short notice. They moan, but they love being included. They love Jerome's unswerving loyalty and affection. Jerome calls Mrs. Jinkens his "white mom" and delights in making a big fuss over her when he runs into her in public places, a black giant embracing this slight Irish woman, sweeping her up off her feet, and planting a big kiss on her cheek, greeting her with "Hi, Mom!" loud enough to turn every head—this still being a community where white moms with black sons raise an eyebrow or two.

The support team had done the best job it could with the limited time remaining—four hundred T-shirts, hot dogs, buns, condiments, Cokes, applications, tickets, advertising. On Friday night, as hundreds queued up outside the Hernando High School gym for the weekend's kickoff event, a celebrity basketball game between the Eagles and the Tampa Bay Buccaneers, Tim had no tickets to sell. He called around and found out that the tickets were in the backseat of Jerome's Bronco, which was parked back at Jerome's house, and, of course, nobody was quite sure where the big guy was. So Tim drove over, found the tickets, and got back in time to avoid unpleasantness.

But things like this are just part of Jerome's charm, evident again in the slapdash course of this whole rowdy day.

"Y'all gonna make me pass out right here!" Jerome pleads as the children press closer.

The mob giggles. The giant isn't feared at home. Everybody down here knows Jerome. He's the most famous kid Brooksville ever produced, and he hasn't changed a bit—white Nike cap worn backward, baggy denim shorts hanging to his dusty knees, oversized ankle-high leather sports shoes worn sockless and untied. Money and fame may have overtaken Jerome Brown, but age hasn't put a dent in him. Down here they used to call him Freight Train for his heroic collisions with fences while playing outfield for the Hernando High state baseball champs, or maybe it was for the way he used to scatter the ordinary schoolboy opponents trotted out during football season to try to block him—nobody remembers which. They would all remember how they had never seen anyone so big, so fast, so strong, whose personality was as outsized as his accomplishments. "We'd just give him the ball sometimes and watch him drag three or four kids over the goal line," says Tim. "In one baseball season, he stole twenty-four bases in ten games. Whatever he did, there was just no stopping him." And for Jerome nothing's changed! Ol' Freight Train just keeps barreling down the rails, his life tracing a path that keeps pushing on and on, farther and farther, faster and faster. He has yet to hit a wall he can't move. Today he's even bigger, quicker, and stronger; hundreds of hometown fans have become millions; the cheers from the high-school grandstands have become the blood roar of tens of thousands, a stage more magically grand than Jerome or his family (lots of family) or friends (lots of friends) could have ever imagined.

But Jerome is still just Jerome. Why change? Just like back in high school, he's still breaking the rules, staying out late, skipping class, juggling girlfriends, drinking too much, driving too fast in any of his six (that's right, *six!*) custom sports cars and souped-up cycles, blasting his music through the center of town, playing poker for stakes higher than any annual wage ever brought home by his truck-driving daddy, vanishing off into the thick Florida veld to loosen up his collection of high-powered automatic weapons, and partying, partying, partying, rolling in snatch. Just watch Jerome for three days on his home turf and you come away wanting to eat hearty, swagger, laugh, boast, stay up late, talk a mile a minute, banish petty worry, and squeeze every sweet moment of life dry. To be Jerome is to practice the art of always making a joyful noise.

"Y'all ain't lis'nin'!"

But now Jerome is beat. "I quit," he whines at a cameraman, here at Jerome's invitation to tape the event so the fans back in Philly can see JB *give something back.* "I don't want to see another kid! I am tee-totally tired."

Hell, he's got all his teammates in town for this. All he wants, all Jerome ever really wants, is to get down to some serious partying, get back to Home Jerome for some backyard barbecue, cold beer, and cards on the shaded deck out by the pool, a chance to show off his race cars and his new sleek fiancée, a fashion model from Miami. His friends have already started back to the house. Out on the high-school playing field you can see Jerome's motor smoking as he tries to finish things up with these kids. They all think his exasperation is an act, but it's not. Jerome has had about enough of this Role Model shit for one day.

"That's it! I quit! Y'all gwan home!"

And, abruptly, he hurls fistfuls of the goodies up in the air, divests himself in one grand gesture, and as the little mob falls on it, Jerome struts off with relief, moving fast. *Let them fight it out* . . . the time-tested Jerome method proved once again. And not a minute too soon. Because back at the house, just a few miles away, things are growing edgy.

OUT ON THE SCREENED-IN PATIO, muscular giants in colorful, state-of-the-art sports gear are draped all over the deck, wisely forsaking the patio furniture, which looks Lilliputian in this crowd. Home Jerome is a suburban rancher ballooned out about four times normal size, finished off with white stucco and painted with purple trim. It sits about two miles north of Brooksville's city limits on a sullen, green ten-acre patch cut out of flat, fly-infested Florida fruit groves—a certified DHM (Dream Home for Mom), the mandatory first major project for every homeboy who gets the million-dollar payday in the big city.

Camp Jerome is really a reunion. The Eagles' '91 season ended badly back in December, short of the postseason play-offs for the first time in four seasons, and most of these teammates haven't seen one another since. That's the way it goes. From July through December they are together night and day, then for six months they go home to heal, step out of the spotlight, and work at being real men in a real world: husbands, fathers, sons, lovers; men with family and friends, with responsibilities, with a future beyond next weekend—what a pain! Gatherings like this one are a welcome respite. Jerome is picking up his teammates' airfare and hotel bills, but most of them would have paid to come.

Once the team is together again, however, it doesn't take long for the old tensions and rivalries to surface. When Jerome is around, these things tend not to get out of hand, mostly because when Jerome is around it's tough paying attention to anyone other than Jerome. But today Big G—as in a raucous "*Gee*-rome"—is delayed, and the usual teasing banter has turned a touch raw. Predictably, it's that Seth Joyner picking on Randall Cunningham again. The team's fierce linebacker can't stand the star quarterback, a fact he's been taking fewer and fewer pains to hide in recent years. And Randall (or "Ran-*doll*" to the less enthralled) has given Seth an opening.

He's done something new with his hair.

"Check out the *weave!*" shouts Seth. Randall is standing just inside the patio door, his rented white monster Mercedes coupe glistening out on the lawn like a sun chariot. He is tall and unusually lean for a football player, especially coming off surgery and months of rehab after blowing out his left knee. He cuts an elegant figure, but his face is rugged; he has uneven skin and a vicious scar on his nose, which earned him the college nickname "Hook," high forehead, blank liquid-brown eyes, moustache, and an underbite that juts his wide, flat lower lip into a natural pout. His hair is shaped in the stovepipe coiffure de rigueur this spring for fashionable young African-American men, the back and sides cropped skull close but with the pillbox top jutting up a good three inches and leveled off clean enough on top to shoot pool. Of Ran-*doll,* who counts "dressing up" among his favorite off-field activities, one expects nothing less. But arching from the dimple at the base of Randall's skull, sprouting from the bump of his first cervical vertebra, the inimitable Scrambling One has this . . . this . . . *tail!* He's let a few strands of hair grow out about four inches, and he's had the spindly thatch twisted into a tight braid that extends the length of a crooked index finger from the back of his long, graceful neck. The tiny braid is fed through nuggets of gold to make this unbearably cute toy ponytail! This is just too, too precious for stone-faced Seth, who has been eyeing the thing all day with disbelief, waiting for a chance to pounce. He begins by clowning, miming wonder, shaking his head. This starts his teammates giggling, but Cunningham, the orphan prince, ever cool and aloof, tunes out the ridicule. He's used to it.

You have to understand. We're diving into the green dragony depths of envy, rivalry, and grudge that lurk beneath the surface of a pro football team.

There's a history here that goes back years.

The way Seth has it figured, he and the Eagles' superb defense have been carrying Ran-*doll*'s skinny, sweet ass now for about four seasons, and whenever they're on the verge of getting somewhere, like at the end of the '90 season when they faced the Redskins in the NFC

Wild Card game, their franchise quarterback folds up like one of those life-sized cardboard stand-ups in front of candy racks back in Philly that offer the new chocolate-covered, caramel-and-peanut-*scrambled* Randall Bar.

But it goes deeper. Randall is odd. There's something about the guy, something so pliant, so sensitive, so . . . *artistic* that somehow he seems not even to belong on a football field. This is the kind of kid usually weeded out in the Pop Warner League (*No offense, ma'am, but are you sure your boy here is cut out to play football? Gits a mite rough out there*). And yet here he is, the highest-paid player on the team and one of the most acclaimed in the league, which, frankly, irks the hell out of many of his teammates.

And Randall doesn't help himself either. He walks around the locker room and practice sessions sometimes for weeks at a time like a man in a fog, saying bizarre things to the press, doodling and day-dreaming his way through coaching sessions, then trying to finesse things on the field come Sunday.

"Being confused has a lot to do with my personality," he says, and if you don't believe him, just listen to what pops out of his mouth over the course of a football season. Randall's soft voice emerges from the labyrinth of his psyche in constant lamentation; he's never happy with himself, he trusts no one, and in the wide silence between Randall and the rest of the world he hears voices: "There's an evil spirit and a good spirit; I lean toward the good spirit all the time, because that's where my heart is, and I know I can be tricked." Just having a wiftbrain like this calling signals for the offense troubles Seth, who is as spiritual as a hand grenade. Seth is a player who has built a terrific career without overwhelming athletic talent, who makes up for what he lacks in finesse with dogged preparation and an on-field intensity that bor-ders on sociopathic. But every time he and his brothers on defense have stomped some opposing offense flat, he has to stand on the sidelines, helmet in hand, and turn the game (*his game!*) over to this fruitcake—who's making triple most of their salaries.

So when Randall does something like show up an hour late for Camp Jerome, which he did earlier this day, and all the kids and parents are asking "Where's Randall Cunningham? How come Randall isn't here? When's Randall going to be here?" it's like poking Seth with a cattle prod.

"What do you expect from him?" Seth growls. "It's just like him to be late. He's such an asshole. He's more interested in being a TV star than a football player."

The crowd, startled by the raw hostility, slowly backs off.

Face it, Randall's the man they most want to see. From a safe distance, one of the fathers asks a newshound, here to record the sweet chaos of Camp Jerome, "Who's that?" pointing across at Seth, who in no time has a corner of the playing field all to himself, better to accommodate the glowing green penumbra of his intensity.

"That's Seth."

"Seth Joyner?"

"Yep."

"Didn't he go to the Pro Bowl this year?"

"Yep."

"No wonder. Is he always like that?"

But even envy and a certain disdain for Ran-*doll*'s fey manner aren't enough to fully account for the depth of animosity toward him on this team. Seth and the others would tolerate anything in Randall if his gifts delivered victory. But they haven't, at least not consistently, and not in the big games. Cunningham is the cynic's quintessential big-money sports star: he has made enough brilliant plays and spectacular scrambles to star in NFL highlights reels forever, and his stats are otherworldly, but in seven seasons he hasn't gotten the Eagles even close to the Super Bowl. This small fact doesn't seem to bother Randall. Pick up, for instance, the *Sports Illustrated* "Weapon of the Nineties" issue with Ran-*doll*'s picture on the cover showboating like the little statue on top of the Heisman Trophy, or read him in another issue calmly classifying himself with the singular superstars of modern sport, calling himself the Michael Jordan of the NFL, the kind of player who can completely, *single-handedly* take charge of a game. And this isn't just some starstruck sportswriter bullshit; this is the stuff in quotes! Randall would later claim he was misquoted, but to some of his team-mates, the quote rings true. After playing with him for years, they believe this is how Ran-*doll* really sees himself! It seems to them that Ran-*doll* fancies himself in the pantheon of black American stardom, the standard-bearers of trend, the black stars of sport and screen, modern media idols; we're talking nothing less than Black Pop Royalty here: that's right, his Airness, Prince, Charles Barkley, Michael Jackson, Whitney Houston, Oprah, and Eddie and Spike and Ice-T and Denzel and Hammer and, the impresario of it all,

✳✳✳✳:::::::::::::!!!ARSENIO!!!:::::::::::::✳✳✳✳

If you're Seth, every time you see Ran-*doll* across the couch on a TV talk show or see him on the front of a supermarket tabloid lounging at some exotic beach resort, rubbing sunscreen on Whitney Houston's back, or read about him hanging out with his good friend, that fairy-chimp-loving-white-skin-worshiping weirdo Michael Jackson, or catch him strutting out on his weekly in-season TV show wearing one of his ridiculous, self-designed outfits with striped pants and gold buttons and *silver fucking epaulets* (in honor of the brave men and women of Desert Storm) . . .

it makes you want to . . .

want to . . .

—well, we're off here into the red zone of Seth Joyner's rage.

So, yes, Seth has this thing about Ran-*doll*, and the little gold-studded toy tail is just the latest . . . well, twist. And once Seth gets the ball rolling, and Jerome is nowhere in sight, the lampoon escalates.

Jumping up in front of the quarterback, Seth begins whirling in circles, whipping his long thickly muscled arms in sweeping chops, pretending he's a character in a martial arts movie, gleefully manufacturing sound effects. "Whack! Thwack! An' when you spin around"—he's laughing so hard now he can barely get this out—"takin' people out with yo' little *weave!*"

Reggie White and Andre Waters and Keith Jackson and Wes Hopkins and Mike Pitts and the rest of them can't help but laugh along—Seth is really throwing himself into it. Randall grins sheepishly, clearly pained. He comes all the way down here, just to be nice, just to show he really is one of the guys, and what's he get?

"Whack! *Hieeeeee-yah!*"

The men are doubled over now, choking with laughter. Randall begins to protest, quietly. "That's enough."

Which is, of course, the worst thing he could do. Especially because there's this writer here, this rumpled white guy with Amazon tree frog eyes, with the ever-present tape recorder and notebook, taking it all in—every word!—just dying to clue the world to his humiliation.

Who needs this? Seth, this joyless grind, this ever-sour, self-appointed team scold, is goosing royalty, right here *in front of the fucking tree frog*—and the rest of his teammates are yuk-yukking.

"You guys are mean," Cunningham protests.

But he is saved.

Just as the moment threatens to turn ugly, in bursts JB, who bangs open the screen door and hulks theatrically across the patio, swinging his black leather briefcase (in which he typically carries his wallet, electronic games, football cards, candy, and so on).

But Jerome stops short.

Who is *that* he spies sitting quietly in the corner?

"It's you," he shouts, dropping the briefcase, arms akimbo, wheeling at the wide-eyed frog.

All eyes turn from Randall and Seth to this new confrontation.

"At my house! On my turf!"

The frog stands. He's been expecting this.

"Mama! Daddy!" Jerome shouts. "Come out here. This is the one. This is the one I've been telling you about. The one puttin' all those things in the newspaper about me! Now I've got you on my own turf."

Devastating pause. Wicked grin. *"Daddy, get my dog! Where's my dog!"*

WHEN THEY TALK ABOUT Jerome's *intangibles*—and there's going to be a lot of talk about them in the coming months—this is what they mean. Just like that, the ragging of Ran-*doll* is forgotten, and the party rolls. Jerome doesn't even know he's done it. It's just Jerome being Jerome. The soul of the group has the keenest eye for a common enemy, and there's nothing like confronting the Beast Without (and a reporter clearly qualifies) to close ranks. This is what Jerome is all about. He's Team, body and soul, from the solid-gold screaming-Eagle necklace he wears to the green color of his beloved Corvette. His teammates have all sorts of ways of taking their images, their careers, themselves, too seriously, but Jerome is there to remind them that they are all just young men getting paid extraordinarily well to play a boy's game. In their twenties, they have, with their heroic size and talent, taken life by storm. They own huge bank accounts and boast fawning admirers, thrilled families, and eager females. They have performed a kind of end run around (or bull-rush through) all the truisms of America's creaking, dusty Protestant ethic, they have proved their parents, pastors, principals, and *every single one* of their grade-school teachers wrong: You can succeed in life, brilliantly, without ever doing homework! They have a million concrete reasons to believe, as clearly as if the Lord God himself had smitten them from a horse in midroad and turned on them with one blinding eye, that they belong to a Modern Elect, a brotherhood of giants at play in a pathetic boobiverse of rejects and underachievers, most of whom would gladly stand in line for hours—even pay!—to get their cap autographed.

It's easy to get carried away by it all. Sure, there is always the righteous and oh-so-upright Bible-thumping free-form Baptist Reverend Reggie to warn against their excesses. But even Reverend Reggie's message doesn't challenge the illusion (if it is an illusion). Reverend Reggie isn't arguing that they aren't chosen—hell, who could argue that? His point is that they are chosen for a reason, that their special status as giants comes with obligations, that they are called upon to be Role Models, Warriors for Christ—Reggie would whisper to an opposing offensive lineman "Jesus is coming!" just before bowling him over on his ass. Reggie's point is that they, as the Elect, are being called to *give something back*. Most of the guys don't even know how. But Reverend Reggie is making real progress with the boys. Even—no, *especially*—with hard-living homeboy Jerome.

Reverend Reggie's message has scored with Jerome. Hell, at least it makes some sense of what has happened in his life. Jerome has even been getting around to emulating Reggie, albeit like a timid bather dipping one toe in the pool. Hence, Camp Jerome. Sure, it's a pain in the ass, nothing really but a hastily organized half-day semiriot, but it's damn cheerful and wholesome; it's a start. Doesn't it have the word "Annual" right up there in the title? And while Jerome hasn't exactly stopped cruising the sinful byways of big-time sports celebrity, he is doing his best by the two boys he had fathered back in his teens—though both the mother of little Jerome IV, now nine, and Dunell, now seven, had spent the better part of the '80s chasing ol' Freight Train through the courts before proving paternity and winning orders for child support. Why, lately Jerome is even current with the payments. Jerome deserves at least some credit. He isn't completely there yet, but he is coming around. Like the camp, it's a start. And he is officially engaged. No doubt about it. Jerome is settling down. His mom, Annie Bell, attributes it all to Reggie's influence and, of course, to Jesus Christ the Lord. It's an answer to her prayers. Her prodigal son is turning toward home.

She can see it.

Why, just that very next morning Annie Bell is bustin' with pride as she inches over with an Instamatic toward the middle of a crowded front pew at the Josephine Street Church of the Living God—a ministry founded by Jerome's grandfather and presided over by his uncle—to capture on film the improbable vision of her youngest son, ninth of the ten children she and Willie called their own (Annie had brought six, and Willie two, to their marriage thirty years ago, then together added Jerome and his little sister, Cynthia), up there before the whole congregation. Annie Bell is cherishing this moment. My God! It is actually happening! There he is in the pulpit—*in the pulpit*—to introduce Reverend Reggie. They couldn't make him wear a tie, but Jerome is up there, swaying back and forth nervously, grinning his neon smile, gripping the plain pine podium like a toy, apologizing for being there, out of place as a rhino in a formal rose garden, wincing every time Annie Bell's flash goes off. Her son, the wild one, the rough one, the loud one, the one who was always in such a god-awful hurry, the one who was so big they wouldn't let him play football and baseball with the kids his own age—"He's always been overaverage," Willie told the enthusiastic Brooksville Little League coaches when they got their first glimpse of the future superstar back in the midseventies—in the pulpit!

Jerome was Annie and Willie's troublemaker, always pushing things too far—but nothing serious. Never anything serious. It was hard to stay mad at Jerome, the way he had of making people laugh. He towered over his mom by the time he was ten years old. When he made her mad, which happened plenty, she'd say, "Boy, I'm gonna knock you upside your head!" And Jerome, he'd come back with his big foolish grin and eyes open wide. "Aaaaw, Mama," he'd say. "Why you want to do that? You can't hurt me," and then he'd offer to go get her a chair, "So you can reach."

"It was always hard to stay mad at him," she says.

Everybody loved Jerome, particularly here in Brooksville. The whole town shared in Jerome's success. And his career just kept on going, like one of those mammoth home runs he used to clout—high-school all-American, '82; freshman member of the national championship Miami football team, '83; two-time college all-American; Eagles' first-round draft pick, '87 (ninth player chosen overall); NFL Pro Bowl, '90 and '91. Jerome's football and financial success made something more of him than he or his hometown had ever dreamed. And, as a consequence, he became the first son of Brooksville to fully bridge the deep, age-old racial divide in this town, which was, after all, named for Preston Brooks, the nineteenth-century South Carolina congressman who became a Southern hero when he brutally attacked Massachusetts abolitionist Senator Charles Sumner with his cane. Jerome just transcended hate. His success was big enough for everybody to bask a little in it. White folks could get as excited about Jerome as black folks could—why, when Jerome's Miami team played in that Fiesta Bowl in '87, his last collegiate game, the town's white folks chipped in to fly Willie and Annie Bell out to Phoenix to see it. Willie was so moved, he just sat down and cried. Neither of them had ever been on a plane.

And despite his fame, Jerome had never stopped coming home, hanging around, keeping up with his old high-school buddies. On the day the Eagles made him their first-round draft pick, Jerome didn't stay in Miami to party with his college teammates; he came roaring back up I-75 to Brooksville, where he loaded Tim Jinkens and his old baseball buddy Tim Simms in his car, then drove back down the road to Tampa to Hooters on Hillsborough Avenue, where he promptly, loudly, ordered a hundred chicken wings and a magnum of Dom Perignon.

"Is he *somebody*?" one of the waitresses asked Tim Jinkens.

Jerome finished the night, of course, gripping the porcelain at his parents' tiny house in north Brooksville.

"It was all the grease on that chicken!" he groaned.

Jerome would always arrive about two weeks after the season ended with money to spend and time to kill. His friends didn't see the six months of seven-day weeks, the injuries, the training-room sessions, the monotony of two-a-day practices and endless classroom sessions, the beating Jerome sometimes took from the Philadelphia press ("fat," "lazy," "undisciplined"). They saw only the cheerful, carefree, eternally adolescent Jerome. His buddies had gone on to getting married, raising families, running their businesses or farms, or punching the clock somewhere, but come spring there was the same Big G, racing around town in his souped-up cars or Ninja cycle, dropping by the auto shop to chat in the middle of the workday, stepping into Tim's Red Mule for a cold one on a hot early summer afternoon. Tim was used to Jerome's stopping in at any time, without warning, for any reason. He'd first hear, growing louder and louder from way up Broad Street, the mighty *whump-whump-whump-whump* of the woofers in the enormous speakers Jerome had mounted on the backseat of his Bronco, or the high-pitched whine of his Ninja screaming down on them like a Zero on a strafing run. One day, soon after Jerome got the bike, he burst in swearing richly.

"Burnt ma fuckin' leg!"

He'd leaned the bare shank of his calf against the hot exhaust pipe and fried a mean pink stripe.

"Help me, Tim? What do you put on burns?"

Tim came out from behind the counter, hunted up some first-aid salve, smeared it on, and Jerome was back out the door, accelerating out of the parking lot with his big body bent low to the handlebars. Tim just turned and went back to work, shaking his head, wondering (as he and the others often did) what it must be like to *be* Jerome Brown.

The whole town was Jerome's playpen. On Sunday evenings, just as shadows started stretching over the dusty shacks and dirt lawns of the Sub, Brooksville's depressed "colored" neighborhood, and the teenagers started assembling in clumps on the street corners, Jerome would pull up in one of his cars and pile as many kids into it as he could fit and take them all to the movies. He'd be the first one to start throwing popcorn, of course. Then he'd take them to Pizza Hut. And the thing was, Jerome wasn't doing this so much as a community goodwill gesture—no way! He was just having fun! It was what he did Sunday night, what he'd been doing since he was old enough to hang out on the same corners.

Not that Jerome was above making goodwill gestures. No, sir. When Marty Shick's daughter came down with cancer and the family's medical insurance gave out, it was Jerome who lent his name to a fund-raising softball game. And who in that town wouldn't fork over five bucks for a good cause and turn out to see Jerome play softball—mouth running a mile a minute, hugging his old friends, chugging around the base paths with the sweatpants over his stretch nylon shorts down around his knees, hat screwed on backward, then he'd clout one so far into the distance he'd remind you of the years he took Brooksville to the state championship, of high-school Friday nights, of youth. In Brooksville, Jerome knew how to be a star. He knew what was expected of him, and he delivered. He wrote a check when a little girl got hurt in a car accident out on Route 50 and wrote another when the high-school football team needed new uniforms and another when a couple of schoolboy track stars couldn't afford to go compete in a meet in Ireland. During the football season, if the camera caught him on the sidelines, sometimes he'd mouth "Hi, Mom!" like everybody else does, only sometimes he'd mouth "Hi, Brooksville!" God, they loved that back at home, hunkered around the big-screen TV at the local bar or in one another's living rooms, pulling in the Eagles game via satellite. Jerome stood for something. When the Ku Klux Klan decided to rally on the courthouse steps, Jerome and his old baseball-team buddies (all of them white) showed up with the Bronco, pulled onto a side street alongside the courthouse, and cranked up Jerome's awful rap music so loud it rattled the dental work of the racists under their white hoods.

So you can see why family and friends are ready to overlook Jerome's little excesses; they have come to be considered simply heroic, a part of himself he could help no more than his greatness. Sure, he drives his cars too fast; but hey, that's just Jerome! Why, ol' Willie even has a funny story about it: "He couldn't wait to drive, that boy. He must have been just about thirteen, and he'd put on my big overcoat and my hat an' he'd jus' ease right on down on the seat of my truck and take off, figurin' the police wouldn't stop him 'cause they'd figure it was me. He was almost big as me then already. I finally said, 'Boy, I better learn you how to drive.' I got him out on 75, you know? Round here in town, he'd spin a wheel, but you git him out on the interstate and he was afraid to drive. Them big trucks would pass him by an' he'd 'bout run off t' road with fright. I said, 'Now, you want to learn how to drive, you better drive or get out from behind the wheel.' And he hit it. Ain't slowed down since."

But he is slowing down. It's happening. Everyone can see it. His very success—not to mention the powerful Christian presence of

Reverend Reggie—is molding this larger-than-life character into a solid family man, pillar of his church and community, Role Model. . . .

In the church this fine spring morning, Jerome fidgets through Reverend Reggie's hour-long sermon, seated up on the dais behind his teammate, trying to look dignified, even though after the first half hour he was contemplating kicking the back of Reggie's knee to get him to wrap things up. "Man, I thought he was going to talk forever," he confesses later, outside the church, where he's obligingly posing for snapshots. The moment is perfect, people in their Sunday best, the church behind, the glorious God-filled azure Florida spring sky, and the cameras are whirring and clicking, Jerome is there with his teammates and Annie Bell, Willie, his sister Cynthia, the Reverend Reggie, and Clyde, and Nicole, his fiancée . . . his fiancée? *Whoaaaa!*

Just a minute, Hoss!

One of these shooters is a pro! Jerome's been in the public eye long enough to spot 'em—khaki flak jacket, ninety-pound Domke bag slung over one shoulder, lenses and light meters clanking everywhere. There's a look of muted panic in Jerome's eyes. He eases on out of the shot and over to a Philadelphia newshound who has accompanied the photographer down and has been taking all this in, of course, and Jerome drapes a great bear arm around the hound's shoulders, and leans in close.

"Y'all ain't going to use that shot, right?"

"What?"

"Me 'n' my fiancée. You're not going to put that one in the paper up in Philly, right?"

Jerome now has a playful but firm grip, between his massive thumb and index finger, on a sensitive spot at the base of the writer's neck.

The writer instantly understands. Hey, you can see the guy's point! A cozy group shot like this with Jerome's fiancée in the picture is just what he doesn't need! Preseason workouts up in Philly just seven weeks away, which means, of course, the party shifts north, where Jerome—need we say more?—has this other little sweetie (her name is Lisa) waiting. Jerome's wedding announcement has been, see, strictly regional. Premature word up north could make for a long, cold, lonely winter.

"Okay?" Jerome whispers.

His smile is pleading; his eyes are a threat.

HE NEEDN'T HAVE WORRIED.

Forty-six days later, on a humid Brooksville afternoon, Jerome pulls his green Corvette into the asphalt driveway of Register Chevrolet and Oldsmobile, just off Summit Road. It rained earlier in the day, and the air is thick. Mist curls lazily from the street. Telling his twelve-year-old nephew Gus to wait for him in the car, he hustles into the humid shade of the corrugated-steel paint and body-repair shop. Inside, his buddy Walter Griffin is sweating over a battered '73 Impala convertible he's rebuilding lovingly for Jerome, panel by gorgeous panel. Jerome plans to drive it north in a week to report to the Eagles' first informal preseason workouts. He's got a quick side trip to the Bahamas planned for Monday, and he wants to make sure his pals are on schedule with the car before he leaves. It's a beaut, beige with a saddle-tan imitation-leather top. Jerome can't wait to show it off to the guys up in Philly. The shop is a big part of Jerome's off-season, a favorite hangout. Hell, with all his cars and the way he drives them, Jerome's repair and tune-up bills help keep the repair shop afloat, which is just fine with Jerome. He admires the work his friends do. He wants the guys in the shop to know how much he's appreciated their company this off-season, so he proposes a big fish fry, for . . . oh, about a hundred people or so, wives, friends, family, children. "Bring everybody," he says, out to Home Jerome before he heads north.

This produces smiles all around. God bless Jerome. It's a mighty slow burg without him during football season. Griffin says he knows a guy who owns a wholesale fish company, so he'll arrange a delivery. "Want to *give something back* before I go to camp," says Jerome. God bless 'im. With that, the big lineman is half sprinting out of the garage, nodding to his buddy Dave Innes, who's working on another car. He quickly crosses the sunny lot and plops his bulk behind the wheel of the low-slung Corvette—zero to sixty miles per hour in 4.3 seconds, fat road-hugging wheels safety tested for track speeds at Indy—and leaves the lot the way he always does, with squealing wheels.

Under a canopy of giant oaks draped in moss that have kept the side street moist, the Corvette starts its skid. Past a red fireplug . . . past palmetto trees and tall wild grasses and a walnut tree . . . a stand of loblolly pine . . . and Jerome tries to pull out (how else?) by gunning the thing—speed and daring are Jerome's friends—only one-half of his car is off the road and one fat wheel grips grass, launching the car, which now straddles a steel guy wire angling up to a telephone pole at the intersection, and suddenly all the power and tonnage of the Corvette's chassis is airborne . . . there isn't even time to scream . . . and the left front end slams into the scraggy trunk of a palm tree as the back end, ballistic, lurches counterclockwise into the telephone pole . . . and the whole howling mass of engine, plastic, metal, and man neatly flips and falls, landing with a horrible thud upside down. Jerome is crushed instantly. Gus lives long enough to smother, the weight of the car collapsing his head into his chest.

Inside the body shop, Griffin hears the screaming engine—nothing unusual there—but then this awful, enormous thud. He drops his tools, and the other men sprint down Hale Street toward the unholy scrambled mass of plastic, metal, and rubber, upside down, barely recognizable as a car.

"Oh, my God!" gasps Innes, who is the first to arrive.

Griffin rips off the flapping back fender and climbs frantically through the shattered back window, shouting, "Jerome! Jerome! Stay calm!"

RON HELLER, the Eagles' veteran right tackle, gets a call that afternoon at his apartment in Tampa from an old football buddy.

"A friend just called and told me he was driving down the interstate and he heard on the news that Jerome Brown was in a car accident."

This prompts a chuckle from Ron. "That doesn't surprise me."

"No, Ron. Apparently this was a *serious* accident. Now, this isn't, like, confirmed or anything, so maybe it isn't true. Let's hope it isn't true. But the report on the radio said Jerome was killed."

"You're telling me Jerome Brown died in a car wreck?"

Ron's wife, Heidi, overhears from the other room and steps into the hall. She shakes her head.

"No," she says adamantly. "A car wreck can't kill Jerome."

When he was traded to the Eagles in '88, Ron had instantly disliked Jerome Brown. He had, of course, heard about Jerome. The big stud from Miami. Ron had played his college ball at Penn State, a few years ahead of Jerome, but he remembered the infamous stunt Miami pulled on the eve of the celebrated national championship game, that '87 Fiesta Bowl, when Jerome and his teammates had donned battle fatigues and snubbed the Nittany Lions by marching out of the ceremonial banquet, refusing to dine with their opponents and accusing (baselessly) Penn State players of making racist remarks. It was nothing but a stunt, of course, a piece of pop theater, but it had introduced an unnecessary whiff of ugliness to Penn State's win the next day over the previously undefeated Hurricanes. Jerome had come off that incident, rightly or wrongly, looking like the instigator. Still, Ron, a man with a Nittany Lion tattooed right on the outside of his right calf, was ready to overlook that. But on his very first day in the Eagles' locker room he watched and listened to Jerome with disbelief. Here was this big, round, profane, wiseass whose mouth never stopped—he remembered it sounded like a high-pitched *yap-yap-yap-yap*. Jerome struck Ron as an obnoxious loudmouth, an undisciplined man with a wide streak of bully in him. At six-five, 280 pounds, the former New York State heavyweight-wrestling champion was hardly intimidated by Jerome, and being something of a hothead beneath the cool and fastidious exterior—this was a man who had been traded by the Tampa Bay Buccaneers after a fistfight with the head coach—Ron figured he and this Jerome Brown were destined to collide.

Which, of course, they did.

Predictably, it was midway through the endless, broiling summer slog of training camp in West Chester, Pennsylvania. The Eagles were grunting through the second of Buddy Ryan's two grueling daily practice sessions. Everybody was stressed to the max, bruised, winded, dehydrated, and exhausted. Jerome had been throwing his weight around all afternoon, his mouth flapping; he was getting on everybody's nerves. When Ron slipped and fell on one play, he instinctively grabbed at the nearest opponent's jersey and pulled Jerome down on top of him.

Jerome jumped up screaming.

"You holding motherfucker!" he said, and lunged at Ron, which, of course, triggered a general riot, with fists and mud flying in from all directions. Players working drills on the adjoining field stopped what they were doing and came running. Ryan (who loved few things more than a serious practice brawl) maneuvered to one side with a bloodthirsty grin and watched as his team merged into a roiling heap at the center of the field. Underneath the pile, Ron and Jerome were pinned together, unable to move.

Finally, Buddy blew his whistle. When practice ended, Ron, as is his wont, sprinted off the field first, up the long, steep stairs to the West Chester University gym, where he quickly stripped off his gear and headed for a cool shower.

He was crossing the locker room when he saw Jerome come in, dragging his jersey, helmet, and shoulder pads. The defensive tackle, not one to stay in top shape during the off-season, looked whipped. Mud and sweat gleamed on his round black face, and his eyes looked bloodshot and vacant.

"Hey, Jerome. You all right?"

"Screw you," said Jerome, not even looking up.

"Hey, come on, man. We're teammates. Everyone was a little hot and bothered out there. You all right?"

Jerome dropped his gear and walked over.

"No, man, I'm not 'all right,'" sneering the last two words, mocking Ron's conciliatory tone. "As a matter of fact, I'm pretty goddamn pissed off!"

That got Ron going again. "Look, man. Then let's finish it now. Let's settle it," putting up his fists.

"You're damn right!" Jerome shouted, moving at him.

By now the locker room was filling up, and teammates crowded in to watch these two behemoths lock horns.

Suddenly, Jerome's face transformed. Breaking through the angry scowl was his neon grin. "Man, I can't fight *you*," he shouted. "Your ass is *buck naked!*"

As the locker room broke out in laughter, Jerome stepped up and locked the naked lineman in an embrace.

Ever since that moment Ron's opinion of Jerome had turned around. He had felt relief when Jerome backed down, but he was also charmed. He realized something. Jerome's profane bluster was for show, and he respected people he couldn't frighten.

Ron's respect for Jerome had grown deeper over the next three seasons. He had known plenty of bigmouthed players who would rag people and complain—when the coaches weren't around. Jerome just didn't care. He was brutal with everybody, right to their face. But his ferocity, talent, and dedication were such that *everyone* accepted Jerome's outrageous ways. Things that would get an ordinary player fined or suspended would be dismissed with a laugh by Jerome's admiring coaches. They knew. They knew, as Ron came to realize, that Jerome Brown was the heart and soul of the football team Ryan had built. He was the kind of player who made everyone around him play better. Ron had been on enough teams—high school, Penn State, Tampa Bay, Seattle, now the Eagles—to know that the kind of motivation Jerome provided was what separated winning teams from merely good teams. Jerome made playing for the Eagles fun. Ron looked forward to coming into work every day, even when the routine of lifting, meetings, and practice became monotonous midway through the long season. And on Sundays, Jerome shone.

No, a car accident can't kill Jerome.

Ron's father calls from New York. The evening TV news up there had run a teaser before a commercial: "There's been a tragedy in Florida for the Philadelphia Eagles. One of their players is dead. More after this. . . ."

"I called right away," Ron's father says. "I almost had a heart attack. How many Eagles players live in Florida anyway?"

EAGLES OWNER Norman Braman is surprised by the funeral. He has flown in from his villa in Grasse, in southern France, and has been expecting a miserably hot, sad affair in a tiny rural black church up in country he regards as more typical of Deep South, cracker Georgia than of the urbane, bustling Florida that buys up his luxury cars by the thousands. But instead of some stuffy shack, his black limo pulls up before Brooksville's showpiece, redbrick, air-conditioned First Baptist Church . . . you know, the one built by the *white* Baptists.

And inside it's even more remarkable. The grand hall is jammed with mourners of every hue and religion. The ceremony is ecumenical, interracial, and (even Norman the old skeptic has to concede) positively inspiring. Music rocks the rafters, the joyous, rhythmic music of African America, that soulful blend of sadness and celebration. All of the Browns' considerable extended family is present, teammates from Jerome's high-school, college, and pro days, including, of course, most of his Eagles brethren (though Jerome's beloved Buddy Ryan is conspicuously absent). In the crowd are Jerome's girlfriends; there's LaSonya (or "Peaches"), who gave birth to William Jerome Brown IV when Jerome was in high school; there is Cynthia, who gave birth to Dunell when Jerome was in college, and Lisa, Jerome's Philadelphia squeeze; and, of course, Nicole, his regional fiancée—the sight of all four together here forces a smile through poor Tim Jinkens's tears (*that Jerome*). Willie and Annie Bell are dressed in white. The congregation's rhythmic clapping is infectious, and as the choir's voices swell, Annie Bell and Willie rise and dance, clapping and singing before the enormous bronze casket of their youngest son, and the smaller blue one of their grandson Gus.

"They have gone," intones Reverend Theodore N. Brown, Jerome's uncle, "to a better place."

Reverend Reggie (who Braman regards as a greedy, sanctimonious brute) rises to deliver a eulogy of heartfelt, earthy eloquence:

". . . He was fun to be with. He and myself were like two kids in grown men's bodies. He enjoyed life. Jerome enjoyed life. It's sad that it ended. But, you know, every time a life ends, there's a purpose to its ending. If we don't grab on to the purpose, we miss out on the whole plan."

"Amen!" someone in the crowd shouts.

"Hallelujah!"

"Jesus is the purpose. For all there is. If we don't take advantage of that, we miss out on life. I hope we learned something from the death of Jerome and the death of Gus. I hope we can open our hearts and find out what God wants us to do. One thing I know is, in the past week, myself, my teammates, and friends, we've lost a special friend. I hope there will be a special prayer. We found out what the purpose of our life is."

And as the church rocks and sways to the gospel song "We're Gonna Make It," Norman is moved despite himself. He feels uplifted, and puzzled. Why are there so many people? In particular, so many white people?

The club's multimillionaire owner doesn't really hold athletes, apart from their athletic skills, in very high regard. They are too young to be interesting, have been pampered through adolescence by a football-crazy society, and are now reaping rewards way out of proportion to their value or accomplishments. He puts up with them, of course, because he is a football fan himself and because they are making him a lot of money. Norman had once, not long ago, considered Jerome Brown to be a fat, disappointing bully.

Take the night before the big Dallas game, '88. It was crunch time for Norman's young team. A win over the Cowboys the next day could mean the team's first trip to the postseason play-offs since Coach Dick Vermeil had retired seven years earlier. The team was having a late meeting at the Summit Hotel in Dallas, and Norman slipped into the room to observe, puffing one of his huge after-dinner cigars. He was still new enough in his ownership of the franchise to get a thrill out of behind-the-scenes moments like these.

He listened briefly, then began to leave.

Before he reached the door, he heard, *"Yo! Norman!"* in Jerome's unmistakable high-pitched voice.

He turned.

"Ain't you gonna talk to the team?" Jerome demanded. "This is the night before the biggest game of our goddamn careers! And you ain't gonna talk to the team?"

It was embarrassing. Norman plucked the cigar from his mouth.

"I didn't mean to be rude," he said. "I didn't think you guys would be interested in hearing from me . . . I've never addressed the team before . . . but if you want me to say something, then I will."

He stepped up to the lectern and improvised a little speech, about how proud he was of the team (they had played way over their heads that season), and whether they won or lost the big game tomorrow, he wanted them to know they had accomplished a lot. It was a dignified, off-the-cuff speech. Everybody was impressed.

Except Jerome.

"Hey, Norman! Cut through the bullshit. If we win tomorrow, are we gonna get more money?"

The owner drew back. He said, "Well . . . Jerome, as things go, I suppose the more you win, the better it will go at contract time for everybody. . . ."

"All right then," Jerome shouted back. "Now git your ass out of here!"

Norman exited to hilarious laughter.

The owner knew this clowning cheek was a cornerstone of team morale, but it was irksome. The laughter that had followed him out the door was like a boot to the backside. And Norman never forgets. The day after he canned Buddy Ryan, Norman had his revenge. He symbolically plucked Jerome out from under Buddy's protective wing and spanked him hard in public. Norman mentioned flab, poor work habits, women, paternity suits, gambling debts, speeding tickets. . . .

And Jerome had gotten the message. His agent (who knew some of what the owner had said was true) hired Jerome a personal trainer and dietitian. Jerome outfitted a corner of the garage at home with about fifteen thousand dollars' worth of state-of-the-art exercise equipment (and a complete drum set in the corner, for good measure). For the first time in his life, Jerome worked hard on his own to get in shape, dropping upward of thirty pounds, struggling through a regimen that made him positively *miserable*. He had come back in '91 to something like his old, dominating, ferocious style of play.

Norman feels he knows dozens of players like Jerome Brown.

But this funeral is saying something else. Here's a whole town wrestling with genuine grief. Here are teammates from every team Jerome had ever played for. Hundreds and hundreds of mourners spill right out the front doors of the church, down the steps and out into the streets . . . *stricken.*

What had he missed about Jerome?

He doesn't go with the small group of family and close friends to the burial. His limo drops him at a small airport nearby, where he encounters a well-dressed businessman waiting to board his own private plane. He had seen the man at the funeral.

"Mr. Braman, my wife and I really enjoy the Eagles," says the man, introducing himself as a childhood friend of Jerome's.

"Tell me something," asks Braman. "That church, is that a black church or a white church?"

"Oh, that's an integrated church."

"An integrated church?"

"Oh . . . see, that was Jerome. Jerome changed this town. . . . Brooksville will never be the same."

. . .

AT THE GRAVE, set on one corner of a woebegone field by a backroad that Jerome used to race down to Tampa (avoiding the state cops on the interstate), Seth weeps inconsolably. His head is buried on Reverend Reggie's broad shoulder. Tears and sweat glisten on Reggie's face. Randall is solemn. One by one the whole Eagles crew, joined by a few of Jerome's old college teammates, steps up silently to the two caskets to say a final good-bye.

One by one, each member of the team removes his colorful silk tie and drops it on Jerome's coffin lid. (Team rule: ties on road trips. Only, Jerome never had one, see, so he was always running around at the last minute, mooching, except this one time, when the charter plane was waiting on the runway at Philadelphia International Airport, players and coaches and trainers inside ready to go, but no Jerome, and Buddy Ryan was fuming, telling them to close the goddamn doors and take off—when all at once, racing down the last five hundred yards of Island Avenue toward the gate, came Jerome's black Bronco, doing . . . oh, a hundred or so. It screeched to a halt and unloaded the lineman, who came sprinting toward the steps, his teammates cheering loudly. He had a big greasy bag of fried chicken under one arm; was wearing a sports coat and . . . well, what do you know? Jerome was even wearing a tie! Only this time he was missing the shirt.)

With his sweat-soaked dress shirt clinging to his back, Reggie stretches over the brass rail around the coffins and taps Jerome's once with his ring.

He says, "Don't let his death be in vain."

When the crowd of mourners moves away, the two caskets are smoothly lowered into the earth, the mound of colorful silk ties descending into darkness.

Out of the nearby woods steps a boy wearing nothing but shorts. He is just twelve, but he has the build of an athlete. His name is Reggie Fagan. He picks two white roses out of a floral display and drops them into the graves, one on each casket.

"Gus was my friend," he says. "Jerome, he was my hero."

2

THE NEXT LEVEL

Everybody knows what Richie Kotite is going to say. They *always* know.

It's halftime in the New Orleans Superdome, January 3, 1993. After eleven regular season wins and just five losses, the Philadelphia Eagles are stalled in a familiar place, losing (17–7) in the first round of the NFL's post–'92 season play-offs. Four times in the last five seasons this team has made it to the doorstep of the NFL's championship series. Three times it has been eliminated in the first round—by the Bears, the Rams, the Redskins—and now, it seems, its fourth attempt will be stopped by the Saints.

Bloodied and a little stunned, the team collects itself quietly in the Superdome's visiting-team locker room, a humid cave with a worn carpet ringed with wood-framed dressing stalls, bathed in soft yellow light, where the odors of menthol and stale sweat have been battling for almost two decades. Right now it is crowded with big men wearing heavy, soggy pads and uniforms of white, silver, and kelly green. Green helmets with silver wings are at their feet. The ceiling rocks with the mirth of nearly sixty-nine thousand New Orleans fans who've been waiting a quarter century for their gaudy Saints' first play-off win.

Today looks like the day.

Before this game began, the Eagles had crowded around a small TV to watch the Buffalo Bills surmount the seemingly insurmountable, overcoming a thirty-two-point deficit (more than four touchdowns and a field goal) to beat the Houston Oilers and advance to round two of postseason play.

There are nods and winks exchanged when Richie, the head coach, launches into the inevitable.

"Ten points! That's nothing! . . . You all saw what Buffalo did this afternoon. . . ."

The Eagles' special teams captain, Ken Rose, just ducks his head.

The thirty-year-old, ponytailed surfer has played eight seasons in pro football, six with the NFL, one with the Canadian Football League, and one with the long-gone USFL. Add in Pop Warner, high school, and college, and Ken, like everyone else in the room, has heard every permutation possible of the motivational halftime plea. There were coaches who ranted, spit, begged, cursed with black fury, cried, laughed, and prayed, coaches who punched lockers and picked fights, coaches who told jokes and coaches who preached sermons, there were even coaches who did all of these things in the same gusty peroration. Ken's never heard one that made a difference. Still, the rituals of sport will be honored.

Equally futile, for that matter, is Norman Braman's thoughtful gesture. In the corner, between the lockers being used by Reggie White and Seth Joyner, the team's equipment men have assembled the JeromeShrine, Jerome Brown's locker, complete with the lineman's old collection of goofy hats—his olive-green pillbox number, a rumpled khaki fishing hat, a telephone company hard hat—piles of shoes, Jerome's gigantic pads and helmet, the green jersey wide enough to be a tent, with its retired white number 99, the cigar safety William Frizzell placed in there when his second daughter was born earlier in the season, the framed tributes, photos, and caricatures, the unopened mail. All of it now stares like an unblinking eye.

It's five exhibitions and sixteen and a half games now, six months and three days, since Jerome's death. Season '92 is down to what could be its last half hour of play.

Back in Philly last summer, Reverend Reggie and the boys had asked that the locker be kept exactly as Jerome left it. In that flood tide of grief it had seemed appropriate, but, as time went by, it started to haunt more than inspire. It gives some of the guys the creeps. Fred Barnett, the team's splendid young pass catcher, thinks the whole Cult of Jerome has gone too far. He tries not to look over at the locker. He isn't the only one. Even Reggie now sees the futility of sustaining momentum on sorrow. But to Clyde and the increasingly insufferable Seth, the locker remains a potent reminder. Their whole season is a JeromeQuest, a tribute to JB, whose initials the team wears on a patch over their hearts. Ol' Freight Train's memory is invoked after every huddle—"One! Two! Three! JB!!" Whenever Seth made a big play in Veterans Stadium, in Philadelphia, he would snap to attention and salute a giant Jerome banner (the one depicting Archangel Jerome cupping his teammates in his hands). They had promised Big G a Super Bowl ring. Now, here they are, three wins shy of the Show, Super Bowl XXVII, on the brink of the abyss.

Not again whispers behind every veteran's ear. Three times the thrill of making the play-offs had fizzled in the first round. This is their last chance to go, finally, to the Next Level, which was the expression Norman had used in early '91 when he fired Buddy Ryan and promoted Richie, Buddy's offensive coordinator, to the top job. Buddy had shocked everyone but himself by getting them into the play-offs in just the third season of his tenure, '88, and had taken them back in '89 and '90. Each time they had stumbled. Buddy had failed. Now Richie was charged with doing better. They had fallen out of contention in '91 after Randall blew out his knee in game one, and then backup Jim "Ming Vase" McMahon quickly crumbled. Still, Richie and the boys managed to win ten games that year on the backs of the NFL's top-ranked defense—*Buddy's* defense. This year, Randall was back, and the defense was in its prime. This was going to be the year for it all. The Eagles had been picked to win the Super Bowl by many of the press prognosticators (never mind that they were virtually *always* wrong). More important, they believed it themselves. They believed it was *their due*.

And why not? In terms of just wins and losses (52–28), the Eagles had been one of pro football's most successful teams over the last five years. They had two blue-chip quarterbacks. They had picked up a used but certified superstar running back in Herschel Walker. Their offensive line was expected to improve with the maturing of right tackle Antone (*An*-tone) Davis, "the Megapick," a mammoth blocker from Tennessee. Ballet-enthusiast Fred, the wide receiver, was poised for greatness, heir apparent to the team's tradition of lanky all-pro receivers Harold Carmichael and Mike Quick. Vicious hitters Andre Waters and Wes Hopkins lent the defensive backfield an enviably ugly reputation—but only if you got past Seth, who played linebacker with a purposeful violence that bordered on pure evil. In front of Seth, of course, was Reverend Reggie, "the Minister of Defense," arguably the finest defensive end in the history of football, and Clyde Simmons, who led the league in crunching quarterbacks. Patrolling the deep secondary was Eric Allen, another perennial Pro Bowl selection, one of the smartest and most consistent cornerbacks in the league. The Eagles were no longer Buddy's talented upstarts; they were older, wiser, shored up by a stronger bench, and desperately overdue. Jerome's loss diminished their front four, but it had hardly destroyed it. It had bequeathed an urgency and emotional purpose often lacking at the pro level.

But lose this game, and the team is done. If this incarnation of Eagles doesn't achieve the Next Level this year—*now!*—they never will. Forever unfulfilled will be the championship destiny Buddy confidently forecast back in '86, when he set to work. Buddy was good at many things, but he was best at assembling a disparate bunch of young men into a Team. Not the mercenary NFL notion of team, a loose confederation of bruisers newly acquired each season. No, Buddy's notion of Team was more primitive, a brotherhood of warriors, a social unit more basic than even family. To those on this kind of Team, money and celebrity were secondary. Buddy connected with the reckless prideful core of a young athlete, with his playful soul. Beneath all the hype and megabucks, the soul was still there. On the field, before that screaming crowd, before the cameras, caught up in the thrilling moment, who thought about lawyers and incentives and paydays? Young men still played to fulfill their destiny. Buddy sang a song that reached them there, where only they could hear it. *He* saw their real potential; *he* believed in the inevitability of their greatness; *he* would lead them to the highest heights. These Eagles believed Buddy when he told them they were the baddest and best. And Buddy hadn't just foreseen *a* Super Bowl, he had talked about winning a whole slew of them. They were going to be the Best There Ever Was! Why, there would be a whole wing devoted to them at the Pro Football Hall of Fame in Canton—Buddy's Boys! Gang Green!

And every year they fell short. When Norman dumped Buddy, no matter. They were going to carry on. Like Moses, Buddy would miss the promised land, but his boys were going there *for* him. Then, in the wild swirl of triumph, when the crowds and cameras spilled out onto the field, they would thumb their noses at their despised owner and instead salute the man who really made it happen, who would be watching in exile, still unemployed back home in his den at the Ryan horse farm in Kentucky, not misty-eyed—not Buddy—but *chortling* with vindication.

Still another year had gone by. The dream was something that could no longer be deferred. Each year the original roster further eroded; old players were waived or retired; newcomers assumed key spots. Buddy's Boys had cohered well since they gelled in '88, but age and injury are relentless, and this year the dawn of true free agency stood poised to disassemble them. They were becoming creaking old-timers, battling bad knees and tricky backs, wrestling with midlife crises, failed marriages, premature arthritis, and facing that prospect most dreaded and dark: Life after Football. They had enjoyed such moments together, moments sweetened by promise. There were games in which they just caught fire, when offense, defense, and special teams were all clicking at once, when they were capable of crushing *anyone.* It was when they achieved this synchronicity, with the crowd roaring and every one of them motoring on love, adrenaline, and conviction, when they were riding a mounting spiral of their own momentum, when they were *bringing the heat*, that the Game became something timeless, pure, and beautiful, something linked to the earliest amateur contests on college greens, something that connected each player with the thrill he felt when he first played as a child, before he knew about playing with pressure and pain. This wasn't just a fantasy either. You could point to the games in which it happened, like when they scored twenty-one fourth-quarter points back in '89 to upset the Redskins, or when they humiliated the Cowboys in Texas Stadium in '91, sacking quarterback Troy Aikman eleven times, allowing no points and fewer than one hundred yards of total offense, or this year, when they crushed that John Elway and the Broncos, shutting them out and allowing them only eighty-two yards of offense. It was always only a matter of time, they had always thought, just one more season together, maybe two, before they could achieve that perfection consistently, play a whole season in that holy zone, sustain it on through the play-offs to a Super Bowl . . . and then another, and another.

Eventually, of course, it would end. But to win a Super Bowl, even just once, meant that no matter what else happened they would always be together. For that season they would be the best of the best— for all time. Jerome's memory would be forever green. There would be the mandatory White House trip, award ceremonies, parties, and then reunions, Hall of Fame enshrinements; their obituaries would read "Member of the '93 NFL Super Bowl Champion Philadelphia Eagles." Win and they would be family forever. Lose, and they would scatter to the winds.

For all this, Jerome's locker is totem. Now, trailing by ten points, unable to stop the Saints or stir themselves, it might as well be Jerome in the flesh, glaring in spooky, decidedly un-Jeromelike silence, daring these blowhards to deliver.

And they're blowing it.

THEY HAD STARTED BADLY.

Weak-armed Saints quarterback Bobby Hebert had come right after them on the first play from scrimmage, launching a wobbly bomb down the right sideline toward receiver Quinn Early.

It was scary, because Early was open. Rookie cornerback Mark McMillian, easily the smallest and least experienced player on the field, was close to the veteran, but not close enough. Only Hebert's imprecision spared the Eagles a touchdown. Up in the TV broadcast booth, CBS game analyst John Madden primed the nationwide audience for a wild one: "They were saying that the Saints have a conservative offense, so Jim Mora [the Saints' coach] says, 'Conservative? We'll show you conservative!' "

Although a failure, the bomb ignites the capacity hometown crowd, living walls of noise rising up on all sides to the Superdome's concrete roof. Football crowds lean toward the bizarre anyway, but nowhere more so than here, the only city in America where cross-dressing is an expression of civic pride. Like the Eagles, the Saints are an aging team of defense-powered underachievers. They're also three-time losers in first-round play-off games (over the last five years). The team that goes down today earns the distinction of being the league's biggest modern disappointment. So the fans, a multitude decked in gold and black sequins and greasepaint, are fired up, lusting for Eagles blood. Homemade signs announcing Saints pride and allegiance to the black and gold hang over every available surface around the field. One of the signs really has Buddy's Boys pissed off. Ornamented with a crude but elaborate painting, it reads JEROME WAS AN EAGLE/NOW HE'S A SAINT. A few of the boys in green were going to tear it down before the game, but cooler heads prevailed—which shows just how serious they are about winning this game.

But the bomb did precisely what Mora intended. It knocked the Eagles' defense off stride. Hanging back more than usual, the secondary was on its heels when fullback Craig "Ironhead" Heyward caught a short shovel pass. Loose in the secondary, the 270-pound runner ("I'm bein' nice with that two-seventy," said Madden) shrugged off the blows of McMillian and safety Rich Miano, both of whom were outweighed by about a hundred pounds. Heyward crossed midfield before a determined John Booty, another lightweight Eagles backup safety (the injured Hopkins and Waters were watching in civvies from the sidelines), rode him down.

Then McMillian screwed up. Instead of following receiver Eric Martin across the middle of the field, the rookie let him go, thinking that Booty would pick him up. But Booty had been assigned deep coverage, so he was fifteen yards away when Martin slanted into a broad empty space in the center of the Eagles' defensive secondary. Martin sprinted down to the Eagles' thirteen-yard line before Booty caught up this time.

So the Saints were in plus territory, inside the Eagles' twenty-yard line. Only four minutes into the game, and their supposedly overmatched offense was pushing the vaunted Gang Green backward in big thrusts on nearly every play. The Dome was vibrating with noise. This was the best of all possible beginnings for New Orleans. Barring a fumble or an interception, they were going to score. If you take the ball on the first possession and march straight down your opponent's throat, you not only take an early lead, you serve notice.

Especially in a game like this. It takes more than talent to win a play-off game. More than emotion. At the beginning of a season, teams approach each other anew. They may be old rivals, but each off-season has brought retirements, draft picks, free agents; strengths bolstered, weaknesses addressed. Aging superstars no longer play the way they once did, and youngsters step up. There's a degree of uncertainty on both sides. By the end of a sixteen-game season, however, both teams know each other well. They know which linebackers can't keep up with tight ends, know which defensive ends with mending knees tend to shy away from low blocks, know which green cornerback is often confused in complex pass coverages. Intelligence counts for more in the postseason.

Tasting blood, the Saints' coaching staff bored in on McMillian. They lined up a three-receiver formation, a triple, which assured a one-on-one matchup between the rookie and Martin, their wily veteran (who was five inches taller than the cornerback and outweighed him by about forty pounds). On the snap, Martin sprinted down the sideline, and, noting that the cornerback was staying too wide, broke toward the center, toward the goalpost. Realizing he was a step too late, McMillian made a desperate lunge and grabbed the back of Martin's jersey. It prevented the touchdown, at the cost of a penalty that gave the Saints first down on the one-yard line.

And Reverend Reggie opened the door. On the first play of the goal-line stand, the star defensive end was supposed to keep his nose down and hold his ground, aiming himself in from his left side of the line toward the center. But even future Hall of Famers goof. Reggie either misheard or forgot the defensive call, because instead of nosing in to his right, he charged out to his left, head up, nearly bowling over right tackle Stan Brock, but leaving an open door behind him to the end zone. Heyward ran across the goal line untouched. The chubby fullback trotted over to a section in the stands for disabled fans and chucked them the ball. This throttled the roar even higher—the *nobility* of it!

Seventy-three yards on the first eight plays of the game! Who dat? Yessir, the Saints were marchin' in! Morten Andersen's extra point spotted his team a seven-point lead, and the fans were dancing in the aisles. It looked like one long Mardi Gras afternoon.

Things got worse. Randall started off shakily, ignoring (as usual) the checkoffs he was supposed to be making on passing downs and missing what the coaches felt would be easy targets. This was frightening, because Randall has a history of playing either brilliantly or abominably, and rarely anything in between. The quarterback fumbled the first time he tried to run with the ball (but the Eagles got a break; officials ruled he was down before he dropped it) and then, in classic Randall form, took off upfield on the next play, ignoring three wide-open receivers. It was the kind of play that infuriates his coaches. He forfeited an easy big gainer by declining to throw the ball, but before Richie and quarterbacks coach Zeke Bratkowski had time to vent their disgust, Randall had high stepped into the New Orleans secondary, slipped two tackles, and, catching and righting himself with one hand on the turf, lunged forward to complete a magnificent fifteen-yard run—the same yardage he might have effortlessly gained by throwing the ball, only that would never have made a highlights tape, the way Randall's scramble would on all the postgame shows tonight (win or lose).

As would the next play, which is the sort of thing Randall did whenever they started thinking he was hopeless. Richie was trying to mix up first-down calls; the Eagles had run the ball twice in a row on first down. This time it would be a pass. He selected a play that involves lining up on the same side of the field two receivers, Fred Barnett and the dour, precise Calvin Williams. Fred and Calvin would run a crossing pattern. Fred lined up split wide to the right, over near the sideline, and Calvin positioned himself between Fred and the right tackle, in the slot. The critical part of the play call was the number 75, which designates the target of the pass to be Calvin, the 7 receiver, and the pass route, a 5 or "sail," which calls for him to sprint exactly 12 yards upfield at the snap and then tear to his right and "sail" toward the sidelines. That was the plan. Only, given a choice between throwing to Calvin or Fred, Randall would almost always throw to Fred, another of the quarterback's standing problems (and one of the reasons that Calvin is so dour).

The moment Randall stepped out of the huddle, he saw he'd made a mistake. It was easy to make a mistake. The quarterback got his play call through an elaborate sequence of hand signals from Bratkowski, the dignified old journeyman, veteran backup from the days of Bart Starr and Johnny Unitas. Intelligent, unflappable, and precise, Zeke stood in the unholy din of the Superdome signing intensely. He had been standing on the sidelines for most of his sixty-one years. He was so used to playing the game in his head that football existed for him like some Zen abstraction—as opposite as one could get from the flamboyantly instinctive Randall. The actual play call in this instance was "slot-I-right, K-44, 75, Z-stop, slow," with each portion of the call fleshing out the play's design: formation (slot-I-right—left flanker Calvin in the right slot, backs stacked in a row behind the quarterback,

tight end to the left side, and Herschel Walker lined up directly behind
Heath Sherman in the classic I formation about three yards off Randall's right shoulder); play fake and blocking assignment (K-44—fake
handoff [hence the *K*] to the 4 hole between tackle and guard, right
side, and the whole line slides to provide left-side pass protection);
target receiver and route (75); secondary receiver and route (Z-stop—
Fred, the Z receiver, runs a stop-and-go); and the tight end's blocking
assignment (slow—Keith Byars, lined to the left, blocks for a few
seconds, then slips out into the flat on a delayed short-pass route). For
every one of these instructions (and this is a relatively simple play,
with no presnap motion, no line stunts, and only two wide receivers),
old Zeke has to make a hand signal; he looks as though he's singing
rounds in sign language. When the old warhorse Jimmy Mac is out
there, he will often just cut Zeke off in midcall, waving his hand
dismissively toward the sideline to indicate "Okay, I've got it," picking
up the whole sequence (as familiar to him as a popular ditty) from
just the first two beats. But Randall, who was sensitive about getting
blamed for screwing up, wanted to make sure he knew exactly what
the coaches wanted him to do at all times, so he demanded the whole
rigmarole. This time, somewhere in Zeke's elaborate sidelines mime,
Randall picked up a "5" for the blocking assignment instead of "4."
As he left the huddle, and watched Calvin trot out to the right-side
slot, it dawned on him that if his play fake was to the left, and his
blockers were sliding toward the 5 hole, he would almost instantly
have two unblocked quarterback-eating Saints in his face.

"Uh, you're gonna want to get out of this," warned center Dave
Alexander, who saw the same thing.

"No, Dave!" Randall shouted, trying to be heard over the crowd.
"Four! Four!"

Alexander started screaming, "Forty-four! Forty-four!" turning
his head to his left, then to his right, adjusting the blocking scheme.

Randall quickly walked back to Sherman and Walker and alerted
them to his mistake. With just two seconds left on the play clock, he
lined up behind the center and took the snap.

Saints cornerback Toi Cook had to make a choice when both
Fred and Calvin started down his side of the field. Cook's free safety,
Gene Atkins, was supposed to help him with deep coverage, so Cook
was keeping one eye on Fred but more closely watching Calvin. If he
could jump the slot receiver from behind, he could pick off the pass
and have a clear fifty-yard sprint to the end zone. It was tempting.
And when Fred came off the line at just three-quarter speed, it reinforced Cook's hunch that this would be a short pass to Calvin on the
out route (which is, in fact, the play Richie called). Cornerback is the

least forgiving role on the football field. With just an eye blink of hesitation—Cook did no more than turn his body a half degree to the left—you were (so to speak) cooked.

Fred had spent some quiet time this morning in his hotel room visualizing just this play. He was always up at about 5:00 a.m. on game days, which drove his roommate, Calvin, crazy. Fred sat up in his bed and made mental pictures, trying to project himself into the situations he would be apt to encounter in the game. It was more than technique to Fred; it was mystical. He knew the patterns he was going to be running in the game. He knew the defenses and the adjustments they'd make. He just fed in the scenarios and ran them like videotapes in his head. And then, during the game, racing downfield in the Superdome, seeing Randall release the long pass, hearing no sound . . . Fred felt a whisper of déjà vu; he had been in this moment before; he was in perfect sync with his mind's eye.

COOK REALIZED A SPLIT SECOND TOO LATE that Fred was Randall's target. He pivoted and turned upfield, but he was already beat. He glanced over for Atkins, but the safety, too, had bought Calvin's out route. They were both out of position.

The pass was a thing of beauty. Zeke had been preaching for years that the place to throw the long pass was not to the corner of the field—where quarterbacks instinctively throw it—but toward the goalpost. When the ball is thrown outside, the receiver has to find and track it over his shoulder. And because the spin on a right-handed passer's football is clockwise, the longer the ball stays in flight on a deep pass to the right, the more it will tail off toward the sidelines and out of reach. Thrown inside, toward the goalpost, however, the ball has a trajectory that draws the receiver into the middle of the field, so he can run toward it without worrying about running out-of-bounds, without craning his neck, without breaking stride, and the spin pulls the ball *toward* the receiver, not away from him. "You make the physics work for you," Zeke told his quarterbacks, who tended to return funny looks. *Physics?*

This pass was a textbook case. Fred saw it rising in silhouette against the roof, and, for a heartbeat, he lost it in the lights . . . then it was back. He hadn't broken stride. He knew he'd left Cook well behind. Fred caught the pass with both hands more than fifty yards downfield and with four long strides was in the end zone, the feeling of déjà vu complete.

South Street Fred was becoming a star.

"If there's one thing I've always said this Eagles offense doesn't do enough of, it's get the ball deep to Fred Barnett," cheered Madden (the lovable, exuberant former Raiders coach is so respected, he has more power than anyone except head coaches to make or break careers, and he's loved Fred since the first time he saw him play three years ago). "He just does that with his speed. Toi Cook just doesn't have the speed to cover Barnett man to man."

But that perfect moment was all the Eagles' offense could muster in the first half, and the defense—the great defense—was struggling badly. It was always that way. For weeks they'd be impregnable, then abruptly turn doormat. The spirit came and the spirit went. It drove the club's defensive guru, that white-haired, chain-smoking fussbudget Bud Carson, to madness. Players and coaches saw the game differently. To players, the game was a physical battle, where the team with the most strength, speed, and agility conquered. To a coach, especially to a wizened pro like Bud, whose "Steel Curtain" Pittsburgh defenses back in the seventies were legendary, the game was a mental contest. On every play, eleven men tried to quickly execute a complex action while eleven other men tried hard to stop them. Every time, players on both sides of the ball screwed up—that was a given. The team that made the fewest mistakes won; that was football from the Coach's-Eye View. Coaches entered a game with the whole thing scripted, a cunningly crafted rout, then the players went out and fucked it up.

So the first half of the Saints' play-off game, from the Eagles' Coach's-Eye View, was a string of little mistakes that eventually added up to two touchdowns and a field goal. The coaches had McMillian's rookie mistakes and Reggie's all-pro mistake to allow the first score. Then Eric Allen, another all-pro, failed unaccountably to stay with receiver Quinn Early, who caught a twenty-yard pass and set up a field goal. Lastly, New Orleans's rookie running back Vaughn Dunbar, their prized first-round pick, had broken free to run the ball deep in plus territory again. Dunbar's-eye view: a brilliant effort by an up-and-coming NFL superstar. Eagles' Coach's-Eye View? Miano let himself get out of position by coming too close to the line of scrimmage and getting walled off by blockers, and then Booty made a pitiful attempt at an arm tackle. John Madden, the old coach, saw it clearly; he might as well have taken the words right out of Bud's mouth: "I tell you," Madden said, "that's where they [the Eagles] miss Andre Waters and Wes Hopkins. Watch when he [Dunbar] breaks through here." Then as the run was replayed in slow motion, Madden noted, "Booty is going to come up and he's going to have a shot"—Booty lunged at Dunbar's legs, arms outstretched—"right there! And he misses the tackle. Hey, if that was Wes Hopkins, that's the end of the run."

In other words, Bud had his players in the right positions; they just failed to make the play. It was like some perverse variation on chess, where outcomes were always uncertain; sometimes knight took pawn, sometimes pawn took knight.

Two plays later, Hebert completed a short pass to Early in the end zone—C-E-V? Eric Allen, instead of playing the receiver wide outside, taking away the corner, was caught underneath, giving Early an open corner for the fade—and the Saints finished the half ahead by ten points in what was supposed to be a defensive battle.

In other words, the Eagles look sunk.

ON THE OFFENSE'S side of the room, Ron Heller isn't feeling darkly sentimental or frustrated. He's feeling good. For weeks he had worried (Ron's a worrier) about facing the Saints' Pro Bowl linebacker Pat Swilling inside the Dome. It wasn't Swilling's excellence alone that concerned the Eagles' left tackle; it was the Dome. More particularly, it was the noise inside the Dome. Ron is obsessive about noise. A full excited house inside a domed stadium means a noise level at which safety engineers would mandate earplugs. But Ron hadn't been worried about his ears; he'd been worried about his pride.

The football team isn't family to Ronald Ramon Heller. He grew up in the lap of a big, loving suburban family on the west end of Long Island. His dad is an executive with the New York Telephone Company. To Heller, football is a chosen career. After nine years as an NFL starter, Ron is making more than $600,000 annually, and while he's not one of the league's big-name stars (few offensive linemen are), he prides himself on being a solid pro, not just one of these mammoth wide-bodies recruited because they're nearly impossible to knock over, but an athlete. He likes to think of his size as a kind of genetic accident, something incidental to his athletic success. He feels insulted when somebody walks up to him and, surveying his Goliath proportions, remarks, "Dang, if you don't play football, it's a waste!" Despite his size, Heller is built like an acrobat, and he works hard year-round to stay in perfect shape. He has a weight and conditioning room built onto his tract mansion down in Tampa and works with trainers and therapists in the off-season to keep his muscular thirty-one-year-old body trim and flexible. He studies things like footwork and blocking techniques the same way an attorney might study a fine point of patent law. Ron is a highly precise individual. His house, his boat, his car, his clothes, his hair—hell, even his wife—they're all like scenes on a cheerful postcard. Out on the football field, where things get messy, Ron always looks perfect. His shirttail never flops; his uniform socks never droop. He wears these triple-wide shoulder pads that, unlike the lumpy armor worn by most linemen, are smooth and symmetrical, flaring to a crisp outer rim over each shoulder that accentuates Ron's broad-shouldered, narrow-waisted frame. He has this way of standing perfectly erect with his feet close together, kind of delicatelike, that can make him look almost prissy out there—truth is, Heller is a bit of a priss.

He plays best when fired with indignation, when convinced that his opponent is playing dirty, and works himself into that state of mind, consciously or not, in almost every game. His teammates know him well enough to help out, pointing out plays in the week before the game, when the line reviews an opponent's game films, noting late hits or cut blocks—"Did you see what that bastard did, Ron?" Not that he needs help. He would find something, seizing upon some small transgression of the man he would be blocking, and start to grumble: "That sonofabitch, I'm gonna kill him!"

Ron is always railing against opponents who refuse *to play by the rules!* After one game against Pittsburgh, Ron pursued Steelers defensive line coach Joe Greene (the famous "Mean" Joe Greene) off the field with his complaints, telling Greene in his earnest way, "I had a lot of respect for you, Joe, as a professional and Hall of Famer, but it's a disgrace the way you're teaching these guys how to cut people from behind and take cheap shots and try to hurt people!"

"I'll talk to my guys," said Greene, somewhat taken aback.

"We're all professionals out here . . . your guys don't have any respect!" Ron raged.

"I'll watch the film," promised Greene apologetically.

Persnickety Ron once even ran over to the sidelines in a red-faced rage during a Dallas Cowboys game (a linebacker had poked him in the eye) and, to what must have been the everlasting amusement of the Cowboys, pointed an accusing finger at coach Jimmy Johnson and bellowed "You should be ashamed of yourself!"—*so there!*

This finer edge to Ron's personality aside, he is a hardened, proven veteran, a man's man. There isn't a fire-breather in the league he can't block, he knows, except—and this is what haunts him . . . except when *he can't hear.*

See, Ron has this nightmare. It is late in the '90 season. The Eagles are playing the Buffalo Bills up in frigid Rich Stadium on a gorgeous December afternoon. The stands, of course, are jammed with screaming Bills fans. Crowds in Buffalo don't need a dome to reach the upper-decibel range, the subarctic air condenses the roar and pools it in the stadium bowl like noise soup, a sustained viscous roar. Out on the field you have to read lips to hear the quarterback call plays. Hearing the snap count is impossible at Ron's spot on the end of the line, where Bruce Smith, one of the quickest and strongest pass-rushing grizzlies in the game, is grinning at him with steam rising through the grille of his face mask. Ron has his feet planted wide, he's bent at the waist, and he's got his arms up; in other words, he's in perfect (we're talking *perfect* here) form to maintain balance while absorbing Smith's initial full-body ram, retreat, and then fend him off. No way Bruce Smith is going to get around Ron Heller, except poor Ron has to look back over his shoulder to see when the ball is snapped. Smith, who doesn't have that disadvantage, is getting this huge jump on every play!

"Look, Randall, I can't hear you out there," Ron complains to the quarterback on the sidelines after the first series.

"I'm using my soft voice," Cunningham says.

"You're using your *soft voice?!*"

"I had this teacher once, and he said that if you want people to really hear you, you should speak softly, because that forces them to listen harder."

"Randall, you don't understand. I'm concentrating. My problem is I can't fucking *hear* you! You've got to be loud."

"Don't worry about it, man," says Randall, seeing that Ron is getting a little worked up about this and all. "If he beats you around that corner I'll"—here he kicks up his knees and swivels his hips— "just scoot up in there."

Terrific. Back out in the noise soup, play after play after play, Smith is just blowing right around him. Ron is being made to look foolish. Then midway through the game—this is the worst—Buddy Ryan yanks him. Benches him! This has never happened to Ron before. The fair-haired wonderchild of Farmingdale High—yanked! Co-captain of the mighty '82 Penn State national champion Nittany Lions—benched! Butt kicked! Do you think it matters a bit to Ron that his replacement, unassuming journeyman Daryle Smith, gets windburns from Smith blowing past him, too, all through the second half? Ron is sitting on the bench in a purple funk. He hopes the goddamn Eagles lose at this point. He's gonna quit this fucking game. He can't figure it out. Sure, Smith was getting a jump, but Ron's always been able to cope at least somewhat with that. It turns out later, when they view the fiasco again on videotape, that not only was Ron at a disadvantage because he had to turn his head, but ol' Soft Voice was unknowingly *hitching his knee* shortly before each snap. They rewind the tape and watch again and again—sure enough! Randall is giving the snap away. Ron didn't have a chance.

Okay, but tell that to the whatever million CBS regional viewers who watched throughout the northeastern United States (including Farmingdale, New York). Tell that to Philadelphia's know-it-all sports writers and columnists, paid sadists, who scour the wreckage of every Eagles loss for scapegoats and mount their heads on pikes. Ron, ordinarily the picture of poise and master of well-reasoned postgame analysis (he's done TV work down in Tampa), loses it postgame when some unfortunate wire-service grind has the temerity to suggest that *just maybe* Ron's not playing in the second half had something to do with the *great day* that Bruce Smith seemed to be having . . . and what did he think about it? Naked, huge, and still flushed bright pink from the cold and the postgame shower, Heller lights into the wretch—*What the fuck do you know, you pussy, about blocking Bruce Smith?* and *Why don't you just come right out and ask what you want to ask?* and such. The noise explanation, and even the knee-hitch, won't do him any good. Sure, Ron, right. We hear you. Tell that to the ignorant gabfest harpies who play host on Philly's sports-talk radio station, the aptly named WIP, who flog the town's pro athletes (particularly the Eagles) twenty-four hours a day, twelve months a year, with razor Lilliputian lashes. Tell that, fer Chrissakes, to Buddy, who can spot the sorry-ass excuse of an offensive lineman below the rim of a West Texas horizon, and who knows damn well that it wasn't *his defense* that lost that lousy football game.

Oh, the injustice!

The humiliation!

The nightmare had, of course, been real, and Ron lives in fear of its happening again. It was the low point of his professional life. Ever since, he has been trying to make coaches take him seriously about noise. It is considered another of Ron's effete concerns. He'd tell Richie, "We've got to do something to prepare for the noise." The coach would just smile indulgently. "Yeah," he'd say. "We've got to *concentrate*." Ron would walk away muttering, "Concentrate, shit. If you can't hear, you can't hear."

Finally, this year, the Eagles had hired a new line coach named Bill Muir, who was eager to earn the trust and affection of his new charges, especially the veterans. Muir, bless his heart, listened. Together they had come up with a new system for the silent count that worked. They'd had a few problems with it against Dallas in Texas Stadium, but in the week before this play-off game Richie had asked the folks over at NFL Films to truck over some speakers and tape and broadcast crowd noise at high volume so they could perfect it during practice. Heller had been so happy it was all he could do to keep from kissing the coach. "Rich, this is the best thing you've ever done," he said. "When we win this game, you get the credit."

And it was working. They had three ways of doing it. There was
the helmet technique, by which, at some point after the line was down
and set, center Dave Alexander would lift up his head, and they all
would silently count to a prearranged number. There was the ball
technique, by which the silent count would begin the moment Dave
leaned over and put his hand on the ball. Then there was the touch
technique—Ron had come up with this one on his own and it was his
favorite. With the touch technique, nobody even had to look back
down the line at the center. The guard just reached over and touched
the tackle's hand, releasing the touch the moment the ball was snapped.
This, of course, left the Eagles' offensive line wide open to potential
leaguewide ridicule—*The Eagles? Ain't they the guys who hold hands?* But
they are using it today, and it is working! Swilling hasn't even been a
factor. Ron is as concerned as any of his teammates about the halftime
score, but more than anything he feels relief. We're talking career
breakthrough.

Unfortunately, that and the bomb to Fred are about the only
things that have worked.

Before the coaches come out of their halftime huddle in a side
room, Dave Alexander steps up to the blackboard. Dave is an amiable
country boy from Broken Arrow, Oklahoma, who loves to play football
and has settled with good-natured discipline into the essential but
glamourless role of snapping the ball. He's the kind of guy who apologizes to his coaches after making a mistake. "It was me, Coach," he'd
say. "I screwed up." This being something of a rare and remarkable
trait at the pro level, coaches were often taken aback. They'd even try
to coach Dave on how to make excuses for himself like everybody else.
They'd say, "Ah . . . well, Dave, the ball musta been all wet."

"No, the ball wasn't wet," Dave would insist. "It was my fault. I
screwed up."

He approaches the game with an honest, cheerful intensity, oblivious to the raging egos and turf wars around him. If he sees something
that needs doing, on the field or off, Dave steps up. That's what he
does now. All through the first half the offensive line has been having
trouble on passing downs. Randall has had two of his third-down
passes batted back at him, and blitzing linebackers have been chasing
him all over. The problem has been handling the Saints' nickel coverage (a five-defensive-back formation). Dave doesn't wait for Bill Muir
to emerge from the coaches' meeting.

"Here's what they've been doing," he says, drawing X's and O's
in chalk. "This is how we're going to block it."

With the diagram, he clearly redefines their blocking assignments.
In nickel, the Saints are positioning their defensive front with rushers

over both guards and tackles and letting their linebackers roam, prob-
ing for a vulnerable spot. The Eagles' blocking schemes are designed
to send the line pushing together either right or left, with the running
back stepping up to plug any gaps. Only, with backers poaching from
a variety of directions, the running backs had started just keying on
them individually, instead of covering the unprotected gaps. Swilling,
when he avoided Ron and rushed from the middle, had been particularly troublesome.

Dave tells running back Heath Sherman, "Look, wherever Swilling's at, the offensive line will be responsible for him. If we've got a
right call, and he's on the left, we'll block Swilling; you just stay with
your regular assignment."

When Muir comes out of the meeting, he walks up to the board
and nods.

"Yeah, that's what we've got to do," he says. "Who drew this?"

The other linemen start nudging the center and teasing, "Coach
Dave! Coach Dave!"

Apart from Ron and Dave, and Randall, Fred, and Calvin, the
only other vested member of what might be called this team's inner
circle on offense is the long-suffering Keith Byars. A devoutly religious, very proper young man, Byars is about four times thicker in
every department than an ordinary human being. Keith's original
nickname with the Eagles was "Sweet Sixteen," because that's what size
shoe he wears, but when Keith didn't laugh along they dropped it.
The former Ohio State star approved, however, of the nickname
"Tank," which is what Richie calls him. It is an apt description of what
his 240 pounds looks like tearing downfield with the ball.

The problem today, as far as Keith sees it, is no different than
the problem most weekends—that is, getting him the football. This
has been the sad theme of Keith's six-year career with the Eagles, and
it got worse this season. When the Eagles' star tight end Keith Jackson
first sat out for eight weeks and then skipped Philadelphia for Miami
in October, Byars, a running back (got that, *a running back*) was pressed
into service on the line. He gets the ball less and less. In the first half
of this game he has one catch—one catch!—for just six yards. Not
that he hasn't been open, mind you. Poor Keith has been out there
jumping up and down, waving his hands over his head, shouting
"Woooo! Woooo!" (which is his way of trying to capture Randall's
attention) all afternoon. One of the things coaches will complain to
Randall about during this halftime is getting the ball to the tight end—
which Randall already knows because Byars has been pleading with
him on the bench for most of the first two quarters. It's just so frustrating for Keith. It isn't all ego either (although it is partly ego). Keith

really believes in himself. He really believes the single best thing this offense could do to get moving is *give him the ball!* Hadn't these guys watched the tapes of what he had done in his glory days at Ohio State? Back when Buddy was coach he had gotten over his disappointment at not being used as the classic tailback he was, instead being moved around the backfield to block on one play, catch a pass on another, carry the ball on another, even though this multiple role had deprived him of the stats he needed in any one spot to win leaguewide recognition. Pro Bowl slots were voted by position. What was he, a tight end? A fullback? A receiver? Byars has long since given up caring how the Eagles use him, so long as they give him the ball. They could dropkick it to him from the Goodyear blimp for all he cared. It seemed so obvious to him. Why couldn't everyone see it? All through the off-season the hue and cry of the so-called experts had been "The Eagles need a running back!" Kotite goes out and drafts *two* this year, using his top pick and a fourth-round spot. What was Keith Byars, wet toast? Runner-up for the Heisman Trophy in '84, second-leading rusher in Ohio State history, first-round draft pick, average of more than one thousand yards gained running and receiving over the four previous seasons? Then the Eagles went and shelled out $1.45 million (a half million more than they were paying Keith) to obtain Herschel Walker, who in '91 had averaged 4.2 yards per carry—Keith had averaged 4.1. Didn't anybody notice these things?

All this weighs on Keith's extrathick brow. His scruples won't allow him to complain—at least not a lot. He has become, in consequence, a brooder. Disappointment envelops Keith Byars like a damp aura.

Herschel, on the other hand, has already had about all the glory and acclaim a body can stand. He has seen the upside and the downside of fame, from the Heisman Trophy to the cover of *Sports Illustrated* to the news stories in Minnesota of his supposed suicide attempt—when all he'd done was fall asleep in the garage listening to music in his car. Most recently he's been making headlines as the marquee member of the U.S. Olympic bobsledding team. Herschel is happy just to be here, playing football. After his troubled sojourn with the Vikings, the Eagles have assumed his mega-salary for a few more seasons, and Herschel is grateful. He isn't looking for glory; he just wants to fit in. He even volunteers to play on special teams. In the first half he's caught one pass (for a one-yard gain) and carried the ball once (for two yards), but he's not complaining.

Alongside Herschel sits Teen Wolf, or just Wolfie, as teammates call Heath Sherman, a taciturn bowlegged little Texan who has become, despite Tank and Herschel and those draft picks, despite all the ambitious plans of owner and coach, the team's premier back in the last half of this season. Heath is the man who runs falling down. He can start falling at the line of scrimmage and not hit the ground until he's thirty yards upfield. With this peculiar, lunging style, Sherman looks like a quadruped cradling the ball with one limb. Until this season, his style worked against him. Head down, he kept running up the backside of his own blockers. But last summer running backs coach Richard Woods suggested a remarkable adjustment—*Son, you need to watch where you're going*—and voilà! Heath was dangerous. He started averaging more than five yards per carry and had broken free for five long touchdown runs in the last half of the year. His teammates had started the wolf nicknames because Heath has a low hairline and a beard that tends to creep up his cheeks toward his eyes, but "Wolfie" partly stuck because of his hungry, four-legged running style. Heath has yet to really cut loose in this game. He's carried the ball six times for just twenty-three yards.

There is one other true insider on the offensive side of the room, but he is a special case. Seated before his locker in pristine uniform is Jim McMahon, the pop cult hero who led the '85 Chicago Bears to football's pinnacle, who still advertises his maverick attitude with punk hairdo, earring, and wraparound shades. Only now, six years on, the look and, to a certain extent, the punk quarterback himself, are anachronisms. With scars scribbled all over his pale frame and braces on both knees, eleven years into his pro football career, Jimbo has become a low-profile locker-room-loving rat, the kind of player who can't wait for training camp every summer. He and his wife have four growing children. The lucrative endorsements, best-selling autobiography, and constant train of media attention are history, but Jimbo is still living and loving the football life, decking his corner space in the Eagles' locker room with crude porn and comical newspaper and magazine cutouts lampooning his coaches and teammates (usually with his own additions in the form of drawn-in appendages or dialogue). Champion of the team's '91 bowling league, ever-ready drinking companion, dead-on domino player, Jimbo doesn't just fit in with whatever football team he joins, he becomes the hub of its wheel. And don't think Randall doesn't notice. After Randall went down in '91, Jimbo had battled his own body through eleven starts, winning eight, including a come-from-behind masterpiece against the Cleveland Browns (341 yards and three touchdowns) despite being so hobbled that he literally had to be carried up the dugout steps to the field at Cleveland Stadium. There are a lot of people in the locker room (Jimbo most of all) who feel he should be playing quarterback in the second half.

One player with no opinion in the matter is Antone Davis, the team's anchor-ass right tackle and Richie's boldest coaching experiment. With Antone's worries, he can't afford to concern himself with anyone else.

Richie, desperate to upgrade his offensive line in '91 just months after taking over as head coach, used both that year's and the following year's number-one choices (he traded his '92 number one to Green Bay to move up in the pickings) to snare Antone—who was promptly christened the Megapick. The ever-gracious Buddy Ryan, who had been silent since his firing three months earlier, wrote a guest article for the *New York Times* that (surprise!) awarded Richie and the Eagles the booby prize for making the "biggest mistake" of that year's draft. Antone hadn't done a lot yet to prove Buddy wrong. He was six-four and weighed in at well over 325 pounds, most of it spread liberally around his upper backside. He had helped make Tennessee's offensive line the most overpowering blocking front in college football in '89 and '90, and on paper and in the highlights film he looked like that rarest of football finds: a natural offensive lineman.

But the pros were a different story. Thrown right into the starting lineup, weighted down with franchise-sized expectations, the poor southern Georgia homeboy with the plaintive, quiet voice had gone through one of the most righteous, sixteen-game public stompings in NFL history. This season had only been slightly better. Antone looked and talked like a man desperate to be anywhere but on a football field, but his enormous size, potential, and paycheck ($1.09 million this year) had him trapped. He had adopted, in self-defense, a surly, diffident attitude toward the game, which infuriated his teammates (not the surliness, the diffidence). But he was improving. In this game, so far, he has only screwed up twice.

The white guys on the offensive line—Ron, Dave, Mike Schad, and backups Brian Baldinger, Daryle Smith, John Hudson, and Rob Selby—gave some of the credit for Antone's slow improvement to new line coach Muir and also to Antone's buddy Eric "Pink" Floyd, the flabby but immovable right guard the Eagles had picked up off the waiver wire that summer. His nickname, of course, came from the pop-music group, but it fit Eric in another way. There was a self-deprecatory sweetness about Pink that was unusual among football players. Eric encouraged the nickname; his huge knee brace was painted that color. Pink wasn't quite as big as Antone, but he dwarfed him in personality. Out on the field he was hilarious. It took every ounce of energy Pink possessed to play a football game, and he whined comically from kickoff to final whistle. This talent for turning reluctance into laughter (instead of scorn) helped Pink hit it off with Antone immediately. That, and being the only black guys on the offensive line. They had a lot in common. They were both from rural Georgia, and in a way, because of their size, both were captives of the game.

Between these offensive players and the defense's side of the room there might as well have been a wall. Buddy had built this team to win with defense, and they remained loyal to his memory and ways. Reggie, Seth, Wes, Andre, Eric Allen, Clyde Simmons, the injured Ben Smith, Byron Evans, Mike Pitts, Mike Golic—these were the black-shoed wonders of the promised dynasty. Richie and Bud Carson had plugged a few holes, but the essence of Buddy's Boys remained. To these players, Richie would always just be Buddy's offensive coordinator (an inherently inferior post), an interloper—and a weak one at that.

Nurtured on the old man's audacious paranoia, they suspected that in Richie's heart of hearts he would really like to dismantle them, good as they were, just to purge Buddy's memory and remake the team in his and the owner's own image, an offense-driven squad with a polite, serviceable defense that would be a credit to corporate white America. Of course, they knew that sort of team would never win. A particularly terrible fate would be to finish out your career stranded on the roster of this bland vision, so everyone knew that with Reggie's departure at the end of this season there was going to be a bottleneck of defensive players all trying to squeeze through at once—*maybe Buddy would land another job!*

But that wouldn't start until this season ended. And this season has come down to this last half game. On this day, Buddy's Boys have themselves to blame for the ten-point hole. They are playing one of the league's weakest offenses, and, so far, they've been—as Buddy would put it—leaning back and spreading their legs.

Seth glowers on his side of Jerome's locker. The linebacker is fired by an inner anger that no one—not his mother, his wife, his teammates, his agent, his girlfriend—can fathom. Seth has an oddly shaped frame: long, thickly muscled arms and a torso built up by weight lifting, balanced on legs so thin he looks like a man who has taken only half the Charles Atlas course. On these overburdened pins Seth combines speed with strength, being one of the few linebackers left in the league who plays full-time defense, on both running and passing downs. He is obsessive about preparations for a football game and has a reputation for rarely, if ever, making a mental mistake, which lends a certain moral authority to his intolerance. Seth has tried to be even more this season—vocal team leader, a role for which he is distinctly ill suited. He wants to play Jerome's old role, but whereas Jerome was beloved, Seth is merely tolerated. In the halftime locker room or on the practice field, where Jerome's flamboyant outbursts made people laugh, Seth's angry eruptions breed resentment. His personality is a cudgel.

Seth doesn't see it. He is hurt by the way his efforts are received. All season he has struggled. And for what? To lose another lousy first-round play-off game? Now their season is dangling precariously, and whose fault is that? Seth hasn't been screwing up in the first half. He sits brooding silently before his locker with a white towel draped over his head, trying to infect the room with angry purpose.

At the next locker, shaved head shining like a wet black stone, is the team's long-armed, unsung middle linebacker and field captain, the amiable and always dapper Byron Evans. Byron is the silent man in the Eagles' outspoken locker room. Not silent in the surly, self-important way of so many prima-donna athletes, but out of some careful inner calibration. Despite his literary name and his college English degree, Byron is simply and resolutely disposed not to speak. He understands better than any of his fellows that in the arena, action is all. Words? Words could only get you in trouble—he had his pal Seth as clear proof of that. One senses that Byron's preferred forum for playing football would be his own field of dreams, a neatly lined patch of well-tended grass 360 feet long and 160 feet wide with goal-posts at either end, laid out somewhere in the desert outside his Phoenix hometown, far from fans, TV cameras, dirigibles, and the pestilent press, where two teams could battle for preeminence before Joshua trees, towering cacti, and the silent watchful eye of God. Byron is fully in the moment, impervious to mood, undaunted by odds, open to opportunity. Thirty minutes left to play? *All right!* He taps his feet (Byron's a terrific dancer), bobs his head, and bides his time until the whistle blows again and he can say whatever it is he has to say.

Clyde is another quiet one. The Eagles' *other* Pro Bowl defensive end has grown up in the league playing on the same line with Jerome and Reggie, so he's learned to go through the season like an extra on a crowded stage. It took the league about two seasons longer than it should have to notice that humble Clyde, a lowly ninth-round draft pick out of Western Carolina University, was making as many or more tackles and sacks than the superstar on the other side of the line. Clyde doesn't seem to mind much. He has a kind of sidekick nature. In training camp he was Jerome's shadow. They roomed together and were so inseparable that teammates made snickering jokes about them.

Jerome, of course, played this to the hilt. Once, as Clyde was leaving the field with a slight injury to his hand during one of Buddy's brutal live-action drills, Jerome hopped up from the pile and, before players and coaches and the press and two thousand spectators gathered on the green slope alongside the field, bellowed, "That does it! Now you made me mad! You hurt ma bitch!"

Mike Pitts and Mike Golic make up the last two increments of the original Gang Green front line—Buddy's famous 46 defense utilized four-down linemen, but he rotated Jerome and the two Mikes in regular shifts to keep the middle fresh, so the Eagles' front four had always really been five. Pitts is a mild, sweet-natured veteran who has been battling creaking knees and a bad back for several years. Golic, whose older brother Bob is a perennial all-pro with the Raiders, is one of the team's most comical players, a garrulous charmer. Being the only white guy on the D-line, Golic has anointed himself an Honorary Black Guy, when he isn't introducing himself as "Bob's better-looking baby brother, the one Mom and Dad liked best." Golic's very sane perspective on the game, coupled with his self-deprecatory wit, have made him a popular TV personality in Philadelphia, which doesn't always sit well with his coaches and teammates.

Eric Allen, the team's smooth, urbane young Pro Bowl cornerback, has been burned for two touchdowns in this game. But you'd never know it. Nothing stirs the smooth surface of Eric's confidence. His consistent excellence and careful preparation for games is legendary, and he is a big favorite with his coaches.

Bud Carson and his assistant, backfield coach Peter Guinta, use a blackboard to illustrate first-half mistakes, offering correction without stressing blame. The last touchdown pass, for instance, the one for which Eric had been too far inside the receiver to prevent the floating pass to the end-zone corner: "That was our mistake," says Guinta. "We put you in a bad spot, Eric. From now on, in the plus-fifteen, play smash corner," a coverage that keeps the cornerback deeper, allowing a clearer view of the play and an opportunity to drive toward a thrown ball, perhaps even intercept. The coaches don't dwell on Eric's other mistake, getting beat down the left sideline by Early. "Hebert made a good throw" is Guinta's gentle analysis. He also points out that free safety John Booty could have been in better position to help Eric deep.

Not that Eric needs to be coddled. From the first day of training camp five years ago, when he arrived as the Eagles' number-two draft pick, the kid from San Diego has had a dream career. He has Hollywood-idol good looks, dreamy amber eyes, and when cameras and microphones approach, he shines. Eric has a degree in broadcasting from Arizona State, and everyone expects he will segue smoothly from the field to the broadcast booth when his playing days are done. A student of the game, Eric has the perfect temperament for cornerback, a lonely position where mistakes are highly visible and very often punishable by touchdown. With two trips to the Pro Bowl and a third pending, Eric can afford the ease with which he acknowledges his mistakes.

"Yeah," he'll say, with a disarming smile. "I let myself get out of position. . . ." as if to say, *It happens to the best of us*, which, of course, it just did.

Not so Mark McMillian, whose back-to-back blunders set up the Saints' opening touchdown drive and got the whole game off on the wrong foot. When you're that much smaller than the other guys, and you're a rookie, you have to play *better* than Eric to earn respect. But Mark's buoyant confidence seems impervious to assault. He receives the halftime analysis ardently and resolves to redeem himself in the second half.

Bud assures this bunch that despite the ten-point deficit, they are not overmatched. The Saints have sprung no surprises.

"Execute," the white-haired professor tells his frustrated students for the ten millionth time.

Then Andre stands up.

Wes and Andre are the center backfield of Buddy's Boys, and both are in street clothes for this game. Hopkins, the senior member of the Eagles and one of its most storied veterans, injured his knee in the second game of the season and has been sorely missed ever since. Waters is the team's on-field mascot, a fiery, undersized, intensely superstitious veteran who plays in an almost trancelike state. He had broken his ankle in Washington during the sixth game of the season, and while he writhed in the hospital fighting a painful infection that set in after surgery, he had read of the Cowboys' running back Emmitt Smith, who told reporters, in so many words, that Andre deserved whatever ill fate befell him. The prospect of meeting this mean-spirited man again in the play-offs, this man who had applauded Andre's pain, had spurred the hotheaded safety through much of the drudgery of healing and therapy.

"You can't do this to me!" Andre now shouts at his teammates. "You can't deprive me of the chance to meet Emmitt Smith!"

The Eagles know that a victory over the Saints today will mean a showdown in Dallas the following Sunday in the second round for a crack at the NFC Championship the following weekend, and then the Super Bowl.

"You can't lose this football game!" Andre pleads. "I've worked so hard."

Speaking in his thick South Florida accent, getting worked up to a full-throated rant, Andre is off on a verbal tear, invoking Jerome, the pain and hardship he had suffered recovering from his broken ankle, fealty to Buddy, what that Emmitt Smith said, how they all knew they could beat New Orleans *and* Dallas, for that matter, and, besides, nobody *deserved* to get injured, and even though he was a Christian and didn't hold a grudge against anybody, far from it, and how piss-poor the New Orleans offense was and how good they could play if they just all got on the same page and how . . . how . . . they owed it to *him*, dammit, if they didn't owe it to themselves . . . all they had been through together . . . and the greater glory of Jesus . . . and . . . can you believe that that Emmitt Smith would say those things?

In general, it's a first-rate, righteous oration, even if it wanders a bit. Some of the guys have a hard time following Andre's eccentric Everglades inflections.

"What's he saying?" a rookie leans over and asks Golic.

"Wants us to win," Golic whispers back.

Compressed into the dank confines of the Superdome locker room, with just twelve minutes to recoup and regroup, they are a colorful mosaic. They come from all over America and beyond—Mike Schad from Canada, return man Vai Sikahema from the Pacific island of Tonga, Andre from tiny Pahokee, Florida—players from upscale suburban childhoods and players who grew up in the mud-stained shacks that pass for public housing in the Deep South. There are perfectionists and wild men, quiet achievers and grand egotists. Fifty young men whose goals and skills have coalesced into this team, this moment, this last chance at . . . the Next Level.

They half listen to Richie's familiar exhortations—*This team has no business being up on us! We've got to take care of the ball. The Bills came back from 35–3; we're down two scores. Let's not go out of this thing by a long shot . . . execute . . . eliminate mental errors!* —waiting for the whistle and for the contest to resume.

Nobody feels the weight of this moment like Reverend Reggie.

He's haunted by more than the ghost of his friend Jerome, who, frankly, they could really use right now in the flesh. Reggie is plunked down heavily on one side of the JeromeShrine. He had learned of his friend's death just minutes before he was scheduled to address a throng at Veterans Stadium as part of evangelist Billy Graham's Christian crusade. He had gone out and delivered an emotional sermon, and afterward, just hours after his teammate's car had crashed, the big defensive end made what he now sees as a mistake: he had tearfully vowed to reporters and fans that this coming season the Eagles were going to win it all for Jerome.

The emotion of that commitment had carried them, Reggie figures, for about four games, and petered out.

Reggie himself had opened the door for the Saints' first touchdown. But he isn't one to dwell on a mistake—*Praise Jesus and watch yer ass on the next play!* What with the intensity of the competition, the ever-present opportunity for serious injury, and the authoritarian grip of coaches, it is the rarest of football players who manages to achieve a strong sense of security about his talent and career. Reggie is one. He and everyone else knows that no matter what the outcome of this game, or season, or the fate of this team, there is going to be a bronze bust of that low forehead, broad neck, goatee, and wide grin on prominent display in Canton.

Reggie is a man of wide-ranging and complex ambition. His dimensions spill outside the frame of football. In ways that his coaches and teammates can hardly imagine, Reggie has already laid the foundation, with his ideas and his millions, for an important and controversial public career beyond football, while at the same time his formidable will and conscience are still profoundly reshaping the NFL. He is the man the NFL Players Association sought out in November to be the lead plaintiff in their lawsuit against the owners, the one that struck down the league's antiquated and unfair restrictions on free agency. In the past, pro football players had been bound by a clearly iniquitous club owners' agreement that effectively shackled them (Reggie always uses slave terminology when he talks about it) to one team—usually the team that drafted them out of college. A player could withhold his talents, he could refuse to sign a contract and sit at home Sundays and watch his buddies bang heads, but if he wanted to use his skills and prove himself on the football field, in other words, if he wanted to have a career, he ultimately had to settle for what the club that owned him was offering. Reggie's lawsuit, joined by hundreds of other NFL stars, had shattered that comfy club arrangement. And the first big-name player to take advantage of the new freedom after this season would be Reggie himself (Keith Jackson had sneaked out a back window to Miami; Reggie was going to drive right through the front gate). Come the end of this season, the Minister of Defense is going to take the definition of "overpaid athlete" to a whole new realm.

But first there is this unfinished business of the Eagles and all those championship rings. For eight seasons, Reggie has been the bedrock of this team. And he has played brilliantly, season after all-pro season. He has thoroughly embraced Buddy's notion of Team. He has developed pastoral feelings for his teammates, whom he tries to lead by quiet example rather than by sermonizing. He watches their petty adulteries and drinking and wild bachelor ways patiently (he, too, had strayed once or twice from the path), confident that Jesus will bring them around. He leads Bible-study classes that attract dozens every Thursday night, players, wives, girlfriends, ex-wives, ex-girlfriends, friends of friends of friends, the circle ever widening. He believes that Jerome's life was snatched away by Satan, because he knew that converting Jerome—he had been *so* close—would have been the key to connecting with Seth and Clyde and Wes and Eric and the rest.

Through all this, his teammates tease him unmercifully.

Ol' Freight Train was the worst. "Reggie, you so full o' *sheee-it!*" Jerome would say.

After a hard-fought victory, Jerome would taunt his locker mate at the top of his voice, "Whatja gonna do to celebrate, Reggie? Go to church?"

Reggie, stooped, removing the tape from his ankles, would ignore him solemnly.

"Come on, Reggie! Tell us!"

"Going home to my wife and kids," Reggie would say.

Long silence, as Jerome waited. "Aren't you gonna ask me what *I'm* gonna do?"

"What are you gonna do, Jerome?"

At the top of his lungs: "Reggie, I'm gonna get me the best blow job of my *whooole* life!"

 Reggie would roll with this stuff. They sometimes call him the Elephant Man, because he seems so much bigger than life, and Reggie just grins and shrugs. On this team he is not just respected, he's loved.

Now, with thirty minutes left to keep the thing alive, it is hard for Reggie not to get emotional. He is the one who constantly reminds his teammates: *This is it! No more next times!* Looking around the locker room now, he doesn't feel this is an ending. Despite the ten points, despite all the mistakes they made in the first half, he smells a win.

But he says nothing. His own thoughts are heavy, and he is wary now of emotion. *To win now,* he thinks, *we need to be hopeful and filled with joy. We need to* bring the heat.

When Reggie sees the official step in and wave the team back out to the field, he stands up and shouts, "Let's go do it!"

ORDINARILY, Norman doesn't like to sit in the owners' box. Even though he and his wife, Irma, usually invite family and friends to the Vet for home games, and he enjoys entertaining before and after, during the game he sits off in a separate box, alone with team president Harry Gamble. There, playing with one of his big cigars, away from prying ears, he feels free to emote like the ordinary fan he is at heart.

Old-guard NFL owners are football men through and through. Most of the new owners are successful businessmen who bought teams as an investment. Norman is a little of both. There's no doubt the Eagles are a terrific investment, but to a greater extent than most of the other newcomers, Norman bought his team for fun, as part of his philosophy of enjoying his wealth. He may just be the first true fan-owner.

Imagine it. He's like the diehard season-ticket holder who, after years of screaming advice at the field and listening to sports-talk radio and poring over newspapers, suddenly has *control*. Partly, of course, Norman knows he's a dilettante, and that, for the good of his own investment, he ought to defer to the pros around him. But in his seven years of ownership, Norman has grown increasingly confident of his football judgment. Some might say dangerously confident. This new confidence, mixed with his natural volatility, can make him insufferable. Irma doesn't like having him around during the game, which is why he secrets himself with Harry, who, while he's too anxious even to eat on game days, is a study in professional cool alongside his boss.

"Why the hell is he doing that?" Norman will ask.

"Why aren't they throwing the ball?"

"Who screwed that up?"

"Why aren't they giving Herschel the ball?"

Harry knows which questions to answer and which to ignore. Who knows how many coaches and players would have been fired over the last seven years without his steadying presence?

But for this game in the Superdome, Norman is stuck in the box with Irma, family, and friends. His daughters and his Palm Beach buddy Irwin Levy are here, as are Jerome's parents, Willie and Annie Bell, flown in from Brooksville as the team's honored guests. So Norman is showing restraint, though he's been at Harry's side the whole first half, pouring a string of urgent complaint into the team president's ear.

As the Eagles fall behind, and Norman's commentary turns increasingly severe, Harry's distress is evident. A gray pallor begins to show beneath the faded freckles on his wide face. During halftime, Harry has to take a break. He paces the carpeted hall outside the owners' box. When he comes back in for the second half, as his players trot out to the field, he sees the boss has moved. Norman is now perched on a stool a few rows up, behind the front-row mezzanine where he had been sitting.

He waves Harry back down to the old seat.

Norman is going to ride out the second half alone.

3

BramanMan

ust give me five dollars of high test, please," says Norman Braman, who has pulled his new black Cadillac up to a gas station in Miami Beach.

It's a noisy stop set on a median between the northbound and southbound lanes of Route A1A, just about a mile in real terms but more like a light-year removed from Norman's home on Indian Creek Island, a lush, guarded tropical sanctuary set in the teal waters of Biscayne Bay.

"Just five dollars," he repeats to the attendant.

The tawny young man in oily T-shirt and jeans looks confused.

"Fieeev dollars?" he repeats—the accent sounds Cuban.

"Five dollars' worth, please," says Norman.

"Hokay."

But the young man remains standing by the open window. Norman bends forward gingerly, leaning his curly white head out the window.

"Want the money now?"

"No," the young man answers.

"Five dollars," Norman repeats, enunciating carefully.

The attendant nods and repeats, "Fieeev dollars."

Now Norman is getting irritated.

"What the . . ." He leans back out. "Plus! Plus!" he shouts.

He settles back into his seat, shaking his head. "That's Miami for you," he says, but before he can begin to lament unbridled immigration's role in eroding the quality of urban life the station attendant bends down to peer in.

"Thee tank," he says, gesturing back toward the locked flap over Norman's fuel tank.

"Open the tank?" asks Norman.

"Thee tank," repeats the young man eagerly, smiling. Cars are now backed up behind the Caddy. It's still morning rush hour.

"It's locked?" says Norman. "Oh, shit."

He's searching now, scanning the dash, bending over to inspect the levers under his seat. The man who has sold America so many cars, proud sovereign of a three-state empire of Braman Rolls-Royce, Braman BMW, Braman Mercedes, Braman Porsche, Braman Aùdi, Braman Maserati, Braman Mazda, Braman Acura, Braman Mitsubishi, Braman Honda, Braman Chrysler, and Braman Cadillac dealerships, is growing frantic, stranded, gasless, two miles from home, victim of an innocent antitheft device.

"Jesus Christ!" he says. "How do you open the goddamn tank?"

It's January 20, 1992, and Norman's tetchiness is forgivable. A little over a year ago he fired Buddy Ryan, and ever since it's been as if there were this (dare we say it?) . . . this *curse*. Buddy always swore he was lucky. It was part of his mystique—*Stick with me, kid, I'm goin' all the way*. If there was any hint of ethnicity about Buddy Ryan it was smothered under generations of Oklahoma barbecue, but somewhere deep inside that wide and weathered good ol' boy hide Buddy insisted there was a Celtic chromosome. It explained, he said, any whopping windfall of good fortune, like an interception in the fourth quarter of a close game, or an opponent's winning field goal try striking the upright and bouncing back on the field. Buddy believed his horses were winners and that fumbles tended to bounce his way. The flip side of that was, of course, you didn't want to go a-messin' with Buddy Ryan. That would be tempting the certain hand of some dark Druidic reckoning.

But Norman is not a superstitious man. You don't get rich two and three times over without tempting fate or by being easily intimidated. Just check out who Buddy was dealing with here.

His mansion on Indian Creek Island is the real-world equivalent of a luxury skybox; it's in Miami but not *of* Miami, separated from the noise and dirt and danger of city streets by a mile of the choppy Intracoastal Waterway, yet visually right smack in the center of it all, a bubble of sublime seclusion in the eye of the urban storm. At night the lights of the city rise up in the distance like Oz, glimmering on the tides. Most of the island is a private golf course, but it is rimmed by extravagant waterfront estates, each secluded behind high walls decked with exotic gardens—the Bramans' features a dozen varieties of palm, citrus trees, hibiscus, mango, avocado, banana, and even loquats and kiwis, tubs of gardenias, and scattered night-flowering cactus. Bay water laps against seawall on two sides of the property, and a polite fence separates it from the yard of a Saudi prince (with his small army of bodyguards). One lot over is the home of singer Julio Iglesias. Braman's two-acre patch of this modern Eden showcases his enviable modern art collection, which is spread out in and around the pool and private helipad. The house is an aggregation of massive rectangular modules cast in scored white concrete that literally sparkles—the stone is blended with crushed white Georgia marble. In '91, when Norman and Irma spent $4.5 million for this place, it was more than anyone had ever paid for a piece of property in South Florida, an act so ostentatious it took Madonna to top it. The house features cavernous, irregularly shaped rooms, a waterfall on the terrace, with sunlight flooding everything through window panels that reach twenty-eight feet to the ceiling, bathing in natural light the Bramans' spectacular display of paintings and sculpture.

It isn't your typical rich burgher's art collection either, a hodgepodge of expensive and unrelated acquisitions. Norman and Irma's collection mirrors their personalities and interests, combining whimsy and romance with, here and there, glimpses of a darker side. The most dominant pieces are Alexander Calder's playful mobiles, Claes Oldenburg's giant *Typewriter Eraser*, Red Grooms's gaudy 3-D assemblies, and George Segal's startlingly realistic life-sized human figures (which more than one houseguest has inadvertently greeted on entering), but there is also Jean Arp's graceful *Resting Leaf.* On the walls, the giant colorful comic-book panels of pop artist Roy Lichtenstein and the eccentric sketches of satirist Saul Steinberg share ample wall space with Willem de Kooning's classic *Bolton Landing*, Jasper Johns's arresting *Two Flags*, and his dreamy, sensuous *Diver* (for which the Bramans paid $4.18 million, the highest price ever for the work of a living artist). To this cheerful mix, Norman has recently introduced (as befits his position with the U.S. Holocaust Memorial Council) a typically discordant note, a haunting collection of works by German artist Anselm Keifer, whose brutal, explosive images on canvas and in sculpture and collage reflect the blasted legacy of Nazism and World War II. Of course, the primary theme uniting all these works is money. Norman and Irma are not out there stomping around obscure garrets and shops, buying the works of undiscovered artists. They choose what they like from within the relatively narrow range of the recognized— artists whose work has been anointed by the high priests of art criticism and, hence, carries a price tag that puts it well beyond the reach of any pedestrian buyer. The collection boasts both wealth and good taste, but wealth first. And the Bramans don't just own this stuff, they *live* with it. They surround themselves with these striking images—a visitor once spotted Oldenburg's six-foot-high soft sculpture *Good Hu-*

mor Bar II (with an estimated value of $400,000) gracing the corner of a nursery (for one of the couple's grandchildren), stuck behind a crib surrounded by a chaos of Fisher-Price toys.

The house, the view, the lavish gardens, the art, the extensive Braman wine collection—all are evidence of Norman's desire to *enjoy* his money. It's what he works at hardest. He stopped enlarging and began drinking his wine collection a decade ago, popping the dusty corks on bottles worth thousands of dollars at casual dinner gatherings. Norman chastened one oenophile, horrified at his lack of reverence before a particularly rare vintage burgundy, with the explanation, "Wine, unlike art, is not forever."

Nothing intimidates Norman. The desk in his high-rise Miami office is wide and mostly bare, the desk of a man no longer troubled with the details of his business empire. An army of people *do* for Norman, right down to Irma, who finds, buys, and packs away the books that her husband will read on their annual summer retreat to Provence. Norman in his seniority presides, mostly via telephone, fielding only the most important questions raised by his far-flung empire, stepping in grumpily (but, in truth, not unhappily) to throw his weight around when needed. From behind his bare desk, if the phone isn't already lit up, Norman will shout to his assistant in the outer office, "Susan, would you get me Harry Gamble on the phone?" or "Susan, find out if Howard is going to be in New York at that meeting next week" or "Susan, where are we going to be staying in Los Angeles?"

This is the man who added the Philadelphia Eagles to his collections in '85 (for $65 million). Norman's idea isn't to sit up in his skybox and admire his new possession from a distance. No way! The idea is to enjoy it, fold it into his life, have some fun.

But it was not to be. Norman's first major act as owner was to hire Buddy, whose first major act as coach was to finesse the car dealer out of his way. It was as though a little painted goon in one of Norman's elaborate Red Grooms constructions had ordered him out of his own living room. Whom did Buddy think he was dealing with? But Norman checked his wrath. For five long and often infuriating years he hung on to Buddy for one reason, because the irritating head coach kept winning—Buddy pitted the owner's tolerance for insubordination against his desire for victory. It was a precarious balance, bound to shift against Buddy eventually. After years of tolerating the coach like a sharp rock in a tight shoe, Norman took genuine pleasure in letting the feisty little bastard go.

Rid of Buddy, Norman was at last behind the wheel. The way he saw it, all the pieces were in place. That off-season, Norman made plans to spend four days of every week during football season in Philadelphia—not that he was going to be telling Richie Kotite and Harry Gamble what to do, see, but the better to oversee his toy. Norman had learned in his six years of ownership. He had confidence in his stewardship, and he planned to be front and center to savor the impending year of triumph.

What he hadn't counted on was the tribal wrath of Erin.

First off, Norman traded a figurative pain in the neck for a real one. While vacationing in Grasse, just months after canning Buddy, Norman sat down on a couch in a shoe store, reached out lazily to drape one long arm over the back, and felt something slip in his neck. He grew dizzy. He couldn't move without pain. Used to running miles on the beach and vigorous workouts in the pool, he suddenly found his arms hung limp. He couldn't even lift his newborn granddaughter. His toes were numb, and his fingers could no longer differentiate hot from cold.

Surgeons told him he had calcium spurs on his upper vertebrae, squeezing the spinal cord. They shaved away bone to relieve the pressure, but there was no guarantee it would take away the pain or restore full strength and sensation. One slip of the knife could have paralyzed him from the neck down.

So instead of savoring a championship, Norman spent the '91 season waiting to see therapists, surrounded by the bent and broken, and being put through a demanding and often painful regimen. Accustomed to keeping others waiting, and giving orders, Norman was at the mercy of health professionals, in whose eyes the Baron of Biscayne Boulevard was just another patient with a pain in the neck. The surgery made his feet supersensitive, so now he ached at both ends. When he managed to get to Philly on a game day, flying up in his private jet, he'd arrive walking stooped and slow on tender toes, his lean, athletic frame suddenly less Astaire than Ichabod, looking, despite his rich golden tan, curly white locks, and handsomely tailored suits, not at all like the vital leader he knew himself to be, but like someone pathetic, infirm, and irrelevant. The neck pain forced him to keep his head cocked at a slight forward angle, accentuating his gaunt profile. In short, he looked like an old man, not the vigorous fifty-nine-year-old he had been, but some caricature of gnarled old age drawn by Daumier or described by Dickens—an image encouraged by the constant whining of his players and their agents, who accused him of being miserly and cold. When *Sports Illustrated* profiled him briefly with other major players in the sports biz, they reported his age as seventy-one. It was deeply humiliating.

And the curse didn't stop there. In the first half of the first game that season, Randall's knee was popped by a lunging Packer linebacker (the aptly named Bryce Paup). Norman's team emerged with its own limp, lurching through the year of high hopes like a world-class miler trying to finish a race on only one good leg. Buddy's marauding defense, fine-tuned and cleverly orchestrated by that maestro Bud Carson, was the best the league had seen in more than a decade, while the Eagles' offense collapsed. It toppled from a Randall-led league ranking of third to twenty-fifth, captained by a succession of quarterbacks—McMahon (who, true to his pattern, couldn't stay off the injured list), followed by a disastrous procession of stand-ins. They went from first to last in the league in rushing yards. There was one four-game midseason losing streak during which the offense scored only one touchdown. The Pro Bowl game in Hawaii after that season resembled an Eagles' defensive convention, with Reverend Reggie, Clyde, Seth, Eric Allen, and, of course, Jerome. Despite the limp, the club won ten games, only to have their postseason hopes dashed by—who else?—the Dallas Cowboys.

It could have been scripted by an evil leprechaun.

Because Buddy, see, hated Dallas. Not that Buddy Ryan needed a reason to despise a rival football club, or anybody else for that matter, but the Cowboys were a special case. In '87, after Dallas had run up the score during one of the godawful strike games (they had nine regular roster scabs on the field against the Eagles' hopeless and reviled "replacement players"), Buddy swore an oath that the Cowboys would *never again* beat his team. This was, of course, ridiculous. Dallas was going through hard times, but they weren't that bad, and, at the time, Buddy's team had yet to post a winning season. But he backed it up. Seven times the two teams met over the next four years, and the Eagles won every game. They won an eighth in Dallas early in '91, after Buddy was gone, crushing the Cowboys 24–0. But during the make-or-break game on a gloomy Sunday in December, Buddy's ghost was in the mist. The Eagles not only blew it, they blew it against *Dallas*.

Diehard Buddy fans, the boys in the cheap seats (well, *cheaper;* in the modern NFL there is no such thing as a cheap seat) are convinced that Norman blew it when he fired the coach. The curse is on and it would stick.

Now, in early '92, Norman is determined to prove them all wrong. He is bitter about Philadelphia's fans. How they had loved him, briefly, when he rode in on his white horse to save the franchise in '85, buying it, so the story went, to prevent the sale to investors in Phoenix. But the honeymoon lasted only a few months. WIPed up by the endless carping of call-in radio, which amplifies the opinions of cranks, Norman has become one of the city's biggest bogeymen. So much so, that

Philadelphia mayor Ed Rendell's pollsters used Norman as a standard for citywide unpopularity when they test-marketed new ideas (Norman was insulted). Part of his original motivation for buying the team had been romantic; he loves his old hometown and has fond memories of growing up watching the Phillies and Eagles. Now Norman couldn't care less. If the club weren't such a good investment (it has more than doubled in value since '85), he'd happily ship the whole enterprise, helmets, pads, cleats, and prima-donna athletes together, to Tokyo for the right offer. That's how he feels some days, anyway. But Norman is also stubborn. Even more than losing, even more than being despised, Norman hates being underestimated.

This year Philadelphia is going to learn. For years he has taken a backseat to that blowhard Buddy; now it's time for people to see what the owner can do.

HE MADE HIS FIRST million in the cut-rate drugstore business. Apprenticing himself to his father-in-law, a gruff Lebanon, Pennsylvania, merchant named Harry Miller, Norman helped develop a chain of discount department stores called Bargaintown USA and then expanded the business into a larger chain of retail drug outlets.

He is the son of a freethinking, self-educated father who had a barbershop on Arch Street in Center City, Philadelphia, and a semiliterate mother who had worked in sweatshops through her teens in order to save the money to bring her relatives to America. Both had emigrated from the Pale of Settlement in eastern Europe, his father from Poland and his mother from Romania. Norman had come up through Philadelphia's public schools and had taken a degree in business from Temple University. He had earned his tuition working two jobs, at a discount store on Market Street and at Food Fair.

Norman at age twenty-two was ambitious beyond the scale of most college men in the fifties. America after World War II had spawned a corporate culture modeled after the military, the great shared experience of the war generation. It was strictly male, hierarchical, and overimpressed with size. Most ambitious young men coming out of college at that time had career goals defined by the corporate ladder. You got your degree, signed on at the lowest rung, and began a steady climb toward middle age and a uniform upper-middle-class dream.

Not Norman. Like most Jewish young men, he regarded corporate America as a largely goyish concern. Besides, he had his sights set a lot higher than a station wagon and a home in the suburbs for the wife and kids. His parents, and the remarkable success stories he saw growing up in Philadelphia's Jewish community, had left Norman the core immigrant belief that *anything* was possible in America. Big corporations? They were other men's empires.

After Temple, Norman took a job in a new marketing research arm of Seagram Distillers, an appropriately Jewish-owned company. It was an opportunity he would later call the most formative experience in his business life. "It taught me how to think," he says. Under the direction of a former University of Pennsylvania professor, Frank Hypps, Norman learned how to do real-world market analysis, traveling all over the country as part of a Seagram's sales-and-marketing team. They would visit bars and liquor outlets and conduct in-depth interviews, note shelf placement of Seagram's products, how and why stores and restaurants decided on a product as their house whiskey. Then they'd write a detailed report to guide company sales tactics. He learned how to rigorously assess and define a market, how to target sales and streamline distribution. Norman would carry Hypps's manuals through nearly four decades of mounting business success.

He met Irma Miller, a slender, blond high-school girl, at Camp Kweebac, a summer retreat for Jewish teens outside Reading, where Norman had worked as a counselor and driver during his last years in college. They were married September 30, 1956. When Norman announced he was leaving his solid corporate job at Seagram's to work for his father-in-law, Irma and her mother were horrified.

Harry was a town character, a burly peddler in an oversized cowboy hat. He was loud, aggressive, and everywhere. In his youth, he had combed Lebanon for surplus merchandise, which he would buy and then sell from the back end of his truck. You never knew what Harry would be selling; you just knew it would be cheap. He seemed born with a knack for knowing, not just what something was worth, but what other people would pay for it. Even when Harry became one of the town's most successful merchants, forsaking the truck for the farmer's market he purchased out at Seventh and Sunset Streets, he remained the gruff hustler. In the town's small and largely affluent Jewish community, Harry was respected, but at arm's length. To Irma, her new husband's prospects, his college degree and urbane manner, were a step up from Harry the Hustler. So Norman's decision to work for his father-in-law came as an unpleasant shock.

But Harry and Norman were soul brothers. The older man respected Norman's education and business insights. Norman respected Harry's up-from-the-back-of-the-truck success and his capital. Money was a means for making more money. And if Harry knew how to hustle, Norman knew how to speed.

One of the first things Harry did with Norman was to send him on a scouting expedition to Providence, Rhode Island. An old factory there had been converted into an unusual kind of department store. Instead of customers approaching a counter and asking a clerk to bring them merchandise, the way nearly all general stores then operated, the owner spread goods out on long wooden tables and let customers wander around the store with a cart.

When Norman liked what he saw, Harry took him down to the bank, cosigned a note so that his son-in-law could borrow ten thousand dollars, and then took the money as contribution to their new partnership—Bargaintown USA.

The first store was in Lebanon, at Harry's old farmer's market. It wasn't fancy—low overhead was key—and the merchandise, true to Harry's reputation, was plentiful and cheap. They ran garish full-page ads in the Lebanon *Daily News* and kept the store open long hours, seven days a week. Harry retained Norman's brother, Leonard, a lawyer, to help battle Pennsylvania's blue laws. Those who knew Norman then remember a gaunt man with dark rings under his eyes, disheveled in appearance, smoking constantly, barking orders, and seemingly camped full time in the cramped offices behind the store. Bargaintown was a hit.

Of course, what worked in one town would work in another. The second Bargaintown opened in Manheim, the third in Hummelstown, the fourth in Lewistown—all places that drew in customers from a wide rural area, but were too small to attract a Korvettes or Alexanders, the giant department-store chains. As the stores thrived, credit came easier and easier, and neither Norman nor Harry was inclined to sit still. Between '57 and '62, they opened six Bargaintown stores.

Branching into discount drugs was Harry's idea. The new stores operated on the same principle—low overhead, high volume, low prices—but they were smaller and less expensive to open, stock, and maintain. Norman especially liked them because he could get them up and running fast. They recruited a successful cut-rate drugstore operator from New York named Mort Klein in '64 and really picked up the pace, opening a new store every two weeks.

Mort traveled the back roads of Pennsylvania, scouting out locations for new stores. He took long coal-country drives, ranging out from Lebanon in ever-widening circuits, stopping in every jerk town they came across with a population of seven thousand or better, places like Sunbury, Uniontown, Shamokin, Kulpmont, Mt. Carmel, Pottsville, Frackville, Shenandoah, Danboro, Bloomsburg, Lewisburg, ranging as far east as Pottstown, as far south as Hanover, north to Shickshinny, and as far west as Monongahela and Aliquippa. He would scout out storefronts with fifteen hundred to two thousand square feet of floor space that could be rented within Norman's parsimonious budget, generally under eighty-five dollars per month. When he found a likely spot, Norman would visit.

Negotiating was Norman's special gift. He had a way of seeming to look right through you, of instinctively sorting out bottom line from bluff. When a landlord in Donora stubbornly refused to accept less than a one-hundred-dollar monthly rent, Norman first balked, then seemingly capitulated. But when the papers were drawn up, the contract called for a ten-year lock on that rate, renewable annually—and here Mort had to admire the audacity—at *Norman's* discretion! Of course, all the landlord saw was the one hundred dollars per month. Norman saw a successful store with a fixed basement-level lease for a full decade.

And just because papers were drawn up and signed, that didn't mean (for Norm) the deal was done. If there was an ounce of advantage down the road, he was patient . . . and ready. Saddled with a rent in Johnstown that he felt was too high, Norman had surprised Mort by pressing ahead. The new store prospered, more than justifying the higher lease, but several months into operation, Norman issued a surprise order.

"Paper it up," he told Mort.

They laid off the employees, locked the doors, and taped brown paper over the windows.

A few days later, the store reopened—with a significantly lower rent.

Most landlords would rather keep a steady tenant at a lower rent than go off looking for a new one. It was a principle with other applications, as Mort discovered. Before he was hired, he had held out for a salary higher than Norman wanted to pay. Harry intervened to secure the better salary, but nine months after Mort moved his family to Lebanon, Norman fired him, then offered the job back later the same day, at a lower salary. Mort took it. It's harder to give something up than to turn something down.

As Norman's expansion plans accelerated, Harry grew anxious. The whole empire rested on his financial clout, so he had a lot more to lose than his son-in-law. And, as the complexity of the enterprise grew, Harry felt its weight shifting from his shoulders. Norman never rested. Store nineteen opened in Bloomsburg. Store twenty opened in Danville. Store twenty-one was getting ready to come on line in Shamokin. There were plans in the works for fifteen more stores before the end of '67—when Harry's foot hit the brake.

Gamble-Skogmo, a retail empire based in Minneapolis, offered to buy Bargaintown. For Harry, the deal would cap a lifetime of success. His son-in-law would go on to further corporate heights; Gamble-

Skogmo offered to make Norman a top exec and move him and Irma to Minneapolis. Harry figured it was too good to pass up. But Norman said no. Irma didn't want to move to Minneapolis, he explained, and, besides, if a retail powerhouse like Gamble-Skogmo was interested, didn't that just prove they were onto something big?

It became more than a professional disagreement. Harry was livid. Who did this kid think he was? Had he forgotten who had loaned him the ten grand to join the partnership in the first place?

The two men stopped speaking to each other. Norman and Irma stopped coming by for family dinners. They split up the partnership; Norman took the discount drug stores, renaming the chain Keystone, and Harry kept the department stores. For several sad years, the family endured a cold and bitter split.

Norman was just getting started.

It was 1967. To further expand, Norman turned to the brokerage house of Butcher and Sherrard (later Butcher and Singer), a bedrock Philadelphia financial institution devoted to the shelter, care, and feeding of money, old and new. Norman was simply dazzled by these men.

And over the next six months, B&S built Norman a conglomerate called Philadelphia Pharmaceuticals and Cosmetics (PP&C). They merged Norman's thriving and still expanding Keystone chain with a troubled venture in northeast Philadelphia called Philadelphia Laboratories; then with U.S. Cocoa Corporation in Camden; with Vitamix, a vitamin manufacturer in Connecticut; and a licorice-extract manufacturing firm in Virginia called F. A. Martin Company. The logic behind the acquisitions was sometimes lost on Norman, but the suits at B&S were delighted. They were predicting annual sales in excess of ten million dollars. Norman was excited. He'd hit the big time.

But his faith in this ungainly contraption lapsed quickly. Despite the impressive array of PP&C holdings, the only one of its divisions making money was Keystone, and the bedrock was starting to crumble. Instead of doubling Keystone's sales in '68, as the wizards predicted, the chain's six-month sales slipped from $4.6 million to $3.6 million. When Norman complained, he was assured that what really mattered was the mounting value of PP&C's stocks, which went up with each new acquisition.

But Norman wasn't impressed by such an abstract measure of success; what he saw was a cumbersome agglomeration of losing ventures. By the end of '68, when B&S proposed adding a concrete company in western Pennsylvania to the mix, he asked out. The suits obliged. They wrote him a check for $1.2 million.

He was thirty-six years old. He drove back to Lebanon that night, and the next day stopped by the Keystone offices waving the check triumphantly. It was a scene no one in Keystone's offices that day would forget.

"I did it! I did it!" Mort remembers him saying. "I never thought I could do it, but I did!"

Norman Braman was a millionaire.

Now he could start making some real money.

A PATTERN WAS BEGINNING to emerge in Norman's career. Twice now, he had formed a partnership with someone older and better established, profited by the association, and then moved on, leaving hard feelings and accusations of betrayal in his wake. Harry Miller was still not speaking to his son-in-law; and the suits at B&S, whom Norman successfully sued after the buyout (he was awarded an additional $838,000), were still smarting two decades later, when W. W. Keen Butcher III, patriarch of the money house, grumped to a reporter, "Mr. Braman cannot be relied upon for informational purposes. Let's just leave it at that."

It's partly a consequence of Norman's restlessness. Every five to ten years he sheds his skin and emerges as a new man. Norman the college kid became Norman the chain-store owner, then Norman the corporate CEO, then Norman the urbane young millionaire ready to sample early retirement.

He would repeat the process again in five years, then again at the end of the decade, and then again five years later. Impatient to succeed, he quickly grows impatient with success. The one constant in this lurching progress has been money. Wherever Norman goes, he makes more.

But dollars aren't enough. Norman has deeper, more romantic yearnings that even he finds hard to define. "I don't know what I want, and it worries me that I don't," a middle-aged Norman told a newspaper interviewer. "I have something inside of me that keeps prodding, that keeps moving, that keeps inquiring . . . a feeling that I'm not fully satisfied with Norman Braman, that I'm not really satisfied with what I'm doing. . . . But what the hell do I really want?"

Politics opened up Norman's next opportunity. As a young millionaire Jewish Republican, he found it easy to make friends in the new GOP power structure in Washington. He was a supporter of Philadelphia senator Hugh Scott, the Senate minority leader, and became close friends with newly elected upstate New York representative Jack Kemp, the former quarterback. When Norman "retired" to Florida, he allied himself with Representative Bill Cramer and became one of a number of young, relatively moderate Miami Republicans who challenged the long-standing upstate-Florida GOP power structure. He became business partners with California representative Bob Wilson, with whom he opened a chain of discount drugstores in Ireland that failed to thrive.

Norman used these connections to pry his way into the business of selling Cadillacs, the foundation for the next explosion in his personal wealth.

It didn't take a genius to see that the hordes of retirees still migrating south were a potentially lucrative market for luxury cars. After the gas crisis of '74, virtually every segment of the car-buying public was looking for smaller, more gas-efficient, less expensive vehicles—every segment except elderly retirees, that is. The folks seeking permanent rest and recreation in the sun were the very people who had made GM and Ford the mightiest car manufacturers in the world. These people liked big cars, cars with fins and chrome and leather interiors and air-conditioning and terrific sound systems. They lived large, craved status, and because they didn't drive all that much, weren't so panicked by escalating gas prices. To someone of Norman's marketing acumen, the business was just idling by the side of the road, fully gassed, keys in the ignition. The problem was how to get behind the wheel.

Norman's reading of the situation was Caddy dealerships did not go to outsiders, and they did not go to Jews. To break down the walls, he needed patrons, powerful patrons.

That's where California Bob came in. Wilson sat down with Norman and some other investors that year and outlined a strategy for a political assault on GM's walls. They recruited Virginian I. Lee Potter, a former Eisenhower administration official and Republican national committeeman, who threw in more than $100,000 of his own money. Wilson borrowed $180,000 from C. Arnholt Smith, a megabucks GOP financier with close connections to Richard Nixon (Smith would later go to jail and be described by one federal prosecutor as "one of the great swindlers of modern times"). Smith loaned Norman $300,000. California Bob recruited the help of his longtime congressional colleague Jerry Ford, who had represented Michigan's fifth district for a quarter century. Norman went to see his old buddy Hugh Scott. Together, they put the squeeze on GM. Before the end of that year, "an opportunity developed," Norman recalls, to buy a silent half of the Sharp-Taylor Cadillac dealership in downtown Tampa. He had his toe in the door.

A year later, Norman purchased his own Caddy dealership in

Miami, on Biscayne Boulevard, and old Bargaintown Braman started teaching GM the art of discount merchandising. He fired the sales staff and hired a workforce that reflected the cultural pastiche of a changing Miami. He ran outlandish promotions, utilizing a cartoon superhero named BramanMan, and turned the area's formerly collegial Cadillac competitors into silly cartoon foils. When the ads started attracting folks who really couldn't afford Cadillacs . . . *no praaaablem!* Norm offered generous installment plans. His marketing strategy stood GM's on its head. Whereas the manufacturer used Cadillac's luxury status to exclude, Norman used the car's status to include: he told people *You deserve to own a Cadillac! If you can't afford one . . . hey, let's talk!*

When the Miami Cadillac shop took off, he did what he had always done with success; he expanded, buying dealerships all over the state, moving into Japanese imports at a time when the industry way still laughing at the Honda, diversifying. Over the next four years, the underdog BramanMan became "Baron of Biscayne Boulevard."

California Bob and Potter were bought out early on, and Smith, whose loan Norman promptly repaid, was doing time when Norman really began to hit his stride. True to the usual pattern, Norman's former partners felt betrayed.

"He's a gifted businessman," Wilson would reflect years later. "I hold him in a minimum of high regard."

But Norman had moved on to new heights. Once merely wealthy and well connected, he was now seriously rich. And true to his life's pattern, Norman again was bored.

HE MOUNTED A BID for the U.S. Senate in '80, hiring professional GOP handlers to build what, as it turns out, would have been an easy walk into Congress. But Norman withdrew unexpectedly at the last minute, discouraged, he says, by the thankless rigors of a politician's life.

Instead, he eagerly accepted an appointment to Ronald Reagan's administration. After serving as vice-chairman of Reagan's Florida campaign and raising nearly $100,000 toward the effort, Norman was nominated by the president to head the U.S. Immigration and Naturalization Service.

It seemed perfect. Son of immigrants assumes top immigration post. Resident of a city besieged by immigration, legal and illegal, steps in to sort out the mess. The agency had been headless for nearly two years and had fallen badly behind the treacherous and shifting ground of immigration issues. Who better to reshape the troubled bureaucracy than BramanMan, a genuine Reagan-era superhero—the archetype really, the take-charge, self-made (twice-over) entrepreneurial genius?

And Norman entered swinging. The day he was nominated, he promised the Miami *Herald*, "I'm committed to a major reorganization of the agency. It needs change." Looking past the little matter of Senate confirmation, Norm explained that he had already begun putting together a task force to plan the revolution. "I think you're going to see changes made within ninety days," he boasted. BramanMan was primed to kick bureaucratic butt.

Norm was so eager he wasn't going to stand around waiting out the mere formality of Senate approval. He crashed INS headquarters in Washington one morning that fall with his administrative assistant and, to the shock and chagrin of the agency staffers, began ordering people around, demanding that the files be opened, computer banks be laid bare, et cetera, and working himself into a full entrepreneurial capitalist lather with the help, when (used to answering to the gentler voice of the U.S. government) they failed to respond as quickly and efficiently as employees of Norman Braman ought. Norman had plans, he explained, to hand a private contractor the job of fully computerizing the agency and to dump at least five hundred people from the Washington staff. Needless to say, the civil servants were appalled, what with Norman having no authorization—*Coming in here like that . . . who the hell does this pompous two-bit car dealer think he is, anyway?*—and in due course (about as long as it took for the door to begin its backward swing when Norm and his assistant triumphantly exited) the feral howl of the frightened bureaucrat echoed through high federal halls.

Rudy Giuliani, associate U.S. attorney general responsible for INS, was somewhat bemused by the teeth gnashing. To his way of thinking, it just confirmed why Norman was going to be such a good INS commissioner. He thought the agency needed to be pounced on by a tiger, and if they had to yank Braman's tail now and then, it was a small price to pay. But, clearly, it was time to yank the tail. This business about a computer contract, though—*Shit, Norman, there are former public officials running laps in minimum-security prisons all over America for things like that!* And Rudy figured somebody ought to warn BramanMan that the seemingly somnolent rank and file of bureaucracy was a vicious beast when riled.

So Norman was invited to stop by Rudy's stately fourth-floor office at Justice a few days later, where . . . well, the idea here was just to clue Norman in on things, a chat between friends in the administration, a little reminder that, in fact, he hadn't yet been confirmed (although the FBI check, completed that summer, had pronounced Norman clean), and that maybe it wasn't a good idea to start throwing his weight around and antagonizing people just yet, especially people he would need, not only to accomplish his sweeping agenda of change, but even to mail a postcard successfully from his exalted new—but still *pending*—office.

Norm exploded. The other men in the room, Giuliani and his deputy Jeff Harris, were astonished. The man was screaming.

"I was appointed to shake this agency up! Nobody's gonna tell me how to do it! . . . You can't tie my hands! . . . If I can't do the job right, I'm not going to do it at all!"

Nobody had ever seen a man—a multimillionaire at that—so eager to assume an onerous, relatively low-profile fifty-thousand-dollar-a-year public job.

Then, abruptly, Norman changed course.

He withdrew.

He retreated to France. His publicist offered reporters, the same ones to whom Norm had been spouting his ambitious designs, a prepared statement with the following lame explanation: "My business is the sale and service of automobiles. With the current depressed market affecting our industry, I have concluded that . . . I cannot now assume a passive role in their operation."

Right.

Some weeks before his withdrawal, a staff member on Strom Thurmond's Judiciary Committee, acting on a telephoned tip (Norm had accumulated a few enemies down the road), produced the name, address, and telephone number of a man, a certain ex-husband of a Braman domestic employee, someone the FBI hadn't encountered in its background check. It seems that back in 1973, Norman and Irma had conspired to arrange a false marriage for a beloved Peruvian maid in order to keep her in the country. Rudy happened to have a speaking engagement in Palm Beach not long afterward, and BramanMan was invited up for Chat II, wherein Norman was advised, just between friends in the administration, that it might look unseemly for the head of the immigration agency to have so cynically sidestepped immigration law.

Actually, Norman didn't wait to be dropped. When he got word of the Justice Department's and the Judiciary Committee's concern over the sham marriage, he was fed up. First they faulted him for trying to get a head start on a difficult job; then they wanted to nitpick him with some minor episode that happened more than a decade ago, in which nobody got hurt and things worked out for the best? Come on! No wonder Washington was in such a mess. No wonder government had such a hard time recruiting real talent. Norman was more disgusted than disappointed. They didn't deserve his help.

When the anger wore off, he was disappointed. His dream of public life, the next great Five-Year Leap, had fallen on its nose.

It was 1982. Norm would be turning the big five-o.

And what besides his $24 million did he have to show for it? What was he going to do with the rest of his remarkable life?

Bob Goodman, the political consultant Norman had hired to help build his aborted Senate campaign, remembers sitting and sipping fine wine with Norm at the villa in southern France that summer. There was no TV in the villa; Norman believed the tube was undermining the art of conversation. So after dinner was served and cleared, there would be long, slow hours on the porch, talking art, politics, business, whatever. Norman confessed his restlessness, and they kicked around a few ideas. One of them was to produce a television program that would give viewers a peek inside the homes and lives of the wealthy—Goodman even approached Louis Ruckeyser, the host of the popular PBS show "Wall Street Week," about being the moderator. But Norman backed away from that, too—only to see Robin Leach develop a similar concept into the hit "Lifestyles of the Rich and Famous."

Another of the ideas that Norman mentioned that night was football.

IT MADE SUCH a lovely story.

Norman Braman, the local boy made good, hearing that the football team he had loved as a child was about to be packed off to Phoenix by that profligate spoiled-rich-kid owner Leonard Tose, who needed the cash quick to pay off his gambling debts, rode in at the last moment with a check for $65 million to save the franchise!

Good old Norm Braman, not the wheeler-dealer car baron Republican kingmaker of South Florida, but Norm, the son of Harry the barber, the skinny Jewish kid who once carried a water bucket for Eagles players during training camp in West Chester, the West Philly kid who climbed fences at Shibe Park to catch a glimpse of his heroes in action. The feature writers loved this stuff. Having gone off in the world to make his fortune, good ol' Norm was now riding back in to save the day. In one interview he referred to himself as "a white knight."

"A solid business deal deeply immersed in sentimentality," he said.

And they ate it up. For a few glorious months, Norman basked in the warm glow of a grateful citizenry. Tose's excesses were legend. He had used the team's value to underwrite his high-rolling, mortgaging it to bankers who were only too eager to shoulder heavy liens on something as golden as a thriving sports franchise in one of the NFL's biggest markets. Like the casino managers Tose would later sue for plying him with alcohol at their gaming tables, bankers kept the inveterate playboy flush with cash. Word among NFL owners (Norman was friends with Dolphins owner Joe Robbie) was that Tose's franchise was about to go bust. Braman made a pass at Tose in late '83, offering to buy the team, but Tose was unwilling to part with control, and Norm wasn't about to bunk on a sinking vessel. When word leaked out that Tose was trying to sell the franchise to a group in Phoenix, the city of Philadelphia moved fast to sweeten the lease at Veterans Stadium and lock the Eagles in for the remainder of the century. When Norman came along to buy the club a few months later, the public still perceived him as the savior, although the only one he saved was Leonard Tose. What Norman got was an incredibly lucrative investment, something to absorb his considerable intellect and ego, and that ineffable something more he found so haunting.

Pro sports would satisfy his itch to be on stage. He liked being written about in the newspapers and noticed on radio and TV. The NFL was a relatively small but high-profile world in which he could publicly throw his weight around, a safe harbor for his grander ambitions.

And the new local hero wasn't just going to keep the club in town; he was going to restore the luster of its storied past! Norman's Eagles, after all, had been the juggernaut team of '47, '48, and '49—two-time league champs. One of his first acts as owner was to invite the old team back to Philadelphia for a reunion weekend. The one-time water boy rubbed shoulders with his old heroes, now flabby, stooped, near-sighted, and gimpy. They presented him with a replica of their NFL championship ring, which Norm would wear from that day forth.

What joy! The glory days were coming back. Only this time, they were going to be *his* glory days. Norman, who had what it takes to succeed in the real world, was going to show these football people a thing or two about winning. After the discount wars in Lebanon, the muscular combat of national politics, the cutthroat world of auto dealing, how tough could football be? It was just a game!

This was going to be fun. Everybody could see Braman had the money, the desire, and the smarts. He was tough *and* idealistic. The players? They were gonna love him. He and Irma would invite them down to Indian Creek Island for dinner, expose them to things, fine wine, art, broaden the boys' horizons—think how grateful they would be. And who better than Norman to dispense helpful, fatherly advice for handling their outsized paychecks? It was going to be one big, happy football family, with Norm as patriarch. It was going to be great. People were going to stop Norman Braman on the streets in Philadelphia just to shake his hand. He'd walk out on the field at Veterans Stadium to the thundering approval of tens of thousands. Norman was going to have a ball!

Enter James David "Buddy" Ryan.

4

BUDDY VERSUS THE GUY IN FRANCE

Larry Sullivant would never forget meeting Buddy Ryan.

It was in 1957, on a sweltering high-school football field in Gainesville, Texas. The new coach, a squat little tyrant with a flattop buzz cut and a jawful of chaw, had been running the boys mercilessly. Thirst was considered weakness. And as if battling fatigue and dehydration weren't enough, this new coach seemed intent on riding Larry in particular, calling him a slacker and a sissy—*nobody* called the high school's star linebacker a sissy! So when a flying cleat opened a gash on the back of Larry's hand, and crimson started displacing sweat and dirt down his wrist and forearm, what Larry felt mostly was relief: maybe a trip to the doctor—first aid and a breather at least.

He trotted hopefully toward the sidelines, brandishing the bloody hand.

"Mmmm, looks bad," said Coach. "It'll need doctorin'."

So the man named Buddy scooped up a handful of dirt. He spat on the wound, then pressed on the dirt, smothering the bleeding.

"That'll do you," he said. "Now git back out there."

Buddy's methods didn't always sit well with the boys' parents, who, despite their enthusiasm for football, tended to draw the line at infection and serious injury, but it had the opposite effect on the boys. Exhausted, browbeaten, and often bullied by their new coach, they learned they could earn his respect. Buddy's heartfelt scorn for those who couldn't take it made the Gainesville team an elite.

Here was the essence of the Game, grasped intuitively by the twenty-six-year-old former army master sergeant embarking on his life's work. He was entering the Pigskin Priesthood, the underground fraternity of coaches devoted to football for its own sake, as a pursuit of manly perfection. Buddy knew where football came from, not the official NFL history-book story of spoiled college brats out for a Sunday afternoon scrum, but from dirt-patch high-school fields like those in western Oklahoma and Texas where he grew up and got his coaching start. Out here, football wasn't just a game, it was a cult. It was part initiation, part religion, a way for roughneck young men to vent their last wild gusts of pure testosterone meanness before settling for the tamer pastures of adulthood and civilization. If one of Buddy's practices ended without injury, he'd line 'em up and force them to run a violent gauntlet, letting them go only after somebody started to bleed. If it wasn't ugly, it wasn't football. The Game was a state of mind, a distinctively masculine state of mind. A team that didn't fight to the last down, in Buddyspeak, "lay down and threw up its skirts." Players who didn't have what it takes, who didn't get it, were nothing short of cowards—Buddy called them, of course, girls. Later, in the pros, weary veterans complained (never to Buddy's face) that his grueling, bloody practice sessions were self-destructive—why risk injury and wear a team down before the season starts? What they didn't get was that Buddy was less interested in practice as rehearsal than practice as boot camp, a rough winnowing, a chromosome check, a way of selecting young men who had the stomach for war. It would take Buddy nearly three decades to ascend to the pinnacle of the coaching ladder, but the basics were in place right at the start.

If the National Football League had become a club of rich, cigar-smoking capitalists who watched the game from Olympian heights in air-conditioned comfort while jiggling ice in their tumblers of gin, the Game remained what it had always been. It demanded total commitment and was rich enough in strategy, emotion, and meaning for certain men to make it their life. At the pro level, the Game demanded years of study and apprenticeship. It could arouse in the devoted all the primal passions of war, of primitive, controlled combat between reckless young men of skill and courage throwing their bodies in harm's way, on a neatly proscribed battlefield, guided by grayheads filled with arcane knowledge of tactics, counterstrokes, and trickery. The Game's violence was real, its victories hard won, its demands brutal and unyielding—there were no fakes on a pro football field. The Game was a brotherhood, a battleground, where the great-grandsons of cowboys and slaves and coal miners and oil riggers and immigrant factory workers and farmers and soldiers proved in each new generation that they, too, possessed the grit that made America great. Out on the dusty flatlands of Oklahoma and Texas, or in the bottom counties of Georgia, Alabama, Mississippi, the Carolinas, Tennessee, and central Florida, places that stirred vague cultural memories of bloody charges, of Sherman's march, segregation, and racist violence, a boy could still make his reputation for life, accomplish things for which he would be better known and remembered at home than for anything, good or bad, that he did the rest of his life.

The high priests of the Game weren't the men in pinstripes up in the luxury boxes; they were the coaches. Coach ruled football completely, more completely than in any other sport. A player didn't cross or question him, because Coach held all the cards. At the high-school level, out of the new crop of a hundred or so eager frosh who materialized every summer, weeks or even months before school opened, Coach decided which kid would be given a shot at playing quarterback (it helped a lot if your father or older brother had played there), which kids looked like linemen or linebackers, and which would go home disappointed. Coach decided whether you were first string or first cut, and every day of your football career from that day forward depended on his judgment.

And who was going to question him? In football, unlike baseball and even basketball, individual achievement is hard to measure. Except for the most visible ball-handling positions, quarterback, running back, and receiver, most football players get lost in the crowd during a game. With twenty-two men on the field at all times, unless they happen to make the tackle or interception on a given play, it is hard to tell whether a defensive lineman, linebacker, strong safety, or interior lineman makes a difference. It is impossible to watch them all. Even with millions tuned in, with slo-mo replays and expert commentary and analysis, the only ones who really know who played well or poorly over the course of a game are the men on the field and Coach—and the players' opinions (as they quickly learned) don't count.

One of the early lessons was that ability and courage weren't enough, not by a long shot. Talent was nothing until Coach gave you a shot. America is thick with potential NFL Hall of Fame running backs and receivers who never touched a football in a real game because they dropped an easy pass in an early practice or fumbled once too often in a high-school summer scrimmage or who back-talked Coach in front of the other boys and were sent packing. Coach decided which players deserved mention when the college scouts did their annual rounds or, at the college level, which players deserved to have videotapes of their heroics packaged with music and narration and mailed to the pro scouts. Coach decided which kid's dropped pass meant he had bad hands or was just having a bad day, which kid deserved a second chance because his head was screwed on straight, and which kid the team would be better off without. Coach wasn't always right, of course, and his judgments weren't always completely objective or even-handed—hence the tendency for black kids to be chosen to play running back or wide receiver (speed, agility, jumping ability) but not quarterback (intelligence, quick judgment), and for white kids to be chosen to play middle linebacker or free safety (field generals) but not cornerback (speed, agility, jumping ability). The racial makeup of position assignments on the NFL football field wasn't just the result of ingrained corporate racism; it reached all the way back to those first playing fields in small towns all over America. It reflected this nation's bedrock prejudices, preserved by the immutable oligarchy of Coach.

The pro coach was a zealot. He had spent years, often decades, studying obscure canons of strategy, of slot-back formation versus single-back sets, of run and shoot versus single wing, of overlapping zones versus man to man, of blitz&burn versus bend-don't-break—things even the most observant fans only vaguely comprehend. Coach invented and preserved the codes and jargon that described these complex stratagems, handed down from one generation to the next with refinements and subtle variations. Each jealously guarded the quirks of his own system. Players joining a new team were novitiates, issued the new playbook like a breviary, learning first the new language before they could attempt the mysterious scriptures traced out in *X*'s and *O*'s. Coach was keeper of the flame.

Most of the NFL's twenty-eight head coaches were former marginal players who became devotees of the cult, unlike the other meatheads who played until their knees gave out and then—*poof*—turned back into oversized job seekers in ill-fitting suits with pathetic pre–middle age limps. Coaches were football's lifers: you stayed on when the money and the cheering died out; you volunteered; you carried water buckets, picked up towels if you had to, until you latched onto an assistant's job at some small college, trying to turn high-school flashes into real football players, getting paid a pittance but still possessing enough of the old pro aura to hold the kids in thrall. That might lead to an unpaid assistant position on a pro staff, then, after a season or two, maybe coach of special teams or tight end or wide receivers, haunting the locker rooms and film rooms and weight rooms, a monk in the sweaty temple of true manhood . . . watching your klutz kid brother, say, the one who always envied you, who used to turn green in the stands watching you don the holy pads for weekend battles, now promoted to his own high-rise office with a secretary and an expense account and his own fucking 800 number, while you're working eighty, ninety, a hundred hours a week in humid, smelly basement rooms under crumbling stadiums, never seeing the wife and kids, enduring the daily tedium of practices, squinting at game films, trying to get these superstars (now half your age) who all make—what? A hundred, a thousand times your salary? Trying to get them to work together well enough to actually execute one or two of the plays that existed with such subtle clarity in your mind's eye. All for the privilege of still being out there on game day, on the sidelines, maybe, but definitely still *in* it, still part of the Game, soaking up the blood-quickening roar of the fans—who individually were the lowest of the low, but who, collectively, were the very fountain, the wellspring of everything that mattered—toughing it out year after year, decade after decade, until there came, at long last, *your* chance, the miter (in this case, a headset) was placed on *your* head, the whistle draped around *your* neck, the ever-present pack of local reporters went to work creating *your* legend, immortalizing your oddities of expression or habit (which later would be shown as proof either of your genius or your unfitness, depending on how many games you could win), and, lo! you had arrived, anointed, one of the twenty-eight NFL head coaches, a High Holy Priest of the Pigskin.

And while the League attended to TV contracts and marketing spin-offs and season ticket sales and expansion and the amazingly lucrative chore of entertaining the masses, coaches tended the flame—the eternal flame of victory, succinctly saluted by the immortal St. Vince Lombardi when he pronounced "Winning is everything." Deep inside the slick multimillion-dollar corporate edifice of the NFL, beyond the salary disputes and media controversies and Players Association lawsuits and free agents' wars, each season coaches labored to assemble forty-seven young men, inspire them with a chance at excellence, urge them to seize the emotional opportunities afforded by another team's public arrogance or their own sense of personal pride (or, in the case of the '92 Eagles, by the loss of a beloved brother), and lift them above the swirl of extraneous ambition and greed just to play—and win. That was what mattered in the end. And Coach? He was the guy who knew how to win. Bottom line.

The two fiefs, League and Game, needed each other. Without the marketing muscle and know-how of the owners, the Game would still be a weekend diversion on scruffy small-town lots. But without Coach, without the wisdom, energy, and will that made the Game authentic, all the slick worldwide marketing schemes of the League would be so much glitter and noise.

There was occasional tension between the two fiefs, but the smart NFL owner had learned to defer Game decisions to Coach, and modern Coach had learned to be diplomatic, polite, and respectful of his boss. The new, corporate NFL coach mingled comfortably at cocktail parties in the owner's living room, learned to salute, at least publicly, the invaluable guidance and support afforded by the commitment of such a successful, worldly gentleman. Corporate Coach understood the necessity of his players wearing color-coordinated socks and keeping their shirts tucked in and having the hue of their face masks match. But the old-timers, the leather-helmet-no-face-mask men, were incorrigible. They viewed owner and team management as unfortunate necessities at best—somebody had to promote the games and sell tickets—and at worst as corrupt distractions. Owners were dilettantes, rich boobs who thought their money entitled them to stick their noses where they didn't belong, men who were owed a certain politeness and occasional audiences and honesty (at least most of the time, except about the real important stuff), but who wouldn't, couldn't, and shouldn't set one toe through the front door of the temple.

And no coach in modern football better personified the latter than Buddy Ryan. He knew exactly where the line was drawn. He knew it back in Gainesville, right when he started—which explains why he didn't last too long. The school board (if not the town) got fed up with him. It fired him at the end of his second season. "They just didn't like Buddy, and he didn't like them," recalled Bill Williams, one of Ryan's original players who went on to become school-board president himself. "See, at that point in time in his life, Buddy didn't have a whole lot of tact."

Then or ever.

Suffice it to say, nothing in Norman's storied past had adequately prepared him for being bossed around by a runty, nearsighted good ol' boy spitting tobacco juice in a paper cup—an *employee*, yet!

Buddy had grown up one of six children in a four-room house on a farm so small it barely deserved the name. His parents maintained a virtually self-sufficient existence just outside Frederick, Oklahoma, during the Depression, growing their own vegetables, slaughtering their own chickens, milking their own cows (that was Buddy's job, every morning). He grew up in a house with no electricity and no indoor plumbing. His mother was German, short and stout the way her most famous son would be, and his father, Red Ryan, was a red-haired Irish house painter who lived fiercely, whether working, drinking, or mixing it up with anybody who looked at him cross-eyed. Buddy played football in high school and helped train quarter horses and never aspired to do anything else.

College recruiters started showing up at the Ryan farm in Buddy's senior year. Red was amazed. He figured football for a waste of valuable working time on the farm, an opinion he repeated often, but events would force him to change his mind. One day a coach from the University of Arkansas paid a visit and explained a scholarship offer.

"Let me get this straight," said Red (as Buddy later remembered it). "You're gonna give my son his tuition and his room and his board? And fifteen dollars a month? And all he's gotta do is go to school and play football?"

"That's right," said the coach.

"That's the damnedest thing I ever heard of," said Red.

Buddy wasn't exactly wowed either. Instead of going to school, he joined the National Guard in '50 after finishing high school and was promptly sent to Korea, where he served for two years and played for the Fourth Army's championship football team in Japan. He came home to a football scholarship at Oklahoma State and played on both sides of the line while earning a degree in education.

Buddy never stayed anywhere long, but his devotion to the Game was unstinting. He signed on at Gainesville after college and then spent one year as high-school athletic director in Marshall, Texas, before latching on as an assistant at the University of Buffalo. He got married there, had three boys, and, demands of the Game being what they are, was divorced by the time he left in '65 to take an assistant's job at Vanderbilt. From there he spent a year out in the Philippines at the University of the Pacific. The New York Jets' Hall of Fame head coach Weeb Ewbank opened the door to the pros for Buddy in '68.

That was the year the modern NFL was born. It brought the retirement of both St. Vince, patron saint of football, and Chicago Bears nonagenarian George Halas, who, legend had it, erected the first goalpost with hammer and nail. It was also the year when, amid the general upheavals of the times, pro football got stood on its head by the upstart American Football League's brash, stylish Joe Namath, prototype of the modern pro quarterback, who thumbed his nose at perennial NFL powerhouse Don Shula's Baltimore Colts and *guaranteed* victory in Super Bowl III. He then delivered a 16–7 victory. Namath got all the press. His success won the AFL's wide-open passing game instant credibility. But it was the Jets' defense (with Buddy coaching the linemen) that held Shula's juggernaut (they were 13–1 that year) to just one face-saving fourth-quarter touchdown. Buddy spent two years ('76–'77) with the Vikings as a line coach before he was hired in '78 to build and run a defense of his own for the Bears.

He was forty-seven years old and had spent a decade in the shadows, watching, learning, and planning for this moment, and he knew exactly what he wanted to do. Buddy had one of the rarest phenomena in modern pro football up his sleeve: a genuine innovation. For nearly a century coaches had been designing different ways to arrange eleven men on a football field either to advance or stop the ball. By the seventies, variations in defenses reflected differing philosophies to an extent, but mostly reflected the strengths and weaknesses of a coach's personnel. As conventional wisdom had it (and football was a bastion of that) there were simply more ways of moving a football than stopping it. Offensive coaches were the game's geniuses, credited with crafting clever new plays and cunning new systems. Success on the other side of the ball was credited to players. They were either big and mean enough to stop the run or they weren't. Either they were quick enough to stay with receivers or they weren't. The defensive coach was responsible primarily for spotting and nurturing talent and rarely got noticed or mentioned when the players on the field did their job well.

But Buddy had come up with a new way of doing defense, a way that reflected his conviction that the soul of the game was not artistry, but guts, aggression, and brawn. You didn't win with strategy and finesse (Buddy saw those as *offensive* traits); you won by *bringing the heat!* He had been watching carefully from the sidelines for two decades and witnessing (it galled him) the growing stature of the overpaid, golden-armed quarterback. Buddy had been with the Jets and Broadway Joe for the birth of this trend and noted the extensive efforts old Weeb would make to protect the linchpin of his aerial offense. Namath may have had a million-dollar arm, but he had dime-store knees. On certain passing plays, Weeb would assign as many as nine players just to block. Well, figured Buddy, if this was the price offenses were willing to pay for their fancy-pants passing game, he was going to exact it in full if he ever got the chance. If it took nine men to protect the quarterback, Buddy would send ten after him. Even if they didn't get there in time to disrupt the pass, the heat was enough to rattle even the most ice-blooded quarterback. His system's basic alignment was 5–1–5, with at least one linebacker taking his place alongside the front four and one dropping back into pass coverage. Two cornerbacks, two safeties, and a linebacker formed the back five, with the middle linebacker reacting in the center, empowered to redirect the forces as he saw fit. But that alignment was just a formality, a way of organizing the defense in your mind. On the field, Buddy would shift personnel all over the place, moving both safeties up to the line sometimes, dropping linebackers into pass coverage if needed, but, most important, keeping the whole squad in such determined motion that quarterbacks and offensive linemen never knew from one play to the next what to expect. Except trouble.

The essence of bringing the heat was, of course, the blitz. Buddy had dozens of variations. There was the 59 blitz, named after linebacker Gary Campbell's number. There was the Taco Bell, named after strong safety Todd Bell. There was the cheeseburger blitz, which was named after Al Harris, a gargantuan outside linebacker who had the nickname "Destroyer" until he showed up for his first Buddy camp. "The only thing I've seen him destroy was a cheeseburger," Buddy quipped, and that was that. Buddy would blitz on first down as readily as on third down. He'd blitz inside his own twenty-yard line as readily as inside the other team's. He'd blitz cornerbacks, safeties, and linebackers, sometimes all at once. He'd advertise his blitzes brazenly, then back his boys off for a play or two, then flood the line with extra linebackers and defensive backs, routinely lining eight eager, ferocious players on the line of scrimmage, daring quarterbacks to get rid of the ball before getting trampled, making them feel . . . *the heat.*

The original man in the middle was Doug Plank, a somewhat undersized but smart, leathery linebacker who wore number 46. Plank's number gave the system its name, but the 46 didn't really hit its stride until future all-pro middle linebacker Mike Singletary began to master it. With Singletary as field general, orchestrating the shifting blitzes and coverages from moment to moment, sometimes changing the defense's alignment three or four times before the snap of the ball, the Bears became a power in the NFL. The 46 defense grew out of Buddy's whole philosophy of life and football (the two being, basically, the same): If you are determined enough and (most important) *tough* enough, you can just plain beat teams into submission. Buddy's swarming rushes wouldn't allow offensive linemen to work blocking stunts and double up on mammoth defensive ends, and the sheer numbers in his banzai frontal assaults clogged rushing lanes. God, how his players loved it! People got hurt playing against the Bears. Buddy didn't disguise his pleasure when that happened. Of all the defenses in the NFL, his was the most feared. His bloodthirsty tactics were considered offensive by most players and coaches, but to Buddy it was just defense.

He downplayed the cerebral aspects of his strategy, just as he kept his own academic credentials quiet. On the Bears' locker-room bulletin board Buddy posted his own homespun summary of Buddy-ball:

TAKE THE SUMBITCH AWAY FROM 'EM INNA HURRY

The attack-dog style reflected Buddy's disdain for the fancier half of the Game, the offense, the squad that put points on the board and excited fans (hence bolstering revenues) and made for pretty NFL Films videos set to neoclassical music and narrated in John Facenda's stirring baritone. To Buddy the perfect football game was a 2–0 affair won with a brutal sack in the end zone, preferably in the closing seconds—the highlights reels would be empty and the training rooms full. Buddy's players loved the system because it elevated them to a breed of toughness apart from normal hominids and because it gave them latitude on the field. From time immemorial, Coach had always sorted out early in that first high-school summer what he judged to be the thinking ballplayers from the dim brutes and sent the brutes over to learn defense. Needless to say (considering the sorters), a disproportionate number of black athletes were assigned to the defense. Buddy loved the brutes, no matter what their skin color. They were the real football players, not the nifty ball handlers who got their pictures on the cover of *Sports Illustrated*. And, my, how the brutes loved Buddy back (especially black players, because Buddy cared about winning more than racist myth and would play the best athlete no matter what). You had to have intelligence and nerve to play Buddyball; you had to gamble and sometimes you had to get beat. But if you played it the way he wanted it, win or lose, he would fuss over you as if you were a future Hall of Famer. He was a champion motivator. Most people didn't know this, and wouldn't guess it, but ol' Buddy had earned his master's degree in education between coaching duties and prided himself on being able to teach the intricacies of his system well enough so that players could make it work out on the field on their own. "We're proving for the first time that it's possible to think and play defense at the same time," quipped Singletary, with evident pride.

There was, however, a weakness. All those bodies hell-bent for the passer left Buddy's defensive backs, especially the lonesome cornerbacks, in a woefully vulnerable spot. A quarterback who was savvy, cool, and accurate enough to fire a pass in advance of the huffing horde could pick away with short slant passes or match up his best receiver one-on-one down the sidelines. Buddy refused to fault his design for these spectacular lapses. The problem, as he saw it, was finding capable cornerbacks. He spent years looking for young men fast and poised enough to handle this pressure, mostly without success—even during the Bears' mighty '85 season, Buddy, with characteristic cruelty, publicly called his cornerbacks, Leslie Frazier and Mike Richardson, "the sorriest corners in the league."

But that was okay. Corners were a little too much like offensive players anyway, small, quick, agile, and pretty. Buddy's ideal player, he always said, was Singletary, who combined quickness and agility with intelligence and size. His defenses were going to give up a few big plays here and there, but they were also going to make big plays—TAKE THE SUMBITCH AWAY. . . . The Jets back in '68 had clobbered the Colts not with dazzling running or Namath's amazing arm so much as with four interceptions and one fumble recovery. Unlike most coaches, Buddy didn't believe turnovers were serendipitous. Turnovers were like the bubbles in water when you turned up the heat. Buddy hated most statistics—he would scoff at reporters who fussed over things like "third-down conversions rates" and "time of possession"—but he held one stat sacred: the ratio of takeaways to giveaways. That ratio was Buddy's rune, a mystical measure of a team's true worth. Bringing the heat was designed to fluster, if not flatten, opponents, to force mistakes—that is, turnovers. He told his boys that a tackle wasn't over when the man with the ball fell down. No way! You kept on tackling the bastard until the ball came loose or the referee forced you to stop. Buddy's were among the first players in the league to practice stripping the ball, launching their helmet right at the pigskin, or slapping at bottled-up running backs' hands. His '85 Bears had the best takeaway-giveaway ratio in football. They averaged three turnovers a game. And once his team stole the ball, Buddy didn't expect the players to hand it timidly back to the offense. His boys would embark on wild adventures; defensive linemen would attempt dazzling open-field jukes; linebackers would pitch the ball back to safeties, who would in turn pitch it back to the quick little corners. It was blitzkrieg football, and as the Bears' successes mounted in the eighties, many people felt it was Buddy who deserved the credit, not head coach Mike Ditka.

When he was hired in 1982, Ditka had been saddled with Buddy as his defensive coordinator after the entire defensive squad signed a letter to Chicago general manager Mike McCaskey begging him to keep Ryan on. McCaskey did, offering Buddy a contract package worth $600,000. Ditka's reward for being upstaged on his own sideline was victory. The Bears won ten games in '84 and went to the play-offs and bowled through the NFL the following year, losing only one game in the regular season, shutting out first the Giants and then the Rams in the play-offs, and then demolishing the New England Patriots 46–10 in front of the whole wide world. And who got carried off the field on his players' shoulders after the triumph?

The fat guy with a crew cut and steel-rimmed glasses. Buddy had arrived, suitably borne on the shoulders of his players.

It was time to anoint a new High Priest.

NORMAN LEARNED about Buddy in the *New York Times*, a longtime Sunday habit around the Florida mansion. The pesky Miami *Herald* was also on the Bramans' table (he was one of the newspaper's biggest regular advertisers), and Norm sometimes enjoyed skirmishing with the local reporters, but for a man of the world, a man who surrounded himself with the best of the best, the last word in daily journalism could be nothing else.

The *Times* article about Buddy on January 6, 1985, page five, column six, started like this: "Almost every season, a new genius emerges."

This from the most sober of sportswriting venues, a full year before the Bears conquered the world, so imagine the heights of journalistic hyperbole that awaited. Sportswriters make a living convincing fans that the obvious is more complicated than it seems—here's the *real* story, folks—so the idea that the mercurial Ditka was not the actual brains behind the Bears played well. As Buddy's star shone brighter in Ditka's shadow, the two men grew testy with each other, which watered the notion. By the end of '85, Buddy had his own nationwide cult.

The *Times* revisited its "genius" on December 1, with the Bears now boasting a 12–0 record. This time he got a long and glorious salute, front and center in the Sunday sports section. The article portrayed Buddy as a humble pipe-smoking perfectionist, a grand master of pro defenses with a stern patriarchal hand.

"My rookies have been pampered all their lives and think they're great football players," Buddy said, explaining why he publicly insulted his players (currently the cream of the league), calling various individuals "dumb" (Otis Wilson), "fat and slow" (Singletary), and "a waste" (William "Refrigerator" Perry). "Some of them are [good players]," Buddy said, ". . . but they have to learn how to play our game before they can compete at this level." Buddy said goosing players in the papers helped cut them down to size before he taught them how to play.

Talk like that was music to the ears of BramanMan, who was growing impatient with his Eagles. The team would lose its seventh game that day under head coach Marion Campbell, making its season record just 6–7 and assuring it would not qualify for postseason play. Norman had decided to can Campbell, a onetime Eagles lineman and a sweet guy who was popular with his team. The new owner favored anointing an offensive specialist, but for the shakeup Norm envisioned, any undefeated coach who held players in such bald contempt was worth considering. He had the story clipped, copied, and sent to Harry Gamble and other top men in the Eagles' front office.

Still, Norman had another coach in mind. For years he had admired Dolphins coach Don Shula, an NFL legend on the verge of sainthood himself. Beyond his friendship with Dolphins owner Joe Robbie and with Shula himself, Norman coveted the steady excellence (and profitability) of the Miami franchise. He saw it as a model for his own. He knew St. Don himself was anchored permanently, but who better to hatch the next generation of football dynasty than the master's own son?

This, of course, was a flawlessly dilettante notion. Never mind that David Shula, a baby-faced twenty-six-year-old assistant on his father's Dolphins staff, would be younger and less experienced than most of the players he would be asked to coach. Never mind that David's pro experience consisted of one year as a lead-foot punt re-turner for the Baltimore Colts (for whom, as the son of St. Don, he was more a novelty than a weapon). Never mind that his apprenticeship in the temple consisted of just three years as an assistant on his daddy's staff. This idea of Norman's showed either contempt or frightful igno-rance of the Pigskin Priesthood, the only true and righteous path to the twenty-eight high holy headsets. To pluck little Davy Shula from the lowest rung of the ladder (which was arguably higher than he deserved to be already) and anoint him with the headset confirmed the worst—the car dealer intended to *mess* with the Game. Where was the man's reverence? Who did he think he was?

Norman was oblivious to this. He would tap into this thorough-bred strain, hire the youngest head coach in NFL history, and commit himself and young Shula to a decade-long experiment in dynasty build-ing. They would learn together. They would have the mutually re-spectful partnership Joe Robbie shared with St. Don, only Davy, being so young and all, would be eager for Norman's guidance.

It was perfect . . . until Davy blew it. The pup had the audacity to negotiate. On the December night he hopped into his Braman Toyota (Norm supplied the Dolphins' staff with cars) and drove over to the mansion for a chicken dinner with Norman and Harry (like a punctilious suitor, Norm had called St. Don and asked permission to court his son), Davy and the Eagles reached an understanding. There were smiles and handshakes all around as Norman loosely outlined the deal, a five-year contract with a five-year Bramanesque option on the back end. Davy left the meeting trembling with excitement. He was going to be the youngest head coach in NFL history.

Impulsive Norman wanted the thing sewn up in a week. He scheduled a news conference in Philly for December 16. Campbell didn't know it yet, but he was to be fired, and Norman was going to shock the world by naming little Davy Shula head coach. Fans would wonder at Norm's audacity and the awesome chance being given the boy. It was going to be, at the very least, terrific theater.

But Davy, like Lot's wife, hesitated. After that chummy dinner and handshake, he looked back. Lawyers were going over the details, he said, and he'd have to talk to his dad about it, and maybe that five-year option on the back end wasn't such a great idea. . . . Davy obviously failed to appreciate he was being offered a gift, a fabulous, expensive, once-in-a-lifetime proposal from an oh-so-romantic—and impatient—suitor. He didn't know whom he was dealing with.

When Davy's lawyers called Norman's lawyers and, like a pack of suspicious pawnshop appraisers, began holding the truly splendid offering up to the light, it was perceived as an insult.

"You're talking ten years of my life," explained Davy, the day before the planned news conference.

Norman scowled. "David, we agreed," he said. "This is a deal breaker."

But, hey, that was just an expression! Deals that break can be mended, right? Davy figured Mr. Braman was just playing hardball. He knew he was going to accept the deal eventually—what idiot wouldn't?—but how would it look if he signed without any posturing? Wasn't that the way the game was played? He didn't want Braman to think he had round heels, did he?

The news conference took place with only half an agenda. Campbell resigned, but no new coach was named to replace him. Fred Bruney, a capable Eagles defensive assistant, took over temporarily and finished out the last week of the season. For more than a month, Davy and his lawyers waited for Norman's lawyers to return their calls and resume tinkering with the contract, to fine-tune Davy's glorious future. He went to bed at night reading the Eagles' media guide. His wife made calls to friends in Philly to start scouting out schools and neighborhoods. It was just a matter of time.

Of course, Davy was already just a pillar of salt.

Three days after the youth's fatal hesitation, the Eagles approached Jim Mora, the Hollywood-handsome coach of the ill-fated Baltimore (formerly Philadelphia) USFL franchise, the Stars. Mora was more like it. He'd served his time in the temple, twenty-three years, first as an assistant and then as head coach at Occidental College in Los Angeles, then Stanford, the University of Colorado, UCLA, the University of Washington, then the Seahawks and the Patriots before accepting a head-coaching job in the upstart league. He'd been college roommates, two decades ago, with Norm's good buddy, Representative Jack Kemp—who was gung ho for Norman to sign him. After back-to-back championships in the new league, Mora was clearly qualified for the headset. But this time Norman wasn't the only suitor, and when he started playing games, reaching a tentative agreement (smiles all around, handshakes) and then deciding to let Mora twist for a few days in mid-January, exercising some leverage (*Maybe we should talk to a few other people, too, just to make sure*), Mora grew antsy.

Unlike Davy, the true monk had options. While Norm dithered, Mora weighed other interests. In New Orleans on Tuesday, January 28, 1986, two days after the Bears won Super Bowl XX, Mora signed a long-term contract to coach the Saints.

Buddy was on Harry's back porch in Haddonfield, New Jersey, the next day.

"IT'S ABOUT TIME" was the new coach's response when his elevation was announced.

Norman got in the spirit. Beaming next to his prize at a press conference, he invoked the mantra: "The next Vince Lombardi of the National Football League." Wow! But Buddy wasn't daunted. The newest High Priest of the Pigskin forecast that the lowly Eagles, under his tutelage, would be a play-off contender next season.

There had been only one stumbling block. Huddling intently in Harry's den, Buddy was happy with the opportunity, happy with the money, happy even with the five-year term, but he wasn't happy at all with the wording that gave Harry (and Norman) final say over any and all personnel decisions. Buddy knew he had more leverage at that moment than he would likely ever have again, and he had always said that if he were head coach, he, and no one else, would call the shots. Everybody in the NFL had heard by now of Norman's courtship of Davy Shula, and the idea of deferring roster moves to the Baron of Biscayne Boulevard was a stopper.

Not to mention deferring to Harry Gamble.

Buddy liked Harry; he really did.

"You're a good judge of talent," he said when Harry first approached him.

But, really. Was a coach of Buddy's stature supposed to submit his decisions for approval to this . . . this . . . *amateur?*

In some ways, Harry and Buddy were alike. Harry was as much a football monk as anyone coaching. He was a gracious, red-haired, self-effacing gentleman with moist gray eyes, a wide square face with a bent red nose, and the broad frame of a former lineman. Both Harry and Buddy were plainspoken charmers who tended to make snap judgments about people (a coach's trait). Harry's story was every bit as authentic, if not as impressive, as Buddy's—it even had its hidden academic side. After playing ball in the army and then at Rider College, Harry tried out for both the Steelers and the Eagles in '48 and got cut from both squads. But he knew by then, in his early twenties, that the Game was the love of his life, and he pursued it faithfully, coaching high-school teams in New Jersey (granted, not exactly the Comstock Lode of football talent) and then at Lafayette College in Easton, Pennsylvania, writing articles in scholastic football magazines to attract attention, and—just in case this football thing didn't work out—earning his master's degree and doctorate in business management at Temple. Harry had even written a book about football, a scholarly tome on the fundamentals and uses of the wing-T formation. It sold ten thousand copies, earning the budding football strategist $2,500 and the kind of credentials, combined with that doctorate, apt to appeal to an Ivy League outfit like the University of Pennsylvania, where Harry was hired as head coach in '71.

Here's where you could start discerning differences between the two men. Buddy wouldn't have lasted a week at Penn, where success wasn't just measured by wins and losses (the priesthood's hard yardstick), but by more esoteric qualities, like effort and character. Presiding over Penn's sleepy football program took patience and tact, suiting up and trying to prepare America's future professional class for their weekly scrums. One thing you can say for the Ivy League, it's kept football in perspective. If you had tossed Penn into the lions' pit of Division I college ball, the players would have been eaten alive, of course, but their roster alone would have brought the division's combined grade point average to respectability. The best thing you could say about a Penn football player was usually something like "He plays linebacker extremely well for a Chinese-lit major." Harry persevered for ten years. When Penn dropped its hockey program, he even picked up a few admits (seats in the freshman class for kids who couldn't meet the school's rigid academic standards but at least didn't look ridiculous in pads). With these recruits, Penn built a team that would dominate the Ivies for the early eighties, but they'd do it without Harry. Years of losses had stirred up even Penn's tolerant alumni, who demanded a change after a spectacularly bad 0–9 showing in '79. The school told Harry he could stay, but that he had to can his staff, and with characteristic rectitude, Harry insisted on going down with the ship. No better measure of the difference between Harry Gamble and Buddy Ryan came at the Penn press conference to announce the firing. Harry told reporters that the winless season, far from being a trial, had been "the most satisfying year of my life."

Imagine!

In '81, Harry took an unpaid job as an assistant on Dick Vermeil's NFC championship Eagles coaching staff. Penn was still paying out the final year of his contract, so he had one year to make himself invaluable, which he did. He got a paying job as tight ends and special teams coach in '82, and when Vermeil unexpectedly retired at the end of that season, Harry became a liaison between the priesthood and the club managers. The team was being run then by Susan Fletcher, Leonard Tose's daughter, and Susan was looking for someone who was in the cult but not *of* it, someone who could carry club concerns to the temple, someone versed in the *X*'s and *O*'s but capable of surfacing long enough to talk about a budget. It's not often that an assistant NFL coach has a Ph.D. in anything, much less business management. The Tose-Fletcher regime was waking up to Harry's full potential; they had just promoted him from administrative assistant to general manager, when Norman swooped in to save Tose and the team from ruin.

Harry was at a league meeting in Arizona when he got word. He flew home expecting the worst. He had never heard of Norman Braman. He met him that day, a tall, slender figure with silver hair and a long, gray overcoat moving enthusiastically around the Eagles' management offices shaking hands and making small talk. Instead of firing Harry, Norman left him in place.

"What would you like to do?" he asked.

"I'd like to do what I'm doing right now. I'd like to be your general manager," Harry said.

"Well, you've got the job."

Harry learned later that Norman had begun looking around for a new general manager right after making the deal, but had encountered, by chance on a plane, former Penn president Martin Meyerson, who had conveyed his high opinion of Harry and explained that Penn's lackluster football program over all those years could not be fairly blamed on the earnest and capable coach.

As Norman's general manager, Harry became guardian of the purse and the boss's chief football adviser. And he wasn't about to abdicate either role to his first major hire. The language in Buddy's contract made it clear that Harry (hence Norman) was firmly in charge. It was, as Norman might say, "a deal breaker."

And it was Buddy who blinked.

"Well, even if I'm not in charge, it has to *look like* I'm in charge," he said.

And Harry bought that on the spot. He could understand where Buddy was coming from. He didn't exactly relish the prospect of disgruntled players trying to get around the head coach by coming directly to him. Both his coaching and management experience counseled against that. So Harry solemnly pledged to maintain the pretense. The issue was adroitly dismissed at the inaugural press conference, with both Buddy and Norman agreeing that the new coach would have "some authority" over personnel decisions. Pressed to be more explicit in coming days, Buddy would say, almost truthfully, "They gave me what I wanted."

What Buddy knew, and what Harry and Norman failed to fully appreciate, was that by promising their new coach the appearance of control, they were effectively giving him control. Both men were novices compared with Buddy. What Harry had in mind was a collegial management-coach relationship, where differences were worked out in private and the organization maintained a united front. It didn't matter to Harry who got up behind the podium. But there wasn't a collegial bone in Buddy's body. And Buddy had been around long enough to understand the role played by the Pack.

Every NFL team has one. By long-standing league practice, the locker-room door is opened for one hour every day, and through it spills a motley collection of amiable parasites, newspaper, TV, and radio reporters, scruffy young to middle-aged men, declining in physique, eager and solicitous in manner, there to collect crumbs of trifle and vapid sound bites to feed the public's insatiable appetite for even the most nugatory information about their team. The tame ones thrilled in equal parts to be sharing space with their football heroes and to be perceived at large as *insiders,* genuine football experts; the ornerier ones were a collection of cynical misfits who, underneath their hard-bitten exterior and unceasing efforts to pry into cracks of team discord, were as thrilled to be in the locker room as the tame ones. Mostly, the Pack was harmless. They wrote reams of adoring prose pumping up the coaches and players and whipping up local enthusiasm for the weekly games. But they were also like the chorus in an ancient Greek play, an extremely annoying chorus standing safely off to one side of the stage and singing praise or criticism after every move the team made. There was a ton of tribute for every feather of fault, but the players mostly hated them anyway. The way players saw it, reporters were a necessary nuisance, glorified fans with a mean streak, all smiles and unctuous goodwill in person, often biting and critical in print or on the air, sticking microphones and cameras in their faces as they tried to gobble a quick sandwich between meetings and workouts, pouncing on them when they were most vulnerable— after dropping a big pass late in a losing game, for instance, or just after being demoted—trying to coax from them comments that could get them in big trouble with their teammates or (worse, and far easier) the coach—*Tell me, Seth, just between you and me . . . don't mind this lil ol' microphone here . . . what do you think about Kotite's play-calling in that game you lost yesterday?* If you took the bait, look out! Your words echoed louder than you'd ever imagined—

SETH RIPS COACH

—and you spent the next week desperately trying to explain your way out of the mess, because once you sounded off, the next wave hit, as the columnists and commentators, the grayheads and round-bellied bigfeet, weighed in, men who never even set foot in the locker room and whom you'd never met, authoritatively psychoanalyzing you in print or on the air and chewing you a new asshole for opening your big mouth, risking the fate of the franchise, and placing your own bigheaded but small-brained self before the team. In a city like Los Angeles, New York, Chicago, Miami, or Philadelphia, this sort of thing happened almost every day. The season was marked as surely by the train of petty tempests in the locker room as by wins and losses on the field. The Trenton *Times*, the Camden *Courier-Post*, the Philadelphia *Inquirer* and *Daily News*, the Wilmington *News-Journal*, the Delaware County *Daily Times*, the Burlington County *Times*, the Atlantic City *Press*, the West Chester *Daily Local News*, the Bucks County *Courier Times*, the Allentown *Morning Call*, the Lancaster *New Era*, the Lancaster *Intelligencer Journal*, the Gloucester County *Times*, the Norristown *Times Herald*, the Reading *Eagle* and Reading *Times*, the York *Daily Record*, the fan magazine *Eagles Digest*, AP, UPI, thirteen separate radio and TV stations—these were just the print and airwave organizations that dogged the Eagles' beat on a regular basis. The Pack regulars numbered into the dozens, all laboring to fill space in the local newspapers and time on the local news programs every day during football season, which now, what with the annual draft, rookie camp, minicamp, training camp, exhibition games, and postseason, took up about ten months of the year. Pro football generated more bad prose and insipid airtime every season than a presidential campaign, and still the stomach of the reading-watching public growled for more. The tidbits mined by the local Pack fed the bigfoot national correspondents and TV-network sports gurus, who repeated it as gospel—no one had time to keep close track of all twenty-eight teams. So an unguarded moment of candor while lacing your cleats before one of these clowns could erupt into a full-fledged national sports crisis, prompting all sorts of dire commentary about your career and the future prospects of your club.

Understandably, most players and coaches labored to say as little of consequence as possible, which suited most of the Pack just fine.

The core of fandom was still hero worship. What the public really wanted was just to glimpse their hero out from under his helmet, or to hear his voice, or to read some tiny insight in prose of what he's *really like*. It didn't matter what he said. As a consequence, pro football had become a sport about which everyone talked incessantly without ever really saying anything—more or less the essence of the sports-talk-radio format.

But the Pack was an essential part of the League, if not the Game, and wise coaches and players understood its power. "Pub" was essential for building your rep in an otherwise faceless game. There were plenty of mediocre players with huge reputations and, hence, huge contracts, but the reverse was also true: a great player with a mediocre rep was apt to have a mediocre contract. What's more, the League encouraged cooperation with the media. There was a little clause in the boilerplate of NFL contracts wherein players agreed to be polite and cooperative with the Pack. Buddy had gotten used to the league's largest and most aggressive Pack in New York during his years with the Jets and kind of missed them up in Minneapolis, when only two or three worshipful reporters would show up for Bud Grant's press conferences. In Chicago, as the Bears climbed to the top of the ladder, Buddy saw the Pack swell to its full frightening *national* proportions, so that by the end of the '85 season there were at least a dozen media types on hand for every player and coach, and the locker room became a surly mob of cameramen, sound engineers, desperate print reporters, and other hangers-on generating controversy and excitement about virtually everything, from how many Super Bowl tickets were hoarded by the Bears' owner, Mike McCaskey, to the slogans on Jim McMahon's headbands.

The Pack was there about one hundred strong on the day the Eagles unveiled their new coach, and Buddy worked the room like the old pro he was, feeding the monster with a steady stream of barbed one-liners, showing off his down-home hauteur, promising to give the boys plenty to write about, which was, of course, all they ever really asked. Veteran reporters could whip a little controversy out of almost anything, but Buddy went them one better; he *fed* them—ripping his own players, for instance, or (with a mischievous glint in his eye) encouraging his own legend.

"Buddy, how did Mike Ditka react to your decision?"

"Mike who?"

The Pack roared with appreciation. His whole performance that day was exquisite. Give a sports reporter a quote to wrap a story around and you've made a friend for ... well, at least a week. Whenever

Buddy said something certain to make somebody else mad (this was just about every day), the Pack loved him all the more. And why not? Editors and producers back at the shop loved this guy. After the ardently vanilla Vermeil, who segued neatly from his football career to one as a corporate TV pitchman, and Campbell, a nonconductor of electricity if God ever made one, Buddy gave off sparks. Buddy was such a vivid character that it hardly mattered what he said. He could pronounce, "The sun was dern hot today," and the Packmen would be elbowing one another, winking and chuckling over what that rascal *really* meant.

In time, their stories about Buddy earned him such a reputation for cutting comebacks and snappy one-liners that people started thinking of him as a comedian, which he wasn't. Buddy was funny because Buddy was funny, not because he tried to be that way. He told the truth crudely and often, and coupled with his country drawl, it made people laugh. He wasn't a raconteur or master of the crisp rejoinder. Most of the time Buddy didn't even know he had said something funny until people laughed. If you took him out of his element, took the whistle off his neck and put him in front of a camera, and expected him to turn into a witty conversationalist . . . well, good luck.

That's exactly what a TV crew tried one afternoon, late in Buddy's tenure. They arrived, looking very arty and hip—long hair, bandannas, earrings (male and female), colorful sneaks—at training camp in West Chester to tape some promotional spots for Buddy's in-season TV show. He agreed to give them a few minutes after the morning practice.

With makeup on his face, the coach perched like a toad on a high stool beneath the bright lights, scowling at the fruity bunch buzzing all around him—oblivious to his disapproval. The job of the director, who looked rigorously Spielbergian in his beard and baseball cap, was to prompt the coach. He plopped down in front of Ryan on a crate off camera, determined to provoke the dry wit people had come to expect from Buddy. The idea was to capture some authentic Buddy-isms on tape and edit them into a series of promos for his show. But Buddy has a good 'ol boy's sixth sense for being made to play the fool; he didn't like the look of this bunch.

"A lot of football expressions have found their way into the language," began the director cheerfully. "So I'm going to say a few terms, and I want you just to free-associate. Suppose, for instance, I said 'Offensive line.' And you said something like, 'The girl at the bar last night told me that was the most offensive line she'd ever heard.' That kind of thing."

"I wouldn't say anything like that," said Buddy.

The director nodded. "But you get the idea," he said, optimistically. "Let's start with that one—offensive line."

"Well, I think our line is going to be real strong this year. We have a couple of returning veterans . . ."

Buddy spoke earnestly for a few moments about the strengths of his blocking front, about the general fine character traits of offensive linemen, and the director listened patiently until he was done.

"Okay," he said. "But that's not what we're fishing for here."

Buddy was growing impatient. He took a long, pointed look at his watch.

"Let me ask you this," the director said. "If Big Al Meltzer [a local sports anchor, cohost of Buddy's show] was a football player, what position would he play?"

"I've known Al for a long time," said Buddy solemnly. "Going all the way back to Buffalo thirty years ago. I've never seen him as somebody who would play football."

"Okay, but let's just pretend that this is, say, twenty years ago, Al is younger and faster, and he's a football player. Do you see him as, say, a lineman? Or a quarterback? A water boy?"

"Well, I'd probably put him somewhere where he wouldn't get hurt. So I'd say water boy." Another long look at the watch. "Come on," Buddy complained. "We're not making a feature film here, are we? This is for a commercial, right?"

It went on like this for about twenty minutes. Then Buddy abruptly hopped off the stool, demiked himself, thanked one and all, and split.

No, Buddy was no TV star, but he understood the Pack. You let them stand on the sidelines during practice and you fed them a steady stream of verbal stingers, and you reminded them at least once or twice a week that they really knew jackshit about football (this was true), and before long they were eating out of your hand. Once Buddy had them eating out of his hand, Harry and Norman were screwed. Since they had agreed to give Buddy the *appearance* of control, all he had to do was sound off to the Pack, and where would that leave the boys upstairs? After introducing his new head coach as the next St. Vince, how was Norman going to publicly reverse him? And right away, if it came down to a popularity contest in the sports media between the meddling Miami car dealer and the new patron saint of smash-mouth football, who do you think would win? The little sumbitch had 'em hog-tied before the new Philadelphia Eagles ever played a game.

Buddy's trump card was, of course, Norman's supposed absentee ownership. If BramanMan had a failing as owner, it was a tendency to get *too* involved (as Eagles fans would discover in coming years), but Buddy turned that perception on its head. Most big personnel decisions were made in summer, when Norman and Irma were away at their villa in southern France. Of course, Norm had a telephone and a fax machine over there. He was in constant touch with Harry and made all the club's big decisions, but Buddy intuitively seized upon the symbolism afforded by the Atlantic Ocean—and, you know, that fruity fer'n culture—and thus Norman, the take-charge NFL owner bent on gratifying his public ego, became, to his deep and lasting chagrin, the Guy in France.

HARRY KEPT his promise to Buddy, even with the regular zingers about the incompetent dabblers upstairs. It started before the Eagles' first training camp. Harry was charged with minding Norman's wallet when bargaining with players through the summer. Corporate coaches, who respected the larger realities of the League (not to mention the folks who signed their paychecks), rarely whined about holdouts. Clearly, no club—no small country—could afford to pay a full roster of pro football players what they thought they were worth. So the task faced by Harry and his minions was to deflate the expectations of an athlete and bring his contract demands back down to earth (and in line with Norm's budget). That meant pointing out all the unpleasant things blustery agents overlooked—*So, let me get this straight, you think that even though you've had two major knee surgeries in four years and led the league in fumbles the last time you played a full season, we should be paying you more than Joe Montana?* While this process went forward, it didn't help when the head coach told the Pack that if those bean counters upstairs didn't get off their duffs and sign some people soon the team would be swimming upstream all season. Buddy routinely sang the praises of players who were holding out, provided they were among his favorites. And, oh, how they loved him for it! Buddy's attitude was strictly Us versus Them, the Game versus the League, the noble dedicated player (and coach) versus the penurious Guy in France. Wins were player triumphs; losses were club failures—"It would help if we could get our guys in here" was the standard Buddy lament.

Then there was the way Buddy acted. It was tough for Norman and Harry to take. Granted, Norman was no choirboy. He'd kicked butt himself in the corporate jungle, and he wanted a head coach who knew how. But Buddy went too far. He taunted opponents, insulted players who couldn't measure up to his standards; he behaved badly—

which was one source, frankly, of his appeal. As Norman saw it, Buddy appealed to the wrong element. He was the hero of the Id-people, the *ugly* football fans, the lowest common denominators. The Id-people were hate-driven fans, who were drawn to football more than any other sport (except maybe pro hockey).

Richie and Norman and the players preferred fans who rooted rationally, who showed up Sundays decked in green and silver and cheered their heads off and then—buoyed by victory or disappointed by defeat—returned to their lives refreshed, pleased with the memory of an exciting afternoon. Norman was convinced most fans were like this. But the most visible and vocal fans were those whose self-worth seemed to hang on the Eagles' fortunes, fans for whom winning was not just a preferred outcome on a fall afternoon, but something owed, by the players, the coaches, ultimately by Norman Braman himself, presumably in return for the cost of their tickets or, for the hardest cases, as a Philadelphia birthright. The Id-people came out on game day, thousands of them, for some primitive venting ritual. They howled abuse and hatred at the enemy—anyone they perceived as an obstacle to victory. They reveled in the violence of football, would cheer when hated opponents (or sometimes hated members of the home team) were carried bleeding, mangled, or unconscious from the field. They were like the throngs who cheered the dismemberment of Christians in Roman coliseums or who turned public hangings into social events. The sheer unthinking brutality of these fans connected vaguely with Norman's Jewishness, summoning disturbing ancestral echoes of murderous mobs, of pogroms, and Kristallnacht.

Needless to say, Id-people were Buddy's biggest backers.

In his character and coaching style, Buddy had tapped into one of the basic underlying themes of American football, and it was a little bit scary. In our Judeo-Christian society, the central dichotomy was Good versus Evil. Buddy's worldview was Homeric. He grasped intuitively that one of football's attractions in our intensely moralistic society was its devotion to a more primitive standard: Victory versus Defeat. Not goodness, but winning (as St. Vince said) was the highest virtue. Who gives a shit how you play the game? The NFL was kind of embarrassed about this, actually, and went to great lengths to promote the good works done by its coaches and players. The underlying theme of virtually all the League's public relations was this effort to overcompensate: *Yeah, we're brutes on the field, but we're supercitizens off it, just a bunch of devoted Christian family men making an honest buck playing the Game.* Slick corporate PR, along with the efforts of the hero-worshiping Pack around every club, not to mention the self-importance of the coaches themselves, whose ghostwritten autobiographies and homilies fed their legends while milking their popularity, had together made coaches like Dallas's Tom Landry, Washington's Joe Gibbs, San Francisco's Bill Walsh, and Don Shula in Miami into secular saints, exemplars of virtuous achievement, models for the modern corporate CEO, molders not just of championship football teams, but of men.

To Buddy this was all a crock. He was a football coach, plain and simple. He answered to no higher calling than winning. He wasn't molding young men; he was looking for football players, mean, fast, strong, smart ones. Did he care that Jerome Brown had been apprehended by the law once or twice in college for toting serious automatic weaponry? Did he care that paternity suits were piling up in local courtrooms in New Jersey naming his players? Did he care that his married players were flying bimbos all over the country to rendezvous with them at hotels when the team was on the road? Buddy's measure of his players began and ended on the gridiron. In his experience, certain off-field excesses often went along with greatness. And if success was important enough to obscure a man's flaws, no collection of virtues was sufficient to offset failure. Failure was the worst character flaw.

Take the case of Dabby Dawson. A short, solid running back from Wichita, Kansas, Dawson was one of the scores of talented football players overlooked in the '90 draft. At the University of Wyoming, he had shattered school records. He was a well-spoken, polite, determined kid, who, after playing schoolboy football with future Lions all-pro Barry Sanders, had prepped for two years in junior college before getting his chance to enroll at Wyoming. Dawson knew he had almost no chance of sticking with the Eagles that summer, but he was out there in the broiling August heat, giving it his all.

He lasted only two days. In a routine seven-on-seven drill, Dawson and quarterback Jim McMahon bungled a handoff, and the next thing the running back knew he was being led off the field by Eagles personnel director Joe Woolley. Ordinarily, when players in training camp are cut from the team, Woolley (in team parlance, "the Turk," bearer of the broad, curved sword) knocks on their door early in the morning, and they are gone before the team suits up for practice. While it makes for more than a few sleepless nights among the rookies in the dorm, the procedure is swift and humane. But in Dawson's case, Buddy wanted to make an example. So he had him led right off the practice field in his pads.

"That got our attention," said Fred Barnett, a rookie draft pick on the field that day. "We'd never seen a coach do that before, humiliate a guy like that."

After practice, Buddy had this chuckling explanation for the Pack: "We had to git rid of number thirty-nine; he's lackin' in some stomach muscles. This stuff is contagious. We have to git him out before it rubs off on other guys."

In other words, Dawson was a coward.

"He ran the ball like a hen—you know, two steps and then squat," explained Woolley, getting in the spirit. "Didn't want to run into people."

The kid never got this or any other explanation. By the time practice was over, Dawson was at Philadelphia International waiting for a flight back to Wichita, wondering what went wrong. He was crushed. On the play before he was given the boot, he hadn't even gotten the ball. The way he saw it, he had never even had a chance!

Maybe they were right about Dawson, thought Harry. After all, both Buddy and Joe were time-tested experts at judging talent. But why publicly embarrass the young man? And then gloat about it to the Pack? It was unseemly, and neither Norman nor Harry liked it. Stories like that traveled fast in the NFL and tarnished the image of the team and the league. Harry complained to Buddy about it, but the coach wasn't backing down. Dabby Dawson had failed Buddy's test, and that alone made the kid not just inadequate, but somehow despicable.

"I didn't want him around here anymore," Buddy said. "Because he made me sick, and he made the other people around here sick."

To Buddy, it was simple truth. He disdained the euphemisms commonly employed by coaches—"He's a good kid, just got caught up in the numbers game." That was the kind of line handed out by the Corporate Coach.

"They make me want to vomit," Buddy said.

Buddy's measure of a football player had nothing to do with decency or honesty or any other of the conventional virtues. Niceness was particularly disdained. Football players weren't supposed to be nice. "I've got two nice kids at home," he once said, referring to the younger two of his three sons, "but I wouldn't want 'em playing for me." Once, after a spring session with a new crop of hopeful rookies, Buddy was pulled aside by a young player and then came walking off the field shaking his head, laughing to himself with disbelief.

"Handed out Eagles caps to 'em all today," he explained. "Kid just wanted to thank me for the hat."

Something about this tickled him so much he had to turn away and take a deep breath to stop laughing.

"What a nice kid," he said, not in an approving tone, but expressing mild scorn, even sadness, as if to say, *Kid don't have a prayer.*

Harry endured it. He even endured Buddy's overt contempt. He knew that the coach had his Pack and most of the public convinced that he, Harry Gamble, was a certifiable football ignoramus, toady for the Guy in France. But Harry was patient and humble to a fault. He could tolerate Buddy's abuse, he could even accept the whole dynamic of Us versus Them, so long as it paid dividends on the field. It wasn't exactly a bargain with the devil, but sometimes that's what it felt like. Harry felt honor-bound, if not to Buddy himself, then to their agreement. He was even willing to put his own hide on the line to save Buddy's. Which happened about once a year.

One of the worst times was when the Players Association went on strike in '87, and the League decided to make a travesty of the Game by insisting on playing out the schedule without the players. They would try to lure players to break ranks and cross the picket lines and, failing that, hastily recruit NFL wanna-bes off the streets to play. It would have been comical if it hadn't been so pathetic. Buddy's immediate response was to tell his boys either to stay or walk, but to stick together.

It was good advice, the advice of a coach working hard to assemble a team and mindful of how the stresses of an extended labor action might tear it apart. It was also advice guaranteed to make the players' strike against the Eagles 100 percent effective, because anyone close to an NFL locker room knew that a vast majority of players supported the strike—which challenged the detested free-agency system, the League's way of preventing players from selling their talents to the highest bidder. The League's whole strategy was to undermine team unity. They were counting on individual players' (a selfish lot used to living week to week on a relatively large paycheck) breaking ranks. Buddy's advice made that *a lot* more difficult for Norman's team, because breaking ranks for an Eagle now meant betraying, not some loose coalition of pro players trying to forge a union, but their own friends and teammates and, more important, Coach. Buddy's advice effectively signed on his entire roster for the duration. Of course, he hadn't asked for Harry's and Norman's guidance on this matter, and by the time the guys upstairs found out, their team, down to the last man, was on the picket line.

And what could Norman do? He'd propped the fat Okie on such a high pedestal it was near impossible to get him off. And Buddy's move just made him more popular in a union town like Philadelphia, where striking players holding out for the chance to push their six-figure contracts into seven figures were joined by throngs of meaty Teamsters, pipe fitters, and roofers, men who wouldn't make in their lifetimes what some of the players were making in one season.

Buddy didn't stop there. Abruptly teamless, the club began hastily assembling forty young men willing to brave the picket lines in order to wear Eagles uniforms for a game against the ersatz Bears five days hence. While Joe Woolley and Harry's assistant, George Azar, were rounding up bodies from the shards of that summer's training camp, Norman was predicting a long strike.

"If we gave the players the right to select the team they desired to play for, the balance we have created over the years in making football the number-one sport in the United States would absolutely be jeopardized," he told the Pack. "So, much as I hate to say it, the issue of free agency is something that we're not prepared to surrender on."

Breaking the strike meant fielding scab teams every Sunday and, even if it really wasn't particularly good football, insisting that it was to the suckers still watching. The League figured most fans couldn't tell the difference anyway. The idea was to package the junker like a Rolls (right up a car dealer's alley, right?).

"Our strike players are individuals who have extensive backgrounds in football," Norm announced. "A number of them, or all of them, were in camp, either our camp or someone else's camp—we'll have a good product."

Buddy, to his credit, refused to play used-car salesman.

"We might have the worst bunch of guys together we've ever seen," he said in his mandated weekly telephone hookup with the visiting team's Pack, in this case Buddy's old Chicago group. Yukking it up with his old pals, Buddy couldn't help himself. "I don't know what anybody else has, but I'd trade mine with anybody's, sight unseen."

Out in the parking lot before Sunday's game, Norman was appalled. The savior of Philadelphia's franchise, the white knight, had to run a gauntlet of abuse to enter the stadium. He later compared the scene outside the Vet to "hooliganism and mobsterism."

"The only thing missing today in Philadelphia was the Ku Klux Klan," he said. The ingratitude of this city! The effrontery!

Buddy's team lost 35–3, and meeting afterward with the Pack at the obligatory postgame press conference, his tongue was firmly in cheek: "I think that, no question about it, we got soundly outcoached in every phase of the game," he said, with a wink. "The Bears staff did a super job, and Ditka, they outcoached the heck out of us. Our guys tried hard. They gave it great effort. It's just we couldn't make any plays on defense, and our offense had trouble making plays," which just about covered it.

The scab team lost to Dallas the following week, and after they dropped their third and final game against Green Bay, Norman paid a visit to the locker room. He kicked a stool, interrupting a postgame prayer session, apologized to the strike players for Buddy's attitude, and, at least according to some of the soon-to-be ex-Eagles in attendance, referred to the next St. Vince as an "asshole." Norm denied calling Buddy a bad name, but was pissed enough to write out in longhand a diatribe against the local Pack and his onetime hometown. Cooler heads (Harry and Irma) prevailed on him to tone it down.

As angry as Norman was at Buddy when the strike fizzled (it was a big victory for the owners) the coach's behavior had endeared him to his players and Philly fans. In the first months after taking over the team, Buddy had bruised a lot of player egos. Reverend Reggie, for instance, considered the new coach arrogant and even a little stupid. But after the strike, players warmly embraced the squat tyrant. He had stood by them at personal risk through the ordeal. Norman, of course, had accomplished just the opposite. The strike hastened a process Buddy already had under way: the Eagles had become *his* team, and no one else's.

Still, he wasn't finished. When the Eagles finished that season with seven wins and eight losses (three of them courtesy of the strike games), and fell short of the postseason play-offs for the sixth straight year, Buddy preempted any effort to assign blame by opening his annual postmortem press conference with some theater.

Calling Woolley to the podium, with the cameras rolling and the Pack hanging on every word, he presented the team's laconic personnel director with two ridiculously oversized brass rings.

"We went to a lot of expense, the coaching staff and equipment people and trainers all went together, and put in a lot of money and bought Joe and George [Azar] a couple of scab rings for all they did for us to get that scab personnel."

In other words: *Y'all don't blame me.*

Woolley, a big, easygoing Arkansan with a healthy sense of humor and acres of self-confidence, shrugged the whole thing off, and if he had been the only target of Buddy's darts the whole thing would have ended there. But by singling out Azar, Buddy had indirectly insulted Harry.

George Azar had been Harry's shadow for more than twenty years. Harry had hired him in '65 when he was coaching at Lafayette, taken George with him to Penn, and, after being named Eagles general manager, brought George in as his assistant. He was a short, muscular man (he had been a state wrestling champion as a Johnstown, Pennsylvania, schoolboy) with a graying crew cut, and nobody was quite sure what George's role was with the Eagles, other than, as the club's media guide put it, to "assist Harry in numerous club matters." George was ostensibly charged with some scouting responsibilities, but the scouts chuckled when asked about it. George was like a wagon hitched to Harry's rear bumper. A shot at George was a shot at Harry.

And Harry was furious. Most people never saw Harry lose his temper. His manner was so genial and upbeat, it was hard to picture him mad. But cross Harry, and you confronted the unholy wrath of the righteous. The smile vanished, and that soft face hardened. Without the twinkle, Harry's gray eyes were like steel bearings. The effect was dramatic.

"Why would you *do* something like that?" he asked Buddy.

"It was just a joke."

"I don't get it," said Harry. "It's such poor judgment . . . to humiliate people and point fingers . . . it reflects badly on the organization."

"I didn't mean it that way. I never thought it would be taken seriously," Buddy protested.

When Norman found out, he said, "That's it." He was going to fire Buddy once and for all.

But Harry talked him out of it. No one was madder at Buddy about the incident than Harry. It was, he felt, unprofessional, cruel, and just plain lousy. He had told Buddy so to his face. And, yes, Harry didn't like Buddy Ryan. But as crude as Buddy's methods were, he got results. Harry was convinced that, without the strike-game losses, the Eagles might have squeaked into the play-offs. In just two years, Buddy had used the draft to acquire Seth Joyner, Clyde Simmons, Keith Byars, Cris Carter, and Jerome Brown (future all-pros), as well as productive starters Anthony Toney, Byron Evans, and Dave Alexander. The team was moving in the right direction. Harry could see the players' newfound respect for Buddy. Something was happening with this group. Dumping the head coach now could be disastrous.

"Look, if Buddy doesn't have a winning season in '88, then kick us both out," Harry said.

Norman considered that option quietly for a moment. "No way I would do that to you, Harry."

So Buddy stayed and didn't change one bit. But to an extent he didn't fully understand, the strike year had clarified the terms of his tenure. So long as the team continued to improve, Norman would wait. But if the team stumbled or stalled, it was going to give him pleasure to show the pompous little smart-ass the door.

The Eagles won the NFC East division the next year with ten wins and six losses and lost a fog-bound play-off game against Ditka and the real Bears. In '89, Buddy won eleven games and lost only five, but again lost in the first round of the play-offs. In '90, the final tally was ten wins and six losses, and the Eagles faced another play-off game, this time against the Redskins. And this time, while no one except Norman knew it for sure, the Eagles would be playing for Buddy's job.

BUDDY HAD STARTED OFF '90 badly. At the end of a third-straight winning season, and with one year remaining on his contract, the coach announced he'd like to renegotiate. He had reason to think his position was strong. Always a firm adherent of the MEAT principle (Maximize Earnings at All Times), Buddy's wide, four-eyed mug had become ubiquitous in Philadelphia. He endorsed products, everything from diet food to caps to cars, had his own weekly in-season TV show, a radio call-in show, and a 900 number. His paid public appearances were much in demand. He even charged the kid who came by once a week to interview him for the ghostwritten "Coach's Corner" column in the weekly fan magazine, *Eagles Digest*. There hadn't been so much excitement about the Eagles since Vermeil's heydey a decade earlier. In four seasons, Buddy hadn't delivered on his Super Bowl boasts, but everybody believed it was only a matter of time. Buddy felt secure enough to put the squeeze on BramanMan.

He told the Pack that he might not honor the remaining year of his contract unless it was extended.

Norman summoned the coach upstairs. When he means business, Norman moves in close, eyeball to eyeball, and speaks bluntly.

"I read your remarks," he told Buddy. "I might have before, but now I promise you, I'm not even going to talk to you about your contract until it's up. And let me give you some advice. I've learned this all through my business career and I know it's accurate: *Never shit where you eat*. And that's precisely what you've done. We'll talk about your future here *after* this season is over, and not before."

Buddy was all *aw shucks* about it, and the matter of a contract extension was never mentioned again.

Then came the Keith Jackson episode.

This is what pushed Norman over the edge. Keith was one of the triumphs of Buddy's drafting acumen, a tall, wide Oklahoma tight end with the size of a lineman and the hands and speed of a wide receiver. Buddy picked him first in the '88 draft, immediately appointed him a starter, displacing the Eagles' popular veteran John Spagnola (the Pack loudly disapproved), and Keith responded with a hellacious rookie season, catching eighty-one passes for 869 yards (Spagnola caught five for 40 yards with the Seattle Seahawks). Keith finished as rookie of the year and was the NFC's starting tight end in the Pro Bowl.

In addition to his obvious physical gifts, Jackson was a charmer, a witty dancing bear of a man who played the cello and aspired to become a rap star—among other things. He was a breezy egotist, outspoken and admired, kind of the offense's more polished answer to Jerome. Everybody liked Keith, from the Pack to the ball boys whom he teased at practice to the receptionists who answered the phone upstairs to Harry to . . . hell, even Norman liked Keith.

Liking players was a temptation owners indulged at their risk. If a player did well, he would ask for the moon when his contract was up, and if he did poorly, he would ask for the moon anyway. The closer you got to a player, the harder it was to stay objective. This was a common coaching failure. Owners knew and fully expected Coach to grow fond of particular players and try to keep them beyond their usefulness. Business dealings with players had to be hard-edged; there was a lot of money at stake. So Norman and Harry avoided getting too cozy with anyone on the roster. But Keith was hard to resist. He had earned his degree at Oklahoma in just three and a half years (many pro players lacked enough credits to graduate after five years), and shortly after joining the team he opened a retail clothing store in Edgewater Park, New Jersey, called Keith Jackson's Silk, Leather and You. He was bubbling with talent, energy, and ambition. He played hard with a broad smile. He lit up a room.

Norman invited Keith down to Indian Creek Island after that rookie season. He took an interest in Keith's family, offering to help them out of a jam once or twice. When Keith suffered painful back spasms in a Monday night game in Chicago, Norman and Irma accompanied him to Northwestern University Hospital and stayed at his bedside until early the next morning. If there ever was an Eagles player destined to enter Norman's inner circle, Keith was the man.

Except—Keith had this little problem with his contract.

The deal Jackson signed in '88 reflected that year's going rate for a first-round draft pick, thirteenth chosen overall. It was a four-year deal, worth about $2.5 million in all. Keith collected an $800,000 signing bonus upfront, and his salary (with a $62,500 payoff for making the team each year and about $100,000 in incentives) would go from about $350,000 in his first season to $400,000 in '89, then $450,000 in '90, to more than $500,000 in '91. It was a fair salary, and Keith was happy with it until he turned out to be a better football player than anyone expected—including him and his agent, the pugnacious Gary Wichard. By the time he made the Pro Bowl for the second year in a row, happy-go-lucky Keith was feeling disgruntled and underpaid.

And for Gary, this meant failure. It wounded his pride. We're talking about Mr. Upfront here, the agent who made University of Oklahoma linebacker Brian Bosworth the best-paid, most famous multimillionaire in football with a ten-year, $11 million contract *before he even suited up for a pro game!* And then, when the Boz flopped big-time (he ended up playing in only twenty-four games, rather unspectacularly, before retiring with a shoulder injury), Gary had neatly segued his career into Hollywood, signing him to a string of atrocious action pictures that were box-office flops but that made Bosworth (and Mr. Upfront) at least briefly famous.

Now comes Keith, an opposite case. Drafted in the same year as the Boz, Keith was already a two-time all-pro, and he's making less than half a mil per annum? Think what this meant to the image of Mr. Upfront.

When Gary, a motormouth anyway, cornered Harry in Hawaii after Keith's second Pro Bowl appearance, he should have been wearing a warning sign that said CONTENTS UNDER PRESSURE. Armed with stats and projections, fluent hyperbole and a ton of legitimate gripe, Gary launched into the same spiel he would later repeat to any reporter whose phone number was within reach.

Mr. Upfront was all worked up.

"You are not going to get a Rolls-Royce and pay Honda prices," reaching for a Bramanesque metaphor. "And don't tell me my guy isn't as deserving of a new deal as Randall was [Norman had renegotiated Randall's contract in midseason '88, locking in the quarterback with a five-year, $12 million deal], and don't tell me it's because Randall is a quarterback and deserved it—I find that to be very discriminating to a football player . . . Keith Jackson has done things that no other player in the history of the game has done at that position . . . third-highest vote getter in the all-NFL, great guy in the clubhouse, great guy off the field . . . what are we talking about here? You talk to me about the sanctity of a contract? In the NFL? Let's talk about that every cut-down day! There's no such animal! That's pie-in-the-sky nonsense. There *is* no contract. Go talk to some of these guys who are down and out, who have been cut. Contracts don't mean crap in this league. These guys are interchangeable parts. But you can't interchange anyone with Keith Jackson, not anyone in the game. . . ."

Somewhere in here, Gary paused to take a breath, and Harry said something crisply responsive, like "No way."

And that was that. Keith showed up for minicamp in May, and then again in July for Buddy's annual voluntary camp, but on day one of the '90 training camp, the team's Pro Bowl tight end was missing.

"I don't know where he is," said Buddy, adding, predictably, "We need him in here though."

And the standoff began.

From Keith's perspective, there was no excuse for him to be underpaid. Things had never looked better for the NFL. Under the league's new TV contract that year, the Eagles were guaranteed $28 million before they sold a ticket. That income alone was $5 million more than the team's total player payroll and was up from just $17.8 million the year before, a lump $10 million increase in revenue that profited Keith not one penny. The Eagles would earn another $23 million in ticket sales. Add $6 million more for skybox rentals (under a sweetheart deal with the city designed to keep the Eagles in town), another $1.2 million in program and yearbook sales—the grand total, when you added in concession income, royalties, insurance proceeds, and other revenue sources, was just about $61 million. When you subtracted the team's expenses, it turned out the Eagles were the NFL's most profitable franchise—one would expect nothing less from BramanMan, whose firm grasp on a dollar was legendary.

The trick to profitability (if not Super Bowl victories) was holding down expenses. Norman's execs, scouts, and coaches were making some of the lowest salaries in the league. Scouts scouring the hinterlands for talent weren't allowed one penny of entertainment expense; they wooed college coaches out of their own pockets. Richie Kotite, in his year as offensive coordinator, was called on the carpet by the folks upstairs for making daily phone calls to his ailing parents in Miami. "Take it out of my paycheck!" Richie fumed. The Eagles' locker room, training room, and weight room (in contrast to the snazzy practice and training facilities other teams built for themselves) were shoehorned into the basement of the Vet, plagued by moisture, bugs, and rats. Players arriving from deep-pocket Big Ten college programs, used to state-of-the-art facilities, indoor and outdoor practice fields, arena-sized gymnasiums, gleaming training rooms with mirrored walls and separate high-tech machines for seemingly every muscle and sinew in their bodies, were appalled to discover that a gloomy closet-sized weight room with—get this—*barbells* and a few antique early-generation Nautilus machines was the destination of their life's ambition. *This is the big league?*

They were even more shocked when the Eagles' equipment manager, Rusty Sweeney, demanded payment for their practice cleats or an extra pair of white socks. Players who could obtain boxfuls of such athletic accoutrements gratis from the sporting goods manufacturers—salesmen vied for their endorsements—found themselves bargaining to replace a worn-out jock.

"Where's the old one?" Rusty would ask.

"Jesus, I threw it away!"

"Where?"

"I don't know. In the trash!"

"If you want another one, you have to return it."

And off the young millionaire would go to root through the bin.

Well, Ebenezer Bargaintown Braman might think he was one tough old boot, but he hadn't yet matched wits with Mr. Upfront.

The owner, of course, was going to eat Mr. Upfront like an after-dinner mint. Norman had always been very, very good at knowing exactly where he stood in a negotiation, and, in this case, Keith didn't have a prayer. He had signed a contract, and that was that. The rules, so exquisitely weighted in favor of the League, were clear. Keith could honor the original deal, or he could carry bags for the Boz and watch football on TV.

"We're not going to renegotiate, and that's all I have to say about it," said the Guy in France, polite but more than a little miffed to be disturbed by a reporter at his villa that summer about something so trivial.

Like an ant trying to move a house, Gary huffed and puffed.

"Keith's prepared to sit out the whole season," he warned.

So Keith sat. All through the Eagles' five-game exhibition season and training camp, Keith sat. The week before the Eagles' first regular season game, the club signed former Pro Bowl tight end Mickey Shuler, who had just been released by the Jets. Shuler was penciled in as a starter. For weeks the club wouldn't even talk about Keith until Norman, reluctantly, agreed to address the issue once more before the season opener against the Giants. Just in from the villa, looking cool and unflappable in a dark blue business suit, he stood on a chair, squinted into the klieg lights, grimaced, and calmly upped the ante.

"Keith's contract basically states, in fact it actually states, that his $800,000 signing bonus is based on $200,000 for each year of the four contract years. We feel that if Keith Jackson is not going to fulfill his end of the contract, then a portion of that money for each game that he is not present should be returned to the Philadelphia Eagles."

Norman wasn't just going to let Keith sit. He was going to sue his young pal. But he left the door open for Keith to come home.

"I find the situation particularly regrettable," he said, looking genuinely sad. "I've had a close association with Keith. When Keith was hurt in Chicago last year, Irma and I spent the whole night till five o'clock in the morning at his bedside. It was as though my own son or daughter had been injured. And I think that Keith has been victimized by bad advice, and I'm hoping that he will come back into the fold, join the Philadelphia Eagles, and contribute to what we think will be a very successful season."

The Eagles lost to the Giants that night (Shuler caught five passes for fifty-four yards) and then lost their second game of the season to the Cardinals (Shuler caught six passes for sixty-three yards).

Still Keith sat. The Eagles didn't call. Philadelphia Eagles, Inc., versus Keith Jackson was set in motion. Not only was Keith receiving no paycheck, and pissing away his chance of posting the kind of numbers he would need to make the Pro Bowl and his other contract incentives, but the Sit was now in danger of costing him. The lawsuit contended he owed Norman $12,500 per game. *It's harder to give something up than to turn something down.*

"As far as I'm concerned, there is no Keith Jackson," said Norman the day after the second loss. "We are not going to renegotiate the contract. We are very happy with the job being done by Mickey Shuler."

Mr. Upfront began to panic. Earlier in the summer, he had stayed coolly aloof, neglecting to return phone calls from the Pack for weeks at a time. Now, unbidden, he started phoning selected newshounds and columnists. He'd call right on deadline, and you couldn't get him off the phone.

"After the game Sunday, Keith was shocked," said Gary, in a call after the Phoenix loss. "He's starting to panic for the team. Keith's not sitting back and saying, 'I told you so.' He's really concerned about Buddy and about Buddy's job and his teammates. Norman and Harry are a bunch of tough guys. When they take a stand they mean business. They sure put me in my place and they sure put Keith in his place and they're sitting there watching an 0-and-2 team go down the tubes. They sure know how to take care of business. Unbelievable. Unbelievable. They're not talking to the right people. If you talk to the right people maybe you can get something done. My attorney doesn't need to talk to their attorney, what do they have to do with the Philadelphia Eagles? Norman says there is no Keith Jackson? I know there's a Keith Jackson. I think last year there were twelve catches and three TDs the second game of the year. I know there's a Keith Jackson. If they don't want to acknowledge it, that's their prerogative. It certainly is reflected in what's going on over there. I don't understand what the whole deal is. Norman has skillfully, in an astute, businesslike way, painted himself into a corner."

Well, one thing was right. Norman wasn't going anywhere. At this point, people were starting to feel sorry for Keith and his agent.

Two days later, the holdout cracked. Gary announced that Keith was coming back. Mr. Upfront had just been kicked in the ass, hard, and was he mad.

"Keith's decision to come in doesn't have anything to do with that egomaniac Norman Braman," he whined. "Braman may know how to hustle cars in Miami, but he doesn't know a thing about professional football. A smart businessman would never paint himself into a corner the way that Braman did. I should include Harry Gamble in this— they're the Abbott and Costello of professional football."

That was all well and good. Norman and Harry would get a good chuckle over the Abbott and Costello line.

And the episode would have ended right there, except for Buddy. All through the holdout, Buddy made it clear he wasn't buying this Mickey Shuler bullshit. He pined publicly for his tight end every chance he got. When Keith abandoned the Sit, Buddy sent a white stretch limo to the airport to pick him up. And when the prodigal son got to the Vet, Buddy sat down beside him for a highly unusual press conference (Harry and his staff didn't even find out about the little séance until it was over).

Keith's theory was this: Norman wasn't just indifferent to whether his team won or lost, he actually *wanted* his team to lose. *See, there was this conspiracy* . . .

And Keith, the loyal soldier, wasn't going to let that happen. All that was missing was Keith's cello to provide a dramatic sound track.

"I'm back for the team and for Coach Ryan," he said. "I heard rumors that there was some conspiracy going upstairs to get rid of Coach Ryan, and I figured if I come in and we win, there's no way they can get rid of him."

Knowing Keith's importance to the team, see, Norman and Harry had deliberately refused to come to terms with him, anticipating that the team would then lose, and they would have the excuse they presumably needed to fire Buddy. In other words, Buddy and his boys were the only ones in the club interested in winning, and they would continue to try despite the efforts of management to thwart them.

"Have you learned anything from this, Keith?"

"Yeah, it's a big difference between the first floor and the fourth floor," he said knowingly, arm around his head coach.

Buddy beamed.

This time, Harry knew as he threw himself in front of Norman's wrath that it would be the last time he could get away with it. One of Norman's star players had sat there with the coach and announced he, Norman Braman, was conspiring to *lose* football games? When Harry confronted Buddy about the impromptu press conference and the conspiracy theory, Buddy played innocent. He was just trying to welcome his boy home, he explained. He didn't know what Keith was going to say, for God's sake. It wasn't his fault. Who believed that shit anyway?

That's how it was with Buddy. The Eagles' president would feel the kick from behind, but when he'd turn around, Buddy was all innocence—*Hey, Harry, that wasn't me done that . . . leastways, not on purpose.* For all his legendary toughness, Harry found Buddy decidedly nonconfrontational off the field.

Well, a confrontation was coming. After this one, Harry wasn't even sure a Super Bowl would save Buddy's job.

ON JANUARY 5, 1991, the Redskins crushed the Eagles 20–6 in the first round of the NFC play-offs.

After the game, as sixty-five thousand disappointed fans exited the Vet, Norman stood tall at the center of the Eagles' basement locker room with his long arms folded, shoulders slightly stooped, head high, chin thrust forward and slightly off center. Norman had a look of bemused discomfort on his face, like a man having a wart removed from his heel. His crossed arms exposed a heavy gold watch on one bony wrist. There wasn't a whisper of wrinkle in the smooth blue fabric of the suit coat that stretched across his back. Under soft fluorescent lights, the back of his neck was crimson between silver curls and stiff white collar.

He had nothing to say. For such a notorious hard loser, the Eagles' owner seemed to be taking this latest play-off loss pretty well.

The first had been a disappointment, the second a surprise. This time, to all but those whose lives were caught up in the quasi-religious fury of this game, it had a faint aura of comedy. Buddy's team was like one of those early NASA rockets that kept toppling off the pad at launch, going *poof!* Around Norman was scattered the wreckage. Dirty, sweaty players peeled off layers of blood-specked padding and tape, lost in the first stage of grief—spacey, disbelieving. Maneuvering fiercely around them was the Pack, swelled with out-of-town reinforcements, elbowing like scavengers on a giant carcass, vying to ask all the obvious painful questions.

Norman had, of course, already decided to fire Buddy. As if losing alone hadn't sealed it, Buddy disgusted his boss one last time by deciding, late in the game, to yank Randall (whom Norman considered one of the premier players in all football) and replace him with McMahon, a move guaranteed to rattle and demoralize the emotionally fragile starter, whose nightmares about being replaced by the former Bears star were well known. The dramatic gesture was made especially pointless when, after Jimmy Mac flopped in one clumsy series, Buddy stuck Randall back in. This accomplished three things that Norm could see: (1) blew an offensive series; (2) sent a clear signal of Buddy's desperation to the Redskins; and (3) fatally jarred what little poise Randall had left, aborting any slim chance of a comeback.

"Care to comment, Mr. Braman?" a hound asked.

"I'm disappointed, the players are disappointed, the coaches, and, of course, the fans," the owner said, grimacing. "It's a kick in the ass."

As for the coach's status?

"Nothing's changed," Norman said. He would pick the moment.

At about the same time, across the dark hallway, Buddy was making his way toward a podium through an aisle clogged with reporters. There was a buzz in the air like the mood in an arena before a prizefight. Buddy's five-year deal with the Eagles was up. There had been no Super Bowl trips, not even close. And few in Philly were unaware of the ill will Buddy had so brazenly sown upstairs. The scent of the crusty blowhard's blood was in the air.

Ryan's round face was obscured by the microphones.

"It's hard to win a ball game when you don't block anybody," he said, speaking in a calm, measured tone. Full of feisty brag in victory, Buddy was mellow in defeat; he reacted more with disgust than anger.

His decision to insert Jimbo was just an act of desperation. "I thought a different pitcher might get us something going," he said.

"Buddy, what are your plans now?" boomed a voice from the back of the room, trying to coax comment on his status.

"I want to meet with the squad at eleven o'clock tomorrow, and then I'll start looking at Plan B people, getting that ready," Buddy said, refusing to concede any doubt about his rehiring.

So the Pack bored in harder: "Are you as optimistic that you will be back here next season as you were a few weeks ago?"

"Yeah. You're not?" Buddy grinned knowingly. The room erupted in laughter.

"The thinking is that throughout the season we've been hearing you had to win to stay," said another reporter, picking up the ball.

"I don't know who thought that, but a lot of people don't realize it's a tough thing to even get to these play-offs."

"We saw Norman talking to you as you came to the locker room. What did he say?"

"He said, I believe it was something like this, 'Sorry, Coach. Tough loss.' The only place that Norman and I don't get along is in the newspapers."

"Buddy, if everything can be worked out, do you want to come back?"

"Oh, you know I do. I built this team. Why would I want to let somebody else come in and take all the bows?"

On Sunday morning, Norman had breakfast with Harry.

"We've got to get rid of him," he told the club president. "I've told you before, get rid of him, and I've let you talk me out of it. This time, I'm not going to let you talk me out of it."

Norman then went to New York. He went to the Whitney Museum to see a Robert Rauschenberg show that featured a painting loaned from his collection. Then he went to the William Doyle Gallery to look at some porcelain that was coming up for auction. He and Irma had dinner that night with Elie Wiesel, the Nobel Peace Prize winner, and his wife, Marion, who had been their guest at the game on Saturday. On Monday morning Norman had NFL business on his schedule.

While at the league's New York offices, Norman took a call from Robert Fraley, Buddy's agent.

"When are we going to get started on Buddy's new contract?" Fraley asked.

"The truth is, before that starts I have to make up my mind whether I want Buddy back."

Norman promised to give Fraley an answer fast.

He took Amtrak back to Philly that evening and dined with Harry and with the team's public relations director, Ron Howard. He asked Ron to prepare for him, overnight, a survey of recent head coach hirings in the NFL, looking at which teams promoted coaches from their own staff and which went outside the organization to hire a new coach and then contrasting their records. He told them to summon the Pack for a four o'clock press conference.

That night he had a long conversation on the phone with Jack Kemp, who was skiing in Vail. Kemp told him the transition would probably go better for his team if he promoted an assistant coach, which meant Norman would have to decide on either offensive coordinator Richie Kotite, who had been with the team only one year, or Jeff Fisher, the young former Bears defensive back and punt returner whom Buddy had brought in as his defensive assistant. Norman made up his mind that night to hire Fisher. Buddy had built a primarily defensive team, and the transition would go more smoothly, he thought, by elevating the defensive assistant.

When he came to work at nine on Tuesday morning, Norman dropped his coat and briefcase in his office and chatted briefly with Harry. Howard's hasty survey showed no advantage to hiring an outsider or promoting a new head coach. Norman explained his preference for Fisher. Harry asked him to reconsider.

"Keep an open mind about Richie Kotite," Harry said. He urged Norman to interview both Jeff and Richie before making up his mind. Harry said he thought Richie ought to get more consideration.

"I'll take care of Buddy for you," Harry told him.

"No way," said Norman. "I'll take care of Buddy myself."

He rode the elevator downstairs, walked into Buddy's office, pulled the door shut, and slumped into one of the chairs across from the coach's desk.

"I've decided, without any prodding from anyone, that I'm not going to extend your contract," he said.

"Why?" asked the coach. To Norman, Buddy looked stupefied.

"You aren't the type of person I want to have around here," the owner said.

Norman chose not to elaborate. He said the team seemed stuck. They needed someone who could take them to the Next Level.

"Well, it's your football team, you can do whatever you want to," said Buddy sadly. " 'Course, I believe that I can take a team to the Super Bowl. I've been to three of them with three different teams."

"You know, Buddy, your record should speak for itself," Norman advised. He then added a threat. "You had better get your act together. You have to learn to be part of an organization. You can start today. If you go out of here with some class, I think you can get another job in this league. I hope you can get a job. If you go out of here with no class, I don't think anybody will touch you."

And that was that. Norman went back upstairs, feeling immensely relieved, happier than he had felt since the day he bought the team. Buddy's agent, Fraley, was on the phone within minutes. Norman expected the agent to launch into a defense of Buddy, but instead Fraley suggested that Norman consider Howard Schnellenberger, another client, as a possible replacement. Norman said no thanks.

Word spread immediately through the coaches' suite and then out the telephone lines to the rest of the city. Some of the veteran assistants, anticipating the usual wholesale bloodletting that follows the ousting of a High Priest, began cleaning out their desks. Lew Carpenter, the white-haired, gimpy receivers coach, had his belongings in a box when he stepped into Richie Kotite's office.

"I enjoyed working with you," he said.

Richie told him to hold on. Harry had by then told both him and Fisher that they were being considered for the top job.

Buddy called his own press conference later that morning, before clearing out his desk and leaving for good. There was a good crowd, but on such short notice, hardly a full turnout.

"I'm a little bit disappointed," Buddy said. "The crowd is not as big as it was when they hired me five years ago, but I guess this'll have to do. I just wanted to thank Norman Braman for giving me the opportunity to coach a pro football team, to do a good job, I believe that we're a lot better team than what we had when I came here, and that's about all there is to it. I'm sorry I didn't get a chance to finish out, but I think that everybody is proud of the Eagles."

"What reason did he give you?"

"Reason? That he didn't think we'd go on to the next level, whatever that is."

"Were you surprised?"

"Well, really, I was. You know, I've been fired before, but usually it's for losing. I've never been fired for winning before."

"Are you angry?"

"Hey, I got a great opportunity. I think I did a great job, and hopefully I'll go somewhere else and do a great job. In this business, you don't feel sorry for Buddy Ryan. I knew what this business was like when I got into it."

"If you had it all to do over again, would you have done anything differently?"

"No. Well, I wouldn't have drafted a couple of guys . . . but everything else, you've got to be yourself, I think. Otherwise people will see through you and you're a phony."

"Would you change anything about your relationship to Norman?"

"I don't think we had that many problems. You'd have to check with him."

If Buddy was, for once, determined to be magnanimous and discreet, Norman on the subject of Buddy Ryan was like a boil waiting to be lanced. Buddy had shaken his faith in St.Vince's credo. Sitting behind his clean glass desk upstairs the next morning, he let five years of frustration rip.

"Buddy disproves the saying, 'Winning is everything.' He places an individual on a border. He comes as close probably as George Allen did in taking the fun out of winning. Read the obit on George Allen in last week's *New York Times*. The man was miserable to be around, a tyrant! And Allen was a little more polished than Ryan. . . . Sitting in my seat, you get to that point of really saying to yourself, Is winning worth it? Is winning worth it? Or winning at what price? At the price of ridiculing your opponents, at the price of ridiculing decent people, and the price of being just a big asshole, of not acknowledging the support of other individuals who help you win? I won, but it's always somebody else's fault when I don't win? . . . I mean, if I had a Super Bowl coach, maybe I could live with it, his mouth, the remarks, his not shaking hands with the opposing coach . . . who needs all that crap?"

Of course, none of this feeling had come through at the press conference the previous afternoon, when Norman named his new head coach. He said he expected a new level of harmony between front office and coaching suite. He said he expected a new measure of discipline and class on the field. And he said he expected his new coach to take the Eagles to the Next Level.

That night, Norman did something he hadn't done in the five years he had owned his own football team. He went out to dinner with his head coach, the newest High Priest of the Pigskin, Richie Kotite.

5

COACH UPTIGHT

Bald, tan Richie Kotite, the crown of his head framed by a faded pink eyeshade, stands on the gridiron, cigar jutting strenuously from his clenched teeth, surveying the crowded practice field like General MacArthur in the prow of a landing craft. He is a wildebeest of a man; he looks assembled from spare parts: short thick torso mounted on long skinny legs with broad shoulders and long powerful arms. With the pink visor—which allows his dome to go brown as the rest of his face—aviator sunglasses propped on a liberal Levantine schnoz, the cigar (a Cuban big enough for an Al Capp cartoon), softening belly, outsized limbs and colossal trilbys, the effect is solid but lubberly.

It's the first day of Eagles voluntary camp, two weeks of workouts without pads on the green fenced-in field off the parking lot outside the Vet. On the grass, leaning with youthful ease into limbering exercises, are more than eighty young men, warming up to the serious business of trying out for the '92 Philadelphia Eagles. Veterans, draftees, and free agents are all out there together, presumably equals at this starting gate, but actually not. There's a core group of forty or so established veterans who will make the team. The rest are all competing for about six or seven roster spots, and even that competition is already stacked in favor of Richie's draft picks. This year he's selected two hotshot running backs, Siran Stacy of Alabama and Notre Dame's Tony Brooks, who now warm up alongside Norman's latest million-dollar free-agent acquisition, Herschel Walker. Randall Cunningham is readying for his comeback, jogging up and down with a shiny black brace on his surgically rebuilt left knee. Buddy's Boys are back, too—Reverend Reggie, Seth Joyner, Clyde Simmons, Andre Waters, Wes Hopkins, Byron Evans, Eric Allen, Mike Golic, Mike Pitts, and Ben Smith, although Ben is still standing around on his bum knee. Most of them had taken off the first two days of workouts, still grieving—

it was just days ago they buried Jerome. Someone has traced number 99 in lime on a corner of the practice field.

It is a sunny hot morning in early July. The nearby skyline of Center City trembles in a bright thermal haze, but the green, silver-winged helmets and numbered jerseys already herald the approach of autumn. Just beyond the north fence, some of the big rigs that roar past on I-676 lean happily on their horns to hurry on the season.

Richie enjoys the truckers' salutes, but that's about as close as he wants fans to get. Richie doesn't like to be watched. When he's working in his office, he keeps the door shut. One of his first public acts as the Eagles' head coach last year was to close off the Eagles' practices to the public and Pack. Buddy's practices had been social events. Avid Eagles fans were free to wander up and down the sidelines, gaping, cheering, snapping pictures, shouting encouragement. Buddy would stand, legs apart, belly forward, rim of his cap pulled down to the top of his glasses, silently twirling his whistle at the precise center of his world, oblivious to the commotion. Richie is, in contrast, a study in anxiety. He paces and shouts and sticks his head in huddles and watches the sidelines like a wary mother hen, annoyed even when the boys pulling water jugs get too close to the action. Out at West Chester University, during the team's official monthlong training camp, a thousand fans or more show up for every practice, morning and afternoon, camped out on blankets and folding chairs, trying to catch glimpses of their favorite players, getting familiar with the top draft picks, and sizing up the free agents trying desperately to impress. Club executives escort groups of season ticket holders and corporate sponsors right down to the sidelines for these sessions, so they can hear the players swear and grunt and see the blood, sweat, and spit fly. It had become such a beloved tradition that, much as Richie hated it ("I found one asshole standing right next to me in the huddle one day," he'd say, with disgust), he had no choice in the matter—how would it look for Norman, whose boyhood water bucket–carrying episode in West Chester was now legend, to wall off his team from the masses? But these two weeks of voluntary camp and the rest of the season up in Philly were Richie's call, and he kept them closed to the public.

People hadn't minded so much in '91. They just nosed up to the fences, which were only about ten yards from the field. But this year Richie has ordered a green tarp draped around the perimeter, and while he works out his troops in private, there is angry milling outside the fence.

"Hey, Kotite," bellows one of the disappointed, a familiar rude male rumbling, voice of the riled Philly fan, "Buddy let us in!"

Richie rips the cigar from his teeth like he's been waiting all week for this moment. In his angriest coach's bellow, he thunders back, "I don't give a shit what Buddy did!"

"Asshole!" the fan shoots back.

Richie takes a couple steps toward the fence now, making eye contact with the retreating heckler through an opening in the tarp. Waving his cigar angrily, he shouts, "Get the fuck out of here if you don't like it!"

Then he turns to a writer standing near the gate, and says, "Don't print that."

Defining boundaries has been a problem for Richie ever since becoming head coach. It is a rule of human behavior that those with the least power flex it most, and Richie wields his with gusto. A pro football team is an organization about the size of a typical Wal-Mart. A head coach can tyrannize a roster of about fifty players, about two dozen assistant coaches, trainers, film technicians, equipment managers, and office help, but that's it. Although his true sphere of influence is actually quite small, public adoration, press clippings, and weekly performances before millions can make an NFL head coach seem (in his own mind, anyway) like a major public figure, a great man. Hence this tendency Richie has of giving orders to people not on the payroll.

He's actually a nice guy, an aggressively nice guy, if he likes you. He's honest and loyal to a fault. And even though his mind is racing a mile a minute about football, twenty-four hours a day, twelve months a year, Richie remembers his friends and keeps his promises. He's adamant about that. His preferred method of social interaction is the telephone. He carries a folding cellular one in his pocket at all times, even on the practice field: it's his lone, static-filled link to the larger world beyond the tarp-draped fence. It wasn't always like this. As an assistant coach, Richie had more time for people. His internal rhythm was about ten beats slower.

But right from the first hours of his elevation, Richie began to change. The pressures of the job inflated some traits and deflated others. The cigar, which he used to light up by himself back in his office, was suddenly with him always, a prop. Richie immediately struck a deal with a Cadillac outlet, and the coach's parking space just outside the front entrance at the Vet, which had long sported Buddy's four-wheel-drive Bronco Rancher, now displayed a gleaming luxury cruiser. Always a busy, solitary man, Richie grew paranoid and brusque. Buddy, whom he had served loyally for a year, became the author of everything wrong with the Eagles. In conversation, Richie was suddenly opinionated to the extreme, announcing his take on things in that preemptive way the insecure have of assuming agreement. "We think alike, right?" he'd say, then press on without pausing for response—interested now in audience, not dialogue.

This, anyway, was the Richie most people saw. He remained the relentlessly upbeat character who had this jocular way of calling grown men "kid," who would never cut a player from his roster without sitting down with him to commiserate—"You're looking at a guy who was cut four times! Four times!" He took time to phone patients facing brain surgery (as he had thirteen years before) to offer advice and his own robust style of encouragement: "You let the doctors handle their part, but you have a job to do, too . . . you have to fight it, get on with your life . . . survive!" Away from the pressures of his job, Richie was as decent and nice a guy as you could ever hope to meet. Only now, as a certified High Priest of the Pigskin, Richie was nearly impossible to get out from under. Not that he complained. No way. Richie was doing exactly what he'd always wanted—at least since he stopped playing football himself. Most people didn't know or didn't remember that Richie had been a player, a tight end and special teams demon for the Giants and Steelers. His old aggressiveness and athleticism were obscured now by the bald head, the glasses, the rounder contours of middle age. The former boxer and tight end now looked almost bookish, especially on his TV show, where he sat on a stool looking roundshouldered and uncomfortable, glasses reflecting the stage lights, head defensively scrunched into his shoulders. Around reporters, Richie (not without reason) looked like he expected at any moment to get bonked on the head from behind. The Pack, annoyed at being locked out of practices, promptly dubbed him "Coach Uptight," and the name stuck.

Once he was anointed, the take-charge tough-guy side of his character was unchained. The full-throated bullhorn of a voice he once reserved for the practice field (the players had nicknamed him "Horn") became more and more his natural tone of voice. The Brooklyn accent had always been there, but now emerged the full-blown Brooklyn Slouch, a way of carrying himself with his shoulders hunched and his head cocked, exaggerated hand gestures to accompany the guttural streetwise palaver—the whole urban tough-guy shtick. Richie's standard posture at a press conference was combative. By the set of his shoulders, the belligerent look on his face, his thrusting hand gestures, he came across like an unrepentant school bully—*Yeah, that's what I did, so what?* Now, when he called you "kid," it sometimes came off in an impatient, patronizing way that not everybody appreciated. When he punctuated his sentences with a rhetorical "Okay?" or "All right?" or "Am I right?" as he always had, the effect was now sometimes like a quick left jab to the nose, keeping you off balance, setting you up. He would be charming one day, growly the next. At his best, he would stop and chat with strangers, kid around with the Pack, or telephone an old friend out of the blue just to say hello. At his worst, he had begun to transmogrify into a self-important bore, a man who now moved so fast there wasn't time for him to really talk to anybody, who formed snap judgments about others (whom he tended to see as either wholly friends or wholly enemies), who could be darkly critical of people behind their backs, who bullied those who worked for him (and even some who didn't, like blowing up at the crew that produced his weekly TV show), profanely chewing out reporters who dared criticize or lampoon him—and all the while promising everybody, unsolicited, with loud authority, "Richie Kotite's not going to change!" and "I'm still gonna be the same old Richie!" Only nobody could remember his thinking that "being Richie" had ever been such a big deal before.

LIZ CORKUM WAS always impressed by how hard the guy worked to *just be Richie*. She was a teenage sophomore at Wagner College on Staten Island when she met him. Growing up as a happily sheltered only child, a good Catholic girl, a cheerleader and Catholic Youth Organization trooper, Liz discovered in Richie a remnant of the college life she thought she'd find when she started school in '70. Instead of proms and mixers and pep rallies, she found herself surrounded by hippies and radical feminists. She didn't like it.

She met Richie at a campus bar. He was a tall, dark, muscular graduate student who drove a nice car, wore his hair short and neat, and dressed nicely—and he played for the New York Giants! Liz liked the fact that he was about ten years older than she was, because she felt about ten years older than her contemporaries. His personality, politics, and values had survived the sixties unscathed—my God, it was as if the guy had been in a time capsule for a decade!

Some of this was not so good. Along with Richie's gracious, old-fashioned manners, he was as unambiguously male as a silverback gorilla. When he was driving, for instance, nobody was allowed to pass him on the road. It was as if his car were his team, and the other cars were all the other teams, and anybody who butted in front or sped past in the outside lane tapped a savage competitive reflex. Another thing: Richie was a friendly guy, but he was almost pathologically brusque. He was always preoccupied and in a hurry. Conversations with Richie of more than ten or fifteen seconds were rare and difficult. Once you got past the pleasantries—he was good at those—he was ready to move on. Richie was like a fast-moving rig on a long interstate run. If you were interested in him, he wasn't about to slow down; you had to find a way to grab on as he motored past.

Liz grabbed on. There would be time to work on all these things, and besides, Liz admired Richie's determination to be his own man. It was tough being a silverback in the Age of Aquarius.

Within a month of meeting her, Richie mentioned marriage.

"I've never really given it a lot of thought before, but since I met you, I've been thinking about it," he said.

Liz's first thought was sarcastic—*Does he plan to ask me what I think about it?*—but she liked the idea. She would make him wait until she earned her degree, and she was enough influenced by the bra burners that she had no intention of becoming a full-time housewife for some superjock, but Liz had no objections to being swept off her feet.

Richie loved to tell people he was from Brooklyn, and he had the whole Slouch down, the loose but burly sidewalk strut and familiar *hey-yo-I'm-talkin'-to-you* growl of the tough city kid. But Richie's Brooklyn wasn't the rough-and-tumble neighborhood of yore; he grew up in fashionable Bay Ridge, a park-rimmed shoulder of carefully landscaped suburbia fronting on the Narrows north of Fort Hamilton, spreading out like a slice of the American dream to the northeast as you pass over the Verrazano Narrows Bridge. Richie's view of Brooklyn streets was from the window of the bus that took him to private school. His father, Eddie, son of a Lebanese immigrant, had carved a lucrative niche for himself in the booming world of advertising in postwar New York. He and his wife, Alice, whose parents had immigrated from Syria, were well off enough to buy a winter home in Miami and to enable Eddie, an avid sportsman, to own a few racehorses and even sponsor some heavyweight fighters.

Richie was born in '42, his sister, Barbara, a few years later, and they formed a close-knit family. Long after they had outgrown it, Eddie still called them by the pet names he had given them as babies. To him, Richie was still "Mummy," even when he had grown to a strapping six-three and weighed well over two hundred pounds. Once, when he took his brother-in-law out to watch Richie's football practice at Wagner, the boy's uncle complained when Eddie kept using the pet name.

"Why do you keep calling him that; you're embarrassing him."

"Look, Uncle Charlie," said Richie, looking down on both men. "I *like* him to call me Mummy, okay?"

The father insisted that Richie call him Eddie, not Dad. He wanted to be his son's best friend. Richie had been a shy, overweight boy until Allie Ridgeway, a trainer Eddie had hired to work with some of his fighters, began teaching his boss's son to box.

As his body grew tall and firm, and his boxing skills improved, Richie's confidence swelled. The discipline he learned in the gym, along with his growing stature and bulk, turned chubby, unhappy Dick Kotite into a prep-school sports star. He was a good athlete, not a great one. He excelled because he worked at it. Winning meant more to Richie than anyone else. To his old schoolmates, the enduring memory of him is that of a lean, tawny kid with a smile on his face and a ball in his hands. Years before it became fashionable, Richie would run with weights around his ankles to improve his speed, and on Friday nights, when his friends went on dates or to dances, Richie would ride the subway up to his father's office on Madison Avenue, and Eddie would take him to more boxing lessons, first with trainers at the New York Athletic Club, then to the famous Stillman's Gym.

Wagner offered Richie a football scholarship, but he had his sights set higher. He enrolled as a freshman at the University of Miami. He planned to try out as a walk-on for the school's Division I football team that summer.

To stay in shape (and maybe catch a coach's eye), Richie entered a campus invitational boxing tournament and fought the first formal matches of his life. He had been sparring for years without actually having a fight, and he surprised even himself by knocking out four opponents straight to win the title Heavyweight Champion of the university. Eddie, who attended every bout, was thrilled, but he knew enough about fighting to know that his Mummy would never be more than an amateur. Richie, then nineteen, got a chance that summer to spar with real heavyweights, even with young Cassius Clay (before he became Muhammad Ali). Richie would later recall that Clay "hit me about five times before I had a chance to react."

When he failed to make Miami's football team, Richie reconsidered the scholarship back up on Staten Island. He transferred to Wagner in time to play football in '62, and over the next three years became a standout tight end, winning Little All-American honors and attracting pro scouts—which didn't happen often at the small private school. In '65, Richie was drafted by both the AFL Jets (during that league's red shirt draft for longshot players to round out their practice squads) and the NFL's Minnesota Vikings (eighteenth round).

The Jets, who had just signed Joe Namath to a then-amazing $427,000 contract, offered Richie $15,000. Eddie was escorted by head coach Weeb Ewbank upstairs to see the big boss, Sonny Werblin, who felt Richie from little Wagner College down the way ought to be sufficiently in awe of so generous an offer to sign that day. Eddie said they had promised Jim Finks, the Vikings' general manager, that they would at least meet with him in Minnesota before Richie signed with the Jets. Werblin was theatrically aghast. He told Eddie he couldn't believe what he was hearing. The kid was going to turn down $15,000?

"I don't know what Richie is worth," Eddie argued, "but a promise is a promise."

Eddie didn't like the way Werblin was talking to him. Who did this guy think he was? Did he take him for some kind of rube? Eddie was a successful businessman and sportsman in New York City, a promoter, a dealer—he was *somebody*—he sure as hell wasn't going to let his son get buffaloed by some two-bit upstart football league. It was insulting. He and Sonny exchanged some hot words and Eddie split.

Father and son flew out to Minneapolis together. Eddie liked Jim Finks right away. Even though the Vikings only offered $10,000, they took the deal. Now all Richie had to do was make the team. Eddie stayed at a motel near training camp, and he would come out to the practice field every day to watch. He would chat up anybody on the fringes of the facility who would talk, scrounging for clues about how the coaches felt about his son. He got all excited one day when the caterer told him he had overheard Norm Van Brocklin and the other coaches saying nice things about his Mummy.

But Richie blew out his Achilles tendon, and he was history. In those days, a club could just drop a player if he got hurt, which happened a lot. Back at the motel room, nursing his sore tendon, Richie was inconsolable.

"What did I do wrong, Eddie?" he kept saying. "What did I do wrong?"

But he wouldn't give up. As a low-round draft pick who didn't make it, the best Richie could hope for was to become what about half of all pro football players are, a grunt, a hardworking, low-profile battler who enters every summer training camp easily expendable and hangs on by working twice or three times as hard as everybody else, mastering the unglamorous parts of the game and impressing coaches with his attitude and intelligence. If he made it, he could expect to earn just a moderate middle-class wage from week to week (the average salary of an NFL player in '70, *after* the first collective-bargaining agreement, was $23,200; which means the grunts were making well below $20,000). Richie wasn't above playing any angle. One day, when former Giants defensive back Emlen Tunnell, then an assistant coach, heaped praise on Richie's expensive suede jacket, the kid took it off and handed it to him without hesitation.

Richie got cut four times, and every time he got mad, not at the coaches or the team that cut him, but at *himself*. He would tell Eddie, "I'm going to learn from this. I'm going to make it next year." It was no coincidence that many future coaches came from the ranks of the grunts. They were the guys working hardest, the ones playing for neither money nor fame, but for love. They were the ones who woke up one morning at age thirty to find that their life had become the Game.

Richie's playing career lasted seven years, most of it sitting on the bench and hustling downfield on kickoffs and punts with special teams. He got a chance to play some tight end regularly in '71, when Giants starter Bobby Tucker was injured. He caught ten passes for 146 yards and scored two touchdowns, but as soon as Tucker was well, Richie was back on the bench. He felt disappointed and frustrated. "I know I can start in this league!" he would complain to Eddie and Liz, but he wouldn't get another chance. He hung through the '72 season with a dislocated shoulder, determined to complete the five years needed to qualify for an NFL pension. He was thirty years old when that season ended, and he had long since known football was going to be his life. His master's thesis at Wagner concerned the impact of TV on development of the NFL. He and Liz were married the following summer, after she graduated from Wagner with her English degree.

Both she and Richie expected he would be trying out for the Giants again that summer, when Joe Morrison, the Giants' running back/wide receiver, was offered the head coaching job at the University of Tennessee, Chattanooga, and invited Richie to be his assistant. So when the Kotites got back from their honeymoon, Richie went to see Wellington Mara, the Giants' owner, and retired as a player. Liz found a job as publications editor in the university's PR office, and the two diehard New Yorkers headed south.

They didn't like it. Some of the women Liz worked with were openly suspicious of Richie's dark complexion.

"What is Richie?" one asked, after Richie had stopped in Liz's office soon after they moved down.

"What do you mean?" Liz asked.

"What *is* he? What's his race?"

"Well, he's Arab."

"Is that like being a mulatto?" the woman asked.

It made Liz feel uncomfortable.

For Richie, the problem was working with kids. It was hard to make them take football seriously. He was dealing with hotshot high-school all-stars who had better things to do than listen to some coach tell them they had to work hard at something that had always come so blessedly natural. And Richie wasn't the kind to nurture a relationship or spend a lot of time getting to know anybody. He had been to the mountaintop; he was a *pro!* And now he was supposed to teach and motivate these children?

What he hated most was recruiting, and it was a big part of the job. In the off-season he'd spend months traveling the rural backroads to meet with high-school wonders Tennessee was trying to recruit. Richie's way was to walk in, lay the deal out in about thirty seconds, and conclude, "You want to come or not?" Any hesitancy or posturing was enough to send Richie right back out the door—*Who needs this?* Of course, this technique wasn't going to be terribly effective with the most-sought-after kids, who had piles of recruiting letters and obsequious college suitors waiting in line. Richie was appalled to learn he was expected to *woo* these teenagers. Imagine it. You sit down in a tiny living room with, like, four dozen trophies and plaques and game balls on the shelves and on the walls alongside the framed portraits of Jesus and Martin Luther King, Jr., and JFK, and the parents are crowded around the eighteen-year-old kid on the plastic-covered sofa with his shoe box full of recruiting letters, all of them hanging on every word . . . and waiting, waiting for just one thing, for you to pucker up and kiss his tight little high-school all-American ass. Richie couldn't bring himself to do it. He could barely understand most of these people, with their slow, down-home, cornbread drawl, and they sho-nuff had trouble with his Brooklynese.

Who needs this?

He stuck it out for four years before resigning and volunteering as an unpaid assistant with the Saints under Hank Stram. One year later, when Stram was fired after New Orleans went 3–11 in '77, Richie followed fellow Brooklynite Sam Rutigliano (who had been Stram's receivers coach) north to Cleveland. Rutigliano had just been named the Browns' head coach, and he hired Richie to coach his receivers.

Liz hadn't followed Richie to New Orleans. She was pregnant when he left, and she wanted to be with her mother in New York to have the baby, a daughter, whom they named Alexandra. She rejoined Richie in Cleveland after almost a year of living apart.

It hardly mattered. By now, Richie was a full-fledged football monk. He lived at the training facility seven days a week, putting in thirteen-, fourteen-hour days. He handed Liz his paycheck every week, and all he asked for back was a little golf money (he'd sneak out sometimes at four in the morning to play by himself at sunrise and be back at the training center in time for an 8:00 a.m. start). Liz and her mom, Stella, had become inseparable. They lived back on Staten Island half of the year and spent the other half in a suburban house near the Browns' training complex. The house had a room for Stella. All the normal chores and burdens of family life—the mortgage, raising the kid, shopping, banking, the church, friends, the neighborhood, the schools—fell to Liz. Richie's part of the deal was . . . well, just to

be Richie. His life was football, football, football. When he started
complaining on the phone to Liz in the summer of '81 about his vision,
she assumed it was from watching so much game film.

Richie first started noticing it when he went jogging. He ran with
some of the other coaches every afternoon, and on one jog he could
no longer see the guys beside him—it felt as though he were wearing
blinders.

Playing on special teams with the Giants twelve years earlier,
Richie had gone to the hospital with a mild concussion. The skull
X ray had turned up a peculiarity, what the doctors dismissed (without
any other symptoms) as an abnormal thickening of his skull near the
pituitary gland. This, of course, prompted lots of jokes about Richie
being especially thickheaded, but when this vision thing started the
old joke started haunting him. The thick-skull notion was just a theory.
Another possibility was a tumor.

When he was driving back to the Browns' training camp after
Cleveland played its exhibition opener that summer, Richie's vision
blurred. He stopped by Sam Rutigliano's room in the dorm that night
and mentioned it.

"You probably just need new glasses," Sam said. But to be sure,
he advised Richie to make an appointment with the doctors at the
Cleveland Clinic, the leading medical center in the area.

He went for tests on Wednesday morning. That afternoon, before
Sam went out for practice, he got a call from Richie, from a phone
booth.

"They found a mass, a tumor," he told Rutigliano, just as matter-
of-factly as a man calling his boss to say he'd gotten a flat tire on the
way in. "They're gonna take it out."

Richie checked into the hospital that day. Sophisticated CAT
scans revealed the "thickening" to be a tumor, grown now to about
the size of a walnut, close to his pituitary gland. The doctors said
Richie had probably been born with it, and that it was almost certainly
benign—although the only way to be sure was to take it out and check.
Left alone, it would continue to grow, and it would press harder and
harder against Richie's optic nerve (as it had begun to do) until he
eventually lost his sight. The operation was risky. It involved a delicate
procedure that had a long list of potentially disastrous, even fatal,
consequences and would mean cutting into his brain by going up
through his nose. "Hey," said Richie, "at least you'll have plenty of
room to maneuver!"

He was unbelievably upbeat about the whole thing—although he
was scared to death. Sam and his wife visited Richie at the clinic that

night. Liz and Stella and the baby were still in Staten Island. The Rutiglianos sat by Richie's bedside and prayed, and Richie kept on his stubbornly positive face.

"Don't worry, Sam, I'm gonna be back, all right? I'm gonna be back."

Liz flew in for the surgery. She thought the worst thing was having to listen while the doctors ticked off the dire probabilities—this much chance of blindness, this much chance of disfigurement, this much chance of paralysis, this much chance of death. Richie sat through the recitation unmoved. Football coaches were experts in a business that got no respect; every fan felt free to second-guess a football coach, and many felt sure they could do the job better, which, of course, they couldn't. So expertise was one thing coaches learned to respect in others. Richie figured, if these guys were as good at their job as he was at his—hey, no sweat! Right? What more could you ask? Let's kick off!

Liz was a wreck. Sam and his wife kept stopping by to sit at Richie's bedside and pray with them, which was sweet and thoughtful, but a little portentous, too.

The operation took nine hours. The tumor, as the doctors had predicted, was benign.

Thirteen days later, wearing a Cleveland Indians batting helmet, Richie was back on the practice field. He was out there for the Monday night season opener, a 44–14 pounding by the Chargers. It was like nothing had ever happened. Boy, was Richie proud of that. In later years, he'd save that story for the in-depth profile interviews, the ones in which the reporter tries to get at what really makes Richie Kotite tick. Sure, a guy proves he has stones when he makes a pro football team and bangs heads with the big boys, but staring down a brain tumor, going to sleep for nine hours on the operating table with at least a decent chance of never waking up again, that shows stones of a different order. And you don't spend twenty years around football fields without knowing what it takes to forge your own legend. The Indians' batting helmet was Richie's badge of honor. Back less than two weeks after facing down the Big C. What a man!

Actually, after thirteen days of no game film, no practice, no hanging out with the guys eating pizza and poring over game plans until all hours, thirteen days of sitting home through endless quiet summer days, looking for something on the TV, reading and rereading the sports page, hanging out with Liz, Stella, and the baby, my God, Richie was about to go nuts!

The worst thing was, at least for the first few weeks, Richie wasn't allowed to drive. So Liz had to take him everywhere. In the passenger seat, he was impossible. It was like Liz had never driven before. She was coached every step of the way.

When a car passed her on the expressway, Richie would growl, "He just made you look like a jerk."

"Like I *care!*" Liz would say.

As Richie rebounded to a full recovery, the Browns started to slide. Rutigliano would last for another season and a half in Cleveland, but the Browns were clearly headed into a down cycle when Richie got an opportunity to move back home. Joe Walton, who had helped coach Richie when he played for the Giants, had just been named head coach of the Jets. The first person he offered a job was his former backup tight end.

For Liz it was a homecoming. They bought a little Cape Cod with a swimming pool out back that adjoined the backyard of her parents' house, the house where she had grown up. Richie would spend the next seven seasons with the Jets, while Liz sent Alexandra to the same schools she had attended. The Kotites felt settled. Liz lived in the lap of her family while Richie toiled in the temple. He was named offensive coordinator in '85, although Walton continued to supervise game planning and call the plays on Sundays.

Which was fine with Richie. He was a Corporate Coach through and through. The new High Priests were highly paid executives in the sports-entertainment business, an international industry with an image to maintain. Like corporate men everywhere, they knew the value of networking, of getting along with others, of handling the press and public with professional charm, and (most important) of showing mutual respect within the walls of the temple. They even respected the guys up in the booth tinkling the ice in their gin, or, if they didn't, they learned how to pretend real good, because it was easy enough to get axed for losing without thumbing your nose at the guy in the black hood.

Richie's pro football journey had begun with refusing a fifteen-thousand-dollar offer from Sonny Werblin. Now he was just one step away from the high holy headset in the Jets' organization. He'd gotten there not just by knowing the Game and building a reputation for success, but by cultivating goodwill with everyone he met within the temple (Buddy would call it kissing ass). You never knew, from year to year, which coaching legend would be out on the street, and which eager novitiate you met on the sidelines of the Senior Bowl would be the next to be anointed, wearing the headset, assembling his very own staff.

It was these things, even more than any coaching success, that led to Richie Kotite's ascension.

GIVEN THE CIRCUMSTANCES of Richie's sudden elevation in Philadelphia, there was bound to be talk. Sports fans love intrigue as much as the next person, and for those under the impression that Buddy was really running the club, his firing and Richie's hiring in the space of about seven hours was a palace coup. And the first thing to understand about a palace coup is that the official story, of course, ain't it.

Rumors flew. The "real" story began to emerge in the days immediately after. Richie, see, had been in on this all along, plotting with Harry and Norman. Randall had been in on it, too. Randall was key. Randall provided the only real scrap of evidence. Ever since Norman had voluntarily renegotiated the quarterback's contract in '88, extending it five years and paying the quarterback millions, the owner had wedded his club's ambitions to Randall's remarkable (if erratic) talents. To the conspiratorialists, of course, the plum contract had made Randall a rival prince, a player with too much power to suit Buddy. Buddy liked his players subservient and grateful, not rich, opinionated, and tenured. But all this would have stayed idle speculation if Randall hadn't been saying some pretty odd things in the days before Buddy's firing. After Buddy benched him for three plays in the Redskins play-off game, Randall told the Pack he had felt insulted and confused. Then the next day, cleaning out his locker, he had gone off on one of his unrehearsed riffs into some hound's microcassette tape recorder: "We just hope Richie's here next year, because I'm sure he's going to get some offers as a head coach on other teams, too. He's got a lot of experience, and changing offenses again would be tough on this team. Of course, I want to see Buddy come back. Buddy's a good coach. I mean, Kotite's a great coach."

Buddy good . . . Richie *great?*

Granted, Randall was always saying pretty odd things, but, to those inclined to suspicion, there was something ominous here, it was as if *he knew.* And then there was the report—from somewhere, something somebody *inaposition* to know told somebody else, which was good enough for somebody *inaposition* to broadcast as the Real Truth to many thousands of listeners—that led one to believe that Norman, Harry, Richie, and Randall had been seen suspiciously lunching or dinnering together (accounts varied) in *New York City,* that Gomorrah, two days before the coup. A plot! After he got fired, Buddy performed the last of his weekly radio programs at a bar crowded with raucous supporters, and while Buddy wasn't *inaposition* to know and wasn't exactly gonna confirm anything . . . well, hell, it stands to reason when a guy like him gets canned after winning all them football games and going to the play-offs three times in three seasons, it don't take no *Phi Beta Kappa* to figure out *somethin' kinda fishy's* been goin' on! If Buddy believed there was a conspiracy, that was good enough for most folks, and . . . ponder the implications here. Hadn't that Keith Jackson warned everybody about this? The Eagles had just fallen flat on their face in that Wild Card play-off game against the Redskins. The defense, of course (Buddy's Boys), had been superb, but the offense, particularly Randall, hadn't done squat (two field goals were it). Kotite, offensive coordinator; Randall, quarterback. Hadn't Buddy gotten so fed up with Randall's lackluster showing that he yanked him in the third quarter, put in his own boy McMahon? How long had they been plotting against him? You had to admire it, the neatness of the coup, complete with conspiracy, cunning, and betrayal. There was even Buddy's shocked pirouette at the moment of the kill—"I've never been fired for winning before."

Only one thing wrong with this version. None of it was true.

What was true was that Richie owed his job with the Eagles not to Buddy, but to Harry Gamble.

They had met back in '77, when Harry was still coaching at the University of Pennsylvania. After messing around with the wishbone offense with only moderate success for a few years, Harry was looking for a way to jazz up his passing game. With Archie Manning at quarterback in the late seventies, the Saints had one of the NFL's better passing games, so Harry made a trip to New Orleans that off-season for a few weeks of tutoring from receivers coach Sam Rutigliano and his young unpaid assistant, a helluva good guy named Richie Kotite.

Back in Philadelphia in the summer before the '78 season, Harry got a surprise phone call.

"Howyadoin', Harry?" came a gust of loud, upbeat Brooklynese. "It's me, Richie. Richie Kotite. How's the new system coming?"

Harry was pleasantly surprised. He told Richie that they had been working hard on the new passing game, but that he still had some questions.

As Harry's mind started trying to frame the questions while he had his buddy from the pros on the phone, Richie volunteered, "Great! Would you like me to come down?"

"Oh, no, Richie, I couldn't ask that."

"Don't be silly; we're friends, right? I'm up here on vacation in Staten Island, you're only . . . what? An hour and a half away?"

And Richie drove down—helluva guy!

Harry never forgot it. As his own career took its startling trajectory over the next thirteen years, he watched from a distance as Richie moved to Cleveland and then New York. When Norman demanded a change in his offense after the '89 season (against Buddy's wishes), Harry told his head coach, "Do you know who would be a helluva guy who could come in here and be offensive coordinator for us?"

Of course, Buddy knew who Richie Kotite was. Within the fraternity, everybody knows everybody else. But Richie had never coached with Buddy before, and if there's one thing about coaches, they prefer to look out for the guys they've coached with before.

"I don't know anything about the guy," Buddy said.

"Well, I think he's got a helluva feel for the game," said Harry.

"Let me look into it," Buddy said.

Days later, when Richie was hired, Harry read a quote from Buddy in the *Inquirer* that said former offensive coordinator Ted Plumb had recommended Kotite. Buddy also said Richie had been given a rave notice by Joe Namath. There was no mention of Harry. Harry just shrugged off the slight—wouldn't look right for Buddy to admit that the *Ivy League guy* upstairs had had a good idea.

Richie had lost his job in New York as part of a clean sweep when Walton got canned after winning only four games in '89. It came as a blow to the Kotites, who were now deeply rooted on Staten Island. Richie had been lucky. He knew coaches in the NFL who had picked up and moved more than twenty times over the years, and here he had been able to work for seven seasons in the pros just a short drive from the neighborhood where he grew up. His daughter, now thirteen, was looking forward to following her friends to nearby Notre Dame Academy. Still, Richie knew what he had to do. True monks go wherever they must go. He got a call from Joe Bugel, offensive coordinator for the Redskins, who was considering head coaching openings in Atlanta and Phoenix, so he and Liz were waiting to hear about that when Buddy's secretary called and invited him down to Philadelphia.

The Eagles signed Richie to a one-year contract, so after what had just happened with the Jets, they didn't even consider moving. Richie would stay at the Hilton Hotel in Mt. Laurel and come home for dinner after practice on Fridays—not for the whole night, mind you; Richie drove back to the hotel that night. Liz and Stella would come down for the home games on Sunday, and they would all go out to dinner afterward. Otherwise, Richie lived in the basement of the Vet, trying to develop rapport with Ran-*doll*, studying films, working up game plans, supervising offensive practices, and going home alone every night to the Hilton.

Richie had considerable freedom to run the Eagles' offense. He was mostly left to develop game plans and pace his half of the squad in practice, but Buddy was often a pain in the ass during games. All the coaches were connected by intercom and carried on a running dialogue throughout the action. The ones in the booths up on the mezzanine relayed intelligence and suggestions down to the sidelines, asking questions, kicking around ideas. Buddy listened in on all this and usually didn't have much to say unless there was a decision to be made. Buddy was good at making decisions. He made 'em fast and he made 'em often. He didn't like to discuss 'em, before or after; he just made 'em. "Actions speak louder than words" was one of his favorite truisms. He wasn't terribly sensitive about the artful twists and careful logic of Richie's game plans either. He'd just weigh in when he wanted something done. It was annoying as hell.

"Run the damn ball," he'd say, leaving the details to Richie.

Then "Run the damn ball again."

Or when he did let Richie call a play, "What the fuck are you running that play for?"

Buddy sometimes would forget to inform Richie when he had made a decision. Richie would look up from his neatly color-coded, laminated play list to see running back Thomas Sanders brushing past to head out on the field.

"Where the fuck are you going?"

"Coach Ryan told me to go in," Sanders would say.

Richie scowled. "Then get your ass in there."

That would have happened because Sanders, a former Bear, was a guy Buddy had brought in. Richie had little success developing players *he* brought in. One big project in '90 was Roger Vick, a running back Richie had fallen in love with and convinced the Jets to take with their number-one pick in the '87 draft. Vick had never proved to be anything other than a lackluster running back, but Richie hadn't given up on him. When New York waived Vick in '90, Richie convinced the Eagles to sign him—even though Buddy felt he already had a surplus of backs. Vick would carry the ball just sixteen times that season, mostly because Buddy didn't share Richie's enthusiasm for the kid.

"What's forty-three doing in there?" he'd ask, if he noticed Richie had slipped Vick in. "Twenty-five [Anthony Toney] and twenty-three [Heath Sherman] know this offense better than he does, git one a' them [Buddy's draft picks] in there."

Richie would reluctantly wave Vick off the field. Vick was waived right off the team before long.

Despite these game-day squabbles over personnel and plays, Richie knew he had a mandate that transcended Buddy's fiats. The club was paying him $99,000 that year to whip Buddy's talented but undisciplined offense, led by their talented but undisciplined three-million-dollar-plus (per annum) quarterback, into a more consistent scoring machine. After the '89 season, even Buddy had to admit that his approach to offense—just give Randall the ball, a couple of receivers, and a decent running back, and turn them loose—wasn't going to cut it. Buddy's Boys on defense were damn frustrated by the other half of the locker room. Randall always produced a play or two, either all by himself or with one of the Keiths (Jackson or Byars) that would be on the weekly highlights show, enough to bolster the quarterback's fame and fortune, but come crunch time for the team, the offense would stall. Deep in his own territory, with the whole field in front of him, Randall was virtually unstoppable. But as they drove into enemy territory, and the room to maneuver shrank, it was harder and harder for Randall to produce. He was completing only about half of the passes he threw, and without his improvised scrambles (which got harder to do when the team moved within scoring range) the Eagles had no running game to speak of—subtract the team-leading 621 yards Randall had gained in '89 and the Eagles were at the bottom of the NFL in rushing. That didn't diminish Randall's accomplishment, of course. He was the best running quarterback the game had ever seen. But it meant that when the team was in a tight spot, at third down and short yardage, or trying to batter its way into the end zone, other teams had only to key on Randall to stop the play.

Just as Buddy's defense reflected his personality, Richie's way of trying to move the ball mirrored his hidebound style. Richie's system hit Randall Cunningham like a bucket of cold water. Over a series of meetings that began in the spring of '90 and lasted through the summer, Richie, the former grunt from the Giants special teams squad, toiled to hammer home the ABCs of his humdrum ethic to one of the game's flightiest and most flamboyant players (who, mind you, after piloting his team to eleven wins in the previous season and making his third trip to the Pro Bowl, who had just posed for the *Sports Illustrated* cover that proclaimed him the "Weapon of the Nineties," saw no pressing reason to reinvent himself in the first place):

> You win by being fundamentally sound, by having a full understanding of what you're trying to accomplish on every play, and by being disciplined. . . . You talk about the great teams that have ever played offensive football—go way back to the Packers—they had a handful of runs and passes. They didn't fool anybody. They said, "Hey, here we come, you stop us." Am I right? . . . The point is that we're

trying to establish a group of plays, runs, passes, play action passes, screens, and draws that we're going to be able to put our stamp on from week to week, and we're going to run 'em and run 'em and run 'em until we get better and better and better. . . .

Randall moped around all summer whining about the change— "I knew the old system inside and out. Now I have to learn a new system." It was more than just the work involved that troubled him. Ted Plumb had started letting Randall call a lot of his own plays on the field in '89, a point of pride with the young black quarterback who was sensitive about the standard phrase uttered in his praise: "the greatest *athlete* ever to play quarterback." This, of course, not only fell short of recognizing him as the greatest quarterback, but included a whiff of the old racist stereotype: *Why that colored boy, he can sure run and throw the ball, but he's too dumb to call plays.* Richie came flat out, day one, and said, "I'm calling the plays." Period. Randall was a cog— albeit an important one—in a machine designed by Richie Kotite.

Randall went on whining into the season as the Eagles lost their first two games. The quarterback ducked any blame for the slow start, complaining that the new system prevented him from "making things happen," that it trapped him in the pocket, took away his genius for improvisation—until the results started speaking even more loudly for themselves. With newcomers Fred Barnett and Calvin Williams catching deep passes and the Keiths catching shorter ones, with Heath Sherman and Anthony Toney taking turns pounding out one-hundred-yard rushing totals, by midseason the Eagles' offense was outperforming the defense. Randall would finish '90 with the best numbers of his career. Several organizations voted him the league's most valuable player. He threw for thirty touchdowns, completed just under 60 percent of his passes, and was starting quarterback in the Pro Bowl. Midway through the season, he found it impossible to stay mad at the bald guy who called him "kid" and who called all the plays and who kept insisting that he needed to concentrate harder on his mechanics.

Not even Randall could argue with results. Grudgingly, the relationship between perfectionist coach and proud quarterback thawed. It got so they could even kid each other. In the thirteenth game of the season, a game the Eagles lost in a squeaker against Miami, Randall trotted off the field after a failed third-down play to confront a furious Rich Kotite on the sidelines.

"What did you call!" Richie demanded. He had signaled in a play called, in part, fifteen-B-choice-right.

"Fifteen-B-choice-left," Randall said.

"I wanted choice-right!" Richie bellowed, his nose almost touching the quarterback's face mask.

Randall, frustrated and angry, feeling incapable of argument, just screamed back in his coach's face, *"Aaaaaaaargh!!"* Then he went to the bench, took off his helmet, and sat moping by himself.

Richie let a few minutes pass before walking over. He bent down to Randall with his face up close so that the quarterback could hear him above the din in Joe Robbie Stadium and asked with a show of serious concern, "Did we forget to brush our teeth this morning?"

ON THE MORNING that Buddy was fired, Richie had driven to work feeling down. That was unusual. But could you blame him? His team had just watched their season wash away in one big loss against the Redskins. Richie's offense, which had seemed to pick up speed as the season progressed, had flopped badly in the big game, and he felt responsible. Rumors were swirling about Buddy's future, and that meant his future, too. Richie had just been through this the year before with the Jets. There was a depressing aura of déjà vu about the whole thing.

Richie knew he was under consideration for a head coaching job in Cleveland, where his friend Bud Carson had gotten fired midway through the season. But that was a long shot. Liz was frazzled. Richie planned to spend a few hours in the office and then drive home to Staten Island at midday—take a few days off, hunker in, and wait to see what happened. He knew he would land on his feet, no matter what happened, but he hated the uncertainty.

Making matters worse, his alarm didn't go off on time, so he woke up in his Hilton Hotel room at seven-fifteen instead of his usual six o'clock. He had promised Tom Brookshier (the former Eagles defensive back) that he would answer a few questions on the telephone at eight-thirty for Brookshier's and Angelo Cataldi's comically barbed morning sports-talk radio program (which Richie hated—imagine, poking fun at football). Now he knew, what with rush-hour traffic over the Walt Whitman Bridge, he would never make it to the office by eight-thirty. He also knew Brookshier would ring the hotel if he couldn't find Richie at the office. There was nothing he could do but eat breakfast and sit around waiting for the call.

So he was already in a bad mood when he got to the office, late. It was about a quarter after nine. He dropped his imitation-pigskin-covered briefcase (pimpled just like an official NFL football) on his desk, wandered out to draw himself a cup of coffee, and was startled

from behind by Norman Braman. Buddy stepped out of his office at
the same moment.

"Hi, Richie," the owner said, shaking his hand warmly. Then he
walked into the head coach's office with Buddy and pulled the door
shut.

Richie stood in the hall with the steaming coffee cup in his hand,
staring at the closed door. He walked back into his office, shut the
door, and phoned Liz.

"It's going to happen today," he told her. "Can you believe it?"
In his voice was the deep chagrin of one who always expects the best,
confronting the worst. "Twice in one year!"

But there was still hope. Sometimes head coaches get fired and
the staff stays, he told Liz. That's not the usual, but it happens. It
crossed Richie's mind that he might be considered for the head coaching job himself—Cleveland's interest in him had been in all the papers—but there was no indication that was so. Far more likely was
that he would be out of a job. He didn't want to say that to Liz, though.

"They'll probably want to keep some continuity with the systems,"
he said. "There's at least a chance they'll keep me."

As word spread, the buttons on all the phones lit up with incoming
calls. The other coaches huddled in the hall. Richie kept the door to
his office closed. He was sitting there smoking a cigar and wondering
what to do next when there was a knock on his door. It was Harry.

"Mr. Braman would like to talk to you upstairs in about ten
minutes," he said.

"Okay. Why?"

Harry explained that both he and Jeff were being considered for
the top job. "Norman's going to make a decision today, after he talks
to you both. What time is it now?"

"It's ten after eleven," said Richie.

"Okay, come on up in about ten minutes, okay?"

He called Liz and told her that.

Richie hung up the phone at about the time he was supposed
to head upstairs, but before he left, the line from upstairs lit. Harry
again.

"Look, Richie, listen. Could you come up in about an hour and
a half?" he asked. "Jeff's up here right now."

What torture! He relit his cigar and started to pace in his long,
narrow office. He ignored the phone. Jeff had been closer to Buddy
than just about anyone on the staff. Buddy had brought him over
from the Bears and was grooming him. But, then, nobody could argue
that Richie hadn't done great things with Randall and the offense in
'90. He had been toiling in the temple now for damn near two decades!

For a real football man, there was no choice here at all! But who knew what Norman would do? Jeff was only thirty-two years old, and he'd never coached anywhere but with Buddy in Philadelphia . . . but, on the other hand, Richie remembered reading about Braman's interest in that Davy Shula when Shula was . . . what? *Twenty-fucking-six years old?* That didn't bode well. At forty-eight, Richie was a much more solid investment than Jeff, some might say more suitable for the job, and there was his longtime friendship with Harry; that had to help. You had to figure that in the Eagles' organization right now, being allies with Harry would carry a lot more weight than being Buddy's protégé. Then again, there were other ways of sizing it up. . . .

This went on until Harry called down about an hour later and invited Richie up. Richie rode the elevator to the fourth floor, and Harry walked him into Norman's office.

The owner did most of the talking. He said some complimentary things about the organization, about how much Buddy had been able to accomplish, about how much Richie had done over the last season. But he also talked about some of the things he didn't like—the lack of discipline, Buddy's Bad-Boy image, the favoritism Buddy showed certain players (most notably Jerome Brown), the disdain for other coaches in the league, the way Buddy talked about players (and owners) in the press, and so on. And it didn't take Norman long to see that, in Richie, he had found a kindred soul. Richie had kept his thoughts to himself all season because Buddy was his boss and he took loyalty seriously, but there had been lots of things about the team that Richie hadn't liked one bit. They were a lot of the same things that Braman didn't like—the way Buddy would insult kids trying to make the team, the way Buddy never gave anybody on the staff upstairs any credit, the way Buddy treated the other coaches around the league (members of the blessed Brotherhood!), all the theatrical bullshit (his defense players had taken to wearing black shoes, hanging black towels from the waists of their silver pants). Jerome was the worst. Jerome would drive ninety miles per hour across the parking lot on his way to practice and ignore and razz assistant coaches on the practice fields, guys just trying to do their jobs. Jerome once had told defensive line coach Dale Haupt "Fuck off," and Buddy just shrugged and laughed about it . . . *that Jerome.*

Why, in training camp that last summer, Richie had nearly gotten in a fistfight with Jerome. The lineman was clowning around, sticking his head in the offensive huddle, when Richie barked at him, "Get your fat ass on your own side of the ball!"

Jerome charged toward Richie, "What you say to me?"

"Listen, you fat bag of pus," bellowed Richie, who squared off to teach the big lineman a thing or two about the manly arts. Team-mates piled in and pulled off Jerome before blows were exchanged, but Richie never forgot the lack of respect—or the fact that Buddy did nothing about it.

"Oh, that's just Jerome," he said. Buddy thought it was kind of funny, actually.

So Norman didn't have to scratch hard to discover that what he had, sitting right there in his office, was someone who understood exactly his concerns about the team—*Win, lose, or draw, you have to act with class*—a perfect broad-shouldered, polite, righteous, respectful, articulate specimen of the modern NFL Corporate Coach.

"Listen, Richie, I want you to go downstairs," said Norman. "I want you to stay in the building."

The Pack had begun to assemble in force in the hallways under-neath the Vet by the time Richie got downstairs. He ducked into the coaching suite before he could be cornered, closed the door to his office, relit his cigar, and began pacing through another excruciating hour and a half.

Harry finally called down, "Can you come up, Richie? Mr. Bra-man would like to see you again."

He slipped once more past the Pack, who were heading upstairs now for the announced press conference, rode the elevator, and stuck his head in Harry's office. No one was there. Harry's secretary told him to go on in and wait, so Richie sat down on a chair opposite Harry's desk. Then Harry came lumbering in with Norman on his heels.

"Richie, I'm going to go with you as the head coach," said Norman.

Richie let out a huge sigh of relief, letting his shoulders sag so dramatically that Harry and Norman laughed.

There was a brief preliminary discussion of contract terms—Richie would earn $250,000 in his first year, close to $300,000 in his second, and the club would have an option for a third year at about $350,000.

"Why don't you call your wife and your parents," Norman sug-gested. On the speakerphone, Richie dialed up Liz.

"They offered me the job," he told her.

There was a silence on the other end of the phone for a long moment, and then Liz blurted out, to the amusement of the men in the room, "Well, you're going to take it, aren't you?"

HIS APPOINTMENT LANDED in the middle of an explosion of team anger. Buddy's Boys were furious.

"It's ridiculous, man," said Seth Joyner. "I think it's the most ridiculous thing I ever heard. Unfuckingbelievable. . . . Well, I just think, I've talked to Keith [Byars] and I've talked to Jerome and I can just tell you right now, it's just going to cause a real bad situation. I don't care who they bring in here. It's like all the positives about the team are just gone out the window right now."

Keith Jackson called Norman a moron.

"I think everything is crazy right now, everybody is going crazy around here, the players are going crazy," he said. "I don't want any ties to this team anymore. I don't want to be here anymore. I think a lot of other players will say it, too. We don't want to be around here anymore."

Richie waited out the mutinous blasts, lying low when Norman's cutting remarks about Buddy and the team's image and Jerome hit the press—even though he agreed with them. Especially the stuff about Jerome. He hadn't forgotten the scuffle with Jerome on the practice field. Jerome forgot about that kind of thing minutes after it happened (he had even been impressed with how Richie had stood up to him), but not Richie. The disrespect galled.

"I'm not exactly sure what Jerome's problem is, but he can't respect himself very much, being the way that he is," the new head coach said, pacing in his office, filling the stale air with cigar smoke. "Out of control with everything he does and says. It's cute and entertaining early on, but it gets old. Because if it's not addressed, the other players, especially the younger ones, they think it's right. I think that in coaching you have an obligation to teach the players that they are in public all the time. . . . You don't just perform on Sunday as a coach or a player and then the rest of the week do whatever you want. I've seen Jerome walk by a little kid holding out a piece of paper and a pen, and brush them away with his hand saying, Out of my way!" Richie balls his fist with anger, and says to the absent Jerome, "You son of a bitch, that ain't right! To some little kid whose father is encouraging him to have enough courage to go up and ask for an autograph? He has to understand, it's not going to be that way with me. I'm a fair guy, but you have to act right. You have to have a certain amount of respect. You have to understand that coaches are here to help you, and that they are coaches, and they're not here to take shit. That's how I feel. Without having an ax to grind. I don't want anyone coaching with a knot in their stomach. That's how I feel."

Like all true monks in the temple, Richie knew—*without question*— what's right. He'd been preparing for this moment for twenty years. He was not about to do some kind of talent search to fill out his staff; that's not the way the priesthood works. Richie already had his own staff picked out, guys whom he had worked with over the years, guys who thought the way he did, guys whom he'd told from time to time, shooting the bull the way coaches do, *When I get the headset, I want you to work with me.* Bringing them in now was a macho thing, proving not just that Richie remembered his promises, but that he had the muscle to make them happen. Within the year he had assembled his crew: Bud Carson as defensive coordinator (they worked together with the Jets from '85 to '88), Zeke Bratkowski as quarterbacks coach (Jets '85–'89), Jim Vechiarella as linebackers coach (Jets, '83–'85), Jim Williams as strength coach (Jets '82–'90), Richard Woods as running backs coach (worked with Richie back in New Orleans in '77). The following year he would reel in Larry Pasquale as special teams coach (Jets '81–'89).

But the one part of the team he inherited that Richie couldn't remake in his own image was Buddy's defense. Theirs would be a tenuous relationship at best. The hot tempers cooled when reality settled in—after all, what choice did these players have? They could play for Richie and earn their six- and seven-figure salaries or join the American workforce in a sluggish economy. And Richie couldn't cut these guys; they were, after all, the best defense in the NFL.

Through the '91 season, after Randall went down, the defense couldn't really fault Richie too much for the team's struggles—although the head coach was hardly blameless in the string of quarterbacking disasters on his side of the ball.

But by the beginning of the '92 season, Buddy's Boys are getting restless. They still see Richie as Norman's boy, and he still sees them as a foreign camp in his own locker room. When he talks about the offense it's "us" or "we," but when he talks about the defense it's always "those guys" or "them."

"They" are the best defense the league has seen in more than a dozen years. And it is pretty clear to everybody that Richie needs them more than they need him.

6

THE SLUICE

Jerome had his own way of opening training camp. He usually
arrived last.

Throughout the day, players would pull up the curved
driveway in front of the tan brick, nine-story Gertrude Schmidt dormitory at the southwest corner of the West Chester University campus,
a steady parade of Broncos and sports cars and Jeeps and BMWs, and
big men would unload armfuls of clothing or a travel bag and then
the bulkier vital cargo: electronic equipment, three-feet-tall speakers,
amps, TV sets, and the tangled spaghetti strands of wiring for their
video-game hookups.

Jerome would show up at about five, as the curfew clock ticked
down into fine territory. As his black Bronco made its way through
West Chester, you'd hear the woofers of his car's megaspeakers a half
mile away, *whump-whump-whump-whump*, like a cotton bat to the brain.
So guys would be hanging out of the windows watching by the time
he drove up front. Jerome would jump out, and then bellow:

"Fuck West Chester!"

And camp was under way.

Four weeks of brutal, two-a-day practices down in the twin humid-
ity sumps outside Farrell Stadium, four weeks of living crammed into
brick Gertrude, tossing on narrow mattresses, coping with roommates,
listening to the howling all-night video tournaments or the card games
called Punk and Broo or the game they played with dominoes called
Bones, four weeks of getting banged around just to get used to getting
banged around, of tolerating rookies, fast and strong and driven,
looking to take your job, four weeks of practical jokes, aches and
bruises, cafeteria dining, of dodging the Pack, which hovers outside
every building and on the practice field sidelines with notebooks, recording devices, and cameras at the ready, and the fans, who swarm
everywhere you show your face, four weeks of meaningless exhibition

games, hollow, meandering contests with all the risks of real combat and none of its rewards—all of it through a stretch of summer that sits on your chest like a three-hundred-pound wrestler, with locusts whining in the dense campus greenery and yellow jackets buzzing around your helmet, air so thick it feels like you have to scoop it into your mouth with both hands. You battle through the practices soaked with so much sweat, from the crown of your helmet to the toes of your socks, that you wonder at how human tissue could lose such rivers of fluid. The only leavening for all this is camaraderie, getting back together with the guys and escaping the off-season's full-court press of family and real-world responsibility; gettin' back down, in short, with Jerome.

But this year, 1992, there is no Jerome. Seth and Clyde and even Reverend Reggie are still reeling with grief. That training camp rat, Jim McMahon, and Eric Allen, Byron Evans, Roger Ruzek, Calvin Williams, Andre Waters, and Keith Jackson are all holding out for bigger contracts (Keith is angling for $6 million over three years—payback time). Buddy is long gone, and killjoy Kotite's in charge. Richie's practices aren't as brutal, but the bastard actually *enforces* the 11:00 p.m. curfew, even for *veterans,* and he's sooooo serious. He actually made the guys hand over their supersquirt water guns because they might damage the dorm—*Shit, coach, with brick floors and walls?*

Little of the old playful mood is evident as the team checks into Gertrude this August, despite the fact that lots of folks are predicting that this team, even without Jerome, could go all the way. Quite a few of the players and coaches feel that way, too. But that's part of the problem. As a young team on the make, it was fun every summer getting ready to take the NFL by storm. Now the Eagles have arrived as a power. Instead of training camp commencing as a time of unburdening and rebonding, it rolls in heavy with expectation.

Camp is one of the rituals of pro football, an annual rite of questionable value but profound significance in the culture of the game. Sequestering the army prior to battle, removing them from their women (ostensibly) and children, from all the domestic comforts, hardening them with rigorous discipline—these were all conventions of the ancient manly art of war. It fuels anticipation for the approaching sixteen-game regular season, just as a week of planning, drill, and hype precede every game on the schedule—a season is, after all, mostly preparation and anticipation, punctuated at weekly intervals by several hours of violent action. In the past, the main purpose of camp was to whip players into shape. Old warriors reported flabby and wheezy after a long off-season of overeating, smoking, drinking, and other indulgences. There are still a few backsliders on NFL rosters, but not many. Today's pro athletes, with such big dollars at stake, are often in better shape when they report to camp than they will be for the rest of the year, what with the cumulative toll of nicks, pulls, bruises, and sprains of the modern twenty- to twenty-five-week schedule. Despite their reputation for wild living, very few players can long afford a profligate life in the competitive world of the NFL. All the vices of modern society are present, of course, but serious depravity is present to a lesser extent on a pro roster than in society at large.

Veteran Ken Rose, for instance, a backup linebacker and captain of the Eagles' kicking squads (their special teams), works as a professional trainer in Los Angeles during the off-season. His compact, thickly muscled body looks chiseled out of jet-black granite, with every oblique, pec, dorsi, subscap, deltoid, trapezius, et cetera, etched in stark relief. Alongside him even the fittest of his teammates looks vaguely slothful. Ken is probably the most extreme example, but he is not alone among players who are far better educated in, experienced with, and committed to the modern science of bodybuilding and physical training than any of the coaches who are supposed to be guiding them. After ten years in pro football, Ken maintains a dietary and workout regimen in the off-season that inside a week would probably kill the pizza-gobbling occasional joggers and weekend golfers on the coaching staff. In the off-season, he is up every morning at four-thirty to jog before driving to UCLA, where he is an assistant strength coach, for an hour of serious track work, doing sprint intervals, and (several times a week) endurance training. This is followed by four hours of intensive weight lifting—maintenance reps, auxiliary lifts, power movements. Then after driving home for lunch and a rest at midday, he undertakes an hour-long martial arts workout. Ken finishes off his day by either running the hills behind his suburban home in Thousand Oaks or surfing on the beaches of Santa Monica Bay. And that's his off-season regimen. Ken hates the off-season. He counts the days till training camp. He'd play football every weekend of the year if he could—in fact, one year he nearly did, finishing up a full training camp and season with the Saskatchewan Roughriders of the Canadian Football League in time to plunge into the then-Oakland Raiders' training camp three days later. He remembers the experience fondly. To him, the spartan dorm life, fellowship, and unrelenting physical demands are soul cleansing. He has his training camp mentality, which is like living blindered, or what Ken thinks of as serving a short prison term, where the entire focus of his life becomes football and Team. He and his roommate and protégé, second-year linebacker William "Willie T." Thomas, have two TV sets in their dorm room, and each TV has two video games attached, so their space is the primary game room in Gertrude, where energetic contests often stretch into the wee hours. They hop up after two or three hours of sleep, eat a big breakfast (Ken has the cook whip up special protein-enhanced dishes), then spend the day supplementing the two-a-day practices and meetings with Ken's weight-training routines; over two seasons, Willie T.'s physique has begun to resemble Ken's uncannily, same bulging trapeziuses and deltoids, same proportions of chest, arm, and leg muscles—as if they'd been assembled in the same factory.

The one irreplaceable benefit of camp, even for the supremely fit, is the chance to play football. You can work alone till you drop, but to play honest-to-goodness football, you need twenty-two guys, pads, helmets, and a staff of trainers to patch everybody up when you're done. Old-timers like Ken know there is being in shape, and then there is *playing* shape, and the only way to achieve the latter is to play. Ken is always eager to see if some new off-season training technique he invented actually enhances his play. He has a very methodical mind and plans to coach someday—either football or physical fitness or both—and his body is his lab.

Beyond that, the tradition of herding the entire roster, along with about thirty draft choices and free agents into a cloister—that's more ritual than necessity.

Living arrangements are why most players, unlike Ken, Jimmy Mac, and a handful of others, hate camp. The university tries. It outfits Gertrude with extralong mattresses and window air conditioners and gives the club the run of its campus. West Chester itself rejoices to receive them. The Eagles' arrival every summer is a major event here, a leafy village three miles square dominated by the campus and a redbrick Georgian center. About thirty miles southwest of Philadelphia, West Chester is the government seat of Chester County, a traditionally rural but increasingly suburban province where Amish farms and tony Republican suburbs coexist in a landscape captured by the paintings of Andrew Wyeth. During camp, the village becomes a minor tourist destination, with thousands of football fans crowding in daily for an early glimpse at their fall warriors.

What they see are mostly unknown rookie free agents, an annual batch of hopefuls, survivors of the Sluice, the extensive sifting mechanism for the Great American Cult of the Pigskin. It works just like the winnowing device at a gold mine, washing raw material down a network of chutes, passing it through an ever-narrowing series of gates, until out of the tons of dross are strained a few nuggets of pure ore. The Pigskin Sluice has arms reaching into every city and small town in every county in every state in America, with Coach manning the gates at every narrowing level of the chute. At the Pop Warner level, just about every teenage boy in America gets a chance to play the game, so that's where literally millions of youngsters splash into the mouth of the thing. High schools provide the first great winnowing, where Coach sorts the hundred or so boys who show up for tryouts into prospective behemoths (linemen), monsters (linebackers, tight ends, and big running backs), and artists (quarterbacks, receivers, defensive backs, return men, and pretty little running backs). Through a few weeks of hard workouts and sadistic gut checks, he sifts the raw material with potential to his roster. There are roughly 14,000 high-school football teams in America, which means about 600,000 boys each year make teams, and about half that number earn starting jobs. Four years on comes a much narrower gate. Only about one in every 23 of those boys (approximately one starting player per high school) will ever start for a college football team. There are about 2,000 four-year colleges in the United States, and roughly 600 of them field football teams, making a college pool of first-string players numbering about 13,200—each of whom may be assumed to possess some real football talent. Out of this number, the 28 teams of the NFL each chose a dozen (the draft would shrink to just six rounds in '93), or a total of 336 (about one in 40 and, remember, these are all *starting* college players). Fewer than half that number will ever actually play pro ball, and fewer than half of that total will ever be starters in the pros. Broadly estimated, out of every 2,000 high-school heroes, one will someday hold a starting job in the NFL.

A large percentage of those chosen are black, which for some tends to buttress racial stereotypes about black males; but, in fact, when you look more closely at most of those who succeed, players like Wes Hopkins, Seth Joyner, Byron Evans, Andre Waters, Ben Smith, and others, the distinguishing feature is more often tenacity than sheer talent. With few exceptions (on the Eagles the exceptions are standouts like Randall Cunningham, Reggie White, Fred Barnett, and Eric Allen), the player who makes it to the pros was not the best athlete in his high school, or even on his high-school football team. He is, rather, the most determined and focused. These are young men who decided at a very young age exactly what they wanted to do in life and pursued that goal for a decade or more with ferocious, even foolhardy, intensity. In a sense, you can only make it by refusing to admit what to everyone else is obvious—that you almost certainly *won't* make it. Most don't. For every player who does get all the way to a pro training camp, there are literally thousands of players with the same dream who don't. Of course, the ones who do feel certain they made it by virtue of superior talent and desire. But talent and desire are only part of the story. A boy also needs luck, a lot of it. Luck is the one essential component of success that players rarely admit to themselves. To make it through a gate is to leave all those other poor bastards behind and to further inflate your own legend, building confidence you need to pass through the next gate, and the next. So those who do make it to the final gate tend to exhibit truly breathtaking vanity. It is, simply, necessary. That fearless, can't-touch-this mien has become one of the distinctive features of the modern pro athlete, encountered in every locker room and virtually every postgame show, infecting youth culture everywhere. The fact that a disproportionate number of these undeniably remarkable and very fortunate young men are black says more about paucity of opportunity and the heroic impetus of desperation than it does about haunches and animal reflexes.

For the pro sifting, NFL clubs rely on scouting services that rate virtually every college football player in America. For the Eagles, it is NFS (National Football Scouting), which divides the country into eleven regions and employs scouts (usually former college coaches) to evaluate every college player in their region. This is done by attending a lot of football games, but mostly by—what else?—schmoozing college coaches. Each player is assigned a value between one and nine by NFS; those rated lower than eight wash right out of the Sluice. The eights and nines are herded into the annual scouting "combine," a critical gate, where they are asked to run, jump, and perform a wide variety of tricks designed to measure the skills that could translate into success on the pro gridiron.

It's an honest effort to turn what is ultimately an art into a science, and most football players think it's just ridiculous. Anyone who has ever played the game knows that the fastest man on a track often isn't a particularly good running back or receiver, just as the strongest man in the weight room isn't necessarily a good blocker. The only way to tell how well a kid plays football is to *watch him play football* . . . but, of course, this isn't possible. Even if it were, you'd have to weight a prospect according to whom he has played against, and not just what teams, but what individual players on those teams. A mediocre wide receiver playing against a lousy cornerback can look like Jerry Rice for an afternoon. So scouts weed out most college players in conversation with coaches. The rest they try to watch and then test with their own methods. The most agreed-upon methods are tried at the combine, where prospects demonstrate agility, vertical leaps, speed, strength, and other easily quantifiable things. The art of judging talent reaches its most eccentric levels when scouts follow up on the combine results by personally visiting the players who interest them most. That can get weird.

Dave Alexander, the Eagles' veteran center, remembers one visit from a Packers scout when he was a senior at the University of Tulsa. Dave had been through a number of these sessions. Each scout wanted to see you do something different. Some were happy just to recheck the combine results on their own, timing you in the forty-yard dash— as if *that* had a lot to do with how well you could hold off a charging three-hundred-pound lineman—measuring your jumps or seeing how much iron you could bench-press. Some would time you through an obstacle course of their own devising, usually an arrangement of orange cones, hurdles, and tires out on the practice field. The guy from the Packers wanted to see Dave's pass-blocking technique, but there was nobody around for him to work against, so the scout had Dave pass block the stadium wall. He had him assume a three-point stance, and then lunge at the wall with his hands up. What the guy hoped to divine from this performance was beyond Dave, but being an obliging fellow, and playing in the NFL being sort of a goal . . . well, Dave obliged. He just hoped nobody was watching. Then the guy showed Dave, who had been snapping the football now for nine years, how to hold the ball. "It was some dumb way of holding it," Dave would remember later. "It was silly. I couldn't get a decent grip on it. I snapped it a few times like that for the guy but it would just dribble out on the ground or go flying over his head."

In '92, the league drafted just 335 college players (the Cardinals broke precedent by picking Eric Swann, a defensive lineman who had skipped college to play in a regional semipro league). So the young men who show up with their overnight bags and stereo headphones in West Chester in August—a dozen draft picks and twice that many free agents (either the cream or the most determined of the undrafted)—represent the paltry pebbles of gold nugget that make it into the straw-thin sphincter at the ass end of the Sluice.

And they still haven't made it.

At that final gate stand the High Priests of the Pigskin, presiding over the last four weeks of a decade-long process that isn't, at any of the Sluice gates, particularly objective or even fair. Coach is forced to make snap judgments about kids every step of the way; in fact, one of the traits of a true temple devotee is total faith in his own judgment. It is essential. Every rookie in a pro football training camp, even the most unknown free-agent hopeful, is a damn fine football player. Now, sorting out which of them possess that extra something, which of these hunks of precious ore are 99 percent gold and which are only 98 percent, is no more scientific than the process was at the start.

Every pro team has scores of top draft picks who never amount to anything on the pro gridiron, so it's at least arguable that an equal number of kids who washed out by flunking some bizarre scouting test or failing to catch Coach's eye could have become starters. Buddy didn't have much faith in the process. He used to swear he could tell just by looking in a kid's eyes, not only whether or not he could play, but often what position he should play. Richie made no special claim to prowess in this area. He handled evaluating talent the way he handled everything else—he wasted as little time on it as possible and never looked back.

For these four agonizing weeks of two-a-day practices and nightly film sessions, the rookies, all the superstars of Wherever, U.S.A., went to bed every night and woke up every morning listening for the footsteps of the Turk in the hall, waiting for the knock on the door.

Dave arrived in West Chester in '87 as a fifth-round draft pick, unpacked his bag, and sat staring at the brick walls wondering what to do with the rest of his first evening in camp, when there was a knock on the door.

"Coach [Bill] Walsh wants to see you downstairs," said a ball boy.

Shit, I've been cut and I haven't even had a chance yet to put on the damn pads! he thought. Turns out the coach wanted the center to try playing tackle.

You stayed on edge until the final cuts were made. In the nightly meetings you could see the mistakes you made (there were plenty of those) and the things you had done well, and you could tell how hard a look the coaches were taking by how many reps you got in practice (how many repetitions of the day's agenda of plays), but it was rare for anyone to pull you aside and say, *You're looking good, rook, keep it up and you might make this team!* If you did well, you were threatening the job of some esteemed veteran. If you did poorly, you were held in contempt—no matter how many touchdowns you had scored or passes you had picked off back in those blessed rah-rah afternoons at the alma mater. Even the sunniest pinnacles of collegiate glory, just a few short months behind you, counted for nothing. Casey Weldon, the Florida State quarterback whose twenty-two touchdown passes kept the Seminoles and Bobby Bowden ranked number one in the nation for twelve weeks the previous fall, who had been favorably compared in a long and flattering profile in *Sports Illustrated* to none other than Joe Montana—what, just six months ago?—now sits on his helmet on the sidelines alongside the water boys, watching veterans David Archer and Jeff Kemp battle for the dubious distinction of being the Eagles' third-string quarterback.

Weldon's college exploits, along with those of top draft picks Siran Stacy, Tommy Jeter, and Tony Brooks, virtually guarantee at least a year on the roster, but for most of the rookies, training camp is high drama, a moment in which your fabulous football career—

Pop Warner superstar, high-school all-American, college standout—knocks up against the final gate of the Pigskin Sluice, and some distracted bald guy with a cigar and pink visor who never once even looks at you or calls you by name decides on the basis of a few dozen chances on a broiling practice field or, maybe, one or two chances in an exhibition game whether in September you'll be desperately looking for an entry-level job in the recession economy or, in some screaming concrete bowl of a football stadium, throbbing with excitement, you'll be acting out the fondest dreams of your young life.

But for this one month, all eighty guys are Eagles, from Reverend Reggie to Randall to the last lowly free-agent camp invitee. The draft picks and free agents get to bang helmets with Seth and Andre, they get to pass rush Randall, tackle Herschel, and try to run with Fred Barnett. Afterward, they get to share tables in the cafeteria with these guys and then hang out on campus or in the dorm. They get to peek at the characters behind the wall of celebrity.

Keith Byars, who rooms with neat-freak Randall, has such elaborate video hookups that their room (to Randall's chagrin) rivals Kenny and Willie T.'s as video central. Players are up until three and four in the morning battling against each other in electronic baseball and football. Electronic barks and beeps from the tube compete with the real-life taunts, shouts, laughter, and anguish of the contestants, who compete . . . well, the way they always do, as if their lives depend on it. Keith is a video junkie. At home in New Jersey he has three setups, in the basement, in the living room, and in the bedroom. For away games, he packs a system in his suitcase and hooks it up in his hotel room—he even does this when the team stays in the New Jersey hotel the night before home games. On the plane, he brings sophisticated handheld versions. In camp, Keith is the Commissioner and draws up charts for the tournaments, meticulously penciling in the totals, orchestrating the competition throughout the four weeks to a final championship, which he wins in baseball, and linebacker Willie T. wins in football. Seth is the champion in golf, which he plays considerably better on the screen than on the links.

Living in the rec room is tough on Randall, not just because it's hard to sleep, but because he is inordinately fastidious about his things and his space. He's like every college freshman's nightmare roomie. He accuses Keith of snoring and farting too much, which makes everybody laugh, but Ran-*doll* is serious. He's got this spray can of room deodorant that he uses liberally, and more. David Archer is playing video games with him one evening when he hears the sound of something plastic hitting the tile floor under the desk across the room. It's a room deodorizer that has come unstuck. Randall hits the pause button,

crosses the room, and affixes the thing back up underneath the desk.
They resume playing, and Arch hears another thud. This time, Randall doesn't even hit pause. He reaches down deftly to scoop another
deodorizer off the floor and jab it back up underneath a bookshelf.
Before he leaves, Arch counts two more of the things in the room.

The accommodations are a big comedown for the veterans, whose
standard of living began climbing at warp speed after they signed their
first pro contract. Mike Schad, the veteran left guard who has missed
almost all of the previous season with a bad back, who has spent months
with chiropractors, MDs, and team trainers to nurse himself back into
playing shape, wakes up after his first night in the dorm with a stiffness
in his spine and panics—he gets excused from practice (which is risky
in this competitive environment) and drives into downtown West Chester, where he locates a bedding store, bursts in, all six-five, 290 pounds
of him, and announces, "I'm Mike Schad of the Philadelphia Eagles
and I'm leaving here with the best mattress you've got!"

Sleep is critical for the big men, who feel the toll of two-a-day
practices much more than their smaller teammates. Midway through
camp, linemen are snoozing all over the dorm whenever there's a
break in the schedule. Defensive backs, receivers, ballcarriers, and
quarterbacks may have time for video-game tournaments and extra-
curricular pursuits, but the big guys are wrung out.

If there is one person who loves training camp without reservation it's Jimmy Mac, who finally arrives two weeks late after settling
unhappily for a one-year $846,000 deal. Jimbo comes equipped with
a well-traveled giant air mattress that about covers the floor of his
dorm room from wall to wall. Once he arrives, a running game of
Bones ensues that lasts, between practices and meetings, for the length
of his stay—and none of the rookies are safe. The veteran has a devious
arsenal of ploys for delivering water, shaving cream, and sundry other
unpleasant surprises to unsuspecting victims, buckets rigged to spill
over opened doors, water balloons delivered from high angles, shaving
cream lathered inside shoes and helmets—every annoying adolescent
stunt five years of life in a college dorm and eleven pro training camps
can teach.

Camp means open season on rookies. It's annoying having to
practice with these cocky kids hell-bent on making the team, so veterans
more than even the score. On the field, the old-timers consider it their
duty to initiate the youngsters to authentic NFL violence, so the few
who make it know what's in store, and those who don't can further
amplify the legend—*Man, you don't know what being hit is until you've
had Wes Hopkins take your head off coming over the middle.* But the on-
field hazing is just part of it. Sure, there's the simple and time-honored

humiliation of having to stand on a plastic chair in the cafeteria and warble through your school fight song, with the veterans throwing food at you, and there's the standard dodging of spitballs and wads of paper throughout the evening meetings. But there are also other hazards, like groin wraps laced with stinging heat balm, a friendly offer of some chaw spiked with hot pepper, getting your pockets picked in Broo and Bones by wily veteran operators (often working together), or being carried out to the practice field to be ceremonially taped to the goalposts and used for target practice by the kicking team. Former backup quarterback Matt Cavanaugh, a veteran of more than a dozen pro training camps, would post an official-looking sign outside the locker room that read HELMET RENTAL FEE . . . $12.50 and do a brisk rookie business until the new guys found out helmets were one of the few things the club issued free.

There's not much leisure time, but more traditional all-American recreational pursuits also thrive. In the three hours between the end of afternoon practice and the mandatory evening meeting there are enough bars and restaurants near campus to afford at least an early and abbreviated nightlife. The window of opportunity here is small, but doable, and into it step eagerly the deliciously contoured, full-breasted, blow-dried fräuleins who sprout like lively wildflowers along the paths trod by pro athletes.

These are the Sis-Boom-Bimbos, the sorority of athlete-worshiping females distantly related to the juicy cupcakes in matching sweaters and bouncy skirts who grace every high-school, college, and pro sideline in America, only these girls have graduated from pom-poms and backseat postprom humps to meatier pursuits. White ones, black ones, ones in shades from beige to sienna to mahogany, ones with quality soft-porn chests and taut, silky thighs, all of them straining with diet and exercise and makeup and elaborate coiffure to achieve that ultimate Platonic ideal of American Goddess, guaranteed to make any red-blooded young male citizen of these United States leap at first sight to . . . well, if not love, then full priapic salute.

It's an accepted part of the Great American Cult of the Pigskin, with roots in the ancient chauvinistic rituals of rape and plunder— *We win; we lay your women.* The glamorous sweeties huffing and puffing in full makeover and glittering cleavage-and-buttock-baring costume on the sidelines of every NFL game are just modern vestiges of the age-old sexual-spoils contest. In Philadelphia, as in most cities, these cheerleaders are actually skillful dancers who work through professionally coordinated routines and keep up an active roster of off-field public appearances, most of them hoping to parlay the exposure and experience into some more serious level of stardom. They are discouraged from fraternizing with players and are all but ignored as they grind through their numbers on the sidelines, through rain, sleet, and snow, heedless of the score or the mood of the hometown fans. But they remain inexplicably popular, for no other reason than that, at bottom, their role as symbolic plunder gives them a certain boosted erotic appeal. Note the glossy cheerleader calendars sold by nearly every NFL club, posing members of the squad in minimal attire before Vaseline-smeared lenses in effusions of soft light, a cleaned-up but clear knockoff of *Playboy*'s pulchritudinous flavors of the month. We love our exploitative sexual fantasies in America. It's no coincidence that the Cowboys' cheerleaders are a standard part of touring USO shows for our military boys based overseas. The young women grow indignant at the suggestion—as do cheerleaders everywhere—that they represent nothing more than ripe, erotogenic prizes for the oafs out there banging heads, but there you have it. Surviving well into the second generation of NOW and postfeminist liberation ideology, we have, in Odessa, Texas—as detailed in H. G. Bissinger's profile of the Permian High School Panthers, *Friday Night Lights*—the Pepettes, high-school girls "assigned" to specific members of the beloved local high-school team for a full season, required to minister to their needs, in practice good clean fun, for sure, but a ritual with sexual implications that are plain. (Eagles linebacker Britt Hager, a graduate of Permian, is married to his former Pepette.) The pornographers who made *Debbie Does Dallas* zeroed right in on the theme, cutting through the proprietous haze, turning the salacious power of the premier Sis-Boom squad, the Cowboys' cheerleaders, into a feature-length hard-core romp, which did predictably boffo box office and is now almost as standard a feature in American hotel rooms (courtesy of in-room video) as Gideon's Bible.

It's no coincidence that most of the wives and girlfriends of the players cultivate the same glamorous, flaming-haired, taut-haunched, pert-breasted, wholesome but hardly virginal look of the professional cheerleader, or that the real camp followers of the sport (out of which at least some of the wives and girlfriends ascend) follow suit. The true Sis-Boom-Bimbos, as opposed to the symbolic ones, offer wares that are far from symbolic. They specialize in making fantasies real. They know exactly where to be and when, usually the same dozen or so girls in every city, some of them not too choosy about which of these burly prizes they commune with from night to night, some of them actually vying to improve their totals as the summer wears on, sort of a XXX-rated version of the football-card craze. They come after players as aggressively as the street whores in Third World capitals, positioning themselves to literally latch onto an arm or a jacket as a star player emerges from the stadium or hotel or front door of any advertised public event. The richer and more famous the player, the more determined the Sis-Boom-Bimbos become. David Archer spent a year watching the trials of Jimmy Mac when they were both on the Chargers' roster in '89. His most vivid memory is of exiting the Hoosier Dome directly behind Jimbo, on their way to the team bus down a path cordoned off through the usual crowd by the police, when a woman, the familiar type, aurora hair, leather pants, probably a looker when she wasn't in full carnivorous heat, jumped out in front of Jimbo and grabbed a fistful of his neatly pressed, button-down oxford. "Jim, just let me—"

A cop jumped out and grabbed the woman's arm, but she refused to release Jimbo's shirt. The cop was dragging her, but she kept her grip on the shirt until *bam!*—the quarterback smacked the woman smartly on the forehead with the palm of his right hand, and she let go and just folded into the arms of the cop.

"Works every time," Jimbo confided on the bus.

The more sophisticated Sis-Boom-Bimbos find out a player's home phone or address and bombard him with mail, flowers, phone calls, fetchingly lewd photographs, candy, balloons, and so on. Needless to say, it is the rare player, married or unmarried, rookie or veteran, who maintains a perfect record in this regard. For the long list of rookies, most of whom are attending their first and last pro training camp, the Sis-Boomers are one of the quality perks of summer. If you walk into the bar with Randall or Seth or Jimbo or any of the team's other big stars, you are going to get laid that night, and not just by some let's-get-this-over-with Molly, but by one of the wildest and sweetest male-fantasy squeezes of your young life. If you go alone, it might take longer to establish your credentials, especially if nobody in the Pack has noticed you and written or aired a report about you, but even then your chances are good—certainly a helluva lot better than they would be back in Podunk, Nowhere, stocking shelves at the Piggly Wiggly.

Beyond the pickup trade, some of the veterans have their standard training-camp chippies—a step up the ladder for every self-respecting Sis-Boom-Bimbo—girls who live out here in sleepy Chester County, or who move in for the summer to offer a little fleshy solace to the hardworking boys, condemned to months of sleeping alone, away from wife (or regular girlfriend) and family, locked in that silly dorm. Many of the veterans, those with homes nearby or girls waiting for them in the local motelry, wink at the team's so-called curfews, and so long as they get back in time for morning practice sober and able, what's a couple-hundred-dollars fine to a guy making a half million or more a year? The players' wives know that camp is the most hazardous time of year for their marriage—a precarious thing at best with these guys. Many kiss their men good-bye and really don't want to know what goes on out there in West Chester, with all those pro hormones percolating under pressure inside old Gertrude.

Richie tries to keep the lid on, but who can watch all these guys twenty-four hours a day? He, of course, devoted football monk that he is, loves camp. Always has. Four weeks of total cloister, up at the crack of dawn, a small army of young men in his thrall, two sessions on the practice field broken by film study and planning sessions, piecing together the team for another assault on the league—what's not to like? But in this, his second training camp as head coach, Richie seems to be withdrawing from the close-knit coaching circle. He has his good buddy from Staten Island, Matty McEntyre, who lives in his shadow now the way George Azar lives in Harry's. Matty, a cheerful retired electrician with a belly big as a keg, just moved on down when Richie became head coach (every High Priest needs his loyal factotum) and does what Richie's wife, Liz, never could—he shares the temple life. Matty isn't on the payroll, but he travels with the team, attends practice (balancing his own oversized Havana), bunks in Gertrude, stands alongside Richie on the sidelines during games dressed in full Eagles regalia—he even flies down with Richie and the other coaches on their annual trip to the Senior Bowl, helping (unofficially) to scout talent for the draft.

When the other coaches and scouts get together in the evening to toss back a few beers, discuss strategy, kick around observations about personnel, Richie is often by himself up in his room or hanging out with Matty or off somewhere in his Caddy. Sometimes he leaves after dark, slipping out alone, and shoots out Route 202 to the strip mall at Painters Crossing to see a movie by himself (his favorite way to go).

His associates note this growing aloofness about Richie, budding paranoia, perhaps, an unwillingness to confide in anyone other than Harry and Norman (and Matty), a tendency to become suspicious whenever he sees one of them talking informally to a Pack hound— Coach Uptight has issued orders, which everyone ignores, that no member of his staff is allowed to speak to reporters without his permission.

About the team and its prospects, though, he's his usual upbeat self. Summer is the season of potential in football. The kid you drafted in the twelfth round really looks like he might be a find, or some free agent out of nowhere looks like he *can really block*, and every veteran is poised to have the season of his career—what could go wrong? Of course, the answer to that is *everything,* but at least not until the season starts. Richie enjoys the opportunity football affords to start fresh every summer, discard the guys who don't fit in and plug the holes with new talent, fit the pieces back together just so, tinker with the offensive system, add a few wrinkles, play out the scenario for victory in his head.

First you have to believe . . .

IT'S NOT HARD to believe this year. When Richie and Harry met with Norman last winter down on Indian Creek Island, amid the Calders and Mirós and Lichtensteins, the owner was in a boisterous, commanding fettle, eager to shake the Curse of Buddy once and for all. Buddy was still pining away unhired on his Kentucky horse farm, and Richie had impressed all but the former coach's most fervent backers by coaching the team to seven wins in their last eight games (even if that one loss was the big one to Dallas). Randall's rehab was progressing nicely, so there was every reason to expect his return. The pain in Norman's neck had eased. Some of that old BramanMan swagger was back.

"This is the year," Norman would tell a visiting hound that month. "The philosophy that I'm approaching this season with is we're not building for tomorrow anymore. Tomorrow is not the goal. Today is the goal. If we can pick up an older player who may have only a year or two left, we're going to do it. And if he's a high-priced player it doesn't make a difference. So if there's somebody out there on Plan B that can come in and help us now, we're going to go after him as hard as we possibly can. Hopefully, we can obtain a quality running back. . . ."

Norman had rarely talked like this publicly with Buddy around, but his take-charge tone didn't bother Richie a bit. Hey, it was his team! You had to respect the guy. You don't make gazillions in the business world without having some clue about things—things in general. Buddy had always scorned advice, anyone's advice, but Norman's in particular. This business about a running back being a case in point. Norman, the press, and the fans had been braying for years about how badly the Eagles needed a fancy-pants running back. To Buddy it just proved his point: none of these people had a clue how to win football games. With Randall running for 600 to 900 yards per season, why did you need a high-priced running back? With the scarcity of roster slots on a football team, you looked for multidimensional guys to free up positions elsewhere. If Randall was both a quarterback and the team's top running back, what luck! One less running back needed.

Richie had gone along with this philosophy as offensive coordinator, even defended it vigorously. It was Randall's 962 yards that had made the Eagles the best ground gainers in the NFC that year. Without Randall in '91, they had fallen to tenth among the division's fourteen teams, but now Randall was back. Buddy would have just listened to Norman vent on the subject of a running back, and then tell Joe Woolley to go out there and find him another corner or linebacker— but Buddy was gone. Hallelujah! Norman loved the way Richie really listened, the way he nodded, the way he jumped on board. By God, if the owner thought this team needed a running back, then Richie was going to give him a running back.

And not just one!

On draft day, months prior to this training camp, Richie thought he'd hit the jackpot. Without a first-round draft pick (they'd dealt it away in '91 to get Antone Davis), they'd nevertheless landed Siran Stacy and Tony Brooks. Siran had been the most exciting collegiate back in the country before blowing out his knee in his junior year. He'd played well in his senior year, but not well enough to dispel doubts about the knee, which was why he was still there in the second round—*You should see the videotape on this guy!* And then Brooks, what a windfall that this big, fast back was still there in the fourth round. And Buddy thought *he* was lucky. All through rookie camp, even though his backfield coach Richard Woods was less than impressed, Richie glowed with enthusiasm about his baby backs. One of these guys was going to start!

Except . . . Norman had this other idea.

"What do you think of Herschel Walker?" Harry asked the coach one morning that spring.

What little Richie knew, he didn't like. Walker was a big, very fast back with no moves to speak of, hyped to high heaven by the media when coming out of college in '82 (third in the Heisman balloting as a freshman, second as a sophomore, first as a junior), celebrated as MVP of the fledgling but doomed USFL, but, except for one outstanding season with the Cowboys seven years back, he had been nothing more than a mediocre running back in the NFL for the last five years. Dallas had traded him to Minnesota in return for about five years' worth of top draft picks, and as a result the Cowboys were now a nascent dynasty and the Vikings a laughingstock. Richie never had liked the way Herschel ran, short mincing steps, no lateral movement, virtually upright. He was strictly a straight-ahead guy with speed. He couldn't make a blind man miss. The vaunted Herschel had rushed for exactly three yards and fumbled twice the last time the Eagles played the Vikings. Then there were those stories about his kookiness, the supposed suicide try, bobsledding, and all that. Suffice it to say, Richie was deeply *un*interested. *"You* are more likely to play for the Eagles than Herschel Walker," he told one startled, asthmatic, middle-aged hound that spring.

Of course, Richie didn't know yet where the Herschel idea had originated.

Norman had looked up to few men in his life, but one of them in recent years was Al Davis, the colorful and controversial Raiders' owner. Davis was a damn-their-eyes kind of guy who strode the public stage unafraid and who unabashedly managed his club with both hands. Of course, Al had the credentials. Long before he became owner of the team, Davis had been a Pigskin High Priest—nobody could accuse Al Davis of dilettantism. And Al, a dinner friend of the Bramans', had told Norman that there really were only two veteran running backs worth buying who would be available this off-season. The Raiders had evaluated both Herschel, whom the Vikings were shopping around desperately, and Eric Dickerson, the petulant former Colts star. The Raiders had gone with Dickerson, but Al said it had been a tough choice; Herschel was neither a fluke nor a flake.

"I think he could really help us," Norman told Harry.

Harry passed out tapes of Herschel in action to Joe Woolley and the coaching staff, and from the temple there arose an unequivocal chorus of naysaying.

"I don't think he can run," said Woolley.

"Neither do I," said Harry.

Richard Woods, the running backs coach, who had his plate full with five returning veterans and Richie's two baby backs, also gave a thumbs-down. What Herschel seemed to do best, and most, in recent years, was run up the backside of his own blockers and fall down—and fumble. The most damning description pro coaches ever apply to a running back was being used to describe Herschel. "He squats," they said—in other words, *Give 'im the ball an' he makes like a girl goin' t' pee.*

Harry got the message.

"They don't want to touch him," Harry told Norman.

"Why?"

"Well, we looked at the film, and . . . ," Harry enumerated the objections.

"Look again," Norman suggested.

Meanwhile, WIP, the Eagles-obsessed nonstop local sports-gab radio station, had mounted a crusade for the club to sign Herschel. It had people jamming the Eagles' switchboard and driving around the Vet with their headlights on, honking for Herschel. People were

standing on the row-house rooftops during minicamp shouting down
to Richie, "We want Herschel!" which annoyed the hell out of him—
Wonder if we can get rid o' those houses? As usual, announcers at the
radio station, assuming a lot more than they could possibly know,
had the story all wrong. They blamed Norman. Angelo Cataldi, the
morning drive-time clown, had taken to chirping "Cheap! Cheap!
Cheap!" in the background whenever the owner's name came up,
which was about every sixty seconds even during the off-season.

After his talk with Norman, Harry dropped the Herschel tapes
back on Joe's desk and said the owner wanted further scrutiny.

"Norman thinks we should sign this guy," he said.

So Joe looked, and Harry looked, and Richard Woods looked,
and they all looked again with Richie, and lo! A miracle gradually
began to take place. It didn't happen all of a sudden, like Paul being
struck from his mount on the road to Damascus, but if you looked
real hard at those tapes of Herschel Walker . . . well, by God, gradually,
ol' Herschel started looking not so bad after all. Sure, he wasn't a
shifty runner, but damn if he didn't seem to grind out those yards. It
wasn't fancy, but the sticks moved. And that move that looked like a
squat? Well, you know what? It turned out to be this determined little
jukelike thing, Herschel dropping down low to evade and squeeze out
an extra yard or two. Even in his worst years as a flop in Minnesota,
Herschel maintained a steady four-yards-per-carry average, which was
pretty damn good, once you thought about it twice. Woolley was still
a lot more impressed with the potential of the draft picks Stacy and
Brooks, but as the coaches looked harder, he began to hear them talk
about ways they might be able to use a running back like that Herschel
Walker.

"Well, if y'all have a way you think you can use him, and you
have in your mind a plan, and you know his limitations . . . well, then,
that's up to you" was the personnel director's halfhearted verdict (Joe
did have this vaguely troubling way, Richie and Harry noted, of not
exactly coming *on board*).

But Richie, even with Norman behind it and all, still wasn't completely sold himself. He just couldn't get past those bizarre things he
had read and heard about Herschel. It was hard to put his finger on
it exactly, but it sounded to Richie, like . . . well, "He doesn't sound
like he really wants to play football," he told Harry.

So Richie and Harry resolved to see for themselves. They ducked
out of the offices on Tuesday, June 9, and met Herschel at his in-laws'
house on a wooded lot in Verona, New Jersey. With Herschel was his
wife, Cindy, and her sisters and her parents. They all sat around in
the living room and had a nice long chat. Herschel was smaller than

they expected. Out from under his giant shoulder pads and helmet, he was built like a gymnast, a compact, solid, well-proportioned young man with a thick, muscular neck, clean-cut, soft-spoken, intelligent, and exceedingly deferential (Herschel certainly had learned, in his twenty-year journey from tiny Wrightsville, Georgia, how to woo Coach). "Don't believe everything you read," he assured them. He had always pursued a variety of athletic venues in his off-season, from martial arts to dance training to, more recently, bobsledding. It had never detracted from his game. He admitted his frustrations in Minnesota, where he had never fit in. He said some of his casting around for challenges outside football resulted because the Vikings had used him so little he had this *excess* of competitive energy to deal with. He was about to explode with the desire to play football again. All he wanted was another chance. He'd do whatever they wanted him to do, even play on special teams. He *wanted* to play on special teams. He was good at it.

As they got up to leave, Herschel's mother-in-law asked if Richie and Harry would pose for a snapshot with the family star. Harry put his arm up around Herschel's shoulder, and he was stunned.

"I mean, my golly! It was like steel," he told Richie back out in the car.

The coach, too, had been impressed. "Hey, this guy can play!" he said.

They drove back to Philly, working themselves into a righteous coachly froth over their coup and phoned Norman with the happy news. Imagine how pleased Norman was—his bit of intelligence had panned out. They worked out the details and signed Herschel two weeks later to a two-year, $3 million deal.

Richie had done a complete about-face. It wasn't an act, either. He didn't feel like Herschel was being foisted on him. Not for a Staten Island minute! Back when the Vikings sold the store to get Herschel and then dumped him on Jerry Burns, there wasn't much Burns could do but grumble and press on, making it clear to everyone (especially Herschel) that it hadn't been *his* idea. But Richie wasn't the least bit disgruntled. He was genuinely excited about signing the back Norman had wanted—and he hadn't. That was one of the good things about the modern, corporate NFL head coach. He was flexible. He didn't just go along with what the owner wanted—why, he was capable of *adjusting his attitude* if necessary.

"I'm thrilled to have him; we all are," Kotite told reporters (some of the same ones to whom he had disparaged Herschel privately just weeks before). He predicted that with the addition of Herschel and the second coming of Randall the team would field the best offense since he had signed on in '90. "He's going to help us make a run for it," Richie said. "Once you get Herschel through the line of scrimmage and he sees an opening, nobody can catch him. He just screams into the secondary. He runs . . . what? A sub-4.3-[second] 40-yard dash? You know how fast that is? I drop you down a mine shaft and you don't do 4.3. . . ."

Hallelujah!

MAKING IT WAS the real drama of training camp. For high-priced superstars like Herschel and the Eagles' veteran starters, camp was just a time to tune up and focus in. But for the rookies, every day of practice was a chance to make the dream come true. Your chances diminished according to the round you were drafted and just about vanished as you dropped past the seventh or eighth round and on into the virtually hopeless region of the free agents. Most training camps ended by adding only five or six new players to the active roster, and Coach was predisposed to keep players he selected in the draft— the club had already paid them hefty bonuses to sign, so cutting them not only made his judgment suspect, it was costly. Nevertheless, almost every summer, some blazingly talented bottom-rung draft pick or free agent (all but overlooked completely by the guardians of the Sluice) would make the miracle shot, overcome all of these odds, and o'erleap the system, prove the whole hired juggernaut of scouting expertise blind.

One of the best recent examples concerned a forthright, fast-talking charmer from Willingboro, New Jersey, named Marvin Hargrove.

On Tuesday, June 12, 1990, Marvin borrowed his brother's Ford Mustang and drove across the Betsy Ross Bridge and down I-95 to Philly's sports complex. Buddy was opening the Eagles' voluntary camp that morning, the first day of informal practice for the upcoming season. Marvin planned to just watch, stand on the track inside old JFK Stadium along with the several hundred other fans that typically showed up for these early practice sessions. That was the idea, anyway. Marvin wanted to see what a pro practice looked like. Tossing his cleats onto the backseat was an afterthought.

Eventually, see, Marvin planned to play pro football himself. He'd been a star receiver at Willingboro High School and had attended the University of Richmond on a football scholarship. He had played well in college, but he was one of the tens of thousands who washed out of the Sluice on draft day. Richmond was a small school that played ho-hum against just mediocre competition, so Marvin's receiving stats were suspect. What's more, the school's offense had collapsed in his senior year, and Marvin had pulled his hamstring, so his numbers tailed off badly, eroding any slight interest out there. Marvin was small for the pros, just five-ten and about 175 pounds, and when he had run the forty-yard dash on the injured hamstring for visiting pro scouts, his time of 4.7 was subpar. Still, he'd gotten himself an agent, who was downright sanguine about his prospects. Even though none of the scouting guides listing the top one hundred or so players at each position in the country even mentioned his name, Marvin had heard from somebody *inaposition* to know that he might go as high as the sixth or seventh round.

On its face, this expectation might seem highly fanciful, but such is the nature of kids who make it; they believe in themselves *beyond* reason. After having been a big star for roughly half of his twenty-two years, it was harder for Marvin to believe his status would abruptly end than it would somehow, against the odds, continue. Come draft day, he was ready, positioned by the phone, watching the early rounds on ESPN, just waiting for the call. And waiting. And waiting.

Through all twelve rounds of the draft, a two-day process, the phone was silent.

That was two months ago. By now the other seniors who graduated with Marvin were shopping around with résumés in the real world, but he wasn't ready just yet to put his criminal justice major to work. The way Marvin saw it, the NFL had made a huge mistake. Why, there were guys drafted high up whom Marvin knew well, guys whom he *knew* he could outplay! What was this system they used, anyway? So what if he ran a forty-yard dash a few tenths of a second slower, as long as he knew how to maneuver in the violent chaos on a football field, and had terrific hands and heart, and, with a football in his hands, had never been caught from behind by anyone, *ever?*

Marvin's dad, a Greyhound bus driver, had owned Eagles season tickets in the three-hundred level of the Vet for years. It was the team Marvin had grown up watching on TV and from the stands. He had called the team's personnel office to see about a tryout, and Tom Gamble (Harry's son and the team's assistant personnel director) had tried to discourage him. Tom was trying to be nice—and realistic. After all, the team had drafted three wide receivers in April: the highly touted Mike Bellamy from Illinois in the second round, Fred Barnett from Arkansas State in the third round, and Calvin Williams from Purdue in the fifth. They already had Pro Bowl receiver Mike Quick, expected back from a leg injury, and Cris Carter, who had finished third in the NFL in touchdown catches last season. Anthony Edwards was a solid backup who also returned punts. And, supplementing these riches, they had invited several other collegiate wide receivers with promise to training camp. Most teams only kept four, five at most.

"It wouldn't be fair to bring you in because you wouldn't even get a good look," Tom explained.

Scouting the situation at other pro camps, Marvin figured his best shot as a walk-on was in New York, but his dad urged him to go to the Eagles' first practice anyway.

"Why don't you just go see what they've got?" he told his son. "See what an NFL practice looks like."

Marvin parked the Mustang on the lot outside the dilapidated gray stadium, set just south of the newer Vet and used as an outdoor practice field by the Eagles. It was an eerie setting, this enormous empty arena, famous for heavyweight-title bouts, rock concerts, and the annual Army-Navy football games, fallen into grand disrepair. The last major event here had been Philadelphia's leg of the worldwide Live Aid rock concert, and pieces of the cheerful banners and hand-painted wooden signage, now weathered and partially in shreds, flapped against the outside of the old press box and TV platforms above, haunting the place with souvenirs of fleeting pop glory. Rows of empty metal benches ascended evenly up to a gray, drizzly sky. For almost two hours, Marvin paced on the track, silently mingling with the other gapers as the players and prospects, who wore helmets and numbered jerseys but no pads, stretched and jogged and ran passing and blocking drills. He tried to measure his own skills against theirs from a distance, but there was no way to do that. He picked out Bellamy, Barnett, Williams, and a few of the free-agent receivers and watched as Randall and Jimbo took turns zipping precise passes at them. The more he watched, the more anxious Marvin became. He decided he had to do something.

As the team left the field, the veterans dashing for cars they had parked inside the stadium just off the track, the rookies trudging off across the acres of parking lot back to the Vet, Marvin positioned himself among the clump of fans waiting outside the tall gate at the northeast end. When Buddy walked up, and the fans pressed in for autographs, Marvin stepped in front of the coach and looked him squarely in the eye.

"Excuse me, Coach Ryan?"

Buddy reflexively reached out his hands, expecting to be handed pen and paper.

"No," said Marvin, waving away the coach's hands, still looking him in the eye. "My father always told me that if you wanted anything done, then you go to the boss, and since you're the boss, I just want to tell you that I'm a wide receiver, I graduated from the University of Richmond in May and I'd like to play for your team if I can have a tryout."

Buddy took a half step back and eyed Marvin up and down quickly.

"Can you run a forty for me today?"

"Yes, sir."

"Come on. We'll time you."

Inside the Vet about a half hour later, Marvin stretched and ran for Joe Woolley, who timed him at 4.5 seconds over forty yards. Woolley said the time was good, not great, but that he liked his stride.

"You get in shape, that time will come down," he said.

But that was all he said. He walked Marvin back inside, and they rode the elevator up to the Eagles' offices in silence. Joe told Marvin to have a seat on a gray leather couch in the waiting room outside the executive suite and then disappeared inside for a few minutes. When he stepped back out he said, "How do I spell your name on the contract?"

Of course, Marvin knew all he had done was secure a chance to run around on the field with the rest of the free agents. He was the lowest of the low on a preseason roster creaking with dead weight. It was like being invited to play the first hole in a golf tournament, where you could stay only if you hit a hole in one.

But the next day, and the next day, and the day after that, Marvin hit holes in one. He lit up the practice field, one amazing catch after another. His bubbly personality was felt all over. If a frustrated defensive back gave him a quick shove from behind as he leaped to catch a pass, Marvin would hang on to the ball as he went flying to the ground, roll, pop up, and give the surly defender a playful pat on the rump as he ran back to the huddle. By the time the team had checked into Gertrude and donned pads in August, Marvin was a favorite with the fans sitting on the grass by the two practice fields.

He made an impression on his teammates, too. The voluntary camp drills were no contact, which put defensive backs at a disadvantage covering the smaller, faster receivers. In a game or "live" drill, defenders could even the match by slamming the receiver as he came off the line or by hitting him so hard as the ball arrived that he couldn't hang on—or, if he caught it, wished he hadn't. Without pads, without *violence*, nimble receivers could win the battle all afternoon. After one such session, Seth and Andre and Wes invited Marvin out for a drink (teetotaler Marvin would accept only a Coke). Afterward, he wasn't sure if they were befriending him or needling him—probably a little of both.

"Keep doing what you're doing," Andre said. "I need that challenge. I'm gonna bust your ass in training camp."

All through the weeks in West Chester, Andre would grin at him on the field, reminding him of the promise. It gave Marvin pause. Waters's concussive torpedo tackles were feared throughout the league.

"Ah, you'll never get a chance to hit me," Marvin bragged.

They loved this kid's daring. Once, in a full-pads live drill, when Seth thought Marvin's feeble attempt at a crack-back block was aimed too low, he came charging at the rookie, 240 pounds of ferocious linebacker, flattening the slight receiver and then pummeling him. Andre came over and added a few kicks to Marvin's ribs—all in good fun. It lasted until Reverend Reggie and Mike Golic pulled the two veterans off. Marvin hopped up unbowed, swinging his fists (careful to let Golic hold him back), challenging Seth, "You want more?"

Which made everybody laugh—including Seth, which wasn't easy.

Meanwhile, obstacles began to shift fortuitously. Quick's aching knees wouldn't allow him to practice much. Barnett and Bellamy were busy for the first weeks of training camp doing what top draft picks do, holding out for a better contract, and when they did return, they both promptly popped hamstrings. That gave Marvin lots of chances to impress the coaches, the quarterbacks, and please the fans up on the hill. The Pack, always desperate for a story line in the long, aimless preseason, fell in love with the Marvin story, turning him into something of a camp sensation. After practices, Marvin would draw knowing chuckles from the veterans by hanging around in the parking lot, sweat streaming from every pore, signing his name with a flourish for all comers, "Marvin Hargrove, #18," savoring every minute of his new pro status.

Up in Gertrude, Marvin's cocky way made him the favorite rookie target of the season. When he suffered a minor groin pull, the team's trainer, Otho Davis, gave him a couple of pills and rigged one of his famous menthol heat balm wraps that set Marvin's nuts on fire—as intended.

That night, when he got up to urinate, Marvin's stream was bright blue. He screamed.

Down in the training room, having frantically awakened Otho and his assistant, David Price, Marvin squirmed as the trainer, with his slow-talking sincerity and basset-hound face, told him that blue pee was a symptom of a rare and dreadful form of the clap, and it probably served Marvin right.

"But I haven't been sleeping around!"

The trainers rolled their eyes.

"It's true! Ask the guys. I go to bed early. I don't go out drinking at night. I've got a steady girlfriend back in Richmond!"

Otho considered this gravely, nodding. Then he said, with grim authority, "Well, it's very rare to get it this way, but it is possible to get it just from showering with somebody who has it."

The trainers said they could remember one other case. Long-term consequences could be dire.

"Sometimes a vasectomy can stop the swelling," said Otho.

"Get the hell out of here!"

"No, it's true," said Price. "Your balls swell up on you. They have pictures of African tribesmen with, like, elephantiasis of the pecker and balls."

"But usually the vasectomy stops it," reassured Otho. "If it gets too far, though . . . well, then they have to castrate."

Everybody was in on it, coaches, players, equipment guys—everybody. People were walking up to Marvin the next morning (he was still peeing blue) telling him how sorry they were for him. Marvin was ready to cry that afternoon when Otho and Dave couldn't hold in the laughter any longer. Otho explained that the pills they had given him to help "cure" that groin pull were actually Urised, a medication that acidifies the urine and produces a numbing effect in the urinary tract. It was harmless and had this startling little side effect . . . damn if those little pills didn't work every time!

Buddy named Marvin a starter for the first preseason game against the Jets, but as the draft picks signed contracts and reported to camp, he dropped perilously on the depth chart. Fred Barnett's size and speed and leaping ability quickly distinguished him as the prize catch of the draft, and Calvin Williams impressed with his good hands and an ability to run pass routes with machinelike precision. Buddy then abruptly dumped Cris Carter at midsummer, a move that surprised everyone, especially Carter, who would go on to a long and distinguished career with the Vikings—Buddy just didn't like him, something about the look in his eye. Quick's knees weren't getting better, and Mike Bellamy, the most expensive and highly rated of the bunch, pulled a groin muscle after his hamstring healed and immediately landed on Buddy's shit list. Marvin was cut in the final week of training camp, but Buddy told him not to worry.

"Wait by the phone," the coach said.

When Bellamy (who was waived after his first year and never

caught a pass in pro ball) reinjured his groin in the season opener, Buddy called Marvin and placed him on the roster as a backup receiver and punt returner. Marvin wasn't about to tell Coach he had never returned a punt in his life.

On Sunday afternoon, September 16, twelve weeks and two days after tossing his cleats in the backseat of his brother's Mustang, Marvin Hargrove stepped out into the giant sunny bowl of Veterans Stadium wearing a Philadelphia Eagles uniform with the number 80 on his back—Cris Carter's old number. The Eagles were about to play the Cardinals. His father and brother were watching up in the three hundred level. He felt charged with destiny.

"This is were I belong," he said.

Buddy sent him in to catch the Cardinals' first punt of the afternoon, but the ball bounced way short and rolled out-of-bounds without Marvin's touching it. On the Eagles' first offensive series, Randall ran a little flea-flicker, handing the ball off to Keith Byars, who took three steps forward, turned, and pitched it back to the quarterback. Randall then threw deep to Calvin, who was wide open. The ball was underthrown, so Calvin had to double back for it. Instead of a touchdown, the Eagles got the ball on Phoenix's thirty-four-yard line. The crowd, watching their team's first home game of the season, was on its feet, filling the stadium with an expectant roar.

Buddy sent Marvin in as a third wide receiver.

Richie signaled a running play, so when Marvin trotted out wide right, he expected just to be running a decoy pattern downfield. The Cardinals sent veteran cornerback Cedric Mack out to cover the rookie one-on-one, and Mack positioned himself about five yards off the line of scrimmage. Randall, looking over, could see that Mack intended to bump Marvin as he came off the line and try to run with him. The quarterback had been throwing to the rookie all summer, and he knew Marvin's surprising speed, so he changed the play, giving a hand signal that Marvin knew meant he was to run a fade route to the end zone.

The pass was perfect. Marvin caught it in full stride and stepped unmolested across the goal line. Few of us will ever have a childhood fantasy so vividly, literally, and publicly fulfilled. And there in the throttled-up roar of his home stadium, football in hand, Marvin felt the glorious shared thrill of sixty-four thousand fans cascading down from all sides, catching him in a momentary confluence of dream and destiny, where he was at once a cheering fan in his three-hundred-level seat and the player who now crumpled beneath the happy mob of teammates in the end zone.

After the game (which the Eagles lost), Marvin stood in the spotlight before his locker wearing a broad smile and nothing else and gilded the performance with charm.

"In Philly they're calling you Rocky, the guy who comes out of nowhere and becomes a hero," one hound said, working his lead.

"Well, I hope I get as many sequels as Rocky," quipped Marvin.

He didn't. It was the last pass that would ever be thrown to Marvin Hargrove in the NFL.

He lasted six more games, returning punts and kickoffs. He did well, but not spectacularly so. A few times Marvin seemed close to breaking loose on a return, but never did—which is the nature of the job; even the best return men break loose only once or twice a season. When Quick's knees continued to ache, Buddy started Fred and Calvin at wide receiver and used Quick as a third receiver and sometimes put Marvin out there as a fourth, but he was never thrown a pass. When the Eagles tried to shore up their paltry running game with Thomas Sanders, a former Bear, Buddy decided to use the bigger veteran for kickoff returns, which shrank Marvin's role. In the locker room, the Pack started to ask the kid if he was afraid of getting cut, which made him worry all the more about getting cut—*Why are they asking me that? Do they know something I don't?* He couldn't sleep at all the night before games.

Disaster struck in the seventh game of the season, in a 48–20 win over the Patriots on a (for a return man) treacherously windy afternoon. On his first try, surprised by a weak punt, Marvin let the football bounce in front of him and then roll past. The Patriots downed it on the Eagles' seventeen, at least twenty yards behind where it would have been if he had stepped up and caught it. On his next try, playing short this time, Marvin saw the ball fly over his head. He backpedaled furiously on the turf, only to stumble and fall as the ball bounced into his chest. This time the Patriots recovered the fumble on the Eagles' twenty-four, and four plays later scored their first points of the game.

Buddy didn't say anything. As Marvin came off the field after the fumble, the coach just took his arm, pulled him close, and looked intently into his eyes.

Anthony Edwards was sent in to catch the next punt. Marvin sat dejected on the bench as his teammates came over to offer consolation and advice. Andre told Marvin his problem was the snazzy long-sleeved spandex black body shirt he was wearing under his uniform; it was making his arms slippery and that's why he was having trouble hanging on to the ball. Marvin knew he'd yet to even get his arms on the ball, but he tore off his jersey and pads and removed the shirt anyway.

Edwards had his own troubles with the wind. He fumbled the

next punt, then, at the end of the next Phoenix series, bobbled another one. A penalty annulled the play, and as the teams sorted out for the rekick, defensive back William Frizzell confronted Buddy.

"It's Hargrove's damn job. Put Hargrove in the damn game!"

Buddy, now furious with Edwards, too, waved the veteran off the field and gave Marvin another chance. He caught the punt and returned it twelve yards, nearly breaking free. He caught one more punt, and, when Buddy stuck him back in with the kick return team, broke loose for sixteen yards, one of his best returns yet.

It wasn't enough. Summoned to the coach's office Monday morning, Marvin took the chair opposite Buddy's desk.

"Yesterday, when I looked into your eyes, you know what I saw?" Buddy asked.

"No. What did you see, boss?" Marvin always called Buddy that.

"A tired kid."

"Yes, sir."

"This is what I have to do," Buddy said. He explained that Harry was impatient for him to use Mike Bellamy. Bellamy was, after all, a second-round draft pick, the receiving end of the fabulous passing stats accumulated by quarterback Jeff George the year before at the University of Illinois. Bellamy had been paid a big signing bonus and was pulling down a salary of $170,000—almost three times what they were paying Marvin. And, so far, Bellamy was just watching. Truth was, Buddy didn't like the kid and didn't intend to use him, but Bellamy's groin pull was healed, and he had to take him off the injured list.

"So I'm going to put you on the practice squad and let you get some rest," Buddy said. "And when you're ready to go again, I'm going to put you back on the roster."

It was sugarcoated, but it was a demotion. Marvin was angry, mostly at himself, but also at Buddy for not giving him more of a chance. The roster maneuver required placing Marvin's name on the waiver wire for twenty-four hours, giving other teams an opportunity to claim him. Buddy told Marvin to report back after he cleared waivers and re-sign for the practice squad.

If I clear waivers, thought Marvin—anticipating a crush of interest from other teams. He called his dad and then phoned his agent and asked him to call around, let other teams know that Marvin Hargrove of the Philadelphia Eagles was going to be available.

He'd show Buddy.

That night he drove his girlfriend, who had witnessed the disaster, back home to Richmond. Tuesday was the players' day off, so Marvin stayed in Virginia all day, still in a bit of a pique. He didn't hear from his agent, and he didn't bother calling home. He drove back early the next morning, getting to his new apartment in New Jersey at 9:00 a.m., and telephoned his agent, who wasn't in yet. Having heard nothing, Marvin reluctantly concluded that another dreadful oversight had occurred. So he phoned the Eagles' front office to see about coming in. As he would long remember it, first George Azar came on the phone sounding bothered.

"Marvin, where have you been?"

"I just got back in town."

"You've got to get in here right now, Buddy has been looking for you. It's important!"

Marvin hung up and headed for the door, when the phone rang again. It was George.

"Hold on a minute, Marvin, Buddy wants to talk to you right now."

The call was patched down to the coach's office, and Buddy's familiar drawl came on. The coach sounded peeved.

"Where have you been?"

"I was on my way down there right now, boss."

"I told you, when you cleared waivers, be here to sign the new contract for the practice squad."

"Right, I'm going on the practice squad."

"Well, seven o'clock last night is when you came off the waiver wire," Buddy said. "I was looking for you at seven o'clock."

"Did you call?"

"Now, why should I call you? You're the one who wants a job, aren't you?"

"Well, yes. You're right, boss."

"I didn't know what to think," said Buddy. "I thought you got pissed off because you got released and figured, 'Fuck it.'"

"No, I would never do that, boss. I told my agent to call and find out when you needed me. . . ."

"No agent called here."

"I told him to call."

"You need to get rid of your agent, son. You didn't need an agent to get you here, you sure as hell don't need one now."

"Okay, okay. What do you want me to do now?"

"Now you're gonna have to wait."

Buddy had signed Tyrone Watson, another of the free agents at camp that summer (who happened to be represented by Buddy's son, a player agent) to a practice-squad contract. He told Marvin that he would put him back on the roster as soon as there was an opening.

But the opening never came.

The season ended, Buddy got fired, and Marvin Hargrove is still waiting. Unless he beats the odds again, he has earned the nickname "One-for-One-for-One" Hargrove, one pass, one catch, one touchdown.

And so he shall remain.

FOR FRED BARNETT, the toughest gate in the Sluice wasn't the last one—landing on a pro roster—it was the first. He couldn't get anywhere in football until he got past his mom.

He still winces at the memory, a dozen years back now, of his mom, Earlean Barnett, showing up on the Rosedale, Mississippi, High School football field on the first day of summer tryouts. Fred was warming up with a group of his junior-high friends. They were too young to play for the high-school team, but the coaches invited the younger boys out to practice to scout them for future seasons. Attending these practices was what you did if you aspired to suit up with the big boys in a few years. Fred was eager to show off his skills. But before practice had gotten fully under way, he saw the beige Plymouth pull off the highway in the distance. Earlean got out, her dress billowing like a mainsail as she strode purposefully across the field. She spoke to the coaches, then Fred saw them looking for him.

Earlean had forbidden Fred to play football. She had lots of reasons. For one, she was a devout Jehovah's Witness, and the violence disturbed her. For another, Fred had been doing poorly in the seventh grade (he would eventually have to repeat it). But beyond those reasons, football stood for all the foolish things people put before their relationship with God. She had seen how crazy her small Mississippi riverfront town got over the high-school team, how the boys who played got special treatment from football-obsessed teachers, alumni, and . . . *girls*.

She knew if her Fred played football he'd be good. He had it in his blood. Fred's uncle, Johnny Barnett, had been good enough to play halfback for the L.A. Express in that USFL, and his father and other uncles had all been big stars at Rosedale High. From the time he could walk, Fred was just like them. His father and uncles would throw him the ball and compliment the way he could hang on, the way he could run and jump, filling his head with visions of glory. But Earlean and Fred, Sr., were divorced shortly before Fred started junior high, so this tendency to be just like his father and uncles became a sore subject with Mom. She was a tough woman, working in a factory by day and taking care of her children at night. She was determined that her Fred would *not* be like his father and uncles. One way he was *not* going to be like them, he was *not* going to play football.

Her Fred was going to grow up strong in the Lord. He was going to be a good student. He was not going to hang out or go to parties where they drank alcohol and smoked dope—and where girls got pregnant. Which is not to say she didn't have doubts. Fred was such a daydreamer, and the game was so important to him. At the dinner table he would break up the food on his plate and arrange it in football formations. As a little boy, when he went to bed at night, he would take the stuffed animals on his bed and pretend they were football players, crashing them into one another. Earlean saw all that. But then, when she thought again about the pitfalls, she was sure once more that football, while not so bad in itself, would open the door.

She had given in once. Fred (with her accent, the name came out in two distinct syllables, Fray-ed) had cried and sulked until she let him play on the junior-high-school team. In the first game he played quarterback and ran the ball for a touchdown and angered his coaches by performing a dandy spike in the end zone—*That's rubbin' it in their faces, boy, you don't do that!* (They were clearly happier with the points, he noticed, than angry with the spike.) On the way home, the bus made a sudden stop, and Fred was thrown forward. He cracked his front teeth on the steel back of the seat in front.

One look at Fred's broken and bloody mouth, and Earlean wasn't in the mood for explanations.

"This is what I was tryin' to tell you about football," she said.

"Oh, Mama, it wasn't football," Fred pleaded. "The man hit the brakes on the bus!"

"If you hadn't been playing football, you wouldn't have been on the bus," pronounced Earlean, with airtight parental logic. And that was that. No more football. When Fred defied her by going out to the preseason practice, Earlean drove to the field to fetch him.

He thought about running, but what good would that do? He hung his head with shame as his mother led him by the arm across the field and back to her car. It would be five long years before Fred would get another chance to play. Five years of writhing with envy in the stands, watching boys with lesser talent romp in the glamorous floodlit Friday-night world of schoolboy football. Fred would play in pickup games with these guys and run rings around them. The high-school coaches knew about Fred. They saw him play in intramural basketball. He could leap so high it was startling. He had hands twice the size of most kids his age. And speed? Nobody in the school could keep up with him. He had the lean, fluid moves of a natural. The talent was raw, but unmistakable. Fred had a totally undisciplined, showboat style on the court. Playing with the other boys, he wouldn't even bother with passing or outside shots or the finer points of the game. He just wanted to dunk. If he scored thirty points in an intra-mural game, twenty-six of them would be gaudy, soaring dunks, which was funny, because off the court he seemed so shy.

After phys-ed class one day, Fred started fooling around at the high-jump pit. He had never tried it before. He just set the bar up near the top of the frame and jumped over it. Just like that.

Then he went in, showered, and got dressed. On his way out, one of the gym teachers asked him how high he had jumped.

"I don't know." He pointed to the rung.

"That's six-three," the teacher said. "I don't believe it!"

By the time Fred was in his junior year, his cousin Tim, who was a year younger, was a star on the high-school football team. That really bothered Fred. But he had given up arguing with his mom.

"The Bible says, 'Do unto others as you would have them do unto you,'" she would say. "There are times in tackling when you hurt people. Do you want to be hurt?"

"No, I don't want to be hurt; it's just a game."

"You think of how many people have been hurt in that game."

"But you don't try to *hurt* people, you try to tackle them. It's just part of the game."

Earlean wouldn't budge. She felt good about her decision. Fred was getting better grades now. He didn't hang out and party with the other teens. He was different, just the way she wanted him to be. And that was a good thing, right?

As Fred grew older, she began to wonder. He seemed to spend most of his free time alone in his room. After supper, he would close the door to his bedroom, lie across the bed, and fantasize—elaborate, detailed daydreams—about playing football. He didn't visualize him-self just playing high-school ball. In his mind's eye he was on a pro field, with tens of thousands of cheering fans, announcers in the booths upstairs, cameras, and he would be racing alone down the field, leaping for the ball, closing his hands around it. . . .

"Are you okay, Fred?" Earlean would ask through the closed door.

"I'm fine, Mom."

"If something is bothering you, you would talk to me about it, wouldn't you?"

"Yeah."

And then back to the daydream.

Two coaches from the high school launched a campaign to change Earlean's mind. They called and stopped by the house. Earlean heard them out politely and then just shook her head.

The thaw came only when Earlean reconciled with Fred's father.

The boy was a junior then, and Willie Thomas, an assistant coach at Rosedale, saw an opening. He knew some of Fred's uncles, and they were all dying to see the kid play. He went to work on Fred, Sr., who resisted at first—no sense making more trouble between him and Earlean.

"It's not up to me."

"Why not—he's your son, isn't he?"

"Yes."

"Well, I don't think you're being fair to Fred. The boy is really hurting."

When Fred, Sr., explained Earlean's worries, Thomas promised he would personally drive Fred to and from practice every day.

Fred, Sr., and Earlean reopened the issue, looking at it every which way. Fred wasn't a little boy anymore. He was old enough to drive a car. He had just one more year of high school left. She wasn't going to be able to shelter him forever.

Earlean sought advice from her meeting hall. She was told that Jehovah gives each individual a life, and there comes a time when parents have to stop making decisions for their children.

One of the elders told her, "It's not like you haven't already done the basic things that Jehovah requires of a parent, which you have."

At first, Fred was allowed to go out for the track team, where he quickly bettered his six-three leap of that afternoon. He would jump six-eleven in his senior year, bettering the competition by more than a foot. When Earlean let him play on the football team in his senior year, despite his inexperience, Fred was the school's star safety on defense, making eight interceptions. As a receiver, Fred caught five touchdown passes. While his cousin Tim was the bigger star, Fred's play in just that one season was enough to attract recruiters at Arkansas State, three hours away.

Five years later (after sitting out one year with a knee injury), Fred was drafted in the third round by the Eagles, the seventy-seventh player taken in that year's NFL draft. The following year his cousin Tim was drafted in the third round by the Chiefs, also the seventy-seventh player taken.

By then, true to those pictures in his head, Fred was a star.

AS THE REST of the team is moving into Gertrude, five of the Eagles' starters head home to settle in for another NFL summer ritual, the holdout.

Eric Allen flies back to the lush hills of San Diego, for what he figures will be a long stay with his in-laws, not far from the neighborhood where he grew up. Middle linebacker Byron Evans heads home to the modern house he has built for himself in Arizona, up in the stark brown Salt River Mountains, south of Phoenix. Through the still desert haze of late summer, looking north over the patio and pool and towering cacti, he can make out the rooftops of the South Broadway projects where he grew up, where his older brother Buriss had been shot and killed five years ago, and, beyond that, rising abruptly from the flatness, the glass-and-steel towers of downtown. Kicker Roger Ruzek returns to Ogden, Utah, where he'll golf some and bowl, and maybe squeeze in some trout fishing. Receiver Calvin Williams drives south on I-95 in his white Wagoneer to his new, mostly empty neocolonial home outside Baltimore, set on a hilltop in a green western suburb that empties every morning when his neighbors all drive off to work. Serious and businesslike, Calvin will adopt a daily schedule here to mirror training camp, rising early to eat breakfast; running by himself on the track at Randallstown High School, zipping past the usual midday assortment of daytime joggers as if they were standing still; then eating lunch and doing a second workout in the afternoon, running up and down hills wearing a weighted khaki vest; having dinner and then going to bed early.

For strong safety Andre Waters, the trip is to Tampa, where he plans to do some jet-skiing in between his regular workouts. This will be Andre's fifth contract negotiation. None of them has been pleasant, but at least the process has become predictable. He figures it will take . . . oh, about three weeks. He'll be back in time for the last two exhibition games.

There's a logic to signing holdouts, even if fans can't understand it. The club has its payroll budget, about $32 million, and it tends to sign players in ascending order of salary, and, hence, of importance. Rookies, with the exception of the first two or three picks, would all be signed by the time training camp started. The veteran backup players would come to terms early in camp, then the top draft picks. The veteran starters would be the last ones in, divvying up what remained of the pie.

Tight end Keith Jackson and quarterback Jim McMahon are special cases. Keith's grudge with Norman runs as deep as his salary demands go high, and he is set on an independent course that, in just a month, will enable him to slip the League's hammerlock on players' careers. Jimbo, by virtue of the special status of quarterbacks and his own celebrity, is holding out for a salary almost double that of an ordinary NFL backup—and will get most of it. He is also looking for a commitment from Richie that he will get a chance to compete with the returning Randall for the starting job—he will get the commitment, but not the chance.

Apart from these two, Andre knows the drill. The holdouts will return in order, with neatly ascending salary figures, from Ruzek on up to Allen, with one exception—Andre will be the exception. Allen, the most valuable player missing, will sign last ($1.3 million), just days before the first game of the season. Andre will sign second from last, befitting his position in the team's pecking order, but he won't sign for the second-highest salary. On August 19, Williams ($400,000), Ruzek ($450,000), and Evans ($825,000) will all agree to terms. Two days later, Andre, the second most-valuable player holding out, will cave in for $685,000.

Andre is sick and tired of being the exception. It's an old feeling, a bad feeling, one linked to his childhood, to a place called the Muck.

That's what locals call the great expanse of Palm Beach County real estate that opens out as you head west from the Atlantic Ocean on Route 98 toward Lake Okeechobee. The Muck is the north end of the Everglades, saw-grass swamp drained a century ago to open up five thousand square miles or so of farmland, land so rich and moist it looks alive, shining, like the black back of some great slumbering reptile. This soil—Frost Free! Cultivates with Ease!—was reputed to grow fruits and vegetables of such Olympian size and miracle sweetness that it provoked a stampede of veterans after World War I, a kind of Ag Rush. Things grew prodigiously all right (although not to the proportions promised), but the amateurs were thwarted by the pre–refrigerated trucking challenge of keeping crops fresh en route to distant markets. The few farms that lasted became huge agribusinesses, nursing orange groves and fields of celery, corn, and sugarcane (which boomed after Fidel Castro closed off Cuba's crops). The growing business demanded lots of cheap, unskilled labor, which prompted the Muck's second tide of immigration, thousands of poor blacks willing to work with their hands for low wages under the hot Everglades sun. The wealthy growers built their estates back east in Palm Beach and Lake Worth, while the field hands huddled in concrete barracks and mud-stained shacks in the lakeside towns of Belle Glade and Pahokee.

Andre was born in Belle Glade, the eighth child of Willie Ola Perry, a sturdy twenty-seven-year-old field hand with a mystical Christian bent who liked her bed warm and her work steady. She worked seven days a week, ten hours a day to support her still-growing brood. In all, Willie Ola would have ten children (and adopt one more) by four different men, all of whom had wanderlust in common. Andre's father, Henry B. Waters, left when he was three. Willie Ola just labored on. She would have two more children by another man (who also left) before she was done. She didn't expect too much from men.

With his mother off working, Andre spent many of his early years living with relatives. He remembers summer days working with his cousin to find enough discarded soda bottles to raise the quarter they needed for an afternoon at the community swimming pool. One of his earliest memories is of playing with the ducks at his aunt Mary's farm outside Tampa, where his mother took the children every year at Christmastime. Andre desperately wanted to take a duck home with him as a pet.

"I'm not gonna give you one of my ducks until you move off the Muck," she told the boy.

He never forgot the promise, and when Willie Ola moved her brood to Pahokee, ten-year-old Andre thought his time had come.

"Auntie, Auntie Mary, we don't live on the Muck no mo'," he told her that Christmas. "We done moved to another place."

"Boy, you still on the Muck," she told him.

Moving off the Muck came to mean something much more as the children of Belle Glade and Pahokee got older. It meant getting a high-school diploma and going off to college or the army. Most of those who stayed wound up working in the fields by day and hanging around the barracks and shanty towns getting drunk or high by night, raising the next generation in the same squalor they had known—or worse. In recent years, Belle Glade has become a pathetic symbol of the ravaging potential of AIDS, with a death rate from the disease triple that of most big cities.

Moving off the Muck became an obsession to Andre. As he entered his teens in the midseventies, he had the example of older brothers and sisters who had escaped, and some who hadn't. All had finished high school and some had even gone to college. His half sister Irma, unmarried with six children, was still living in Belle Glade, as was Monica, who had married and was raising a brood that would eventually number nine. His half brother Harry was an army officer. His half sister Sandra was working for her college degree in social work. Anthony, another older half brother, had joined the air force.

Andre had his own plan. Like millions of boys who grew up watching the NFL come of age on TV, Andre was going to be a pro football player. In his last few years of elementary school, he had hero worshiped with the rest of the town as Pahokee High went to three straight state championship games led by a strapping tight end named Rickey Jackson. Sought after by colleges all over the country, Jackson had chosen the University of Pittsburgh, where he would star as defensive end and get drafted in the second round in '81 by the Saints (and still be giving Antone Davis fits at the end of the '92 season as a Pro Bowl linebacker). With only a child's understanding of how remarkable, how literally one-in-a-million Jackson's course had been, Andre was determined to trace his steps.

When he showed up for tryouts in the summer of '76, the year after Jackson graduated, Andre was a skinny, hyperkinetic fourteen-year-old, with a gigantic Afro, whom everyone called Spanky. "I guess because I used to get so many whippings," Andre says. Coach Anton Russell almost sent Spanky home, and probably would have, if he hadn't needed every kid who showed up. Little Pahokee High competed against schools from the more affluent eastern side of Palm Beach County, where coaches had the luxury of sorting out boys by size and skill and assigning them suitable positions. Coach Russell had to work with whoever showed up. Typically, his linemen were as small as other teams' defensive backs. Coach Russell looked for intangible assets, things like boldness and heart.

The younger brother of the kid who played quarterback the year before had that job sewn up, and Coach had most of the other glamour jobs parceled out to boys he had seen play before, so Andre, small as he was, got lumped in with the linemen.

He was determined to make up in ferocity what he lacked in size. And he made a good impression on his first day, especially in drills where he had to pull from the guard position, sweep around end, and launch himself at would-be tacklers head-on. Andre showed reckless enthusiasm for this. He took visceral pleasure in violent contact. The coach was impressed. When Andre told his brother Anthony about the practice, though, Anthony had some sage advice.

"Don't play so good there," he said. "If you play the line good, they'll end up keeping you there, and you're too small to play that position in college."

The next day, Andre slipped and fell a lot. His pulling move slowed, and he kept missing the blocks on his sweeps around end. He played so badly, Coach banished him from the offensive squad, telling him to go work out with the defensive backs, where his quickness and surefooted play were miraculously restored.

Coach Russell didn't have the biggest or the fastest or the most talented athletes in the county, but he always had some of its best football and track teams. Many of the boys who played for Pahokee had never seen a weight room and had never run on a track, but they had grown up, like Andre, working in the fields and groves and in the packing houses. Russell never had to worry about bulking his boys up or getting them in shape. Pahokee boys were poor, tough, and wild. When they played against the bigger schools, it was class warfare. They were small, but they were *feared*. Boys from the suburbs rationalized their fear by calling the Pahokee players dirty.

Andre set out to be the toughest of the Pahokee tough guys. He had grown up this way. If they played soccer, Spanky wanted to be goalie, so he could come tearing out and dive at the feet of attacking players and snatch away the ball. In baseball, he liked playing catcher, getting dirty down behind the plate and standing in tough when some bigger kid tried to bowl him over at the plate. Now, on the football field, opposing players and coaches would complain that the little cornerback was hitting people late, aiming for their knees and ankles—*trying to hurt people*—and Coach Russell would defend him, saying, "He's just a hustler; he wants part of every play," and then wink at Andre—*Never hurts to make 'em afraid.*

On the weekends and holidays, when football games were scheduled, Andre would have to work in the orange groves. It was hard work up on ladders, wearing long sleeves to avoid the thorns, a burlap sack over one shoulder, picking fruit for hours. Coach Russell would tell the boys to take it easy during the day and come out to the high school to stretch and warm up before home games, or board the bus early for away games. But there was no taking it easy for Spanky. Sometimes the coach would have to hold the bus, waiting for the trucks to return from the fields. Andre would hop off the back end of the truck and jump on the bus. The coach toyed with the idea of speaking with Willie Ola about it, seeing if she would let the boy take a day off now and then, especially when there was a big game coming up. But he thought better of it. He knew other women like Andre's mom. Andre's work helped keep her family fed and housed—what was a football game weighed against that?

Willie Ola had never seen her son play football. She saw all the stories in the local papers when his team won or lost, and she knew lots of people in town got all worked up over it, and, frankly, she thought it was all a bit much. All that fuss for nothing. She knew it was important to Andre—too important, really—so she tolerated it. It gave her some of the leverage a mother needs to keep a rambunctious teen in line. She'd tell him, "If you don't do this . . . ," or "If I ever catch you doing that . . . ," it would mean the end of his precious football career.

One afternoon, coming home from practice, Spanky and five of his teammates were picked up by the Pahokee police for stealing oranges off trees in a backyard.

Willie Ola got the phone call at home late that afternoon, after a long day's work.

"You'll have to come down here and pick him up, ma'am," said the cop.

She didn't have a car, so she had two long miles to stoke her wrath. Among the things in which Willie Ola took great pride was the fact that none of her many children had ever gotten in trouble with the law. When she got to the station, she had to sign her name in a book that recorded Andre's offense: petty theft.

Confronted with the offender, Willie Ola uttered the three words she had been practicing to herself with every step:

"No more football."

Andre started to cry.

"Mama, please," he said. "Whup me, do anything to me, but please, let me play ball."

"No more football."

At that point, one of the police officers, moved by Willie Ola's harsh, swift justice, intervened. He lied.

"With all due respect, Mrs. Perry, I don't think your boy was one of the ones who actually *took* any of the oranges. He was just with the others."

Willie Ola relented. She reduced the sentence to an undetermined period of house arrest.

She left on foot at a stern pace, with Andre walking just a few steps behind. As they walked, he reached back and dropped the oranges he had stashed in his backpack, leaving a guilty fruit trail down the road. "If she turned back once, I'm busted, " he would remember, laughing. "But she was too mad to turn around and look at me."

By his senior year, Spanky Waters was a local star, feared by opponents as a mean, dirty little player, but beloved by his teammates and his school. Off the field, he had a sweet, decent way about him, but on the field, he became *someone else*. He worked at it. Before the game he would don his pads and jersey, carefully wrap his forearms, pull on elbow pads, affix his helmet, transforming himself into someone bigger, faster, and stronger, psyching himself up for the violence of the arena.

Andre was good, but not good enough to attract Rickey Jackson–sized interest. Size, speed, and state championships drew college scouts, not intensity and a flamboyant field personality. Coaches use the word "scrappy" to describe a player like Andre, which means *The kid makes the most of limited assets.*

Still, Coach Russell had connections. Every year he had players like Andre, players with lots of heart and big dreams but minimal prospects. The idea was to sell these kids to Division II schools, use football to get them in the door, and hope they came out four years later with a degree—their ticket off the Muck. He was able to swing Andre a partial scholarship to Alabama A&M and an invitation to try out for the football team at Cheyney State, in Pennsylvania. Cheyney's coach, Andy Hinson, had spent twenty-two years coaching in Florida, and he knew Pahokee players tended to play better than their size and speed would indicate. With no scholarship money, Coach Hinson could hardly compete for sought-after high-school players. So when he got a call from Coach Russell, who said he had this scrappy boy who deserved a chance, Hinson sent Andre an invitation.

Actually, the Alabama A&M offer was better. They had a bigger program and a tougher schedule. Andre probably wouldn't get a chance to play much until his junior year, but he'd have time to learn, and if he did grow into a decent college player, he'd get more exposure playing in the football-crazy Southeast Conference. But Andre had his heart set on Cheyney. First, he was under the impression that he had been offered a full scholarship—he hadn't bothered to read those letters Hinson had been sending him, the ones that explained that Cheyney State had no scholarships to award. Hinson had assured Andre that all he had to do was get himself north to the school and the rest would be taken care of, but "the rest" involved room and board and tuition *loans*, not scholarships. All Andre heard, of course, was the *just-get-yourself-up-here* part. To him, that meant a scholarship. Second, Andre had this friend who told him that all the football games played by Cheyney, which was just a few miles outside the big city of Philadelphia, were on *television*. The magic word for an ambitious young football player is "TV." Just as TV had turned the NFL into a multimillion-dollar industry, for a player, one big game in front of the cameras could make a pro football career. Andre figured he could intercept the hell out of the ball at Alabama A&M without a scout ever noticing, but if he could get on *TV!* Weighing a full scholarship—and TV—against the partial deal at Alabama A&M ... well, in his mind, it wasn't even close. Andre (with typically inflated notions of his own talents) figured Coach Russell was pushing Alabama because he'd made promises to coaches there and didn't want to disappoint them.

"Spanky, man, why do you want to go all the way up to Cheyney?" Coach Russell would ask him. "Don't you know how cold it gets up there in the winter?"

But the coach knew that arguing with a kid like Andre was hopeless, once his mind was set.

Of course, both of Andre's assumptions were false.

When Andre got a letter from Cheyney requesting a fifty-dollar room deposit, he was puzzled. He called Coach Hinson and asked, "What's this?"

"Don't worry about it," the Cheyney coach said. "Just pay it and we'll see about reimbursing you once you're up here."

Hinson knew the hard part was getting the kid to show up. Competing against schools who had money to give away, it would have been unwise to unduly stress that Cheyney did not. They sent out all the information, and it was all spelled out clearly for any kid who was paying attention. But kids, being kids, often weren't paying attention. For a poor kid like Andre, it would take his family every penny they could scrape up to send him north. Once he arrived, he'd have no way of getting home even if he wanted. And it wasn't like some kind of evil scam, either. Hinson all but adopted the boys he recruited for his program. He took care of the loans and financial-aid packages just as he promised. The kid and his family didn't have to put up a penny until the kid had his degree, and was presumably in a position to pay. His boys got a chance to play football and they got a college education, and Hinson got a football program that could compete against other schools in his division with more to offer.

Andre had only himself to blame for getting almost everything about Cheyney State wrong. He had looked it up in an encyclopedia in the high-school library. It didn't say anything about having a big-time football program, but it did say that the school was a small black college in the Philadelphia area. Andre had this image of attending school in the big city, an exciting, magical place full of beautiful sights, gleaming towers, and glamorous people. After a lifetime on the Muck, out in the middle of nowhere, Andre was ready to go someplace big, someplace where important things happened.

Instead, Cheyney turned out to be set on a wooded campus in the remote rural outskirts of Chester County . . . in the *middle of nowhere!* Then at the first meeting of the football team, Coach Hinson got up and started telling the guys how to apply for their bank loans. Andre thought, *Well, he be talkin' to these other boys 'bout gettin' bank loans; I'll wait till after the meeting and talk to him 'bout my scholarship.*

So afterward he stepped up to Hinson. "Coach, you know, how do I go 'bout gettin' my scholarship?"

"Son, Cheyney doesn't give out any scholarships."

Andre felt like crying. More than a thousand miles from home. All he had in the world was the change of clothes in his traveling bag. They had put him up in a small dorm room with Keith Banks, an offensive lineman. There were two beds with a small table between them and a radio alarm clock on the table.

"Man, I got to leave," Andre told Keith.

He called home. Willie Ola was off on a picking trip north, so he talked to Anthony.

Anthony told him to stick it out. He figured if he scraped together enough money from his brothers and sisters to buy Andre a train ticket home, the kid would come back, get a job in the fields making two or three hundred dollars a week, and be satisfied with it—and stuck. Anthony called Coach Hinson the next day and got the straight scoop Andre would have gotten from the start if he had been paying attention. He then called his half-brother back and laid out the situation plainly. Cheyney State played Division II football. There was no TV. Chances of a pro contract when he was done were remote, at best. There was no scholarship. While he was trying out for the football team he could share a room in the dorm and take his meals in the cafeteria, but books and tuition money would all have to be borrowed.

"Don't worry about football," Anthony told him. "Get an education. If you get a good grade point average in the first semester, and you still want to come home, I'll help you transfer."

Andre stayed. He went out for the football team halfheartedly, expecting to be cut every day that summer—looking forward to it, actually. He was playing against grown men now. Cheyney may have been Division II, but just about every man on the field was better than anyone Andre had ever played with or against. He felt that he didn't measure up, and, what was worse, he wasn't sure he even cared anymore—*no TV, no scholarship, no pro scouts!* In his mind, he was putting football and the dream behind him. He told his roommate, "I'll be glad when they cut me. . . . I'm going to go ahead and get my education and then transfer."

But Andre was making a better impression than he thought. He made varsity as a freshman, as a backup to a senior cornerback, and when the senior snapped his thigh muscle in the first game of the season, Andre became a starter. They called him Batman because of the bat wings he drew on his elbow pads, and because of his dark reputation as a hitter. Andre was still small—he stood well under six feet and weighed around 180—but that trancelike violent state he achieved during a football game was something else.

When he finished his four years as a starter at Cheyney, even after earning honors on the small-college circuit, Andre was no closer to playing in the pros than he had been to playing in college after his last game in Pahokee. Once washed out of the Pigskin Sluice, which Andre was in any ordinary sense when college recruiters had ignored him, it was hell getting back in. Andre's success at Cheyney wasn't even that remarkable. While his eccentricities and desire made him a favorite with his teammates and the fans, he was still just a scrappy ballplayer. Coach Hinson didn't even consider Andre the best cornerback on the team, that distinction went to a junior named Terence

Capers. When you're the second-best cornerback on a Division II football team with a losing record . . . well, your light isn't just hidden, it's out. Time to knuckle down and get that degree.

Which is pretty much how Andre sized things up in the winter of '83. It's a tribute to the extensiveness of the Sluice that pro football paid any attention to Andre at all. He wasn't invited to any of the NFL's pro scouting combines, and none of the teams inquired about him—Cheyney not only lacked the elaborate promotional apparatus of the publicity divisions in major college athletic departments, it didn't have a publicity division.

But after all those years at Penn, Harry Gamble, then working as an Eagles' scouting assistant responsible for evaluating local talent, had a soft spot for overlooked players from smaller colleges with losing records. He liked what he saw of Andre in films of Cheyney's games. So Eagles defensive assistant Fred Bruney showed up one afternoon with a stopwatch and a receiving prospect named Willie Tolbert, and put Andre through his paces.

The Eagles didn't draft Andre, but they invited him to attend their training camp as a free agent.

He never unpacked his travel bag up in Gertrude that summer. The team roomed him with Evan Cooper, a defensive back from Michigan who was their third pick in the draft that year. Cooper knew he was going to make the team. He arrived with three big suitcases full of clothes. Before cut-down days, Andre would lie awake in his bed all night, watching Cooper snore, meditating on the injustice of it all. When he would drift off for a moment, Harry, who was then the Turk, would knock at the door and ask, in that pleasant way Harry has, "Andre, are you ready to go?" Then Andre would wake up. He'd check the door and hall just to make sure he had been dreaming. When his alarm went off he'd suit up and spend another hot day throwing himself around on the practice field like a man possessed. West Chester isn't far from Cheyney, so Andre would slip out when he got the chance and escape the foreboding to spend the night back in his old dorm with his friends.

He escaped that way after the Eagles' last exhibition game that summer, a Thursday night game, taking off with a group of his buddies for a long Labor Day weekend at the beach. Andre felt good about having lasted through the summer, and he spent the weekend convincing himself that he should be happy with that.

Come Monday morning, he saw Harry standing outside the locker room and, trying to postpone fate, slipped silently across the hall hoping not to be seen. Harry said nothing. Next he went to his locker, and his things were still there, everything as he had left it after the game. His name tag, a slip of cardboard with WATERS #20 scrawled on it, was still in place on top. Moving tentatively, he undressed and pulled on sweats for that morning's weight-lifting session. As he walked into the weight room, tortured with anxiety, he approached strength coach Tim Jorgensen.

"Tim, I don't want to get started lifting weights if I ain't made this team," Andre said. "How do I know if I made the team?"

"Aren't you dressed?" asked Jorgensen.

Andre nodded.

"Did anybody say anything to you?"

"Not yet."

"Then go lift weights," Jorgensen said. "Until somebody says something to you, you're on the team."

"Well, I don't want to be in here lifting weights and have somebody come in and pull me out of there in front of everybody," pleaded Andre.

Jorgensen grinned. "Go ahead in there, kid. You're all right."

None of the Eagles' draft picks that year amounted to the kind of football player Andre Waters would become over the next eight years. Wide receiver Kenny Jackson, their number-one pick, hung on in the NFL for a decade, primarily as a backup receiver and special teams tackler. Cooper lasted for three seasons, as did placekicker Paul McFadden, but all twelve of the draft picks deposited in West Chester that summer by the Pigskin Sluice are well into Life after Football eight years on, as Andre camps down in his Tampa condominium waiting for the Eagles to come to terms on what is likely to be his last contract, the one he hopes will finally pay him what he deserves.

Fat chance.

The peculiarities of the NFL's salary structure ensure against it. Inside pro football, the laws of supply and demand get distorted like a three-hundred-pound tackle in a fun-house mirror. For instance, Siran Stacy, the Eagles' top draft pick in '92, who will conclude this season without once carrying the ball in a regular season game and get cut from the team the following summer, will make more money than Andre, one of the team's established veterans, a starter for six consecutive seasons, one of the top tacklers in team history, a player easily ranking among the top-ten safeties in pro football.

That's because the Sluice not only selects out blue-chip talent for the pros, it determines the baseline value of a football player before he ever plays a down of pro ball. To sign first-rounder Kenny Jackson in '84, the Eagles gave him a $1.5 million bonus and a four-year contract with a first-year salary of $175,000 and an '87 salary of

$300,000. As an unknown free agent, Andre began life in the NFL that same summer grateful to sign for the NFL's minimum wage of $60,000. Of course, Kenny had been a star receiver at Penn State and was a much brighter prospect than Andre, so his potential value was greater. The problem is that no matter how mediocre Kenny turned out to be, and how terrific Andre turned out to be, they would continue to negotiate from the same baseline salary—Kenny, $175,000; Andre, $60,000. Kenny the millionaire played in eleven games and caught twenty-eight passes in his rookie season and scored one touchdown. Andre played in all sixteen games, made twenty-two tackles, and also scored a touchdown—a thrilling eighty-nine-yard kickoff return. Kenny got a 14 percent salary increase the following year, bumping his salary to $200,000. Andre got a 16 percent increase and collected $70,000.

It took Buddy to bring out the full potential in the kid from Pahokee. The new coach and Andre (whom teammates dubbed "the Dré Master") were made for each other. Andre's Pahokee tough-guy reputation suited Buddy perfectly. "I'm an animal, I admit it," Andre told one reporter. "If people are afraid of me, that's good." He started all sixteen games in '86, playing shoulder to shoulder with players earning five to ten times his $85,000 salary and has held on to the starting job ever since.

He finished the '91 season as the team's leading tackler for the fourth consecutive year and was named first-team all-NFC strong safety by UPI. Statistically, Andre had a better year than the Bears' Shaun Gayle, who started in the Pro Bowl. His pay had grown steadily. Andre's salary that year was $510,000, and by meeting incentive goals in his contract, he was paid $625,000, which was about what the Eagles paid Jesse Campbell, a rookie safety drafted in the second round to be groomed as an eventual successor to Andre. Campbell spent most of the season on the injured list and practice squad and would be cut early in '92 before ever playing a down in an Eagles uniform.

In the spring of this year, the Eagles had offered Andre a contract with a base salary in the first year of $550,000. He was insulted.

"They could at least start with what they paid me last year," he told his agent, Jim Solano, a local accounting professor who represented about a half-dozen Eagles players. Solano, a chubby, curly-haired man who wore nice suits, drove an expensive foreign car, and spent most of his time baby-sitting his clients—he showed up every Thursday at the practice field with bags of candy and gum—had been through hundreds of contract negotiations with the Eagles, enough to see contract issues from both sides. He knew that the team would probably come up from the $550,000—probably to about $600,000—but he knew that number would still seem fundamentally unfair to his client.

"Andre Waters is a very good safety," argued Bob Wallace, the club's lawyer and chief negotiator. "We're willing to make him one of the top-ten best-paid safeties in the league."

Solano told Wallace that Andre deserved to be ranked among the top-five safeties in the game and had the stats to prove it. Besides, he told Wallace, Andre was due for a break.

"This guy has a history," he told Wallace, who had just joined the Eagles in '91. "His first contract he was underpaid. Second contract he was underpaid. Third contract, fourth contract underpaid."

It was the old free-agent dilemma. Because Andre hadn't been drafted, his earnings were forever stuck in a lower caste. Of course, the way the club saw it, that was the idea. The Eagles, who were no different than any other NFL team, readily admitted they were overpaying some players and underpaying others. Unfairness was central to the system. For every overpriced draft pick who flopped, there had to be an unheralded free agent who excelled. The system demanded six- and seven-figure bonuses for top draft picks, and of the team's top twenty-four draft picks since Andre signed on in '84, only six would be starters this year. That's a lot of bonus money out the window. You made up the difference down the road when free agents and low-level draft picks, players like all-pros Seth Joyner (eighth round) and Clyde Simmons (ninth round) panned out. Just as the fans loved to see an unknown free agent step out to become a star, so did the club. The fact that the Eagles had gone out and discovered the inimitable Dré Master on their own would work to Andre's detriment, and the team's benefit, till the last game of his career.

So Andre's holdout is pretty much pro forma. Just as Solano predicted, the club ups its offer to $600,000 before training camp starts. Andre goes golfing in Tampa.

He is making more than a half-million dollars a year. He has built a beautiful modern home for his mother in a swank Palm Beach development, where Willie Ola now lives alongside doctors and lawyers and other professionals (and still goes off at age fifty-seven to pick celery and corn in the fields). Andre has gotten his college degree and has saved and invested enough money, with Solano's help, so that he will most likely never have to worry about supporting himself again—but he still feels, at least symbolically, that he hasn't moved off the Muck.

"I want to be traded; I'm fed up!" Andre shouts into the phone to a reporter one day after Byron Evans signs for $825,000. By almost any measure (except maybe Byron's agent's) Andre is the more valuable of the two players—more experience, more tackles—but the Eagles are still offering him $225,000 *less* than Evans, a fourth-round draft pick in '87. Andre's goal in this negotiation is to be paid with the top-five safeties in the league and on a par with his backfield partner Wes Hopkins (who will earn a $750,000 base salary this season). Andre has played as Wes's equal or better for six full seasons now, but Hopkins was a second-round draft pick back in '83 who made the Pro Bowl in his second year. Whenever Solano brings up the Hopkins comparison, the Eagles' negotiators point out, "But Wes made the Pro Bowl."

But that was eight years ago. Andre can't help the fact that he wasn't elected to the Pro Bowl. He can't help it if his menacing reputation has made him less than popular around the league—players and coaches elect the Pro Bowl team, and they let offensive players vote, too.

Solano points out that Byron has played three years less than Andre, has also never made the Pro Bowl, and did not even become a starter until '89, yet he has settled for hundreds of thousands more than they were offering Andre.

Andre blows like a force-nine tropical gale, words rushing out so fast he hasn't time to completely form them.

"I mean it. I'm fed up! I think I've proved myself over the last six years. I've led the team in tackles over the last six years. Me and Wes were the best two safeties in the league last season. I think our stats prove it. . . . I mean, I know they say this is a business and you're not supposed to take it personal, but at some point in time you have to take it personal, business when you get down to it *is* personal, and what they're offering me, and the things Bob Wallace has been saying about me are degrading to me, and I do take it personal; honestly, I don't think I want to play again in an Eagles uniform anymore."

Two days later, Andre signs. The Eagles up their offer by $85,000 and include another $100,000 in incentives—an additional $50,000 if Andre makes the Pro Bowl and additional dollars for tackles, interceptions, fumbles caused, fumbles recovered, and touchdowns, that could total another $50,000. He will finish this season earning $714,000, or about $100,000 less than Wes, $250,000 less than Byron, and less than half of Herschel's salary.

Boy, you still on the Muck.

POOR MARK MCMILLIAN figures he's blown it after the Rookie Show. Whose idea was this anyway?

It's an annual end-of-camp ritual, a chance for the poor schmucks at the low end of the roster to poke fun (supposedly with impunity) at their tormentors. Earlier in the week, the veterans had held a meeting with them to explain how the Rookie Show is supposed to go.

"Everybody is fair game," explained tackle Mike Golic. "Coaches, owner . . . even us!"

The club rents the second floor of a local bar for the night, the doors close to the press and fans, the beer flows, and the laughs come easy and loud as the rookies entertain. The highlight of this year's show is twelfth-round draft pick Brandon Houston's cunning impersonation of Richie. They've set up the stage like an episode of "The Dating Game," with Pumpy Tudors, a goofy little punter from Tennessee, all dolled up in a blond wig, balloon boobs and a dress, and Houston (as Kotite) playing one of three bachelors on stools separated from the prize date by a partition. He's perched on the stool, waving an oversized cigar, doing a Texan's best approximation of brazen Brooklynese—it isn't so much the things Houston says as the way he says them, bragging of his sexual prowess in language punctuated by plenty of Richie's pet phrases: "Without question!" and "Am I right?" and "Okay?" and calling everybody "kid," until the slightly juiced audience is rolling in the aisles. Casey Weldon attempts a disastrous number, trying to lure Richie onstage for a "magic trick" that's supposed to end up with the coach unknowingly smearing soot on his face, but Richie, of course, won't step on stage and sends his buddy Matty, who has already seen this one (like, back when he was maybe nine), so it flops. Weldon is booed off stage.

Next comes Mark, with professorial clipboard and pointer, in a skit poking fun at Bud Carson. Mark is a tiny (five-seven, 162 pounds) tenth-round draft pick from Alabama whom people tend to mistake in the locker room for somebody's little brother—on Mark's first day, Reverend Reggie had actually asked, "Who are you here with, son?" Despite his size, Mark has been impressing coaches all summer with his pilot-fish genius for staying with receivers, even though Bud Carson tells him almost every day, "You played like shit today. You're gonna get cut." "Don't worry," assures Wes Hopkins. "Bud says worse things than that to the other guys." Chosen to play Bud now because of his diminutive size (the elderly Carson is dwarfed by the players he coaches), Mark does his best to imitate the professorial fussiness and virtual deafness of the veteran defensive coach and pokes fun at Bud's obvious fondness for the still-missing Eric Allen, who is portrayed by one of the other rookies as an obsequious teacher's pet. Exaggerating (but not by much) the typical evening meeting with Bud, the class tumbles comically out of control. The skit gets some laughs and polite

applause, but not from Bud, whose pale complexion flushes pink—
and it's not just the beer.

On the practice field the next morning, the defensive coach
strides up to his tiny rookie cornerback and tells him he didn't appreciate the humor.

"You ought to work that hard at playing football if you expect
to make this team," he says.

Mark is dismayed. Just a couple days earlier, he had seen a newspaper story in which Bud was quoted as saying "Mark McMillian is
the best cover man I've ever seen." He was starting to think things
were looking up.

"Man, don't worry so much," counsels Mark's new buddy, the
returned Andre Waters. "At least you was drafted."

ALL DAY THURSDAY, August 27, Richie's mother-in-law, Stella,
had been complaining about the heat. It was a disgustingly damp late
summer day. She and Liz and Alexandra had driven down from Staten
Island, as they always did, for the Eagles' game that night, the team's
final preseason game. But it was so unpleasant outside the air-conditioning that Liz understood when her mother said she didn't want to
go this time.

Liz left the TV on in the den, tuned to channel 3—Stella hated
fooling with the remote control—and as she left the house she shouted
upstairs, where her mother was lying down, "I'll call you after the
game. Make sure you get something to eat."

The team loses, which is no big deal, since the exhibitions are
more a testing ground for personnel than a contest. Richie has a few
tough decisions to make, so he's preoccupied, as usual. It has been a
rough summer for him. His parents, Eddie and Alice, have been terribly ill now for months. Richie has flown down to Miami four times
this summer, and every time he's just jumped in a cab at the airport
and gone straight to the hospital. Out on the practice field, he's often
off to one side talking intently on his portable phone, nodding his
bald head slowly, gesturing with the cigar in one hand as he speaks.
The Pack assumes he's cooking up some kind of deal for a big-name
defensive lineman, but it's just Mummy checking with Eddie for an
update.

Now looms the final cuts, decisions Richie hates to make. Among
other things, it looks like he is going to have to cut Jesse Campbell,
his second-round pick the previous season. Bud doesn't like the way
Campbell moves on the practice field, and he really wants to keep the
little cornerback—nice kid—McMillian.

Richie is always trying to placate Bud, but the old man is all knotted up like a fist. Bud gets like this before every season. How's he supposed to win football games with this defensive line? He's lost a Pro Bowl tackle (Jerome), veteran starter Mike Pitts is out with a bad back, and second-year tackle Andy Harmon, who's being thrown in over his head as it is, has a broken hand. His middle linebacker has only been in camp a little more than a week, and his Pro Bowl corner-back is still unsigned. And they're opening against the Saints in just over a week! Richie, of course, always sees the glass half-full. But he respects Bud, and he heeds him. So the defensive coordinator's worries become Richie's worries. He's monitoring frantic efforts to land a solid defensive lineman, accepting Harry's assurance that a deal with Eric Allen is close. On his own side of the ball, he's checking the waiver wire for a backup tight end (there's little hope of Keith Jackson's returning anytime soon). . . .

Still, this is family night. The plan is usually to head out for a late dinner together with Liz and Alexandra, give it a rest for a few hours.

But Liz has changed her mind.

"I've been calling, but there's no answer at home."

"Maybe she turned off the phone," says Richie.

Liz said she didn't think her mom would do that. She knew it was probably silly, but she was worried. Stella hadn't been feeling well all day.

"Let's just go home and check on her," she says.

So they cruise in Richie's Caddy across the Whitman Bridge and back home to Mt. Laurel. The house is dark. When they come in the front door the only light they see is the TV still on in the family room. Stella isn't in there.

"Why would she leave the TV on?" says Liz.

"Stella!" booms Richie's big voice.

No answer.

He walks upstairs, still calling, "Stella!"

She lies clothed and perfectly still on the bed.

"Stella?"

No answer.

"Stella!"

Richie goes over to her and lays his hand on her wrist. It's cool to the touch.

"Oh, my God. Stella!" he shouts.

Then, downstairs, Liz hears him bellow, "Call 911!"

7

HAMMER TIME!

Three days later, the day after his mother-in-law is laid to rest, Richie is back at work, getting his team ready for the Saints in the season opener.

He's edgy.

When one of the local TV stations decides to snoop on practice by pulling its van up to the tarp-draped fence, setting its camera on top of the van, and shooting down, the coach explodes.

"Get the fuck outta heeyaah!" he says, red-faced with rage, chasing the crew off the lot, sending renewed ripples of indignation through the Pack, prompting protests from the local NBC affiliate—and stirring things up for the PR types upstairs.

Can't we be a touch more diplomatic about these things, Rich?

But Coach is adamant. His turf is his turf. Hey, what do these guys want from him? Richie makes time to answer questions from the Pack after every game and *every fucking weekday* in his office after practice. Still, Richie is unpopular with the Pack. Oh, how they pine for Buddy's old bite. Richie, by comparison, is a compendium of coaching banalities: *The Saints are an excellent football team, without question, it'll be a tough football game,* and so on. Every once in a while, with the one or two hounds he feels he can trust, Richie will drop his professional reserve—*We're off the record now, right? Completely off?*—and then disappointingly deliver exactly the same sentiment: *This is a great football team we're playing . . . you hear what I'm saying?*

He never lets down his guard, never lets the hounds get a whiff of doubt, concern, or subtlety. The secret of winning over the Pack, of course, is to occasionally and selectively allow them a peek behind the tarp, let them at least *feel* like insiders. Richie doesn't have time for it. He can't understand their need to keep trying.

He's still fuming in his Caddy later that week, driving out the

Schuylkill Expressway to tape the first of his weekly in-season TV shows. The car is about the only place you can get him to sit still for a few minutes to talk about himself.

"I'm a friendly person," he says, defensively. "My best friends are cabdrivers, waiters, waitresses, busboys . . . and I try to help people and everything, but what I can't stand is when somebody has a big set of balls and pushes all the time."

Coach Uptight is off and running in his second season, and nothing, not Stella's sudden death, not the annoyance of pushy TV crews, nothing is going to throw him off stride. Richie prides himself on this. If you're sick, if somebody dies, if you win, if you lose—whatever— you don't break stride. He has often told with pride the story of how, four or five years back as an assistant with the Jets, he had repeatedly promised his daughter that he would attend her school play, only to get stuck with some blocking-scheme crisis or other on the appointed evening and miss it. "She took it like a trooper, and she was only eight or nine!" he would say, proud Papa—until someone pointed out, *Gee, Richie, that's just an awful thing to have done to your kid!* So he dropped that anecdote from his repertoire. But, hey, this is the NFL. Richie can't help it if people don't understand the pressures the way Liz and Alexandra do.

The season is a race down a track with sixteen hurdles. Each game on the schedule is a jump. Like all good hurdlers, the coach has the steps between each one counted—Monday, review game tapes and critique; Tuesday, game plan (players off), first-down and second-down plays; Wednesday, introduce players to first- and second-down game plan, work up third-down and plus-twenty plays (plays twenty yards or less from the opponent's goal line); Thursday, major team practice sessions, running through the game plan (drive out and tape "The Rich Kotite Show"); Friday, light practice and more classroom work, drilling home the plan; Saturday, walk-through in the morning and either travel or sequester the team in a New Jersey hotel to prepare for: Sunday, game. The idea is to maintain stride, whether you clear the hurdle clean or trip, whether you win or lose.

"The important thing in this profession is avoiding the highs and lows," says Richie, balancing his cigar between two fingers over the steering wheel. "Regardless of how you feel inside, you've got to stay level, stay focused."

Richie's going to need that approach to survive in this city, where fans are every bit as rabid as those Richie grew up with in New York, except—at least right now, September '92—football is the only game in town.

Beyond the Id-people, whose neuroses have no rational basis, impatience and vexation rule the pro sports scene in Philly. Maybe it is the thirty-year wait between Phillies World Series trips ('50–'80), or the thirty-one-year wait for the Eagles to win a league championship (since '60). Some local pundits say it's a legacy that dates back to the British occupation during the Revolutionary War, or to Philadelphia's losing its status as the nation's capital afterward, bequeathing lasting municipal insecurity, aggravated today by the city's location between Washington, the power center, and New York City, the money (hence style) center, and the way most traffic on the interstate highway system manages to bypass Philly completely on the three-hour drive back and forth. Whatever the source, the citizens of this fifth-largest of American cities "love" their sports teams like overbearing parents, who, disappointed with their own lives, place unrealistic demands on their children—and are, consequently, forever frustrated.

No amount of success is enough. The Phils have been to the Series twice in the eighties (and would make it again in '93), the Eagles played in the Super Bowl in '81 and have been a solid, exciting, and improving team now for six years, basketball's 'Sixers and hockey's Flyers have both been in their league championships three times in the eighties—the 'Sixers won it all in '83—but Philly fans still seethe with discontent.

In a perfectly balanced sports world, a fan could fairly expect their team to play in the Super Bowl or World Series once every thirteen or fourteen years. In Philadelphia, they expect annual contention and success at least once every three or four years. By this standard, their pro franchises are forever falling short. Booing is a civic art form. Mike Schmidt, the greatest third baseman in baseball history, three-time National League MVP and easily the best player ever to wear a Phillies uniform, was routinely booed at the Vet. Ron Jaworski, the quarterback who led the Eagles to the Super Bowl, who played so hard he used to sustain (on average) three concussions a season, was hooted unmercifully, including once as he was being carried off the field on a stretcher, bleeding from the mouth. Philly fans have razzed presidents, mayors, opera stars, pop singers, small children—you name it. They even booed Santa Claus at a '68 Eagles halftime show—although, in fairness, players remembered "it was a pretty horrible Santa." Combine this rude tradition with the Id-people and the cold-weather ritual of getting tanked up in the parking lot before games—drunkenness at the Vet had gotten so out of hand in recent years that the team had stopped selling beer in the second half—and you had a weekly prescription for riot. The most enduring image of World Series victory in '80 wasn't relief pitcher Tug McGraw leaping for joy off the mound after the final out, it was the cordon of snarling police dogs and mounted police who hustled out to prevent the melee in the stands from spilling out on the field.

Of all the athletes who are paid to wear Philadelphia uniforms, football players find this prevailing public mood hardest to take. Football players are used to coaches being hypercritical, but not fans. They grow up playing before adoring crowds. High schools and colleges don't turn on their teams in defeat. But in the City of Brotherly Love, it's win *or else*.

GAME ONE OPENS with an orgy of sentimentality over poor Jerome. Television viewers catch a video tribute to the fallen tackle on "The Randall Cunningham Show" (slo-mo shots of Jerome in action to the plaintive strains of Madonna's hit "This Used to Be My Playground"), then catch another tribute on "The Rich Kotite Show" (Jerome in slo-mo action narrated by Reverend Reggie with intermittent strains of the lively gospel singing at the funeral), then again on CBS's "NFL Today," where they show portions of the pregame memorial to Jerome, complete with tearful speeches from Reggie and Seth and another tearjerk tribute video up on the big stadium screen (the Madonna one), followed by the retirement of Jerome's number, which is presented to Willie and Annie Bell with Norman standing stiffly alongside in the rain. By the time all this is done the mood in the Eagles' locker room is as wet with emotion as the field is with rain.

"Don't get your heads down now," barks Seth. "We need to get up and get ourselves together and get ready to play! It's too quiet, we have a game to play! Jerome is gone, we honored him, and we can't bring him back. He'd want us to go on and play, play hard and win this game."

All the Jerome stuff distracts from the return of Randall, who is starting his first regular-season football game at the Vet in more than a year and a half, wearing a knee brace. He drives the team downfield against one of the league's best defenses for a seemingly sweatless opening touchdown. The drive instantly dispels some of the biggest doubts about the offense. Just about every one of Richie's plays works. Herschel sprints off Antone Davis's shoulder into the right flat for eight yards; Randall completes a quick six-yard hitch pass for a first down; another hitch route the other way for eight more yards, and Herschel plows to another first down. Moving now into the Saints' half of the field, Randall takes off across the slick green carpet for ten more yards, high stepping out-of-bounds (brace and all!); Herschel breaks through the left side this time, hurdling his own blockers and throwing off tacklers for a thirty-two-yard run (that's forty-three yards for the Eagles' prize acquisition in the first six minutes of the season—who says this guy is washed up?); Randall runs again, leaping heedlessly into two tacklers just short of the goal line (so much for any hesitancy because of the knee); and then Randall fakes a handoff, spins, and floats a two-yard touchdown pass to—Herschel!

Wait, it's not over. The rattled Saints now fumble the kickoff right in front of the big Archangel Jerome banner. They recover the ball, but in three straight plays manage to move it only three yards. They're forced to punt from the back end of their own end zone; the stadium is a maelstrom of glee.

Then things settle down.

Randall fumbles the ball away on the next offensive play. He goes on to fumble the ball away two more times. Herschel fumbles it away once more. Placekicker Roger Ruzek misses two normally automatic extra-point tries—a collection of mistakes that would doom most efforts. But Herschel goes on to bash out seventy-two more yards, and Fred Barnett catches a twenty-yard touchdown pass in the fourth quarter. He falls over backward theatrically in the end zone, both arms held high. This, coupled with their stubborn and nasty defense, gives the Eagles a two-point lead, which they are still clinging to in the final three minutes of the game.

Ball control is central to Richie's philosophy—*they can't score if you don't give them the ball*—so the idea here is just to hang on, grind out first downs, and let the clock run out. If New Orleans gets the ball back, even with less than a minute on the clock, all they need is a pass or run that puts them within fifty yards of the goalposts for their superb placekicker, Morten Andersen, to boot the winning three points. Richie is pacing the sidelines in a fumble-prevention frenzy, gesturing to Randall and Herschel and Heath, cradling his arms, begging them to hang on to the ball. But the offense, once again, looks inept. Randall is sacked for a six-yard loss on the first play from scrimmage (the sixth time he is sacked this game), and Herschel is swarm tackled in the backfield on the next play. But having attained the critical third-and-long advantage, the Saints now doom themselves with two consecutive penalties—offside and pass interference—that spare the Eagles' having to earn first downs.

At the two-minute mark Keith Byars clinches the win when he catches a screen pass and chugs his tanklike frame downfield twenty-one yards, fending off five Saints tacklers fighting to push him out-of-bounds to stop the clock. The play consumes nearly fifty seconds, gives the Eagles a final first down, and allows them just to fall on the ball for two plays until time runs out.

So they narrowly win a game it would have been discouraging to lose, after the emotional Jerome homage and dedication. Even Richie, ordinarily deeply reserved about inflating his team's prospects, had bought into the JeromeQuest. After the video tribute on his own pregame show, the coach had said, in what for him was a moment of daring self-revelation, "We want to go to the Super Bowl; I'm not afraid to say that. I think Jerome Brown is going to have a lot to do with that."

WHEN THE FINAL gun sounds, offensive line coach Bill Muir heads for one person in particular. He meets and embraces 330-pound right tackle Antone Davis.

On Keith's big run, Antone's block had cleared the way. Pulling out from his slot at right tackle, he was charged with flattening the first tackler in his path, who happened to be Saints linebacker Sam Mills. Mills is smaller and a lot faster than the massive tackle, and appeared to have already raced far enough upfield to nail Byars. Antone, showing remarkable agility for a man his size, had dived at Mills's feet and, catching just the lower half of the linebacker's left leg, sent him flying.

It's the kind of play the team hoped Antone would make when they used two first-round picks to get him last year, only up till now the investment hadn't exactly paid off. Nobody knows this, of course, better than Antone, a sad-faced giant with quizzical eyebrows, a deep horizontal furrow permanently creasing his brow, a tiny voice, and a manner so retiring he seems ever ready to apologize for taking up so much space. In the year and a half Antone has been with the Eagles he has gone from cocky to angry to stone miserable.

Up until this block, Antone has stood as a kind of on-field martyr to Norman's and Richie's impatience. He was obtained by the Eagles in the '91 draft, three months after Buddy got the boot, in just the kind of bold Bramanesque move that Buddy would never have allowed.

Without Buddy to inhibit him, Norman showed up for draft day that spring with an entourage of family and friends, threw open the bar, and put on a show.

The NFL college draft is a twenty-eight-team conference call, with coaches and owners holed up in war rooms all over America before blackboards listing all the top college players available, broken down by field position (quarterback, tackles, guards, centers, cornerbacks, linebackers, safeties, et cetera). The rankings of the players under each category differ slightly from war room to war room; it's the end result of each team's yearlong scouting effort. The Eagles' personnel director, Joe Woolley, had written in players under each category ranked according to his and the coaching staff's appraisal of their potential. With the worst club choosing first and the best club last, the draft rolls a dozen times through all twenty-eight teams. The whole process is spread over two days and grows increasingly confusing to the casual observer when clubs start wheeling and dealing, swapping choices, or trading up.

Wheeling and dealing is, of course, Norman's thing. It taps that old entrepreneurial strain in him, the desire to move-move-move, make things happen, worry about tomorrow tomorrow, seize the day! In '91, coming off their 10–6 season, the Eagles weren't scheduled to choose in the first round until eighteen other teams had taken their pick. This hardly rattled an old-timer like Joe. He had been to about twenty of these, enough to know that the hard part isn't making the first three or four picks—every team in the league knows who are the two or three most likely prospects at each position—it's knowing whom to choose down in the middle or lower rounds that proves a scout's mettle. The pace of the day seems frenetic to those watching ESPN's coverage of draft central in New York, but to the men at work in each war room, the day unfolds slowly, with long waits punctuated by brief flurries of action when their fifteen-minute turn comes up.

Norman was fine during the brief flurries of action; it was the long waits in-between that were the problem. Joe found the guy annoying. For one thing, there was the party atmosphere the owner introduced to what was, frankly, the most serious and important day of the year for Joe and his staff. All their efforts, all their traveling and interviewing and thousands of hours of squinting at videotapes, all of it built toward these two days—and here was this car dealer with his drink in one hand, his wife, Irma, daughter Suzi, and her husband, all yukking it up loudly with Harry and George and Richie.

Throughout the long day, Norman would insist:

"Make a deal!"

"Move up!"

"Do something!"

Or he would shout, the way he did to his executive assistant in Miami with the little office outside his door, "Get me Jerry Jones on the phone!"

In the past, Buddy was the buffer. He'd spend most of his time huddling with Joe and the scouts, and Norman didn't interfere. If he tried, going off about how he wanted to do this or that, Buddy would listen quietly and come over and whisper to Joe, "Don't pay any attention to him. Here's what we're gonna do."

Now Joe felt like he was working in the middle of a fucking cocktail party.

He was on the phone with the war room in Detroit, and the guy on the other end complained, "Jesus, what in the hell is going on in the background?"

And Joe, who had just about had it by then himself, pulled his six-six frame out of his chair, cupped his hand over the phone, and shouted, "Men, we cannot operate like this! I can't hear what's going on on the phone."

The room went coldly silent. Norman turned a stare on Joe that raised the fine hairs on the back of his neck.

"Don't you ever talk to me like that again," the owner said, and then strode out the door, muttering, "I don't know why they can't do it here like they do it in Miami."

Slowly the room emptied, and Joe sat down uneasily and went back to work.

Norman and Harry—and Richie!—were desperate for a big offensive tackle that year. Buddy had neglected to build a first-rate offensive line in his five years as head coach. Again, it reflected his philosophy. To Buddy, an offensive lineman was a big body without fire in his eyes. The true thoroughbred linemen were the flashy hard chargers on defense, and Buddy had outdone himself there, inheriting Reggie but drafting Jerome and Clyde and picking up Mike Pitts and Mike Golic. But instead of using top draft picks to build an offensive line, Buddy was always trying shortcuts. He traded to get Ron Heller, Ron Solt, and Mike Schad, players other teams had found wanting (only Heller had really panned out), drafted Dave Alexander in the fifth round, a move that had paid big dividends, but otherwise Buddy kept trying to plug the big holes up front by taking guys who couldn't cut it on the defensive side of the ball and trying to turn them into blockers.

The approach showed Buddy's basic lack of respect for the position. In fact, in recent years offensive tackle had become one of the most important specialties on the field. There were ever-shifting trends on the pro gridiron, and one of the big movements in the eighties had been the emergence of blazingly quick pass-rushing linebackers and defensive ends—the prototype being the Giants' Lawrence Taylor. Players like Taylor, the Saints' Pat Swilling, the Packers' Tim Harris, the Bills' Bruce Smith, and the Eagles' Seth Joyner weighed in fifty to seventy-five pounds less than an offensive tackle, but combined extraordinary quickness and strength with power surprising for their size. They could often just blow right around the slow-moving big men trying to block them or use sudden cutback moves to throw the big men off balance and then club them out of their way. If rushing the passer required remarkable physical skills combined with wild abandon, blocking these fire-breathers demanded comparable physical skills and a calm, disciplined demeanor. The modern offensive tackle had to have not only size and strength, but quick feet, tremendous balance, a solid grasp of blocking (and holding) fundamentals, and an overabundance of poise. Buddy's efforts to turn slow, earnest former defensive lineman Reggie Singletary, and lately a towering, eye-poppingly muscular but stiff former pass rusher named Cecil Gray, into offensive tackles condemned these poor players to years of agonizing frustration and had kept the Eagles near the top of the NFL in sacks allowed for several seasons. At some point, the Eagles knew they had to stop trying to make a premier offensive tackle and draft one.

So the first order of business this draft day was to land a blue-chip offensive tackle. Joe had two big tackles topping his list, Antone Davis and Charles McRae, two young giants who had been so overpowering on either end of the Volunteers' offensive line in the '90 season that they'd been dubbed "the Tennessee Valley Authority." Most teams had the same two names at the top of their tackle list, with McRae listed first, but Joe liked the twenty-seven-inch vertical leap Antone demonstrated at the scouting combine and the almost comically dainty way Davis moved—like the toe-dancing hippos in *Fantasia*.

But the way things shaped up that afternoon, the Eagles wound up eleven picks away from their turn, with at least three or four other teams ahead of them interested in a big offensive tackle.

Norman told Joe, "Call Green Bay."

The Packers had the eighth pick. Norman wanted to trade up.

Joe got Packers' vice-president Tom Braatz on the line and asked what it would take to buy his number-eight slot.

"We've been offered two number twos," said Braatz.

"Hold on a minute," said Joe. He relayed this information back into the room. Joe knew something drastic was required. If Green Bay had turned down two number twos (some team offered them not only their second-round pick in this draft, but next year's, too), then there was only one better offer to make.

"Only chance we've got is to give 'em next year's number one," he said.

Norman, Harry, and Richie all immediately agreed, just like that . . . one, two, three.

"Go," said Norman.

Joe turned back to the phone.

"Would you switch places with us for our number one next year?"

"Hold on," said Braatz.

They waited in silence while Joe held the phone. He turned on the speaker so everyone could hear the response. For once the Eagles' war room was silent.

Then came Braatz's amplified voice, "We'll do it."

Moments later, Tampa Bay, as expected, snagged McRae, and the Eagles got their man.

He's six-four and, fully padded and shoed, weighs more than two ordinary men—much of it centered toward the rear. With the explosive power provided by that million-dollar ass (Eagles teammates would nickname him "Twin Cheeks"), Antone looked like a sure thing. Richie proudly told the Pack, "He's a prototype. . . . The guy was at the top of our list—the top of our list."

Pro teams often boast about their exhaustive scouting methods, all the clever ways they have of ensuring their picks are sane, solid, and superior. But ten minutes of candid conversation with the guy they just spent two number-one picks (and soon a few million bucks) to get would have told the Eagles they were drafting trouble. Antone, see, has this problem. *He doesn't seem to like playing football.* He's learned the mandatory mean face of the pro blocker, and he's big enough and quick enough on his feet to do the job if he has to, albeit reluctantly. With lots of enthusiastic hard work, Antone could even turn out to be a great blocker. But one long look into those brown eyes, soulful as a calf's, and one long listen to that soft, intelligent voice talking about going for his master's in education, and it's clear that while Antone's mind is impressive and highly active, it's elsewhere. Leave him alone and he'll hack away on his home computer, hang out with his adoring young wife, read a book on urban planning, fly his nifty remote-control model planes and helicopters around a parking lot, or whip up a gourmet meal—he's a great cook. Football is way down on his list of preferred activities. But when the Great American Cult of the Pigskin happens on a Goliathan teenager who's amazingly light on his feet . . . well, it can have a mighty and smothersome embrace. Particularly with a boy growing up aimlessly in a sleepy rural backwater like Fort Valley, Georgia.

He was the last of Daisy Davis's eight children. She had seen to that. She had watched her own mother bear sixteen and then die trying to bring forth one more, so after her Tony was born in '67, she took steps to halt the assembly line. Daisy grew up on the "colored" side of the tracks in Fort Valley, a small shopping and banking center deep in the heart of Peach County, Georgia, about one hundred miles south of Atlanta. Her father had worked as a night watchman and jack-of-all-trades at nearby Fort Valley State College—he had literally helped build the place—and spent his life trying to build a bridge to a better life for his brood. He bought a four-bedroom house from a family in Fort Valley proper, disassembled it, and then rebuilt it on a woody plot east of the Georgia Central Railroad tracks, the town's color line. The dirt road that led to the house was called Davis Street because theirs was the only house on it.

Heeding their father's promptings, most of Daisy's brothers and sisters made it out of Fort Valley and into a different way of life. Her older brother Richard was a member of the famous black squadron of Tuskegee pilots during World War II. Another brother became a lawyer, another a school administrator, another an accountant. But Daisy fell into the cycle of child rearing that had captured her mother—she calls herself, with weary resignation, "a fast breeder." Much to her father's disgust, she bore three children when she was still an unmarried teen. She met Milton Trice in the early sixties, and with him went on to have five more.

Times were hard for Milton and Daisy as they struggled to raise their large family. Milton learned brick masonry and helped build houses when he could, but he was afflicted with the sleeping disorder narcolepsy, which few foremen understood. They'd find him sleeping and he'd find himself out of a job. Daisy did some sewing and now and then took work at a local textile plant, but there were nights Antone remembers going to bed hungry. He grew up bitter about his predicament, about the way his mother and father failed to measure up to the rest of his impressive extended family.

He remembers picking peaches for thirty-five cents a bucket— the fuzz would stick to his skin and itch—and doing odd jobs at his uncle's store. He was a skinny, eager thirteen-year-old when Dave Rowell opened the R&R Quik-Stop out on Route 341, about fifty yards down from where Daisy and Milton were living on Fagen Street. The job became Antone's second home. He started as a floor sweeper and in time was virtually running the place. He quit school to tend the cash register, stock shelves, and cook up the barbecue chicken, ribs, and sandwiches they sold from a counter in back—one of the store's biggest attractions. Being underage, Antone earned less than the legal hourly minimum, but it was more money than he had ever seen—he earned enough to buy himself a twelve-speed bike!—and he was allowed to *eat*. Boy, could the kid eat! Rowell would remember the skinny kid attacking heroic portions, three or four plates full of barbecue, sausage dogs, crackers, potato chips, whole boxes of cookies. He ate while he worked and he ate some more after he worked.

And he started to grow. He grew so fast that one day he complained to his mother about a painful swelling around his nipples.

Daisy spent her last thirty dollars on an appointment with the white doctor in Fort Valley, who examined Antone and determined that the swelling was just the boy's glands working overtime.

"It's nothing to worry about, he's just growin'," he told Daisy.

Working behind the counter, slinging burgers, ribs, and beans, Antone just kept on growing. "Folks around here blamed it on the barbecue," says Daisy, chuckling. "They said he must be eatin' more than he was sellin'." But Daisy had some size on her side of the family, and several of Milton's brothers and sisters were exceptionally tall. Still, nobody was as big as her Tony. Before long, Barbecue Tony behind the counter at the Quik-Stop was a local legend. By the time he was fourteen, Daisy was handing up the clothes her Tony outgrew to his older brothers.

In time, Antone realized the Quik-Stop was a dead end. He would sometimes sit with the fruit pickers and unemployed who gathered daily outside the store drinking cheap wine. One day, one of the men sighed and said he wished he could go back to school, which got Antone thinking. After missing a year of high school, he decided to go back. He liked the idea of playing for the Peach County High School football team, but the coach, while admiring Antone's size, told him that he couldn't because he hadn't come out for the summer tryouts and practices.

Antone didn't bother with football for a long time after that. He went to school and worked afternoons and weekends at the Quik-Stop, getting bigger and bigger. It wasn't until the summer before his junior year, after a friend teased him about not being able to make the football team—"A boy your size!"—that Antone got mad and showed up for summer practice. He played center for one season, as a junior, but was too old to play for the team in his senior year. Still, word had gotten out. There were college recruiters in the stands for a few of those junior-year games, and when a football player from the University of Tennessee stopped in the Quik-Stop one day to check out the local legend of Barbecue Tony—Antone was six-four now and closing in on three hundred pounds—he remarked, "Boy, you that big? I'm gonna tell my coach 'bout you."

An assistant coach from Tennessee came knocking on Daisy's door. He recommended a year at the Tennessee Military Institute, where Tony could play on the school's football team and shore up his academic credentials. If he did well, on and off the field, there would be a full four-year scholarship waiting at Tennessee. The boy wasn't sure. He wasn't really dying to play football. He had already decided to join the army. Daisy, remembering her father's admonitions, encouraged him to give school a chance.

"Just try it for a little while," she said. "If you don't like it, you can come home."

He went and he never looked back. He endured the year at TMI—he remembers it, unkindly, as "a private school for rich derelicts"—and then moved up to Chattanooga—and a new life. He excelled on the field and in the classroom. Barbecue Tony became *Antone*, the star lineman with a degree in city planning and an adoring coed girlfriend named Carrie, whom he would marry after graduation. He was already taking graduate courses when the Eagles made him a high first-round pick and a millionaire. Antone wasn't really any keener on playing football than he had been six years earlier, but how does a twenty-five-year-old recent college grad turn down the million-dollar payday, and the promise of lots more, just to keep on doing what he'd grown accustomed to? His size and agility had made him overpowering in the All-Southeast Conference; there was no reason to expect he wouldn't continue to dominate opponents in the pros. Certainly the NFL thought so. Antone had been contracted by just about every team in the league, and he had some of the biggest player reps in the country begging to handle his affairs. Richie Kotite had called him a "prototype." On draft day, he pulled out a book of floor plans for new houses he had been leafing through and dropped it on Daisy's lap.

"Start looking them over," he told her. "You can have any one you want."

Now, as Antone is starting the second year of his pro career, Daisy and Milton are living full-time in the DHM (Dream Home for Mom), an L-shaped brick house with about ten times more space than they know how to use. They tend to live mostly in the kitchen and den off to one corner of the place, as if unable to inflate their lives to such grand dimensions. Daisy doesn't turn the air-conditioning on because she's not sure how to work it and isn't convinced it's healthy. On a typical summer afternoon you will find her parked on a worn couch (from the old house) in the den, fanning herself with a magazine, the head of a sleeping grandchild in her broad lap. In the corner, a TV provides a splash of color, a bright window on a distant world. The satellite dish outside brings in all of her Tony's games, which she watches without full appreciation or understanding. Mostly she just watches her son and prays he doesn't get hurt.

Tony doesn't come home much anymore. One whole wing of the big new house is for him, and it's empty.

With the million-dollar bonus and $3 million–plus salary over four years, Antone's got it made. He and Carrie divide their time between a lovely suburban home with a pool in New Jersey, a place in Knoxsville, and a condo down in Chattanooga. When Antone isn't playing football, he and Carrie have nothing to do but relax and travel and plan. He has been playing with a new computer program called Atlas that calls up maps and demographic information for anywhere in America. He and Carrie are searching for the perfect place to eventually settle down, build a big house, and raise their own family.

So far none of the places they're considering is near Fort Valley. Antone finds it increasingly difficult to go home.

"I don't even call it home anymore," he says with pride.

Not all the players on the Eagles' roster have risen rapidly from the depths of poverty. Many, like Randall, Dave Alexander, Mike Schad, Ron Heller, and Ken Rose, were raised in comfortable homes. But the conventional image of the black kid rising from urban projects or stubborn rural privation to a six- and seven-figure salary holds true for quite a few, players like Antone and Andre, Seth, Byron Evans, Herschel Walker, Ben Smith, Calvin Williams, Mark McMillian, Siran Stacy, and others. Sudden financial success at a young age sometimes makes it awkward for even the formerly middle-class players to relate to their parents, siblings, and hometown friends. Ron Heller, for instance, has brothers who did far better than he had in school and who have gone out and found good jobs after graduation. They are in their early thirties now, raising families, paying their bills, doing fine by any conventional measure, but they are all making maybe one-tenth or less of the $661,000 Ron will earn this year playing football. Did you offer them money or would that offend their pride? If you invited them down to go fishing with you on your cabin cruiser was that showing off? If you started giving away money, where and how did you stop?

For players escaping real poverty, the problem magnified a hundredfold. Many had large extended families, parents, siblings, half siblings, stepsiblings, uncles, aunts, nieces and nephews, cousins, and second cousins. Add in old high-school teammates, college teammates—once the big payday arrived the size of a player's "intimate" circle exploded. "People come up to me, and they say, 'Remember I did this for you?'" says Ben Smith, who was the team's number-one draft pick in '90. "And I say, 'Gee, I always thought you helped me because you liked me, or because you were a nice person, not because you've been waiting around for me to pay you back.'" And it isn't just money. It's the life players now lead. After four or five years away at college, several years of living the life in the social circle of a pro football team, travel, marriage . . . the boundaries of a players' world enlarge beyond the comprehension of those trapped in the old life.

Part of what had made Jerome unique was his ability to keep his hometown connections, although even Jerome, in an interview shortly before he was killed, said he did not intend to eventually settle back down in Brooksville, citing the usual complications. For Antone, the gulf between then and now has become too wide to comfortably bridge.

"People are always telling me to remember where I came from," he says. "Well, I remember."

A man finely attuned to the smallest slight, Antone remembers the way his supposed "friends" and extended family treated his parents, him, and his siblings—the store that milked interest payments from his poor mother for nearly a decade for a tricycle she bought him on credit, the relatives who ignored Daisy when she couldn't feed her children, the man in the neighborhood who made a show of feeding his dog steak, yet would say no when Antone and his brothers came down the street offering to wash his cars for five dollars, the college weekends when Antone couldn't find anybody to drive him back up to Chattanooga, so he would be forced to drive up with his father, which was dangerous, because then Milton would have to drive back alone, and he couldn't stay awake on the long stretches of country road. There was the man who gave Milton a truck (or so he thought) upon hiring him to build a house, which Antone's father did, virtually at cost, only to have the new homeowner demand the truck back when the work was done—even though Milton had understood it was the main part of his payment. This same man, fallen on hard times, stopped by the house on one of Antone's first trips home after signing with the Eagles. He asked for some help in meeting a mortgage payment so he wouldn't have to forfeit the house.

"No," said Antone, without apology or explanation.

An old college buddy called up and asked Antone to buy him a car. Just like that.

Another wanted two hundred dollars.

"Just two hundred dollars," he pleaded. "What's two hundred dollars to you?"

What was Antone supposed to say? He couldn't say he didn't have it.

"Is it going to be two hundred a week, two hundred a month, or what?" he asked.

"Just two hundred, that's it."

Antone asked, with disgust, "If I give you the money, are we still friends? If I don't give you the money, are we still friends?"

One of his best college friends had a decent entry-level job with an auditing firm in Atlanta, making about $35,000 a year. Antone called him just to say hello.

"You're big-time now, you're really big-time now," the guy kept saying.

"What do you mean?" asked Antone.

"You're too big to talk to me now."

Antone knew the guy was just joking, but, in another sense, he wasn't. It poisoned the whole conversation, introduced an issue that, as far as Antone was concerned, wasn't even there.

He hardly even calls home anymore. He gave all his brothers and sisters a gift of several thousand dollars when he signed, and now they all come to him for advice, treat him like some kind of father figure—he's the youngest! He knows that no matter how well they do for the rest of their lives, unless they hit the lottery, they'll never catch up to him. It's awkward. When Antone and Carrie vacation in Hawaii in the off-season, should they send a postcard home, or is that rubbing it in their faces? He's worked hard for his success, harder than most people realize. He feels he's earned his money. Still, he feels guilty.

But that's not the worst of it for Antone. What's worse is what happens out on the field.

The Megapick is thrown in at right tackle his rookie year with the weight of the entire franchise strapped to his broad backside. He's less a sacrificial offering than a sack pass for the NFL's left-side rushers, gift-wrapped in an Eagles uniform with the number 78 on his back so that the fans in the stands and at home watching TV can more easily track his travails. The Eagles yield 20.5 sacks to left-side defensive ends and outside linebackers that season, which is almost half the team's conference-leading total. It's on-the-job training, complete with stop-action, slow-motion analysis and critical commentary on regional and frequently national TV. These guys he's trying to block in the NFL are nothing at all like the opponents he faced in the Southeast Conference.

The worst was his fifth game, against Washington, on ABC's national telecast "Monday Night Football." Daisy and Milton and all of Antone's family and friends from Fort Valley, millions of home viewers, including just about everyone he's ever known, were watching as Barbecue Tony lined up to do battle with Pro Bowl defensive end Charles Mann. And it was the most exorbitant whacking they'll ever see. In a 23–0 Eagles loss, Antone turned in what just might be the worst performance by a pro player ever documented on network TV.

Boy, did they document it.

On the Eagles' second offensive series, Antone was called for holding Mann, a loss of five yards. On the next play, Mann just bulled him over backward; Antone hung on as he toppled, pulling Mann over with him, and was called again for holding.

"That's the daily double for Antone Davis!" said Al Michaels (close-up on frowning Antone).

On the very next play, Mann beat Antone and sacked Jimmy Mac. "What a start for the rookie!" said Michaels.

"Remember last time how Mann went inside and overpowered him?" explained Dan Dierdorf excitedly (they show the play now again in slo-mo, camera isolated on Antone and Mann). "This time, like all great defensive ends, he goes with a change-up and goes upfield and beats Davis around the corner!"

On the Eagles' next possession, Antone let Mann blow right past him and chase Jimbo off the field—the quarterback twisted his knee on this play and wound up missing the remainder of this game and the next two (an absence that prompted the quarterback debacle that ultimately doomed the '91 season).

"Again, Charles Mann just came in unheeded, just unimpeded," said Dierdorf. "McMahon just had to get out of the pocket. He had no choice."

(Close-up of Jimbo screaming at Antone and the rest of the offensive line in front of the bench.)

On the next Eagles' possession, Redskins lineman Fred Stokes sacked replacement quarterback Pat Ryan for another eight-yard loss. Who was the culprit? (Slo-mo replay of Stokes running right past Antone.)

"It's been a long night already for Antone Davis, the rookie right tackle," said Dierdorf, chuckling (close-up on a scowling Antone). "Antone Davis just gives him the corner . . . that's just poor technique."

Consider that just one or two big plays on "Monday Night Football," the one game each week that *everybody* who watches football sees—most important, other players and coaches from around the league—is enough to elevate a player to stardom. A night like Antone's, with all the commentary and slo-mo replays? It was enough to destroy his reputation for good.

Out on the field, Mann never said a word to the rookie. Antone had heard coaches in pregame meetings whetting the appetite of a pass rusher matched against an inferior opponent: *You're going to have a field day with this guy.* Well, that night Charles Mann was having a field day with him. Throughout, the rookie was haunted by images of his family and friends watching him on TV. His teammates offered him little solace—most of them didn't like him much or resented his salary. Mann would blow him away, line up for the next play, and blow him away again. Every time Antone jogged back out on the field for a new offensive series, he asked himself, *What are you running for? In a hurry to get your ass kicked again?*

The second half began with another holding call on the rookie, who had now become the broadcast's primary subplot.

"Did you see what Antone Davis did to Charles Mann?" asked Dierdorf (slo-mo replay to make sure everybody did). "I mean, we're dealing with a major league mugging [close-up again on fuming Antone, hands on giant hips]. Antone Davis, the big rookie right tackle, is having an unbelievable tough night." (Laughter in the booth as they replayed the holding call again.)

"This has to be so frustrating for the rookie first-round draft pick out of Tennessee," said Michaels, who, you could tell, was starting to feel sorry for Antone.

(Close-up on Charles Mann.)

"We've see him physically overwhelm Davis and we've seen him beat Davis around the corner," said Dierdorf.

On the next play, Mann again eluded Antone's block and nearly sacked Ryan in the end zone for a safety.

"Charles Mann again!" shouted Dierdorf. "The time he went *over the top* of Antone Davis and almost got the sack!"

(Close-up on confused and angry-looking Antone.)

"Antone, it'll get better," said Dierdorf, addressing the pathetic image on the screen. "You're a rookie and it's going to take a while."

On the next series, another holding call.

"I don't even want to say who that's on," said Dierdorf.

"How about a hint," said Michaels.

(Close-up on distressed Antone, brow knotted inside the gridwork of his face mask.)

"It's been tough enough," said Dierdorf.

"That's why he gets paid the big bucks, right?" said Michaels.

"He got some big bucks. Number-one draft choice. High one at that. Antone Davis continues to learn."

When the game ended, Antone half expected Mann to search him out on the field and thank him. He figured he'd just helped get the Redskin's star in the Pro Bowl for the fourth time; the least Mann could do was run out and shake hands.

Then he had to sit through the embarrassing game tapes with his teammates the next day. Antone figured, what was he supposed to do? Cry? Apologize? So instead of wilting with shame as the tape replayed his public disgrace, Antone made jokes about it. He used the one about "The least he could have done is come over and shake my hand." Antone saw it as leading the laughs on himself, but his teammates saw it differently. This was their livelihood on the line here. Why was the rookie laughing? He got his ass kicked on national TV, helped blow an important game, lost Jimmy Mac, maybe the season, and he thought it was funny?

Antone's sad-sack personality didn't help either. After the third game of that season—the Eagles had just drummed the Cowboys 24–0, so the boys were feeling pretty good—Antone was in the shower with tattooed, ponytailed Dennis McKnight, a nine-year NFL veteran. Antone sighed and reflected wistfully, "Man, I'm glad I'm not going to have to play as long as you have."

"What?" asked McKnight, not believing his ears.

"With my bonus and everything, I'm gonna finish out my four years and that's it," Antone said. "I ain't gonna play this damn game for that long."

"You aren't going to make it four years with an attitude like that," said McKnight. It was enough to make a guy pissed off. Not counting the million-dollar bonus, Antone was making about $62,000 per game (McKnight, after his nine seasons, was pulling in about $16,000). The least the fat-ass rookie could do was keep his ennui to himself.

Antone wasn't about to get any sympathy, partly because of the money thing, partly because of his attitude, but largely because, as his line mates saw it, he refused to work at the game. All of the veterans on the line—Ron Heller, Mike Schad, Dave Alexander, McKnight—put in long hours in the weight room to keep their big bodies from going slack, but not Antone. He whined every week about his knee or elbow or back being too sore. Rob Selby, the team's third-round draft pick from Auburn, while less visible to the public (he wasn't a starter), was having just as hard a time playing at the pro level as Antone, but, boy, did Selby ever work at it. He'd be in the weight room early every morning and in the classroom late every evening. Out on the practice field he had a million questions, and he volunteered for every chance to work at his game. When Selby screwed up, in practice or in a game, he got so angry that his round pink face inside his helmet looked as if it were about to blow out the earholes. But Antone didn't ask questions, and tended to shrug and joke about his failures. Veterans like Ron and Dave had to take extra reps with the scout squad because Antone refused to honor the long tradition of rookies handling the extra practice load. Antone seemed to feel they were dumping the extra load on him because he was black.

"Antone, get in there, you've got to take the reps," Ron would say.

"Why don't you give a brother a break?"

"Listen, *brother*, it's got nothing to do with that. You get your ass in there and pay your dues."

"No," Antone would say, and just walk away, as if to say, *You think they're paying me millions to run with the scout team?*

When the offensive line coach would remind Antone to take his playbook home for some extra study, the Megapick would snicker.

The other linemen could admire Antone's natural ability, the way he was so light-footed and quick despite that huge frame, but they could also see he was playing like shit. Yet the kid was apparently convinced, what with his millions and megastatus, that all he had to do to get better was show up. And nothing bad that happened to him seemed to disabuse him of that notion. Even after Charles Mann turned him into a human turnstile, he was *still* impressed with himself!

What they didn't understand was that laughing about his failures was Antone's way of coping—he was feeling embarrassed and uncomfortable, so he pretended not to care. But his teammates just saw the smirk. Through his rookie season Antone became more and more isolated and brooding. He had the furtive eyes of a man looking for some way out.

Antone then made things worse. He did what many frustrated and angry pro football players do; he turned on the Pack. And not without reason. From day one they'd been feasting on his hide.

Antone was dubbed the "Tennessee Turnstile" and the "Saloon Door." One writer suggested he might as well be wearing a "green light as a green helmet."

After the Redskins game, the Philadelphia *Daily News'* sports columnist Bill Conlin wrote, "Antone Davis not only won the ears, tails and an autographed Sonny Jorgensen cocktail napkin last night, the Eagles rookie right offensive tackle has been invited to lead next year's running of the bulls in Pamplona."

Assessing Davis's performance later that year and returning to the bull theme, Conlin gibed, "When confronted with the NFC East's premier pass rushers, the mammoth rookie right tackle should have been issued a red cape . . . nah, cancel that. It would have been too tough to hold and execute a Veronica at the same time."

Philadelphia *Inquirer* writer Ron Reid noted pointedly (and correctly) after one atrocious outing that "Antone Davis allowed more sacks than Herschel Walker had yards."

After that particular preseason game, Antone strode right into the den of the beast, the pressroom in West Chester, and asked the Eagles' PR director, Ron Howard, to show him his press clippings—something players never did. It was considered bad form ever to admit that you had read a newspaper article, although there wasn't a player on the team unaware of the smallest slight in the lowest paragraphs in the sports pages of even the most obscure tabloid. With the Pack quietly working away on deadlines at desks around the room's perimeter, the sounds of their laptop computers madly clicking, Antone plopped his leviathan bulk onto a worn sofa and silently tortured himself with the neatly stapled stack of notices, the ones with all the clever nicknames, and afterward harrumphed that he would henceforth not be responding to questions from the press.

It made matters worse. Shutting up seemed a natural and intelligent reflex, but in dealing with the Pack, as Antone would learn, it was a tactical error. So long as a player was still stopping to answer questions, the Pack had an incentive to accord him at least a measure of decency. But when he stopped talking—screw him.

A TV reporter stopped Antone the next day as he emerged from the cafeteria.

"Antone, you got a second?"

"No, I don't," the big tackle said. "I'm not talking."

"Why not?"

"I just don't have anything to say right now."

"Well, you talked last year and you didn't have anything to say then."

But the Saints game, game one of Antone's second season, ends on an up note, that acrobatic game-saving block to spring Byars. Never mind that the rest of the game has been the usual string of embarrassments. The Saints' superb pass rushers, Rickey Jackson and Wayne Martin, had spun the big tackle every which way.

Antone ends the game responsible for three of the six times the Saints sacked Randall. After the game, he sits brooding before his locker enveloped in a dark cloud. At this point, no one dares disturb him. He can just picture what horrific press clippings this new season will bring.

Only, in the next day's newspaper, Antone is the hero! One headline actually reads:

DAVIS & CO. GET IT DONE!

Antone is shocked. He had a horrible game. One nice block at the end of a dismal outing, and he's suddenly point man for the whole team?

"There you have it," says one of his coaches. "Proof positive the assholes don't know what they're talking about."

ANDRE WATERS's ordinarily robust spirits are even gustier than usual after the opening win. He had made a diving interception, a wonderfully good sign, interceptions being serendipitous enough to be considered acts of God. Andre remembers the long dry spell of '90 when he was being tested or had somehow fallen out of divine favor and *not one* pass fell into his hands.

"Hey, Eric, who'd I say was gonna get the first interception?" he asks Eric Allen in the next locker.

"Eeeh," groans Eric, who returned to the locker room just three days before the game with his $1.3 million contract in hand, the last piece of Bud's defensive puzzle to fall in place. His teammates had clapped and cheered on his return, feeling fully invincible once more, chanting, "Hammer time! Hammer time!"

"See? Y'all didn't believe me!" says Andre. "I tol' y'all I was gettin' the first interception and y'all be laughin' at me."

"That'll be your only one, too," teases Eric.

"Y'all be jus' laughin' at me."

Andre is the last of his teammates to have seen Jerome alive. They had gone jet-skiing in Tampa. Jerome had a souped-up wave runner that could go faster than everybody else's, of course, and he would take off on the thing without a flotation vest—of course. Andre's last vivid memory of his friend was watching him wipe out spectacularly in the bay, his mammoth black body spread-eagle, flying through the air, head over keester, and then having a moment of panic remembering that Jerome wasn't wearing a vest—only to see his wide grin pop up and hear his high-pitched laugh come rolling out across the water.

"J'rome, man, you get hurt, you messin' with my money!" Andre scolded him.

Weeks later Jerome was dead, and that joking concern for his importance to their chances (and wallets) was real. Shaking his head now, pulling off gear before his locker, shouting to be heard in the din, Andre offers an impromptu, heartfelt State of the Team Address to stray members of the Pack:

"I think that everybody thought that last year the defense was a hoax, and that, especially now with the loss of Jerome Brown, we wouldn't be the same. We might not finish one across-the-board, but I guarantee you, if we continue to play the way we been playin', we can finish near the top. . . . I mean, we wanted to get this game, we wanted to get the first one, we want to get to the Super Bowl, you know? We dedicate this season . . . first, all of these people in here, dedicate everything they do to the Good Lord up above. Secondly, Jerome. We want to take them one at a time. We got one down, we got fifteen more to go. We want to go all the way to Pasadena and win it all for Jerome, you know? I know he's somewhere up there smiling. Maybe he got that first down for us when we needed it."

. . .

OUT ON THE FIELD at Sun Devil Stadium in Phoenix the following Sunday, Ron Heller can't believe the heat. A big thermometer set up by TNT, which is televising the Eagles-Cardinals game nationally, reads more than 120 degrees Fahrenheit. No wonder Phoenix games are the most poorly attended in the NFL. Nobody sane leaves air-conditioning unless there's an emergency.

Ron knows what it's like to play in heat, to play until you grow dizzy and you can't focus your eyes, which sting like hell because you're so dehydrated your sweat has turned mostly to salt. He was taken by Tampa Bay in the fourth round of the '84 draft and was a starter down in that tropical climate for three seasons. He liked the heat. He had built his house down in Tampa and would gladly have stayed there for the rest of his career—if not for this little run-in he had with former Buccaneers head coach Ray Perkins.

Having played for Perkins, Ron understood better than most football players how ugly the Tyranny of Coach can get. Years later he remembered his experience with Perkins vividly, every escalating incident and slight, scenes he had played over in his head so often they came back to him word for word.

Ron had fallen in love with the deep-coral-and-salmon dusks over Tampa Bay, the chrome-blue waters, the fertile smell in the air after a spring shower, the year-round blossoms and balmy nights on that side of the state, which offered the same climate as Miami without the severe, sun-bleached flatness, and without the bigger city's tumult and grime. Granted, the team was lousy, but Ron never even thought about leaving. The Bucs had drafted him, and he felt loyal to them. When he heard guys grumble that they'd rather play for a contender, Ron would challenge them, "Do you want to get traded the night before the championship game or do you want to earn it?"

When he cleared $100,000 of bonus money and started earning an $80,000 salary in his rookie year, he felt like he had a fortune. His four years at Penn State had been wild ones—living in a dorm or in hotel rooms on the road, wearing the same clothes sometimes for days, playing ball, partying, going to class, partying—at the center of rowdy good times on campus. College had been a blast. But now it was time to get serious, get to work. Ron bought himself a pair of sneakers and jeans, a condo, and a fishing rod, paid his father back the money he had borrowed to buy his Ford Bronco, kept enough pocket money to support a little barhopping, and sunk the rest of his earnings into treasury bonds. Ron liked things neat and regular.

In his second year he made $125,000 and met his wife, Heidi, a Bucs cheerleader who had blond hair, a dancer's body, and the cool head of a finance major. He saw her at a bar in Tampa, recognized her from seeing her around the sidelines, couldn't think of anything to say, so he just grabbed her—which, fortunately for Ron, was something Heidi didn't mind. Seems she had noticed him around the ol' gridiron, too. They hit it off. Ron and Heidi were planners. They'd postpone having kids until Ron was finished playing football. They'd invest their money, build a home, and lay a solid foundation for Life after Football. Ron was not one to waste time. Off-season, as he saw it, was opportunity. He got his real estate license after one season and an insurance license after another. He took a job with a beer distributor in the winter after Tampa's abysmal '86 season (they were 2–14, the worst record in football).

That was the off-season when Perkins was hired to turn things around. A lean, blue-eyed former wide receiver (Alabama and then the Baltimore Colts), Ray had the weathered, creased countenance of a tough Mississippi cracker and the personality to go with it. He had a dour and imperious manner that scared most people, including his players, but he had a history of getting results. As head coach with the Giants in the early eighties he'd turned a 6–10 team into a play-off contender in just three seasons, and at Alabama, where he had succeeded his beloved mentor Bear Bryant, he'd compiled a highly respectable winning record over three seasons (32–15–1). Ray had willed himself into an all-American at Alabama in the sixties after nearly dying in his freshman year of a blood clot to the brain. He was an authentic member of the Pigskin Priesthood, acolyte and successor to the Bear, one of the Game's saints, with connections to such NFL blue bloods as Johnny Unitas (whose passes he caught) and Don Shula (who had coached him). His years coaching the Crimson Tide further burnished those credentials. He arrived in Tampa Bay as a savior to the NFL's worst franchise. Owner Hugh Culverhouse made the obligatory nod to St. Vince, anointing Ray as "the next Vince Lombardi." It would be hard to overstate the impact his arrival had on this sleepy franchise. Ray lent instant credibility to a team whose incandescent red, orange, and white uniforms and swishy symbol, a swashbuckling pirate with a Zorro mustache, a dashing feathered cap, and a dagger clenched in his teeth—*en garde, big boy!*—looked like they belonged more on a stage in nearby Disney World than mixing it up in the trenches on a football field. You didn't mess with NFL graphics, so there wasn't much Perkins could do about El Zorro, but he planned to toughen up the team's fruity image fast.

Which Ron found out when he stopped by the club offices in

Jerome Brown on the sidelines of a night game in 1991, his last season

Richie Kotite earning his nickname "Horn" (short for "Bullhorn") as Buddy Ryan's offensive coordinator at a winter practice in 1990

Club president Harry Gamble (left) and Norman Braman immersed in the mandatory post-loss locker-room gloom after a 1988 game

Buddy Ryan and Norman Braman passing like ships in the night in the locker room after Buddy's last game as head coach, a play-off loss to the Redskins, January 5, 1991

Buddy Ryan cheerfully serving a daily helping of Buddyisms to the Pack after a 1990 summer practice

Bud Carson in his obsessive quest for perfection on the sidelines of a 1991 game

Ballet and jazz enthusiast Fred Barnett, the gifted receiver from rural Mississippi who emerged as an NFL star in 1992

Marvin "One-for-One-for-One" Hargrove, the charming walk-on from Willingboro, New Jersey, who talked Buddy Ryan into letting him try out for the team in 1990. He made it in the NFL long enough to have one pass thrown his way, which he caught, for a touchdown.

The smiling Andre Waters, as opposed to his evil game-day alter ego, the Dré Master

Reggie White arrives for the first day of training camp at West Chester in August 1992. He's moving his gear into Gertrude Schmidt dormitory.

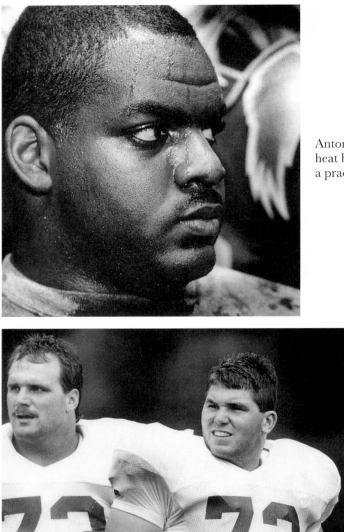

Antone Davis feeling the
heat before his locker after
a practice session in 1992

Ron Heller (73), Dave Alexander (72), and Mike Golic (90) on the practice field
in 1992

Locker-room rat and training-camp joker Jim McMahon mugs for the camera during a practice in 1992.

Jerome Brown (99), Randall Cunningham, and Keith Byars (41) douse Reggie White at practice.

Wes Hopkins cooling off during a practice session

Seth Joyner *being Seth* on the sidelines before an early-season workout in the summer of 1991

Keith "Tank" Byars offering typical encouragement and moral support to Randall Cunningham during a 1992 contest

Ben Smith writhing on the grass after blowing out his knee against the Cleveland Browns on November 10, 1991

Randall Cunningham at home in his Fortress of Solitude. In the foreground is one of the suits of armor from his collection.

Randall Cunningham bites his lip and sheds a tear on the sidelines of the Monday night Eagles-Vikings game, October 15, 1990, as home fans boo his first-half performance and chant "We want Jim!"

Reggie White clowning on the practice field

Keith Jackson hams it up on the practice field in 1991, his last year as an Eagle.

Andre Waters being carted off the field after breaking his left ankle during the October 18, 1992, Redskins game at RFK Stadium. Trainer Otho Davis (right) and assistant trainer David Price give a hand.

Reggie White (foreground) and Seth Joyner show their disgust with the performance of the Eagles' offense during the punchless 16–12 loss to the Redskins at RFK Stadium, October 18, 1992.

The ordinarily sedate Herschel Walker (34) celebrates in the end zone after running for one of his two touchdowns against the Cowboys in the big Monday night showdown on October 5, 1992, won by the Eagles 31–7 at Veterans Stadium.

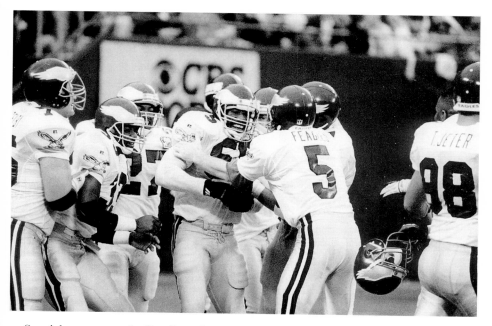

Special teams captain Ken Rose (55, center, clutching the ball) is congratulated by punter Jeff Feagles (5) and his teammates after blocking a punt by Giants kicker Sean Landeta, recovering the ball, and returning it for a touchdown on November 22, 1992, at Giants Stadium.

Seth Joyner (59) sprints to the end zone after picking off a pass by Minnesota Vikings quarterback Sean Salisbury on December 6, 1992, at Veterans Stadium. The fourth-quarter play clinched a 28–17 home victory. He's being trailed by cornerback Eric Allen (21).

In classic form, Randall Cunningham takes flight over Seattle safety Robert Blackmon in a December 13, 1992, marathon game at the Kingdome, which the Eagles won in overtime 20–17.

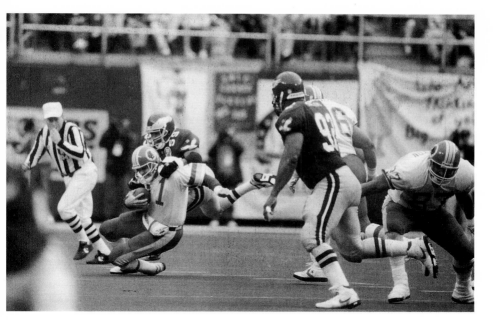

Seth Joyner (59) drags down Redskins quarterback Mark Rypien in a pivotal December 20, 1992, game that the Eagles won 17–13 at Veterans Stadium, clinching a play-off spot.

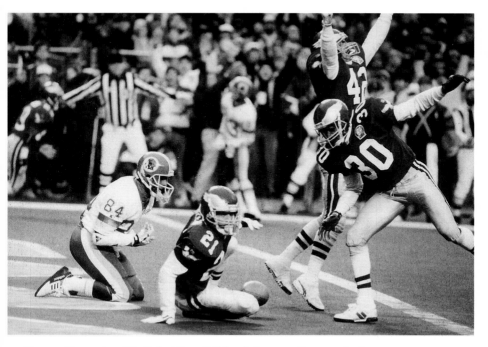

Also on December 20, Eric Allen (21) lands just a split second after a game-saving, season-saving play. He had just dived and slapped the ball away from the outstretched hands of Redskins receiver Gary Clark (84), kneeling in the end zone. Otis Smith (30) was beaten on the play. John Booty (42) celebrates.

January to introduce himself. He took a morning off his work for the beer distributor and was looking pretty sharp in his business suit, all fair-haired six-six, 280 taut pounds of him. Ron was trying to make a good impression, show the new coach what a straightforward, serious-minded kind of guy he was—he figured Perkins would be impressed that, just three weeks into the off-season, he was already at work, wasn't just pissing his time away.

"What're y'all dressed up for?" asked Ray.

Ron told him about the job, and how he'd taken the day off and all.

"How the hell are you gonna work out if you've got a job?"

"When I start my workouts I plan to do them in the mornings and only work afternoons with the company."

"*When* you start?"

Whatever Ron hoped to accomplish by introducing himself, he achieved the opposite. Ray was going to strike the fear of God into this pathetic football team. He ripped into Ron: *You play for a wind-sucking, weak-backed team that goes 2–14, exactly when do you plan to start getting in shape? . . . You want to play football or do you want another job?*

Ron had played for Joe Paterno at Penn State, and Paterno could be tough, but it was always an intelligent, even avuncular, toughness. You always felt no matter how hard Joe rode you, he had your best interests at heart. And Ron had had a terrific rapport with John McKay and Leeman Bennett, Tampa's previous coaches. They had a losing team, sure, but Ron had been treated like a winner, someone the team could build on for a few years. Right from that first day, his impression of Perkins was sour. The new coach seemed neurotically combative, *out to get him!* You couldn't get close to somebody who treated you like the enemy.

"Hey, Coach, how ya doin'?" he asked that summer when work-outs started, showing he didn't hold a grudge.

"Why do *you* want to know?"

"Well, I don't want to know," Ron said, peeved. "I was just trying to be nice."

"Well, if you don't want to know, why don't you just mind your own business."

Of course, ol' Ray was just trying to send a message early to these candy asses. He wanted them to know that things had changed. That summer, in Florida's stifling July heat, he started them on a spartan, pre–training camp regimen of three-a-day, full-pads, rock 'em–sock 'em practices. Ray knew the three-a-days were harsh, but harsh was what this team needed. Ron didn't see it that way. What he saw were guys dropping with stupid practice injuries and wearing themselves down. Ron figured, *Fuck this!* It was hard enough surviving five weeks of training camp and a sixteen-week season intact; he wasn't going to invite injury. He thought Perkins's approach was foolish, self-destructive. (The team did, as it turned out, run out of gas before the season ended, winning four of their first seven games and then losing the last eight.) Shortly after camp started, he asked to be traded, all his happy long-term plans sweated and beaten right out of him.

"Why do you want to be traded?"

"Coach, I don't think we're going in the right direction with these three-a-day practices."

But Ray wasn't about to trade Ron Heller. Ron was the kind of player he needed. He saw him as a potential team leader. But it wasn't Ray's way to flatter a young man into playing hard. He applied the spurs. He told the lineman, in so many words, he was a lazy, overpaid, barhopping pussy who didn't know what real football was.

Ron was miserable. Right on through that summer, and then on into the season, not a week went by without his asking to be traded.

By the thirteenth week of the season, having lost four straight and any chance of making the play-offs, Ray benched veteran quarterback Steve DeBerg, and started his first-round pick, the prize of the '87 draft, Heisman Trophy–winning, undefeated national champion Miami's superquarterback, Vinny Testaverde.

SuperVinny made his debut as a starter on December 6, appropriately in the Louisiana Superdome, against the Saints, who were playing to clinch their first-ever play-off berth. Vinny fumbled the ball away on Tampa's first two possessions, setting up two New Orleans touchdowns in the opening minutes, but then gained his poise. The Bucs battled back to within four points of the Saints at halftime. It was a wild, emotional game. Vinny was on his way to the best passing debut in NFL history (369 yards on twenty-two completions). Saints fans were rocking the Dome, urging their team to hang on, hungry for that first-ever taste of postseason glory.

Ray was understandably wound up in the locker room at halftime. The Bucs still had a shot at a decent, turnaround kind of season at that point. A game like this, coming from behind against a play-off-caliber team with their new, franchise player at the helm—it was the kind of win you could build on. It was a turning point, a moment every fired-up cell in his body told him was pivotal, and he was throwing his whole weight onto the scales, working his Bear Bryant–Don Shula heritage for all it was worth, afire in full-throated philippic, when the ref peeked his head in to say, "Wrap it up, Coach, we need you."

"All right," Ray shouted. "Let's go out there and kick their ass!"

And as the team jumped up, everybody yelling blood oaths and whatnot, Ron was moved by the heroic mood to shout, "Come on, guys, don't quit!"

He was about to finish off with something banal like "We can do it!" when the coach wheeled around and punched him—*bam!*—flat in the mouth.

As he reeled from the initial shock, the big tackle's arms went up, and the coach continued to flail at him.

Ray was shouting *"Quit!? Quit!?"*

Even though he'd just been punched in the mouth, when Ron realized he'd been misunderstood, he started to laugh.

Still fending Ray off, he said, "No, Coach, wait . . . ," trying to explain.

But Ray wasn't about to listen. He was raining blows on Ron's head and chest. Ron again pushed him off.

"I didn't say 'Quit,' " he shouted. "I said, *'Don't* quit'!"

"You can't even *mention* that word in my locker room!" raged Ray.

It was like a superstition with him, that word, but there was nothing spooky or mystical about it. The point was—to the extent that there had to be a point—it was not permissible for the concept "quit" to flash even briefly through the gray matter of a true champion. It was hard as hell to win at this level. The difference between the best and worst teams in the league wasn't that great. And every coach knew you could field the best team, enter a game with the best game plan, and still get stomped. It was, of course, one of the things that made the game so great. You never knew how the ball would bounce. So you assembled the best team you could, prepared them as best you could, and then . . . well, some coaches had lucky hats or pregame rituals or special prayers they said, but with Ray, the secret was to shift to a whole new level of effort, willing yourself (and the team) into a winning frame of mind, and for that you had to banish all negativity, beam the light on every little shadow, chase the very seed of defeat from your mind.

So it didn't matter what Ron *meant*. That was beside the point. He had uttered the word! He had, even indirectly, *introduced the concept*. Punched a pinhole of doubt into the brilliant, blinding vision of victory.

There was, of course, no time to explain any of this—not to say it worked on a logical plane anyway. Ray had reacted instinctively. He would beat the shadow away. It wasn't even Ron Heller he was attacking; it was the idea, the word. He was trying to make a point.

By now, the team had responded the way you would expect football players to respond to a seriously interesting halftime locker-room brawl between player and Coach; they were standing on benches and crowding around, elbowing one another and leaning in to get a better view.

"We need you! We need you!" came the voice of the ref, trying to get the team back on the field.

SuperVinny stepped up and tried to restore order. He grabbed Ray by the back of his sports coat and started dragging him toward the door.

"Jeez, what was that all about?" one of Ron's teammates leaned in to ask.

"I don't know," said Ron, shaking his head and still chuckling a little about the misunderstanding, when he heard someone shout, "Heads up!"

Ron looked up in time to catch the coach, having wriggled out of the sports coat, charging back for more.

Bam! He popped Ron again, right in the face. This time, the lineman slipped and fell, and as he tried to get up on one knee the coach was pummeling him, so—pissed now—Ron wrapped one ham hand around Ray's throat and held him at the length of his very long and thickly muscled arm, digging his fingers into the coach's neck. Ray was still swinging—no give in this guy—but Ron's reach was so long the blows just glanced off his shoulder pads.

"You want to fight? Let's fight," said Ron, the former state heavyweight wrestling champion of New York, releasing his grip on Ray and balling his fists.

The ref was still shouting.

Ray seemed to snap out of it. He took a step back, eyed the two very large padded fists, collected himself, and turned away.

"Let's go," he told the team.

Ron stayed in the locker room. He was confused. One part of him said to hell with this, but the other part said, *You don't go out there now, it's going to hurt your career bad.* Ron had been around the league long enough to know that a fistfight with the head coach—grappling with a High Priest of the Pigskin right inside the temple—could not only get you fired, it would likely get you blacklisted. So would refusing to finish a football game. But the way he was feeling—how could he ever play another down for this asshole? He was still debating with himself when he walked back out. The Saints had already fielded the second-half kickoff and the Bucs' defense was playing. Ron stood with his teammates, holding his helmet, arguing with himself about what he should do, when Ray walked up.

"Hey, man," he said. "Are you all right?"

Ron glared at him.

"I just want you to go out and have a good second half now, all right?" the coach said.

"Don't worry about me, you asshole."

"What's the matter? What's the problem?"

"Fuck you," said Ron, and started to walk away.

Ray grabbed his arm. "Are you all right? I didn't hurt you, did I?"

"Hurt me?" said Ron, trying to laugh. "You didn't hurt me, but I could tell you were trying."

Ron played the rest of the game. What else could he do? The Bucs lost, 34–44. As they filed off the field, Ron thought maybe Ray would apologize. The team had a few private postgame minutes with the coach before the Pack descended. He figured Ray would say something like "Sorry guys, I lost my mind there for a minute." But the coach said nothing, just "All right, hit the showers, let's go."

Ron wasn't about to leave it at that. He stood up and addressed the team, imploring them to keep the halftime altercation to themselves. He was worried about how it would look for him, about getting a reputation for fighting with his coach.

"What happened stays here with the team, okay? We're trying to accomplish something here. If the media gets hold of this, it could only be a negative."

Ron was the last one in the shower room when Ray walked in, fully clothed.

"Hey, I ought to tell you why I did what I did," the coach said, getting thoroughly soaked.

"Yeah, Coach, why's that?" the tackle said.

"You mentioned quitting, and I've never put up with quitters. I hate that word, and when I heard it, I went off. I just won't have it."

Ray was trying to apologize (not an easy thing for a head coach to do to a young player). He felt like he was apologizing anyway, trying to explain that he hadn't meant to attack or insult Ron personally— it was the word, see—but Ron wasn't on the same wavelength. The player felt insulted and unfairly accused. Ron, a highly rational young man, wasn't sure how to cope with such an irrational charge. Everybody knew he hadn't suggested that the team quit—the charge was ridiculous! What kind of damn fool would do a thing like that, even if he did feel that way?

"Wait a minute," Ron said. "Is this an apology?"

Now the coach had his back up again. If Ron didn't recognize an apology he wasn't going to beg.

"Look, I'm just telling you why I did what I did. You seemed to be confused."

"Look, man, I wasn't talking about quitting."

Ray shrugged and walked off. On the plane home, Ron noticed that the coach's hand was iced and bandaged. He had smashed two knuckles. He told the Pack that he hurt his hand when he slipped on the wet floor in the locker room.

Ron finished out the season, and Ray reluctantly agreed to trade him. Tampa dealt him to the Seattle Seahawks for defensive lineman Randy Edwards, who failed to make the Bucs, and a sixth-round draft pick in '89—Ray chose South Carolina linebacker Derrick Little, who likewise failed to make the team. Ray himself got canned in '90, after compiling a distinctly un-Lombardi-like 19–41 record with the Bucs.

Ron, on the other hand, prospered. This Cardinals game, five years later, would be his 117th pro start, his 60th as an Eagle. He would earn $660,000 this season, and he'd be a free agent when his contract came up at the end of the year (he'd make more than $1 million the next year, playing in Miami for Perkins's old head coach Don Shula). He and Heidi built their house in Tampa, an elegant two-story stucco home with a spacious, airy interior, a thirty-foot central ceiling, pool room, state-of-the-art audio-video setup, pool, detached two-car garage with a personal exercise center on its second floor, and just a few blocks away was the marina where Ron kept his boat.

The heat—nah, the heat doesn't bother Ron Heller.

By GAME TIME , shadow has fallen across Sun Devil Stadium's grass and the temperature has dipped to a merely stifling one hundred degrees. A Cardinals night game has a surreal quality. The modernistic stadium has been scooped out of the desert between two stark sienna buttes (one of which is tall enough for locals in beach chairs to perch on for a free view down at the action). The field, a patch of perfectly groomed, almost spongelike prescription grass on a layer of sand and dirt, is the greenest thing in five hundred miles—it's so out of place it seems plastic. Phoenix citizens quickly lost enthusiasm for their fugitive franchise, which has played four losing seasons (and is embarking on its fifth) since fleeing here from St. Louis. The neat rows of silver benches rising high around the field are only about half-filled—just over forty thousand attend, and the majority of them are more watchers than screamers, still waiting for this franchise to show some fire. There's just a fraction of the usual din. When the Eagles open the game with a long, pounding drive of fifteen consecutive plays, setting up a thirty-three-yard field goal, it silences whatever scattered enthusiasm exists. For the last five minutes of the drive, it feels like they're playing with the volume turned off.

Ron checks the game clock overhead—6:25. He does some quick math to figure out how long they held the ball to open the game—eight minutes and thirty-five seconds! He is disappointed they didn't push all the way in for the touchdown, that they had to settle for three points, but the drive was satisfying. They've sent a message. In each of the last two seasons, Phoenix, a lesser team by any measure, has beaten the Eagles in the season's second game. The boys were starting to feel a little spooked about these guys with the funny cartoon redbird heads on the sides of their white helmets. But to open the game just hammering the ball at them downfield like that asserts control.

That's the game plan. If you positioned all four of Phoenix's linebackers on the line, the Cardinals would still be more than 100 pounds lighter than the Eagles' offensive front, reinforced by two tight ends—Pat Beach outside Ron, and Keith Byars outside Antone. So that's what Richie has decided to do. It's steamrollerball. Time to give the revamped front line some confidence, especially the heavyweight right side, where pudgy 330-pound free agent Eric Floyd now lines up inside Antone. To further tip the scales, Richie inserts a *third* tight end, Rob Selby, a wide-bodied 286-pound lineman who ordinarily plays guard. The idea is just to keep ramming your way upfield, grinding out yards, eating up the clock—*They can't score if we don't give 'em the ball.*

Ron loves it. What lineman wouldn't? Their game isn't the stuff of highlights films, the glorious diving catches, the dazzling Gale Sayers–like open-field dances, the splendid gravity's rainbow of a football captured in slo-mo in the stadium lights, spiraling to its distant target. The lineman's game is the loud smack when helmets and pads collide, the hammer, the sudden jolt of contact that stings flesh and bruises bone and sends a dull shock wave down the spine. If there is one thing that separates football players from normal human beings, it's a bit of neurochemical confusion in some obscure hypothalamic juncture where the brain sorts out pleasure and pain. Asked to explain the sensation of a brutal hit, most pro players, even the most articulate, struggle for the right words, but it's clear that they are groping for a way to describe pleasure. Most people recoil from violent contact, the hammer, the nanosecond of blackout as the wet sponge of your brain whacks the inside of your skull, and the subsequent aftershock vibrates down your spinal column to pelvis, femur, fibula, tibia, and toe. The best football players seek it out, dream about it, relish it. For linemen, this is practically the whole thing. A football game consists of sixty or seventy collisions, the initial crack of helmets and pads colliding hard enough to stand two huge men upright, and the brief and artful wrestling match that ensues. Their game is mud and mouthfuls of grass, poked eyes, scraped elbows, blood smears on tight silver pants, fingers crushed between two helmets, or some scrambling 250-pound linebacker landing with his cleats on your arm; it's swearing and pushing and kicking—pulling out of a struggling heap and craning to see where the play has gone. And it's here that Richie is determined to beat the Phoenix Cardinals. *Mano a mano*, brute force against brute force—Hammer Time! It's a strategy designed (and this is part of what Coach is after here) to prove the mettle of his offensive line.

It's Herschel into the right side for three yards, Herschel into the right side seven yards, a quick eight-yard pass out to Fred (keeping them honest), then Herschel into the left side for five yards, Herschel into the right side for two more. . . . Herschel carries the ball eight times on the opening drive and grinds out twenty-five yards. Randall gets thirty-four more on four short passes, the Cards chip in five on an offsides penalty, Ruzek boots the field goal, and the Eagles have a 3–0 lead with more than half of the first quarter gone. They have the upper hand.

The Cardinals had played in sweltering Tampa heat the week before (and lost), and in the game films you couldn't help but notice how spent they were in the second half. Richie figures that if they force Phoenix to spend a second consecutive week playing hard football in a sauna, they will wilt and die. When the Cardinals fail to score on their first possession, the pounding resumes. Working mostly out of the same steamroller formation, again it's Herschel for six, Herschel for three, Herschel for four . . . and just when the Cards figure out this could go on all night, Randall fakes the handoff to Herschel, drops back, and fires a gorgeous fifty-one-yard bomb to Fred. Three plays later, after two more runs, Fred catches a seventeen-yard touchdown pass.

"What a great sequencing of plays!" remarks Pat Haden, the color man for TNT's evening broadcast.

For once on this team, it's the offense that has seized control of a game, and the defense that is having troubles. Despite knocking Phoenix's young starting quarterback, Timm Rosenbach, out of the game with a separated shoulder, the defense struggles in vain to stop backup Chris Chandler's pinpoint passing. Showboat receiver Randal Hill catches a forty-four-yard pass, and then Chandler completes a pass to the end zone. They score again on a forty-six-yard Chandler pass, pulling ahead 14–10 near the end of the first half.

Mindful that hardly a game goes by without Buddy's Boys reminding the offensive line of its inadequacy, particularly that Seth Joyner, Ron leans toward his buddy Dave Alexander on the bench as the kick sails through the uprights and jokes, "Well, I guess I'll have to go down and take a walk by the defensive side of the bench and tell those guys they're not tough enough."

But the Eagles score again before halftime, and after that the game is never in doubt. Boosted by an IV injection of fluids at halftime, Fred catches another touchdown pass in the third quarter, this one a seventy-one-yarder, racing the last fifteen yards into the end zone, holding off beaten cornerback Aeneas Williams with a humiliating straight-arm to his face mask.

"I love Fred Barnett," enthuses Haden to the national TV audience. "I *love* Fred Barnett. He has some very strong hands. He just snatches the ball, and then he gave Aeneas Williams a straight-arm for the last fifteen yards. That's seven catches tonight, 183 yards. And we're still in the third quarter. Seventy-one yards and it's in-your-face!"

The camera also loves Fred. After all those teenage nights of dreaming himself at work on the football field, Fred has all the moves choreographed. He doesn't just play, he performs. After a touchdown catch he poses with feet together and both arms outstretched, holding the football high in one gloved hand, more like a lead dancer stage center at the Met than a receiver doing some personal variation of the touchdown boogie. His first touchdown catch as a rookie, in a Monday night contest against the Vikings, was unforgettable. Fred performed a kind of interpretive dance, later described as an "electric glide," or a "moonwalk," which involved dragging himself into the end zone in slow motion, like a mime stepping through an invisible window, holding the ball in one hand at arm's length and, with a final flourish, dragging it artfully across the "plane of the goal," which is what must officially happen for a touchdown to be scored. In tonight's game, he pops up after one long catch and comically pats the rump of safety Tim McDonald, whom he has just beaten. McDonald responds with a distinctly uncivilized shove and a very rude remark. When cornerback Robert Massey manages to knock a potential third long touchdown pass from Fred's hands in the end zone, the receiver bounces up and leads the scattered applause, clownishly clapping gloved hands together with both arms fully extended. Fred finally leaves the game with severe leg cramps in the middle of a nine-and-a-half-minute fourth-quarter drive, ending a career-best 193-yard, two-touchdown performance, which does a lot, on this national telecast, to spread his growing reputation.

Fred's last touchdown catch and the extra point puts Phoenix down by ten points, so they need to score twice—but Richie's steamroller approach won't give them the ball. The stadium is sullen and the air feels like it's on fire. This being Fan Appreciation Day at Sun Devil Stadium, the team handed out cardboard Cardinals fans on wooden sticks to everybody at the gate before the game. As it becomes apparent that the Cards just can't stop this drive and aren't going to get the ball back in time to catch up, the cardboard fans start flipping out onto the field, and the two-legged fans start heading for the gates.

This is football the way Richie most likes to play it, the Brooklyn Slouch translated into a football strategy, aggressive, fundamental, and demoralizing—*Hey, here we come, whaddayagunnadoabowdit?* By the final quarter of this game, the Cardinals are whipped. Ron can see it. He remembers the feeling from his years in Tampa, where losing was a way of life. The coaches down there would always say, *These guys coming down here aren't used to this heat,* as if it would work to the Bucs' advantage. Ron never bought it. He always figured, these bums just have to finish this game and they're out of here, we're back out practicing in this soup all week, playing in it all year. After losing in Tampa last week, now playing in this home scorcher, the Phoenix defense must feel as if it's descending through the rings of hell.

The drive goes on and on. After the sun sets, the desert sky flashes with lightning like a strobe, but there is no thunder and no rain, which adds to the twilight zone feel. Out on this platform of grass under the lights, the sky flashing, the cardboard fans on sticks whirling down in slow motion like crippled Frisbees from the emptying stands . . . the grim Cardinals players have even given up yelling at each other.

For Ron, the game's best moment comes at the beginning of this final drive. The play doesn't even count; it gets called back on a holding penalty, but it's still Ron's favorite. The Eagles call it the counter OT ("Counter" means the back makes a fake and then runs in the opposite direction of the line's blocking; and "OT" means the offside tackle and guard both pull up from their normal blocks, reverse direction, and race around to run interference for the back downfield.) It isn't one of the Eagles' regular plays, the ones they repeat over and over and over again in practice until they are hard-wired into their brains. They've run it only once or twice in the years Ron has played for Philadelphia.

"Man, I'm glad we repped this," Ron quips to Mike Schad as they break huddle.

But it works like a charm (except for that flag). To Ron, *this* is football. For once he gets to pull out of the trenches, be an athlete instead of a stone. He and Schad churn around the right corner in front of Herschel like runaway earthmovers, Schad flattening a safety and Ron running downfield full speed, scoping the field for someone to hit, and finally unloading with enervating force on a mismatched linebacker, who goes flying. Herschel picks up eleven yards. It feels so good Ron doesn't even care when the refs walk it back.

Then it's back to grinding out the win. The heat, even with the sun down, is unrelenting. Poor big-bellied right guard Eric "Pink" Floyd, his jersey soaked with sweat from his collar to the thick round folds that spill out over the waist of his tight silver pants, feels like he's going to pass out.

"Tone, you gotta help me, you gotta help me," he gasps as they line up to run a sixth consecutive running play.

"You can do it!" Antone urges.

After the play, Pink is down on one knee, breathing hard, gulping the molten air. Dave Alexander urges him back into the huddle.

"You okay?"

"I can make it. I can make it," says the big man, trying to convince himself.

Pink's predicament strikes the other guys as hilarious, mostly because they're winning, which always lightens things up. But it's partly because Pink is always poking fun at himself, at his fatness and slowness and overall seeming unfitness for the role he's being paid so well to play. Pink had proved to be the perfect antidote for Antone's overpaid ennui. Physically, he's like a caricature of the Megapick, carrying the same bulk, but with his distributed mostly in an ample, soft midsection, rather than a million-dollar butt. Unlike Antone, who had been handed big money and a starting job at the gate, Pink had battled every step of the way. He wasn't even drafted coming out of Auburn, and he got cut when he tried out for San Diego in '88. The following year he impressed coaches only enough to be carried on their development squad (translation: he made a good blocking dummy in practice). But Pink persevered. He made the Chargers in '90 and '91, and even played a little. He wasn't taken seriously enough for the team to "protect" him at the end of the '91 season. His size attracted the Eagles' attention early this year when they were shopping around for offensive linemen. When Pink started the Eagles' training camp in summer, a job was by no means assured. But he had made it. After Antone and Pink started four preseason games, coaches liked the way 660 pounds looked together on the right side of the line. And the chemistry worked. For as bored and disheartened as Antone could be, Pink was thrilled just to be around. Nothing bothered him. If he screwed up and the coaches jumped all over him, he'd grin and shrug and work like hell to do better. "Doesn't that bother you when they chew you out like that?" Antone would ask, and Pink would look astonished, "Shit, Tone, they're paying me this kind of money [he made $371,000 in '92]! They can call me any damn thing they like."

Pink was the kind of guy you rooted for, so his struggles in the heat at the tail end of a winning game . . . well, in a way they warmed your heart.

"Antone, you gotta keep me goin'," he pleads, as they line up again.

"Okay, Pink, you can make it," Antone says, wondering what good saying so could possibly do.

They crash ahead for the next play—Herschel runs right behind the two big men, pushing the ball into the Cardinals' territory again.

"Can you make it?" Antone asks Pink, herding him back toward the huddle.

"I can make it," he says, but then, in the next breath, he turns to Alexander and blurts, "I can't make it!"

"Okay, Pink, man, go on out," says Dave, but before he can even finish the sentence the big guard is sprinting for the sidelines like an elephant galloping downhill—the fastest he's moved all evening. They can all identify.

Except Herschel. Herschel seems inhuman. He's on his way to gaining one hundred yards for the second week in a row—for only the second time in his NFL career, and nothing, not the Cardinals, not the heat, *nothing* is going to stop him. During training camp some of the guys made fun of Herschel's excessive work habits. Two grueling practices a day weren't enough for this guy; he was up at 6:00 a.m. every morning to run two miles by himself before breakfast, and in his room, seemingly on the hour, day and night, he would drop to do a hundred sit-ups and a hundred push-ups, accumulating thousands of each over the course of every day. Tonight, they see those efforts paying off. Herschel seems as fresh and eager in the fourth quarter as he was in the first. The Eagles will give him the ball twenty-eight times tonight, and he plays like he wouldn't mind if they gave it to him twenty-eight more. During the clock-eating drive, he carries the ball at one point on seven consecutive plays.

Even some of the guys most skeptical of Herschel when Richie and Harry signed him this summer now find him an inspiration. The Cardinals' linebackers, who outweigh him by fifty pounds, are hitting him for all they're worth, taking out frustrations, piling on, trying to shake the ball loose. Herschel just pops up with a little smirk and says, "Let's go fellas, isn't this fun?" His eyes widen in the huddle as Randall conveys Richie's next play call, to Herschel again.

There is an air of greatness about him on the field. He looks bigger, more formidable, in his uniform, more like the figure who once graced the covers of all those sports magazines. Boundlessly energetic, eager, unfailingly polite—on one of his slams up the middle, he runs full speed into Alexander's backside, knocking the center forward, but keeping his footing and pressing on, and as he churns past to pick up another four yards, he finds time to say, "Sorry, Dave."

His attitude is infectious.

"Get ready, Ron, here we go," he says to the big tackle as they prepare to give him the ball again.

There are just over three minutes left when Phoenix gets the ball back, and Seth Joyner puts the game away. Seth has been having an awful game, one of the worst he's played in years, missing tackles, blowing coverages, drawing penalties, getting outrun by receivers. In the third quarter, running back Larry Centers steps right through Seth for twenty-eight yards. But he rescues his whole off-key performance in the final minutes of the game, as he blitzes and chases down Chandler, drapes his long arms around the quarterback, and slaps the football up and out of his hands—where it is snared by Reverend Reggie right out of the air. Reggie sprints thirty-seven yards for the game's last touchdown—final score 31–14—and Seth is vindicated.

All week the grumpy linebacker will be accepting congratulations on his great game from fans who don't know better. He confesses to friends that an amusing side effect of making the Pro Bowl, and being designated a "great player" on TV, is that it becomes virtually impossible to play a bad game! Fans see, at least in part, what they want to see.

"People been tellin' me all week how great I am," he tells his wife, Jennifer, on the phone later that week. "I can't believe it. I played like shit."

Ron Heller is not among those congratulating Seth. Neither is the rest of the offensive line.

INSIDE THE TEMPLE , Bud Carson is a legend. Long before he had ever been anointed with the headset for a sad, brief tenure in Cleveland, the little white-haired man with the hearing aid and perpetual worried look had already left behind an enviable record as a defensive coach. One of his defenses, the Super Bowl champion Steelers of '75 and '76, was regarded as the best ever, and another, the '79 Rams, rivaled the Steelers' excellence. Bud was a revered master in the temple long before Buddy Ryan began bringing the heat, and long before Art Modell chose him to be head coach of the Browns in '89.

In his first year as head coach, Bud took Cleveland to the AFC championship game, where they were dismantled by the Broncos' sensational quarterback, John Elway.

Bud still has nightmares about Elway.

Denver's quarterback is one of the game's great masters of come-from-behind heroics, a sturdy, smart quarterback with a powerful arm and a gift for avoiding trouble in the backfield, complete with the wholesome corn-fed look of the high Pacific plains, the sandy mop of a teen idol, and a bucktoothed smile that is positively Kennedy-esque.

In Denver's Mile High Stadium, for that AFC championship game on January 14, 1990, the defensive guru and his young, surprising team took on the superstar, and when it was done, Elway had played the game of his life. He threw for 385 yards and three touchdowns, pacing three dramatic second-half drives of 80, 60, and 80 yards to a 37–21 victory.

It wasn't just losing that bothered Bud so much—although that was enough. It was the way he lost. The bucktoothed wonder had embarrassed Bud's defense. The Broncos hadn't won on a few fluky plays, the way many football games are decided, but on a systematic dissection of the Browns' coverage strategies and personnel. When Bud got fired nine games into the '90 season (after losing seven) by the fickle, meddlesome Modell, everybody knew that the critical step over which Bud had stumbled was Elway. Elway had passed Bud Carson out of the job of his life.

That is all fresh in the coach's memory. Only twenty months have elapsed since that game, and twenty months is like yesterday to Bud, who has been coaching football since Khrushchev was pounding tables with his shoe. Bud had signed on with Richie just weeks after Buddy Ryan got the ax. He was a sour and angry man in '91, his tenure as High Priest untimely ended, when he took the rowdy talent Ryan had assembled and coached them into the league's best defense, a defense to rival the legendary ones in his past—rival, mind you.

It was fun that year watching the Pack's efforts to coax hyperbole from Carson over his new team. Buddy Ryan's approach had been to huff and puff an inflated image for his squad and then dare them to measure up. Carson worked the opposite way. His fussy perfectionism was *never* satisfied. If Buddy had huffed and puffed his team's reputation, Carson's very presence was deflating. This green bunch had yet to win a play-off game. In his first weeks on the job, Carson called safeties Wes Hopkins and Andre Waters slow and out of shape and questioned the work habits of the Eagles' defensive line. Even after Gang Green finished the '91 season with the rare trifecta—first in the NFL overall, and first against both the run and the pass—Carson stubbornly (and correctly) refused to compare them with the great defenses in his past: "This is a very good defense," he conceded, "but they haven't been to any Super Bowls yet."

Not yet, anyway. But Bud Carson has a lot more to work with in Philadelphia than he had in Cleveland in '90.

Now Elway is coming to Philadelphia, and Bud is worried. It's been nearly half a century since Bud actually played football as a defensive back in North Carolina, so the game for him long ago drifted away from the physical realities of the field. Bud doesn't even picture football the way most people do. Fans watch from the relatively low angle of seats in the stadium or, worse, from the narrowly framed action on their TV sets—beneath layers of often unreliable commentary. To Bud the game is best viewed from directly overhead, in silence, from enough distance that the whole field of play can be seen. From this Coach's-Eye View, players can be distinguished only by number and position on the field. They move—or are supposed to move—in a carefully choreographed pattern, reacting to the play as it unfolds, surely, but reacting within carefully proscribed limits, holding their positions. The goal of the offense is to draw or knock defenders out of position, fool them or tempt them with indirection and fakes, or hammer them down with a bone-rattling block, but if the players are strong enough and smart enough to hold their positions and make the plays when the ball comes their way, the offense will not only fail to score, it *won't even be able to advance the ball.*

Chain-smoking in his windowless office as he pores over computer breakdowns of opponents' tendencies, moving salt and pepper shakers and napkins around the table over dinner with his wife, preaching precision to defensive backs in front of a screen in a darkened meeting room, scratching his head on the sidelines when he encounters something unexpected . . . Bud's game is an abstraction, a live-action chess game in which the pieces don't always move the way they're supposed to, and where checkmate ideally comes with a punishing hit. Bringing the heat is an important part of Bud's philosophy—essential, really—but only a part. It is equally important to learn where, how, and when the heat should be applied. Buddy Ryan is connoisseur of the blitzkrieg, Bud Carson is battlefield technician.

Let's see . . . there're eleven guys on offense. Five of them have to block. That leaves a quarterback and five players to mind. How many ways can a team use those six players to move the ball? What's the best way to arrange your eleven people to stop them? How does this particular team usually try to move the ball? On first down? Second and long? Second and short? Third and long? Third and short? In the plus-twenty? Deep in their own half of the field? When it lines up three wide receivers on one side, how often does it run? When it passes, where do the passes usually go? If the running back lines up two steps to the right, does that mean the team is more likely to run the ball? If so, where?

Angst-ridden, fidgety, obsessed, Bud's goal every week is to think of everything, and after twenty-one years of coaching NFL defenses, he's pretty sure it's doable. His requests for the computer folks who help the Eagles create each game plan are notoriously voluminous and specific. Many of the older coaches (Bud is sixty-two) disdain heavy use of the computer, relying on their experienced feel for the game. Not Bud. The computer was made for Bud Carson; it enables him to do better what he's been doing successfully for so long, dissecting offenses so thoroughly that, by game time, he's inside the mind of the opposing coach—and quarterback.

All week Wes, Andre, Byron, and Seth, the field generals of Bud's secondary, and the front line of Reggie, Clyde, Mike Golic, and newly acquired former Bills lineman Leon Seals have been listening to Bud fret about Elway. The last time the Eagles faced Elway, in '89, the bucktoothed wonder scrambled for forty-five yards and one touchdown and threw for 278 yards and two more touchdowns!

Yeah, Coach, but we intercepted him three times and we won the game!

But that was three years ago. Elway has gotten smarter, better! Besides, how many times can you expect to win when you let a guy gain 323 yards and score three TDs? Bud has hammered home the four basic tenets of Stopping Elway 101: (1) Don't let him escape the pocket; he's most dangerous when he can buy time by fleeing the rush. (2) If he does scramble, it's imperative that defensive backs *stay on their receivers*. (3) If he breaks out of the pocket, don't let him run to his right; he's right-handed and can throw with accuracy running that way. (4) If he starts running to his right, don't let him set his feet— otherwise, he'll kill you deep.

The guys have to chuckle about how nervous Bud is. After all, Elway and the Broncos haven't exactly been lighting up the league in their first two games this year. They won both, but just barely, and their running game is ranked near the bottom of the league. But right up until just minutes before game time he's still at it, back in his smoke-filled space fiddling with coverages, checking the computer analysis one more time, trying to think of *everything*.

And this time Bud very nearly does. Elway never even gets started this Sunday. Game three, a dazzling autumn afternoon so mild that most of the crowd at Veterans Stadium is in shirtsleeves, is one of those rare football games that goes almost exactly according to plan— Bud's plan, that is. It's a study in defensive perfection, a window into the mind of a defensive master.

On his second play of the game Elway completes a pass to Victor Jones, who races for sixteen yards before Eric Allen drags him down— and it's all downhill for the Broncos from there. Denver is stopped short on the next two plays, so they need eight yards on third down, a sure passing situation. Bud sends in his dime squad, a formation featuring six defensive backs and only one linebacker. The Broncos line up three receivers split wide to the left and one split wide right— and they shift their sole running back about three steps to the left of Elway; it's this that catches Seth's eye.

This is one of the clues Bud mined last week from his exhaustive study of Denver's offense. When the running back shifts left in this formation, it means he nearly always will be running a pass route to the left flat. Because the left side (seen from Elway's perspective) is already flooded with three pass catchers, tying up the left-side coverage scheme, it will force Seth to pick up the fourth, a wide receiver, in this case Mark Jackson, if he comes streaking across the middle of the field. The back half of the strategy exploits coverage on the right side. The standard third-and-long coverage of the sole receiver split right will require the safety (Andre) to pick him up short with help from the cornerback deep. If you send the right side receiver racing straight upfield, which is the plan, then both Andre and the cornerback, Izel Jenkins, will be drawn deep. Denver's play, in a nutshell, is designed to bottle up most of the defensive secondary to the left while matching a speedy receiver one-on-one with Seth, a bigger, slower man, angling upfield to the right. If both Andre and Izel can be suckered upfield in coverage, Jackson should have plenty of room to run if he can outpace Seth and catch the ball.

Only, Seth spots Bud's clue (the running back split left) and, as instructed, starts shouting "Bronco! Bronco!" kicking his right leg to get the message out to the teammates split wide. The call frees Andre from helping out with the right-side receiver, dropping him into the deep middle zone, where he's free just to move to the ball.

The play works perfectly. Jackson races across, easily outpacing Seth, catches Elway's perfect short pass in stride and . . . Hammer time! Andre will roll his eyes with pleasure describing the hit later on. He had awakened this morning with a wicked crick in his neck and had been trying to work it loose ever since. Jackson sprints across the middle like an invitation for a spinal adjustment, Andre just hanging back in the deep middle, admiring the angle he has for a shot on Jackson (blind side, just over forty-five degrees, allowing maximum impact with minimum warning), so perfect he's afraid to believe Elway will actually let this happen—*No, he's not goin' to throw the ball to this man*—and then seeing the ball caught and just launching himself from a running start, elbows up in front of his face, eyes closed (gone ballistic now), he arrives at Jackson's head just a split second after the ball. Jackson crumples as if he's been hit by a locomotive, two yards short of the first down, and recovers his wits just in time to relocate the ball, which has popped free. The stadium erupts with a scrotal roar, the defense swarms Andre, pounding him on the head—*Hey, the crick is gone!*—and the Broncos have to punt.

Andre's neck adjustment sets a vicious tone. All afternoon Bud has Elway off stride. Seth slaps away his first pass on the next series, and when the Broncos next try to run a simple running play up the middle, they are met by a defensive line stunt that has both ends taking one step back and swinging around inside their own tackles, screwing up the running lanes and blocking assignments so that Reggie, Clyde, and linebacker Byron Evans all meet the running back in the middle—*crunch!*

Faced with third and eight, the Broncos line up four receivers, and the running back shifts three steps to Elway's left. Again, this alerts the defense that the back may be running a short pass route to the left flat. This time, it's Andre who changes the call, shouting "Key! Key!" to announce that he will pick up the running back. If the back doesn't come out, Andre becomes a free man in the short secondary policing against the run. On this play, the back stays in, and when Elway shovels the ball to receiver Shannon Sharp on a running play, Andre again is primed and ready. Diving through the phalanx of big blockers, the safety performs one of his patented submarine tackles, hitting the six-two, 230-pound Sharp at the ankles and literally upending him. The picture will be the centerpiece of tomorrow's sports page, the big receiver flying through the air upside down, with Andre, prone on the turf, looking back over one shoulder, admiring his work.

Again and again, throughout the game, Bud's defense anticipates Elway's moves and, with complex, shifting pass coverages and occasional line stunts, shuts down play after play. Nothing Denver does works. The defensive guru is pacing the sidelines the whole time, nervously consulting his play list, muttering to himself and conferring with his assistant, Peter Guinta, who's in the booth upstairs. If Bud is taking any pleasure in this, it doesn't show. On their third possession, the Broncos lose two yards—punt. On their fourth, they can only gain eight yards in three plays–punt. On their fifth possession, five yards—punt.

Meanwhile, the Eagles' offense is having another big day. Randall is putting on a stylish show, the best he's looked so far this year, taking off on one classic, swivel-hips open-field run for twenty-nine yards and throwing two touchdown passes in the first half, one to Fred and the other to Calvin Williams. Richie has forsaken the steamroller this week, the three-tight-ends formation that he used against the Saints and Cardinals. Today the offensive workhorse is Keith Byars, who moves back and forth from tight end to running back from play to play, allowing the Eagles to change formations without changing personnel—which doesn't give defenders time to react. At the end of the first half, the Eagles lead 17–0.

In the NBC-TV studios in New York, during the halftime show, who should appear behind the desk to deliver news and analysis but Buddy Ryan, in white shirt and red paisley tie, his round face looking tense, his straight white hair surprisingly long and combed over to the side—which, on Buddy, manages to look like a pathetic attempt to tart himself up for the camera. With his reputation for being a comedian, Buddy has been invited in by the network for a few tries at commentary like this. They are, in a sense, screen tests. The network sports execs figure a guy like Buddy can't miss, just sit him in front of the camera and let 'er rip! Right? But just as the crew of youngsters back in West Chester had learned a few years back, Buddy's wit is entirely situational and often inadvertent. Away from his role on the sidelines or in the locker room it fades. On camera now, he looks stiff and uncomfortable, out of place. When he does speak, he says something obvious. He sounds dumb—which he isn't.

What he has managed to do at every public appearance, however, beginning with the ghostwritten column in the *New York Times* on the day after the '91 NFL draft, is make the case that Richie is mishandling his old team. Of course, with the Eagles having won their first two games this year and now soundly thumping the undefeated Broncos, it's getting harder and harder to do.

Today the old coach is on his best behavior, and it takes an experienced Buddy watcher to discern the subtext.

"You can't say enough about the Eagles' defense, of course. On offense, the first big play they had was a scramble by Randall to set up the score. So both sides of the ball are doing well in Philadelphia. The defense is just smothering." (Subtext: *They're winning because of my great defense. The offense is doing well because they have Randall Cunningham, not because Richie Kotite is doing anything special.*)

Elway gets his chance on the first possession of the second half. Punt returner Arthur Marshall sprints forty-seven yards to push the Broncos into the Eagles' half of the field for the first time in the game—jump start for yet another Elway comeback . . . Bud can just see it. Positioned on the Eagles' twenty-eight-yard line, Denver is already in range for a forty-five-yard field goal (the posts are ten yards behind the goal line, and the kicker lines up about seven yards behind the ball). But it's not going to happen.

First and ten on the Eagles' twenty-eight: Denver lines up three wide receivers, which would ordinarily force Bud to deploy his nickel defense (five defensive backs). The nickel trades linebacker William Thomas for a smaller, faster defender, Otis Smith, so it improves pass coverage at the expense of muscle against the run. Only, Bud knows the Broncos like to run from this formation, especially deep in an opponent's territory, so he gambles. The Eagles go with "regular people," their normal four down linemen, three linebackers, two cornerbacks, and two safeties. And the Broncos, confirming Bud's hunch, try to run. Seals fends off his blocker and wraps up the ballcarrier after a two-yard gain.

Second and eight on the Eagles' twenty-six: Now the Broncos have to pass. They line up three receivers, two split wide to Elway's left, one wide right. The Eagles must also cover a tight end and the running back lined up in the backfield.

The play demonstrates the complexity of pro schemes. Bud breaks down the defense into four parts, left-side pass coverage, right-side coverage, middle coverage, and the pass rush. In this case, left-side pass coverage consists of three defenders playing a combination of man-to-man and zone. Cornerbacks Eric and Otis each have a receiver man-to-man, with Andre playing farther upfield, defending the deep zone in case one of these two receivers breaks upfield. On the right side, Izel is all by himself; he has man-to-man coverage on his receiver all the way upfield. In the middle, coverage is man-to-man: safety Wes Hopkins will cover the tight end if he comes out on a pass route, and Byron Evans will pick up the running back. As for the rush, Bud has called a blitz. He's going to send Seth after Elway on the right side. And the line, just to mix things up further, will try a stunt—instead of rushing straight at the quarterback, Reverend Reggie will swing around from his position on the end (Elway's right) and attack up the middle.

The play takes about five seconds to happen, but to the men in the thick of it, time slows. Much happens in five seconds. On the snap, Elway drops back and checks his receivers, all of whom are covered (two seconds). Seth's rush from the right forces him to step up in the pocket, which is supposed to make the middle linebacker charge, leaving the running back, who has slipped out on a pass route, wide open. Only, Byron doesn't bite. He wheels around and hangs back, so Elway still has no open receiver (two seconds). The tight end has stayed in to try to block Seth, so Wes is free and is now zeroing in to put the hammer on Elway. Clyde, who all afternoon has been beating the rookie tackle trying to block him, collapses the pocket to Elway's left, so the bucktoothed one scoots right, only to confront Mike Golic, who has fought off his blocker. He dodges to his left, right into the arms of Reggie, who—remember?—has swung over to the middle (one second). The quarterback is sacked for a three-yard loss, which is actually a good thing for Elway, because if Reggie doesn't grab him,

Wes is about to arrive with a full running start from the front, and Seth, having shaken off the tight end, is about to unload from behind— Seth ends up having to hurdle Reggie to avoid hitting Elway late.

Third and eleven on the Eagles' twenty-nine: Bud sends in his dime squad, taking out Byron and substituting smaller, faster John Booty and substituting Andy Harmon for Mike Golic (Harmon is smaller and less experienced, but a better pass rusher). Again, there are complex pass-coverage assignments to the right, center, and left, mixtures of man-to-man coverage and zones. All week, Bud has stressed the importance of not allowing Elway to break away from the pass rush and scramble to his right and has stressed that *if this does happen,* defensive backs must bump their receivers and hang on tight.

This time, desperate, Elway does break free and does scramble to his right, athletically slipping away from what appears to be certain tackles by Reggie and Andy Harmon, and scooting toward the sideline with Clyde in hot pursuit. And in one of the rare Eagles' mistakes this game, Andre fails to stay with his receiver, Mark Jackson. Andre catches a glimpse of Elway breaking free, so he turns back to pursue, and Jackson races upfield, wide open, waving his arms in the air to catch Elway's attention. Izel, who has a deep middle zone, spots the mistake and races after Jackson, arriving just a split second after the pass, which is caught on the one-yard line before Jackson's momentum carries him out-of-bounds.

But the play is called back. Bud is standing on the sidelines gesturing frantically at the scrimmage marker. Elway, fleeing Clyde, had stepped across the scrimmage line before throwing the ball. The pass comes back, so instead of taking over with a first down on the one-yard line, Elway loses the down and is penalized another five yards, which pushes the Broncos back to the Eagles' thirty-four-yard line, and out of field-goal range.

Denver is demoralized. Ever gracious in victory, the Eagles' defense taunts the Broncos gleefully as the clock winds down. As the orange-jerseyed players break huddle and approach the line, they're greeted by a chorus.

"Come on, run at me!"

"Hey, try that stupid slant play again, I like that one!"

"Yo, Elway, that ain't gonna work!"

"Don't bring that shit this way!"

The Eagles score again on the next possession and then intercept Elway when the Broncos get the ball, and Randall throws another touchdown pass . . . the game turns into a rout. Denver coach Dan Reeves throws in the towel when the score reaches 30–0, sending in his second string.

Bud waits until there is less than a minute in the game before he removes his headset, smiles, and congratulates his players on the bench. "We figured he wanted to wait until he was sure we had it," jokes Golic. It is only the second time in Elway's career that he has been shut out.

"They're known for their great defense, and they proved it today," Elway calmly acknowledges afterward. "They just manhandled us."

The highly credible Bill Parcells, the former Giants two-time Super Bowl–winning coach who is now working as a commentator for NBC Sports, validates the emerging stature of this '92 Eagles team, now 3–0 in the season.

"This team is definitely capable of beating anybody in the National Football League," he says. "In the past, once in a while, they would self-destruct and give games away and lose to people that they shouldn't lose to, but I see a greater sense of purpose here with the Eagles this year."

Lying in wait for Bud as he emerges from the locker room is a TV reporter, determined to extract a rare mote of high praise from the defensive master. One can only imagine—nostalgically—what verbal excesses Buddy Ryan might have reached after a rout like this. The Broncos were not only shut out, they were held to eighty-two yards! Surely now, after this performance, Bud would be ready to acknowledge that this Eagles defense deserved to be considered with the very best that ever played the game.

"This is truly amazing," the reporter says, priming the moment for the home audience, diminutive Bud squinting up at the camera alongside him. "To hold a team like Denver, and a quarterback like Elway to just eighty-two yards, isn't that a first?"

Bud grimaces, the face of a man who knows too much. "Well, maybe it is *here*," he says.

There isn't time to go into it on the air, see, but what about the time his '79 Rams held the Seattle Seahawks to a grand total of minus-seven yards? *That's* the NFL record. Sure, today was pretty good, but, you know, it wasn't perfect or anything. Andre had missed that tackle in the first series, and where was Otis on that second-and-ten play in the fourth quarter? And on that play when Elway scrambled, what was Jackson doing open down there on the one? Sure, it got called back, but mistakes like that can hurt you down the road. Bud still hasn't figured out what happened there.

He's going to have to talk with these guys.

8

IS DADDY'S BRIDGE BROKE?

Erika Hopkins knows what this is. The ultimate betrayal.

In the private lounge for the Eagles' wives, girlfriends, and family, she has just introduced herself to this luscious cookie as the wife of veteran free safety Wes Hopkins.

"That's strange," says the woman.

After nine seasons in Philadelphia, Wes is one of the team's best-known players, and Erika, a chatty, stylish woman with a lively wit, is president of the Association of Eagles' Wives. She makes a point of greeting newcomers to the wives' lounge at the Vet before games. Outside on the street-level concourse thousands of fans are in motion, buying food and beer, meeting up with friends, getting ready to find their seats for the Eagles-Broncos game. This being only the second home game of the season, Erika hasn't seen all the new faces yet.

"What's strange?" she asks.

"Oh, it's just that . . ." and the woman hesitates, sensing she might be stepping in something.

"What?"

"Oh, it's just silly. But I just saw a girl out in the food area and some guy was trying to hit on her, and she turned around and said, 'Look, you don't know who you're talking to. I'm Wes Hopkins's wife.'"

Erika wants to laugh—you know, *Isn't that just rich!* She actually gets out, "You've got to be joking!" But she knows the rest of the women—her friends—standing around watching now aren't fooled. They sense the anguish; they catch the flush in her cheeks. They know.

That's what's so excruciating about this, see? *They all know!*

"Who?" Erika asks. "I mean, what did she look like?"

"Blond white girl."

Erika exits, a short, buxom beauty with big brown eyes and smooth skin the color of cappuccino. Erika looks fabulous, copper-colored hair, subtle makeup, gold earrings and bracelets, ivory lace vest, and gold-tassled pinstripe blazer over black stirrup pants and black ankle boots. But, hey, they *all* look fabulous. All the female ornaments of the young gods about to do battle, assembled here on the green-and-silver furnishings in the wives' lounge, all of them are stunning—drop-dead slender in tights or designer jeans, colorful sweaters or leather jackets, glittering jewelry, stylish ankle boots or sleek gator-skin cowgirl boots (the white girls lean toward Western chic), their exquisite features perfectly painted, framed by a nova of hair that's been teased, sculpted, tinted, and set with all the cunning of modern hairdressing arts. These are the women who share the dream, the cover-girl lovelies who share the family portraits in the glossy NFL *GameDay* magazine, life partners of these men who own the top rung of the chaw-chomping, testosterone ladder of red-blooded American manhood. These women are the real thing, not the symbolic trophies down there jumping around on the sidelines in skimpy out-fits with pom-poms and titties bouncing, not the camp-following Sis-Boom-Bimbos, these are the she-gods impressive enough to tame and bridle these men's men and lead them to the altar, bear their robust children, share their suburban tract mansions, their luxurious foreign cars, public appearances . . . their whole glorified, charmed lives.

Holding on to these boys, however, has its price.

Erika goes straight to the will-call ticket window next door.

"Hi, Erika!" says the girl behind the counter—everybody around here knows and likes Erika.

"Wes and I have some friends coming in for the game today, and I didn't write the ticket numbers down. Could you look them up for me?"

Armed with section and row, Erika strides out into the busy concourse and locates the section. It's about a half hour before kickoff now; Wes is out on the field with his teammates, stretching, running perfunctory drills—*There he is, number 48!*—only Erika is not watching the field.

She walks up the ramp, and standing on tiptoe, counting down the rows, she locates her husband's complimentary seats. Blond white girl and guy. The girl is . . . she's terrific, early twenties, perfect petite Anglo features. How many times has she heard Wes say it about white girls? *If you gotta have it, it better be gorgeous.* So Erika knows who this is.

She walks down the steps and stops right in front of the young white couple.

"Excuse me, is your name Amy?" she asks.

The blond smiles. "Yes, it is."

Amy.

It's been three months since Erika found the envelope lying on the passenger seat of Wes's car. On the outside, in loopy, hyperfeminine script, was written "Wesley." Erika opened it.

"I'm so looking forward to our trip away"—Wes was leaving to do a weekend football camp for a friend in Indianapolis in two days— ". . . I'm going to love you morning, noon and night . . . I'm sorry I've been fussing at you lately, but my mother told me that you need to make a decision. . . ." *A decision?*

Erika had to drive her mother home before meeting Wes. It gave her time to think before she confronted him. As she would remember it, she pounced as he stepped into the car.

"Okay, what the hell is this!" brandishing the note. "Who is this person? What the hell are you doing?"

Wes didn't lie. Cool Wes. Cold Wes.

"It's nobody."

"Oh, so nobody is writing this!" She waved the note at him. "Nobody is going with you to Indianapolis?"

There was silence for a moment as they drove. Then Wes said, calmly, "Her name is Amy."

"Amy what?"

The last name sounded German, or Norwegian.

"She's white?" Erika was shouting.

"Yeah, she's white."

This was trouble. This was different than the other times. Erika knows Wes has had women before. Since they were married, back in February of '87 out in L.A., there has been a string. It has torn her up. But what could she do? He was Wes Hopkins of the Philadelphia Eagles, number 48, Pro Bowl free safety, handsome, successful, smart, well-to-do (actually not, but more on that later).

And the Sis-Boom-Bimbos were everywhere, in the bars where Wes liked to hang out one night a week with his teammates—Erika allowed that; she was no tyrant—in the hotel lobbies when they traveled, at the public appearances where Wes signed autographs. It was part of the life. The athletes expected it, the way they expected their gear to be laid in their lockers on game day. Wes and Erika had never fully worked through the issue of other women before they married. It hadn't seemed necessary. Their wedding had come after Wes's injury, when his career was in jeopardy and his finances in ruins, when he had temporarily fallen off the golden chariot.

WES HOPKINS HAD two faces. If you met him out of uniform at a bar or at one of his public appearances or even in the locker room, he had a ready smile and charming sense of humor. He had thick eyebrows over intelligent eyes, a mustache, a distinctive widow's peak that came to a point at the center of his forehead. Wes wasn't a giant, and his body wasn't especially well built. He had bandy legs, particularly his surgically repaired left knee, which looked as if it had been reset at the wrong angle. His warmth and social ease stood out in a group that was distant, surly, and self-important. The Pack loved Wes. You could hold an easy conversation with him. In a pinch you could call him at home. He made eye contact. He was generous with his time and insights; he treated the hounds like people. And, God, were they grateful. They bestowed their annual Good Guy Award on him in '91.

But on the field and to those closest to him, Wes was also something else. On the field he was feared, a vicious hitter who seemed to take a lifetime's anger out on anybody who entered his space. His teammates, even players who prided themselves on the violence of their play, would describe him as "mean"—and not just in the admiring way football players do, but earnestly, touching on something deeper than professional toughness. "Understand me," one confided, "Wes is truly a mean man." Oddly, this was the side of his personality that Wes would sometimes show those closest to him, his family, his wife. They used the words "silent" and "cold" mixed in with the softer "shy" and "private." "He'll never have a big phone bill," says his mother, Maggie. "He never stays on the line for more than about fifty seconds." It was as though Wes, who could be so jovial with strangers, resented intimacy and guarded his inner self as jealously as he guarded the passing lanes in the Eagles' secondary.

Like so many of his black teammates—Byron, Seth, Andre, and Clyde—Wes was raised by a devoted, strong, willful single mother. Maggie worked as a practical nurse and sent her three children to Catholic schools in Birmingham, Alabama. Maggie says that she never sought or received a cent of support for her children—she would have considered it demeaning. She worked double shifts to pay the bills, leaving the children with her parents. She made it on her own.

Wes was her baby. She saved pictures of him in thick albums, as a toddler, wearing a dress, sitting on a potty, in his altar boy cassock and surplice, in his football uniform, and in the pink leisure suit and giant Afro, posing with his date at John Carroll High School's senior prom. He was, she says, a silent boy who loved just one thing, playing football.

He was a good football player in high school, but not great. He owed his career to his uncle, Maggie's brother, Jimmy Lee. Jimmy is a tall, dapper smoothy, a former executive with IBM and Xerox with an entrepreneurial soul. Uncle Jimmy would visit several times a year and, at Maggie's urging, took an interest in his fatherless nephew. Jimmy seized upon Wes's love of football as common ground and, seeing a spark of talent and desire in the boy, blew it into real fire. He watched Wes play running back for the high-school team and told his nephew he thought he could play college ball, maybe even pro. On one trip to Birmingham, Uncle Jimmy bought the boy jogging shoes and a sweat suit and helped him map out a daily routine of running and lifting.

Jimmy had credibility in this area, because while living in Dallas as a recruiter for Xerox, he had gotten to know some of the town's pro athletes. He introduced Wes, then a high-school freshman, to Cowboys receiver Drew Pearson. Just being able to meet someone like Pearson brought the dream more within reach. It made a big difference. And when no recruiters came to Wes during his senior year, sweet-talking Jimmy set out to promote the boy.

He encouraged Wes to apply to Southern Methodist University in Dallas, and when Wes was turned down for academic reasons, Jimmy put on a full-court press. He argued with the university about their admissions standards, and through a friend who was a major alumni supporter of SMU's football program, he convinced Ron Meyer, the new coach, to take a look at his nephew. Jimmy brought Wes in to run some time trials, and Meyer wasn't impressed. Too slow, too small. "Are you kidding me?" he asked Uncle Jimmy.

It's a tribute to Jimmy's persuasiveness that he worked a deal with SMU to enroll Wes in summer school, and if he could earn a C-plus average, he would be allowed to enter as a freshman. Meyer said the kid could try out for the team, but not as a running back. He said he would work with him as a defensive back, and if Wes could make it . . . well, then they would see about a scholarship. Wes moved to Dallas that summer and assumed a supervised regimen of schoolwork and physical training. Jimmy drove Wes to school in the morning and picked him up in the afternoons—*You've got something to prove to these people, Wes. They don't think you can make it. You're going to have to become a student of the game . . . learn it, not like a player, but like a coach.* Back home, Maggie borrowed from everyone she knew to pay Wes's tuition until he earned the scholarship. She was betting on him.

Wes made it. He was awarded the scholarship that freshman fall.

Maggie started paying people back. In his sophomore year, Wes started at free safety and shifted to strong safety in his junior and senior years. He wasn't particularly fast, but he played smart, and when he hit somebody the player had a hard time getting up. He impressed pro scouts in his senior year when SMU beat Pitt in the Cotton Bowl, virtually shutting out highly regarded quarterback Dan Marino (Pitt scored just three points).

Maggie was working in the day-surgery clinic, catching glimpses of the NFL draft on TV, the day Wes was picked in the second round by the Eagles. With Uncle Jimmy handling the deal, he got a $175,000 bonus and a four-year contract with a starting salary of $120,000 and a final year salary of $200,000—the total package was for almost $800,000! He left school without collecting his degree (promising his mother he'd go back) and bought himself a condo and a Porsche, which Uncle Jimmy helped him drive up to Philly. Jimmy found it hard to leave him alone like that in the big city; the kid had come so far so fast . . . he seemed unformed.

Jimmy Lee had started to notice something about Wes and the other kids who played college football—even some who made the pros. They didn't grow up. Through his recruiting work, and from his own background as a college basketball player, Jimmy Lee knew many athletes, but mostly basketball and football players. The football players were different, he thought, more vulnerable, particularly the black ones. Basketball players came from more diverse backgrounds. There were as many from big cities as there were from small towns, as many from middle-class backgrounds as from the projects. A higher proportion of the football players came from stark poverty, from the high-school football mills of the Deep South. A disproportionate number had been raised without fathers. Basketball teams were small, just five guys on the court at one time, so each man had a stronger individual identity. It was the more glamorous of the sports, attracting the best athletes and awarding them with a very high profile—so, in time, they tended to develop poise. Football players, on the other hand, were seen only from a distance, encased in helmets and pads; their identity was more team than individual. The appeal of football was as much *belonging* as doing. There was something in the nature of football, maybe it was the violence, that grouped players in herds. He had thrown corporate recruiting parties and invited young men who played both sports, and, for the most part, the basketball players blended well. No matter what their origins, they became more confident and articulate with each passing year. But not the football players. They arrived, stayed, and left as a herd. They'd be off in the corner joking with one another, enjoying themselves, but when you pulled one away from the group, he'd close up, turn awkward, sullen, and forlorn. The seniors were often as bad as the freshmen. They depended on one another. With fifty or more players on a roster, there were more football players than any other athletes in the athletic dorms, so even there they tended to form their own community . . . or, the more Jimmy thought about it, their own family. For some of these boys, Team was the only family they had known.

This family was a fraternity of cocky, isolated, indifferent young men whose strongest attachments were no longer to Mom or Uncle or brother or girlfriend or wife, but to one another. The herd was managed carefully by the school's athletic department. In the dorm their rooms were picked up and their laundry cleaned; their meals were waiting in the cafeteria; for out-of-town games they were steered to buses and led to planes by handlers, then herded back on buses and assigned hotel rooms—there were players who, after tens of thousands of miles of air travel, hadn't a clue how to get to the airport, check luggage, buy a ticket, find a gate, book a hotel room, and get to the hotel when the plane landed. Team handled these things, just as it arranged for study halls and tutors to coax players through the minimal academic load required by the NCAA and found them "jobs" (this was usually a laugh) donated by gung ho alumni as an excuse to give the boys walk-around money and a nice car. For the lucky few who went on to the pros, the pattern continued. The club helped them find an apartment, a car, handled all travel plans, set their work schedule, and even booked their public appearances. Consequently, many of these young men remained virtually helpless outside the herd. You couldn't get close to football players who were in this mode, couldn't interest them in thinking beyond next week. So there was no way to prepare them for the inevitable fall. Inevitable, because the football team—especially the pro team—was no conventional family. It was strictly an arrangement of convenience, ruled by Coach. There was nothing permanent about your status; in fact, your standing with Team could (and usually did) end abruptly, without warning, because of injury, a new coach, a younger player who was better, or just a change of Coach's mind.

Any worries Uncle Jimmy had about Wes that day, when he dropped him off in the big city, evaporated fast, because Wes was an even bigger hit at the pro level than he had been in college. He became a starter after the second game of his rookie season, in his second season was voted first alternate NFC safety to the Pro Bowl, and in his third was the team's MVP and went to Hawaii that winter to start for the NFC in the Pro Bowl. Wes was twenty-five years old and at the top of the game. His new contract with the Eagles would make him a millionaire.

Erika met him that winter on a blind date. She living in L.A., where she had just graduated from Loyola Marymount, and was dating Malcolm Barnwell, a former Raiders wide receiver, when her friend Simone called and asked if she would join her on a casual date with two pro players in town, Harvey Martin and Wes Hopkins—*Hey, forget Malcolm, this guy Wes is starting in the Pro Bowl!* Wes was in California to see the Super Bowl in Stanford. He and Erika were a couple instantly. Wes had a girlfriend back in Philadelphia, but it was Erika who went with him the following week to Honolulu for the Pro Bowl game. She was a handful. Pretty, funny, and brassy, Erika had the self-esteem to stand her ground with a big football star. She had a sarcastic wit that kept Wes slightly off balance, while at the same time attracting him. They talked on the phone every day that spring, commiserating over the problems he was having with his then girlfriend (of course, Erika was quickly becoming the main problem), the financial troubles brewing with Uncle Jimmy in Dallas, the inexplicable hostility of this new head coach they'd hired in Philadelphia . . . Erika listened and joked and advised, bucking up Wes's spirits. Presently, Erika became his primary road squeeze—she flew around the country for a series of romantic rendezvous.

The new coach, of course, was Buddy Ryan, who promptly served notice on the batch of boobs, malingerers, and losers who had compiled the Eagles' 7–9 season in '85 that their days in green and silver were numbered.

At first, none of this bothered Wes. Of all the returning Eagles, he felt the most secure. What team wouldn't want Wes Hopkins on its roster? He had youth and proven talent. Aside from the Pro Bowl start, he had established himself as a serious student of the game, a player with strong work habits and a vicious game face that seemed to suit Buddy's style perfectly. But the timing was bad. As Buddy came wading ashore in full St.-Vince-straight-from-the-Super-Bowl-kickass mode, Wes was loafing on the beach threatening to sit out the season, demanding a contract extension.

Buddy gave Wes the nickname "Wallets."

When Wes secured the contract extension, giving him a $200,000 bonus for the '86 season and a three-year $1.5 million deal beginning in '87, he reported to summer training camp on time. But Buddy seemed set against him. The new coach told the Pack that Wes, the Pro Bowl starting free safety, wasn't really suited to play that position.

"He's too big a guy to stand back there."

This, of course, made no sense, but Buddy was at that point a certified genius (it said so right in the *New York Times*). Wes hurt himself further when he pulled a hamstring and had to watch a week of practices. "All I've seen him do since he got here is kill grass," the coach quipped. "I imagine carrying that big wallet around helped him pull it."

None of Buddy's barbs came to Wes directly. He got them, like everybody else, from the newspapers. Still, Wes was back at free safety when the Eagles started the '86 season and probably would have won his way into Buddy's graces if he hadn't blown out his left knee in the fourth game, against the Rams. He set himself on his left foot before latching on to former SMU teammate Eric Dickerson, and as his body turned with the tackle his foot stayed planted on the plastic turf. Surgeons repaired the torn joint, but it would be two years before Wes could play again.

It was then he discovered the hard truth about the family of Team—when you can't play, you don't count. Every day Wes would hobble on crutches into the Vet for therapy. He faithfully attended team meetings and practices—what else was he going to do? And every day he was ignored. It was like he didn't exist! From the time he was injured until the summer of '88, when he was ready to resume playing, Buddy didn't say more than three words to him. This kind of thing takes its toll. As the months go by, injured players start to get the silent message (intended or not) that they just ought to go away. Under the modern, less exploitative NFL employment regs, teams can't simply drop an injured player, but they can sure make a guy feel like a malingerer. In time, it is easier to go than to stay. Sometimes the assistant coaches or a teammate would ask how Wes was doing, but they were clearly distracted, just being nice. It drove him crazy. He was a ghost, sentenced to haunt the locker rooms and meeting rooms unseen. He wanted to shake people by the shoulders—*This is me! Wes! The Pro Bowl starter! I'm still here!* At the end of the '86 season, when the coaches asked team members to vote for the season's MVP, the award Wes had won himself the year before, they didn't even give him a ballot. The coach walked up and down the rows of desks dropping ballots on them, but when he came to Wes's desk he just passed right by.

Becoming a ghost would have been bad enough, but at the same time Wes's playing career hit bottom, so did his life. Uncle Jimmy had steered the bulk of Wes's funds into a condo complex in Dallas—*A great deal! A surefire moneymaker! A can't-miss opportunity!*—which went sour. It seemed every lawyer in Texas was looking for him. Uncle Jimmy filed for bankruptcy, and investors in the condo deal won a

$225,000 judgment against Wes. Coinvestors scattered. He ended up holding twelve properties in his own name that he couldn't afford to keep and, in the slumping Dallas economy, couldn't sell. Wes owed the tax man and just about everybody else. It was a mess.

It was at this point, feeling like an outcast and a failure, that Wes asked Erika to marry him, and she did. Erika had been an honors student at Loyola and had a lot more patience and aptitude for Wes's predicament than he did. She spurred him to sever his financial ties with Uncle Jimmy and worked closely with his new agent, a Philadelphia lawyer named Harry Himes, to sort through the mess. While Wes the Ghost concentrated on rehab, Erika was on a mission, writing letters, attending meetings, returning phone calls, balancing bank accounts, and insisting he save money. Their credit was destroyed, and when it was all worked out, Wes had virtually nothing to show for his spectacular success in pro ball; but they had each other, and their feet were on the ground. All Wes had to do was get back out on the field.

He returned in '88 to discover he was way behind in his understanding of the 46 defense. The coaches all suspected he couldn't play like his old self, and Buddy seemed wedded to Terry Hoage, the smart, rangy former Georgia safety who had stepped in after Wes's injury.

Despite feeling less than fully healthy, despite a head coach who offered no encouragement, Wes started every game at free safety that season, matching or bettering his Pro Bowl–year stats. But Buddy refused to call him a starter, referring to him as a "platoon player" with Hoage. That's what it said in the media guide that year, with its player-bio summaries shaped by the dictates of Coach. Wes was described as "part of a very productive free safety platoon" with Hoage. "Together," the guide said, "they accounted for . . . 177 tackles."

Now, there's no denying Hoage had one hell of a season playing free safety in the nickel that year. He had eight interceptions. But fair is fair. One hundred and forty-six of those 177 tackles were made by Wes Hopkins.

At home, Erika called Hoage "Prince Free Safety."

Wes asked to be traded. If he couldn't prove himself to Buddy on the field, he should be allowed to make his way somewhere else. But the team wouldn't hear of it. With rapidly escalating players' salaries, the $450,000 they were paying Wes in '89 was a bargain.

Through the following season, Wes once more posted numbers comparable to his Pro Bowl year. He felt he had finally mastered Ryan's defense. He had intercepted no passes, but, overall, Wes's teammates and coaches were impressed. Near the end of that season, Erika gave birth to a daughter, whom they named Montana.

Buddy even thawed a little. In their regular one-on-one, end-of-season chat, the coach was uncharacteristically complimentary. He told Wes he had squarely won back the starting job and that his comeback had been impressive. He said the Eagles had big plans for Wes in '90, his seventh year as a pro.

So the first months of that year were secure and happy ones for Wes and Erika. They had climbed together out of the hole. The Eagles were now a top NFL contender, his agent was negotiating a new contract that would up his annual salary to $655,000, plus incentives, and Wes could envision topping his football career with four or five more seasons as one of the better-paid players on the team, and maybe even grabbing a Super Bowl ring or two. Wes was excited. His years as a ghost, the collapse of his finances, his marriage, his baby daughter had all changed him. He wasn't as cocky as he had been when he first came up. Having glimpsed how fickle and insubstantial Team was as family, he had carved out a family of his own, one that would outlast his career. He was careful with his money—he was now driving a little Dodge sports car (an Eagle), not the Porsche, and he and Erika were living in a conventional, two-story Cape Cod on a postage-stamp lot in a workaday New Jersey development.

Playing pickup basketball with his teammates that winter, Wes found that his left knee even started feeling normal again, for the first time in three years. He told Erika and his teammates he felt that he had another Pro Bowl season in him—Wes was back!

Then Buddy drafted Ben Smith.

Free safety is a prize role on any football team. Lined up behind the other ten defensive players, often without direct responsibility for covering a specific zone or receiver, the free safety is "free" to observe and react to an unfolding play. On passing plays he is the last line of defense and often the defender with the best chance of intercepting the ball. On running plays, he is, again, the last line of defense, but the player with the best opportunity to lower the hammer, preferably with a swift running start. Given this responsibility for hitting, most free safeties are bigger than cornerbacks, whose job it is to go one-on-one against small and speedy wide receivers. Ideally, though, a free safety should combine the speed and agility of a cornerback with the size and strength of a linebacker. Wes had an extraordinary feel for the game, and, brother, could he bring the heat, but his deficiencies in speed and quickness had always kept him suspect in Buddy's eyes—with reason.

Buddy's 46 was a swarming, all-out attack on the quarterback that stranded cornerbacks and the free safety on a high wire without a net. The system turned linemen and linebackers into legends, and pass defenders into goats. Now that he had Byron and Seth plugging holes on the line, he was looking for a man at free safety who was smaller and faster than Wes, which is why Hoage was thrown in on passing downs even after Wes regained his starting job. Of course, Wes bought none of this logic—not that Buddy ever tried explaining it to him. The way Wes saw it, no matter how well he did, Coach seemed determined to get rid of him.

Yet Wes survived. Experience worked to his advantage, because Buddy's defensive backfield had to think on its feet, often shifting position rapidly two and even three times between the opponent's break from huddle and the snap of the ball. With all these players shifting around, the backfield relied heavily on the free safety to direct traffic, which wasn't easy on the floor of a concrete bowl with sixty to eighty thousand fans screaming for blood. Wes was pretty good at it. He excelled at another part of Buddy's system, too. In some formations, Buddy's free safety had to step up and effectively play linebacker, colliding with 300-pound linemen and 250-pound running backs. Wes's 215 pounds and fabled mean streak enabled him to do both with some success.

So when Buddy named a 183-pound rookie to replace him, it took not only Wes but the team's coaches and players by surprise.

Wes had heard about Ben Smith. Playing for the University of Georgia, Ben was one of the premier college safeties in '89, and everyone projected him as a first-round pick that spring. But he was regarded as too small to be an effective free safety in the pros. Even Ben was looking forward to playing cornerback in the pros; he saw himself as a cornerback. When Buddy faced the cameras and microphones to announce Smith as his first pick, one of the hounds remarked, "Well, Buddy, I guess you've got your new starting cornerback."

The coach said, "No, I've got my new starting free safety."

Those involved in selecting Ben assumed he'd play left corner. And even if Buddy was determined to play him as free safety, the way to do it would be to bring him along slowly, groom and educate him, especially at such a key position . . . unless you were desperate. The Eagles were hardly desperate. Wes was regarded as one of the best in the league. He got the word from a reporter by phone at home and felt ill, as if he had been kicked in the stomach.

It was not just a matter of wounded pride either. Buddy's announcement had immediate practical consequences for Wes and Erika. Wes was looking for a salary of more than $655,000 that year. The Eagles' initial offer had been $550,000, but when summer rolled around, and the team ticked through its signing priorities, the amount would surely come up—Wes knew the dance. Only, when Buddy drafted Ben, the step changed.

Harry Gamble knew the difference between a second-string player and a first-string one. Instead of improving on the initial offer, Harry told Hopkins's agent, Harry Himes, that unless Wes signed before June 1, the day league rules required the team to make an offer, $100,000 would be withdrawn.

Himes didn't believe it. This was not the way the game was played. The initial offer was always just a formality.

But Harry was as good as his word, and on the appointed day, the Eagles lowered the offer to $450,000—literally the minimum NFL wage for a player of Wes's experience.

Wes stayed up late that night and made a call to Norman Braman's villa in southern France. The club's maneuver had shaken Wes's faith in the basic fairness of things; surely Norman, who had always been so cordial with him and Erika, wouldn't approve of such a thing! And Norman was gracious. He told Wes that he tried not to involve himself in player negotiations, and that any decision on the matter would have to be made by Harry, but he did promise to look into it and see what he could do.

And the next day, the $100,000 was back . . . but with a contingency. The club offered to pay Wes $6,250 extra for every game of the '90 season in which he played in at least 50 percent of the defensive plays. Of course, Wes had no control over that. Buddy decided who played and who didn't.

The Eagles wouldn't trade Wes, so under the existing NFL rules restricting free agency, he was stuck. After passing a disgruntled training camp, he was given an ultimatum by Buddy. He could either agree to suit up as Ben Smith's backup and keep his mouth shut about it, or he would be cut from the team. Wes swallowed his pride and assumed his place on the bench.

The Eagles lost three of their first four games. Two of the losses came against teams considered to be among the worst in football, the Cardinals and the Colts. In a game as complex as football, no one player makes the difference between victory and defeat, but to veterans in the Eagles' secondary, one major problem was obvious. The proof was right there on tape: cornerbacks waving with frustration at Ben in the center of the field, waiting in vain for the call that would tell them what coverage to play; Ben lining up in the wrong spot on the field; Ben wasting an opportunity to slow down a sprinting running back in the open field by trying to bowl over a blocker to make the tackle himself, only to be knocked flying by a 280-pound lineman. These were all rookie mistakes, the kind even the best young football player makes, and Ben was doing a lot of things right, but his inexperience was making Gang Green look bad.

Buddy clung tenaciously to a decision once he had made it. Having made such a show over replacing Wes with the rookie, how would it look for him to back down now? He'd be admitting a mistake, and mistakes were what those damn fools on the other side of the field made.

Then Izel Jenkins, the cornerback everyone had earlier assumed Ben was drafted to replace, popped his hamstring and gave Buddy a face-saving solution. Ben moved to left corner against the Redskins in the sixth game, and Wes returned to his familiar spot. He responded with eleven tackles and was named the defensive player of the game. Despite missing most of those first five games, Wes went on to lead the team with five interceptions that year and averaged seven tackles per game. The Eagles won eight of their last eleven games.

Still, Buddy stubbornly refused to admit his mistake or give Wes credit (which would have amounted to the same thing). Wes finished the season as starting free safety, and the club even coughed up the full $100,000 in incentives, although Buddy hadn't allowed Wes to earn it. Toward the end of Buddy's tenure, Wes felt he had won a measure of grudging respect. At a team meeting before the Redskins' play-off game, the coach made a comment, in passing, to the effect that they had "one of the best free safeties in the league."

He didn't elaborate, just pressed on with his remarks, but a few of Wes's teammates turned around with wide eyes. When Buddy was fired three days later, Wes wasn't among the Eagles' players shouting imprecations, venting anger, and predicting doom. He heard it on the car radio on his way into the Vet and felt like rolling down his window and shouting for joy.

THE INFIDELITY Erika endured was an occupational hazard of NFL marriages. More of the other wives she knew had been through it than had not, white, black, newlywed, or long hitched. Her best friend, Jennifer Joyner, was going through it now with Seth.

Jennifer's nightmare had started in February, when Seth flew both her and his Puerto Rican girlfriend, Wanda, to Honolulu for the Pro Bowl. Jennifer discovered Wanda when she kept phoning their hotel room the night before the game. The phone rang right in Jennifer's ear, on the table next to her pillow. Wanda called again before sunrise.

Seth, alongside Jennifer, took the phone and held it to his ear. Jennifer could hear the woman on the other end complaining loudly, rattling on and on, with Seth just nodding—"Uh-huh . . . no . . . uh-huh."

"Who is this woman?" Jennifer demanded. "She must be pretty important if she has the nerve to call you and yell at you in your own hotel room at five o'clock in the morning with your wife in the room and your child sleeping in the next bed!"

Seth was now getting it in both ears.

He handed the phone back to Jennifer and rolled over silently, an inert black mountain. Jennifer had high hopes for this trip. She and Seth had gotten in a huge fight over his mother the summer before, and he had left her and his daughter behind in El Paso when he flew back to Philly for the season. He had sworn to her that he wasn't seeing anyone else, that he just needed some space. When he made the Pro Bowl, he had invited Jennifer and her parents out for the game. Her parents were going to take Jasmine, their four-year-old daughter, back to El Paso at the end of the week, and then she and Seth were planning to spend a week together on Maui. She saw it as a time to heal their marriage . . . long afternoons on the Wailea sands, luxurious dinners, champagne nights . . . just what the doctor ordered to rekindle romance.

Now this.

When Seth woke up at dawn, he pulled on his clothes silently and made for the door. He knew Jennifer was angry, and, with her at least, avoidance was Seth's major tactic in interpersonal conflicts. Jennifer had spent many long days and nights seething alone over some issue like this, waiting for Seth to phone or return home. *This time*, she thought, *by God, I'm not going to sit around wallowing in anxiety all day*. She scooped up Jasmine from the next bed and ran out into the hall after him.

"You are going to talk to me," she said.

She was in her nightgown, her blond hair all tangled and pillow tossed, their child in her arms.

"What the hell are you doing?" he asked, and kept on walking.

"I'm right behind you," said Jennifer. "You are going to talk to me!"

He stopped at the elevator.

"Go back to the room," he said. "I'll be back."

"I've got to talk to you right now."

"You're embarrassing me!" said Seth.

"Oh, you don't know yet what real embarrassment is like."

She followed him into the elevator, and they rode down silently. Seth wouldn't look at her. When the doors slid open, he headed straight out across the lobby, apparently assuming Jennifer wouldn't follow farther. There were men working in the lobby, spraying plants, buffing floors, getting ready for the day. Jennifer plunged on behind Seth, stepping gingerly in her bare feet over the hoses and wires. When he saw she was still behind him, Seth turned and glowered.

"Will you just sit down and tell me what is going on?" she asked.

"Go upstairs," he said. "You're embarrassing me!"

"Okay, Seth. Today is Pro Bowl day, right? When's that? Three o'clock? If you don't talk to me right here, right now, you're gonna see embarrassment on national television."

There was just enough resolve in her voice to break through. He shrugged, and they sat on a couch in the lobby. Seth insisted the phone calls were just a misunderstanding. It was some girl he had met a long time ago, and she knew he was in Honolulu for the Pro Bowl with his family, and she, this girl, was obviously just calling to try to stir up trouble for him.

"Oh, the hell with you," said Jennifer. "This is the reason you didn't want us to come up to Philadelphia."

Seth spent most of that off-season traveling to golf tournaments and public appearances, and when the '92 season started that summer, he came back to Philadelphia by himself again, his issues with Jennifer still unresolved. She and Erika talked on the phone almost every day. Seth was out with Wanda all the time. Everybody back in Philly knew Wanda.

Erika knew of dozens of other similar cases with players on this and other teams. The women all lived in fear of it happening to them. They coped with all sorts of rationalizations. The temptations were ever present; men like Seth, Wes, and others had grown up without fathers, without normal family structures, so they didn't understand how to keep a family together; the game and its sophomoric fraternity atmosphere, hanging out with guys who were mostly single, the travel, the bars, the money, the celebrity, the Sis-Boom-Bimbos, it went to the men's heads—or pants. With the single guys, the stories were of paternity suits or of lewd parties where two or three women entertained and ministered to the star's (presumably heroic) sexual needs at the same time. Jerome was the champ, but he had lots of competition. Siran Stacy, the team's top draft pick this year (and something of a disappointment) was in the process of being successfully sued by two women, a former high-school girlfriend and a former college girlfriend, each of whom had borne him a child. The college girlfriend, a white from southern Alabama who had become estranged from her family as a result of the relationship, had recently flown north to confront Siran at his new Philadelphia condo with the baby, provoking a scene that led to the rookie's arrest on assault charges—he had faced similar charges in Geneva, Alabama, where the local police called him "Siren" Stacy for his frequent run-ins with the law. Clyde Simmons was living in his own apartment in Philly, about a fifteen-minute drive away from his wife, Sandra, and their children, yet still picked them up every Sunday to bring them to the Vet for games, as if everything were hunky-dory.

No, marrying into the NFL was a hazardous step. And it wasn't just the Sis-Boom-Bimbos either. Even if your husband was loving and faithful, in many cases an equally vexatious problem was Mom.

Wes and Seth, like so many of their brethren, had especially close ties to their single moms, ties bound to cause serious trouble when they married or started living with a woman. A successful pro player, having rescued himself and Mom from the projects and spread a little good-feeling money around among siblings and stepsiblings and other various family members, overnight became Shahanshah, Lord Bountiful, hero and chief home buyer.

The DHM (Dream Home for Mom) is often more than just a nice house or condo on the posh outskirts of whatever community bred the fledgling NFL star; it is also a kind of shrine to the upper-middle-class dream family he never had. In it, Mom preserves an ideal of the former fantasy life; only, for Mom, it becomes reality. She lives there every day, usually in a house three or four times bigger than what she needs, kind of waiting for her boy to come home. Wes's mother, for instance, lives in a big suburban rancher with wooden shingles and a spacious deck out back, a Jacuzzi, a swimming pool, a complete bar and rec room in the basement, the walls and shelves loaded with her son's pictures, plaques, trophies, helmets, game balls, et cetera—only, see, Maggie doesn't know how to swim, so the pool stays covered year-round, and she doesn't drink, so the bar stands empty. Like most young men a year or two out of college, the busy young NFL star comes home to visit a few times a year, leaving Mom alone in the DHM like some kind of well-dressed, well-fed prop in a tricked-up Natural History of Suburban American Childhood diorama.

Resentment percolates in this kind of arrangement, particularly with moms who have this history of men leaving them behind. And one of the easiest targets for this resentment becomes Mrs. NFL Star. You can imagine how the moms feel. They have labored for years working long hours at low-paying, scumbucket jobs, coming home to rat-shack housing, struggling to be both father and mother to their brood, and when one finally hits the jackpot, the million-dollar payday, he's suddenly off splitting the wealth with some leather-booted, blow-dried tart with a board up her ass. This isn't just a matter of sharing

Junior's time and affection either. Once the tart reels in her boy and wears the ring, suddenly the family fortune is split in half!

In short order, the ugliness flows both ways. It's just swell when a single guy decides to shell out $400,000 for a DHM and put his beloved mom on a generous monthly stipend. But when it's your husband talking about shipping that kind of money out of the family bank account—*Hey, can't we talk about this? Aren't we trying to build a family of our own here? What about college for the kiddies down the road?* There is usually a yawning culture gap, too. Your basic NFL superstar isn't likely to meet and marry someone from his mom's general social circle and educational background. No. He marries one of these college-educated sweeties with upper-middle-class values. Take Jennifer Joyner, for instance. She's not just white, she's amazingly white, green-eyed, blond—*Dutch,* for crying out loud! She speaks three languages, has a college degree, speaks her mind about everything under the sun; she's the embodiment of every black mom's worst Aryan-bitch daughter-in-law nightmare! The NFL wife tends to show, if not contempt, then certainly an aversion to the basic staples of American po'-folk lifestyle. Little things like greasy-fingered diets laden with fat and cholesterol and gooey sugary treats, baby-sitting toddlers with game shows and TV soap operas, Mama's gun-toting alcoholic con-man boyfriend, plastic coverings on the furniture, and an alarming tendency to haul off and whack a fussy two-year-old, in public! *Honey, you aren't really thinking about leaving Junior with your mother for the weekend, are you?* In the worst cases, a subliminal tug-of-war goes on, with Mom functioning as a kind of rival for her boy's affections and, in some cases, actually working to undermine her darling superstar son's marriage.

Erika and Jennifer, who both had served as vice-president of the Association of Eagles' Wives, were shocked sometimes comparing notes on their predicaments, how similar they were, the moms, the bimbos, the avoidance . . . right down to their husbands' pulling the sheets up over their heads.

"Seth does that, too?" Erika said.

Even players with moms who didn't meddle were influenced by this outsized role as Shahanshah, Lord Bountiful. It gave them tacit license to flaunt their disdain for the normal rules of marriage and family. Within the brotherhood, it was neither unusual nor especially frowned upon for a married guy to show up at a nightclub or a party with a girlfriend on his arm, or to leave with one. There was even a certain amount of macho grandstanding involved. A married player could demonstrate his regal stature by flaunting a Sis-Boom-Bimbo without it causing any outward domestic stress, as if to say, *Look at me,*

I'm such a stud the normal rules don't apply . . . the wife doesn't dare give me shit. And, sure enough, the dutiful and adoring wife would be there in the lounge on game day, as usual, and on the star's arm for any serious public occasion, like an awards ceremony or an NFL-sponsored United Way commercial (which would portray the player as a great humanitarian for showing up to hold a disabled kid on his lap long enough to make a sixty-second commercial) or an antidrug lecture (Erika had seen players give antidrug lectures who she knew were users themselves). Wives were useful whenever it was important to preserve the club's image, to present the clean, upright, all-American NFL family front.

Erika could live with the facade. She was no innocent. She had grown up in south-central L.A. in a family that made money on both sides of the law and had a cynical sense of humor about the more extreme illusions peddled by the NFL. But she, unlike some of the other wives, could not cope with infidelities.

She had almost walked out several times. But Wes would always swear it had meant nothing. What really galled her, though, was this attitude that she couldn't shake in him, this notion that *she* was somehow oppressing *him* by objecting to his dalliances. *What's the big deal? What did you expect from me?* He was never exactly contrite. He would act as if the problem were with her!

"Aren't you at least sorry for it?" she would say. My God—how easy she was willing to make it for him, *advertising* her willingness to forgive.

And even that didn't do it. The best he'd come back with was this sarcastic, "Yeah, Erika, I'm sorry."

Wes just didn't get it. As Erika saw it, deep down, he thought he was a terrific husband and father. After all, he had given them his name; he came home every night; he supported her and Montana; he worked hard at his job; he was somebody they could be proud of . . . what more did she want? It was one helluva lot more than his father had ever done for him and his mother! And his mother, Maggie, she never complained. She had never expected anything from the man who had fathered Wes. What was Erika's problem? What strapping, healthy young man didn't sample the other wares now and then? Did she expect him to be a saint? Why couldn't she just let Wes be Wes?

Erika had stuck around hoping that he would grow up. He would be thirty-two this year. His career wouldn't last much longer. Surely he realized what he had in her and his daughter was more valuable than any fleeting pleasure he got out of playing superstud in a night-club or hotel room. Sometimes Erika found herself looking forward to it all being over, to Wes's retiring and withdrawing from this goddamn fraternity/family of Team, so that the two of them could be a real family, live a normal life.

Except, Erika did love to watch him play. She lived for the sunny autumn and chilly winter Sundays, the gathering of the wives in the lounge, all of them looking so terrific, and watching the game together out in the stands, cheering their men on, then getting together afterward for nice dinners out on the town, where they would be received like royalty at local restaurants. She called football season "my time." Game days were what made all the bad things worthwhile.

When Erika first found the letter from Amy on that drive in mid-June, Wes told her all about it . . . again, *What's the big deal?* To her, the timing couldn't have been worse.

They were on their way out to do a walk-through of the new house they had built, the final preliminary before settlement. The house was a half-million champagne stucco beauty on a wooded corner lot in a swank New Jersey development, with a grand entranceway and huge sunny living room and kitchen under a twenty-foot ceiling; it was their triumph, tangible evidence of how far they had come back since Wes's injury and ruin. To Erika, the house was a symbol of everything she had meant to Wes, and a cornerstone for the rest of their lives together.

And now comes this Amy.

"Wes, it's the forty-eight on your back," she said. "You know that's why they want you, the number forty-eight on your back."

"No, it's not like that," he said.

"What's this 'decision' you have to make?"

"It's nothing. She can't do anything for me. I just have fun with her."

Erika told him to get rid of her. They went ahead with the walk-through that day, but her heart went out of the project. She was going to leave him. This business with Amy, his attitude . . . it showed he wasn't changing. He was getting worse. It was only partly the girl. Ever since he had worked his way back into the starting lineup and regained his old form, Wes had been feeling more and more strongly the pull of Team. It was like he had forgotten his years as a ghost. He had gone back like a pathetic kicked puppy. He couldn't get enough of them. During the season he was off at dawn and didn't come home until late. He would spend all day with the guys, and then they would stay late to study film and then retire to one of the hot-spot bars they liked to frequent, Mahorn's in Jersey and, in Philadelphia, the Cat Club and the Ritz. On his day off he'd go golfing with them. During the off-season it was more of the same, weekend trips out of town to golf tournaments with the guys, nights out drinking at the clubs—they couldn't get enough of one another. Wherever they assembled, there was the magic of Team, the stir of excitement, the thrill of stardom—it was like a drug. This, Erika knew, was her real enemy, not Amy. Amy was just a symptom. After Amy it would be somebody else, and somebody else.

"When this is all over," Erika's mother said, "Wes will be looking for you with a candle in daylight, he's going to be looking for you so hard."

Erika's patience and pride had just about worn out.

She would ask him, "Why are you going through with this? You've been seeing this girl since January, through the whole time this house has been under construction. Why go through with it? I don't want to move into a house that's just a shell. We're supposed to be building ourselves a home. What is the problem with you? We're working on this, this is supposed to be *our* thing! We've worked hard to have this."

Wes had no answers.

Then Jerome died. Erika had tracked Wes down by phone, pulled him off the golf course, to tell him the news, and he had come home shaken. He told Erika to get him something to drink, so she went out and bought him a bottle of cognac, and Wes sat on the sofa all night getting drunk and talking on the phone. He was inconsolable. She never knew Jerome had meant so much to him.

They all went down for the funeral in Brooksville, that glorious, uplifting, emotional ceremony, and Reverend Reggie and the other fine preachers talked about how fleeting was our time, and about how youth flies and beauty dies and how critical it was for one's soul to see through what was temporal and trivial (though tempting) to the things that were truly lasting and important . . . and they all wept and felt their hearts break and then miraculously mend; they all praised Jesus and sang and held one another close, awash in sorrow and wonder at the savage beauty of life. It was cathartic. No one left unchanged.

How could she walk away from her marriage after that? Wes said he would end his relationship with Amy, and Erika believed him. They settled on the new house and moved in in late June, just a few weeks before training camp opened in West Chester.

Wes had gone off to camp when the phone bill arrived, on Erika's birthday, with a record of toll calls to Newtown, Pennsylvania. Erika knew that this Amy lived somewhere northeast of Philadelphia. They didn't know anyone in Newtown . . . it had to be.

She dialed the number.

"Hello?" A young woman's voice.

"Hello, may I speak with Amy?"

"This is Amy."

"This is Erika Hopkins, Wes Hopkins's wife."

"Oh."

"I don't understand what's going on between you and my husband, but I want to ask you one question. At Jerome's funeral he told me, 'That's it.' Is it over between you?"

"No," said Amy. "We haven't broken it off. As a matter of fact, I saw him just two days ago."

Still, Erika wouldn't give up. She drove out to see Wes at camp, an hour and a half away, and when she and Montana had been there for only about fifteen minutes, he asked her to leave.

"I don't want you here," he said.

He swore he had ended his fling with Amy, but when he came home from camp he was obviously unhappy. Something had changed. In the past, Wes would always come around. If he didn't apologize, at least he knuckled under, showed some desire to remain a family. Now his attitude was different, and Erika thought she knew why. It occurred to her that all the profound connections they had made at Jerome's funeral, not just she and Wes but the whole team, had actually been a giant misunderstanding. When she heard the preachers talk about how fleeting was life, how crucial it was to remember what part of the human experience was lasting and truly important, she heard it as a plea to honor family and God and truth. It gradually dawned on her that the message Wes seemed to have taken, and Seth and some of the others, was exactly the opposite. What they had so loved in Jerome wasn't what Reverend Reggie and Willie and Annie Bell Brown saw their beloved teammate and son *becoming*, it was what he *was*, what he had been to them, a wild spirit, fending off responsibility the way he fought off blockers in pursuit of a quarterback, immune to criticism and the opinions of others—heedless of the future. Ol' Freight Train had been about *living life now*, on his terms, while it lasted.

And the big, awful message of that gigantic bronze coffin being lowered into the earth draped with their colorful ties? *Boys, it don't last forever.*

That, she thought, was the root of this new, grim defiance. Wes was drawing a line. Before he had always fudged the issue, tried to have it both ways, but no more. He wasn't even going to hide his philandering anymore. Either Erika accepted Wes the way he was, let him have his Amy and whomever else followed, or she had to walk away.

She grew weary of it, and, for a time, just surrendered. She made him a deal.

"Do what you will," she said, "but, I'm asking you now, don't bring her to the games. That's my time. Just don't bring her to the games."

ERIKA FINDS HER way back to the seat in the wives' section as the Denver game is about to kick off. She is sitting with her sixteen-year-old nephew.

"Wes has his girlfriend here," she tells him.

"Where?" he asks.

Erika points her out, two sections over.

Wes nearly intercepts John Elway's first pass; it goes right through his hands. The crowd groans. Erika walks down to speak with Lynn Allen, Eric's wife.

"Lynn, as soon as Sara gets here, I need to talk to Sara."

Sara White has been a comfort to Erika, a counselor and a friend. Deeply Christian, Sara has prayed with Erika and shared her pain and confusion. They go to Bible study together, and Erika, feeling overwhelmed right now with decidedly unchristian impulses, tells Lynn she needs Sara to help calm her down.

Sara returns minutes later, and when Erika explains, she says, "You're not going to believe this! I had a dream that I had a chance to minister to Amy at one of the games."

Sara asks Erika if she would object.

"No." Erika wants *something* to happen.

So Sara heads up the steps and crosses over two sections. Erika follows, her nephew in tow. They stand at the top of the stairs and watch as Sara, a petite woman who radiates stern intelligence and commitment, marches into righteous battle, down to the row where Amy is sitting.

Erika watches as Sara addresses Amy, and sees Amy stand, and then catches something, something in the way the blonde reacts, the way she reaches and flips her hair—as if she's giving Sara major attitude—and Erika snaps. She comes flying down the stairs full speed, her sails swelled with outrage, maternal, wifely, and just.

She clobbers Amy in the face, and the force of the blow and her charge sends the woman reeling. Amy falls and rolls down nine rows to the bottom of the steps, with Erika right after her, then jumps up without even a look back and flees. She bounds quickly up the stairs, with Erika in delayed pursuit, and turns at the top to look back down and flash a triumphant smile.

At this point, Erika's nephew takes hold of both Amy's shoulders, and says, "Wrong way, bitch."

He shoves her back toward his aunt.

By now, the Eagles' on-field masterpiece is decidedly secondary in this part of the crowded stands. They see a young black man pushing a white girl down the steps, and, in short order, Erika's nephew gets jumped. She's still flailing at Amy, screaming for the fans to get off her nephew, when the yellow-jacketed security guards descend, pulling people off one another. Behind them, running, are blue-shirted city police.

Erika gets grabbed from behind by a yellow jacket, and another pulls her nephew from the pile.

"I'm Wes Hopkins's wife," Erika is screaming. "Get the bitch out of here right now!"

"Mrs. Hopkins, please," the yellow jacket is saying, when she breaks free and smacks Amy once more.

Amy is loose again now, running, only to be met this time by Lynn Allen, Margaret Byars, and several other of the Eagles' wives.

"What's wrong?" Lynn asks Amy.

"That woman is after me!" she says, pointing back to Erika, who is gaining on her again.

"Well, then I'll hold you until she gets here," says Lynn, grabbing hold of an arm.

In the ensuing melee, Amy gets kicked around pretty good. Erika feels this enormous sense of sisterhood with the other wives—helping her out like that—they *all* understand. Erika can feel great gusts of repressed wifely outrage from her friends. She no longer feels humiliated; she feels empowered. *She* hasn't done anything wrong! It's as though she's tapped into some reserve of anger in the group. Something is screwy about this whole NFL Star and His Little Woman thing, this whole hypocritical way of life. It's all grossly unbalanced, sadly out of whack. Erika knows she isn't the only woman here to have been dragged down this road. So many of them have, that now, seeing Erika actually *do something about it,* even something wild, futile, and ugly, they've risen as one to her aid. It's about time somebody took a stand! About time one of them howled loud and long about the goddamn fraternity of Team and the Sis-Boom-Bimbos and the glory ride these young men are taking, oblivious to the emotional havoc in their wake. It makes Erika feel suddenly proud. It gives her courage. And later, when she speaks of this awful day, if there is one thing about this whole thing that will always choke her up, it will be this sense of solidarity with the other wives. They are tired of being victims, of living in fear—you can see it in their faces whenever a new nova-haired sweetie shows up in the lounge on game day; a trill of panic goes through the room. Who's that? Who's *she* with? And how nobody can relax until the woman is properly accounted for. The brawl of the Broncos game has vented some of it, for sure. One of the wives grabs Amy's purse in the scuffle, figuring there might be some useful intelligence inside, and Erika hears Amy complaining to the police about it heatedly, accusing Erika of theft. When the coppers unwisely leave Erika unguarded for a moment, leaving the two women alone in the concourse, she laces into Amy again.

"Please, Mrs. Hopkins. Please," begs the guard, who has come sprinting back, embarrassed *for* her. But Erika is beyond embarrassment now. She has crossed the line. She has had enough.

They lead her back to the guard station. Later, they bring Lynn Allen in, too. Lynn explains how she had gone out to confront Amy again in the lot outside the Eagles' entrance to the Vet.

"I don't have anything to say to you," Amy had said.

"Well, you're going to listen to me," said Lynn, and then laid into her with a vengeance. "Don't you know what you are doing? He's married, he has a little girl. This isn't some kind of game. People get hurt."

Security had dragged Lynn off.

No charges are pressed. As the Eagles finish their triumphant shutout of the Broncos, and Erika listens through the stadium's concrete walls to the cheering and thumping of the happy fans out there on that fabulous autumn afternoon, watching those beautiful young men in their colorful gear play the violent and manly and fascinating game, she knows it will never be the same for her again. It had been foolish to try to hang on to it.

She waits until the cheers die down and watches as the crowds file out happily through the gates. Then she takes the elevator downstairs to wait in the dark concrete tunnel outside the locker room— to wait for Wes.

He is the last person to come out, long after the stadium has grown dark and silent. Erika has to stand down there for hours, being cheerful and pleasant with everybody, reporters, coaches, coaches' wives, players and their families . . . wondering if they know what has happened, worried that her brawl in the stands will make the news reports.

IN THE LOCKER ROOM after the game, Wes is positively bubbling with enthusiasm, about how they shut down Elway and how this game, in all his nine seasons, was the most dominant all-around game he and the boys have ever played.

Wes has reinjured his hamstring, so he has to stay late for treatment. Out in the damp and gloomy concrete corridor, Erika has lots of time to think through what she's going to say. She rehearses it in her mind, coolly, slowly.

She has made a decision.

Erika is standing alone when her husband emerges through the twin green metal doors, limping slightly on his bowed legs.

"I have to go get an IV," he tells her.

She can't tell if he knows or not.

"Okay, I'll go with you," she says, forcing a smile.

"You follow me," he says, which means he plans to head off on his own someplace afterward.

"No, we can go in one car," says Erika.

She is going to confront him, but she has to wait for the right moment. Wes is a runner. If she starts in on him with something he doesn't want to hear, he just jumps up and leaves, gets in his car and drives off. So Erika rides with him to Methodist Hospital, a few blocks up Broad Street, and waits until the nurse hooks him up to the IV.

Only then does she start. "You know, Wes, I just beat your girl-friend's ass," she tells him.

He grimaces.

"You know, Wes, I've been through a lot with you. I've been behind you in everything you've done, and, you know, I don't deserve this. I don't deserve to be humiliated like I was humiliated. I was put in a position today where I reacted. I regret that I reacted the way that I did, but, you know what? I'm totally within my rights to have done it. Do you have any idea how hurtful that was . . . finding her there at the game? That was the one thing I asked of you. This is supposed to be *my* time. I'm well respected in the organization, and with the wives. These people are my friends, Wes. And you have to flaunt this girl in front of them? You don't disrespect me like that. You have to have more feelings for me than to do something like that. You could see this bitch six days of the week, but she didn't have to go to the game."

Wes just listens glumly, tethered to the IV.

"I want you out of the house," Erika says.

"I'm not moving out of my house."

"Wes, yes you are."

"No, I'm not."

"Well, either you come and get your things on your own, or when you go to work tomorrow you'll come home and find all the locks have been changed. I want you out of there."

When the IV bag has finished draining, replenishing the fluids he lost in the game, they walk together out to the car, a minivan that Wes is driving as part of a promotional deal with a local car dealer.

"I'm taking the Lexus," he says (Erika had driven the new luxury car to the game, and it was parked back at the Vet).

"No, you're not," she says. "That's my car. I'm taking the Lexus."

Wes doesn't come home that night. He shows up the next day and loads the minivan with his things.

ERIKA DOESN'T KNOW how to explain all this to Montana, so initially she doesn't try. Whenever her daughter, soon to be four, asks about Daddy, Erika says, "Daddy's at work, honey."

Montana understands work. She has driven with her parents over the big bridge across the Delaware River, the Walt Whitman. The giant stadium where Daddy works is on the other side of the bridge.

Wes stops by to visit his daughter every few weeks. He comes in and parks on the sectional sofa, bounces Montana around for a few minutes, and then loses interest—at least that's the way it seems to Erika. Wes comes by for Montana's birthday party and is over again for Christmas—but Montana knows something big has happened. She misses him.

After the Eagles win a big game at the end of the year—Erika and Montana had watched it on TV—Montana says she wants to buy flowers.

"So Daddy will be happy at me."

"Tana, Daddy is always happy with you," Erika says.

So they go out and buy flowers, and when Erika talks to Wes on the phone—they still talk almost every day—she tells him about it and asks him to stop by for them.

But weeks go by before Wes comes, and the flowers wilt. They stand dead on the foyer table for days, but Montana won't let Erika throw them away.

"How come Daddy didn't take my flowers?" she asks. "Is Daddy's bridge broke?"

9

BETTER THAN SEX

Defensive tackle Mike Golic is driving south on I-55, cruising the great thundering tangle of expressways through Philly's sprawling New Jersey suburbs, when he sees an eighteen-wheel rig up the road clip the back end of a car.

It's like a cow flicking a fly off its rump. The car flips up and off the road at high speed, airborne into the median, where it touches down on one side and does three violent rolls before coming to rest, upright.

It's Monday afternoon of D-Day, Dallas Day, about seven hours before kickoff for what the local Pack has facetiously dubbed the "Game of the Century," the ABC-TV "Monday Night Football" spectacular Battle of the Unbeatens between the Eagles and Cowboys. Both teams are 3–0, and both had last weekend off, allowing for a two-week build-up of suspense . . . and hype. Mike has dutifully spent Sunday night at the hotel in Mt. Laurel with the team. They had meetings all morning, and now, with a long afternoon to kill before reporting for work, he's heading home to the wife and kids.

He pulls onto the median, jumps out, and runs toward the wreck. The car's windows are all blown out. He can see the driver, bleeding and slumped over the steering wheel, and, as he approaches, hears the unmistakable sound of WIP coming from the radio. The station has been featuring a pregame show since dawn this morning, broadcasting from a tent across the street from the Vet, where a beery crowd is already deeply in the mood.

Mike leans in the window on the driver's side. The driver has his seat belt on, and a gash on his forehead.

"Man, you all right?" Mike asks.

The poor man stirs and looks up, and a look of startled recognition comes over his bloody face.

"Hey!" he says, grinning. "You're Mike Golic!"

He reaches to release the seat belt and maneuver himself out from behind the crumpled steering wheel. "I'm going to the game tonight!" he says.

"No, no, no," pleads Mike. "Sit still!"

"Man, how do you think you guys are gonna do tonight?"

Mike can't really blame the guy (who did, he learned later, emerge from the emergency room braced and bandaged but in time to take his seat in the seven-hundred level for kickoff). Two weeks is too long to wait in a town as football-mad as Philadelphia has become. One week is bad enough; two weeks amounts to fan cruelty.

The NFL instituted these midseason byes in '90, a nod to mounting injuries and player complaints, because the league's profit-driven schedule had expanded beyond the bounds of human tolerance. Back in the days of the so-called Iron Men, heroes like Y. A. Tittle, Otto Graham, and Johnny U., pro teams played a neat twelve-week season. The first game was played at the end of September and the last before Christmas. Today, it isn't unusual for players to report for pre–training camp workouts early in July and finish their season in mid- to late January. Making it to the Super Bowl can mean playing twenty-five football games in six months (five preseason, sixteen regular season, three play-off games, and the big one). Midway through this slog, pro training rooms look like the outpatient ward in a MASH. To Richie and his players, the bye is like a thirty-second breather in a marathon, but to the devoted followers in Philadelphia, fresh off that 30–0 Broncos rout, it amounts to (this being a Monday night game) holding their breath for fifteen days.

While the teams rest, the hype mills work overtime, with every newspaper, radio, and TV station in Philly's huge media market milking the upcoming contest for all (no, *more than*) it is worth. This being a nationally televised showdown, it attracts the bigfoot national newshounds. The matchup has become a megaevent that transcends mere sport. It's a national happening.

It is featured on the cover of *Sports Illustrated*, on nightly national news programs, in weekly news magazines, dissected from every conceivable angle in the burgeoning literature of pro football tabloids and newsletters, and is even discussed in the high cerebral zones of National Public Radio. It may be the most celebrated early season battle in NFL history. Locally, Monday, October 5, 1992, might as well be a city holiday. Philly hasn't been this giddy since those Phillies hosted the Orioles in the '83 World Series.

Radio station WIP is cashing in, of course. They've been egging on Id-people all day, seeding the airwaves with bellows, grunts, and other simian-display noises, culminating in a ritualistic smashfest of

Cowboys' paraphernalia. Put it all together, a genuinely good early season matchup, the decade of rivalry, a mountain of hype, the city's desperate wish for a champion, and the endless two-week wait . . .

"A supercharged air of excitement!" is how ABC announcer Al Michaels kicks off the evening broadcast.

THE EAGLES TAKE special pride in arriving at this pinnacle of expectation without two of their star players, Jerome and tight end Keith Jackson.

Their cello-playing, would-be recording star—*nom de rap* K-Jack— had been sitting once more, through the summer and first month of the season. Despite their differences, Norman (you know, "the Moron") had made Keith a liberal offer—$3.6 million over three years, which would have made him the highest-paid tight end in football. But K-Jack was holding out for the sky. He and his agent, Gary Wichard, that Mr. Upfront, had a score to settle with Norman. Keith wanted $6 million over three years, and he wanted the contract guaranteed.

This, of course, was perceived by the Pack and the general public as the height of arrogance. Keith was a twenty-seven-year-old man whom the Eagles wanted to make a multimillionaire to play a game! And he was scoffing? Who did he think he was?

But look at Keith's take on it: A career in pro football is like no other. It lasts (on average) four to eight years, can end at any time, and demands that team and player agree on its value beforehand. Keith's initial four-year contract for about $2 million assumed he would be a starting tight end and a good one. No one foresaw that he would become the best in the league in his first year and then have to play for three more years being paid far less than players of comparable value. *So what?* says the cynic. *This time the Eagles got a bargain; he'll catch up with his next contract.* The trouble is, there may not be a next contract. Every time a player suits up for a game, it could be his last, or it could result in an injury that will never again allow him to play at the same level. For four years and sixty-three football games, Keith ran the risk of finishing his career without ever earning his true value—and it's safe to assume he would never earn as much money doing anything else.

You had to see him on the basketball court to fully appreciate his skills. At six-two and 250 pounds, his size approached that of an offensive lineman—with a bulk-up diet and lots of weight training, Keith could probably approach the 280-pound playing weight of Ron Heller. But on the basketball court he moved with the grace and quickness of a point guard, dribbling, passing, driving to the basket, making flying, one-handed dunks. Tight ends evolved from linemen who could sneak out occasionally and catch the ball. It was considered a low form of comedy watching one try to run with the ball after catching it—as the little cornerbacks and safeties bounced off trying to make the tackle. Even today, teams assign big pass-rushing linebackers to cover tight ends on pass routes. But Keith's speed and agility mismatched every linebacker in the league. He was too quick and fast for the big men, and still so big it was fun watching the safeties and cornerbacks bounce off him—if they could catch him. Opposing coaches literally had to redesign their defense when they played the Eagles, to account for both scrambling Randall and their point-guard tight end.

By dint of talent, luck, and effort, Keith emerged as the rarest of jewels at the bottom of the Sluice—yet he was being paid like a run-of-the-mill lineman. In '91, the last year of his Eagles' contract, he had earned about a half million. Norman and Harry conceded that was less than half his worth. The way Keith saw it, he had years of back pay coming—at least $2 or $3 million—in what might well be the last crack at a pro contract he would get.

In the past, a player had small leverage. He couldn't negotiate with other teams. But this year, while Keith sat out, the NFL Players Association was pressing a lawsuit in federal court to break the chains. Players argued that the league restrictions on free agency violated their rights.

Keith wasn't about to sign a contract with Norman until the court ruling, even if it took most of the season. He knew this next three-year contract would carry him through his prime playing years—if he hadn't passed them already. He would never again be in such a strong negotiating position. In fact (as he knew better than anyone), he had better leverage two years before, when Norman had refused to renegotiate. Despite Mr. Upfront's windy projections two years earlier, Keith's stats showed a steady decline over his four-year career (accelerated by his contractual hassles and injuries). He had caught eighty-one passes in his rookie year and then, year by year, sixty-three, fifty, and forty-eight. His total yardage during that phenomenal rookie season was 869, and then it went as follows: 648, 670, 569. He was still averaging five or six touchdown catches per season, but Keith hadn't made the Pro Bowl since '90. He was, without question, a superb tight end, but he wasn't a player (like a blue-chip quarterback) who could make or break a club.

Four days after the Eagles won their opener against the Saints, U.S. District Judge David Doty ruled in favor of the players, striking down the league's restrictions and ordering both sides to craft an agreement that protected players' rights and the league's competitive balance. Keith and nine other unsigned players promptly asked the court to free them from all restrictions in the interim, and two weeks later, four days after the Broncos game, Doty did. Keith was a free man. The following week, as his old teammates prepared for D-Day, he signed a four-year, $6 million contract with the Dolphins. Even spread out over four years, he stood to make $300,000 more in each year of the contract than the Eagles were offering. Harry had made a last-minute effort to sweeten the deal, shifting a few more dollars into the first year and offering a bigger incentive package, but for Keith, the choice wasn't even close.

"There was clapping and cheering in the background when we called to tell them we were coming here," he said at the Thursday press conference in Miami, beaming under a Dolphins cap and standing alongside a new teal-and-orange jersey bearing his number, 88. "In Philadelphia, I think, even if they came up with the money, it would have been a bitter situation."

Bitter and probably frustrating. Because every bit as important to Keith as the money was the way he was likely to be used in Philly. The slide in his stats over four seasons was less a reflection of declining skills than it was of games missed and other teams figuring out how best to stop him—and how the Eagles, subsequently, adjusted their use of him. As the team's offense improved, with the addition of wide receivers like Fred Barnett and Calvin Williams and the emergence of a stronger running game, Randall had more options for advancing the ball than scrambling around and dumping it to his talented tight end. And they needed more options, because Keith wasn't a big surprise anymore.

So despite the perfunctory nods to Keith's talent ("You always hate to lose a player of that caliber," says Richie) and the obligatory player shots at ownership ("It should never have come to this," says Keith Byars), Jackson's defection to Miami barely causes a ripple on the surface of this confident, surging team.

Which suits Norman and Harry and Richie just fine. Winning solves all problems. Norman has weathered a spate of terrible publicity, ever since documents released during the players' lawsuit revealed that the franchise was the league's most profitable, and that he had paid himself $7 million out of the Eagles' profits in '91—this despite years of claiming that his team wasn't a moneymaker, a claim used to justify hiking season ticket prices and playing hardball with salary demands. The documents did nothing to dent the growing and errone-ous public perception (fragrant of anti-Semitism) that the owner was a lying cheapskate plundering the franchise. They showed that Norman spent less money on management, coaches, scouting, equipment, and other peripherals than any other team in the league, and that his player payroll was slightly above average but not at the top. Losing a Pro Bowl tight end and one of the team's biggest offensive weapons just underscored the Shylock image. The stories during the lawsuit had neglected to note that expert testimony showed the most successful NFL franchises, at the till *and on the field,* were not those with the heftiest payrolls, but those that kept expenses to a minimum and paid players in the moderate range. In other words, victory wasn't just something you could go out and buy. Teams with huge payrolls tended to be loaded with veterans and expensive free agents, and those at the bottom tended to be younger, rebuilding teams. The recipe for sustained success was a well-balanced roster that mixed savvy but injury-prone veterans with eager young talent. By an accountant's reckoning, Norman was doing things right, for himself and the fans. Even the $7 million "salary" was more complicated than it seemed. News stories played it up as if the owner had been caught in a lie (he *had* fudged on how unprofitable the club supposedly was). But all the $7 million really amounted to was a tax maneuver familiar to most business owners. Corporate taxes being stiffer than personal income taxes at that point, it was beneficial to draw out as "salary" as much of the team earnings as the law allowed in order to take advantage of the lower rate. It made sense in another way. If Norman had not paid himself the profits as salary, the club's $7 million would have been taxed twice, first as corporate earnings, and then as dividends, which are personal earnings. In fact, Norman had no intention of keeping the money for his personal use—he hardly needed it. He produced canceled checks showing he had churned the money right back into the club. But few of the Id-people and talk-show comedians followed the intricacies of the transaction. It was a lot easier and more fun just to hate Norm the *cheap!-cheap!-cheap!*-skate.

Truth is, Norm wants to win so bad he can hardly sit still on game days. His pride is on the line, and that is at least a match for any profits the football club earns. After losing Jackson, after enduring the endless ignorant abuse of the Id-people and the press and those "goons," as he called them, on WIP, every victory is an ounce of sweet revenge. He's in Philadelphia days before the Big Game, as restless and nervous as any of his coaches or players.

After Keith's defection, the Pack turns out in full local and national force in the Eagles' locker room to solicit what will surely be great blasts of vitriol, outrage, and anguish on the eve of the Game of the Century. They are surprised to find Keith's buddies are far happier for their friend's good fortune, and for what his court case and subsequent freedom mean for them down the road, than they are concerned about the setback for their team. Eric wears a Dolphins cap to the locker room as a jaunty symbol of solidarity.

"A friend of mine has made a big move and a big statement," he says to the microphones. "What he did has importance way beyond this team or even himself, it's for the whole NFL, for everybody. In the next couple of years we'll see a big change. Nothing is ever going to be the same. What he has done will help every player in this league and every player who comes into the league. . . . Twenty years from now the only people on this team that people are going to remember are Randall Cunningham and Reggie White and Jerome and Keith Jackson. They'll remember them for different reasons. Keith, he's going to be remembered as the one who started it."

THERE IS, however, one exception. If there is one player in the Eagles' locker room with reason to be chagrined by Jackson's defection, it's the long-suffering Keith Byars.

"I talked to him on the phone Monday night," says Tank, his thick body curled up on a stool inside his locker, speaking softly, unable to disguise his disappointment. "It was a business decision. His words were saying one thing and his heart was saying another. I told him I thought he was making a mistake."

The two Keiths were the sliding trick components of Richie's offense. Both big men could block and catch passes. Byars could also run with the ball. Other teams had to send different players out on the field for a pass than for a run, tipping their hand—but not the Eagles. Richie's playbook contained little razzle-dazzle, but with both Keiths in the game, nobody could tell what was coming.

Teamed with Jackson, Byars was on the doorstep of leaguewide recognition. Because his talents were so versatile—he was used as a receiver as often as he was used as a back—his stats never made the top of the lists in either rushing yards or receiving, so he tended to get lost in the statistical shuffle. But people were beginning to notice him. In the four years he had teamed with Jackson, his total yardage had been close to or better than one thousand every season. He was on the verge of carving out a new kind of Pro Bowl slot—the all-purpose back. And with recognition, of course, came superdollars, the kind of contract money K-Jack had just landed down in the land of endless sun.

Without Jackson, Byars, who weighs about twenty pounds less, has been pressed into service as a tight end. He doesn't get to carry the ball, and he doesn't get to go out for nearly as many passes. What he does mostly is block—which is like using a Mercedes to pull a plow. In the Phoenix game, he did not carry the football at all and was thrown one pass, which he caught, for a five-yard gain. So long as the other Keith's return was on the horizon, Byars could endure. But news of the defection means he's doomed.

Again.

Tank is arguably one of the unluckiest men alive (if you can use that term for anyone earning more than $1 million per year to play a game). This is the latest in a long series of setbacks. Son of a Dayton, Ohio, minister, Byars looked to be the second coming of Archie Griffin in his junior year at Ohio State in '84. He had been fast enough to run one of the legs on his high school's state championship 4-by-100 relay team, but was built extra-wide from head to toe. On the football field he was virtually unstoppable. Throwing his solid girth around with peculiar mincing footsteps, he was capable of the kind of performances normally seen only on grainy black-and-white film highlights from the anything-goes, leather-helmet days. Byars's most famous game that year, against Illinois, was like something out of a Hollywood screenplay: with his team down 24–0, he almost single-handedly crafted a 45–38 comeback, running for 274 yards and *five* touchdowns, including one accomplished by reversing direction, losing a shoe, and racing 67 yards in cleat and sock. Big Ten MVP, the nation's leading collegiate rusher with 1,764 yards rushing, another 677 yards receiving, and twenty-four touchdowns, not to mention a thoroughly decent Christian role model who devoted time off-field to do volunteer work in the Dayton community, Byars was a heavyweight contender for the Heisman Trophy that year. The trophy meant, of course, reams of adoring press coverage, two more winter months in the national sports spotlight as he "decided" whether or not to return for one more year at Ohio State (nobody in their right mind would), culminated by the mandatory million-dollar payday in April when some lucky NFL team made him their number-one pick.

The scenario was perfectly predictable until Doug Flutie launched his famous Hail Mary pass, a sixty-four-yard prayer into the teeth of a strong wind to defeat defending national champ Miami (and that Jerome) in the Orange Bowl. It provided a storybook finish to Flutie's storybook college career, and America (and the Heisman judges) fell madly in love with the little quarterback who could.

No problem, Byars was a cinch for '85—everybody agreed—until he broke his foot early in the season and spent the rest of the year on crutches. His value fell so dramatically that Buddy was considered a reckless gambler by many the following spring when he claimed him in the first round, the tenth player overall. Tank paid off the big gamble by breaking a bone in his other foot shortly before his second season.

Now, seven years into his NFL career, he is stuck once more. His contract has $100,000 in incentives for rushing and receiving production. How is he going to accomplish that if they *don't give him the ball?*

Quietly, Byars had gone to Richie to complain after the Phoenix game. He had been given the ball more against Denver—he carried nine times for thirty-one yards and caught six passes for thirty-six yards. The Eagles were considering doing something about the contract incentives, and Richie has promised Tank that against Dallas he would be involved . . . somewhat.

But Keith knows his hopes for a personal banner year are dead.

DAVE ALEXANDER HAS his own reason for looking forward to a showdown with Dallas head coach Jimmy Johnson. It goes back eleven years, to when Dave was a big clumsy Oklahoma teenager snapping the ball for the Broken Arrow High School Tigers.

Dave has a guileless way about him; his personality is as plain and straightforward as his crew cut. To match his double-wide body he has a flat, friendly pan of a face with double-small features and a playful spark in his eye. Dave has never been a star player, even in high school; he lacks the size and strength to be a dominating lineman. But he has the durability and quick mind that coaches look for in a center, the kind of man you need to anchor an offense, the only man on the squad besides the quarterback who handles the ball on every offensive play.

Growing up in Broken Arrow, a Tulsa suburb, Dave and his brother and sister were part of a generation for whom college and a successful white-collar career were expectations, not dreams. Dave's father owned a metal-fabricating company that made drills for oil wells. It boomed with the prosperity of that industry through his childhood and would later fizzle with its decline, but out in the vast flatlands of the tame near West, the Alexanders lived worlds away from the desperate poverty so many of Dave's teammates had known as children. Football wasn't a gate to a better life for the boys who tried out at Broken Arrow High School; it was fun, a chance to emulate the heroics of the athletes who performed on TV. Without a pro team within two hundred miles (Dallas had the closest franchise), the heroes in this football-crazy part of the country performed on college teams, and the top of the line, as far as David and many other tall-grass Tulsa men were concerned, was Oklahoma State University in Stillwater, home of the fightin' Cowboys and their dynamic head coach, Jimmy Johnson.

Johnson had taken over the program in '79 when it was under severe NCAA sanctions for recruiting violations (*Them 'Boys take their football serious*) and had turned them back into a powerhouse in just two seasons. When college recruiters from several regional schools came courting after Dave's senior season in '81, they were wasting their time. Dave knew exactly where he wanted to play.

A recruiting weekend in Stillwater clinched it. Dave was wowed. The school flew him in on a private plane, showed him the facilities, the stadium, locker room, dorms. He was waiting around the coach's office there for the plane to take him home, when Coach Johnson called him into his office for a chat. Johnson was a nervous, pudgy-faced man with a small helmet of fair hair, every strand perfectly in place. He seemed to have the metabolism of a bumblebee, moving around the room quickly, taking small, short breaths, his body taut, radiating energy. As Dave remembered it, here's how the session went:

"We really want you at Oklahoma State and I want you to commit," Johnson told the strapping seventeen-year-old.

"Well, I'm going to catch the plane, and it's only a half-hour flight, so I'll be home in an hour and I'll talk to my parents and call you back."

"No," said the coach. "I need to know now."

"Okay," said the always affable Dave. "Then just let me give my parents a call and tell them what I'm going to do."

"No. I need to know from you, right now. If you're not going to commit to Oklahoma State, then we're going to offer your scholarship to somebody else."

Staring at him across the desk, Dave capitulated.

But it bugged him. Maybe it was the blocker in him; Dave hated to be pushed around. It ruined the weekend. All the way home on the plane he kept getting madder and madder about it. *The son of a bitch wouldn't even let me call my folks?* And then, *What will it be like to play for this guy?*

When he got home he said screw Jimmy Superman and called the coach at the University of Tulsa to accept a scholarship there.

It isn't like Dave to hold a grudge. Dave had played four happy years at Tulsa and met his wife, Kathy, there (they now had a twenty-one-month-old boy). During Johnson's Dallas tenure, his teams had met the Eagles, with Dave playing center, six times, and had lost five. So Dave never had a reason to regret his college decision. Still, something about Johnson rubs him the wrong way.

Old helmet-hair's zeal clashes with Dave's placid, amiable personality, which was one of Dave's strengths as an offensive lineman. Defensive linemen are attackers. They tend to be egotists and hotheads. It is more fun to play on the defensive line—Dave knows this because he had played some in high school. When you made the tackle your name was announced over the loudspeaker. On the offensive line, your name is never announced. You are a wall, a blocker, a nameless bigbody who absorbs blows, who stands in the way. Being an offensive lineman requires humility and tolerance. If you lose your temper, act impulsively, you can more easily be thrown off balance and pushed aside. The ideal is to be impervious, to become, as Ron Heller put it, "a blocking stone." Over the years, the job begins to define a lineman's temperament. Linemen can joke about the game. Writers love them because they observe all the strutting peacocks around them with knowing little smiles. Blockers get blamed when the team loses and almost never get credit when the team wins. Their faces are almost never on the covers of magazines. They aren't paid to endorse candy bars and sweatshirts, and their talents are nearly always poorly understood and ill appreciated, even by the most ardent and knowledgeable of fans. Yet they are literally in the thick of things; their view is from the crowded center of the action. They know *exactly* what is going on. A sturdy veteran like Dave has credibility to match his size. He possesses an almost bovine serenity—it is as hard to rile him up as it is to move him out of the way.

The blocker's mind-set had been illustrated perfectly for Dave in a little scene he remembered from training camp a few years back, involving his old friend and mentor, former Eagles center Dave Rimington, and, as so many of the Eagles players' stories did, Jerome.

The most competitive drill for offensive linemen during training camp is one-on-one pass blocking. The veterans like working against each other in these drills, because none of them has anything to prove—the idea isn't to hurt or humiliate your opponent, but to work on your timing, footwork, and mechanics. Of course, that's not how Jerome saw it. Any opportunity to compete became, for Jerome, a test of self-worth. Boy, how he hated to lose. To let some big-butt Bessie of a flat-footed offensive lineman show him up was enough to ruin Jerome's whole week. Rimington, on the other hand, was a wily veteran, a towheaded Nebraskan weight lifter with, as Dave saw it, the ideal blocker's personality. Nothing bothered Rim. He had been banged up so bad during nine years in the NFL that it was hard for him to raise his thick arms over his shoulders; there were days when he needed help just to knot his necktie. Rim was trying to hang with the Eagles and draw the big paycheck for one last season.

And on this afternoon, he showed he could still handle Jerome.

"Let's go again!" Jerome shouted after getting beat—a personal challenge in front of all the other linemen, offensive and defensive, standing around awaiting their turn.

So Rim shrugged and resumed his stance, and as Jerome recklessly bull-rushed his own full 330-pound frame, the veteran pulled one of his favorite tricks. He met Jerome's charge with a loud smack of pads, and then, as the big tackle continued to churn full forward, Rim took a sudden giant step backward, throwing Jerome so off balance from his own heedless momentum that, with a gentle finishing tug, he planted the flailing tackle's face in the grass.

Jerome hopped up looking for a fight, screaming, "Rim, you holding asshole motherfucker, you ever do that to me again and I'll *kick your fuckin' ass!*"

"Okay," said Rim pleasantly, with another little shrug and a smile, refusing to get riled. He turned and walked away.

Chuckles of appreciation arose from the offensive linemen watching, Dave among them.

"*All right!* You motherfuckers think it's so funny? *I'll kick all yer asses!*"

"Jerome, it's over, man, relax," said Dave.

Offensive linemen were used to small victories and defeats. Dave had been playing football now for more than fifteen years and had never scored a touchdown, caught a pass, thrown a pass, or taken a handoff. He had run with the ball, though, once. It happened in his first pro game, September 7, 1987, at Washington, D.C.'s RFK Stadium, in a loss to the Redskins. Dave was lined up deep in the blocking wedge for a kickoff return, back on his own twenty-yard line, when the Skins kicker shanked one that came dribbling down the grass to his feet. He scooped it up and rumbled eight yards before he was buried. Kathy cut the game story out of the newspaper the next day, with the evidence at the bottom, in agate type:

PUNT/KICK RETURNS: Alexander, 8yds.

As a joke, they highlighted the notice with yellow marker, framed the story, and hung it on their family-room wall.

Now he's a gnarled veteran, playing in his sixth season. His knee has been surgically reassembled. His hands have been smashed and broken so many times he's lost count. His left ring finger, which has been hurting him since, oh, midseason '90, is so lumpy and misshapen than he had to take his wedding ring back to the jeweler to have a tiny hinge put in it—it now clasps around the base of his finger. And in all that time, exactly eighty-two football games, other than beginning each play with the snap, he's never touched the ball.

Walking through final drills the day before the Monday night matchup, Dave confesses to his buddy Ron that he has this peculiar *feeling* about tomorrow night's game.

"I feel like I'm gonna get the ball, Ron. I'm gonna get the ball and I'm gonna try to score with it."

He was only half-kidding. He'd had this dream. It was not a feeling he had often.

"No you're not," scoffed Ron. "I'll score before you do."

"Put a little money on it?"

They agreed on fifty dollars for a touchdown, twenty-five dollars for advancing the ball for a first down, and ten dollars for recovering a fumble.

SEVERAL HOURS before game time, before the stands begin to fill, Jimmy Mac is on the field playing with his remote-control car, racing it madly up and down the turf.

Back in the locker room, he entertains the troops by dropping his pants to his ankles and waddling around the room doing his Richie Kotite imitation, throwing his arm around a teammate and bellowing in his best Brooklynese, "My friend," "Without question," and other Richie-isms, then climbing up on the table in the middle of the locker room, still with his pants down, and striking some of the classical, heroic, mock action poses found on old football cards or in old magazines—one knee up, straight-arm out—which gets a few of the other guys clowning, and before long gales of laughter echo from inside the clubhouse.

Bill Muir, the team's new offensive line coach, peeks in at the mayhem and walks over to Dave.

The coach says, "Well, I guess there's no worry about this team getting too tight for any game, is there?"

"A HAPPENING . . . an electric atmosphere . . . whichever team wins tonight is going to take a big step toward winning the NFC East!" gushes announcer Al Michaels to the nation shortly before kickoff.

(Aerial view of the city ablaze—the chamber of commerce has urged Philadelphians to leave their lights on for the generic panoramic dirigible shot. Lines of traffic can still be seen snaking in from all directions to the great and shining concrete bowl.)

Color man Dan Dierdorf goes Al one better. "Are the Philadelphia Eagles the best team in the National Football League? Randall Cunningham is the NFL's most exciting player, and they have the best defense in football. If they beat the Cowboys here tonight, the answer is yes."

THE GAME STARTS madly. The Cowboys win the toss, and on their first play from scrimmage, before ABC has time to flash the lineup on screen, Reverend Reggie blasts through the Dallas line and chases quarterback Troy Aikman backward about ten yards. Aikman dumps the ball to avoid the sack and draws a penalty, losing both the down and another five yards. At second and twenty-five, now deep in the Cowboys' own half of the field, with the stadium thundering approval, the league's leading rusher Emmitt Smith is stopped for no gain, and then Aikman's third-down pass is intercepted.

Taking over on Dallas's fourteen-yard line, Randall drops back to pass, finds no one to throw to, tucks in the ball, and races down to the Cowboys' three-yard line. Two plays later, he fakes a handoff to the left and swings around, running the ball to his right, outrunning a Cowboys' linebacker and then, with a feminine swivel of his slender hips, dodges a flying safety and slips standing into the end zone. Roger Ruzek's extra point gives the Eagles an immediate seven-point lead.

But Dallas comes right back. Aikman's pass to Michael Irvin is slapped by cornerback Eric Allen, but the Cowboys' receiver reaches back for the blocked pass, bobbles it, but hangs on and races fifty-nine yards before Eric can catch him and haul him down from behind. It's a fluke, but it sets up an Aikman touchdown pass, and just that quickly, the game is tied.

That's all in the first seven minutes of the game. Then things settle down. The Eagles manage a long drive and a field goal, and Wes picks off another Aikman pass in the end zone to thwart a go-ahead Dallas touchdown—he starts to run with it, hesitates, thinks better of it, tries to drop to one knee, but his momentum carries him back out of the end zone. So Randall gets the ball on his own one-yard line. He leads the Eagles out of the hole, but they don't score again, and the score is still 10–7 at halftime.

Randall is not having a good night, despite those two opening runs. In the first half he has only completed three of his ten passes, and he's been intercepted. Nevertheless, his face fills the screen for ABC's halftime show, prepared earlier in the week. He's introduced by Frank Gifford as "the game's most complete quarterback," older and wiser after missing a season with his knee injury.

"In the past, I just tried to lead by example," says Ran-*doll*, in his commanding soft voice. "I'm more verbal now. If a guy makes a mistake, I'll tell him, but in a nice way . . . no feelings are hurt."

After a quick exploration of Randall's, well, *Randallcentric* worldview, Gifford runs down the long list of Randall's off-field activities, the TV shows, candy bar, clothing line, autograph-signing sessions, and so on, and says the quarterback has matured "as a businessman and a player."

As for his coming back from the injured knee, ABC offers up a last, reflective Randallism, a piece of wisdom from the mountaintop.

"When you fear something it can happen," says the Scrambling One. "But if you train yourself not to be afraid of anything, then it won't happen. So I've been confident since my injury."

In other words, Randall feels he can prevent injury by not fearing it (this is actually a common superstition in NFL locker rooms).

Presumably, Randall remains fearful of being sacked, because he gets clobbered moments later, on the first Eagles' offensive series of the second half, and falls to the turf clutching his knee—which leaves the ball skittering free a few feet to his left.

Dave dives for it and comes up at the center of the screaming bowl, square in the gaze of the nation, with a herd of Cowboys closing in, and bellows, *"Heller, you owe me—"*

. . . and the *"ten dollars!"* gets lost in a flattening stampede of three-hundred-pounders in blue-and-silver jerseys.

Dave is having the time of his life, the best time he's ever had on a football field. Despite this setback—Randall jogs around on the sidelines for one play and then comes back in—his team now shifts into its *bringing the heat* zone.

Seth had hyperextended his knee on a play early in the first half and, typically, has refused to come out of the game. He's been limping around ferociously ever since and has been repeatedly victimized by Dallas tight end Jay Novacek, who is hard to cover even on two good knees. But a needle or two of numbing juice at halftime has the Eagles' star linebacker feeling like his old self. On Dallas's third play from scrimmage in the second half, he swoops in on Aikman and slaps the ball into the air, where it is gathered in by Byron.

The Eagles run and pass for a second touchdown—Herschel scores against his old teammates and in a rare demonstrative moment does a fancy windmill spike motion in the end zone, then freezes and lets the ball just drop to the turf. Dallas gets the ball, and Byron forces a fumble, which is picked up by Willie T. This time the Eagles score in just four plays, with Herschel slipping a tackler and losing a shoe, racing sixteen yards for his second touchdown.

Seth is playing like a wild man.

"He's one of those rare football players, he just *makes thing happen* on a football field!" says Dierdorf excitedly.

Reggie sacks Aikman; Andre delivers another punishing hit to poor Emmitt Smith, who will gain only sixty-seven yards (preserving an Eagles' streak of fifty games without allowing a running back to gain one hundred yards). Smith, the Eagles are convinced, is now just taking the ball and looking for a safe place to lie down. Andre is off in his killer torpedo zone, throwing himself around the field with such abandon that he literally knocks himself out on one play—inadvertently spearing headfirst into the padded leg of his teammate Willie T. Andre lies motionless on the turf for a few moments, then tries to stand, only to have his legs fold under him. He's back in the game a few plays later, reoriented and unhurt, wildly cheered by the home fans.

The stadium is in a blood-lust frenzy midway through the fourth quarter, as the home team's 24–7 lead begins to appear decisive. The noise becomes a constant, joyous ringing; on the field it's like a drug, the soundtrack of victory at home.

"Here's a team that *ought to be* in Pasadena!" says Dierdorf, catching the mood, projecting the Eagles into the upcoming California Super Bowl game.

On the last chance Dallas has to get back in the game, Buddy's Boys drive Aikman and the offense backward ten yards in three plays.

Richie is about to explode with happiness on the sidelines, his great foghorn voice blasting nonstop, greeting his players as they come off the field, slapping their helmets and butts:

"All right! All right!"

"Keep it going! Keep it going!"

"Way to go, kid!"

Out on the field, the Cowboys are reduced to bickering with one another, screaming to be heard over the din. As the Eagles hammer out a last scoring drive in the final minutes, Dallas defenders are shouting at each other:

"Hey, that was your gap! You're supposed to make that play!"

"Where were you at, man?"

"What's going on!"

The supreme moment for Dave comes in the final touchdown, a twelve-yard run by Byars—his eighth carry of the night and his first points of the season. Dave lines up across from big Dallas nose tackle Russell Maryland, the Cowboys' number-one draft pick from the year before, a Jerome protégé from Miami.

Dave has had his share of good blocks before. He's caught guys off balance and knocked them flat or met some giant's charge head-on and held his ground and then pushed him backward. But this block, on this play . . . it's the most amazing block of his life.

Maryland lines up on his left shoulder, so as Dave snaps the ball, he turns his head into the bull-rush and drives forward, standing Maryland upright, locking his hands up inside the big nose tackle's shoulders and getting a firm hold of his jersey. Maryland sees Byars breaking out toward his right, so for a moment he stops concentrating on Dave and tries to pull off, which gives the center all the leverage he needs. With Maryland thrown slightly off balance, and Byars turning upfield, Dave now begins to drive the big man backward. They've gone about five yards downfield when Maryland starts bellowing and swinging his arms, trying to knock the blocker off him, but Dave has his face mask buried in the tackle's chest, so the blows rain ineffectually off the back of his helmet, and Dave keeps on driving the big nose tackle back, back . . . back all the way to the end zone.

Ron Heller lets up after Byars rumbles by, and looks up to see the Cowboys' nose tackle locked up and flailing at Dave, so Ron takes a flying leap at Maryland, trying to knock him loose, and ends up collapsing both men. Maryland leaps up in the end zone—twelve yards downfield from the line of scrimmage—cursing up a storm and swinging now at Ron, who gamely lunges right back at him. The ref signals touchdown. Dave is so caught up in the bliss—his touchdown, too—that he just trots back toward the bench, trying to calculate how many yards straight backward he blocked Maryland.

Heller draws a fifteen-yard personal foul, which is assessed on the kickoff.

The Eagles haven't just won, they've romped—31–7. Having lost two Pro Bowl players, Jerome and K-Jack, they seem to have gotten stronger. What team depth! What fire! What mastery!

Just about every Eagles fan packed into the Vet is still in place at midnight as the Cowboys attempt a meaningless forty-eight-yard field goal on the last play of the game. The ball sails wide right, a final image of futility, and the stadium sends heavenward one last winning wail.

The ABC cameras capture a handwritten sign in the crowd, held aloft by a grinning Philly fan in stocking cap and mittens.

The sign reads: ANY QUESTIONS?

The boys in the booth chuckle.

"Nope," answers Michaels.

Dierdorf offers this closing national benediction on the Battle of the Unbeatens: "The Eagles leave the Vet this evening crowned, I think, the early October Super Bowl favorites. Tune in next week."

• • •

THE LOCKER ROOM is mobbed. There's potbellied Dr. Z., *Sports Illustrated*'s football guru Paul Zimmerman, with his thick, well-worn notebook, cornering players and questioning them nose to nose.

There's the clink of metal on metal as ESPN, ABC, and HBO cameras war against those from NFL Films and all the local crews, and the usual pack of printhounds has swelled to almost three times its usual size. The team's mood is definitely ready-for-prime-time, and they turn on their considerable charm.

Wes kids about his "size thirteen" feet peeking out of the end zone on his interception.

"Willie T. tipped it, and I alertly got it," says Wes. "I didn't alertly stay in the end zone."

Andre jokes about about knocking himself silly. "My teammates make the highlights, and I make the 'Football Follies.' "

The Pack has dozens of promotional angles: Byars Gets TD (Who Needs K-JACK?), Randall NFC's Player of the Month (He's Back!), Herschel Plows for Two (Sweet Revenge!), Seth Plays Hurt (Jerome's Best Bud Inspires!), Reverend Reggie Sets the Tone (Divine Intervention!), O-Line Comes of Age (Antone's on Track!)—all will be pursued. Not so Dave's career-best twelve-yard block, his recovered fumble, or any of the other hard-won small victories on the offensive line. But the big guys don't care. They play their own game within the game, and the victory is as much theirs as anyone else's—maybe more.

"It's better than sex! There's no better feeling in the world," says lineman Mike Schad.

At the other end of the room, before a small convention of TV and film equipment and tape recorders, Seth stands with a bowling-ball-sized ice wrap around his right knee and revels in the heroism of his performance, pronouncing himself the prime author of victory.

Recalling the pass he slapped away from Aikman in the third quarter, which was then caught by Byron, Seth says, "That play was really the turning point. It gave the ball to our offense in a position where they could get something done. Turnovers are what it's all about [true Buddy disciple]. That's how you dominate. . . . I love the big games. The only thing that would have kept me out is if I couldn't run and started hurting the team . . . I just told myself to put it out of my mind and play."

There will be talk of greatness in tomorrow's newspapers, talk of a possible undefeated season.

• • •

OUT IN THE PARKING lot in the early morning darkness, long after the fans have departed and the stadium has gone dark, a group of the players and their wives linger, savoring the moment.

Dave describes his perfect block at least three more times, and Pink makes everybody laugh, talking about how scared he got when Randall had gone down clutching his knee—Pink had misheard the snap count, so was left squatting ridiculously in place as the nose guard ran over the quarterback. At the time, Pink had been close to tears on the sidelines. But everything had worked out. Now he could laugh about it.

"Coulda sworn he said 'On two,' " says Pink, which strikes everyone as hilarious.

"That's how I got my fumble," says Dave. "I *knew* I was gonna get the ball tonight. . . . Yo, Ron! You owe me, Buddy. Ten big ones."

And their laughter rises in the cold night air, happy fading clouds of steam.

10

BEING SETH

Seth Joyner, Monday night hero, architect of the turning point, is still in the training room hours after the Dallas victory, getting treatment for his injured knee, when in walks his wife, Jennifer, and his daughter, Jasmine.

Jasmine is a perfect blend of her interracial parentage: she has skin of soft beige, with a wild thick halo of frizzy blond hair. She and Jennifer haven't seen Seth for about three weeks, since catching up to him in Phoenix before the Cardinals game.

The linebacker turns on his baleful, stone-faced stare—blank brown eyes, a crease of scar tracing the ridge of his left cheekbone, black stubble outlining full lips. His features fall naturally, even when he's not angry, into a scowl. Jennifer recognizes the expression, of course.

It's just Seth *being Seth*.

He asks, "What are *you* doing here?"

JENNIFER POPPING UP like this is just the latest thing to go wrong this season for Seth. Nothing he does seems to work out as intended.

Seth is really getting on people's nerves.

He plunged into a funk so deep after Jerome's death that it scared those who knew him best. He got the word when he was out in Los Angeles taping the television show "American Gladiators" and flew back home to El Paso before flying east for the funeral. Jennifer had never known how important Jerome was to Seth. It was like he had lost his brother, or his mother! She encouraged him to call Buddy.

"You need to talk to somebody who cared as much about Jerome as you did," she said. But Seth wouldn't pick up the phone. It was not his way to reach out to anyone.

And now, having dedicated the season to his fallen buddy, Seth feels an obligation to produce a Super Bowl win, to make it happen. If the team needs somebody to step up, fill that leadership void, who better than Seth himself? Only, the idea scares the hell out of everybody else. Anybody who knows Seth *knows* he's the wrong person to shoulder Jerome's leadership role.

Seth's motivational methods are . . . well, crude. Take the Skins game at the end of the '91 season. The Eagles were down 10–7 at halftime, and the offense hadn't done squat. The touchdown had come on an interception by defensive back Otis Smith. Resilient Eagles backup quarterback Jeff Kemp was getting hammered like one of those round-bottomed punching dolls that keeps popping back up with a grin. In the first two quarters, the Eagles had advanced the ball only twenty-six yards. They were averaging just over one yard per play.

So in the locker room at halftime, as the offensive line huddled around a blackboard to watch Dave Alexander draw up some new blocking strategies, Seth stepped in, in one of his glowering fits.

"You sorry sons of bitches!" he growled at them. "Why don't you guys learn how to block? You guys couldn't block my grandmother. You're a bunch of pussies!"

The big linemen were momentarily taken aback.

"Just a goddamn minute!" said Ron Heller. "Seth, that's not fair. You have no right to accuse us. You don't have any idea what's involved here. We're not pussies, we're just trying to straighten things out. You worry about your own goddamn side of the ball!"

Seth retreated, grumbling.

As it happened, the Eagles came back to win that game in the second half, 24–22. Kemp threw a slew of big passes, including two for touchdowns. Seth's insults were forgotten in the general good feeling after that win, until Ron, Dave, and the others read the next morning's newspaper. In it, the linebacker bragged about how his pep talk to the offensive linemen at halftime had straightened them out and made them play like men!

That was the final game of the season, and most of the linemen caught the quotes on their way home. They grumbled over this affront for a few days at home, and the whole matter would have been forgotten by the following summer, except that Seth, in training camp, picked up right where he had left off. Puffed up with this new leadership thing, he was huffing around West Chester like the badass master of the ball field. Richie had named Seth a team captain, which just sanctioned this conduct. Seth as captain began to infect the whole squad with his dark aura.

For instance, when the other team captains—Reggie, Keith Byars, and Ken Rose—go out for the coin toss before preseason games and shake their opponents' hands in the time-honored football tradition of good sportsmanship, Seth stands conspicuously about ten yards off in a black funk, asserting his malice, subverting the ritual, embracing *bad* sportsmanship. This isn't just theater either, like the promotional posturing of heavyweight fighters at the prefight weigh-in. Seth has his own perverse rationale. "The other team is the enemy, man," he says. "I ain't shakin' hands with nobody before a football game. Why would I want to do that? I'm getting ready to go to war against these people."

Another of the newer irritating things about Seth is his insistence that his grief over Jerome is more profound and heavier than everyone else's—walking around all season with "#99" shaved out of the hair on the back of his head. Clyde Simmons is the only other player on the team whom Seth acknowledges as having been "as close to Jerome," although there are plenty of others who could, if they chose to, dispute that. For his part, Clyde maintains a dignified silence that becomes real sadness. But Seth stakes out the high grieving ground as though laying claim to the soul of the team, which isn't itself so bad, except he uses that vantage point to hurl dark thunderbolts.

He criticizes teammates who failed to attend Jerome's funeral. He lambastes the club for not helping out with Jerome's camp last spring, which turns out not to be true—the team had quietly made a thousand-dollar donation for the event and is already making plans to carry out Jerome's plan for a similar event in New Jersey. When Seth learns of his mistake, he faults Harry for not keeping him informed. "It's the same old story," he says. "They never think of us. If they had let us know what was happening, I never would have said anything."

Back in the preseason games, he and the rest of the defense defied league restrictions on altering their uniforms by drawing black outlines around the silver wings on their helmets and penciling in Jerome's number 99. When the league objected (with millions invested in worldwide merchandising of NFL products, the league takes graphics *very* seriously), the team came up with a memorial patch for the players to wear on their uniforms—only Seth then blasted team management in the papers and on TV for not making the patch bigger and more ornate. "It looks like something you'd get down at K-Mart," he growled. The patch was redesigned.

It's hard to believe so much trouble can be caused by one man's mouth.

In practice, Seth would strut over when the offensive line was doing one-on-one pass-blocking drills with the defensive line. He'd grab Clyde or Reggie as they prepared to tangle with Antone and say, "Let me do it, I'm gonna make Antone a man"—apparently oblivious to the insult thus given to both blocker and blockee.

Dennis McKnight, the formidable veteran backup lineman with a badass biker image of his own, got fed up.

"Seth, you are the angriest man I have ever met," he said after one training-camp practice. "I've never met a man with more hate than you. I don't understand it. I've tried . . . but, hey, you're on your own. I don't want anything to do with you. Whatever your problem is, it's not my fault, and you better leave me the hell alone."

More and more, as the season progressed, teammates resented the linebacker's attitude. With Jerome around, Seth's forbidding intensity had been a plus. His brooding persona lurked in the background, helping to set the defensive squad's menacing tone. Jerome would make everybody laugh, Wes and Eric would analyze things, Reggie oozed respectability and excellence, and Andre lent a kind of spooky voodoo strain. Seth had just glowered in the back of the room, an automatic rifle with the safety on . . . until he entered the field. This year the safety is off all the time. With his mouth locked in firing position, Seth has become a danger to his own team, and to himself. Teammates aren't openly critical of him, but there are enough nods, winks, and rolls of the eyes for the Pack to know how most of them feel.

The contrast with Jerome formed a study in leadership. Jerome didn't try to lead and never really saw himself as a leader. Joy just radiated from that dancing, cast-iron-furnace frame and neon grin. Jerome made you feel as if he were on a ride that was just so damned terrific that nobody would want to get left behind. Seth, on the other hand, made you feel like he was slogging through some sort of awful crusade; you could join him if you had the stuff for it, and if you didn't? Well, fuck you.

The way he acted, it made them almost feel like losing sometimes, just to spite him. On the field, Seth was a great player. No doubt about it. But after making an interception and running it in for a touchdown, or after brutally sacking the quarterback, he'd trot back toward the bench with his face set in cement as he passed the offensive players. Some would pat him on the back or helmet—Randall always made a point of running out to congratulate him—and more often than not, Seth would coldly ignore all but his defensive teammates, avoiding even eye contact with offensive players, conveying the sense that they were unworthy to stand with him on the same field.

Ron, who'd had some of the more vocal clashes with the linebacker, went out of his way to bridge this divide. When one of his brothers attended a home game and happened to sit near Seth's mom and sister and brother, he'd snapped pictures of the linebacker's family watching the game. When the film was developed, he sent Ron prints to give Seth, and Ron was delighted. Maybe this would break the ice. He cheerfully crossed the locker room with the photos in an envelope.

"Hey, Seth, my brother took some pictures of your family."

Seth eyed him flatly. "What do I want them for?"

"I just thought you might like them."

"All right, put 'em down."

And that was that. No thanks, no nothing. Who wants to join the crusade of a guy like that?

Seth can feel the bad vibes he's created. But he isn't about to back down. Like him or not, these guys are going to play up to Seth's expectations—or there'll be hell to pay.

JENNIFER SMIT was a twenty-four-year-old senior at UTEP (University of Texas, El Paso) when she met Seth Joyner. They were both living in the dorm for scholarship athletes. Jennifer had been recruited by UTEP from the world track-and-field circuit, where she was a promising heptathlete, which is track and field's seven-event female version of the decathlon, a demanding two-day competition testing all-around athletic ability—distance running and sprints, high and long jumps, shot put, and javelin. Years of strict training had given the impressive female contours of her body an Amazonian edge, an uncustomary hardness and definition, and little about Jennifer's personality softened the effect. There was nothing at all soft about her. She had the courage and self-possession of one who has traveled far and embraced big changes in her young life, and she was fiercely competitive—the kind of person who seeks out challenge and confronts conflict head-on. She spoke an emphatic and highly original English, which she learned first in school in Holland, and then refined on the casual rhythms of African-American dialect mixed with some easy West Texas drawl. She was a true exotic out in the taco desert, strong, fit, bold, and opinionated, and despite her smashing blond good looks, Jennifer was a loner. In this sunny, Freon-addicted, strip-malled, Alamo Republican corner of America, she came off, frankly, as kind of a kook.

Eighteen-year-old Seth, however, had his own priorities where women were concerned. Observing the forbidding long-legged blond track star moving alone through the dining hall every day, he had bragged to his teammates, "She will be mine." This got back to Jennifer, as these things are supposed to in school, and the senior track star's response was, "Yeah, right. Dream on."

But she was intrigued. She started noticing Seth more. He stood out from the other freshman football players because he seemed lost at all times in a dark cloud of lonesome gloom. His gravity and singularity appealed to her. She had been around UTEP for four years now, and the blacks, especially the black football players, moved everywhere in loose, joshing homeboy herds. She learned that this Seth Joyner, a hardship recruit from someplace in New York—a place distant and harsh—was considered mean and a little crazy. One of the senior football players told her that they hadn't dared subject Seth to the usual hazing rituals inflicted on freshmen—the guy was too scary.

Seth was the second son of Pattie Cooper, a North Carolina sharecropper's daughter who had left the farm after high school and followed a friend north to take a job as a practical nursing aide at the Rockland Psychiatric Center in Spring Valley, New York. She would end up working at the center, about a half hour's drive north of New York City, for thirty-five years before retiring in '90, raising her two boys and a daughter, Samantha, by herself. Her oldest, Eric, and Seth were sons of a man she met at church and was involved with for about six years. They had split before Seth was born in '64. Her daughter, by a different man who also did not stay in her life, came six years later.

There was always something, right from the start, rather stark and arresting about Seth. Even as a toddler, Pattie says, he was a peculiarly solitary and independent child. He seemed precociously capable. Most mothers in the low-rent neighborhood where they lived were afraid to let a two- or three-year-old outside by himself to play, because unsupervised older children would bully the babies and sometimes get rough. But this was not a problem with Seth. He more than held his own. Growing up, he spent many hours by himself, developing a dour, silent, proud personality that even as a small boy he wore like an outsized suit. He had a violent temper and was fearless. Pattie would often repeat the story about Seth, the one that she felt defined him best, of how his father had come for a rare visit one day, and how Seth had found him, a large man, sitting on Pattie's bed.

Seth was only six years old, but when he confronted the big man he became fiercely protective, threatening, "Get off my mama's bed!"

"Boy, do you know who you're talkin' to?" asked his father.

"My mama says you're my daddy, but no man sits on my mama's bed."

At church, where Seth worked as an usher when he grew older, people would compliment Pattie on what a fine, big, strong boy she had, but would complain, "He looks like he'd bite your head off!"

"Oh, no!" Pattie would say. "That's just Seth being Seth"—in other words, you either accepted Seth the way he was, sourpuss and all, or you could go fry spit. He damn sure wasn't going to walk around forcing himself to smile just to make other people happy. If people thought he was mean . . . well, that was their problem—*Want to make something of it?*

In school, he walked the halls masking whatever insecurities he harbored with hair-trigger aggression, picking fights with anyone who even looked at him for too long—*Who you lookin' at?* He remembers fighting almost every day. It was who he was; he was just *being Seth*. The absolute worst side of Seth's *being Seth* was on display in any kind of competition. With him, there was no such thing as a friendly pickup game of anything, whether cards, bowling, pool, basketball, baseball— even miniature golf. With some people competition was do or die; with Seth, it was do or kill. He had to win. If he didn't, it was somebody's fault—referees, teammates, opponents, coaches; it didn't really matter. His temper was like napalm, splashing and burning everything in a wide moving radius. It got so that people were afraid to play not only against Seth, but even *with* him, at anything.

He had a caring side, though it was well hidden. His mother leaned on him at home, especially when her widowed mother, Emma Cooper, suffered a stroke and came to live with them. Seth was about eight years old then and was handed much of the responsibility for helping his ailing grandmother. When his older brother graduated from high school and moved away, Pattie depended on Seth to handle household chores while she worked, and he didn't let her down—Seth never let Pattie down—cooking, cleaning, and caring for both his little sister and his grandmother. By the time Emma died, at age eighty-five, teenage Seth had grown extremely close to her. He would recall years later how his grandmother prepared him for her death, telling him that she had lived long enough, and that she was tired. "I've seen all my children grown, and I've seen my grandchildren and great-grandchildren. It's my time." When she passed, Seth missed her and grieved, but he also felt the rightness of it.

Shouldering household tasks at an early age, becoming the man of the house, caring for his grandmother in her years of decline, and watching her die—these are the things Pattie feels shaped Seth into such a serious young man. Sometimes too serious.

"Boy, can't you smile sometime?"

"Mama, this is the face I was born with, I can't help it," he'd say. "I can't be walking around forcing myself to smile all the time just to make other people happy. I can't be somebody else. I'm Seth."

Being Seth was, of course, something Pattie could understand and even admire, but where his mother saw just great seriousness, others saw ever-burning sulfur unconsumed, an unappeasable anger that spilled into every part of his life. He found a legitimate outlet for that fire on the football field, but even there he had a hard time fitting in. As a sophomore, he had latched on to an assistant coach at the high school named Jimmy Pinkston, who had played college ball at the University of Miami. Seth had decided he was going to play pro football—his mother remembers him boasting quietly, *seriously,* as a young teen, "Mama, see these hands? These hands are going to make you a fortune. These hands are going to play in the NFL." It was a common boyhood dream, but there was nothing common about the way Seth set to work at it. Other boys played high-school football for the fun of it, for the status it afforded them at school, for the camaraderie of Team. Seth enjoyed those things, too, but the football part for him wasn't just fun; it was very serious business. He would pump Pinkston for information about the game, practically moving into his house in his early years of high school. It wasn't the kind of attachment Pinkston had felt with other boys growing up fatherless, looking for a substitute. There were plenty of boys like that. Seth was different. He wasn't looking for a father figure; he was looking for a mentor, a guide. He knew where he wanted to go and figured Pinkston could show him the way. Sometimes Pinkston felt the kid was trying to suck him dry. "He damn near worked me to death," the coach recalls. Seth couldn't learn enough about tactics and game planning, about how to study films for clues about an opponent's (and his own) tendencies and weaknesses, and how to exploit what he had learned on the field. He wanted Pinkston to tell him everything he knew about how high-school players landed college football scholarships, and how the pros scouted and recruited from colleges. Pinkston would have to chase Seth away many nights: "Look, son, I've got to go to bed. Either you're going home now or you can go upstairs and find a bed here."

But Pinkston was transferred to another high school, and in Seth's senior year he had to play for coaches he didn't know well, and whom he didn't respect. Even at that point, Seth felt he knew more about the game than they did—certainly more about how to best use himself. Seth thought he was the best player on the team, and probably was, and it burned when the coaches put other players ahead of him. Of course, his resentment just worsened the situation. He started *being Seth* in a big way. When his coaches reprimanded him, Seth just burrowed more deeply into his hole of grudge. He would still complain about it more than a decade later, as a millionaire Pro Bowl NFL linebacker, at a time when dropping old and petty differences would seem both easy and wise. Asked to recall his high-school playing days, something sure to provoke gaudy sentiment and grateful memories in almost any other pro football player, Seth would grouse angrily about ignorant coaches who "treated me like a flunky." He was convinced that he was not allowed to excel as a running back in high school because the coaches preferred other players and had given Seth the ball only when they were in a tight spot and desperately needed yardage. He would pull their nuts out of the fire and come grumbling back to the bench, shrugging off their praise and thanks, having proved his point once again to no avail, wrapped in a cloud of disgust. That's how Seth saw himself as a football player—someone whom coaches disliked and would prefer not to play, but whose talent would not be denied. His attitude, his mother says, was "If you let me play, I'll show you how good I am. If you don't, your loss."

He took the same grudging approach with him to UTEP, where Bill Young, the head coach, had taken a gamble on him. At 185 pounds, Seth was well under the expected playing weight for a Division I college linebacker, and he lacked the academic standing to enroll. But Pinkston had sold Seth's potential to Max Bowman, a coach at a nearby New York junior college, whom Young then hired to help him at UTEP. So Seth was brought in as a grant student, part of the university's outreach efforts to the underprivileged. Young figured that under his guidance, Seth and the other academically underqualified boys he had shepherded into his program could be taught discipline, manners, and work habits to see them through college and life. In return for playing father/adviser, the coach got talented players capable of turning around UTEP's struggling football program. If things worked out, that is.

Seth rewarded the coach's gamble with aggression—on and off the field. Young was an authentic Texas old-school, my-way-or-the-highway, football coach, whose methods borrowed heavily from the military. For instance, he expected his boys to address him and the other coaches with a crisp "Yes, sir!" or "No, sir!"—standard fare on scholastic football fields in that part of the country. Well, it wasn't going to be standard fare for Seth. At an early practice as a freshman, Seth responded with an innocent civilian New York "yeah" to some coachly inquiry and found himself on the receiving end of a whole raft of good ol' boy drill-sergeant-style outrage in front of the whole team. Nothing serious or personal was meant by this, of course. Seth was just the first recruit to give Young the opportunity to hammer home this particular point, but fresh off the plane, still uncertain about how homey was going to play out here in redneck Cowpokeland, Seth took the chewing out as a personal affront, and—Seth *being Seth*—there was no way short of a six-gun to his temple that he was ever going to cough up a respectful "sir" to anyone again.

It started there and just worsened. Used to a high degree of freedom as a teen in Spring Valley, and unused to any kind of paternal authority, Seth balked at the stern efforts Young made to mold his charges into both successful football players and students. The coach enforced a 10:30 p.m. lights-out policy in the dorm, strict curfews with bed checks on game weekends, mandatory study halls—real basic these were, too, such as "Men, see this book in my hand? Any of you ever seen one of these before? This here is a dictionary. Today we're gonna learn how to use it."

Seth felt he was being treated like a child, and he didn't work at disguising his contempt. He had come to play college football, a necessary step on his inevitable trajectory to the pros, and he didn't need or expect a lot of character-molding bullshit from Coach. One of the reasons Jennifer often saw him alone was that the more conscientious players knew that hanging around with Seth (at least until he began to prove himself on the field) wasn't exactly the short path to success on Bill Young's football team. The fact that Young came to see him as a bad apple (actually, this was mostly in Seth's mind, Young would later insist) didn't bother Seth one bit—*If you let me play, I'll show you how good I am. If you don't, your loss.*

Young played him, and Seth showed how good he was. He took over as a starting outside linebacker in his freshman year and grew stronger and more ferocious every season. Young rewarded his efforts by taking him off the grant program and writing him a full scholarship. Despite Seth's surly demeanor, Young discovered that the young man from New York had work habits—at least where football was concerned—that put the rest of his squad, even his starting seniors, to shame. Seth set a whole new standard of intensity, although the coach found the attitude troublingly grim. He'd see Seth slumped in joyless repose at his locker and ask, "What's wrong?" But there was nothing wrong, at least nothing Seth cared to discuss. Just Seth *being Seth*.

When he finally met Jennifer, he made good on his old cafeteria boast, and that, too, became a problem. Jennifer went on the European track tour the summer after she graduated, and when she returned to take an assistant coaching job at the school and to resume her training, she and Seth started seeing each other often. Both had found it hard adjusting to the social circles in the athletic dorms, and both had gone through periods of feeling lonely, isolated, and far from home. In short order, they were inseparable, and what a striking couple they made. Hand in hand, black on blond, ebony and ivory, the emerging young linebacker with the grim look on his face and the stern Dutch wonder woman six years his senior—not everyone on campus had horizons wide enough for the view. Some thought the match wasn't good for the image of the team or the school. Young worried that Seth's romance would distract him from his studies and from football, which had, in fact, happened more times than he could count. And the interracial aspect, that was worrisome, too. Young was infected with that educated and sensitive good ol' boy kind of racial outlook, the sort of second-generation, well-bred, kinder and gentler racism that said, *Hey, kids, this kind of thing don't bother me, y'understand, but everybody ain't as lib'ral as I am.* In fact, Young had seen quite a few of these black player–white girlfriend pairings in his coaching years, and in his experience they nearly always ended up badly. So in his father/adviser role, he pulled young Seth aside one afternoon and tried to warn him away from Jennifer, telling him that chances were better 'n even that there was heartache and a heap o' trouble jus' waitin' for him down the road.

This, of course, pissed Seth off, and when he told Jennifer that night, he touched off a Teutonic typhoon. Jennifer wasn't attuned to the subtleties of American racial politics; as far as she was concerned, Coach Young's warning might as well have come dressed in white sheet and noose. Raised in one of the world's most liberal and tolerant cultures, having competed all over the world with women of all races and backgrounds for more than a decade, she was appalled by the small-mindedness of rural America . . . and now it had come knocking on her door! No way she was going to let what she saw as backward, provincial crackerism interfere with her pursuit of happiness. The next morning, she barged past the secretary in the football coaches' suite to confront Young.

"Have you ever met me?" she demanded.

"No," said the startled coach.

"Well, my name is Jennifer Smit."

"Oh, sure, I've heard of you."

"Oh, you've heard of me? But do you know me?"

"I've seen you around. I've read about you in the paper."

"Oh, that's great. So you've read about me in the papers. But do you know me?"

"No."

"Well, then, I'd appreciate it if you would stop telling your players bad things about me. Because I have nothing bad in mind for Seth. I'm going out with him. I really like him. And it's not your business who I go out with and who he goes out with!"

And that was that. During those college years, Jennifer would recall later, with some wonder, that Seth was devoted to her. She helped tutor him through his classes, worked out diet and training programs in the off-season to bulk him up and increase his strength, flexibility, and endurance. She gave him a twenty-dollar weekly allowance from her paycheck as a track coaching assistant so he could go out to the bars after practice with his teammates. Apart from being his lover, Jennifer became the kind of mentor and partner to Seth that Young could not possibly have been to all of the young men on his squad. Seth rubbed it in by bringing her out to watch practice now and then, which was fun, underscoring his defiance of Coach and, face it, showing off a little. That blond hair and those long internationally competitive legs made it tough sometimes to concentrate on the ol' pigskin.

But Young continued to let Seth play, and Seth continued to show how good he was. By his senior year he had built thirty more pounds on his frame, most of it in the upper torso. He led the team in tackles in his junior year as an outside linebacker, and when Young shifted him inside to middle linebacker in his senior year, he led the team in tackles again.

None of which meant Young had to like Seth. Years later, the coach claimed to have no memory of this, but the linebacker recalled being voted one of UTEP's team captains in his senior year, only to have Coach abruptly do away with the policy of having three or four elected team captains in favor of designating two himself, one for offense and one for defense. He did not appoint Seth.

Little energy at UTEP, needless to say, went into promoting Seth to NFL scouts, and, even at 215 pounds, Seth was considered too small to play linebacker at the game's next level. When he wasn't invited to the national scouting combine, his pro prospects didn't look good.

Again, Jennifer proved helpful. The kind of things scouts could quantify about football players, she noted, were track-and-field skills— mostly running and jumping. And these things were her forte. So she altered Seth's normal training regimen to improve those skills, to build better explosive power in his legs for sprinting and leaping.

Still, on draft day, Seth was disappointed. He watched the first two rounds on TV, without really expecting to be chosen—he had excelled as a college player, but had played on a losing team, and he was undersized. His hopes rested in rounds three through six. When his name wasn't called in those rounds, he just left the house in a nuclear funk. Seth was nowhere to be found when he was taken in the eighth round by the Eagles, and that news, relayed by friends, couldn't chisel a smile in the stone face. His friends and family wanted to celebrate, but not Seth. Big fucking deal. Eighth round. As far as Seth was concerned, in those lower rounds teams were just rolling the dice. The Eagles had chosen two linebackers ahead of him and had some quality veterans already on the roster. What kind of chance would he have? He was *being Seth* all out when he flew back to the East Coast for rookie camp with the Eagles' new head coach.

But if there was one coach in the whole Pigskin Priesthood built to appreciate Seth *being Seth,* it was Buddy Ryan, who never met a sociopathic linebacker he didn't like. Seth epitomized the defensive player Buddy was looking for to fill out what was going to become (just ask him) the best defense the game had ever seen. On the one hand, Seth was a grind, a workaholic, with the intelligence and grim determination to master Buddy's complex and shifting on-field strata-gems. On the other, Seth's lifelong surly mien expressed exactly the image Buddy was after. It was an image that played unconsciously on an American racial myth, the stereotype of the intimidating black male, the myth that black men are inherently more virile and violent than white men. Shit, that's exactly the defense Buddy was after! Scare the nut hairs off them pretty little white-boy quarterbacks. So blackness itself became an essential part of the Eagles' defensive character. Reg-gie, Jerome, Clyde, Seth, Byron, Andre, and Ben all were cut, at least outwardly, from the same mold, Buddy's mold. The fact that Buddy, the Okie drill sergeant, played a classic overseer role . . . well, none of the guys seemed to mind that. Playing defense for the Eagles became a distinctly black thing. Together in their far corner of the locker room, their blackness seemed to suck light right out of the room. The Pack (which was overwhelmingly white) would enter casually and drift down about halfway and then stop, the way white folks would cross the street to avoid a group of black men strolling together up the sidewalk, or the way white motorists would roll up their windows and lock their doors entering *that* part of town. The spell was deliberate. To drive home the message, Buddy's Boys wore black shoes and draped black towels from their pants. They hung out together on and off the field. No one played the role with more enthusiasm than Seth. He loaned his stone face to the whole squad.

Yessir, Seth and Buddy were soul mates. Buddy had to let Seth go at the end of the summer, juggling his forty-seven-man roster and relatively certain that Seth—the eighth-round pick—would not be picked up by another team. He promised Seth he would be back in

Philadelphia shortly. Seth flew back out to El Paso and nearly wore out his new green-and-silver sweat gear; when Jennifer washed it, he'd fish it out of the dryer to put it back on the next day. Buddy re-signed him in time to play in the Eagles' third game that season. After a standout year on special teams, Seth was Buddy's starting left outside linebacker for '87.

EVER SINCE THE SCENE in Honolulu over Wanda, Jennifer and Seth had been estranged. He had flown back alone to Philly for the '92 season, leaving unresolved once more plans for his wife and daughter to move back east with him.

By October, Jennifer is through waiting. There are positive signs. Seth is even pleasant on the phone once or twice. When one of the Philadelphia Pack decides to write a big profile of him, the man who had stepped up and taken a leadership role since Jerome's untimely demise, Seth gives the hound her number—what can he be thinking?

Jennifer plays the game like a champ, telling what a great, loving, sweetheart of a guy Seth really is beneath the laser stare, nuclear temper, and apocalyptic gloom . . . well, yes, he is hardheaded enough to play the game without a helmet and he does hate to lose, but all in all a model NFL superstar husband and daddy underneath.

She flies to Philly the day before the big Monday night Dallas game, D-Day, and, planning to surprise him, she and Jasmine spend Sunday night with Erika, who is still coping with Wes's betrayal. Jennifer watches the glorious win, wincing as Seth tries to keep playing after hurting his knee, cheering when he makes his big play. She and Jasmine sit with Erika and Sandra Simmons, two other members in good standing of the fabulous sorority of Eagles' wives whose husbands no longer lived at home. Wes's girlfriend Amy is back, too, over in that other section in one of Wes's guest seats, prompting much clucking and scorn among the outraged *official* women. Erika has gotten out of her system any need to confront Wes's shameless blond sweetie, who now before the players' wives stands for the whole sleazy, preying culture of Sis-Boom-Bimbohood. Lynn Allen can't resist walking Jasmine and Montana over and presenting them to Amy—*I just want you to see who else you're hurting!*

After the game, Jennifer waits in the Wives' Lounge for Seth, who is staying late for treatment. Erika stays with her.

"You might need the ride," she says knowingly.

After an hour or two, with the stadium drained of its loud and deliriously happy fans, Seth's older brother, Eric, comes in the lounge and ignores her. Then Clyde Simmons walks in, again without a word to Jennifer and Erika, crosses the room to speak with Eric in a hushed tone, and then the two men start back out together.

That's when Jennifer takes Jasmine by the hand and follows. She can't stand waiting around anymore. She has to confront him.

Eric turns as he steps through the door, startled.

"Where are you going?" he asks.

"I'm going in," says Jennifer, in her clipped Dutch accent, a blush of that Teutonic blood in her pale cheeks.

"You can't go in. It's only for men. Here, I'll take Jasmine in," he says, taking the little girl by the hand.

"If women aren't allowed, then Jasmine can't go either. I'm going in."

"Suit yourself," says Eric.

Jennifer follows them into the nearly empty locker room, and then into the privileged enclave of the training room, where (as she would later remember the scene) she now returns Seth's scowl.

"What's your problem?" she says.

"What did you come here for? You know the deal."

Hunched on the trainers' table, the massive plates of his chest and shoulder muscles bunched forward and his long, heavy arms resting on his thighs, Seth looks like some brooding heavy in a gladiator movie. The postgame high of the locker room is gone. He is weary and bruised.

"Tell me, Seth. What is the deal?" Jennifer asks.

"You know the deal between you and me."

Seth is clearly embarrassed, being confronted like this in front of the trainers, on his own turf.

"I don't know. That's just it! Are you still seeing that girl?" Jennifer is getting upset now, starting to feel choked up, which makes her angrier.

"No. That has nothing to do with it."

"Then why are you so upset that we're here? Any normal man would be happy to see his wife and child."

"I thought you and I had a better relationship than this."

"Than what? I just came out to see my husband play a football game!"

"You show up unannounced, sneaking around behind me."

"I'm your wife! I didn't think I had to be *announced*. And I was not sneaking. It was supposed to be a surprise."

That had been the idea. But Seth had been tipped off, of course, by his mother, ever protective of her millionaire son.

"If something has you this upset," Jennifer says, "then maybe there's something you need to tell me."

"Like what?"

"Like if you're involved with somebody else. Maybe you should let me know right now. Is there somebody in your life? If you're so bent out of shape, there must be!"

"I told you, there's nothing going on."

"Then why are you so upset?"

"I told you why I'm upset! I just thought we had a better relationship, that you wouldn't do things behind my back."

"Look," says Jennifer, wanting to cut this short now, sobbing. "Please tell me right now. You want me to leave, I'll leave. Jasmine and I will leave, right now, and we won't be coming back."

"Do whatever you want to do, Jennifer," he says, with that cold unfeeling stare. She hates it when he does this, this in particular, implying that their marriage, their family, their future, all of it is *her decision alone.* And him, with his stone face on, with his regal posture that nothing touches him, he's Mr. Pro Bowl Linebacker Superstar, Seth *being Seth,* and she can flit around further in his blazing aura if she likes, or leave, or whatever; it doesn't matter to him. The mighty trajectory of Seth Joyner's career will just maintain its cool and magnificent arc in the heavens.

JENNIFER, SEE, just doesn't get it.

Football players, and athletes in general, learn early the importance of not looking back. It's a discipline that is drilled into them from the first week of organized play: Forget about what just happened, *that's in the past.* If you catch three touchdown passes and break a school record . . . *that's in the past.* If you drop the winning touchdown . . . hey, *that's in the past.* If you hammered the Dallas Cowboys the last time you played them, or if they ran cleat marks up and down your spine . . . forget about it quickly. Things that happened *in the past,* good things, bad things, whatever, they could only hurt you. They were done, kaput, of no further significance. The important thing is to leave them behind. Unburden the mind and unleash the senses. Think only positive thoughts. Forget value judgments, critical analysis, self-doubt, worry; it's just next play, next game, next season. That's the cold logic of pro sports—*You're only as good as your next game*—and that is how you had to proceed. It is a valuable discipline in sport. If you let yourself get too far up, you're that much easier to bring down. If you let yourself get too down, it is that much harder to get up. The pressures of the game are heavy enough without carrying mental baggage with you out on the field. At its ideal, it's like practicing

Zen. You live entirely in the moment, fully alive and open to new opportunity, unmuddied by the past, unformed in the future.

That's in the past is a powerful mantra. So powerful, in fact, that pro athletes find all kinds of uses for it. If you are arrested for drunk driving or beating up your girlfriend or throwing a small explosive out a car window at a group of fans, you get yourself a good lawyer, call a press conference, and when the bastards turn on the lights and point the cameras and microphones at you, all you have to say is, yeah, it happened, that was me, but . . . hey, *that's in the past,* and then scowl ferociously at those who persist in questioning you about it. One of the true rarities in sportswriting is a feature story about the player who blew the game. Sure, there are plenty of soulful accounts from players reminiscing in retirement about the pitch that blew some long-ago World Series game, or the field goal that might have been, but not many show up as part of the daily report, looking back at the game just lost. It isn't because the Pack is too timid or sensitive to probe a fresh wound—hell, no—it is because questions about the crucial mistake are nearly always greeted by the mantra *that's in the past.* End of story. 'Nuff said. It's the niftiest concept since Confession: *In nomine Patris, et Filii et Spiritus Sancti,* and voilà! Clean slate. You can reinvent yourself over and over and over again. It can apply to all phases of your life, too, like, girlfriends, like *wives.* Almost all these guys had left behind whole former worlds when they made the leap from high school to college and then to the pros, every step a big change, a shedding, a rebirth. Just invoke the mantra.

See, what Jennifer doesn't realize about her relationship with Seth, what is so obvious that he doesn't even feel the need to explain, what is also so appropriate and clearly right that he wastes not a moment of regret or sentimentality or any discernible emotion on it, is that Jennifer, who just keeps popping up, demanding explanations, wondering what the hell is going on, is already inalterably *in the past.*

She accompanies Seth that night to Methodist hospital for his IV drip, and once on the table, he promptly falls asleep. She just sits there watching the fluids shifting in the tube.

Can't she see it?

JENNIFER PERSISTS for the rest of the week, living in Seth's apartment. He spends most of the week ducking her, leaving early and coming home late, frustrating her efforts to understand, to reconcile, to part . . . to confront and resolve whatever it is that has sprung up between them. It's in this frame of mind that Jennifer decides the following weekend, when Seth flies off with the team to Kansas City for game five, to phone Wanda. Since Seth won't tell her what's going on, maybe his Puerto Rican dulcinea will.

It's quite a scene, in its own way more than equal to the drama and violence (emotional, that is) waiting on the field for Seth and the Eagles the following afternoon, and with far more lasting consequences.

They meet at the Bennigan's Restaurant on Route 73. Erika accompanies Jennifer, high officers in the Association of Eagles' Wives. As they enter the place, Erika recognizes Lisa, one of Jerome's old harem, at the bar with this fragile Puerto Rican doll face who just has to be Wanda.

Jennifer learns her husband has been living another life. Wanda has been seriously involved with Seth for more than two years now. She was with him on all those road trips in the off-season of '91, at Jerome's camp, at Keith Byars's camp in Dayton, golf tournaments; she had been with him in L.A. taping the "American Gladiators" competition when he got the news of Jerome! The only reason Wanda hadn't flown down to Brooksville for the funeral, she says, was that Seth had told her how Jennifer had *insisted* on going along.

It's staggering. Apart from the emotional blow, my God! A woman has to start wondering about her health. If there is this much about Seth's life over the last two years she hadn't known, how much else was there? Exactly how vast and colorful is the sweep of human sexual history that her husband invited into her body? There are more revelations—this Wanda is too much—enough to just freeze-dry Jennifer's soul and blow it away. She feels numb. She honestly feels more like laughing at this point than crying. It's the emotional equivalent of having just stepped off one of those monster carnival rides that spins your top and bottom in separate directions simultaneously. Suddenly, her whole understanding of her life for the last two, three—hell, the last decade—is up for grabs.

And Wanda is just bubbling over with information. She knows Amy, of course, Wes's squeeze. Both Lisa and Wanda roll their eyes at the mention of Amy, as if to say *What a bimbo that one is, and she dresses so tacky!* Wanda is just adamant that Seth is a dog and that they are through. "I put my career on hold for Seth!" laments Wanda. *Oh Christ, she's looking for sympathy now!* Among other things, Jennifer learns that Seth is planning to build Wanda a house in Florida—see, because then, that way Wanda would be close to Puerto Rico and she would be located strategically between his daughter in El Paso and his mom, after he built his mom a DHM in North Carolina, where Pattie has decided she'd rather retire (more news for Mrs. Joyner). Jennifer thinks, *The poor son of a bitch never did study his geography.*

The more she listens to Wanda, the more she wonders if she has ever known Seth at all.

WHEN SHE GETS BACK to El Paso she gets a phone call from a Philadelphia jeweler, a man they had both gotten to know over the years, a friend. Seth had a thousand-dollar bill outstanding for some bauble he purchased months ago.

"What did he buy?" she asks.

"I can't tell."

"Was it for me?"

"No."

"Was it for his mother?"

"No."

"Was it for his brother or his sister?"

"No."

"Then you don't need to tell me anything else, do you?"

She decides, what the hell.

The woman who spent hours each week clipping food coupons goes out and buys herself the most expensive BMW she can find.

11

INTO THE BELLY
OF THE WHALE

Luck is the hand of God in football. Preparation, talent, momentum, motivation—all of which the '92 Eagles had in excess five games into the season—can all explode in a moment. A great season is as fragile as a blimp in a field of flak.

As a coach or player, you do everything you can to be successful, and after that it is up to a higher authority. Nobody is more keenly aware of this than Andre Waters.

One thing you took with you, growing up on the Muck, was an abiding sense of the divine. Part of it was the culture of poor working black families, who practiced a Baptist brand of Christianity flavored by ancient African and island traditions, and part of it was just the all-embracing eminence of sky, a landscape that made you feel elevated and exposed, so that, on balmy days, you might feel like the coddled firstborn of creation and, on days when the tropical storms boomed, like a helpless offering on a grand ceremonial plate. If Reverend Reggie's Baptist Bible taught a muscular evangelical Christianity, and Randall Cunningham's offered an esoteric (one might even say chummy, you know, like, celebrity to celebrity) rapport with the Almighty, then Andre's experience was more like Jonah's—*hie thee on that path to Nineveh or beware*. It taught him to . . . *watch out*.

You couldn't be too careful. Andre, with his shaved head and Fu Manchu mustache and wide-set squinty gaze, lives in a world where even the most minor of daily activities is fraught with significance and peril. Luck depends, of course, on God's grace, and that depends on not only trying to live the right way, doing good works, resisting temptation, all that, but also getting dressed in the correct sequence, changing lanes on the expressway on the way to work at the right moment, invoking heavenly tolerance with the exact right words—keeping things regular. There are obviously no guarantees; you can do everything exactly right and God might still smite you—and that was for your own good, too—but you can minimize the chances by making the right moves.

It isn't always easy finding them either. The Lord's path may be plain to the righteous, but Andre makes no such claims for himself. God knows, Andre has slipped up now and then. There is, for instance, the fact of his being widely feared and reviled in the NFL for trying to hurt people on the football field.

This is true, certainly in reputation and partly in fact, and sometimes even Andre will admit it. Even as kid back in Pahokee, his unofficial assignment on defense was to rough up the other team's star player. Playing safety in the pros (for Buddy) gave full license to this approach, since in many formations Andre's job was just to move to the ball. And Andre would make it his business to get in one good hammer—late, low, unnecessarily high, it didn't matter—sufficient to send a message. The message was *You could get hurt out here.*

He had perfected the violent alter ego he had begun imagining before games back at Pahokee High. It had started as a vague notion, an alter ego bigger, stronger, and faster than his poor undersized self. In college, when his teammates called him Batman, the vision was still just half formed. Now, in his ninth pro season, at age thirty, the creative visualization had become very real. When Andre suited up to play, he was no longer Andre Waters, the loving Christian gentleman who greeted callers on his answering machine with gospel music and a sweetly intoned "God bless you," he was someone else, his Overman, someone known to him and his teammates as the Dré Master.

His friend Mike Flores, a second-year defensive end with a flair for comic-book artistry, had drawn the Dré Master just right, a brooding, Dr. Doom–like caped villain. To become this "Dread Master," Andre has to work himself into the right mind-set, and he has an elaborate ritual to help. It starts days before the game, when he comes up with a motivational slogan for for the week, something like "Nothing nice" or "Let's do it" or "I'm for real" or a phrase from the Bible, or maybe the name of someone near and dear. He writes the phrase on the pages of his game plan and meditates on it at every opportunity. On game days he arrives at the stadium two hours before kickoff, gets a massage and treatment for any aching muscles or joints, soaks in the Jacuzzi, anoints a troubled limb with some oil blessed by the pastor of St. Paul Church of God in Christ, Willie Ola's church back in Belle Glade, pulls on his shorts *before* picking up his lucky shirt—a limp, lightweight cotton pullover with blue sleeves that doesn't quite match Eagles' green, but that Andre has worn for games ever since an '88 victory over the Rams that triggered a season-saving seven-game winning streak. Then Andre inscribes this week's slogan on a hand towel and on a piece of white masking tape. The towel gets draped from his belt, the tape he affixes to his forehead. Only then will Andre kneel to pray, not just as Andre anymore, but as the Dré Master, invoking God's help for the game, to protect his opponents, his teammates, and himself from injury. He concludes with an incantation, tried and true, which goes, "and when the dust has settled, may the team that has worked the hardest and deserves it the most emerge victorious."

Then, after invoking heaven, Andre primes himself to raise hell. He looks for reasons to hate his opponent. Say, if he had given up a touchdown against this team in the past, that would suffice, or if some player on the other team had taunted him, or said something in the newspapers. Before the Broncos game, for instance, that safety Tyrone Braxton had dared to compare his team's defense favorably with the Eagles'—*We'll see about that!* Andre could always find something. He enters the arena girded, anointed, sanctified, psyched, and . . . *transformed!*

In this mode, part hero, part villain, Andre plays possessed, so darkly focused that his own teammates will sometimes clap him on the helmet to make sure he doesn't lose himself completely in the dark fantasy. When the game ends, all traces of evil and heroic excess fall off with the gear, and he becomes the sweet man he was before.

To Andre, the division between real self and Dré Master is so complete he's startled when real people, in the real world, confuse the on-field antics with *him*. He's brought some of this on himself, actually, like when he boasted that time—one of these things uttered in an instant to the Pack that assumes a life of its own—"I'm an animal, I admit it." That had been a mistake. Because then the press box pontificators started keeping score, replaying Andre's more questionable shots in slo-mo, where a third-degree misdemeanor looks like premeditated assault. In fact, the decision to hit or not to hit was made in an eye blink, often when running at full speed or airborne, and it was made, not by Andre, but by the merciless Dré Master. One of his most notorious shots was a low, out-of-bounds body chop in '86, aimed at then-Falcons quarterback (now teammate) David Archer. Arch was unhurt, but the shot was so flagrantly late and out-of-bounds that it caused leaguewide uproar. Andre felt compelled to admit he was in the wrong and wrote a letter of apology to Arch—the first one the veteran quarterback had ever seen. But no act of contrition could undo what those slo-mo replays fed into gazillions of American living rooms had done. Andre became an icon of bad sportsmanship, a symbol and scapegoat for every pro player's fear of the career-ending injury. When *Pro Football Weekly* had polled players in '90, asking them to name the "dirtiest" players in the league, Andre topped the list—

not the Dré Master, mind you, but Andre Waters—which, besides hurting Andre's feelings, garnered still more scrutiny. Dan Dierdorf, the capable color man of "Monday Night Football," leaped on the bandwagon during the Vikings game that year, singling out the safety for such a severe tongue-lashing that Andre was fined ten thousand dollars by the league—for plays that hadn't even been flagged on the field!

But how is he supposed to jettison the Dré Master? How can he stop playing the game his way? It has brought him from a mud-stained shack on the Muck to annual earnings in the upper six figures. It has raised his hardworking mother from poverty. It has allowed Andre to do good works—unlike many of his teammates, Andre donates not just money to good causes, but his heart and his time. Besides, Andre's mean streak is by now part of the Eagles' mystique. "If the other team is afraid of you, your battle's half-won," says Seth, who knows a thing or two about intimidation.

Andre couldn't change even if he wanted to. He is successful because of the Dré Master, not in spite of him. So no matter how much his agent Jim Solano polishes Andre's off-field image, the Dré Master will undo it in games. Take the Saints game in '91. The Saints were winning, and Andre was upset. Losing fired up the Dré Master like little else. Andre could feel himself getting sucked deeper and deeper into the vortex, so much so that it scared him. There was one play where he torpedoed the knee of tight end Hoby Brenner, trying to hurt him. Brenner had dived over a pile of players and hit Andre after the whistle on an earlier play, which often happened, no big deal, except he had then pushed Andre's face into the turf. So when a spontaneous instant of opportunity presented itself later, the Dré Master did his thing (he made contact, but Brenner was unhurt). After he did it, Andre felt weird. He didn't approve of what he had just done, but it really, totally, *wasn't him!*

All that afternoon he'd been putting up with the taunting of Saints receiver Eric Martin. The Dré Master was just aching to take a shot at the guy, but the right opening hadn't come along. When the gun went off, and New Orleans had the victory, and Andre was standing dejected on the field near the Saints' bench and saw Martin trotting happily off the field, he felt himself crossing back over to the dark side.

"Eric, pull me in! Eric, pull me in!" he pleaded with his teammate, Eric Allen.

Actually, later, he wasn't sure whether he had really called out to Eric or if it was just his good side crying out from deep inside. What happened next was . . . the dark side just took over.

Before the thousands remaining in the stands, and nearly every player, coach, and official on the field, the Eagles' safety tore down the sidelines and leaped on Martin's back, blue arms flailing. Martin fell, and as his teammates ran to his aid, his attacker fled. Minutes later, in the locker room, his Dré Master gear spilled at his feet and the spell broken, Andre looked incredulous when the Pack mobbed him and asked about the postgame assault.

"Nothing happened," he said.

The Pack had lots of fun with that the next day, running Andre's denial under the caption of the photo, the one showing Andre climbing up Martin's back. There was no way Andre could make people understand, you know, about the Dré Master, and the trance. Certainly not the NFL, which slapped him with a $7,500 fine.

No, Andre knows the Lord's path to be demanding and fraught with danger, so he is cautious. Like, say, with women. Andre enjoys the bounty on the Sis-Boom-Bimbo trail. He sees what happens to many of his teammates' marriages, and he knows why, so he avoids serious commitment with women. He is living the life and enjoying it. Responsibility is waiting down the road, and he'll be ready for it, but while he's living the dream, not getting tied down is fundamental. Independence suits him. Sometimes Andre gets in a mood where he doesn't want to be bothered. That's what killed the one serious fling he had, with a woman from Atlanta to whom he had been briefly engaged. She kept getting upset—and Andre could understand this— about the other women in his life, even though he went out of his way not to rub her nose in it. But keeping things from her only fueled her suspicions. Then Andre got in one of his go-it-alone moods and didn't talk to her for, oh, about two or three months. Women, he learned, were real touchy about that.

Marriage, he figures, is a way of taking one of the great and (with the proper precautions) relatively harmless pleasures in life and turning it into a sin. Andre knows that if he were married, it would only be a matter of time before his very own blow-dried sin came walking into some bar, and that would be that. Why tempt fate?

Because fate, for Andre, is not some abstract concept. Lurking in the waters out over the horizon is the whale, and you never know when it might swoop in on some divine current and swallow you whole. You have to be careful. There are just too many ways to screw up.

Take, for instance, the day he didn't wear his lucky shirt.

It happened in the fourth game of the '91 season, against the Pittsburgh Steelers. Andre arrived at the Vet at the right time, only to realize he had left behind his lucky shirt, the one with the blue sleeves. There was not enough time to drive back home and return to prepare himself properly for the game. Andre's rituals were timed right down to the minute. No, he'd forgotten the shirt; now he was just going to have to deal with it.

Sometimes, when you screw up, you can derail the bad luck by taking some dramatic new step, but only if you can think of the right thing. He got a new pair of socks from Rusty, never an easy task, and the socks were okay. Then he paced through his ritual in the usual way. He wrote his slogan on his towel and on the tape—this week it was a recently deceased relative: "For you, Aunt Rosetta, I miss you." He got the tape in place on his forehead, invoked heaven in the usual way and then hell—he'd missed a ton of tackles against the Steelers in a game three years before—and everything was ready except . . . the shirt.

He was trying to summon the Dré Master, but it wasn't coming.

Andre confided his predicament to Eric, whose locker was next to his.

Eric understood immediately. His superstitions weren't in the same league as Andre's, but he did have his lucky, white long-sleeved undershirt, which his rules forbade him to wear two weeks in a row. With some misgivings, but seeing Andre's fix, he offered it.

"But, look here, Dré. When you get two interceptions in this shirt, don't ask me for it next week."

This, Eric knew, was a serious concern. Andre promised.

But what a disaster! Three times in the first quarter Andre's mistakes allowed big plays. He was mad as a stuck gator. Then on the Steelers' second drive, with Andre scrambling to redeem himself, tight end Eric Green shrugged him off to catch a forty-nine-yard pass. On the next play, Green grabbed a slant pass and ran into the end zone with white-armed Andre, the obviously pseudo Dré Master, flapping helplessly on his back.

Andre came running off the field, muttering to himself, and headed straight for the bench. The network TV cameras caught the moment for posterity as the furious safety jerked off his jersey, ripped at the snaps on his shoulder pads, and in one contemptuous motion peeled off and flung the offending white shirt.

Eric watched with surprise.

"It's the shirt, man! It's the shirt!" Andre said. "I'm going to burn it."

"You don't burn *my* shirt, man," Eric said. "That's my lucky shirt."

"I shoulda never worn this shirt," he said. "You're the reason all this happened."

Eric shrugged. There was no reasoning with Andre when he was like this.

From that point forward, the Steelers not only could not score, they failed to move the ball into the Eagles' territory. Late in the game, Andre forced a fumble.

"Look at me now," he shouted to Eric midway through the fourth quarter, when the Eagles had the game in hand. "I can concentrate now! I'm doing good now. I can think like I'm supposed to think!"

Eric hid his shirt from Andre when the game was over.

"I don't think it works for anyone else," he said.

It had been a close call, but Andre survived the curse. He learned (1) don't forget the shirt, but, of equal importance, (2) don't try to *replace* the shirt. Trying to outguess God, it turns out, was blasphemous, sheer prideful folly. No, if you screwed up, you had to just cope, and hope Bud's game plan pulled you through.

All of the signs and portents are good for Andre after the triumphant Dallas victory. His team is undefeated and on its way. He is tied for the team lead in tackles (twenty-seven), and, surprisingly, the evil rep caused by the untamable Dré Master is even getting a buff job in the press.

Even Dierdorf tosses him a bouquet during the Dallas game, saying "Dirty" Waters had cleaned up his act, that he was still hitting just as viciously, but now his blows were "clean."

Andre isn't buying it, and he isn't in an especially forgiving mood either.

"I'm no different," he tells the Pack, pugnaciously. "Everything I do ain't perfect. Sometimes I make hits that aren't good hits, but so do other people. . . . I'm not going to change. My mama told me to always forgive, but I'm a firm believer that what goes around comes around, and I would hope that no one would ever criticize Dan Dierdorf's kid in front of a national audience, or that his kid doesn't become a victim the way I became a victim of his criticisms, and that he doesn't have to hear things on national TV said about his kid that my mama had to hear him say against me."

He gives the impression, however, that while not wishing it, Andre might not mind too much if some such trial were visited on the Dierdorf clan.

And out in the deep blue stirs *the whale*.

DESPITE HIS PROTESTS that nothing has changed, Andre's supposed "reformation" becomes a hot topic before game five of the '92 season, a matchup with the formidable Chiefs in Kansas City's snazzy Arrowhead Stadium.

The NFL pregame show features a segment on Andre, showing him delivering a bone-rattling blow to that Emmitt Smith, then leaning over and shouting into the flattened running back's face mask (just wishing the young man well, actually, advising, "Don't get hurt out here.").

Terry Bradshaw's upbeat narration says, "While the Eagles are still flying, the yellow flags aren't. That's because Bud Carson has been playing a more disciplined game. Case in point: Andre Waters, who appears to have cleaned up his act."

Andre makes an appearance, wearing his NO FEAR black cap, balling up his Fu Manchu in a scowl, and backs down not an inch— "I'm no angel. I do things sometimes that I'm not particularly proud of myself."

Andre's belligerence is part of a general Eagles' defensive chest thumping prior to this game. Having led the NFL in stopping the run for several seasons now, having topped every defensive category in '91, having won their first four games and just demolished the Cowboys, the Eagles have one foot planted on the platform of legend.

Finally, they're getting respect. Now, facing the Chiefs, Buddy's Boys are going on all week about "strength on strength." Kansas City has the best head-on running game in the pros, with two huge effective running backs, 260-pound Christian Okoye and 242-pound Barry Word. Over the last two years, the Chiefs have been beating teams by using these two giants as battering rams, eventually just wearing down opponents. Their offense has become so predictable even the adoring hometown fans are impatient with it. Well, Buddy's Boys can hardly wait. All week long they're promising "big hits," eager to put their toughness to the test. Wes and Andre are the keys. Bud needs them to step up from the backfield and plug gaps with some spit-splattering hammers. Even Richie tips his enthusiasm for the coming collisions. "Kansas City likes to keep pounding you, but they're playing the best team in the league against the run, so it ought to be interesting," he says on his TV show.

Well, Marty Schottenheimer, the Chiefs' head coach, is no fool. A square-jawed veteran of the Pigskin Priesthood, he's also a jet pilot in his spare time. Coaches are always saying you don't have to be a rocket scientist to understand the Game, but Marty . . . well, with his wire-rim glasses on, he even looks like a rocket scientist.

To Professor Schottenheimer, the Eagles are like a fighter so certain of his roundhouse right that he brags about it. Marty had coached with Richie in Cleveland when they were both monks in the temple, and he knows Richie is many things, but subtle and deceptive aren't among them. If Richie and his team say they plan to meet the Chiefs' big backs head-on ... well, that's exactly what they have planned. It's Richie's style.

So Professor Schottenheimer starts cooking up a lesson plan. All that week, to every microphone in earshot, he laments what a challenge the Eagles pose for his team's running game, and how, with their homely little veteran Plan B quarterback Dave Krieg, they just unfortunately have no choice but to challenge these bad boys head-on—*May God have mercy on our poor blasted hides.* He has his running backs at it, too. Word provides the Dré Master's hate motivation for the week when he tells the Pack, "I'm tired of hearing about the Eagles' defense. We're the runners, they're the run stoppers. We're very physical, so are they. Something's got to give."

The primal smell of barbecued beast wafts over the brim of Arrowhead Stadium, smoke from hundreds of grills set up in the vast parking lots where fans, some of whom drive for many hours from the prairie outskirts to this middle-of-nowhere city to attend weekend games, set up camp four and five hours before kickoff. When they fill the broad, sloping two tiers of the stadium, which holds upward of seventy-six thousand, the stands practically bleed the scarlet color of the home team, with all the Chiefs' sweatshirts, jackets, hats, scarves, mittens, flags, pom-poms, face paint, et cetera. A Kansas City home game on a brilliant fall afternoon is a great, roaring spectacle of Americana. The upshot on the field is, of course, the opposing team can't hear a thing.

And with one final intonation of today's competitive theme by CBS commentator Dan Fouts—"The Chiefs want to run the ball with Barry Word between the guards today"—Professor Schottenheimer steps up to the blackboard.

First play (first and ten on the Chiefs' twenty-eight): Krieg drops back and looses a sixty-yard bomb deep down the right sideline, where receiver Willie Davis is covered one-on-one by Izel Jenkins, who slaps the ball away at the last moment.

"Okay, no problem," says Andre, "he got that out of his system, nice try but no cigar. Now we'll get down to business."

The Eagles aren't wasting any man power deep. Why bother? Everybody knows K.C. plans to sledgehammer its way through the Eagles. Bud's playing both safeties and all three linebackers up on the front line, and the boys are just itching for that first spine-jangling whack—why, on that first play, Wes had tackled Word *in the backfield!* Of course, he didn't have the ball. But it was a helluva hit!

Second play (second and ten on the Chiefs' twenty-eight): A fake handoff (play action) and pass, for a seventeen-yard completion to Davis, who does a little curl pattern covered one-on-one by Eric—the easiest way to come free in one-on-one coverage is to sprint downfield twenty yards, then stop suddenly and come back for the ball. It works like a charm . . . oh yeah, and the boys were all over that poor bastard Word again in the backfield.

Third play (first and ten on the Chiefs' forty-five): Another play-action pass, this time, a twelve-yard gain, another curl pattern matching receiver J. J. Birden alone against Eric. Again Word is swarmed in the backfield, breaking some sort of record for getting tackled without the ball.

By now, the beauty of Professor Schottenheimer's strategy is dawning on the Chiefs' side of the field. Every time Krieg takes the snap, turns, and fakes the handoff to Word, Arrowhead Stadium tilts about five degrees on its horizontal axis, as all seventy-six-thousand-plus fans lean along with the Eagles into the fake. Marty has never seen anything like this before. He's come up with the unspoilable gag, the only fake in the whole history of football that works better the more you use it—because, see, every time Krieg feigns the handoff and then throws, the proud and mighty Eagles are *that much more* convinced that on the next play the handoff will be real, so certain are they of Marty's game plan, so eager are they for the test.

Fourth play (first and ten on the Eagles' forty-three): A screen pass, with the Eagles tripping over themselves scrambling toward the runner in the backfield. Only the long right arm of Clyde Simmons, slapping down the ball, stops a big gain.

Fifth play (second and ten on the Eagles' forty-three): Bud has called a blitz; he's sending cavalry, infantry, and mess-hall staff into the backfield this time (Andre is practically assuming a three-point stance), and he has this nifty stunt going on in front, with the ends swinging inside the tackles to throw off blocking schemes and just snuff that ol' running play with a heavy splash of Clyde and Reverend Reggie, once again leaving Eric and Izel isolated in one-on-one pass coverage. Krieg can see the blitz coming (Christ, the Gang Green is panting and slobbering all over itself in blitzful anticipation), so he changes the play, calling for both his receivers, Birden and Davis, just to flat out challenge the cornerbacks. They sprint off the line converging toward a point near the center of the field and then, about twenty yards out, suddenly alter course and angle back toward the deep corners of the field.

Eric turns adroitly, he doesn't miss a step with his receiver, but Izel (he isn't called Toast for nothing) is distracted for a fatal instant by Krieg's pump fake, and his receiver, Birden, has him by a good three steps. Krieg lays the pass out in front of his man, and the Chiefs have a forty-three-yard touchdown pass to conclude their opening drive. Five straight passing plays—so much for "strength on strength."

But, hey, that was a fluke. Bud's defense comes off the field chastened but undaunted. They figure Professor Schottenheimer is just setting them up for those big backs. These guys can't pass the ball all day—they're *a running team,* for crying out loud!

See, this is the unspoilable gag, the more you use it, the better it works!

Things settle down for the rest of the first half. The Chiefs actually run the ball a few times, with predictably minimal success. But Randall can't seem to get the offense moving. For one thing, in all this noise the Eagles are using the silent count, with all the linemen looking back for center Dave Alexander to raise his helmet, and then counting to themselves, only Randall is once again telegraphing the snap *every fucking time* by jerking his right leg, which is making it all but impossible for poor Ron Heller to block the Chiefs' speedy outside linebacker Derrick Thomas—Ron's nightmare, the Bills Game Redux. Randall does manage to inch the Eagles within field-goal range early in the second quarter, chucking the play as drawn and high stepping for a couple of first downs. So there's just a four-point deficit as the game approaches halftime—where presumably Ron can get the quarterback to keep his silver heels planted until after the snap.

With less than a minute remaining until the half, Richie tries to move into field-goal range with a few passes, but Randall gets sacked again by Thomas (who can't believe how easy Randall is making this), and then again by the Chiefs' star pass rusher, left end Neil Smith, who manages to battle through both big Antone Davis and Keith Byars. So with only forty seconds left, after Eagles punter Jeff Feagles gets off a rare bad kick, the Chiefs have the ball back again, just thirty-one yards away from the end zone.

It's easy to figure the Chiefs' next move: send that big back Word right up the middle for three or four yards, call time out, hammer him into the middle once more, call another time out, and kick a field goal. Easy to figure. The boys are ready.

Krieg fakes the handoff, the Eagles dive for the ballcarrier, the stadium tilts seven degrees this time—and the quarterback throws another pass, this one for a seven-yard gain. Now they're in relatively comfortable field-goal range.

Bud decides to blitz, push 'em back, challenge them. With only twenty-five seconds left, time to get off just one more play before the kick, the Chiefs have two receivers split to their left, where they're guarded by three Eagles defenders. Cornerback John Booty joins Eric and Wes on that side. But Bud's call will send Booty after the quarterback, leaving Eric and Wes to handle the two receivers. They've done this a thousand times: Wes has the inside guy; Eric has the outside guy. Simple. Two smart veterans and a routine adjustment.

Only Booty doesn't do a very good job of disguising his intention. So Krieg can see he'll have two receivers with one-on-one coverage on the left side . . . and then Eric screws up. He follows the inside receiver across, practically colliding with Wes, and leaving the outside man, Birden, all alone down the left side of the field. They had handed the Chiefs a touchdown. Booty pointed Krieg's nose in the right direction, and Eric cleared out to let the quarterback and receiver play catch.

So the Eagles go into the locker room down 14–3 . . . and Richie and Bud are convinced—*Okay, they've gotten away with it twice, lucked out, but now the contest really starts, strength versus strength, don't be fooled, fasten your chin straps tight, boys, they're going to be running that ball right down our throats.*

The unspoilable gag!

And who does Professor Schottenheimer pick for the coup de grâce? Why, Andre, of course. The Dré Master has been so transparently eager to stop the run all afternoon that he's practically been playing a third defensive tackle. Andre had knocked himself unconscious (for the second time in two games) in the first quarter delivering a headfirst shot to running back Todd McNair that prevented a Kansas City first down. He was back in on the next series, bailing out of pass coverage at so much as a hint at the fake.

So on the first play of the second half, the Chiefs come out in triple formation, with a pair of tight ends joining Willie Davis on the right side. Before the snap, one of the tight ends pulls up and moves back to the left side, shifting into what is clearly a running formation, with maximum blocking power evenly distributed upfront. As soon as the tight end goes into motion, the Eagles' coverage changes. Andre's job is to stay with Davis coming off the line. Cornerback Otis Smith (who has been inserted to replace the toasted Izel) is supposed to help Andre if Davis goes deep.

Only—*shit, everybody knows they're gonna run the ball*—so when Krieg turns and fakes the handoff, and the Eagles dive, and the stadium tilts, both Andre and Otis abandon Davis and start toward the backfield. A split second later they realize, of course, that they've been had, but by then Davis is sprinting all alone about twenty yards behind them. Davis has time to slow down and circle under Krieg's pass like an outfielder shagging a routine fly—a seventy-four-yard touchdown pass.

Andre is left standing with his hands on his hips, talking vigorously to himself. How has this happened? (The CBS announcing team of Verne Lundquist and Dan Fouts inexplicably places the blame on Wes.)

Randall gets his act together a little better in the second half, completing a long pass to Fred Barnett to set up one touchdown and steering the offense in for a second after Eric picks off a pass late in the game. But there's too much ground to recover. The unbeaten, but clearly beatable, Eagles fall 24–17, undone by that newfangled invention, the forward pass.

The precise margin of victory, as Andre sees it, was supplied by the Dré Master's gaffe. The fact that Eric's mistake and Izel's mistake or any number of offensive breakdowns were all equally culpable means nothing to Andre. He figures he lost the game. He—or that Dré Master—traded victory for the promise of a big hit. How could he be so stupid!

The next day he has to sit and watch it replayed on film, broken down from the overhead side shot and the end-zone shot, while Bud points out all the obvious adjustments that weren't made—Andre can't remember when he ever played so stupidly. And next Sunday they face the Redskins, always one of the toughest games in the schedule. Andre knows he can't afford to play against those fabulous Redskins receivers Art Monk, Ricky Sanders, and Gary Clark, with his head up his ass the way it was in Kansas City. He worries that Bud will now think he's the kind of player who easily suckers for play action. Remember, Andre is not out there because of his physical gifts; he's out there because of his mind. After aggression, experience is his greatest asset. Getting suckered on play action is precisely the thing that should not happen to Andre Waters. Bud doesn't rub it in. He knows Andre feels terrible.

But Andre is tormented in ways Bud can only begin to imagine. The veteran knows what he did wrong on the field, but for him there is always the more mysterious and troubling metaphysical question: *Why* did he do it wrong? How many thousands of times has he seen right through play action, knowing by the formation, the situation, the *feel*, that the pass is coming? Why does all that knowledge and intuition abruptly fail? What causes the sudden fall from grace? Is this just a slip, or is this the beginning of a more serious slide?

All week before the Redskins game Andre feels . . . *stalked*. He does everything he can. He writes his motivational slogan for the Skins game on all his playbooks, "We love you #99; bring it home for Jerome," and he stays late studying film every day, not leaving the Vet until hours after dark. Working intently at his locker before the game, he uses a black marker to ink in on the white towel and forehead tape "Matt. 6–33" (*But seek ye first the kingdom of God, and His righteousness; and all these things shall be added unto you.*) It is both spiritual reminder and talisman: Andre wants to enter the battle with a pure and righteous heart, no doubt about that, but he's also mindful that this particular chapter and verse was his slogan in the Redskins' season-ender last year, and had produced a satisfying victory.

Yet despite his diligence, Andre has a sense of foreboding. Meditating in the RFK Stadium locker room before the game, Andre has what he will later recognize (too late!) as a premonition. It's a fleeting vision of the horrible (and hence oft replayed) videotape of former Skins quarterback Joe Thiesmann having his right leg cleanly snapped by a Lawrence Taylor tackle. The image doesn't linger, and it doesn't trouble him. Despite his caution, Andre doesn't brood over his fate. The remainder of his verse from Matthew instructs *Take therefore no thought for the morrow. . . . Sufficient unto the day is the evil thereof.*

As the team huddles before kickoff, it is Andre who first addresses his teammates, urging them to be mindful of the lessons learned last week. "We can't give up *anything deep.* Hey, if they catch something short, come up and punish them. Let's not give up big plays. This team can't beat us if we don't give up big plays. So let's not give up big plays."

Then it's "One, two, three, JB!"

It is a cool, sunny afternoon, and the stadium is filled to capacity with loud, hungry Redskins fans. The defending Super Bowl champions have gotten off to a slow start, but a win here will boost their record to 4–2, and they will pass the Eagles in the standings—by virtue of the head-to-head win. An Eagles win will help bury Washington (three divisional defeats) and keep pace with Dallas, which hasn't lost since Monday night. A defeat will completely dash the hopes of early October. They will go home trailing both Washington and Dallas.

Stealing a page from Professor Schottenheimer, Randall and the offense come out shooting, attempting two long-range passes—Randall's arm is truly a magnificent thing, these passes travel sixty yards or more—that skitter uncaught on the grass. The Skins then come out and do, successfully, what the Eagles waited in vain for the Chiefs to do all afternoon the week before. They run the ball right at them, pounding Earnest Byner up the middle in eight consecutive plays, scratching out gains of two, six, two, three, six, five, six, and one yards. Washington coach Joe Gibbs is advancing Professor Schottenheimer's gag, anticipating that the chastened Gang Green will this week be back on their heels, paranoid about stopping the long pass (witness Andre's pregame comments). Quarterback Mark Rypien finishes off the drive with a ten-yard touchdown pass to Gary Clark. On the sidelines, as the Skins add the extra point, Seth paces before his teammates, helmet in hand, "#99" carved into the back of his head, snarling at them to shape up. Seth is wearing a knee brace today—he aggravated the Dallas injury playing against the Chiefs—which slows him down on the field and seems to make him even grouchier than usual.

After Randall leads the offense through three more unsuccessful plays, the Dré Master contributes a big blunder. He's back in coverage six, a two-deep zone the Eagles prefer against the Redskins' passing game, and when the Skins send two receivers wide left, Andre and cornerback John Booty (replacing Toast's toasted replacement, the singed Otis) check off in what they call slide-switch coverage. This means Andre has the inside man and Booty the outside man, unless one of the receivers breaks across the middle. If that happens, Andre is supposed to pick him up—only, Andre finds himself peeking into the backfield again, the very thing he has promised himself all week he won't do. So when Rypien fakes the handoff to Byner, the overeager safety involuntarily lurches forward—he can just *feel* the hit vibrating those subcortical synapses—at just about the time Monk, the NFL's all-time leading receiver, goes flashing past across the middle ("I was in space at that particular moment," Andre, with typical candor, will later explain). He catches Monk from behind thirty-four yards upfield.

Seth jumps all over his teammate. "Andre, you can't make that dumb mistake! You can't do that to us, Andre. You looked at the film. You know you've got to read your key. Keep your eyes on the key!"

Andre walks back to the huddle hanging his head, hands on his hips, muttering to himself—*What is this? Why is this?* Back in the huddle, he says to the furious linebacker, "Seth, I promise you, it won't happen again."

They manage to stall this Skins drive on their own fourteen-yard line. Chip Lohmiller, the normally reliable Washington placekicker, misses the field goal, and Andre can breathe easily again. Still, there is something ominous about this run of bad luck. He's got on his blue-sleeved shirt; he's wearing the towel, the slogan; the pregame stuff went well. *What gives?*

But Andre starts to feel more like himself on the next drive. He crashes into the backfield on a third-down running play to tackle Ricky Ervins for a two-yard loss. He's so happy he leaps up to do a victory dance, but can't decide on which step, so he does this backpedaling improvisation, waving his hands like he's discharging six-shooters. It looks pretty silly, and Andre knows he's going to get teased about it tomorrow in the film room—such a sloppy display!—but this is the first time he's felt right on the football field in two weeks.

Both teams manage field goals before the half is over, so the Eagles come out for the second half trailing by seven points. Randall is having a terrible day, worse than the week before. He hasn't completed a pass for more than eleven yards. Even when the defense intercepts a Rypien pass—Byron picks it off and then pitches it back to Eric, who runs it out to midfield—the offense can't get going. Tank fumbles the ball right back to the Skins.

So Andre and the defense trot back out on the field, Seth grumbling about the goddamn offense and how many goddamn chances do they goddamn need. The Skins open up another long march. The crowd at RFK is growing wilder and wilder—a touchdown here will almost seal victory—and Andre can feel the dark shadow closing in . . . only, he thinks it's just the possibility of defeat.

Ervins carries the ball off right tackle on a second-down play and scoots untouched into the secondary—into the zone of the Dré Master. Andre lowers his helmet and launches himself at the running back headfirst, delivering a satisfying blow, driving Ervins backward, but then someone else slams into Andre from the side, turning his fall so that when he tumbles backward with Ervins on top his left leg stays planted on the grass. As their combined weight hits the grass, Andre feels and hears a sudden *pop* in his lower left leg, down around the ankle. He reaches down and feels the foot at an awkward angle.

"Eric, I broke it," Andre says, as his friend leans into the pile.

"Don't move," says Eric. "Don't move."

"It's broke."

So far he feels no pain. Otho Davis and Dave Price sprint out to the field. They reach for the foot as Andre tries to straighten it—now he feels a jolt. Otho and Dave don't say much.

"It's broke, Otho," says Andre.

The old trainer nods. He and Dave scoop Andre up and carry him from the field, setting him gingerly on the bench, and already Andre is calculating the damage. Broken ankle, does that mean the whole season? Maybe it's not so bad. Maybe it'll just be a few weeks. How long does it take the bone to heal? Pain is starting to mount. The ankle is starting to swell already, which is a bad sign. Andre can't move his toes. He's loaded on a small truck, which motors toward the ramp at the far end of the field that leads back under the stands.

As the Skins kick another field goal, the truck steers toward the gaping exit, and Andre, helmet off, foot elevated, prostrate and in pain, is swallowed by the cavernous darkness.

AFTER THE GAME, he sits in his wool parka and black cap on a folding chair at the center of the visiting team's locker room. His left leg, shot full of painkillers, is propped on a second chair. A dripping bag of ice is balanced on his lower leg. The X rays, taken on the

premises, show he snapped his left fibula, the more slender, outer
bone of the lower leg. The break is near his ankle. After the swelling
goes down, in a day or two, team physician, Dr. Vincent J. DiStefano,
will fasten together the broken bone with a metal screw. His most
optimistic prognosis? Six to eight weeks, depending on how fast Andre's bone heals. Andre has never had a serious football injury before,
so he doesn't know what to expect. He's dazed and depressed, deep
in the belly of the whale.

He hasn't even bothered to watch much of the remainder of the
game, which has played out on a small color TV screen in the corner.
The Eagles' offense had come alive at last in the fourth quarter, scoring
nine points to pull within four of the Skins. But it was too little, too
late, just as it had been the week before.

His teammates file in glumly. Having risen to such dramatic
heights two weeks before with the Monday night win, the Eagles'
fortunes have plummeted. The Cowboys have won again, defeating
the Chiefs. The Eagles have gone from being the undefeated leaders
of the NFC East, and every reputable prognosticator's pick for Super
Bowl victory—*Hell, let's just skip the next twelve weeks*—to a lowly third
place in their own division.

The locker room after a loss is a study in gloom. Even those
players who don't especially feel it, like the guys who didn't even play
and who might, in their heart of hearts, actually be rejoicing at the
failure of the players who started in their stead, wrap themselves in a
funereal funk. Steam rises from the showers and gradually fills the
crowded windowless room. Balls of white tape cut from ankles and
wrists adhere to shoe soles. Wet towels and discarded gear litter the
floor and chairs. The Pack enters wearing matching long faces—it's
important not to let the boys think you *enjoyed* their humiliation, that
you might relish tomorrow's sprinkling of acid prose into the open
wound.

Richie is subdued and says what losing coaches say.

"We had some missed opportunities," he says. "We're all disappointed that we came here and played the way we played . . . put
ourselves in a hole . . . just didn't get the job done . . . it's going to be
a close race . . . our destiny is still in our own hands . . . this team has
always bounced back. . . ."

The ever forthright center, Dave Alexander, his broad square
face still flushed, stands naked, a crush of reporters pinning him at
his locker.

"We've had two tough games in two weeks at away stadiums
against two good defenses. It's not time to jump off the bandwagon.

We're still the same group. We had our chances, but we just got started a little bit too late."

Any nastiness is well under wraps. All the mandatory postgame mea culpas are general and restrained, but on the defense's side of the room a familiar theme begins to emerge: these guys are tired of playing their asses off and then watching Richie and Randall's offense fall short. In the Chiefs game the defensive breakdowns had temporarily eroded the ground under Buddy's Boys' soapbox, but in this game they had allowed the Redskins only one touchdown. They intercepted a pass and set up the offense with excellent field position again and again.

"Anytime you're forced to play defense all day, that's not a good sign," says Byron, who rarely speaks, much less complains. "It either means the offense is doing great or it isn't doin' nothin'. I think it's pretty obvious which it was today."

There are comments of a similar, vague tenor coming from Wes and Clyde and Reverend Reggie and Eric, enough to flavor the steam with the general drift, so that in short order every camera, notebook, and microphone in the room are assembled around Seth, who doesn't have a vague bone in his body.

He scowls up at the crowd.

"I don't want to point no fingers at anybody, because I know everybody comes to me for the controversy," he says. "But I've made up my mind this year that I'm going to try to stay as positive as I can. Whatever gripes I have, we're gonna keep it between us as a team.

"*But . . .*"

And Seth proceeds to break his personal vow. First in line to take it on the chin is Richie Kotite.

"It just seems to me that whichever team wins is the one who can better outsmart the other. Quite often in that department we come up on the short end of the stick."

But Seth has venom enough to go around. Special teams?

"Special teams looked like garbage."

Defense?

"We gave up too many plays."

But, of course, the prime beneficiary of the linebacker's blame is the offense, and, in particular—who else? Ran-*doll*. See, in one of the quarterback's regular meandering exercises with the Pack the week before, Randall as much as admitted that it had been four seasons since he had mounted a good game against the Redskins, and that Washington, more than any team in the league, seemed to "have our number."

Well, they sure as hell didn't have Seth's number.

"You can't expect to play well if you don't challenge people. You can't go into a game thinking, or being afraid to challenge somebody! I don't care who it is! . . . Offensively, it just seems like when you say 'Washington Redskins,' we just fall to pieces."

It would be unkind, and probably a little unfair, to point out that the sum total of Seth the Scourge's contribution to today's battle had been one tackle.

No one does.

THE PROBLEM worsens the following week, back at the Vet, when the Eagles squeak out a 7–3 victory over the Cardinals. But what a paltry victory! Randall completes fewer than half of his passes, and while Herschel again pounds out 112 yards on the ground, the best the offense can muster is one touchdown. They are playing the weakest team in their division, one of the weakest teams in the league (with a 1–5 record), a team ranked third from the bottom in defense, a team that the Eagles beat handily just weeks before, and this is all they can do? The defense holds the Cardinals to one fourth-quarter field goal, and the thing goes right down to the wire?

For Seth and the rest of the defense (John Booty is now playing for Wes, and Rich Miano for Andre), the whole game comes down to one series near the end of the first half.

After picking off one of Randall's passes, the Cardinals get the ball on the Eagles' three-yard line. Seth and the gang trot out sullenly past their offensive colleagues.

Then with their back to the end zone, framed by the giant flag of Archangel Jerome, the defense draws the line. They put on the most amazing goal-line stand any of them have ever seen. The Pack will dub it "the One-Yard War." Even jaded Bud will later concede it's the best he's ever seen.

Seven times—six from the one-yard line—the Cardinals slam the ball straight into the Eagles' line, trying to push into the end zone:

Play one (first and goal on the Eagles' three): Computer and film studies of the Cardinals' tendencies this close to the goal line show that Phoenix nearly always tries to run the ball in. Coach Joe Bugel had been an offensive line coach for years before being anointed with the headset, and an offensive line that can't advance the ball three yards doesn't belong on a pro football field. Once or twice in past years the Cardinals have run a surprise passing play, but not often. A coach facing the Eagles' number-one ranked defense (the Gang has yet to allow a rushing touchdown this season) has two choices. He can concede the Eagles' strength upfront and go for razzle-dazzle, or he can try to prove how tough his team is by going nose to nose, pushing them back. Bugel likes to call himself a tough guy.

Bud sets up to stop the run. He sends in his jumbo goal-line defense, six linemen (Reverend Reggie, Clyde, Pitts, Harmon, Tommy Jeter, and Mike Golic), four linebackers (Seth, Byron, "Willie T." Thomas, and Britt Hager), and one safety (Miano), who sets up on the end of the front line and keeps a close eye on the tight end.

The Cards come out in their power I formation, eight men down in front and a fullback and tailback lined in single file behind quarterback Chris Chandler. They run into the left side of their line, away from Reggie and toward Clyde, Golic, and Pitts. The fullback tries to hit Willie T. and move him out of the way, and a pulling guard is supposed to lead tailback Johnny Bailey into the hole, banging Byron backward and clearing the path. The play works well. It's stopped short of the end zone because Golic gets enough penetration with his surge off the ball that the pulling guard is delayed. Both Byron and Seth stop Bailey on the one-yard line.

"Too much! Too much!" shouts Seth angrily as the pile untangles.

"We got to tighten up!" pleads Byron.

Play two (second and goal on the Eagles' one): Now the Eagles can't afford to give an inch. Any backward movement on the front line will allow a ballcarrier to fall into the end zone or just reach the ball across the line. They shift to jumbo goal-line gap all-out, their last-ditch defensive formation, with calls for every man on the front line to plug a gap between blockers. The six linemen just drive low and hard at the snap, plugging their gaps and leaving the four linebackers to dive up and over the roiling mass of bigbodies and make contact with the runner.

Chandler keeps the ball himself, but the surge from below knocks his feet out from under him, and he can't jump. Instead he tries to reach the ball forward, but in the process it is slapped away, and out of the green tangle of clutching Eagles in the end zone, Pitts emerges with a beatific grin, holding the ball.

The ref signals the fumble recovery, and Pitts and his teammates parade triumphantly toward the sidelines.

But the celebration is premature. Another official had thrown a flag before the fumble. Linebacker Hager, out on the far right side of the play, had jumped offside. The ball is inched a half yard closer to the end zone, and the Cards are back in business.

"It's not just Us against Them, it's Us against Them and the Referees!" growls Seth as the defense shakes off its disappointment and reassembles in the end zone.

Play three (second and goal from the Eagles' .5 yard): The Cards come back to the same play they ran from the three-yard line. This time Willie T. slips the fullback's block, and Clyde manages to push the tight end trying to block him into the backfield. So the pulling guard can't get into place, and as Golic wraps up Bailey's legs, Byron delivers a thrilling, concussive hit on the smaller running back, who winds up going three yards backward.

Byron extricates himself from the pile—his mouthpiece has popped to the turf; his bald black head is shining, his helmet is embedded down in the pile in Bailey's abdomen—and begins a loose, gloating dance. The stadium is now roaring with pleasure.

"You don't have to say a word, just turn up your hearing aids and listen to this!" enthuses CBS commentator Matt Millen, a former linebacker, as he replays the massive hit on screen. "If that doesn't get you wanting to play football, nothing will!"

The hit fires up the defense to near frenzy. All the pride they feel in being number one, mixed with all of this season's emotion, their grief for Jerome—they suddenly feel immovable. They are convinced the Cards are not going to score. They will not allow it to happen. When the officials spot the ball on the one-yard line, where Byron first made contact, instead of back at the three, where Bailey came to rest, even that's okay. It just doesn't matter anymore.

Play four (third and goal at the Eagles' one): the Cards go back to the same play again, only this time Miano is in perfect position to stop it. Before the snap of the ball, the tight end goes in motion, first right, and then back to the left. Miano mirrors his movements behind the line and sees the ball snapped just as he's over the hole on the left side. He dives in to grab the runner's legs as again the linebackers unload.

This ought to force the fourth-down play, only the Eagles have drawn another flag. Hager is called for jumping offside again. So the Cards get the play back, and the ball is once more inched up half the distance to the goal line.

Play five (third and goal from .5 yard): the Cards try another quarterback sneak, and this time they have even less success than the first time. Harmon and Golic drive their blockers straight backward, Miano wedges himself underneath, and Chandler doesn't gain an inch . . . but there's another flag! This time, way out on the left side, Willie T. had jumped.

Play six (third and goal from .25 yard): Pitts has to go looking for his helmet, which was torn off in the previous pileup. Seth and Byron are hopping up and down in the end zone, banging their helmets together, screaming incoherently.

The faces of the Cards' linemen now show disgust as they line up over the ball. It's hard to tell if they're angrier with themselves or with their coach, who has grimly decided that they *must* move these Eagles players backward. Anyway, everybody on the defensive side can tell at a glance that the "tough guy" on the sidelines has called for another straight-ahead running play, and that his players are none too pleased.

"Run it at me!" screams Seth, straining to make himself heard over the savage roar from the stands.

Again the Cards try to lead with the fullback, left side, pull the guard, and slam in, only no one on the Eagles' defensive front is pushed back an inch. The surge is now so powerful that, again, the guard can't get around to make the block. Bailey anticipates Byron's hit this time, so he dives back toward the center of the field, only to be met in midair—180 pounds meeting 240 pounds—and with a decisive smack is driven backward yet again.

No flags!

Bugel calls time out.

Play seven (fourth and goal from the one): Everybody knows he's got to go for it. No field goal, no tricks. Six times in a row he's lined his big boys up against the Eagles' big boys, and six times in a row the Eagles have won the battle. Later, Bugel will explain, "This is the NFC East. If you can't run it in from there, people will laugh at you." The stadium is rocking. This is one of the great macho moments of football. One group of eleven men trying to move the oblong pigskin forward one yard; another group of eleven men straining to stop them. Bugel is trying to build some pride in his 1–5 squad. Pride turns on moments like this.

Bud warns Miano on the sidelines to be wary of the pass, but he's the only one on the field even considering it.

"Joe Bugel says he's a tough guy; he's going to try to prove it right now," says Millen up in the booth.

They try to run at Reggie this time, and the Reverend doesn't budge. Two men arrive to block him before Bailey gets there. Reggie just hurls 266-pound tight end Walter Reeves backward. Reeves's backside collides with Bailey, who is immediately crushed by Reggie and Hager and then a flood tide of green helmets and jerseys—short of the line.

"Eagles win the battle," says Millen.

FEELING FORLORN, Andre watches all this on TV from a bed at Graduate Hospital, about a half mile away. Afterward, he phones his replacement, Rich Miano, to congratulate him. But it's getting harder and harder for Andre even to think about football.

The broken bone in his left leg has turned from something routine and uncomfortable into something far worse.

After Dr. Vince had screwed the broken fibula back together four days earlier, Andre went home to heal. But three days later, he was in such pain he could hardly bear it. When he checked back with the doctor, he was told that blisters had formed around the fracture in his torn ankle ligaments, and they were slowly, painfully working their way up through the skin. Dr. Vince checked Andre back into the hospital, where he lay with his leg elevated, suffering the worst pain of his life. The hospital was concerned about controlling infection, which would threaten the limb, and Andre was no longer thinking about when he'd get to rejoin his teammates, about the Dré Master and big hits and biting on play action.

The throbbing was unbearable. The Eagles' ferocious strong safety, the man with the Fu Manchu mustache and dark reputation, was reduced to begging the nurses for his regulated doses of painkilling injections. But the shots only took the edge off it. They wouldn't shoot him up more than once every four hours, but the drug wore off after about one. Andre sometimes just laid in bed weeping.

Willie Ola flew up to be with him the next day. Together, in the hospital, they prayed for fortitude and deliverance.

I cried by reason of mine affliction unto the Lord, . . . out of the belly of hell cried I. . . . One week after surgery, Andre's blisters have healed sufficiently for him to go home, but he's still in terrific pain. Lying on his back with his foot elevated, Andre is getting only about one hour of sleep a night. Willie Ola cooks and takes care of the house, feeding him in his upstairs bedroom. Otis Smith, who shares Andre's condo, keeps him up on the day-to-day developments with the team. As the Eagles prepare for game eight, their rematch with the Cowboys in Dallas, it's Otis who brings news of the comment Emmitt Smith made to reporters there about Andre's injury.

"He's hurt," said Emmitt to a clutch of newshounds around his Dallas locker. "Keep doin' bad, and bad things will happen to you. I guess bad things finally caught up to him."

As if Andre *deserved* what he's going through! Emmitt Smith becomes the focus of his recovery. If the Eagles make the play-offs, which they almost certainly will, then it seems increasingly likely that they will face the Cowboys a third time in January. So while Andre sends his supplications to the Lord, the Dré Master chews on a vision of the Cowboys' all-pro running back. It's hard to say which inspires him more.

The worst of his ordeal is over after three weeks—*And the Lord spake unto the fish, and it vomited out Jonah upon the dry land.* Willie Ola flies home, and Andre resumes daily trips to Veterans Stadium to speed his rehab.

During those lost weeks, it was as though Andre had dropped off the earth. He sees Otis because they share the same condo, but other than that, Andre hears not a word from coaches or teammates.

There is one exception. He hears from Ben Smith.

12

WHERE'S BEN?

Ben Smith had been a ghost now for more than a year.

His fall had come late in the second quarter of a November 10, 1991, game in venerable, gusty Cleveland Stadium. He knew the instant his knee gave way that the injury was serious. Nobody had even touched him. The twenty-four-year-old cornerback's leg just buckled, and down he went, alone at the bottom of the arena with eighty-thousand-plus local fans cheering wildly for Webster Slaughter's seventeen-yard gain. Ben didn't try to get up. He just lay clutching the knee.

He started to cry.

One day you're at the top of the world, playing on TV, reading your name in the newspapers, driving your fancy foreign car, signing autographs, and then—*poof*—you're gone. More than in any other pro sport, football players roll the dice with their entire career every time they step on the field. Years of single-minded devotion to the game, all the off-season workouts, summer training camps, high-school and college glory, the chance to become a great pro, to win financial security for yourself and your family for a lifetime . . . all of it is on the line every weekend, every play.

A limp is one of the distinctive features of an old football player. A quick injury tour of the Eagles' locker room confirms that the game hasn't grown gentler: Jim McMahon, football's equivalent of a crash dummy, has already willed (in his '86 book, *McMahon*) his battered remains to the Smithsonian Institution as the world's foremost collection of scar tissue; Randall Cunningham is coming off knee reconstruction, the second of his career (and he'll miss most of '93 with a broken leg); Dave Archer, a veteran of multiple shoulder surgeries; Fred Barnett, knee surgery in college (and he'll go back under the knife in '93 with a blown knee); Calvin Williams, who missed four games in '91 with a separated shoulder; Andre Waters, veteran of multiple minor knee surgeries; Wes Hopkins, totally reconstructed knee joint; Rich Miano, total knee reconstruction; Seth Joyner, multiple knee surgeries; Britt Hager, neck surgery and a hip condition called necrosis encouraged by taking so many painkilling injections as a high-school player; Reggie White, knee surgery; Mike Golic, knee and ankle surgery; Mike Pitts, knee surgery and nagging back problems; Keith Byars, multiple bone breaks in his feet, one so severe he required a bone graft from a piece of his hip; Ron Heller, broken hand, severe eye injury (after being poked in the left eye by Viking Al Baker, whom Ron sued), knee surgery, foot problems; Dave Alexander, knee surgery and foot problems; Eric "Pink" Floyd, ankle break in college (and knee reconstruction coming in '93). These are just the starters, and one of the reasons they are starters is because they are particularly durable.

Usually it's a knee. The joint is a marvel of anatomical engineering, a complex interface of muscle, cartilage, and bone, an elegant organic hinge with both strength needed to support the full frame of the body in motion and sufficient pliability to enable flexion, extension, and even a few degrees of rotation. Unflexed, the knee allows an accomplished athlete to seemingly defy gravity with sudden, fluid, powerful motion up or down, sideways, backward, and forward. Flexed, the joint performs a small screwing action that locks the upper and lower parts of the leg so tightly it assumes the stability of solid bone. Surrounding the ball and socket of the femur and tibia are wrapped layers of muscle, cartilage, tendon, and ligament, superbly capable of absorbing a lifetime's worth of walking, running, climbing, leaping—but woefully incapable of absorbing the sudden and violent twists, whacks, and tortuous hyperextensions of football.

This is the remarkable but fragile vessel on which players hazard all.

With Ben, the trip to that painful moment on the grass at Cleveland Stadium began when he was just eight years old, throwing the football up in the air as high as he could and then racing down Flanders Drive in front of his father's tiny house in Warner Robins, Georgia, trying to catch it before it hit the ground. He'd do it for hours, all by himself. He'd been a solitary boy ever since his mother, Doris Louise Bailey, had left five years earlier, moving off to the "fast life" of Macon, about a half hour's drive north.

Doris couldn't cope with the increasingly strict and stubborn ways of Ben's father, Bennie Joe, an illiterate but proud, ambitious, and colorful man who frightened people with his intensity. Bennie Joe was the oldest of twenty-two children (his second cousin is Antone Davis's father, Milton Trice, which makes the teammates fourth cousins, al-

though they hadn't met until they were both playing for the Eagles),
and he had assumed a patriarchal role in his enormous family at an
early age, after his father, drunk, had managed to flip over a piece
of heavy farming equipment on himself and die in a horrendous ball
of flame. Bennie Joe helped raise his younger brothers and sisters and
earned a license for operating heavy road-construction equipment.

He and Doris had five children, and Ben, the last, was only three
when his mother accused Bennie Joe of seeing another woman, and
went to live with her mother. The children stayed with their mother
for a short time, but then Doris took up with a man from Macon and
left all her children with their father. Looking back on it, she says she
was just fed up with the rural life, with Bennie Joe, and with raising
children. If he was so determined to hang on to his children, she
thought, she'd let him have them. All five of them. She felt her husband
was better suited to raising them anyway, with his strictly sober ways
and steady wages. A frank woman with few pretensions, she would
recall years later with a trace of a smile that at that point in her life
she "went a little wild," falling in with a bootlegging ring in Macon,
spending her days and nights "out and around."

Growing up a Smith meant being poor in worldly goods but rich
in family. Bennie Joe built his house at the north end of Warner
Robins, a splash of suburbia adjacent to Robins Air Force Base, a
bustling modern oasis on a landscape of sprawling cotton, soy, and
peanut land. A multitude of Smiths populate Houston, Bibb, and
Peach Counties in Central Georgia, and as a motherless boy, Ben
remembers being passed from aunt to aunt to aunt while his father
was away, sleeping on blankets or on a mattress tossed on the floor
alongside his brothers and sisters and cousins. The first time he remembers sleeping in a bed was when he was fourteen years old, when
his older brother Lorenzo got fed up with his father and went north
to live with Doris in Macon.

Ben remembers his father as a "wild man," feared in the neighborhood and in the family for his strong opinions and fiery temper,
but also admired for his stern competence and character. Angered
after being robbed at gunpoint when he stopped for a hitchhiker on
one of his long road trips, Bennie Joe brought himself a nickel-plated
.38 Smith and Wesson, got a license for it, strapped it to his belt, and
carried it with him everywhere except to church. It got so nearly
everybody in town knew who he was, the intense, compactly built black
man in work clothes and bandanna with the nickel-plated pistol on
his hip. When one of his younger brothers was stabbed to death in a
fight by a man named Earl, Bennie Joe swore revenge on the man,
and it was common knowledge in the town's black quarters that it was

only a matter of time before Bennie Joe—who was known as a man who did not make idle threats—would follow through, plant Mr. Earl deep in the Georgia clay, and land himself behind bars. Bennie Joe thought so himself, although he worried about what would happen to his children. His conversion to a strict and evangelical Baptist Christianity showed him another way. Forced by his pastor to assist with door-to-door missionary work at the south end of town, in the very neighborhood of his intended victim, Bennie Joe arrived one afternoon at Mr. Earl's door, with a Bible in his hand and the pistol on his hip. He heard a scornful voice, he says—*Now look at you. How can you go and witness to somebody when you're carrying around this grudge like a dead weight?* And in that moment he saw the light. He had to chase down Mr. Earl, who fled out the back door at his approach, but Bennie Joe held out his hand and apologized once he caught up. Not long afterward, he stopped carrying the gun.

But Bennie Joe's rebirth as a lay preacher came as an unbearable shock to his teenage brood, who one by one left him to live with their mother. Ben left when his dad forced him to quit the junior-high-school football team because it was interfering with events at the church.

Ben felt sorry for his dad. He explained that he intended to play high-school, then college, and then pro football.

His father scoffed. "I hate to disappoint you, son, but you're too little to play football."

But Ben had it all figured out. He had taken something from both his strong-willed parents. He looked just like his father, with his dark complexion, square jaw, and small features, but he had, at least outwardly, none of his father's unbending and aggressive personality. People thought Ben's personality, so outwardly easy and fun loving, resembled his mother's. But beneath his ready smile and seemingly feckless ways, Ben at age fifteen was already as hard and focused as a diamond bit. He knew where he was going, and he was prepared to be stubborn about it if necessary. He *was* small. He stood only about five-five and weighed fewer than 130 pounds entering high school, but he was still growing, and he was agile, quick, and tough.

Ben had made a study of football, mostly from watching it on TV. There was room for a small, fast, hard-hitting player, even in the pros, in the defensive backfield. Central Georgia even had a reputation for producing some of the finest defensive backs in the country.

He also knew that his only chance of making it to the college game, at his size, was to become an excellent high-school cornerback. Macon was the best place to get noticed. It was a small city with old, well-publicized high-school rivalries that produced many of the athletes who went on to play at Georgia State and the University of Georgia. His plan was to move in with his mother, not just to enjoy the looser atmosphere and the fun of city life (although that was appealing, too), but to play football—no, not just football, but *corner-back*—for prep-school powerhouse Northeast High.

He moved in with his mother to finish out junior high and went out for the football team at Northeast in his freshman year. He was placed on the scout team, which was where most first-year players expected to go . . . except Ben. He watched the older boys in practice and felt sure he could outplay them if Coach would let him try. But there was a protocol to these things. Freshmen just didn't shoulder established players aside, unless they had grown up in Macon and caught Coach's eye playing on a junior-high team, or unless their older brothers had blazed a reputation. Ben felt unknown and unappreciated, and after a season on the bench, he told his mom he wanted to move back in with his dad, play for Northside High School in Warner Robins.

He moved back to Flanders Drive and was MVP of the junior varsity team as a sophomore at Northside, where they used him at cornerback some, but mostly as quarterback and running back . . . which Ben didn't like. He wanted to play *cornerback*. But Coach (as Coach will) had his own ideas. When he seemed insufficiently concerned about the fifteen-year-old's playing preferences, Ben balked. Working out in preparation for the annual spring football game, an off-season exhibition designed to keep the team focused and in shape, Ben refused to participate in a rigorous one-on-one contact drill near the end of practice—he believed in saving his body for the game (or, from Coach's-Eye View, he was *too good to practice*).

"I'm all tired out from being asked to play so many positions," he told Coach.

So when the spring game was played, Ben was on the bench. Coach waited until the closing minutes before waving Ben out to the field.

Ben declined.

"You don't have to worry about me playing for this team anymore," he said.

See, Ben wanted to play *cornerback*. Period. He had the whole thing scoped out. He wasn't interested in school, and the only career option at that age that was marginally attractive to Ben was going to work in the numbers racket—he had lots of older relatives who got along fine doing that. But that kind of life seemed to teenage Ben so *ordinary*. Football was a far more attractive avenue. It was exciting and glamorous and you could get rich without looking over your shoulder for the law! His father and friends and coaches all told him his chances were next to none, but that didn't deter him one bit. Just like Doris and Bennie Joe, once young Ben had his mind set on something, step on out of the way.

If he couldn't play where he wanted at Northside, maybe they would wise up at the south end of town, at Warner Robins High. The only problem was that to play on the south end he had to live on the south end. Bennie Joe and Doris agreed to drop their parental rights, and an uncle who lived on the south end adopted Ben.

And at Warner Robins, they let Ben play cornerback. Northside High's coaches mounted a brief legal effort to block the move, and Ben had to sit out the first few games of his junior year while the schools wrestled in court, but the maneuver worked. Ben wasn't the best athlete at Warner Robins; he wasn't the fastest boy on the track team or the most gifted player on the football team. But nobody could match his intensity. After an amazing game in which he picked off three passes in an overtime victory over Lyons County High, Ben was named the Atlanta *Constitution*'s high-school defensive player of the year in '85. He spent a long, lonesome year at a junior college in Oklahoma getting his grades up enough to satisfy the NCAA rules, and then accepted a full scholarship to play for the University of Georgia Bulldogs—all according to plan.

EVERYTHING ELSE had gone according to plan, too, including top collegiate football honors and a first-round draft selection by the Eagles. Georgia and then Buddy Ryan had tried to turn Ben into a free safety, but by mid-'91, halfway through his second season with the Eagles, Ben was what he had planned to be all along, a starting NFL cornerback.

He was patrolling the left side of the Eagles' number-one-ranked defensive secondary, opposite Pro Bowl cornerback Eric Allen.

And, as Ben quickly learned, Eric was something else. A poised, articulate young man with a deep golden complexion and amber-colored eyes, Eric was as a San Diego high-school superstar whose trajectory through college and into the pros was as clean and untroubled as a play on a blackboard. Excellent Allen, or EA as his teammates knew him, was Buddy's second pick in '88, the player he took right after Keith Jackson. He started at right cornerback the first game of his rookie season, was named to the NFL's all-rookie squad, earned his first trip to Honolulu after his second season, and had gone every year since. Eric was married to his sweetheart from Point Loma High School—you could look up their picture in the yearbook, Eric with an Afro the size of a bowling ball. He was the image of grace and ease, whether intercepting a pass on the field or pointing his Hollywood smile at a camera and offering commentary like a seasoned network veteran. Eric was golden. He made it look easy.

But what Ben discovered about Eric was, beneath that unruffled exterior, the man was a devoted craftsman . . . a *grind!* Eric was one of a handful of NFL cornerbacks who were so good at what they did that they were redefining the position in the pros. He and the Steelers' Rod Woodson, the Redskins' Darrell Green, the Falcons' Deion Sanders, and a few others formed an elite corps within the community of NFL cornerbacks, players who weren't just cornerbacks, but Cover Guys. It wasn't just a matter of prestige either, although that was important. These players, Eric included, commanded salaries comparable to the league's top receivers, more than $1 million a year. And they were worth every penny. Teams without an excellent Cover Guy had to resort to conservative zone coverages. Their corners needed deep help and assistance in the middle of the field, which would tie up both safeties in pass coverage and give opposing quarterbacks a set-piece defense to play around with, dropping short passes or running the ball when the zone set deep, and then lobbing over the top of it when defensive backs pulled in closer. But a team with a great Cover Guy had a lot more flexibility and punch. If you had a guy with the speed, quickness, and savvy to play one-on-one with a receiver like Jerry Rice all afternoon without getting fried, it freed up a safety to rove the secondary looking for trouble, or blitz the quarterback, or move up with the linebackers to stuff the run. A team like the Eagles, with two excellent Cover Guys, Eric and Ben . . . well, it helped explain why the Eagles in '91 were far and away the best defense in the league.

A Cover Guy was a single-combat warrior, out there on the corner all by himself, dueling play after play, *mano a mano* with the league's best receivers, with the stakes very public and very high—failure more often than not meant a touchdown. And we're talking more here than having your mistake witnessed by a packed stadium of sixty thousand or seventy thousand, or even the millions more watching at home. When a cornerback got beat, it produced one of the most exciting plays in all of football, the long touchdown pass, which made the highlights reel for tens of millions of viewers the night and week after the game and then went on to have an NFL Films life of its own, replayed on videotapes and football anthology programs . . . it was a fair bet that your great-grandchildren would be watching it someday.

It took a special kind of person, someone with the assurance of an Eric Allen, to handle the job with aplomb. First, you had to have the physical skills not just to keep up with the league's top receivers, but to stay with them running backward part of the time, keeping one eye on them and one eye on the quarterback, and then be able to leap with them and wrestle with them, if need be, to keep them from catching the ball. Second, if you had the physical skills, you had to know more about receivers, pass patterns, tendencies, and opposing quarterbacks than they knew about themselves. Eric and most of the others, Ben discovered, kept their own little books on receivers and quarterbacks, gleaned from experience on the field and hours and hours of film study. You had to know all the little moves receivers liked to make (they were all different), which foot they liked to jump off on, how they used their hands, and what opposing teams tended to do out of certain formations. Third, you had to fit all these skills and insights into a reliable set of techniques. Eric approached the line on a given play aware not only of the person he was covering and the quarterback who might throw him the ball, but of down and distance and offensive formation, which dictated how much room he could give a receiver coming off the line and what the man was likely to do with that space. Eric had eight different specific coverage techniques, roughly falling into the categories of playing off the man or playing bump-and-run. "Off" coverages relied on savvy, eye, and the quickness to close on the ball once it was in the air, getting to it before it reached the target. "Bump" coverages meant slamming the man coming off the line, trying to throw him off balance and interfere with the timing of his route, while maintaining your own balance and position.

Ben went to school on this stuff at the end of the '90 season and then into his second year. He learned the delicate art of jamming a receiver and getting his arms up inside to gain leverage. If you did it right, the receiver couldn't break off the jam, and you'd have taken him out of the play. If you did it wrong, you drew a holding flag and gave the other team free yards. He was learning all the subtle ways veteran receivers have of pushing off a cornerback; a gentle shove at precisely the right moment was all it took to get enough separation for the catch. Ben learned countermoves, how, when the push came, to latch onto the inside of the man's jersey, away from the referee's line of sight, so that the receiver couldn't pull away. Most of the time, though, staying with a man was just timing and technique, getting in that bump, keeping your balance, reading the route, closing on the ball . . . it was like a dance, and Ben was getting good at it.

His salary was $352,000 in '92, about a third of Eric's. But Ben had made the NFL's all-rookie team in his first year, just like Eric, and midway through his second year the Pro Bowl didn't seem out of reach. The Pack still speculated from time to time that Ben would eventually play free safety. But Ben had seen the light. He wasn't just interested in being a cornerback anymore, he was going to be a Cover Guy. He couldn't wait for Sundays.

But now it was over. It was as though he had been struck by lightning. He was done, certainly for this season and part of the next, maybe for good. One second it's you and Webster Slaughter, precisely the kind of receiver only a true Cover Guy can handle one-on-one, the next minute they're rolling you off the field on a little cart.

TEAM DOCTOR Vincent DiStefano called it "the worst knee injury we've seen around here in many, many years."

Which is saying something. Dr. Vince, as the players knew him, had been the Eagles' team doctor for twenty-one seasons, and as such had seen as many orthopedic injuries as a battlefield surgeon sees trauma. A Philadelphia native, graduate of Temple University and Hahnemann College Medical School (both in Philadelphia), chairman of the orthopedic department at Philadelphia's Graduate Hospital, and a well-known authority in the growing field of sports medicine, the short, precise, curly-mopped, sensationally tanned Dr. Vince, father of eight, was by any measure a fine surgeon. Dr. Vince told Ben his anterior cruciate and medial collateral ligaments were badly torn, that he had severely sprained the posterior cruciate ligament and torn both the lateral meniscus and medial meniscus cartilages—in other words, the equivalent of a small bomb had gone off in the joint.

Ben tried not to imagine the mess inside his throbbing, swollen, discolored knee. Twenty years or even a decade earlier, Ben's career would have been over. Maybe Joe Namath could extend his career limping around inside a pocket of blockers with braces on both knees, but a cornerback's livelihood depended on peak speed and agility. With the advances in surgical knee reconstruction over the years, there was at least a fair chance he'd fully regain use of the knee, said Dr. Vince, who was prepared and capable of opening the joint up and piecing the shreds back together. But, as Ben well knew, even a slight diminution of strength or flexibility would kill his Cover Guy plans. If he went under the knife immediately, with hard work and good luck, he could be back on the field in eleven months, midway through the '92 season. But there were no guarantees.

The world of pro football had changed dramatically in the twenty-one years since Dr. Vince started haunting the Eagles' sidelines, harvesting injuries. As players' salaries mounted, and as agents became a bigger and bigger part of players' lives, the concept of team doctor had gradually grown suspect. Whose doctor was he, Team's or the player's? Their interests weren't always the same.

Injury is a central part of the culture of football. In the old days it was simple: you played *with* pain, *through* injuries, and proved your mettle as a man by *sucking it up,* doing *what it takes.* Sacrificing your body was expected, encouraged, and, with a growing arsenal of alluring painkillers, ably assisted. In the old days, a football club's medical staff had one purpose: Keep the show going, patch 'em up, pat their rumps, and get 'em back out on the field. A player who insisted on healing properly was quickly branded a malcontent or, worse, a sissy. Boys learned this from the first day they donned a helmet and started crashing into people. You proved yourself worthy by hopping right up, tearless and fearless, after a bone-crunching tackle. The other boys would crowd around you when you were gasping or bleeding on the field, dozens of little-boy eyes peering intently down, pushing and shoving to get a better view, staring—not with concern, but to see if you cried. Every schoolboy athlete in America knew legends were made by popping dislocated fingers back in place and stepping right back into the huddle, or spitting out a tooth and calling the next play. In the beginning, in a sense, this was *why* men played football. Absent the heroic myth of the battlefield to test the strongest and ablest, America took a perfectly elegant and ageless sport and turned it into a brawl. In the good old days, pro football was just the meanest, biggest, grandest brawl of them all. Go back and check how bitterly the old pros resisted wearing helmets, then face masks and other protective gear; it was an affront to the awful dignity of the game!

The modern NFL has, of course, come a long way from the old standard, at least on the surface. For one thing, a club's multimillion-dollar investment in a star athlete would be ill served by heedlessly exposing him to injury. A decent argument could be made (and often was) that it was in the enlightened best interests of both player and club to make sure a player was well cared for and fully healed before plugging him back into the lineup. But, medical opinions differed. Why go to the doctor who represents the Team when you can go to a doctor who represents you, and only you?

For Dr. Vince, being team doctor was a lot easier back when he started. It was a no-lose deal, especially for a football fan—which the good doctor was. Ministering to pro football players was not only interesting and lucrative work (Lord knows he had a guaranteed steady supply of patients who all could pay their bills), it gave Dr. Vince a high profile and considerable prestige—*Hell, if the Eagles go to him, he's the guy for me!* Dr. Vince attended all the Eagles' games, even those on the road, watched from the sidelines, and repaired the mounting damage as the season unfolded. What a deal! After more than two decades of this, he had written scores of papers and articles on sports-related injuries in medical journals and served as officer or consultant in several prominent sports-medicine centers.

But increasingly, the good doctor was encountering something new. A cynical virus had invaded paradise. Instead of the misty-eyed gaze of grateful respect he once got from repaired athletes, more and more he was getting looks that were outright skeptical and accusing. Increasingly, Dr. Vince was getting the cold shoulder—athletes publicly demanding second opinions before submitting to surgery or treatment, or flying out of town to be operated on by their own doctors. The truth was that Dr. Vince was as respected and admired as any doctor in his specialty, but gradually his official designation as team doctor began showing a dangerous new downside.

How do you think it looked when Randall, the most closely watched player on the team, chose to fly back out to California and put himself under the care of his own orthopedic surgeon, Dr. Clarence Shields, after being felled with a knee injury in the first game of the '91 season? There was a growing list of players in the Eagles' locker room who wouldn't even consider placing themselves under Dr. Vince's care, not because he was any less skillful with the knife, but because with so much riding on their career (and with cynical agents whispering in their ears), players no longer felt comfortable just placing their fate in the hands of Team.

Ben's case was going to ably illustrate why.

HIS AGENT, Dick Bell, urged Ben to seek a second opinion. They lined up an appointment with a renowned specialist in Denver, and Bell even booked Ben a flight. But the knee was throbbing so badly on the day he was supposed to leave, Ben just skipped it. He was impatient to get the surgery done and get the healing process under way. Maybe he could beat the eleven months of rehab forecast by Dr. Vince and be ready to start the '92 season. Seeing the second doctor in Denver would either confirm what he had already been told, or it would force him to make a decision—and, no doubt, mean further delays.

What was he going to do with himself if he couldn't play football? Sure, he'd continue to get paid, but Ben had all the money he needed. He didn't know what to do with all the money he had; in fact, it had created a whole set of problems in his life that he had never even imagined before. In that sense, Ben's sudden success had been deeply disillusioning.

He'd started off enthusiastically, buying himself clothes, a car, the mandatory DHM in Macon, buying Doris a new car, buying Bennie Joe his own backhoe, giving away thousands of dollars to that huge extended family of his down in Houston County, paying off his college loans, purchasing insurance and paying his taxes . . . until he discovered, to his chagrin, that about half of his bonus was gone. Dick had helped him set the rest aside.

When it was all done, Ben came face-to-face with the fact that his life wasn't all that much improved. Sure, he had *things*, a house, cars, clothes. He could take exotic vacations if he liked, but, when he really thought about it, he'd had more fun being penniless in college. The money he gave away didn't make other people happy either. His mom didn't like the DHM in Macon that much. It was a two-story structure with pillars in front like some kind of suburban echo of plantation life—didn't suit her. His father was jealous of how lavish Ben had been with his mom. "She gets a house and a new car and I get a backhoe?" Bennie Joe complained, "I guess I'm used to being the underdog in this family."

Like so many of his teammates, Ben found it difficult to go home. Many of his high-school friends were adrift and unemployed. Some of his classmates were already dead or in jail. Everybody wanted money. *Ben, I got this great idea to start a business! Ben, I just need it for one car payment until my check comes through. Ben, we're gonna lose the house if we don't pay this bill.* His uncle was in jail, arrested for armed robbery trying to keep up a crack habit. His disgruntled father was hard to be around—he still wouldn't tolerate swearing or alcohol, so how could Ben invite a few of his old buddies over for a beer?

Ben himself had managed to emerge from one year of junior college and four years at Georgia with the literacy of a grade-schooler, although he was clearly intelligent and capable of learning almost anything—even a driven achiever when it came to football. But his ideas of what life held for him after retiring from the game consisted of a vague plan to build a big house on a lake and take kids fishing. It was easy to see why Ben quickly was possessed by one overriding impulse—fix the knee and get me back on the field.

He reported to Graduate Hospital on Friday, November 15, for six and a half hours of surgery by Dr. Vince, who replaced Ben's anterior cruciate ligament with one from a cadaver and repaired all the other tears and breaks.

In the week he spent lying around the hospital, he was visited by only one of his teammates. Andre Waters stopped by to drink a beer with Ben and play Nintendo. Ben didn't forget.

THE TROUBLE started about five months later, when the knee was feeling strong enough for Ben and the Eagles' trainers to begin putting stress on the joint, trying to build it back up. It didn't feel right. To Ben, apart from the pain, the joint felt wobbly.

"I don't think this is supposed to be like this," he complained to Otho, who assured him it wasn't unusual at this point in rehab.

Otho had been around forever. A big, gruff man with a face that seemed one size too large, framed with dark hair, and accented by bushy dark eyebrows, Otho walked with a permanent lazy slouch and spoke with a low Texas drawl still intact after twenty-one years on the East Coast, first with the Baltimore Colts and then, since '73, with the Eagles. Longevity like that was rare in football. Otho had seen whole generations of players, coaches, managers, and even owners come and go. He was a repository of down-home wisdom and NFL anecdotes and knew just about everybody who had ever worn pads and a helmet at this level. His lair, a suite of windowless rooms adjacent to the locker room and off-limits to all but those on the club payroll, was cluttered with massage tables, exercise equipment, relaxation devices (including a flotation chamber into which Otho once crawled and fell asleep, awakening late at night in an eerie, vacant stadium), workout charts, reference books, training schedules, tape, wraps, pads, orthopedic braces, shoe wedges, painkillers, needles, pills, and a positively legendary assortment of homespun ointments, balms, and potions that lent Otho an almost Merlinesque reputation for pasting football players back together and getting them back out on the field. A consummate yarn-spinner and practical joker, Otho was a gray eminence, not only with the Eagles, but throughout pro football, since many of the trainers working for other teams had served an apprenticeship with Otho or with someone else who had. In short, if Otho told Ben what he was feeling was normal, then, by God, who was going to argue with Merlin himself?

But at age fifty-eight, after more than a quarter century ministering to athletes, Otho was most definitely of the Old School when it came to sports injuries. Real men scoffed at pain. Although Otho and the other trainers on his staff knew enough not to encourage players to risk further damage to frayed limbs and swollen joints, they considered themselves frontline experts on what constituted a "playable" injury.

Pain was part of the rehab process, too. An athlete in a hurry to repair a damaged joint couldn't afford a painless rehab schedule (nor could the team, although insurers picked up the big paychecks of injured players). To a certain extent, the old ethic of playing with pain lived on most vigorously in the training room, where the idea was that real men regularly pushed their aching, surgically repaired body parts right up to the edge of human endurance in their determination to get back out on the field. By this standard, Ben was something less than a real man.

"It doesn't feel right," he kept complaining.

Part of Ben's problem with the trainers predated the injury. He had always been something of a fussbudget with trainers. He'd come back to have his ankles or wrists retaped two and three times before a game, complaining that they didn't feel just right. Little aches and pains would convince Ben he ought to skip practice, when Otho and the trainers knew damn well he could play—*too good to practice*. These were little more than annoying eccentricities so long as he was playing well.

But once Ben became Otho's ward, his attitude became a major problem. As the trainers saw it, one purpose in pushing the damaged joint through painful exercises was to break down the formation of scar tissue from the surgery, which was essential for regaining full range of motion and his old speed and agility. But to Ben, pain signaled danger. He wasn't buying Otho's strategy. So the team kept sending Ben back to Dr. Vince. In March '92, the surgeon performed a follow-up arthroscopic examination and surgery, cleaning out some of the scar tissue himself. In another session, Dr. Vince sedated Ben and then vigorously manipulated the knee himself—a procedure the doctor and Otho felt a more dedicated player ought to be doing for himself. Despite these efforts, as summer approached, and the '92 season, Ben was still complaining that the knee didn't feel right.

It didn't help having Randall working away like a rehab god right alongside him. Randall's injury, while severe, had not been as extensive as Ben's, and he was much further along in his recovery. The surgery with Dr. Shields had obviously gone well. Randall was King Fucking Rehab himself, running, lifting, jumping, getting measurably stronger every day—putting on a dazzling show for Otho and the boys, and saying helpful things to Ben like "You've got to *want* it" or "Time to get down to *business*."

Ben could sense a showdown brewing. Hanging around on the fringes of a team minicamp in June, Ben told one of the hounds that he didn't think his knee would be ready to play on until the '93 season.

Given that Richie and Harry, Otho, and Dr. Vince were all still projecting Ben's return for early in the '92 season, this was news. Asked
about it, the club's brass wasn't about to budge.

"Ben is a young player who has never been through this before,"
explained Richie. "So it's not surprising that he gets discouraged. It's
not easy to work back from an injury like that. But Otho and the
doctor still think he's making good progress. We expect to have him
back this season."

That was the public line, anyway. Privately, the club was getting
fed up with Ben. Dr. Vince said he wouldn't get better until he started
working harder with the knee. But the damn thing felt so unstable;
Ben was convinced the knee was going to pop apart every time he put
weight on it. The word "malingerer" was being whispered around—
Ben was being tagged a gutless slacker. During training camp at West
Chester, Ben was up in the dorm with everybody else. He had therapy
every morning at 7:00 a.m., and then Otho would tell him to get out,
run, push himself up and down the steep hills around the practice
fields, and Ben tried, halfheartedly. When the trainers found him just
idling around the practice field, they scowled and reported him to
management. When Ben skipped a weekend therapy session, taking
a break from training camp while the rest of the team was out of town
for an exhibition game, the club fined him $3,000. By midsummer,
the team was considering taking Ben's case to the league's management
council and trying to get released from his contract. If he refused to
work himself back into playing shape, they could refuse to pay him
his salary. Nobody confronted Ben directly, but he heard the whispers
around the locker room and on the practice field—*won't work, poor
work ethic, won't take advice, coward . . . doesn't want to play.*

Doesn't want to play?

Ben had gone into a long depression the previous winter after
the knee surgery. He was a lost soul. He stayed home playing Nintendo
all day and went out drinking at night. He would lie in bed until noon
and then roll over and play video games until his eyes started to blur.
His appetite went away, and he dropped nearly thirty pounds from
his once-impressive frame. Gaunt, big-eyed, his head shaved, Ben
showed up in the Eagles' locker room late in the '91 season looking
so bad it frightened some of his teammates and friends. To the Pack,
he had been transformed from a cocky, muscular millionaire athlete
into a frail, insecure teenager. He was, of course, a ghost, no longer
a member of the family of Team, cut off from his family and friends
back home (his mother was afraid to fly, so she couldn't come up to
be with him, and his father was always working). Ben watched the

Eagles games on TV, and when the announcers sang the praises of the team's number-one-ranked defense, or mentioned the temporary absence of this or that key player, the name Ben Smith never came up. He had started ten games for that number-one-ranked defense in '91, yet it was as though he didn't exist! He felt as if he had not only lost his future, but his past.

Ben had weathered all that. He had bulked himself back up and regained the cocky twinkle in his eyes. It hadn't been easy. And the club thought he *didn't want to play?*

It came to a head at the end of summer, when Dr. Vince and Otho acknowledged that the knee was still loose, but that it was strong enough. They suggested that he tape the knee, brace it, and try running on it. How else were they going to find out what he could do? To Ben, the "suggestion" had the ring of ultimatum.

He said no.

"Somebody is going to tell me what's wrong with my knee," he said. "Y'all do what you're gonna do; I'm gonna talk to my agent."

When the Eagles' pass defense started to slip so badly in Kansas City, Bud Carson kept trying to patch the weak spot on the left corner. After Izel Jenkins was repeatedly burned, he inserted Otis Smith and then John Booty, with similar results. Waiting anxiously on the sidelines was rookie Mark McMillian, but the kid was only five-seven and as green as the color on his uniform. Bud didn't dare just throw Mark in. The locker-room chorus became "Where's Ben?" Hadn't Dr. Vince and Otho projected his return for October of '92? Here it was almost November!

Ben was on the road with his agent, for three independent evaluations of his still-wobbly knee.

The first was with Dr. Michael Fagenbaum, a noted orthopedic surgeon in Raleigh, North Carolina. Fagenbaum took about ten minutes to examine and assess the progress of Ben's knee and pronounced a stunning verdict.

"I can't see you playing on this again."

According to Fagenbaum, the donor anterior cruciate ligament had not taken properly (which happens in a certain percentage of these surgeries), and as a result the medial collateral ligament was unstable. As Ben and his agent understood it, if Ben played on it, the knee would almost certainly be seriously reinjured, and the question would no longer be one of playing pro cornerback, but of walking.

Fagenbaum said he could take it apart and put it back together, but the chances of Ben's being able to regain anything like his former speed and agility were only fifty-fifty.

"Let's not panic," cautioned Bell to his stricken client. "We've already learned that different doctors can have different opinions. Let's see what the other ones say before we panic."

"But, Dick, why would he say that?" Ben was distraught.

Next they flew to Atlanta, to consult with Dr. Blaine Woodfin, another noted orthopedist.

Woodfin examined and tested Ben's left knee, and, as Bell remembered it, pronounced Dr. Vince's surgery a "failure." He agreed with Fagenbaum's assessment of the problem, but held out slightly more hope. Woodfin said he could reconstruct the knee himself, and Ben had a good chance of playing again, but there were no guarantees. He gave better odds. Woodfin said there was an 85 percent chance he could get Ben's knee back in playing shape.

Next they flew out to see Dr. Shields, whom Ben had been eager to see after witnessing Randall's miraculous resurrection. And the California surgeon, the first black doctor Ben had consulted, just swept the nervous young athlete off his feet.

"This is what we have to do," said Shields, confidently, reassuringly. He explained how he would repair the damage. "You'll be fine," he told Ben. "Don't worry about a thing. You're gonna play football and you're gonna play corner again."

They scheduled the resurgery for December.

Ben and his agent were furious with Otho, Dr. Vince, and the Eagles. No one was seriously questioning Dr. Vince's surgical skills (though Eagles players now began to eye him with unjustified apprehension). It was a given that knee repairs were tricky, and that they didn't always work out. What surgeon could guarantee total success every time? But for months Ben had been complaining that things weren't right, and all he'd gotten in response was whispered scorn, threats, a fine, and an ultimatum . . . to do what? All three independent doctors felt playing on the knee without further repairs would have been disastrous—Ben would almost certainly have blown it and his career. Of course, their opinions were no more valid than Dr. Vince's. Chances are, all three were wrong. Dr. Shields and Otho had easily seen and worked with as many or more injured knees than the other doctors. But for Ben, judging by the way the knee felt, there was no question who was right. The way he saw it, Dr. Vince's surgery had failed to restore the knee—Ben could *feel* that! And then, either out of incompetence or out of some misguided refusal to admit he was wrong, he had urged Ben to play on it. For months he had endured suspicions that he was shirking rehab, that he *didn't want to play* anymore. Now he felt completely vindicated, and angry.

The only scientific measure of the joint's stability, and this was hardly the last word among experts, was provided by a machine called a KT/1000 that ranks tension in the joint on a millimeter scale—the lower the number, the more stable the knee. Any knee loose enough to be ranked over 3.5 millimeters is considered a candidate for reconstruction. Woodfin's measure of Ben's knee was 6.5 millimeters! Why hadn't Dr. Vince used the KT/1000? What was more important, pushing him back out on the field or making sure the knee was fully healed? So much for the team doctor!

Dr. Vince was surprised by the other surgeons' findings, particularly by how poorly Ben's knee had responded to the KT/1000 tests. He had inspected the joint back in March, when he scoped it, and it had looked fine. That was a far more reliable way to check on the success of his reconstruction than strapping Ben's leg into a KT/1000, which is why Dr. Vince hadn't used the machine. It wasn't like he was unfamiliar with it. Hell, he had been one of the first sports-medicine experts in the country to use it! But given such poor readings from Ben's knee, it was clear to him that something had happened since he had last looked at it. Since Ben hadn't run on it, and had resisted any kind of strenuous rehab, he could only conclude that the knee had been reinjured in the manipulations he had been forced to perform— a more violent therapy than the daily rehab sessions with Otho would have been.

The way Dr. Vince saw it, Ben had only himself to blame for the poor progress he had made since surgery, and for the football season he would now miss. Of course, that's not how Ben and his agent saw it. Three weeks after Ben told his story to the Philadelphia *Inquirer*, all but accusing the doctor and the team of what amounted to malicious incompetence, Dr. Vince resigned as the Eagles' team doctor. It was a step he had been considering for some time, given the changing climate. He had even discussed leaving with Harry Gamble months earlier. Ben's case, and this new round of bad publicity, just sealed it.

When Dr. Vince had signed on as team doctor all those years back, he hadn't bargained on it so regularly taking a public bite out of his ass.

BEN FLEW OUT to Los Angeles in November and Dr. Shields redid the knee, a little more than a year after he crumpled to the grass in Cleveland Stadium.

Days after the surgery he had regained the flexibility it had taken him two or three months to regain after the first operation. Less than two months after the procedure, Ben's knee measured a 3.0 on the KT/1000 at the Kerlan-Jobe Orthopaedic Clinic. He felt his career had been robbed of a year. The first year he chalked up to the injury, but the second year he blamed on Dr. Vince and Otho and the Eagles. Sure, they were paying him, but no one could ever give him back a full season's joy in doing what he did best, and the ground he had lost proving himself Eric's equal in the secondary. His contract would be up at the end of the '93 season. How much more valuable would he have been with another full year of playing time, and maybe that trip to Honolulu? He and Bell were optimistic about his winning back his starting job in '93, but what if he couldn't? If Ben didn't make it all the way back, they were going to come looking for Dr. Vince and ol' Merlin Otho with lawyers. Ben had bad feelings about the Eagles. He wasn't sure, frankly, he wanted to play for them anymore.

Ben had a lot of time to weigh these things as he recuperated out in L.A. He checked into a Hilton near the airport and got the hotel maintenance crew to hook up his Nintendo to the TV, and for a month and a half, while his team fought through a rocky period of uncertainty and conflict, Ben went to therapy sessions in the morning and hung around his hotel room for endless hours playing video games, trying to read Magic Johnson's book (he got through part of it), staring out the window at the planes coming and going, chalking up huge telephone bills, ordering out for pizza, drinking beer, and counting the days until weekends, when he could watch football on TV.

During those long, lonely weeks, he got one call from the Eagles. Bud Carson phoned one afternoon to see how he was doing and wish him well. It meant a lot to him. Ben started thinking, *Maybe playing for Bud again wouldn't be so bad.*

13

RANDALL AGONISTES
(The End of the World)

It is a peculiarity of the football field inside Texas Stadium that players sitting on one bench can see players standing on the opposite sideline only from the waist up. This is because the stadium designers went a little crazy with the concept of a "crown," building up the middle of the field from goalpost to goalpost so that the green plastic turf slopes down toward the sidelines—in this case, the drop-off is a foot and a half, steeper if you continue down toward the benches—which makes someone standing on the center ridge feel like king of the hill. The contour facilitates drainage when it rains through the giant rectangular hole in the roof (the one TV viewers peeked through all those years in the opening credits of the TV show "Dallas"), but to an extent that can only be appreciated by playing here, it means that a quarterback throwing a pass to a receiver running a sideline pattern must literally throw the ball downhill.

Eagles quarterbacks coach Zeke Bratkowski thinks that might explain why Randall has opened this game so badly off target.

On their first possession in this game, which is their eighth of the '92 season, Randall hadn't thrown the ball. He nearly had his head taken off trying to make the third-down play—by himself, of course—diving for the first-down marker with two tons of Cowboys in heavy pursuit, only to be met in midair by cornerback Larry Brown with such a resounding smack that it sent a gasp of pleasure through the sixty-five-thousand-plus hometown fans. And when Randall bounced a pass toward Calvin Williams to abort the second series . . . well, that was because Calvin slipped. Randall threw the ball to the right spot.

But there's no excusing what happens next. The ornery and increasingly impatient defense forces a fumble—Clyde Simmons reaches up to slap the ball away from Dallas quarterback Troy Aikman from behind, and Eric Allen pounces on the ball at the Cowboys' thirty-yard line. The defense has been doing this all season, rising to the occasion in big games, handing the offense choice scoring opportunities again and again. Especially over the last three games, Richie's offense has fallen embarrassingly short.

And this time Randall blows it on the very first play. He throws a bad, bad, bad pass—bad read, bad decision, bad throw. Richie had signaled in an 81, a play that sends both Fred and Calvin, split wide to either side, on quick little out routes—it's a safe, high-percentage, short pass (this one to Calvin) designed to gain five or six yards on first down. Only, as Fred and Calvin line up, the Cowboys' cornerbacks guess the patterns and move up close, which pretty much closes off the quick out. This maneuver calls for an automatic countermove that both receivers and Randall know without even signaling one another or changing the play. Instead of running five steps and turning out, they will both take their routes slightly deeper, fading into the dead space behind the cornerback and in front of the safety. Randall's job is to lob the ball in over the corner's head or, if the receiver is sandwiched tightly between the corner and safety, to throw the ball away—or, in Randall's case, the ever-present third option: kick up those gold-tipped shoelaces and scoot.

First, a bad read—Calvin is sandwiched, but Randall forces the pass. Second, bad decision—first down deep in the Cowboys' territory with the whole game left to play is no time to be taking a risk. Third, a bad throw—the pass floats softly into the blue number 24 on the front of cornerback Brown's jersey for the easiest interception of his two-year career. Bad, bad, bad. On the sidelines, Zeke, the old pro, just shakes his head.

You can see the deep clouds of disgust on the faces of the defense as they come back out. What could Randall have been thinking? What's wrong with the guy?

Randall sulks off the field. There is a delicate grace to Randall that seems out of place on a football field. His long, lean body seems fragile, even with the pads on. There is refinement even in the way he reaches in with spidery fingers to extract the plastic toothguard from his mouth, carefully thread it through the bars of his face mask, and then insert it in his wristband, a fluidity that seems almost effeminate. But the face behind those bars doesn't match; it's a blunt, hard expressionless mask—the face of a man determined to show nothing. Randall doesn't stop to consult with Richie or Zeke or anybody, just walks back to the bench keeping his thoughts and feelings zipped, pulls off his green, winged helmet and sets it on the turf, then pulls his black, self-designed and -marketed I'M BACK SCRAMBLING hat over his mussed-up flattop—the helmet does weird things to the 'do—and when the sideline cameras catch the hat . . . bingo! . . . sales leap.

Zeke walks over to commiserate. Sometimes in the early going it's hard to get used to the slope caused by the crown.

The Eagles hate to play in this place anyway. The partially enclosed ceiling collects and redirects noise down toward the field, and the fine citizens of Dallas and surrounding Cowboy country reserve a special loathing for the Eagles. Notwithstanding the wholesome image bequeathed this city by Tom Landry, Roger Staubach, and the other members of "America's Team," its fans are among the league's most bellicose. No fans are more surly than Philly's Id-people, of course, but Dallas is a worthy rival. It gets ugly inside Texas Stadium. Eagles players trot out to the field through an entranceway hung with abusive slogans, beneath a clump of regulars who arrive especially early just to rain spit, insults, and ridicule on opponents. There is one fan, present at every home game, who taunts opponents by dangling a ridiculous effigy in their faces as they emerge—today it's a scrawny rubber chicken dressed in a tiny Eagles uniform, complete with a cardboard silver-winged helmet, dangling from a noose. The players wonder what kind of person has the time and inclination to sit at the kitchen table during the week for hours fashioning such a thing. What kind of weird negative energy does it express? Should they be afraid of such a person? During the game, there are Dallas fans who crowd along the railing just behind the Eagles' bench, who neither watch the action nor cheer the home squad, but spend the three and a half hours hurling coarse, personal invective.

"You fairy, Heller! You suck cock!"

"Whazzamatter, Randall, you pussy!"

"Fuck Philadelphia!"

"Philadelphia sucks!"

"Go home, you candy-assed motherfuckers!"

That sort of thing. To turn around, even for a split second—and sometimes you are just dying to catch a glimpse of what kind of idiots these might be—just wrenches it all up a notch or two and brings it raining down on you personally. So the players just keep their eyes on the field and trust that the local cops, patrolling the narrow space behind the bench, will intercept anything actually dangerous aimed at their backs.

Today, the home crowd is even more worked up than usual. With the 31–7 pasting their 'Boys took at the Vet a month earlier on national TV, still the only loss of the Cowboys' '92 season, civic pride is on the line. The teams have gone in opposite directions since the Monday Night Superspectacularama, but a win today by Richie's struggling squad will not only pull the Eagles' 5–2 record even with Dallas's, it will put them ahead once more in the standings, thanks to two head-to-head victories. While it's still too early in the season to call this game critical, psychologically, at least, Gang Green could use the lift.

But to win, you have to score points. And to score points, your quarterback has to make things happen. For the better part of three outings now, Randall has looked terrible. He's bouncing passes to receivers, running when he should be throwing, and throwing when he should be running. The Scrambling One, easily the most mercurial and important player on the team, has not looked like himself. During the four-game winning streak in September, he was named the NFL Player of the Month, but even then, to the knowing eye of his coaches and teammates, Randall's performance looked spotty at best. Great plays alternated with blunders, touchdowns with turnovers. Starting with the Chiefs debacle and up through last week's stilted effort against the Cardinals, Randall has slumped terribly.

This is obvious to everyone except the quarterback himself, who has something of a blind spot where his own performance is concerned—which annoys the hell out of Richie. For three years now he has been coaching Randall, and the pattern is clear. In victory (and sometimes even after he has made a few showstopping plays in defeat), the quarterback is all smiles, amazing *even himself* with his intuitive on-field genius. But in defeat, he's invariably poor Randall, the miracle worker hog-tied by the rigidity of Richie's offensive system. There is a vacancy in the self-critical quarters of his brain. A play doesn't work because (a) it was the wrong one for the coach to call; (b) the line didn't give him a chance to set and throw; or (c) a receiver ran a wrong route. The line "I threw a bad pass" or "That was my fault" is not in Randall's vast store of postgame ruminations. Statistically, he looks great, ranked second in the NFL so far this season behind the 49ers' Steve Young, but then Randall always looks great on paper. He is the best running quarterback in NFL history—during the Skins defeat two weeks ago he had surpassed in just seven seasons Fran Tarkenton's all-time record for yards gained by a quarterback (3,674), a record it had taken Tarkenton seventeen seasons to compile. Running removes from Randall's stats the deliberately errant passes other quarterbacks frequently throw when receivers are covered, which keeps his completion percentage high. His ability to scramble around and buy time for his receivers to shake loose downfield gives him an always-strong average of yards gained per throw. These are, of course, real advantages on the field, but they also give the Scrambling One an edge in the complex equation used by the league to rank quarterbacks every week of the season. High rankings mean high profile, high salary, and high off-field earnings. But his teammates and coaches couldn't care less about Randall's stats and money—they are sick of hearing about them. The only numbers that count for them are the ones on the scoreboard. They are still in the race this season *despite* Randall, not because of him.

Nevertheless, Richie defended Randall in the week before this second Dallas game. The Pack had discerned the winds of discontent blowing from the back end of the locker room. When a hound had the temerity to ask what it would take for Randall to "snap out of it," Richie hunched his shoulders, gave his bald dome that belligerent tilt.

"I don't think he's in a trance, first of all, okay?" he said, punching his big cigar toward the offending questioner. "So I don't think he has to 'snap out' of anything. . . . We have very high expectations for number twelve. You people do, the fans do, everybody does. But he's not Superman. He doesn't have to be Superman. He has to do what he's supposed to do and let the other guys do what they're supposed to do."

Okay, or as Richie liked to put it, *without question*. But that was just Richie's public face. Privately, he had confronted Randall.

"What's the matter with you?" he asked. As Randall would later recall it in his ghostwritten autobiography, *I'm Still Scrambling*, the coach insisted, "We have to get things going. Your timing is off, your focus is off. What's the matter with you?"

Randall had nothing to offer. When things go badly, he turns sullen and withdrawn. He has a slight underbite, so his face falls quite naturally into a pout.

Like in today's game. The Eagles' defense is stopping Troy Aikman, Emmitt Smith, et al. cold, and Randall looks like he's sleepwalking.

John Madden, analyzing the game for CBS, makes note early in the game: "Randall Cunningham is, I think, suffering a little from lack of confidence. Maybe not lack of confidence in himself [Madden knows the Scrambling One well enough for that], but lack of confidence in the offense, what they're doing, the guys around him. He's really been in a slump, and I think if he's gonna get out of this slump, he's going to have to have some success . . . Richie Kotite was saying last night that Randall has to get into sync with these guys, and he hasn't gotten in sync here early."

Randall is violently sacked the next time he tries to throw. He has no chance. His receivers haven't even turned out of their patterns downfield before he's hit from both sides simultaneously. It feels as if his arms are being taken off. Back to the bench, draw out the mouthpiece, face blank, helmet off, black cap back on.

Randall is pissed. Okay, so the line can't block. He's lived with that his whole career. What bugs him is the confining way Richie insists on blocking for him. Richie, the former tight end, likes to "max-protect," that is, insert two or sometimes even three tight ends into the game . . . *and* leave the running back in the backfield to help block. The idea is to give Randall time to read the situation downfield and get rid of the ball. Only, with so many guys in blocking, there are too few targets downfield. And, besides, Randall doesn't mind coping with a dangerous pass rush. He *likes it* when all hell breaks loose in the backfield and he has to flee. That's when the reflexes flip to warp speed, and Randall the Rocket can make things happen, either dodging around in the backfield and waving his receivers deep for the bomb or taking off for one of his celebrated open-field sprints, dodging tacklers, hurdling bodies. That's what he's better at than anyone in the whole storied history of football—you could look it up! Only, with so many guys in blocking, Randall's escape lanes are all clogged. He doesn't have a chance. He has nowhere to throw, and nowhere to run. Then he gets crushed . . . and everybody blames *him!* What do they expect? What do they want from him?

On into the second quarter, the defense is still shutting down the Cowboys cold. But Randall opens the Eagles' first drive of the second quarter by bouncing a short pass at the feet of Fred, who is open. By now, it can't just be the crown. On third down he ignores an open primary receiver farther downfield and tries to dump the ball instead to Keith Byars, who has slipped off a block and is waving his hands, shouting his "Whoo! Whoo! Whoo!"—begging for the ball. The short pass is batted down.

Again Randall sulks off the field, draws out the mouthpiece, removes the helmet, dons the cap. Same blank look. The quarterback is radiating frustration. To his teammates it's disheartening. *He's back in the tank.*

Again the Eagles' defense holds. Richie calls for a naked bootleg to start the next offensive series, a play that Randall likes, because it gives him a chance to run with the ball and throw on the move. He executes it well, too, completing an eight-yard pass to Tank that results in the biggest gain of the day. Then Keith bulls out three yards up the middle for the first Eagles' first down of the half. But just as it seems momentum is building, Randall bounces a third pass at the feet of an open receiver and the minidrive dies.

They go into the locker room at halftime trailing 3–0. Dallas's top-ranked offense has been able to muster only a thirty-five-yard field goal. Randall and the offense have been given the ball six times in the first half. They've managed just one first down, failed on every third-down play, gained just twenty-eight yards running the ball and—get this—*thirteen yards* passing! Add in the stats from the second half of the Cardinals game the week before, and Richie's offense has now played four full quarters without scoring a point, having gained a total of just twenty-four yards by air. *It don't take no Phi Beta Kappa* to sense mutiny brewing in the locker room.

And, in fact, Richie has decided on a drastic remedy. After huddling briefly with his assistants, he summons both Randall and backup Jim McMahon into a side room. Randall can sense what's coming. He stares glumly at the wall.

"Randall, look at me," the coach says. "We're going to go with Jim in the third quarter. Be ready to go back in the fourth quarter."

Randall's gaze returns to the wall. No expression.

"Randall, look at me," says the coach.

"Fine," says Randall. "Good luck, Jimmy, I'll help you all I can."

The switch has the desired effect. It shakes the team up. Word spreads through the locker room quickly before an announcement is made. "He's goin' with Jimbo" is whispered from locker to locker. Most welcome the news. They can see how much Randall is struggling. In the huddle, the quarterback seems lost, hurried, and confused. There was a time, not too long ago, when the whole team had an almost giddy sense of confidence in Randall. He had this aura. They really felt that with him on the field, *anything* could happen. But the aura is gone. There has been a detour on Randall's path to greatness. In fact, most of these guys think Randall's benching is overdue. Hell, if they're not getting the job done, they expect to get yanked. It's happened to almost all of them at one time or another. But Ran-*doll* has always been this special case, the designated franchise player, even though his mood swings are notorious. Just as there are days when it seems that nothing can stop him, there are days when it is obvious to everybody around him that he just *doesn't have it.* If it is so plain to the players, why isn't it plain to Coach? Playing him when he's like this is like taking your hands off the wheel and letting the car roll over the cliff. Still, it's as if there were this mandate from on high, from Norman himself, that no matter what happens, no matter how desperate the situation and how dismal his performance, Randall remains the Man. Look what happened to Buddy after yanking him for just three plays!

So Richie's move earns instant approval on both sides of the locker room. His stock has never been so high with Buddy's Boys. And when Jimbo comes out in the second half and drives the offense eighty yards in eight plays for a touchdown, giving them a 7–3 lead . . . well, shit, maybe this Richie Kotite has some balls after all!

Randall makes all the right moves. He's the first guy out on the field to congratulate Jimbo as the battle-scarred veteran comes waddling off in his bulky flak jacket and two knee braces. But the expression on Randall's face has found a new shade of blank.

This is his private hell.

WHEN THE EAGLES took Randall Cunningham in the second round of the draft in '85, it was considered a gamble. Few doubted the kid's raw talent. He had thrown for more than 2,500 yards in three straight seasons at the University of Nevada, Las Vegas (only the third collegiate quarterback in history to do so—the others were Doug Flutie and that Elway), gained a mind-boggling 8,290 yards rushing, *and* was one of the premier college punters in the nation. Randall's punts were legendary, Promethean—*On top of everything else, he can kick!*—great towering parabolas that hinted something about this kid went beyond any normal measure. His college coach, Harvey Hyde, told the story of how Randall had begged to be allowed to punt the ball in a game, and when Hyde finally relented, "The thing was launched like a satellite! The coaches in the press box were screaming in my headset, 'Holy Cow! It's above us!' It drove the receiver to his knees." The punts gave Randall a mythic quality, nudging him into Jim Thorpe–Paul Hornung territory. If most pro football players had not been the best players on their high school or college teams, Randall was the exception that buttressed the stereotype. He was the Natural, a living, breathing football version of Roy Hobbs. If his gangly but lithe twenty-two-year-old frame looked incomplete, it also hinted at unlimited promise. Already he had moves on the football field like no one else's, and an arm that could launch a precise pass sixty or seventy yards, without even planting his feet. When he threw the ball, his body uncoiled like a rope, a loose, smooth, wave action that began at his heels and concluded with a whipping motion at the end of a long, rubber arm, the way a Disney cartoonist might draw it. The throwing style was so unique that hidebound scouts—their minds patterned to seek out Unitas, Namath, Marino—took one look at it and said, *The kid'll never make it. Throws like a fuckin' windmill. Takes him too long to release the ball.* Randall's success, they said, could be chalked up to his playing for UNLV—*It's a basketball school.*

There was this other (deeper) current of skepticism. See, Randall is *black.*

The racism was, of course, smothered in generations of horseshit. Football had its own subtle code words and rationalizations. It was anecdotal wisdom run amuck, self-perpetuating and blind to itself. Blacks made great running backs and receivers and defensive players (the dim brutes theory) because . . . well, even if you weren't prepared to buy the speculative observations of armchair physiologists and theoretical geneticists (thicker haunches, better animal reflexes), and even if you scorned the Grand Dragon logic that placed dark-skinned races closer to monkeys on the evolutionary scale—*Shit, man, all you got to do is open yer eyes! Just look at how many of them are playing those positions in the college and the pros! And how many o' them darkies do you see playing quarterback?* In truth, the Great American Cult of the Pigskin was set up to steer black players into so-called athletic roles and preserve for white players the so-called strategic roles: safety, quarterback, center, middle linebacker, not to mention head coach. In '84, Randall's senior year, three decades after the desegregation of schools and twenty-one years after Dr. Martin Luther King's "I Have a Dream" speech, there were no black head coaches in the NFL, and only one starting black quarterback (Warren Moon). While black players were making inroads at safety and middle linebacker, the unwritten racial code remained. Never mind that the complexity of the game in the pros demanded a high level of strategic thinking at almost every position—how could Eric Allen's mastery of cornerback be considered purely an *athletic* accomplishment? There wasn't a responsible person in any consequential position in the NFL who would think of defending these racist distinctions, but the Pigskin Sluice itself kept racism alive long after most overt traces of it were gone from the upper echelons of the Game. As with most aspects of American society, racism was hardwired into the system. The pattern was still set back on the hometown playing fields, where Coach (usually white) tended to choose for field generals those kids he knew best and felt the most comfortable with (also usually white). By the time players made it to the college level, they brought with them years of schooling at their specialty, and by the time they were being picked by pro teams, they had become accomplished specialists. The pattern set back at the mouth end of the Sluice was still visibly in place throughout football the year Randall's name came up in the draft, completing the circular logic—*how many o' them do you see quarterbacking in the pros?* There wasn't an overt racist in the room when the Eagles were considering Randall in the draft that year, but the question, of course, came up: *Is he intelligent enough to play quarterback in the NFL?*

Add to that the unorthodoxy of Randall's style, and the flip side of Randall's Promethean promise was risk. The subtext of the concern for Randall's throwing motion, powerful but loose and undisciplined, was the old *athletic* versus *strategic* bugaboo (he was black, not white). All that running around he did? That was *athletic* ability, not the disciplined, cerebral, *strategic* skill of a pro caliber quarterback (he was black, not white). To their credit, the Eagles' scouts put at least one of these concerns to the test. They broke down films of Randall's remarkable throwing motion frame by frame and discovered that despite how it looked, he actually took no longer to release the ball than most NFL quarterbacks. Besides, here was a guy you had to catch before you could sack. As for his running ability . . . well, that could be a plus if channeled the right way. Ted Marchibroda, then the Eagles' offensive coordinator, was known as an innovator (he would later introduce Buffalo's no-huddle system), and Marchibroda was the kind of coach who got excited about a player who was different. Backed strongly by his assistant, Lynn Stiles convinced head coach Marion Campbell to ignore the naysayers.

Randall quickly disproved all the doubters. He was intelligent, all right, and he could play the position like few others. Which is not to say he didn't pose the Eagles some problems—*unusual* problems. They had little to do with his race, and everything to do with his singular personality. To understand Randall's problems meant trying to understand Randall.

If thinking is a problem with the Scrambling One, it's that he thinks too much, and always about the same thing—himself. Randall is a prisoner of self. He's like a man serving a life sentence in solitary, who counts his breaths and takes his pulse every few minutes, forever watching himself watching himself watching himself. . . . It explains the ever-shifting ground of his conversation, which doubles back in on itself again and again, as Randall assesses what he is saying while he's saying it and then corrects himself in midstream, modifying his statement, then remodifying it, until he sometimes ends by directly contradicting himself—*Being confused has a lot to do with my personality.*

In one of his better inadvertent witticisms, Buddy once said, "Whatever Randall said, he didn't mean it." The phrase should someday be chiseled on the quarterback's tombstone.

"Randall to me is like a catfish in a pond," says Andre Waters, who has played with him now for seven seasons. "I reach in to grab him and he slips right out of my hand. I could not begin to explain Randall because he is so moody, so indifferent. One minute he's this way, the next minute he's the next way. He means well, I know that. In his heart, he means well, but the way he comes out with things, it doesn't seem right."

Whereas other players, after arriving at the big payday, buy the fancy foreign car and then DHM, Randall, who has no mom, signed his five-year, $20-million-plus deal in midseason '89, bought himself a white Mercedes coupe, and set about building a DHS (Dream Home for Self). It rose on a collection of flat lots in Moorestown, New Jersey, after more than a year of planning, a $1.4-million, twenty-six-room, ten-thousand-foot Fortress of Solitude, surrounded by high fences and adjacent to a quarter-million-dollar empty field that Randall bought and had bulldozed, grassed, and lined into his very own private football field. And what better portrait of the superstar could there be? It's an austere study in monotone, all white, gray, and black, surrounded by a tall cast-iron fence. It has a gigantic posh white leather sofa that no one is allowed to crease with their buttocks, a white kitchen crammed with every utensil, dish, goblet, pot, pan, and mechanical and electric cooking convenience you would need to feed a football team three meals a day, a room filled with wires and keyboards and speakers for Randall to compose synthesized music (perhaps when his friend Michael Jackson drops by), a room filled with pinball and video games, a viewing and listening room with a fifty-inch TV screen and a retractable wall-sized mirror to cover a small mountain of electronic apparatuses, a billiards room with a sleek modern table designed by Gucci, a twenty-foot-long bedroom closet and dressing room chockfull of full-length mirrors, where Randall can indulge his fetish for "dressing up" (in his extensive collection of military uniforms, for instance—note the Michael Jackson cum Sgt. Pepper influence).

Up through the designing and building of the house, Randall had been living in a more modest Cherry Hill home with his girlfriend Rose, a light-skinned, slender woman who had worked as a beautician and dyed her hair red and wore contact lenses that turned her brown eyes green. Randall liked his women skinny, so Rose threw herself wholeheartedly into a diet that reduced her to a skeletal shadow of her former self. Living with them was Rose's son, Bruce, whom Randall insisted call him Daddy, and whom for a season or two, he introduced as the most important person in his life. Randall had other women friends on the road, of course, although he was not one to travel the Sis-Boom-Bimbo trail—his requirements were more strict. When the Fortress of Solitude was finished, Randall—to Rose's shock—announced he would be putting her and Bruce up in an apartment. They continued seeing each other for a time, Rose and Bruce in the apartment and Randall up in the Fortress of Solitude. The house was for Randall and Randall alone, although he did have guest bedrooms fully furnished awaiting visits from his very good friends. It was significant that these *special* friends, special enough to have their names tacked on the door of their own bedrooms, were not teammates or old high-school or college buddies, but peers in Randall's special fantasy celebrity kingdom—there was the Eric Dickerson room, the Whitney Houston room, the Michael Jackson room. . . .

Las Vegas was where Randall built his second house, for his Aunt Nettie. Nettie, his mother's sister, was a kind of adopted mom, and

Las Vegas was Randall's adopted hometown, and a perfect one it was for him, too. Tinsel City, the Money-Obsessed, Something-for-Nothing Capital of the Free World, it beckoned the quarterback from his peripatetic existence in the off-season, a neon-painted glitter palace at night that in the cold light of dawn was revealed to be nothing more than the largest contiguous strip mall on the planet.

Randall came here after high school to play quarterback, because most of the big schools wouldn't let him play that position at the college level—*See, what the boy has, that's what we call* athletic *ability*. Randall wasn't ready for the way his blackness would play in the rest of America. He says the first time he confronted overt racism was as a student in Las Vegas, when a stranger shouted "Get out of the street, nigger!" at him from a passing car. He was every bit as much shocked as insulted.

Santa Barbara, where he grew up, had such an easy blend of Hispanic, Asian, Anglo, and black that Randall never developed any special sense of race. His neighborhood was a pleasant, tree-lined suburb of single-family, low-roofed ranch houses with attached garages and fenced-in backyards. His father, Sam, had been a railroad porter until ill health kept him from working. He was a huge man, tall and thick, weighing more than three hundred pounds. People called him Heavy. Randall's mother, Mabel, worked as a practical nurse at Goleta Valley Community Hospital. The house was a gift from Randall's half brother Sam, who had starred at Santa Barbara High School in several sports before playing football at the University of Southern California and then for the Patriots. The house was not fancy, but its location on the city's oceanfront mesa was idyllic, bordered to the west by the Pacific Ocean and to the east by the red-brown cliffs of the Santa Ynez Mountains, where hang gliders take daring leaps into the hazy California sky and coast down like Day-Glo butterflies. It was just a short walk for Randall to the Arroyo Burro Beach, where he learned to surf. He spent long summer days on the beach, greasing down his board with Sex Wax and slathering his long, skinny limbs with Coppertone just like the white boys.

He would say things sometimes that confused the hounds, not knowing where he came from. He said, for instance, on first arriving in Philadelphia, that one of the things that was hardest for him to get used to was "being around so many black people all the time." And there was the time he remarked, without the slightest outward irony, that after spending many hours studying game films seated between his receivers, Calvin and Fred, he "felt just like an Oreo cookie"—*Whoaa, partner, ain't the filling white?*

Randall doesn't see himself so much as a black man (if he sees himself as being black at all) as a celebrity. He has been a celebrity all his life. As a grade-schooler, he was Sam "Bam" Cunningham's little brother, Sam being the best young athlete the city had produced. Randall and his other two older brothers would visit the USC Trojans' locker room after Sam's games, soaking up the atmosphere and collecting autographs and keepsakes from their collegiate heroes. Randall played Pop Warner football wearing an elbow pad signed by USC stars. By the time he was in junior high, living in the house Sam bought, he was the younger brother of a famous pro football player, and an emerging talent in his own right. As a senior, Randall quarterbacked the high-school football team to a 13–1 record, losing only in the finals of the regional championships. Grainy black-and-white films show a wiry boy lost in helmet and pads doing the same tricks that would later make him famous in the pros.

Within two years after that senior season, both of Randall's parents would be dead (Mabel of cancer, Sam of a heart attack a year later). His older brothers had all moved on. Randall was swept up at this vulnerable point in his life by a tide of personal celebrity that he has been riding ever since. He was named starting quarterback at UNLV in his sophomore year, which made him an instant twenty-year-old celebrity in Glittertown, which loves its ramblin' Rebels. The place suited him. There are two ways of earning status in Las Vegas—money and celebrity. And, it turns out, the kid from Santa Barbara is an exotic flower that only blooms under just those lights. Before he was out of school, he received a $3-million offer from the USFL (and was awarded a $650,000 breach-of-contract penalty when that fell through) before signing with the NFL for a somewhat smaller but still multimillion-dollar sum. He had been a celebrity all his life, and now he was a rich celebrity. If Randall belonged to a subculture, that was it—the Culture of Rich Celebrities, more particularly (in this still racially divided society) the Culture of Rich Black Celebrities. Hence the special Eric Dickerson, Michael Jackson, and Whitney Houston bedrooms in his house, the appearances on Arsenio Hall, his chummy ties with Boyz II Men, Jaleel White (TV's Urkel), MTV's and HBO's "Downtown" Julie Brown, and an assortment of other *best friends* Randall collects like sequins on a tacky dinner jacket.

Even God is a kind of celebrity *best friend*—top dog of the ultimate in exclusive clubs. In Randall's book, he recounts how he was "saved" in '87 at Spanish Trails, a posh golf course in Las Vegas. After Randall finished a round of eighteen holes with an old friend, as they were heading back out to the Benz, his friend asked, "Have you been saved?"

"What does being saved mean?" Randall asked.

His friend explained about having a personal relationship with Jesus Christ the Lord. "Do you want to be saved?"

"How long will it take?"

The quarterback says that conversation kindled an interest in the Bible, where he found a never-ending source of parallels with his own situation. He began tithing 10 percent of his considerable earnings to his church, the fantastically fortunate St. John Baptist in Camden, New Jersey, where, needless to say, Randall became the ecclesiastic equivalent of an overnight sensation. He read that those who were saved, and led a righteous life, would enter the kingdom of heaven, where the streets are paved with gold—sure sounded like Randall's kind of place.

The great thing about his celebrity *best friends* was, apart from sharing his status, they didn't want anything from him. It was this precise quality, in fact, that first attracted Randall to South African dancer Felicity De Jager (pronounced "De-Yaga"). Well, actually, the first thing that attracted him to her was her beauty and celebrity. He met her after watching her perform as a featured dancer with the Dance Theatre of Harlem at a charity fund-raising banquet called "The Night of 100 Stars"—Randall's kind of people. He was living with Rose and her boy at the time, but he asked to be introduced to Felicity backstage, and they began seeing each other whenever he was in New York City, according to the Scrambling One's autobiography— "One of the first times we were together we went to the mall," he says. "I'm a very generous person [got that?] and I like to buy my friends things—especially beautiful clothes. I saw this beautiful orange outfit and I asked Felicity to try it on. She looked so fine in it; she had it going ON!"

But Felicity refused to let him buy the dress. Thought Randall, "This is a very honest, beautiful, respectful person. She is a dancer, doing her own thing, and she doesn't need me or my money."

By the fall of '92, as Randall's quarterbacking is cooling off, his romance is heating up. Felicity has the thin, leggy look that Randall preferred (a reflection perhaps?) and shares his passion for high style. Most important, she has class, that is, she is, by virtue of her growing status in the chic dance world of New York City, a certified member in good standing of the Culture of Rich Black Celebrities. As for the Great Club of God and eventual residence in that city where the streets are paved with gold . . . well, Felicity had taken care of that. On her first visit to St. John Baptist with Randall this summer, she heard the preacher's call and stepped lightly to the fore to pledge her soul. Leaving the church with her that day, hand in hand, with the congregation clapping for them, Randall says he decided to propose. All Felicity lacked was riches, and Randall could supply that. Late in the football season (Rose is back at work in the K-Mart beauty shop) he will announce his engagement to Felicity . . . where else? On Arsenio!

All this, the Cult of Self and Celebrity, has built a wall between him and his teammates higher than the one around his Fortress of Solitude. You can't, for instance, get Randall on the phone. He is the only player on the Eagles' roster who refuses to leave his home number with the team's PR office. They get hold of him like everybody else, by leaving a message with his appointments secretary and waiting to see if he'll call back—an iffy proposition at best. No one ever drops in on Randall; one is never quite sure where to find him. Randall, like royalty, awards petitioners audiences, so that even when you hung around with him "casually," you felt like you were being indulged, and that you were on probation. Old teammates, childhood friends, even Randall's brothers complained about this.

You could only approach him as an equal if you shared his celebrity status, or if you had as much money as he had—more money, of course, made you an object of his respect and genuine admiration. Randall conveyed his obsession with money and status in ways big and little. He would tease teammates about the kind of car they drove, the jackets they wore, their pants, sweaters, shoes—"Been shopping at K-Mart again, Andre?" When he teased his teammates he was just kidding, of course, but some of the guys took real offense. Each cute gibe was just another reminder—*Hey, turkey, I'm richer than you are.*

Randall has erected quite an elaborate edifice on the cornerstone of self. This off-season alone, he had worked on a pilot for new syndicated TV game show called "Scrambler," endorsed a candy bar and snack-food line now being regionally marketed in his name (proceeds to charity), produced and starred in an hour-long prime-time TV interview program called "Randall Cunningham's Celebrity Rap" (which featured, among other things, one of the all-time truly great suck-up interviews with *best friend* Donald Trump), helped promote a new line of leisure apparel called the Quarterback Club, backed by himself and several other starting NFL passers, posed for several national magazine covers, and managed his self-promotional business, Scrambler, Inc., which booked moneymaking public appearances and designed and marketed T-shirts, caps, and trinkets featuring Randall's name or likeness. He spent many hours in the offices of Scrambler, Inc., signing mountains of memorabilia, surrounded by boxes and boxes of color portraits of himself, helmets, footballs, T-shirts, and so on. The office walls were decorated with blown-up images of himself. Even Randall's charitable work was in part self-promotional, from the new youth center in Camden he helped build in memory of Jerome (Randall pictured at a gala groundbreaking, turning over the first shovel of dirt), to the $100,000 he dropped in the collection basket one Sunday at his Baptist church—word of which found its way into the newspapers the next day. If he donated money to buy pads for a local Moorestown little league football team, the team was featured on his in-season TV show, "The Randall Cunningham Show." He would make a point of telling reporters that there were lots of other charities he helped support, but then decline to elaborate, citing biblical injunctions against drawing attention to your good works (which, of course, he had just done). He existed at the center of a thriving commercial cult of self, wherein virtually every act he performed outside the high monotonous walls of the Fortress of Solitude was in some way self-promotional.

If ego is the root of embarrassment, imagine the redwood of shame Randall shoulders out to the field in Texas Stadium for the second half of the Cowboys' game. In his I'M BACK SCRAMBLING cap ($17.95), arms folded, for the entire second half, he watches Jimbo steer the offense through a seesaw battle with the Cowboys.

Jimmy Mac is playing well, doing what he does best, reading defenses, hanging in the pocket forever, taking hit after hit, but always pulling himself back to his feet, always moving the team downfield. God, how Richie likes this guy! They speak the same language. Randall is outside looking in as the head coach, Jimbo, Zeke, and David Archer huddle between series, comparing notes, planning strategy. And Richie isn't hectoring Jim, he's *listening*, nodding, agreeing ... it's a rapport Randall can only envy.

The score is tied 10–10 late in the third quarter, with the Cowboys deep on their own side of the field, when Reverend Reggie makes the fatal mistake. The defensive front is supposed to be performing a stunt, with ends Reggie and Clyde swinging inside the tackles and charging up the middle. It's the perfect call for what the Cowboys have planned, too, because Dallas's play is a draw to Emmitt Smith. If the stunt works right, Smith gets smothered by the two premier defensive ends in football. But Reggie doesn't get the call, or he forgets, or whatever, because instead of swinging around inside, Reggie charges out to his left, which opens up a airplane hangar–sized door for Smith, who dances around gimpy Wes ten yards downfield and races forty-one more before Eric can catch him from behind and push him out-of-bounds. This sets up a field goal to give Dallas a lead that they don't lose.

The final score, after the Cowboys add another touchdown, is 20–10. The fortunes of early October are reversed. Now the Cowboys own the spotlight, and their path to postseason seems as wide open as that hole Reggie offered Emmitt.

Meeting with the Pack immediately after the game, Richie doesn't even wait to be asked about his quarterback move.

"I just thought that to have only one first down in the first half is to have your defense out there for too long," he says. "It took its toll in the second half. I felt that we had to make a change, try to get something clicking. . . . Randall is still the starter."

But that would change the next day. On the flight home, Richie changes his mind. He calls in Randall first thing in the morning and tells him Jim will start the following week against the Raiders.

"I'm going to start you again the following week," the coach says, explaining how the week's layoff should do him good, get the pressure off his shoulders . . . just the thing to shake off the slump. Randall isn't even listening. He isn't going to start next week? He, Randall Cunningham, the Weapon of the Nineties, the Michael Jordan of the NFL—second string? He leaves the coach's office without saying a word.

What's there to say? It's Richie's call. But the decision to bench Randall isn't just a simple personnel move, it pulls the plug on a ten-thousand-watt flashing beacon every bit as gaudy and grand as any marquee along the Strip. Who buys the second-string quarterback's candy bar? T-shirt? Cap? Autographed portrait? Football card? Jersey? Sweater? Jacket? How many second-string quarterbacks sit across the couch from Arsenio? Interview Donald Trump? Dance with "Downtown" Julie Brown? Who watches the second-string quarterback's weekly TV show?

For Randall, this is a crisis of soul.

HE MAY BE a hothouse flower that blooms only under the lights of money and fame, but Randall is also a revolutionary.

Pro football has become a conservative game. "You can't reinvent the wheel" is a favorite coachly saying at the pro level—Richie says it all the time. "There are no geniuses in this game" is another—Richie says this a lot, too. Football attracts conservatives. Maybe it's the martial parallel. The Game is chocked with Silverbacks, men for whom the old rules of Western culture work. Flamingly creative souls simply do not end up coaching football teams. And the Pigskin Priesthood turns already conservative men into overmentored, blindered traditionalists. Money and hype nurture this natural hidebound bent by investing every season, even every game, with such career significance for both player and coach that no one dares fail magnificently. With only one

or two exceptions, the tenure of a High Priest is no longer charted in
eras, it's measured from year to year. And when the cost of failure is
high, daring dies. There hasn't been a dramatic offensive innovation
in the game since Eddie Cochems introduced the forward pass at
St. Louis University in 1906. Sure, the monks still tinker with the
fundamental offensive scheme, a few teams have gone recently to
a heavy passing strategy (the run and shoot, or what Buddy Ryan
contemptuously calls the chuck-and-duck), and Marchibroda has the
Bills hustling through a no-huddle attack, but the game is played week
to week with offense and defense lining up in the same basic ways,
running the same timeworn play sheet of twenty or so runs and passes,
both teams armed with careful, computer-assisted analyses of tendencies and percentages. On the sidelines, Coach no longer thinks in terms
of *How can we fake these sumbitches out of their shoes?* He thinks something
more like *Okay, it's third and long, we have an 85 percent tendency to throw,
15 percent tendency to draw, they blitz 30 percent of the time in this situation,
they didn't blitz last time, we ran the draw last time, so they'll most likely be
coming after the quarterback expecting us to throw, so. . . .* College football
still offers Bobby Bowden's trick plays, which he calls "Rooskies," and
foolhardy acts of derring-do, but the pros have become careful to
excess. It's almost a lock that each Super Bowl, the most heavily
scripted contest of the year, will be dull as a commencement address
at a college of podiatry. Caution has fashioned a straitjacket for the
Game.

In this world, Randall is a subversive. Writers have dubbed him
"Quarterback of the Future," but Randall is really a throwback. With
his flair for thinking and throwing on the run, he has more in common
with Walter Camp's college boys than today's pros. The kneejerk, racist
interpretation of Randall is that he is more *athletic* than *strategic*, but,
in fact, his skills are both mental and physical. He has a genius for
football. He is a scat singer busting out of a Gregorian chant. He is
intuitive, not analytical; spontaneous, not programmed; inspired, not
predictable—he's right brain to the NFL's left brain, in short, a breath
of fresh air.

Philadelphia fans who caught their first glimpses of him in action
in his rookie year, making atrocious blunders and amazing moves,
couldn't get enough of him. His presence on the field meant something
unexpected and, hence, exciting was going to happen. In his pro
debut, a preseason game against the Jets, Randall threw six passes and
completed three and took off with the ball five times, gaining eighty-
six yards. Teammate John Spagnola, a veteran tight end, saw right
off that this kid had a different way of doing quarterback—"He took
a very sophisticated position and narrowed it down. . . . If the receiver

is covered, he just takes off and runs fifty yards. Maybe we shouldn't worry so much about strong and weak zones and everything else."

Indeed! If Randall is a round peg, then fix the square hole! Why not scrap your traditional offensive schemes and come up with something wild and different, something that exploits Randall's strengths and protects his weaknesses, something on the order of Marchibroda's no-huddle system but even more drastic? Why not breathe real inspiration into the well-ordered recipe of the game? Why not a new offense that would be maddeningly difficult for the crusty defenses of the NFL to dissect, anticipate, and stop? Send Randall in on fourth and long and let defenses figure out what to do against a player who can kick the ball sixty yards, throw it sixty or longer, or just take off running that far? Confuse them! Tie them in knots! Randallize them! How many times does a player with this mix of talents come along? The traditionalists are always asking *How many different ways can you use eleven men to advance a football against eleven other men?* Well, who the hell knew? Try something different! What's the worst that can happen?

Of course, the worst that can happen is you lose a whole peck of football games and get fired. Not just you, but the whole coaching staff, maybe even the front office. To attempt something bold and new demands trial and error, maybe several seasons' worth. Even the forward pass had a hard time breaking into the repertory of pro football. Despite the immediate success it brought Cochems's St. Louis squad, which trounced all comers, including much higher-ranked teams, it was received the way brilliant new ideas have been down through the ages—established coaches ignored it for years. Most monks in the pro temple sniffed at Randall's college numbers. Maybe he could play the game that way in college, but not in the pros.

The other way was to try to make the round peg square.

The Eagles hired Sid Gillman, the most famous of NFL quarterback gurus, to tutor the wunderkind in his rookie season, and Gillman got fed up. Randall would listen intently in the classroom, ask questions, argue fine points of strategy, and then, on the field, the moment the ball was snapped—presto—the plan went out the window. Failure didn't seem to bother Randall at all. He seemed to have been born with a gift for the *that's in the past* mantra. No matter how lopsided the score, no matter how deep the hole, young Randall never lost heart. With him it was always *The next play, I'll make something happen.*

"I don't believe this guy studies," Gillman complained one day to Harry. "I give him film to study. I tell him, do that, do this . . . and he doesn't do it."

Harry said that was a pretty serious allegation, maybe the young quarterback was just a slow learner. Maybe he had a hard time remembering things. Gillman said, no, Randall is as intelligent as they come. It wasn't that he couldn't learn the material, he wouldn't. It just didn't seem important enough to him. And Gillman set out to prove his charge. He inserted a torn slip of paper inside a roll of game film and gave it to Randall to take home and study overnight. If Randall played the film, the slip would drop out. When the quarterback returned the film, the old coach unrolled it at his desk, and out floated the slip.

Gillman was gone with the rest of Marion Campbell's coaching staff at the end of Randall's rookie season, when Buddy took over. And Buddy was, more by default than design, the perfect head coach for Randall. As a defensive coach, Buddy saw Randall's combination of skills for what they were, a defense's nightmare. The kid had the damnedest talent Buddy had ever seen. There was no telling what he was going to do when he got hold of the ball. Buddy brought in Doug Scovil, a laid-back, rangy old quarterback who had been Buddy's boss years before at the University of the Pacific. Scovil worked with Randall on his throwing motion, helping him to quicken his release of the ball, but he deemphasized all the classroom work on reading defenses and bought heavily into the revolutionary aspects of the kid's game. Buddy's plan was to assemble the best defense the NFL had ever seen and give Randall the ball on offense. It didn't bother Buddy if Randall fell on his face nine out of ten times, so long as the quarterback gave him "five big plays a game." Buddy wasn't that concerned about developing a powerful offensive line, because the way Randall could move around with the ball, defenses didn't dare risk the temporary mayhem of an all-out rush. Buddy used the draft to acquire Keith Jackson, Keith Byars, and Anthony Toney, big men who could throw a block when Randall took off, but who were also skilled pass catchers, giving Randall additional targets. Ted Plumb developed the game plan, which served as a kind of rough outline, the chord changes over which Randall extemporized. Scovil's job was to pat Randall's ego, especially when things went awry. "Don't worry about it," Doug would say. "You're the best. You're the man."

They started off using Randall only on third downs. Ron Jaworski, the old veteran, would steer a conventional offense on first and second down, and on third down, in would trot the kid and the defense would start scratching its head—*How do you defend against this guy?* Randall was electric. He was easily the most exciting player the league had seen in years. He started five of the last six games of the '86 season, and in '87 he was the Eagles' offensive MVP and was named to the Pro Bowl. Randall started in the Pro Bowl in '88, won multiple player-of-the-year honors, and took the team to their first play-off game of Buddy's tenure (along with Buddy's defense, that is). He had become such a valuable player that Norman didn't even wait for his contract to expire. The club renegotiated and re-signed him to a five-year deal early in the '89 season, staking the franchise on him. By the end of that season, Plumb was letting Randall call the plays himself in some situations. Scat quarterbacking had arrived. No doubt about it, Randall, age twenty-six, was the Man.

It was a strategy that played dangerously to Randall's self-obsession. Doug Scovil's mantra, *You're the Man*, placed the quarterback above criticism on the squad. His central place in the offensive scheme, his huge new contract, it all fed a growing public perception that the team *was* Randall. In postgame analyses, Plumb and Scovil would lavish praise on Randall's clever moves and crisp passes—*You're the Man*—and excuse or roll right past his mistakes. The other guys had never seen anything like it. There would be a play, for instance, where Randall ignored open receivers downfield and ran for a small gain. On the screen you could see the open guys jumping up and down, waving their arms, pleading for a pass. And instead of slamming Randall for ignoring his checkoffs, Coach would say something like, "Uh, you might want to note, for the future, Randall, these other options on that play." And that was it! On to the next play! When the team lost, in the absence of any fair assessment of blame by the coaches, the locker room assessed its own blame in whispers and grumbled asides. Like any sore left to fester, it grew. Key players on defense would stay late after practice every day to bone up on opposing teams and prepare themselves to the hilt. And where was Ran-*doll*? Off at some public appearance or taping his TV show or radio show or participating in some fashion show or flying out for an appearance on Arsenio, for Crissakes!

Norman began to lose patience with the quarterback after the second opening-round play-off loss in '89, to the Rams. The impatient owner was hearing whispers from the temple: *Buddy's winging it with that kid . . . that's fine for the regular season, but not the big games. The best teams are too smart, too fast, too well coached. They're not going to get beat with that improvisational bullshit, they're not going to let themselves get Randallized.* Buddy didn't agree. Hell, they were gettin' so close he could taste it. But Norman wanted a smart guy running his offense. He wanted a solid, dependable, structured offensive attack that employed Randall, but didn't lean on him. Doug Scovil had died of a heart attack late in the '89 season. After the Rams loss, Buddy bowed to the pressure from above and let go of his low-key offensive coordinator Ted Plumb. It had been Harry, of course, who came up with the name Richie Kotite.

And so, in the late winter of '90, Randall the Man was introduced to his new handler, and the days of rump-pat, high-flying scat quarterbacking ended.

Which is not to say Richie wasn't impressed. The Eagles' new offensive coordinator was, simply, amazed by Randall. Talking to a friend in the summer of '90, the new offensive coordinator was genuinely in awe of the quarterback's talent. "His ability to create something on his own because he's had to . . . sometimes I can't believe what I'm seeing. It's just tremendous. I've always known how dangerous he could be when he's in space, when he starts running with the ball—he's one of the most dangerous pure runners in the league—but I never realized until I started working with him every day what an accurate passer he is! I've seen him throw passes on the run that no other quarterback I've ever seen could have thrown, and right on the fucking dime."

But right from the start, these incredible talents were to Richie, the Silverback, strictly peripheral. Richie believed in running the same twenty or so plays over and over and over again until the offense could do it blindfolded and in a trance. He disguised the plays by running them out of a shifting pattern of formations, making it tough for teams to guess exactly what was coming, but the Richie offense was high Gregorian all the way, an eleven-man choir working in a limited tonal range, scripted to the max.

"The premise we're going by is to be fundamentally sound, to be as disciplined as possible," he said the summer he arrived. "The thing you try to do is get them where they are believing in themselves, synchronized, and regardless of what happens during the ball game they keep working hard and pecking away and eventually good things will happen."

Fundamentally sound? Synchronized? *Pecking away?*

Nobody in the NFL had a squarer hole than Richie, and Randall, the remarkable round peg, was going into it.

Randall told Richie that he liked to call his own plays.

"I'm calling the plays," said Richie.

Randall said there was a core group of plays that he and the Keiths particularly liked, that worked well for them—couldn't they just add them to Richie's offensive scheme?

No go.

"Whatever you were doing before, there are similar things in the scheme we're going to put in. Relax, you're going to like it."

Randall didn't like it.

As for being the Man, Richie's line was, "Randall, you're not out there alone; you do your job and let everybody else do theirs."

He took to calling Randall "Arsenio," an unsubtle dig at the quarterback's celebrity status and a backhanded reminder that he was supposed to be part of a team. As for kicking up his heels, making things happen, Randall's on-field genius for escape and action . . . well, that was okay, said Richie, but only when all else fails: "Take the snap, do your drop, step up in the pocket, check off your receivers, and if there's nothing there, *then* take off!"

Sure, that sounded great, like Johnny Unitas with a surprise fifth gear. Only everybody knew that by the time Randall did the traditional quarterback thing, he'd either have to throw the ball or get knocked on his ass.

The conflict between Randall and Richie was, at heart, the standard clash between talent and experience, between the chaotic rumble of the action and the calm wisdom of the playbook. Players believed they were the only ones who could win football games. The Game wasn't some dry abstraction, *X*'s and *O*'s on a blackboard or the silent overhead camera of the Coach's-Eye View. It was a the thrill of action, of making sense fast out of a jumble of hurtling bodies, sensing which direction to turn, where to throw. It was easy to see, later, projected on a screen from afar, all the options and obvious pathways. Randall's special genius was living in that chaotic, instinctive moment, on the field. He wasn't some programmed warrior acting out a script prepared by computer-assisted Coach. He was an artist!

When Richie arrived, Randall was at the top of his game. Before Richie ever signed on with the Eagles, Randall had started fifty-three games. He'd led the Eagles to victory in twenty-one of his last thirty-two starts. After just five seasons, he was the fifth-leading rushing quarterback in NFL history, behind only players who had played the game twice and three times as long as he had. He had been to three Pro Bowls.

Richie insisted his offensive system was an opportunity for Randall, a chance to make even more of his skills. Randall saw it as a threat and an affront. Who was this guy? A failed tight end from the olden days (*Were they still wearing leather helmets then?*), a former assistant with the Jets? What could Richie Kotite possibly teach Randall Cunningham about *making things happen* on a football field? And Richie was neither tolerant nor tactful. He had more than the usual coaching tendency to treat players as interchangeable parts.

Then things got worse. Buddy picked Jimmy Mac off the waiver wire and signed him to a one-year contract. Randall and Jimbo made a big show of togetherness at first, but no single thing could have done more to shatter the mantra. Jimbo completed the scenario Randall could see shaping up. First comes Richie with this Neanderthal offense that demands a windup, pocket-passing quarterback, and they bring in Buddy's old pal from the '85 Chicago championship team to run it. Jimbo was everything Randall was not. Skip the fact that he was white. He was an acknowledged master of running a conventional offense, reading defenses, making adjustments on the field before the snap, and hanging in the pocket until the last possible microsecond before releasing the ball. Jimbo was also an immediate hit in the locker room, popular with all the guys, whether it was dominating the bowling league, playing golf on his day off, maintaining the constant running game of Bones, playing a practical joke—Jim, the traditional, honky, tested quarterback with the Super Bowl ring on his finger was, face it, exactly the kind of player Richie needed to pilot his *synchronized* offense.

Randall did the only thing he could do. With Buddy acting as a buffer (the head coach still preferred his "five big plays" theory, but Norman had demanded a change), the scat quarterback and the Gregorian choirmaster got along. Randall still cut loose pretty much when he felt like it, and when he failed . . . well, Buddy would intercede to protect him. And Richie tried to accommodate Randall with lots of rollouts and half rollouts, which he called waggles. The quarterback's game hardly fell apart. He had the best season of his career. With two extremely talented new receivers, Fred and Calvin, and with everyone running the crisper, more predictable pass routes Richie scripted, the offense (and Randall) posted its best performance in years. They finished the season ranked third in the league.

But it wasn't enough. The offense was shut down again in the first-round play-off game, the infamous Redskins loss that prompted Buddy's firing. Randall was just awful. Injuries had shredded the Eagles' offensive line, and the quarterback, with the experience of two consecutive play-off losses behind him, was leaning more heavily than usual on Richie's script at precisely the time he needed to cut loose.

It was after this game that the festering resentment of Randall spilled out. The vehicle, of course, was Seth. After that game, standing half-naked in front of his locker, bitterly disappointed, the linebacker vented a long tirade against an unnamed teammate, whom he blamed for the defeat. Of course, anybody who knew this team knew exactly whom he was talking about:

> You commit yourself to something; you commit your-
> self to winning. You commit yourself to achieving your goals.
> And don't half-ass commit. Put everything you got into it.
> If you don't want to do it, fine, then find something else to
> do. Because there's a lot more guys here than to just, you

know, be selfish. If you want to be selfish, if you want to think about yourself, go be a damn ice skater, run track or something or play golf or something. People just have got to take into consideration that they're not the only person on the team. . . . Until guys realize that, until guys grow up and realize that this is your job, sure you make great money at it, but at the same time, if you don't love the game and you're not playing to become the champion, then you just really shouldn't be in it. I just think that certain areas, you know, *certain guys,* they just need to grow up and realize you either commit, do something 100 percent, or just get out of it, because it's more than just themselves that they're hurting. There's nothing you can do. The coaches can sit there and say, you need to study, you can take a horse to the water but you cannot make the horse drink. That's all it comes down to. It's desire. You either want to be a champion, you either want to be the best at what you do or you don't.

As Randall collected his pile of postseason honors in early '91, he was far from a happy man. Doug Scovil, Ted Plumb, and Buddy were gone. His teammates' resentment had spilled into the open.

Randall told one hound that off-season that he felt like he was in a coffin, pushing up to keep the lid from being closed on him. He saw it all as a trial, a test of his faith and mettle. He sat stoically through a painful preseason meeting with his teammates, who one by one stood to dump on him their suspicions, envy, and disappointed expectations. Seth accused him of not preparing hard enough for games and for caring more about himself than his team. Keith Byars said he needed to forge a better relationship with his teammates, invite the guys out to dinner now and then at the Fortress of Solitide. Keith Jackson complained that he didn't check off his receivers—that is, he didn't throw Keith Jackson the ball often enough. Much of it was petty, self-serving, and unfair, but Randall just took it. Afterward, he thanked everybody for trying to make him a better quarterback and person. It ended the session on a weird passive note.

Worst of all, the scat revolution was over. Despite all that production in '90, much of the joy had gone out of Randall's game. When Richie said, "You're not out there alone, kid," the coach meant it in a nice way; he was trying to take some of the pressure off Randall. What Richie didn't realize was that Randall *liked* being all alone out there, at least figuratively speaking. He liked the pressure. He liked being the Man. But now no one would stand for it. His teammates had risen up against him. He knew that Richie would have little patience if he tried to make something happen on his own and failed—and failure was necessary! To succeed with this head coach, Randall would have to don the traditional robe and take his place in the choir. Richie had no feel for Randall's game. And if Randall didn't sing the right notes on cue? Waiting in the wings was Jimbo, just dying to do exactly what Richie wanted.

So long as the team kept winning, this was all okay. Randall entered the '91 season professing his loyalty to Richie and his enthusiasm for the offensive system. He looked terrific in preseason games that summer, running the offense according to Richie's script. Then he blew out his knee in the first game of the year. After he had battled back from surgery and rehab, his start in '92 had been unsteady, but the team was winning. It was only when things started going bad, as they had now with four flat outings in a row, losses to the Chiefs, Redskins, and Cowboys, and the narrow escape from the Cardinals, that Randall had a chance to air the old chestnut "They won't let me be me!"

With all that it entailed.

IT STARTS in the clutter, bustle, and steam of the Dallas locker room after Randall's benching.

The Pack crowds in around the quarterback as he stuffs his travel bag. Randall is glum.

He complains that he just hasn't been able to get in sync. He waves off a suggestion that maybe playing with the knee brace is hindering him, or maybe there's something wrong with his arm.

"I'm fine," he says.

"Is it something mental?" a hound asks.

"It's not me, man. It's not me. All I can do is go out and do what I'm told, it's that simple. I'm going with the structure of the offense, trying to make it work the way they want it done. It's that simple. That's why I'm here. I don't run this football team. This is Richie's team and you've got to do it his way."

Then as the Pack drifts off, Randall asks one reporter who lingers nearby, "You tell me what you think the problem is."

"No joy," says the hound. "You're not having fun playing the game anymore."

"You saw it," says the quarterback, nodding. "Jim went out there and did the best he could, still, he couldn't do anything. They did get that one touchdown, but not much else. I just can't get in sync with this. I haven't been in sync for three or four weeks. As much as I want to just take off and run and do all that stuff, I'm confined. I can't do what I want to do."

There you have it.

Richie makes things worse the next day, when he announces he's changed his mind about starting Randall next week against the Raiders. He's giving the superstar a week off. Suddenly, the main action with this football team is no longer on the field; it's in the locker room.

Randall arrives at his locker every morning this week to face the full national Pack. O. J. Simpson, whose autograph a nervous nine-year-old Randall once requested in the USC locker room, is covering this for NBC. The other networks are represented, as is ESPN, HBO, the wire services, New York press, visiting reporters for L.A. . . . . All of them supplement the full normal Pack of locals, who elbow in closer with handheld tape recorders to catch his every soft-spoken word, camera lenses zoom in close to capture any small sign of distress (*Is that a tear?*), anger, frustration, or—blessed chance!—insubordination. Richie has handed the hounds one of the staples of the pro football reporting genre, a quarterback controversy! And with Randall, there's no telling where the thing might lead.

And Randall doesn't disappoint.

"It's started, man," he says. "The quarterback controversy has started, so let's get it going."

The following week is a running seminar in Randallisms. He tells the Pack he's a team player, and he'll abide by what the coach says, and in the next breath hints that if Richie keeps him on the bench, he'll quit. He says he can learn a lot from watching Jimbo play, and in the next breath says he won't learn a thing from sitting on the sidelines, and that if Richie believes it will fire him up again, "Then Richie doesn't know me very well." He says he's "a humble person" whose ego can take the benching, and that the coach has every right to sit him down, then he points to the bulletin board where the NFL rankings are posted every week and makes sure everyone notices his quarterback ranking there, second on the list.

And the commentary spins out of control. The Philadelphia *Daily News* banners the benching and follows it as the lead sports story all week: "Pine Time," "Earth to Randall," "If I'm Sittin', I'm Splittin'." The Philadelphia *Inquirer,* on the day Bill Clinton is elected president of the United States, leads the paper with a story about Randall's benching, and the story tops page one on the Sunday after the election. Local TV carries comments from Randall and Richie and teammates every night, and the network sports shows lead off their broadcasts with the "furor." Buddy's face pops up on TV to (surprise, surprise) criticize Richie—"I've benched players before . . . but they were back in there the next week." The old issue of *athletic* talent versus *strategic* talent surfaces again, of course—never mind Randall's five full incredibly accomplished NFL seasons. There is speculation that Randall's taking too long to throw the ball, not reading defenses, throwing poorly, favoring his good knee, taking drugs, drinking heavily, missing Keith Jackson, losing his mind . . . which the quarterback doesn't help later in the week when he decides to put things in perspective with a little lecture to his insistent audience about the imminence of Apocalypse.

"I think the world is confused right now," he says. "We have a new president. The economy is all messed up. You know, earthquakes, hurricanes. I think everybody should get into the Bible right now and do what God wants us to do because this world could be ending very soon and my main goal is to go to heaven and not hell."

Which pushes things deeply into the realm of the weird. Wait a minute, weren't we talking football?

See, up on the mountaintop, things don't happen to Randall on a normal, earthly scale. Randall's scale is cosmic. Later he will insist that he was just kidding, having some fun with the Pack—*Whatever Randall said, he didn't mean it*—but it isn't the first time that the quarterback has drawn a parallel between life and death and a career setback. Randall routinely lumps the profound with the trivial, like when his teammates' criticism made him feel as if he were "in a coffin," or when he invoked the death of his parents in the postgame press conference after Buddy benched him for three plays in that notorious Skins playoff game. This week he talks about a fan, a woman, who waited for him in the rain outside the stadium, and who told him she was a spiritualist who had foreseen his travails, and that she was praying for him, and that God had chosen him to go through this adversity so that his personal strength could be a beacon to others. Randall is buying this. It places the trials and tribulations of Randall Cunningham, quarterback, on a biblical scale, which feels right to him. Indeed, at home, up in the Fortress of Solitude, the lonely, benched, multimillionaire quarterback has found an echo of his own torment in nothing less than the Book of Job:

> Though I speak, my grief is not assuaged: and though I forbear, what am I eased? . . .
>
> He teareth me in his wrath, who hateth me; he gnasheth upon me with his teeth; mine enemy sharpeneth his eyes upon me.
>
> They have gaped upon me with their mouth; they have

smitten me upon the cheek reproachfully; they have gathered themselves together against me.

God hath delivered me to the ungodly, and turned me over into the hands of the wicked.

Mind you, Job here was talking about the loss of family, fortune, reputation, and being covered with boils from head to toe. Still, there is at least a thematic parallel with being benched for a game and a half. It shows how much Randall's whole juggernaut Cult of Self was riding on his status as starting quarterback. And in his hour of need, one to whom he has turned for solace, he tells the Pack, is his very good friend "Downtown" Julie Brown.

"Downtown" Julie Brown?

This is the kind of thing that drives his teammates crazy. Down in the locker room the boys who go to war with Randall every Sunday are shaking their heads. It's typical of the quarterback's problem. What's he doing talking to a TV star when he ought to be talking to his teammates? Why isn't he sitting down with his linemen and receivers and asking them what's wrong? *What can I do to make this work better? How can I improve?* These are the guys who are out there on the field with him every Sunday, whose fates rise and fall with his own. Is this a crisis of Randall's celebrity or a crisis of Team? Above all, he should be talking to Jimbo, to him and to Arch. They sit in all the meetings together, study the same game plans, go over the same tapes. What are their insights? Hell, a guy like Jimmy Mac brings a wealth of accumulated wisdom, eleven seasons' worth, not to mention the trip to the Super Bowl. And Jimbo's insights are not just about things like strategy and technique, the man has played against just about every coach and player in the league; he knows the strengths and weaknesses of linebackers and cornerbacks. Jimbo is a player clearly on the downside of the parabola at age thirty-three; his legs are long gone but he's still making up for it with his head. What an opportunity! Before this ever happened Randall should have been grateful to tap into what his celebrated backup had to offer. He should be picking the son of a bitch's brain apart! Instead he's crying on the shoulder of "Downtown" Julie Brown?

"She told me, 'Just don't worry about all this stuff,' " says Randall. " 'You know how things are, rumors and all that crazy stuff. Just go out there and be yourself.' "

"She didn't say nothin' about looking off the free safety?" quips Arch, who has made it a habit to listen in on these sessions.

Randall had his reasons for staying away from Jimbo and Arch. He could sense enemy vibes over his shoulder, and they were real.

The veteran, traditional, white quarterbacks had played together before, with the Chargers in '89, and they had thinly disguised contempt for Randall's methods. For one thing, Randall's exceptional talent and his philosophy of the position inadvertently played right into the old *athletic* vs. *strategic* racial stereotypes. Jimbo and Arch believed his understanding of the game was minimal, almost childlike. Before the midweek game-planning sessions with Zeke, for instance, Randall would always fetch a clean pad from Zeke's desk drawer and a green and a red pen. He was fussy about the pens, always a green one and a red one. And while Zeke would walk them through the game plan, Randall would often be off in space, drawing up plays of his own he wanted added to it. Mind you, the coaches had been working twelve- to fourteen-hour days since Monday morning poring over film breakdowns, computer analyses, self-scouting, discussing tendencies, twists, clever variations, and Randall walked in cold Wednesday, grabbed a pad and a few pens, and doodled up a better idea? Jimbo and Arch would roll their eyes behind Randall's back. At the end of the meeting, whatever notes, diagrams, or doodles Randall made would invariably be left lying on the desk—so much for boning up on things at home.

Arch and Jimbo got a kick out of what they saw as Randall's remedial-level comprehension of the game's finer points. In the second half of the Dallas game, for instance, when Randall was acting like a trooper, hanging next to Richie and trying to get involved, he ran out on the field between plays at one point and shouted to Jim, "They're playing zone, Jim! They're in zone!"

Arch watched that and just shook his head. To whom did Randall think he was talking? Nobody in the whole NFL was a better game-day quarterback than Jim McMahon. And telling the difference between man coverage and zone, hell, that was high-school stuff!

"Did you hear him when he ran out?" Jimbo asked Arch after the game. And they both had a good chuckle over it.

To these journeymen veterans steeped in the traditions of the game, Randall lacked the leader-of-men profile they felt the position demanded. During a game, one minute Randall would be walking up the sidelines screaming in a childish snit, raving out into the air to no one in particular about how he can't get any time to *make something happen*, the next minute he'd be sulking by himself on the bench, and then you'd look over and he'd be down on one knee praying with Keith Byars. Shit, the quarterback was supposed to inspire! Other players looked to the quarterback to be cool and steady in a crisis. Randall's demeanor was like some peacock actor's pique over how bad he was being made to look because his supporting cast couldn't get their lines straight. And here they both were, getting paid a fraction of Randall's salary, sitting behind him on the bench, mentally noting the opportunities missed out on the field, watching opposing teams take advantage of Randall's unschooled approach to the game.

Jimbo would pull Richie aside from time to time and say, "Hey, why don't you give me a chance to play?"

And Richie would shrug. They both figured the coach's hands were tied. What other explanation could there be?

To his credit, Jimmy Mac low-keys the whole week leading up to his start against the Raiders. He steers clear of the Pack, adhering to his policy of answering questions only immediately after a game in which he plays. He goes about his business the way he always does, playing Bones with his teammates, moving from the training table to the practice field to the meeting rooms with his pale face and pale blue eyes and tousled fair hair, head held high, teasing his teammates and taunting the teeming mass of scribes and airheads pressing around Randall's locker, growling when the Pack intrudes on his small space, which is just two stalls away.

But Jim doesn't have to say anything for Randall to know how he feels. He knows that both of his backups are less than sold on his worthiness as a starter. They are true believers, both of them. They are old-fashioned, drop-back, take-what-they-give-you quarterbacks, not make-something-happen guys. He respects them; why can't they respect him? Randall has watched the Richie-Jimbo chemistry gel during the long '91 season, while he sat out and rehabbed the knee (which, as it happens, he blew out standing in the pocket checking off receivers). He suspects Richie would be a lot happier with Jimbo as his starter, and he is right about that.

Randall believes this benching move is what Richie had in mind all along.

THE GAME SUNDAY, a sunny, cold afternoon at the Vet, does nothing to dispel Randall's fears. Buddy's Boys pounce all over the Raiders' second-year quarterback Todd Marinovich, who skipped his senior year at USC to join the pros and about now probably wishes he could reconsider. His passes are intercepted three times in the Raiders' first five offensive possessions—Eric, Wes, and John Booty all profit—and L.A. coach Art Shell pulls the kid midway through the second quarter before things get worse.

At first, the Jimbo-led offense stumbles around haplessly, managing only to set up a field goal despite being given great field position three times.

"This would tend to support the arguments of Randall Cunningham, that the problems this team has been having are not his, but the offensive system," says NBC game analyst Bob Trumpy. "You can't keep getting field position like this and come away from it empty-handed. The Eagles' defense ought to be able to sue the offense for nonsupport."

But then Jimbo hits his stride. Early in the game, he notices a Raiders' coverage tendency he can exploit. When L.A. lines up with two safeties in a deep zone, it leaves Fred Barnett covered one-on-one by cornerback Lionel Washington for about the first twenty yards downfield. Deep coverage is handled by safety Eddie Anderson. In meetings during the previous week, they had decided they liked the Barnett-Anderson matchup. What's more, the quarterback notices that Anderson will sometimes cheat toward the middle of the field, which is just opening the door for a receiver with Fred's speed. Opposing teams have always doubted Jimbo's ability to throw the ball deep with accuracy. And sure enough, he has Fred wide open sprinting for the end zone but throws an errant pass. The quarterback comes off the field swinging his fists with frustration, but makes a mental note.

And late in the second quarter, in a second-down play, Jimbo decides to try again for the open door. Richie signals in a play calling for both wide receivers to run down-and-in patterns, which Jimbo dutifully calls in the huddle, but then he turns to Fred like a sandlot quarterback and tells the receiver to fake the turn inside, and then break off the pattern and sprint deep.

"Give me an extra second or two on this one, guys," he tells his offensive line in the huddle, "and this is a touchdown."

It's Babe Ruth pointing to the centerfield stands, as far as the offensive line is concerned. They do their part, and Jimbo lofts a beaut, a thirty-five-yard arc that meets Fred perfectly in stride for six points.

"He called it!" the linemen are shouting as they come running off the field.

"He called it! He called his shot," they tell their excited teammates.

It's the stuff of which legends are made. Randall, wearing a green hooded jacket, is among the first to greet his replacement as he chugs off the field, clapping him enthusiastically on the back.

The Eagles take a 17–3 lead into the halftime locker room, and never look back. Their defense allows only one late-fourth-quarter touchdown, which Seth will later blame on Richie for not playing conservatively with a 31–3 lead late in the game and running out the clock. "It was totally uncalled for," he says. Throughout the second half, the TV cameras move back and forth from Jim, on the field, to

Richie, calling plays on the sidelines, to Randall, pacing by himself, sitting on the bench, yawning, looking forlorn.

But when the game is over, Richie reiterates, with one of his belligerent, preemptive announcements punctuated with a jabbing "okay?" that no matter how well Jim performed, Randall will start next week's game against Green Bay. Diplomacy rules throughout the locker room. Jimbo doesn't gloat, and he doesn't complain about the coach's verdict.

"I'm here on this team, part of this team. I'm not here to make those decisions."

"Don't you think your performance today will increase the pressure on Randall?"

What's he supposed to say?

"Hell, the guy's making a lot of money," said the veteran quarterback. "Pressure is going to be on him every day. Comes with the territory."

The only small crack in the wall of happy talk is inadvertent. Center Dave Alexander, obligingly stopping for a chat with a local TV reporter outside the locker room, lets his candor get the best of him.

"What do you think made the difference out there today, Dave?" the reporter asks. "Was at it Jim McMahon?"

"Jim and Randall are almost total opposites as far as quarterbacking goes," says Dave, grinning—the center is blithely wading into trouble here. For one thing, he's one of Jimbo's favorite golf buddies, which makes him automatically suspect in Randall's eyes. He's also a big, good ol' boy from Oklahoma redneck country, another problem. Dave is a confident public speaker, but, as with most linemen, he is not usually high on the Pack's list of interview opportunities. He's used to speaking to the more veteran print reporters, offering valuable insights that will often find their way into print unattached to his name. He likes talking about the game. Now his wide friendly face fills the TV screen as he unwittingly inserts his foot in his mouth.

"Randall is a guy who's gonna run around the pocket, try to make the big play, throw the ball downfield [*athletic*]. Jim doesn't have that kind of ability. He can't run around, can't throw the ball as far. He uses his brain, reads the defense, and gets rid of the ball [*strategic*]. . . . I played with Randall for four years before Jim got here. I've grown up in the league with Randall. Playing last year with Jim, I realized some things could be done audibling the play. Randall is not a big audibler—he likes to go with the play that's called and try to make a big play even if it's not there. If the play's not there, he'll say, 'I'll make somebody miss.' Sometimes that works, and sometimes it doesn't."

This is, of course, simply true. But coming on the heels of Jimbo's big victory—the Eagles have just scored more points in four quarters than they scored in the previous three games—it sure sounds like you could maybe *interpret* what ol' Dave is saying here to mean that the shrewd old white guy gets the job done better than the fancy-pants young black guy, and that fancy-pants, the *athletic* performer, is kind of a hotdog who thinks he can make things happen on his own. *Sometimes that works, and sometimes it doesn't.* Well, hell, everybody sure knows how well Randall's methods have been working lately. Dave doesn't bother putting the two and two together, but the announcer whose face fills the screen when the center moves away doesn't hesitate.

Why, that's amazing, we've just heard the team's starting center practically, by gosh—and you heard it here live on our station just now with your own ears! —endorse Jim McMahon over Randall Cunningham! Randall may be starting next week, but who says this quarterback controversy is over?

Truth is, the controversy will rage as long as Randall plays the game. He's either way ahead or way behind his times.

Dave won't find out until later that he's pretty much screwed up his career-long rapport with the Scrambling One, who will hear what quickly becomes known as the Amazing On-Air Betrayal soon enough.

As for Randall, he emerges the following week, having survived his exile, his Job-like trial, in a relaxed, even chatty, mood. Jimbo is back on the sidelines. Hurricanes, tornadoes, and earthquakes have subsided; the presidential transition is going smoothly; the world has jerked back into joint. A rainbow is on the horizon. The swollen Pack is back down to its normal, local size. Randall now insists that all that doomsaying and spiritual angst last week was a put-on, just something to keep his friends in the media entertained.

"Nice sweater," he compliments one of the familiar faces come to quiz him before his locker at midweek, reaching up to tweak the fabric of the hound's considerable belly between two long fingers. "These lint balls come with it?"

"Hasn't all this furor upset your balance a little bit?" a hopeful voice asks.

"We had fun with it," says Randall. "You guys all sold your papers. The TV people blew it up and took it national, and I had fun with it, but I have to get back to concentrating. I can't do this every week."

"It's over?" a hound asks sadly.

"It's over," says Randall.

"Are you sure?"

"It's over. Because people are getting tired of it. . . . But, hey, that's the most fun I've had with you guys in quite a while."

14

AN UGLY THING

Seth Joyner had been on his best behavior through the week of the Great Benching.

After the Dallas game, he told the Pack, "Not today. If I say anything, somebody will accuse me of running my big mouth."

Ever since the night of that first heady win over Dallas, Seth had been battling through a bad streak both personally and professionally. There was going to be a reckoning down the road with Jennifer. That knee injury he suffered in the Monday night game had lingered. He was playing with a big brace on the joint, which slowed him down. Seth had been less of a factor ever since, and at least part of the reason that the Eagles had dropped three of their last five.

During all the locker-room hubbub over Randall and Jimbo, Seth tried to use his new leadership role to distract attention from the QB controversy by lacing into his teammates on defense, whom he accused of forgetting the swagger of their Buddy (and Jerome) days. This was specious. They were, after all, the top-ranked defense in the league midway through this '92 season. Their excellence breathing down Richie's neck had helped prompt the Great Benching. Whipping up on his squad just then was just a backhanded way of calling attention to the team's offensive failings, as if to say, *If we could just play even more godlike ball, we could carry these sorry asses the whole way by ourselves!* Leadership sometimes demands silence, an aspect of the role Captain Seth hadn't mastered. His teammates rolled their eyes—just more Seth *being Seth*. Still, by benching Ran-*doll* for a week, in what the players took to be defiance of Norman and Harry (actually, Norman thought it was a fine idea and wondered only about the wisdom of promising Randall the starting job back the following week), Richie had earned at least a trace of respect from Seth and the rest of the back end of the locker room. Enough, as it turned out, to last exactly fourteen days.

Because moments after the team literally gives away a game to the Packers on November 15, Seth unloads. Never mind everything else that happened that afternoon in freezing Milwaukee County Stadium, the 410 yards the defense allowed (their worst in more than three seasons), the impressive Randall-led comeback to regain the lead in the second half, and the two game-losing fumbles at the end. Seth is an adept at finding fault, seeing past a confusion of culprits, close calls, and bad bounces to the single quivering shithead with his hand on the very lever of defeat. Locked in his crosshairs this time is the bald, bespectacled face of the head coach.

Seated at the center of the visitor's locker room, clouds of steam forming in the confusion of pipes and cable hung overhead, Seth focuses his critique on the final one minute, twenty-five seconds, of the game, when the offense got the ball on their own eleven-yard line, with the score tied 24–24.

Richie had two time-outs left, plenty of time to drive downfield to within field-goal range and win the game. But backed up deep on his own half of the field, he had to be concerned about what would happen if they failed to get a first down. A punt from that field position would set the Packers up near midfield, close enough for them to drive down with a quick pass or two and kick a field goal—the defense hadn't exactly been a brick wall. Richie's strategy, albeit conservative but arguably wise, was to hammer the ball on the ground, get out to at least his own twenty-yard line before sending in four swift pass receivers and going for the big play. The Eagles had been running the ball well all afternoon—they had already accumulated 110 yards, not counting Heath Sherman's 75-yard touchdown sprint after catching a little screen pass—and, indeed, Herschel slammed out 9 yards on first down, moving the ball to the 20. Then, at second and one, with just under a minute to play, with the Packers' defense spread out all over the field to stop the pass, Richie decided to grab the first down with another run, maybe gain 9 or 10 yards more before going to the pass. The worst that could happen at that point, after all, was for the clock to run out and the game to go into overtime . . . unless Herschel fumbled.

Herschel fumbled. The Packers covered the loose ball with forty-three seconds remaining, let the clock run down to three seconds, and Chris Jackie kicked a thirty-one-yard field goal.

"Real disappointing" is how Richie sees it moments later. Always quick to defend his players in adversity, the coach adds, chin up, "But don't worry about these guys. There was no lack of effort. They'll bounce back. They will. They'll show their character."

Well, Seth's character is now on center stage, and it resembles magma. Before the Pack is allowed in the locker room, the linebacker crashes his helmet to the wet concrete and loudly berates the offense. The offensive line just endures this outburst, partly because they've grown used to Seth's rants, partly because they can't believe how ridiculous this one is. My God, the defense gave up three touchdowns and two field goals! Lord knows there were plenty of games where this defense was blameless, but today? If ever a loss had been well earned all around, this was it!

But Seth's rant isn't just a momentary venting; it's a full-fledged eruption. As the Pack wades in, Seth holds forth patiently on his stool, starting over again for each new wave of eager cameras and microphones. He makes sure nobody misses the message. There's practically a stampede for the Eagles' locker room. Word gets out fast that Seth is "ripping the coach," one of the prized delicacies of postgame reportage. Richie and the rest of the team won't find out until the next morning the full range of Seth's critical insights.

Seth figures Richie blew it by running the ball in the final minutes.

"We should be moving the ball down to get a field goal, you know, score. And we're down there running the ball, playing conservative. . . . You've got the ball back inside the twenty. How far do you think you're gonna get running the ball? And we're running it on first and second down." He bows his head and runs one big hand over the "#99" carved in his hair. "I just don't understand. Is it me? Somebody please tell me."

One of the hounds offers Richie's explanation. "Rich said he wanted to get the first down on the ground and then put it up."

"It doesn't make any difference whether you get it on the ground or in the air, does it? Move the ball down the field. We had two time-outs left, one-thirty left on the clock. Every time you run the ball you eat up the clock. If you get a play down in there where it doesn't work, then you're in a predicament. The thing is, move the ball downfield, put us in a position to win the game."

"Seth, you guys on defense were pretty vulnerable today, can you explain what's wrong there?" asks a hound, gently cautioning the linebacker that he's standing on shaky ground here. But Seth doesn't even blink.

"You're just gonna have your days, you know? The most important thing is, we had an opportunity to win and we didn't get it done. You got to understand, when you're the best defense in the league, teams spend the whole off-season getting ready to play you, figuring out your weaknesses. We played a great game last week. But even though we couldn't stop them all day, we stopped them when we had to and turned the ball back over to the offense when we had to. We put them in a position to go down and get us the field goal.

And we call two running plays. You've just got to have some balls about yourself. You got to play the game all out. We [Richie] just didn't handle things in a smart way at the end. You can't play not to lose. You got to have some guts and nuts about yourself. Step up and call the play! Call the unexpected play!"

Some players standing near Seth begin parroting the theme. Fred Barnett uncharacteristically adds his voice, frustrated that he didn't get a chance to perform any last-minute heroics. Even silent Byron jumps in, seeing his buddy Seth out there on a limb all by himself.

"You can't play not to lose," seconds Byron.

Seth had exploded his grenadelike personality on the seam of the great rift in the Eagles' locker room, exacerbating the strain between the Buddy loyalists on defense and the supposed slackers on Richie's offense. Even in the best of times, the guys in the back end of the locker room merely suffer sharing the same green uniforms with Ran-*doll* and the pussies upfront. Seth may have chosen the wrong moment to unload, but his sentiments are shared in varying degrees by most of the defensive players. Even Reverend Reggie, the most mature, solid player in the room, agrees in general, although he's much too mindful of preserving harmony to speak up.

Richie reads the morning papers in a stew. He knows he can't bench Seth. It would hurt the team, first off, and just make things worse. Why, just the week before, during all the Randall/Jimbo nonsense, he had told the Pack he wasn't about to silence his players. On his own pregame TV show, aired just before the Packers' debacle, he was asked if he had considered muzzling some of his players, and he had said, "I don't do that. I don't believe in doing that. I think a lot of them talk because they care a lot themselves, and they want other guys to care as much as they do. This team is used to playing with a little bit of controversy. They don't talk now anywhere near as much as they used to. I don't want a bunch of Boy Scouts playing for me."

Well, a Boy Scout Seth's not, but even Richie knows he can't have his players so openly mutinous. And that line "You got to have some guts and nuts about yourself" is a direct challenge to his Silverback manhood! It violates Richie's code. One of the things he hated about Buddy was the old coach's habit of publicly insulting players. As prickly as Richie can get with the Pack, that is something he never does. Never. Richie defends his players in public, even while he is excoriating them in private. He remembers what it was like to be a pro player, which is something he had that Buddy could never touch. Sticking up for his players is one of the ways Richie asserts his own status and his higher claim to loyalty than Buddy ever deserved. And this is what he gets in return?

During the previous two weeks, all the WIP goons and print columnists and TV windbags have been chewing over the quarterback controversy and how the Eagles are a divided, squabbling team of egomaniacs. Okay, they'd gotten through that. It had been a distraction, but never as much a one as the Pack seemed to think—the hounds tend to exaggerate their influence on things as a rule. Randall had performed reasonably well against the Packers, so maybe that shit would all die down. Now Seth has set the wheel spinning again. It's all over the papers, radio, and TV—everywhere! Coach Uptight losing control of his locker room. The dread Attitude Problem creeping up. Ghost of Buddy haunting the practice fields. The whole goddamn alphabet circus—ABC, NBC, CBS, ESPN, HBO, CNN—will be back in town, with cameras and microphones prying at the cracks of the rift, throwing fuel on the flames.

But all that is not what really gets to Richie. He can deal with the Pack jackals. He does that every day. That's part of the job. No, the thing that gets Richie is Seth's effrontery. The linebacker is way out of line. His rant shows he doesn't understand the code. It demonstrates his misguided and lasting loyalty to that asshole Buddy, who was ultimately responsible for this behavior. Buddy had never taught these guys how to act.

So in the team's Monday morning meeting, Richie stands up before the roomful of players, in full Brooklyn Slouch, as angry as his team has ever seen him. He doesn't address Seth in particular, but everyone in the room knows exactly who is his primary target.

As several of those present would reconstruct it, here's what Richie says: "I read in the paper this morning where a few of you guys got some things off your chest after yesterday's game. Fine. There are some things on my chest that I've kept to myself, as long as we're saying stuff. There are a lot of guys on this team who haven't been playing to their capabilities," a low rustling sound in the room as certain players get eyeballed suspiciously. "If you're going to point fingers at me and talk about play calling and what defenses are being called and such, I think we better be sure that the guys who are being called on to make certain plays are getting them done. Okay? When Bud or I call a certain play, we're depending on a certain guy to get his job done. If he doesn't get it done, then what the hell am I supposed to do? I can't get out there on the field and carry the fucking ball myself! Am I right? Before you blame somebody else, you better look in the mirror. Either you get your own jobs done or you can get your asses out of here now! Okay? Because you're doing nothing but pulling us down. And, in the future"—now his voice drops an octave, Silverback challenge tone, and he's glaring unmistakably at Seth—"if you've got a problem with me or this organization, come and see me. Look me in the eye. Be a man. This is an inner circle, a family. We don't wash our laundry out in public. Got that?"

All that morning Bud Carson sticks it to Seth and the rest of the defense as they review film. Bud isn't usually one to dwell too long on mistakes and who made them. His style is more laid-back, instructive (*Now, the right way to handle this formation would have been . . .*) but today he's scathing. And Seth has made a few boners himself.

All that is minor compared with the going over he's getting in the press. Seth has become the Pack's favorite, in a sense. He is, since Charles Barkley left for Phoenix in June, the hottest postgame interview in town. In the locker room, face-to-face, the hounds are one thing. Gracious, grateful, and obliging, a small mob descends on him whenever he sits down at his locker. They stand and nod and smile and hold their little tape recorders and microphones under his mouth for as long as he wants to talk, then prod gently for more. They seem so disappointed when he stops! Only, the next day in the newspaper, Seth would see his comments edited down and strung out between great gusts of critical oratory. He was the mouth that roared, the locker-room scold, the source of division and conflict on a "troubled" squad.

All the Pack needs is a quick glimpse behind the rah-rah, we're-all-a-band-of-brothers facade to brew up a storm of controversy and doubt. Weeks before, after Seth's lament over the Redksins loss, Reverend Reggie had pulled the linebacker aside and asked him to keep it zipped. "If what you say isn't going to help, don't say it," Reggie had said to him. "And say it to the team, not to the press." It hasn't done any good. Seth can't control himself. After a loss, he comes off the field in such a black funk that there's no staunching the bile. Only now, as the season enters the final stretch, Captain Seth is starting to feel like a pariah. Everybody is down on him, his wife, his girlfriend, his coaches, his teammates, the Pack, the fans—who needs it? Suddenly this business of leadership feels like a carbuncle on the ass.

SHUT UP AND PLAY BALL

says a headline in the Philadelphia *Inquirer.*

STRIFESTYLES OF THE RICH AND BLAMELESS

is the headline of a critical Philadelphia *Daily News* column.

Seth's feelings are hurt. So he does something truly drastic. When a familiar hound approaches him at midweek with a question, Seth interrupts, "I'll answer one question."

"What?"

"Ask me why I'm not going to give you guys any more interviews."

"Okay," says the hound, smelling an exclusive. Now here's a headline:

SETH TAKES VOW OF SILENCE

"Tell me, Seth, why aren't you going to give us guys any more interviews?" And Seth vents:

> I'm not doing any more interviews for the simple fact every time Seth Joyner says something, it seems to be wrong. Things are taken out of context. I give a two-minute interview and somebody takes a five-second spot out of that and throws it in and turns the whole story upside down. I'm made out to seem to be the bad guy.
>
> I speak my mind because I care what happens with this team. I want to win. I want to win a championship, and sometimes the frustration is just too much for me to walk around and carry it inside. I've never been one to point the finger at anybody [referring here to the care he takes not to actually name the victims of his verbal assaults], and I've always been the most critical person of myself [well, not always]. If I was wrong or did something wrong I was always the first one to raise my hand and acknowledge it. Somehow, through all of that, I was portrayed to be the bad guy. I don't agree with it, and for that reason I'm not giving any more interviews.
>
> I'm not the type of person that I'm going to say something and then I'm gonna go back and apologize for it. How I feel is how I feel. I have to be me, and the way I think about a situation and the way I feel about a situation is *me*. I don't agree with the way I came across . . . I wouldn't say it was the correct way. But by no means do I apologize for what I said. So I look like the bad guy. If that's the kind of grief I have to take for stepping up and caring what happens, then I'm going to keep my mouth shut. Therefore, *this* will be the last interview that Seth Joyner gives anybody for the rest of this season.

The lead in the next day's *Inquirer* article reads: "Mt. Seth blew for the last time yesterday."

You could almost hear the sigh of relief from the locker room, coaches' suite, management offices, and from fans throughout the city. Only one group is distressed—the Pack.

"Isn't there a clause in players' contracts which says they have to cooperate with the press?" complains one of the veteran hounds—football reporters, as a group, having been coddled for generations by the NFL, believe far more strongly than your run-of-the-mill news-papermen they are *entitled* to have their questions answered.

"Is there?" says Richie, who recognizes a positive development when he hears one. "I don't know anything about that."

And he's damned unlikely to check.

THE EAGLES ARE ENTERING the pivotal months of the season. Winter is the endurance test, the gun lap, when just about every player on every roster is nursing some nagging injury, when cold hardens the plastic turf ("It's like playing on concrete with a bedsheet pulled over it," says Dave Alexander), and every game is a test of will and stamina.

Richie's squad has a respectable 6–4 record, even with Randall's struggles, and is relatively healthy. Andre is back on his feet, limping around the locker room and predicting a return of the Dré Master in time for the play-offs, which is his way of urging his teammates to *make* the damn play-offs. Wes nurses his knee all week, then hobbles out to play and reinjures it every weekend. He plays until the pain gets bad. Each game the pain comes sooner. It needs surgery, but Wes knows what it's like to be a ghost, and he isn't going back if he can help it. At this point, he knows if he sits down, he may never get back in the game. Seth is playing with that brace on his left knee. Ron Heller is limping around on a very sore strained arch in his left foot. Antone Davis has what they call turf toe. "I don't know what it is, it just hurts like hell," he says. But compared with other teams, they're in relatively good shape. They've only lost two starters.

Nevertheless, they're floundering. They are lost in Yo-yo-ville, up and down, up and down—a loss to Washington, a win against Phoenix, a loss to Dallas, a win against L.A., a loss to Green Bay. . . . If it continues, they could finish out of the running.

They've squandered their early fortune by losing four of their last six, but in four of the remaining six games they're favorites. The first of these supposed mismatches is in Giants Stadium, a concrete wind tunnel set out in the northern New Jersey swamp. It comes on a cold, gloomy afternoon, so socked in with fog and rain that you can't even see the low-flying jets coming and going from Newark International Airport next door.

The Giants have begun to self-destruct. Their head coach, Ray Handley, inherited the great team Bill Parcells had nursed to one last Super Bowl on the last legs of proud veterans. It's now a mix of disgruntled old-timers and raw talent, with many of the former taking potshots at the coach on TV and in the papers, and the latter making mistakes on the field. All week the national Pack has billed this game the Battle of the Malcontents, flipping back and forth between clips of Lawrence Taylor calling his coaches and teammates quitters, Seth ripping Richie's play calling, Pepper Johnson saying he's going to ignore the game plan, Fred Barnett saying "If I were calling the plays, it'd be different."

With forty-seven men on the roster, the personality of any football team is far more diverse and multifaceted than any of the caricatures drawn by the Pack. All through this season, with its rabbitlike 4–0 start, then its rocky midterm, the most visible drama has been between its disgruntled defense and its struggling, mercurial offense, with Seth and Randall playing the lead roles. But not all the true leaders of this team are obvious. The undergirding of any team is its cadre of grunts. Most of these players, old-timers eking out one season at a time and youngsters hoping for a shot at a starting job, are herded into special teams, the men who take the field for kickoffs, punts, and extra points. On the Eagles, the king of special teams is Ken Rose, and it's Ken, on this saturated Sunday in the New Jersey swamp, who will pick up this squabbling, uneven football team and point it back toward the play-offs.

Ken took some grief when he reported for work in the Eagles' locker room in November of '90. Mostly it was the thick, black ponytail, which hangs a good foot or more down the center of his back.

"Whooo-hoo! Who's this?" shouted Jerome, as Ken paced across the room for the first time, carrying his gear to his locker.

"Love the tail!"

"Ain't that sweet!"

"Where'd they get this one?"

But any who felt Ken Rose might be intimidated for one second had a lot to learn.

He makes a striking appearance even without the ponytail. His skin is so black that in a certain light it has a bluish sheen, and his hair, instead of the tight black curls of African inheritance, is thick and wavy—freed of the ponytail, it hangs down past his shoulders. There is a hint of aboriginal Australian in Ken's face, but his features are leaner and smaller. When he smiles, beneath his thick mustache the grin seems too large for the face, with a row of oversized teeth broken only by a gap between the top front incisors.

Ken is one of the few intellectuals in the locker room, with eclectic reading habits that range from comic books to serious nonfiction— just now he's lugging *A History of the Moors* on road trips. Ken is the team's liberal conscience. He spent a good part of this season trying, without much success, to persuade his teammates to vote for Bill Clinton. But given that the Democratic presidential candidate was talking about soaking the wealthy, that is, those earning more than $200,000 a year, it's a little bit like trying to sell speed bumps at a NASCAR convention.

"Who are you going to vote for, Mike?" a hound asks polite, sweet defensive lineman Mike Pitts one morning, within earshot of Ken.

"I'm votin' for Jesse," says Pitts.

"Jesse Jackson?"

"He's my man."

"Mike," says Ken, looking up at the giant, "Jesse Jackson isn't running for president this year."

"I knew that."

"Don't you want to make your vote count?"

"Yeah. Well, I guess I'll be voting for George Bush then."

"*George Bush!*" says Ken, half-agitated and half-amused. "Now you tell me how in hell a man can have Jesse Jackson as his first choice and *George Bush* as his second choice? That doesn't make any sense at all, Mike!"

Pitts gives a pained little frown, as if to say *Jesus, how did I get into this?*

"I just don't feel like I can trust Clinton," the lineman says, apologetically.

"You can't trust Clinton? Hell, Bush and Reagan have been running this country now for almost twelve years, you *know* what the people can expect from them!"

Ken's secular humanism polices Reverend Reggie's fundamentalism by pouncing whenever it strays too far from provable fact. For instance, when Reggie confidently asserts that federally funded abortions are a government plot to eliminate the black poor, Ken will jump in with the fact that most abortions performed in America are performed on women from the middle and upper classes and that black women are not using the procedure disproportionate to their numbers in the general population. "If anything, poor black women are the ones more inclined to *have* their babies!" he says. This kind of exchange, of course, prompts a heated round of sociological and theological posturing, which sends both Ken and Reggie home vowing to produce indisputable data to back up their assertions. It makes their teammates giggle.

Ken played on the same team at UNLV as Randall, whom he remembers arriving as a stripling—"He was obviously gifted, but so immature he was clumsy." The door to the pros opened for Ken only after five years of determined effort. He played for one season on the wide fields of the Canadian Football League with the Saskatchewan Roughriders, another for the USFL's Tampa Bay Bandits, and he tried and tried, without success, at NFL camps. He was cut five times by NFL teams. He never once considered giving up.

The door opened for him at long last when the NFL players went on strike. Ken got a hurried call from New York the night the players walked, and he jumped. He had knocked his helmet up against the unfairness of the system for so long that he had no sympathy whatsoever for the striking regulars—they were just guys who'd gotten a break he hadn't. Playing with a ragtag crew of wanna-bes, before disinterested and surly fans, Ken Rose finally played a pro football game, in Giants Stadium, on October 4, 1987. The Jets' scab team lost, lost again the following week, and then beat the Dolphins' irregulars in an exciting game (quarterback Pat Ryan threw four touchdown passes). Bud Carson, then the Jets' defensive coordinator, and Larry Pasquale, the special teams coach, finally got a chance to see that Ken, who was considered too short at six feet, and too small at two hundred pounds, played like a Tasmanian devil, hard and fast. He was the star on defense for the replacement team. When the Jets invited about a dozen scab players to stay on when the regular players returned, Ken was among them.

Scorned by the regular roster players, Ken and the other remnants of the scab team were ejected from the Jets' regular locker room and assigned space in a racquetball court at the Jets' training center in Hempstead, New York. With no lockers, they hung their clothes on rolling metal coat racks and deposited their gear in a heap on the wooden floor. The coach had promised to give them a shot at making the team in earnest, but for Ken and the others, it felt as if they were marking time, satisfying some club need to proffer at least a display of loyalty toward the players who had crossed those ugly picket lines and upheld the NFL banner. A bond developed among the guys in that room, and Ken, a hardened veteran of exclusion, became a leader. His undying faith in himself was infectious. Just having him around made the other guys feel like . . . well, maybe it *was* possible, despite everything. When defensive lineman Scott Mersereau became the first of their number to be invited to join the regular squad, there were handshakes and backslaps all around, and Scott moved his gear out of the racquetball court and into the locker room. Ken was invited next, only he refused to move. He kept his gear right there on the wooden floor, in a heap.

"I'm stayin' with my boys," he told Pasquale.

Ken stuck. In '88, when injuries felled one defensive end after another, at the end of the season Bud placed Ken—the man considered too small to play linebacker—at one end of the Jets' defensive line. In just two games, Ken, looking like a hyperkinetic midget alongside the behemoths lined up to block him, sacked the quarterback five times—three times in a December 12 game against the Giants. But even a performance like that wasn't enough to break down the rigid job specs of today's highly specialized NFL. As soon as a less productive but larger, more appropriately sized player was healthy enough to play again, Ken went back to his role on special teams.

And there he stayed, with the Jets ('87–'90), Browns (with Bud for the first six games of '90), and then the Eagles. Ken has never lost his conviction that he can play linebacker (or defensive end) with the best of them, but he's a realist. At age thirty, after all this time in the league, he knows he's pigeonholed but good. So Ken has applied his remarkable will and intelligence to mastering special teams.

He never laments his backup status. Ken radiates a serene joy, the pleasure of someone who *made* his life's dream come true. It makes him steady as a structural pile. Over these five and a half seasons, he's become one of the best special teams players in the league. He jokes about being a blue-collar guy, and it's true in a sense—compared with veterans of comparable experience on the roster he's making a lot less. But $257,000 is hardly a blue-collar wage. Ken and his wife have built themselves a spacious, sunny hillside home in Thousand Oaks, and among the relatively small circle of game cognoscenti who appreciate the subtleties and importance of special teams, he's a legitimate star. He is one of a handful of kicking-team specialists in the running for the Pro Bowl every year. He hasn't made it yet, but once Ken sets a goal . . .

Through all the high drama of the Eagles' up-and-down '92 season, the running-back controversies, quarterback controversies, coaching controversies, Ken Rose just quietly goes about his work. Just last week, Reverend Reggie lamented to a TV reporter, "Since I've been in Philadelphia, it's the most negative atmosphere I've ever been around." But none of that touches Ken. The Pack hardly ever bothers with him, though he's one of the most intelligent and friendly voices on the team. Ken is looking forward to this week's contest in New York because he still gets excited about big games, and he still has fond, fond memories of Giants Stadium—showing that broad, gap-toothed grin, remembering his breakthrough games with the Jets, his three sacks of Phil Simms, he says, "Good things always happen to me there."

Only, on this monsoonlike day, it doesn't start off that way. Veteran kick returner Vai Sikahema, the Eagles' sage little return man, springs a forty-one-yard punt return late in the first quarter that sets up the team's first touchdown of the game, but Roger Ruzek, the kicker, boots the extra point wide right. It's an important point, because the Giants had jumped out to a 10–0 lead. Without the extra point, ordinarily a routine thing, the Eagles can't catch up with a field goal. Ruzek comes off the field muttering to himself, "How can I miss that?"

But that setback is nothing compared with what happens next. Ruzek kicks off to the Giants' return man Dave Meggett, and Meggett races ninety-two yards for a touchdown, water splashing up from the heels of his flying cleats. Ninety-two yards! This is the worst, the worst. With that one stroke, the Giants are up 17–6, and special teams, which have played so well all season for the Eagles, are suddenly guilty of the worst kind of incompetence.

"My God!" screams Larry Pasquale, Richie's former associate with the Jets who now coaches special teams for the Eagles. He's pacing the sidelines shouting to himself, "How could he possibly run through eleven guys? How can this happen? This *can't* happen! Eleven guys?"

Pasquale is one of the league's premier special teams gurus; his squads have routinely led the league in statistical measures, with the Jets, Chargers, and now with the Eagles. He hasn't had anyone return a kickoff against one of his teams for a touchdown in more than ten years. It is almost a rule of faith among special teams experts that such things *just don't happen* to a well-coached squad. They happen precisely because many teams fail to adequately coach their kicking teams, because there are still those among the twenty-eight NFL head coaches—yea, the very High Priests of the Game—who prefer to wing it on kickoffs and punts. It's people like Larry, and his field captain Ken, who are busy proving the importance of coaching in this neglected aspect of the game. Now this! It isn't just a serious blow to the Eagles' chances in this game, it is a blow to everything Larry and Ken stand for.

Ken knows how it happened. The way Larry has designed the runback defense, the team sprints downfield when the ball is kicked, fanning out toward the sidelines and then converging toward the return man when he catches the ball. Roger's kick this time was higher and shorter than usual, and it hung up in the air for a long time. So the timing was off. The tackling wedge converged too deep, so when

Meggett caught the ball, they were all racing to a point just behind him. With Meggett's quickness, all he had to do was dodge one or two lunging tacklers and sprint the rest of the way downfield.

When Ken comes off the field, he's the focus of the team's discontent. Larry is staring glumly at the ground.

"Kenny, you've got to get special teams going!" pleads Richie.

Ken feels personally responsible. He'd been one of the first to overrun Meggett. He knows why it happened, and he also knows there's no excuse.

Seth, Clyde, and some of the other defensive players come over now to vent their anger.

"Come on, Kenny, play some fuckin' football!"

"What went on?"

"What happened?"

When Ken first joined the Eagles, this was one of the things he liked about the team. Every other team he had ever played for relied exclusively on Coach for motivation. The players were like children, in a sense, and Coach was the father. When players screwed up, they would huddle together on the bench muttering to one another, waiting for Coach to come over and blow his stack. But on this team, players blew their stack at each other! It was a way of doing things that had started under Buddy, and it was one of the things the Eagles' players meant when they said they appreciated how Buddy had treated them like men. Buddy had created an atmosphere in which every player expected the most out of his teammates and had every right to criticize anyone on the team who wasn't shouldering his load. Seth was, of course, the world's foremost disciple of this approach and had taken it to such bitter lengths that some of the guys were starting to question its wisdom. Ken still thinks it's a healthy thing, although being on the receiving end of it now isn't too pleasant.

He calls together some of his teammates after comparing notes with Larry and gives them a pep talk.

"Look, screw those guys," says Ken, referring to the offensive and defensive starters (although a few of them are also part of the special teams squad). Ken notes that Seth and the others never come over to congratulate them when they do well. "Fuck them . . . Who the fuck do they think they are?"

Seth helps turn things around a few minutes later, pouncing on a short pass to Meggett, catching it and outracing everyone (knee brace and all) forty-three yards for a touchdown. Randall then leads a nifty eight-play, fifty-two-yard drive for a second touchdown, and the score is tied when the halftime gun sounds.

Randall comes into the locker room complaining because Richie had instructed him to toss up a Hail Mary pass toward the end zone in the closing seconds of the half, which was intercepted. Such things put dents in a quarterback's stats.

"Man, I'm sick to death of hearing about your stats," shouts Fred. "We're not out there playing for *you!* This is a team, Randall . . . a *team!*"

In his corner of the room, huddled with Ken and the other special teams guys, Larry says, "They got the big one. We've got to get a big one of our own."

And, indeed, Vai opens the second half with a thirty-eight-yard kickoff return, setting up another Eagles touchdown. That return, along with two other nifty runbacks by Vai in the first half, starts Larry thinking. Veteran backup safety William Frizzell had come off the field after a Giants punt late in the second half with a small piece of intelligence.

"They're not blocking that long," he said.

Punt blocks are one of the rarest of big plays in football, almost as rare as a kickoff or punt return for a touchdown. The kicker stands so far back from the line of scrimmage, and the penalty for bumping him is so severe, that most teams on most punts make only a token effort to block the kick. What Frizzell's intelligence tells Larry is that the Giants' punt team has grown so wary of Vai's returns, they are becoming complacent. They are hurrying their blocks in order to get a fast break downfield to corral Vai.

So, particularly after Vai's thirty-eight-yard runback to open the half, Larry decides to go for the long shot, a blocked punt. It's risky. The Giants are kicking from their own forty-yard line, so if Sean Landeta, their punter, gets off a good kick, Vai will probably have to call for a fair catch deep in the Eagles' territory.

In runback formation, the team receiving the punt usually assigns two men to block the speedsters (Larry calls them hawks) who line up split wide to either side of the punting team's formation. The hawks are the first tacklers downfield and pose the first threat to the return man. So a punter needs only glance to either side before calling for the snap of the ball. If his hawks are facing two blockers, he doesn't have to worry unduly about an all-out effort to block his kick. When a punt-receiving team is desperate for field position, usually late in the game, they'll line up just one blocker on each of the hawks. If a punter sees that formation, he knows he'll have to hurry his kick, because they're coming fast.

Larry has devised a deception. He lines up his punt-receiving team in runback position, with two blockers lined up wide, facing the hawks. But just before the snap of the ball, each of the inside men split wide in this formation creeps in toward the middle and makes a dash for the punter. Frizzell works the play to perfection, waiting for Landeta to check the formation, and then edging in just before the snap. He's unblocked at the line of scrimmage, so the fullback, lined up halfway between the kicker and the center, has to shift over to pick him up. Meanwhile, on the line, the tackle assigned to block Ken sticks out an arm and hurries downfield toward Vai. Ken races right by him for the punter, and with the fullback shifting over to block William, there is no one to pick him up. He leaps in front of Landeta, feels the ball carom off his chest and sees it bounce hard back down to the turf. Ken scrambles to his feet, scoops up the ball, and stumbles into the end zone—blocked punt, recovered ball, touchdown! The first touchdown of Ken Rose's pro career. Good things always happen to Ken in Giants Stadium.

The Eagles now have a 34–20 lead, and, shortly, they improve on it—again because of special teams.

The logic of a football game is fluid. It builds upon what happened before. Teams enter a game armed with plans based on analysis and stats of what their opponent has done in past games, but by midgame each contest develops its own logic. And just as failure breeds failure, success breeds success. With the Giants now back on their heels to protect against a blocked punt, Pasquale reverses the strategy. He lines up his team in punt-block formation, and has them creep back into a runback formation before the snap. This buys Vai all kinds of time to do his thing. Landeta booms a towering punt, which Vai grabs back on the Eagles' thirteen-yard line, and thus has (with New York's renewed emphasis on blocking upfield) about ten yards or more to pick up steam and read the field before any Giants tackler is near him.

In the week before each game, Vai memorizes all the numbers of his opponents' special teams players. He knows how big and, more important, how fast they all are. Usually, there isn't enough time to use this information. You either call for a fair catch or rely on instinct when you catch the ball and tacklers start banging in. But when he has time, as he does now, he's one of the most dangerous return men in the game. He can pick out the lumbering bigbodies among the would-be tacklers, big men whom he can dodge, and structure his return accordingly. After about five steps forward, Vai picks his angle of attack, breaks suddenly to his right, and runs right around number 99, linebacker Steve DeOssie, who (as Vai well knows) doesn't have a prayer of cutting as quickly as the diminutive return man. Downfield, Vai steps inside of Landeta, who makes such a clumsy lunge that he injures his knee, and Vai completes an eighty-seven-yard punt-return touchdown.

The game has become a rout. Seth turned things around, but

this is one game that everyone knows was won by special teams—final score, 47–34. It had been seven years since the Eagles won a game in which they allowed the other team more than thirty-four points. Randall played reasonably well, the defense came up with a few big plays, but the game was won by Larry, Ken, and the rest of the ragtag crew of bit players on this temperamental squad. There's a lesson in this win for the whole bickering stable of superstars, one that Richie will not fail to hammer home.

For Ken, it's bliss. On the bus ride home down the wet interstate, the team watches a videotape of the movie *Deep Cover*, cheering on the violence, laughing at the melodrama. Ken's still got the ball in his hands. His old college teammate Randall may have nearly 150 of them, but Ken's first and only is arguably more satisfying.

MUCH OF THE POISON in the Eagles' locker room seems to have dissipated in the following week. It's Thanksgiving, and a lot of the players have family in town. There is a loose, confident air. The team is preparing to play the San Francisco 49ers, one of the legendary teams in the NFL. It's a chance to prove something to themselves. With the Niners' 9–2 record, they are, as usual, one of the most imposing teams on the schedule. If the Eagles can beat them, or even play them close, some of the lost luster of the first month of the season will be regained.

Wes comes limping out of the training room on Wednesday.

"How is it?" a hound asks.

"The same," he says with a shrug. Against the Giants the week before, he'd taken himself out in the third quarter.

"Wes," interrupts another hound. "The stats say that the 49ers are the best offensive team you've faced so far."

Wes smiles. He has an easy rapport with the Pack. "Yeah? Well, the films say it, too," he says.

"Wes, Thanksgiving is this week," a TV reporter asks—he's walking around the locker room asking everybody this question. "What do you have to be thankful for?"

"My health," he says, and hesitates. "And my family." The Pack nods appreciatively.

Randall is sitting alone before his stall, lacing up a shoe. Tomorrow he will present Felicity with an acorn-sized diamond and ask her to marry him. He has flown in his entire family—his three brothers and their families, his Aunt Nettie from Las Vegas, and even Felicity's sisters from Johannesburg for a Thanksgiving meal—and, if he gets the answer he expects, the announcement.

But here in the locker room, he seems glum. It's rare to find him alone like this. One of the veteran newshounds, who has watched the mercurial quarterback's ups and downs over the years, wanders over to chat.

"Chin up, Randall, you're about ready to explode with a big game."

"You think so?" he says.

"I do. You're due. You've played enough of them in your career, and you haven't had one in a while."

"Why do you think that is?"

"Probably partly because of the way you've been used."

"You guys write that?"

"I have."

"How would you use me?"

Long pause. "I think I would encourage you to have more fun, use your own judgment more on the field."

"That doesn't do it, man."

"I don't claim to be a football coach."

"I respect that," he says. "Man, I like to go out there and just be exciting, that's all. I hate it when I'm not doing that. Joe Montana and I are a lot alike. But in this kind of system, he's had a a lot more experience. He's been able to prove himself with the Super Bowls and all. I haven't been able to achieve that yet. We've made the play-offs, but . . . that problem is deeper than just me."

"If you make a big play out on the field, even if it isn't the one called, whose going to give you grief?"

"You've got to be *allowed* to make big plays. What do you think the best blocking scheme is for me? To get everyone out of the backfield and have five linemen in front of me? Or to leave people in the backfield, extra blockers to protect me?"

"What do you think?"

"Get everybody out of there. Give them all a route, clear them out."

"What's the advantage for you?"

"The advantage is there's a gap, and—shooo!" he makes a sudden motion with his hand shooting forward. "Nineteen-ninety style."

"And you can't do that now?"

"Take a look on Sunday," Randall says. "See it for yourself."

Down the room, Mike Golic, the amiable defensive lineman, is cheerfully bemoaning the fact that the league, on reviewing the tapes of the Giants game, took away one of the two quarterback sacks he had been credited with making—the one that sent quarterback Jeff Hostetler to the hospital. These were Mike's first two sacks of the season, and, given that his line mates, Reverend Reggie and Clyde, are always among the league leaders, they were especially prized.

"When they looked at the film, on the one it showed Clyde came around and made the hit," says Mike. "I say, yeah, right, like Clyde *needs* another sack."

His small audience laughs.

"He did get it. But, hey, they had me with two in *USA Today*, so that's what people think, and that's what counts, right?"

"Do these guys rib you about not getting your share of sacks?" a hound asks.

"Hell, yeah," says Mike. "They always tell me, 'Don't embarrass yourself, Mike. When you do get one, don't celebrate or anything.' "

"Were you ever even close before this? I mean, was there ever any chance of their, like, throwing a charity sack your way?"

"Naah. At least I'm not a virgin anymore!"

The TV reporter has made it down the line of stalls to Andre.

"Andre, Thanksgiving is tomorrow," he says. "What do you have to be thankful for?"

"My life," says the young man from Pahokee, without hesitation, like he's been sitting here for a half hour waiting to be asked just this question.

"Really?" the TV guy says, looking surprised. "Despite the ankle?"

FOUR DAYS and one successful wedding proposal later, the Eagles lose to the 49ers by one inch.

"No, *less* than one inch," corrects center Dave Alexander, who's naked and furious. "We're talking about the width of a piece of paper!"

It's particularly galling because the disputed millimeter depends on where an official decided to spot the football in the final seconds of the game, and because it's the 49ers.

Whenever the Eagles' players get to complaining about Norman Braman and what they perceive to be the money-grubbing, low-rent style of their organization, they always cite the San Francisco club as the way things ought to be. The 49ers are like the older brother Mom always liked best. Closely held financial data revealed in filings during the players' antitrust suit that summer confirmed two crucial things about the storied franchise that many people suspected, but few knew for certain:

1. They lose money every year—$16 million in '89.
2. They have the heftiest payroll in the NFL—$27.5 million in '89.

See, club owner Eddie J. DeBartolo, Jr., isn't all that interested in making money. That was Eddie, Sr.'s, forte. Eddie, Jr., is interested in winning football games, preferably championship ones. That, and hanging around with pro football players, taking them out to dinner, vacationing with them in Hawaii—face it, Junior is living his fantasy. His players report for work to a fifty-two-thousand-square-foot state-of-the-art training facility, with its players' lounge, indoor swimming pool, racquetball courts (Eddie, Jr., likes to bat it around with the boys), glistening modern weight-training facilities, carpets, windows, artwork on the walls, dining facilities (the team employs its own chefs), two natural-grass practice fields with underground drainage facilities (keeps the field dry, which cuts down on practice-field injury). When the 49ers travel, the team assigns each player two seats on the plane (they're big guys, see?), and everybody on the roster gets his own hotel room. In short, the San Francisco 49ers are run exactly the way a football player's dream franchise would be run.

And there is more than just anecdotal evidence that the 49ers' way is the right way to build and nurture a winning team. Even though a thorough statistical analysis shows that, overall, spending more money is no guarantee of winning championships, the Niners are an exception. Four Super Bowl trophies are displayed in the lobby of the Santa Clara training center. Over the last eleven seasons, the 49ers have *averaged* thirteen wins a season. They've captured eight division titles and four conference trophies. The team has fifteen assistant coaches on the payroll and eight full-time scouts, and the club's management is racially well integrated. It is a luxury care-and-feeding system for football players.

Compared with the 49ers, the Eagles are the NFL version of Bargaintown USA. There are no Super Bowl trophies to display in Philadelphia and no training facility to display them in. The Eagles employ ten assistant coaches, and only one of them is black—Dave Atkins, assigned a nominal role as tight ends coach. The team employs just two full-time scouts, the smallest scouting crew in the league. Players report to work every day in the musty gloom of the Vet Stadium basement, contend with Rusty for extra socks and jocks, and practice in conditions they consider primitive. The turf inside the Vet in '93 will be declared unfit for use in the NFL by George Toma, the league's official groundskeeper. They travel one to a seat, thank you, and share hotel rooms on the road. The Eagles don't scrimp on players' salaries; their total payroll is among those of the top teams in the league, as befits the number of accomplished and experienced players on their roster. But very little is wasted making these players feel appreciated.

There is a blind spot in the organization, a failure to nurture or even notice the intangible assets of an institution like this football club. The franchise has the look and feel of something stripped down, efficient, and ruthless. It has no warmth.

In San Francisco, players belong to something, something tangible. The training center is like a shrine to the club's thoroughbred heritage. It is named after Junior's mother, for crying out loud—the Marie P. DeBartolo Sports Center. Sentiment and memory matter here. Players don't arrive, perform, and depart feeling like chattel; they feel like part of something lasting and worthwhile. Even if he weren't paying the highest salaries in the league, Junior would be doing something right.

The Eagles' way of doing things is more typical of the NFL than San Francisco's, but most Eagles players don't know that. Most have never played for another team. From their perspective, the charmed San Francisco franchise is Oz, with Eddie, Jr., as the benevolent wizard, and when you fly out to meet them in Candlestick Park, it's hard not to feel like visiting Munchkins.

Today, for instance, the 49ers' win clinches them another play-off spot—the sort of thing that's become almost automatic out here. And they start out, as usual, by making it look easy. Jerry Rice, the league's most heralded receiver, opens the game by catching his one hundredth career touchdown pass from Steve Young, the league's top passer. The elegant receiver trots effortlessly past poor hobbled Wes on a simple post pattern, and as the Eagles' safety waves frantically and in vain to his teammate, Rich Miano, for deep help, the perfect pass arrives. Rice doesn't even have to trouble his stride—nobody so much as touches him on the play. The catch ties an NFL record, so the action stops for a moment while the stadium and national TV salute the achievement—it feels as if you're playing against royalty, the whole world rubbing the go-ahead touchdown in your face. Then John Taylor, the 49ers' other Pro Bowl receiver, catches a short pass, shrugs little Mark McMillian off (like a Munchkin!), and races downfield for a fifty-one-yard gain that sets up a field goal. The Eagles finish the first half down 10–0, without so much as a rumor of offense—eleven yards rushing and just eighty-three yards passing (Randall looks like Dorothy lost somewhere out there in the poppy field).

Wes takes himself out early in the third quarter. The knee he's been struggling to keep intact all season is finally too far gone. He had gotten Dr. Vince to shoot it with Novocain for this game, and it had felt okay for the first half—he'd even made a few big hits—but he twists it on a play early in the second half trying to stay with the tight end on a pass route. He stays in for two more plays before conceding to himself that he can no longer run. He comes limping off and tells Bud, "I hurt it again."

But something remarkable happens for the Eagles in the second half: Randall wakes up! He completes two crisp eleven-yard passes to move the team into field-goal range and then drops a perfect twenty-three-yard lob into Fred's sure hands in the back left corner of the end zone, laying the ball through the smallest of windows, over the outstretched hands of two trailing defenders, just inside the end line. With the extra point, the score is 10–7.

The 49ers come back with another field goal and then open the fourth quarter with another touchdown, but Randall seems totally nonplussed. It's hard to believe this is the same disgruntled, indecisive performer Eagles' fans have been watching for two months. He throws seven passes, completes six, the last an eleven-yard touchdown toss to Tank.

With the Eagles down now 20–14, Cunningham is the picture of poise and confidence as he leads the offense downfield in the final four minutes of the game. The sixty-four thousand fans in Candlestick watch in tense silence as the quarterback methodically marches the offense toward the winning touchdown. Randall pulls in the ball and races upfield for eleven yards. He zips a sideline pass to Calvin for two yards, then again for seven more—Calvin is flattened after this catch right in front of the Eagles' bench by cornerback Eric Davis, who delivers a blatant illegal forearm shot to the receiver's helmet, which brings Seth howling out to the field in protest to the official, who stands alongside without throwing a flag. "I can't fucking believe it!" Seth screams, storming back toward the sidelines, where another official runs up to caution *him*. Just after the two-minute warning, Randall completes another pinpoint fastball pass to Herschel, which moves the team down to San Francisco's twenty-yard line. The Eagles use the first of their two remaining time-outs. Another pass to Herschel gains three yards, and with fifty-nine seconds remaining, Randall can't find a receiver and is sacked for an eight-yard loss. The Eagles use their last time-out.

With fifty-three seconds remaining, they are stalled at fourth and fifteen on the twenty-five-yard line. Richie confers with Randall on the sidelines and the coach calls a 17-X-corner, which gives the quarterback three do-or-die targets: Fred on the right side streaking for the end-zone corner, Calvin on the left side cutting across the field just past the first-down marker (under the 49ers' deep zone), and Herschel in the right flat. On the snap, Randall checks off Fred, who is covered, and then fires a pass at Calvin, who leaps between two defenders, catches the ball, and lands on the ten-yard line. The first-down marker is also at the ten-yard line.

Calvin reaches out and sets the ball down inside the ten. A first down stops the clock. There's time to run at least three more. But the back judge, arriving moments after the catch, slides the ball back outside the ten-yard line, to compensate for Calvin's hopeful spot. Players mull around the ball, the 49ers arguing that the ball belongs farther back, Calvin and Randall and other Eagles pleading that it should be farther forward. The line judges trot across the field with sticks and chain, and very deliberately stretch the measuring device from the line of scrimmage to the ball. At first, it appears as if the Eagles have it. San Francisco players reel with disappointment. But then, on closer inspection, the referee, on his hands and knees, finds space between the ball and the post. He stands and extends one arm. Niners' ball.

Randall flings his helmet across the grass.

"The 49ers won that game by a spot," laments John Madden in the CBS-TV booth upstairs, disappointed that an exciting finish has been ruined for millions of network home viewers. "I think they [the Eagles] got a bad spot. To me the officials didn't hustle . . . when he [the back judge] got down there, how does he know where to spot the ball?"

What Madden sees as laziness and bad luck, the Eagles, of course, see as further evidence of a leaguewide official plot.

"Everybody on the field thought it was a first down, including the 49ers defense," complains Dave Alexander. "They were hanging their heads. Everybody on the offense was jumping up and down."

"I saw where they marked it, and it was just crazy," says Randall.

"We were robbed," says Wes.

"He leaned the stick," insists Antone.

See, this is Oz and these are the 49ers. And the Eagles? They're those rabble-rousing, braggadocio Bad Boys from Philly, Buddy's old team, the guys who try to hurt people, the team the League loves to hate. Isn't it obvious? Wasn't it obvious last month when the striped-shirts kept throwing flags, giving the Cardinals extra shots at the end zone on that goal-line stand? When they flag Antone for holding three times a game but never see the other team's tackles hanging on to poor Reggie? When there was no flag after that blatant forearm to Calvin's head?

Seth packs his bag, wrapped in dark, silent fury, good to his vow of silence, but when Andre, who watched the game on the sidelines wearing a Cheyney University sweatshirt, says, "Same old, same old," Seth nods with a room-chilling scowl.

"It's getting painfully difficult for us to play a game and have it called evenly," adds Wes.

But Richie takes a different and typically upbeat message from this loss, which once again puts his team's chances of making the playoffs in jeopardy. He's excited about what he saw from Randall and his offense.

When he gets the gloomy team together in the locker room immediately after the game, instead of lamenting the bad break in the final seconds, the coach shouts, "We're back!"

ONE OF THE THINGS defensive tackle Mike Golic does to prepare for the upcoming Minnesota Vikings home game has nothing to do with studying film, knocking heads in practice, or taking notes in team meetings. The big defensive tackle dons a horned helmet, a thick paisley cape with a shaggy collar of bright orange, a brown smock, tights, and boots, and, clutching a broadsword and round shield, spends about four hours on his day off standing in a cold drizzle in the prow of a dinghy on the Schuylkill comically ranting at the varsity crew team from La Salle University.

"Row, you scurvy dogs, row! . . . Lean on those oars!"

The crew team is also sporting horned helmets for the occasion.

"I'm getting in that Nordic frame of mind," shouts Mike, waving the broadsword wildly. "If I can maneuver through the Schuylkill, I can surely maneuver through that Minnesota offensive line. Now I know what it is to be a Viking! What it takes to be a Viking!"

He turns to the camera in the boat alongside and drops the sword and shield to his sides.

"And I don't like it!"

About three years ago the producers of "The Randall Cunningham Show," Mitch Goldstein and Mark Jordan of the CBS affiliate in Philadelphia (WCAU-TV, channel 10), recruited Mike to do an occasional two- or three-minute comedy bit for the weekly program. Mike is something of a born clown, and unlike some of the other funny men on the team, his humor is mostly G-rated.

With 280 pounds distributed haphazardly on a six-five frame, Mike's body looks like something patted together with Play-Doh, topped off with a pudgy potato face and a cheerful, *whazzup?* grin. He'd tell reporters that he was born "on the tenth, eleventh, and twelfth of December" or, after knocking down a pass, explain, "I was crouched behind the line ready with my amazing five-inch vertical leap." "I'm just as good as these guys," he'd say of the more acclaimed members of the Eagles' defensive line (Reverend Reggie and Clyde).

"They just have more foot speed, more strength, better moves . . . and more sacks." Grin. And, he might have added, more money.

On TV, he's golden. Like all natural comics, something about the face and body make you want to laugh. And Mike is willing to do just about anything, which the show exploits by having him make a fool of himself every week in some crazy stunt related to the upcoming football game. Before playing the Redskins' famous offensive front, nicknamed the "Hogs," Mike goes splashing around a muddy pigpen grappling with real porkers; before tackling the Packers, he steals a page from the movie *Rocky* and pounds on frozen carcasses in a walk-in meat locker. Before meeting the Cowboys, he tries his hand at cowpunching, dressed in chaps, boots, Western shirt, and what must be a thirty-gallon hat, wrestling, with some difficulty, a steer to the ground by the horns. "This is *hard!*" he says, in one straightforward aside to the camera, hanging on to the annoyed animal with a trace of fear in his (Mike's) eyes. In one bit, he pokes fun at his own lumpy physique, showing off the fleshy roundure of his own chest ("I was so ashamed when I saw it on tape," he confesses later. "What a *nasty* body! I'm never taking my shirt off in public again!"), climbing into a sweatbox and emerging with a perfectly defined upper torso (loaned, in a close-up shot that left his head out of the frame, by safety Rich Miano). The comic bits are sophomoric and unscripted, which just adds to their charm. The "Golic's Got It!" spots were so popular last season that Mike won a local Emmy. That led to more offers and, as it happened, some trouble.

When Reggie grows tired of his weekly radio call-in show, he recommends Mike as his replacement, so Mike starts doing that. Then McDonald's comes looking for an Eagles player to act in a series of comical commercials. These are a little more slick than the "Golic's Got It!" spots, but in a similar vein.

The idea is that each week the ads will feature an as-yet unchosen Eagles player boasting about the upcoming game, dressed up in an appropriately silly costume—for the Raiders, a pirate; the Redskins, war paint and feathers; and so on. Then the player will tape two alternate postgame spots, one showing him glorying in victory, the other in some ridiculous posture of defeat. He might be shown with an arrow through his head after the Redskins loss, for instance, or trampled by a stampeding herd after the Cowboys defeat.

Eric Allen, Seth Joyner, and Mike try out for the spots, and choosing Mike is kindergarten math. Seth clowning around in a funny hat is like Charles Manson leading a Christmas sing-along. Eric is charming and smooth, but there's a natural dignity about the man as ill suited to slapstick in its own way as Seth's malevolent visage. Anyway, with the Randall show spots, the radio call-in show, the McDonald's ads, and a host of product endorsements—on top of the normal saturation Pack coverage (Mike is a favorite locker-room interview)—by midseason, you can hardly open a newspaper without reading a Golic one-liner, turn on the radio without hearing Mike kidding around with call-in fans, or, on TV, seeing that Play-Doh face mugging on screen. Mike has become one of the top-three most readily identifiable characters on the football team (behind Reggie and Randall), a big, lovable galoot. His high profile just leads to even more speaking engagements, public appearance requests, postseason cruises, all of the goodies waiting at the end of the rainbow of big-time NFL celebrity.

Not everyone is amused. All these extras began dropping in Mike's lap before he was even a starter. The Eagles' front four at the time consisted of Reggie, Mike Pitts, Jerome, and Clyde Simmons. Golic was used as a rotating fifth, inserted to allow Jerome and Pitts a breather. As a backup, his approach to his work—"Yo, guys, lighten up. This is a game!"—was a little easier to take. Reggie, Pitts, Jerome, and Clyde would kid him about being an "honorary black guy." "Only, Mike, you gotta git yo'self a personal trainer this off-season and get to work on developing some *butt,* man," Jerome would say. "You can't be no brother with a flat little honky ass like that!" Mike could cheerfully accept playing behind these guys. It was second string, but not exactly. Mike actually played a lot. Buddy used to call Mike "one of the best fifth defensive linemen in the league."

"I liked that 'one of,' " Mike would say, chuckling. "Like there's a ton of 'fifth' linemen in the league."

Guys like Seth and Eric are not just starters, they are legitimate stars. Each has been to the Pro Bowl. And here's this glorified backup—go ahead, say it—*white guy* hogging the commercial sidelights! Mike is making about $520,000 from the Eagles this season, and his outside work isn't just fun, it's lucrative. He gets paid $15,000 for one day of work on the McDonald's commercials.

Midway through this season, Mike and his wife, Chris, start noticing that their relationships with some of the other guys and their wives have grown cooler. Richie and most of his coaching staff, a generally humorless bunch, are sometimes mildly put off by the fun Mike pokes at himself and the team. In one case, Mike was busy taping a segment at a New Jersey hotel, trying to coax a few laughs out of Richie's decision early in the '91 season (quickly reversed) to do away with the tradition of herding players into a hotel the night before local games. Mitch Goldstein got a call on the set from someone in the Eagles' organization.

"Is Golic there? Rich Kotite wants to speak with him."

Richie told Mike some of his friends from the hotel called and told him what they were doing, and he didn't like the idea. Sounded a little bit like they were fixin' to *make fun* out of him. Plans for the shoot had to be revamped on the spot to keep Mike from crossing his boss.

Mike's outside success has bypassed the status hierarchy of Team. Public recognition, commercial deals, fame, and fortune—these are things that are supposed to flow from excellence on the field. Mike is, make no mistake, one fine football player, but he's no Clyde, Eric, or Seth, which he is unfailingly first to admit. Mike's success off the field is *disproportionate*. There are subtle hints, like when Mike is singled out in the film room for some blunder the day after a game, and Coach says, "Put *that* on your TV show." Or when a teammate on the practice field says, "Some of you guys might think this is just a big joke, but . . . ," looking right at Mike.

He laughs. Everybody laughs. But he also feels the stab.

He's a little mystified when folks fail to see the humor in the McDonald's ads that air after a loss.

"Hey, it's not like I rush out to the studio after the game and tape the spot," Mike protests to a call-in complainer on his radio show. "We taped all those spots at once earlier in the season, one in case we won, another in case we lost. It's just a joke. Look, I hate to lose just as much as anybody!"

Actually, Mike probably *doesn't* hate to lose as much as most of the others, which is not to say he doesn't try just as hard to win. It's just . . . well, Mike isn't a brooder. Everyone mouths the mantra *that's in the past* and does his best to live by it, but there is a protocol after defeat. You mope around for about twelve hours. Many of the players are used to being indulged by family and friends through at least one long night of grumpy remorse.

Well, suffice it to say, there is none of that for Mike, who has a hard time extinguishing that happy glint in his eye even after the most atrocious pasting. It is a good thing, too, because Chris doesn't have the patience for it. After being home all day with their two boys, the tiny titans, Mike's arrival fresh from some thrill or agony means Chris finally gets a break.

"Boy, you guys sure got your butts kicked today," she'll tell him.

"You're all heart," Mike will complain.

And it is time to bounce a kid on his knee. "Mikey and Jacob, they don't have a clue if I won or lost," says Mike, happily.

And everybody knows this about Mike, which makes the McDonald's ads somehow harder to take. They are unseemly, like blowing a kazoo in a funeral procession.

It is irksome, too, because his ascension to the starting role was the first and most tangible team consequence of Jerome's death. Dreadful as it sounds to say it, Jerome's ultimate demise was Mike's main chance, clear and simple. With training camp starting up just a week or so after the funeral—Mike had been one of the pallbearers—he spent a lot of time grimacing and shrugging and saying the right things: "I feel terrible, but all I can do is do my best to fill those shoes"; "Sure, it's something I've always wanted, but it goes without saying, you know, I hate for it to happen this way"; et cetera. It was an awkward role, but Mike pulled it off ably. He struck just the right note of guilty eagerness, conceding he wasn't the player Jerome was, but that maybe, if he played *waaay* over his head, the NFL's best defense wouldn't go completely in the toilet.

And it doesn't. By the thirteenth game of the season, the defense ranks fifth in the league at stopping the run and has allowed only two rushing touchdowns. Mike feels secure in his new role. Even though he has (now) only that one sack, he's leading the D-line in tackles. His quarterback hurries are respectable. Mike has knocked down five passes with his long reach and forced and recovered a fumble. He's a having a good year.

Against the Vikings, however, Mike faces an old nemesis. Back at St. Joseph's High School in Cleveland, in his senior year, he went into the Ohio state wrestling tournament as the favorite to win the heavyweight division. In the first round he went up against a smaller but tenacious opponent from Salem Senior High in Canton named Kirk Lowdermilk, and lost. Lowdermilk went on to win the heavyweight division, and Mike finished third.

Now Lowdermilk is starting center for the Vikings, like Mike a seven-year NFL veteran, and in the five or six times they've met on the pro field, Mike never feels as though he's come out on top. Needless to say, the Vikings' center never misses an opportunity to remind Mike of the wrestling championship. Blocking to Lowdermilk's right is Randall McDaniel, one of the best guards in football. Frequently double-teamed by these two, sometimes by Lowdermilk and left guard Gary Zimmerman, Mike has a long, dark day against Minnesota in the trenches. It's a frigid afternoon at the Vet, the turf feels like prickly concrete, and he just can't seem to work up any momentum. Running backs Terry Allen and Roger Craig rush for nearly one hundred yards in the first half alone.

Nothing Mike does seems to help. On the field he's regarded as a clever player, one who frequently makes up for any deficiencies in speed and strength by correctly guessing plays and putting himself in the right spot. There have been times, for instance, when Mike has been able to read the opposing quarterback's lips in the huddle and tip off his teammates to the general drift of a play in advance. Or he'll sometimes notice little patterns in the way the center or guard sets up, clues to the coming play. But today all his guesses seem to be wrong. At third and goal early in the second quarter, Mike's assignment is to hunker down low and drive forward, push the center or guard backward a foot or two. Only he notices that the guard lined up opposite him, Brian Habib, is set lower than usual, which means it will be virtually impossible to get underneath him. So instead, Mike decides he's going to attack the gap to Habib's right. He knows from the formation the Vikings are in—they've put the lineman McDaniel in the backfield as a lead blocker—that if the run comes to that gap, the lead blocker's assignment is to hit the linebacker. Mike figures he'll surprise 'em, shoot the gap uninvited.

Except McDaniel spots him and delivers the full force of his 270-pound frame right at the crown of Mike's lowered helmet, driving the hopeful defensive tackle straight backward, into the linebacker, and clearing a clean hole for the touchdown run—make that *three* rushing touchdowns against the Eagles this season.

Mike is momentarily woozy, as he gazes up into McDaniel's smiling face.

"Surprised you, didn't I?" gloats the Vikings' blocker.

"Jesus," Mike complains. "You're supposed to hit the backer! Don't you study the plays?"

IT'S A PECULIAR GAME. For one thing, for the first few minutes of it Randall looks shaken and confused. There's a reason for that.

It seems the Scrambling One was discovered to have sneaked out of the New Jersey hotel the night before. Now, Randall may be a subversive in the way he plays football, but he's practically a Goody Two-shoes when it comes to toeing the club line—as anyone getting paid his salary might be expected to be. But this time, the felicitous lure of his newly betrothed had gotten the better of his usual punctiliousness. It was an understandable lapse, and probably would have gone unnoticed, except a security guard posted in the hotel hallway read something else into Randall's departure. He saw Randall walk into Jimmy Mac's room, heard Jimbo shouting and cursing, and then saw Randall furtively exit the room, come down the hall, and leave the hotel . . . and not come back. Lots of the veterans cut out of the hotel after meetings the night before games. They live nearby, think the whole hotel routine before home games is bullshit, and can easily afford the thousand-dollar fine if they get caught. A handsome tip to the security man once or twice a year can generally ensure against discovery.

Only this night, because of the circumstances, the guard thinks that maybe Randall got in a fight with his backup (there being reports, and all, of the two players not exactly being *close*, see), so he does his duty this time and alerts the head coach.

Jimbo gets a call from Richie in the wee hours.

"What'd you do to Randall?"

The quarterback sleepily protests he doesn't know what Richie is talking about.

Richie relates the guard's tale, and Jimbo laughs. He explains that he was hollering, per usual, at the video game, not at the precious Scrambling One.

"The guard says he left in a huff," says Richie.

Jimbo says the quarterback was fine when he left and says he figured Randall had just gone back to his room.

Randall arrives at the Vet about three hours before game time, checks out some film, and heads for the training room. Richie passes him in the hallway and says nothing, doesn't even look at him. Looks as if he's mad about something.

Randall immediately assumes he isn't starting. Richie's giving Jimbo the ball again! The whole spiraling Week of the Great Benching mess starts all over again—world spinning into chaos, Empire of Self crumbling, portents of apocalypse everywhere. . . .

Dave Archer sees Randall walk into the locker room with the face of a man whose bus has just driven off a cliff.

"Has Richie said anything yet about Jim starting?" he asks Arch.

"What?"

Arch knows Randall had taken every snap in practice the week before with the starting team.

"Jim's going to start."

"No, he's not, Randall, you're gonna play."

But Randall walks off to the training room clearly unconvinced.

A few minutes later, Richie finds him and pulls him into the equipment manager's office and closes the door. Randall figures *this is it*.

"I can't believe what you did!" Richie says, as Randall would later recount the story in his book. "I can't believe you, the disciplined person you are, the guy we always count on, could do this."

Randall, who has by now figured out this is about his skipping out of the hotel the night before, is in his blank mode, waiting for the boom.

The coach tells him he's going to have to pay a fine. The quarterback says no problem (chump change for the multimillionaire). The coach stands up, says, "Hey, have a good game," opens the door, exits, and closes it in the quarterback's face.

All through the pregame warm-up, Randall looks like he's in a daze. Is he starting or isn't he? What did Richie mean by that "Hey, have a good game?" Was he being facetious?

But, sure enough, Randall is out there for the Eagles' first offensive series. He hands the ball off to Herschel twice, and the running back grinds out a first down. An offside penalty on Mike Schad pushes them back five yards, and on first and fifteen, Randall fails to see the obvious Minnesota blitz formation, gets swarmed trying to pass, fumbles, and the Vikings run the ball down to the Eagles' nine-yard line. They kick a field goal four plays later.

Arch can see the confusion in Randall's eyes when he comes off the field. So the backup quarterback walks over to consult with the quarterback's buddy Byars.

"Hey, Tank, you better talk to your boy. He looks like he doesn't want to play."

"What do you mean?"

"He thinks Richie's going to put Jim in."

So Byars walks over and bucks up Randall's spirits with an embrace before the offense heads back out on the field.

And, just like that, Randall is back. Stuck on third and fifteen, he takes off with the ball for a classic improvisation, juking and high stepping along the sidelines and out-of-bounds thirty yards upfield. The crowd loves it. They haven't seen much of this from Randall this season. Then, four plays later, this time on a second-down play, he takes off again, for eighteen yards. He finishes the drive with a one-yard dive into the end zone to erase the damage caused by his earlier fumble.

And Randall goes on to have his best day of the season, running for an amazing 121 yards on just twelve carries, carrying the ball into the end zone himself twice, completing 70 percent of his passes for 164 yards, and leading an inspired offensive effort that results in a 28–17 win—this against one of the top-ten defenses in the NFL. Later, Richie explains that the Vikings' all-out pass rush had the unintended consequence of opening up big running lanes for Randall . . . no, this did not mark a coaching decision to unleash the Randall of old, but the game produces a great late-season swell of confidence in fans and team alike—not to mention the quarterback.

Seth is the other big hero of the game, again. Late in the fourth quarter, after a Vikings' touchdown had brought them within four points of victory, with plenty of time and surging momentum, Seth made an announcement to Mike Golic and a few of the other guys.

"I'm gonna make a big play. Watch."

He had said the same thing two weeks before in the Giants game, before picking off a pass and running it back for a touchdown. "When he said it this time, you'd best believe we were watching," says Mike.

The linebacker had observed the Vikings working little screen and flare passes all day as a way of getting around Reggie and Clyde, and he knew from his typically exhaustive film study the week before that on critical drives they liked to spring these short passes on first down, delaying the running back out of the backfield and flipping him the ball over the pass rush. When quarterback Sean Salisbury tried it this time, Seth stepped in front of the receiver. The linebacker was so far out in front of the play, in fact, that he damn near overran the pass. Reaching back with one hand and kind of coaxing the ball into his grasp—a maneuver the stunned Salisbury in postgame interviews would call "unhuman"—Seth raced twenty-four yards into the end zone for the game-clinching touchdown.

Seth had waved away his teammates when they swarmed in to congratulate him and instead ran over to the Archangel Jerome banner behind the goalpost and executed a full formal salute.

That, and Randall's terrific day, tended to obscure the overall poor performance of Bud's defense. In the 28–17 victory, which nudged the Eagles' season record to a highly respectable 8–5, they had given up 219 total yards, 138 of them on the ground, and had allowed two rushing touchdowns. The Vikings had averaged more than 5 yards every time they carried the ball! Randall's performance had put Minnesota far enough behind in the second half that the Vikings virtually had to abandon the run, but other teams would take heart from the way they had moved the ball right through the Eagles' midsection.

Nothing is more embarrassing to a defensive line than an opponent's running the ball right up its middle. Buddy Ryan had a crude and unforgettable analogy for that.

BUT, AS USUAL, Mike is funny about it afterward.

"Those guys [Lowdermilk and McDaniel] were bouncing me into the cheap seats all day," says Mike, in a typically self-deprecatory newspaper interview after the game. "They were having a fun time double-teaming me all over the place, knocking me over one way, and then coming back and knocking me over the other way . . . I admit, it didn't seem too funny to me at the time."

Mike explains in detail for the hound his misstep at the goal line, the one where McDaniel crushed him right on the tip of his helmet and opened a hole for the touchdown.

"I think I'm an inch shorter," he says.

About that embarrassing success the Vikings had running the ball?

"There wasn't much to recommend that first half," says Mike. "They were burying us. They were bringing three tight ends in and doing a good job executing. We were missing tackles, letting them run inside, letting them run outside."

He describes his own missed tackles, the growing irritation of coaches on the sidelines, reveals that one big-play sack by the Eagles had resulted, not from a stroke of coaching genius, but from a seren-dipitous Mike Golic misreading a Vikings play—"What can I say, some-times you screw up . . . and it works out!" It's good stuff. In all, a disarmingly candid look at a terrible outing, in this case leavened somewhat by the fact that the Eagles won the game. But, whatever the circumstances, Mike is one of very few pro football players who would so cheerfully admit he'd been overmatched.

Three days after the article appears, Dale Haupt, the Eagles' defensive line coach, benches him. Mike gets some cold looks from teammates in the locker room, and there's a comment or two, but he's used to that. Then Dale invites him in for a talk in his office.

"I can't believe you did that article!" the coach says.

Mike is flabbergasted. "You can't be serious."

They're in Dale's tiny space, across the hall from Bud's. Both are big men; they look jammed into the space on either side of the coach's desk. As Mike would recall later, Haupt says he's starting Harmon and Pitts—maybe *they* won't be so chirpy about getting humiliated.

"Listen, you're the one . . . how many times have you told us, don't believe what you read?" protests Mike. "Look, I'm the first one to admit that I got my butt kicked. I told reporters after the game that I did. What am I going to do? Sit there and cry about it? Sure I was pissed about it! If we played them again, I'd sure as hell want to do better, but I'm not going to whine about it, so I joke about it. That's what I do. If some people get mad at me because I don't carry a loss around for five days . . . screw 'em!"

"Those things you said . . ."

"All right, maybe it wasn't the smartest thing for me to do, doing that article, but that's the kind of guy I am. I'll joke about it, but I don't take it lightly. I got my butt kicked, but I think benching me is unwarranted. Look at the last six games!"

"I think your play has been slipping," says Dale.

"Go back and look. Count the tackles. As much or more as any other lineman!"

"You're probably right."

"Then how can you say I'm slipping?"

"Well, you only have that one sack."

"But look at my hurries. I'm right behind Seth and Clyde."

Dale won't budge. The decision has been made—and with it, thousands of incentive dollars awarded Mike for every start.

Put that in your TV show!

EVERYBODY'S SENSE of humor is strained at this point in the '92 season. The Eagles are locked in a second-place tie with the Redskins in the NFC East, both teams with an 8–5 record, and only one of them is going to the play-offs. Richie's squad cannot afford another misstep. It's time for the big-money players to step up. It's time to bring the heat.

Unfortunately, the heat arrives Sunday morning, December 13, in the gift shop of the Marriott Sea-Tac Hotel in Seattle, in the form of the *New York Times*.

Seth has been pretty good the last few weeks. He always plays well, and ever since he took his vow of silence there's been a noticeable loosening of team tensions. Until now. It seems Seth has made an exception to his gag rule. Because right there on the front page of the sports section of the *Times*—Richie's hometown newspaper—is an action shot of the stone-faced Pro Bowl linebacker, under the headline:

JOYNER HITS AS HARD AS HIS CANDOR

"Joyner," writes *Times* reporter Thomas George, "who turned 28 this month, is the epitome of the National Football League player of the 1990s, who speaks with bluntness and conviction and who attempts to balance his individuality with team unity and team goals."

Uh-oh. One senses, with that reference to "bluntness and conviction," that this is not going to be one of those times.

> "I have opinions, I am not afraid to state them and this causes people to be critical of me. Well, so be it," said Joyner . . . , "The truth is an ugly thing to a lot of people, but I accept it about myself, too. It's not that I don't have

any faults or that I don't make mistakes. But don't attack me for caring about winning. I want us to win a Super Bowl, this Super Bowl this year, badly. Maybe by everyone taking a closer look at what's happened here and being honest about it, we can."

Oh, shit. The pisser is that the line "caring about winning," is actually Richie's. It's the one he used publicly to defend Seth when everybody jumped all over the linebacker for running his mouth after the Packers game. After letting off steam before the team, he'd come up with this "caring about winning" line, which was pretty good . . . kind of turned the whole poisonous episode into a positive. Until now.

"Buddy drafted and crafted a team in his image," said Joyner, who was part of Ryan's first draft. "He built the identity of a team that would beat up on other teams and intimidate people. Intimidation goes a long way in this game. Under Buddy, the players were vocal, the coaches were vocal, everybody was vocal. But we had unity."

Seth is uttering the unspoken gospel, in public! In the fucking *New York Times*! Coaches and players like to say that they don't pay any attention to the things written and said about them—one way of asserting the pocket-lint status of the Pack—but they read and listen to every word. The only things that ultimately matter, however, are the things actually said by players and coaches. It's hard to strive together toward a common goal when a member of the team keeps shouting to onlookers *This'll never work, I'm playing with a bunch of idiots*, which is a fair description of what the linebacker is doing here. And at this critical moment in the season, Seth has decided—what happened to the vow of silence anyway?—to air Buddy's Boys' take on the new-look Norman/Richie Eagles.

"Buddy had built this team from the dumps and wanted certain things to push it over the top," Joyner said. "Buddy cared about winning, and Braman cared about making money. Buddy did not get the chance to complete the job. Braman wanted a puppet [that would be Richie] and that's what he got. Much of what Buddy said has come to roost. We lost Keith Jackson because of money. Free agency is coming and this team could be ripped apart."

Having sacked his coach, Seth moves on. He trots out the old figment about Randall's role in the palace coup.

". . . Randall lobbied for Rich to Braman and deserted Buddy," Joyner said. "Buddy gave Randall the chance, as a black quarterback, that no other coach in this league would. Buddy built the entire offense around Randall. I told Randall that he would pay for what he did, and I don't know if him missing all of last year with the knee injury was it, but God works in mysterious ways."

Well, so much for that business about balancing "individuality with team unity and team goals." Seth reiterates his criticism of Rich for running the ball in the final minutes against Green Bay—"screwed up the game"—and basically leaves no old grudge unvoiced in the lengthy article.

Richie doesn't see it until after the game. Harry Gamble reads it in his hotel room that morning, seething, but then it's time to leave for the Kingdome and play a big football game. He thinks it best to deal with this one later.

It turns out to be the longest game in the history of the franchise, more than four hours' worth, dragging through four quarters and an overtime period that ends with a winning Eagles' field goal just three seconds shy of the full fifteen minutes.

During the marathon, Richie's team is flagged with penalties seventeen times, for 191 yards, the second-highest total of penalty yards in *NFL history*. Clipping, holding, offside, personal fouls, defensive pass interference, offensive pass interference, illegal use of hands, illegal backfield motion, delay of game, illegal block . . . the play-by-play later reads like an NFL referee's catalog. All through the game, the Eagles keep handing Seattle chances to stay in the game. Poor Vai Sikahema has two spectacular runbacks annulled by penalties, a 66-yard kickoff return and a 52-yard punt return—plays that would have made Vai the leading return man in the NFL, would probably have snared him another Pro Bowl spot and doubled or tripled his salary—flagged, walked back, and erased.

Through it all, though, Richie's offense keeps moving the ball. Herschel rushes for 111 yards on twenty-three carries. Keith Byars almost single-handedly saves the game, rumbling for one big gain after another in the overtime period to move the team into field-goal range. Randall plays well, completing 60 percent of his passes, scoring one touchdown with one of his patented soaring, headfirst leaps into the end zone, engineering a long scoring drive late in the fourth quarter to tie the game, and then coolly conducting the long march (complete with a couple of nifty, improvised numbers with Byars) at the end of the overtime period to set up Roger Ruzek's game-winning 44-yard field goal.

Mike Golic gets sent in as a sub late in the first half and promptly bulls his way into the backfield and sacks Seattle quarterback Stan Gelbaugh.

"Eagles coaches went out of their way last week to say that the lack of intensity was not Golic's fault," points out CBS commentator and former NFL coach John Robinson, then adds, knowingly, "Golic, nevertheless, was the guy they dropped from the starting lineup."

The narrow, 20–17 win enables the Eagles to keep pace with the Redskins, who upset the Cowboys today. So the Eagles have now earned a one-game, do-or-die contest next week at the Vet against Washington—winner goes to the play-offs, loser only maybe. So the air in the postgame locker room is giddy with relief and expectation. They've narrowly escaped blowing the whole season, and they know it.

"All I can say is we're sure happy to have the win under the circumstances," says Richie. "Any time you make seventeen penalties and give the other team one hundred and ninety-one yards and *still* win a ball game . . . well, the only thing you can feel is damn lucky."

Richie won't say it publicly, but he blames the referees for the flagfest. He's beginning to buy into the notion that the league's officials have it in for his team.

"The officiating in this league is high school, strictly high school," he says afterward, away from the Pack. "It's a disgrace."

Larry Pasquale has his own theory. Many of the penalties today were on his boys, and those annulled runbacks of Vai's . . . well, suffice it to say, they would have done more than propel the return man's stats to the top of the charts; they would have put his special teams squad up there, too. Larry is bitter, and he has a theory: he thinks the Seahawks were doing it on purpose.

"It looked like, sometimes, when our own man was in a position to hit them, what they were doing was, they were *diving* to the ground, on their stomachs," he explains to one or two startled newshounds. They've heard many a postgame rationalization, but this reaches a new imaginative height. "So that when our guys hit them, it gave the impression of a clip, a push from behind! It's a terrific trick, I just have never seen it used before!"

"So you think they were *trying* to draw penalties?" one of the hounds asks, giving Larry a chance to back in off this ledge. But the coach is fired up.

"I think they were," he says. "Because twice there were calls for clipping where we never hit the man. James Joseph [a backup ballcarrier who plays mostly on special teams] got called for clipping one time and he never even hit the man. The man was already down and sliding on his stomach when James came up."

"The guy took a dive?"

"Yeah"—the look on Larry's face says *Why aren't these guys getting this?*—"because he realizes he's blocked. See, our man has position on him, and just as our guy approaches, their guy just dives on his stomach. So the refs gets the impression it's a clip or a push. See, at that point, their guy can't make the tackle, but he can still draw the penalty."

Richie later says, "You can't take Larry seriously some of the time; he gets mad, he goes a little crazy."

Seth is angry, too. He's seen the article, and he knows the timing is atrocious. He's going to catch holy hell for this one. The vow of silence is out the window anyway; he's going to have to talk his way out of this. Sitting shirtless before his locker, he's a man who has been run over by his own truck.

"The interview was supposed to be more of an interview on Seth Joyner than an interview about Randall Cunningham, Richie Kotite, and Norman Braman," he says, with the Pack crowding around, delighted to have the infamous mouth roaring once more. "So, once again, I make myself accessible to the print, and this is what happens. Another big deal, something being blown all out of proportion, because someone has been misquoted. And then, here we go with this situation all over again, man. I should learn my lesson . . . not to just say anything [literally, this would be good advice, but what Seth means to say here is "to say nothing"], because it's amazing how you guys take little bits and pieces out of what I say and piece it together the way you want it, man. I ain't doin' any more interviews, man."

Of course, far from being misquoted or having his remarks distorted, all Seth had done was share with the public an opinion held by many of his friends and teammates on defense. It's fair to say that they all wished he'd keep it to himself, but the sting in Seth's remarks comes from this body of silent agreement in the back end of the room. Buddy had attended a team function honoring Jerome the previous week, the former coach's first visit with his team since the firing. Richie and Harry avoided the former coach. "All that son of a bitch has done since he left is run me down, and all I've ever done is say nice things about him," complains Richie. There was no proving it, but Richie is convinced that Buddy's visit with his old crew has prompted Seth's ill-timed remarks. It smells like sabotage. Richie has been laboring mightily for two years now to bridge the divide between *his* offense and *Buddy's* defense, and just as Richie has the team on the verge of going to the play-offs for the first time in his tenure, Seth lobs another grenade into the fault.

Richie reads the remarks on the bus on the way to the airport. Through the long flight home he fights the urge to confront the linebacker right there on the plane. But he's torn. Personally, he'd like to take a swing at the guy, but he's also got the team to think about. Next Sunday's Redskins game is the most important one of the season. It's his job to hold things together, not tear things apart.

But, Christ, it makes Richie mad. Especially that part about him being a puppet. And the stuff about Randall? It's all fiction! But what's he going to do? Seth is a vital part of the team. A college coach will sit a defiant player down, figuring his authority is more important in the long run than any particular game. But in the pros, as St. Vince said, winning is everything. Especially now. Sitting Seth down just now, on the doorstep to the play-offs, just cuts everybody's throat.

The plane deposits the team back in Philadelphia at about 3:00 a.m., and Richie drives home to sleep on it for a few hours. He doesn't feel any better when he wakes up.

"I wanted to kill that motherfucker last night," he says, venting confusion and frustration in his office early the next morning. "Nobody in this league has the fucking authority I have, except maybe Shula and a couple of guys like that, the authority without interference. I don't go around telling people I'm in charge every fucking second like that asshole Ryan did. Did you hear what I said? I'm sick and tired of it! Especially when it takes the focus of the team away. I mean, come on! He's supposed to be a team guy? Come on! What's going on here? The whole thing is . . . look how many people aren't here from last year [he's lost Jerome, Wes Hopkins, Andre Waters, Ben Smith, and Keith Jackson]. And we're still 9–5! Against one of the toughest schedules in the league! How many teams have a tougher schedule than us? This is disgusting. And I bit my tongue last night. I'm gonna say something to him, obviously. But I'm not going to make a big public show of it. I have the team to think about."

Gusts of words pour out of Richie, who typically spends very little time reflecting on things. He's strictly an action guy: problem— *boom!*—solution. But not with this one. Seth's dark aura has spread over everything . . . it's poison, but how do you get rid of a Seth Joyner when you can't afford to lose a football game?

"What's going on here?" Richie is thinking out loud. "He has this *distorted* view! How can they perceive this shit? Because of that son of a bitch Ryan, that's how. . . . I'm sick and fucking tired of it. And he [Seth] had four penalties on him yesterday! And I'm trying to hold this together. . . . But I'm not going to ruin this football team. I'm just trying to get to the play-offs. You know what the weird thing is? I know Seth Joyner. I don't know what it is that's motivating him right now, but, basically, one-on-one, he's a good fucking guy! I don't know what's doing it. I don't know if it's Buddy, who was here last week, or what. But I'm telling you something . . . this is too, too . . . he [Seth] won't let go! Buddy's been gone for two years now! I mean, how many times do I have to get hit by a falling piano walking out the door?"

Richie is still asking himself these questions the next day. He's in conference with Harry, as a matter of fact, kicking around ideas for what to do about Seth, when the loose cannonball rolls in the door on its own. Seth presents a wholly unexpected solution. He apologizes. He admits he crossed a line, and at the worst possible time. He says he really didn't mean those things he said, the reporter twisted his remarks, that *was* how he felt, way back when, right after Buddy got fired, but no more (never mind that much of what he said had to do with *this* season). The reporter had gotten it wrong. He says he'll hold a press conference and apologize publicly.

"I wouldn't hold a press conference," advises Norman when he's consulted by phone.

But Seth wants to go ahead, and Norman says, "Suit yourselves. I still think it's a bad idea."

And that afternoon, the surly linebacker who has vowed not to give another interview again this season, and vowed to never apologize, sits in front of the assembled and somewhat amused Pack on his day off and does both (the former for the third time).

"It's really important for my teammates to understand that I'm not trying to stir up anything," he says. "I wanted to come forward and let my teammates know—and I will speak to them—let them know that . . . hey, I want to be a leader. And I mean a leader in a positive way and not a negative way."

He is somewhat less abjectly apologetic in public than he had been in private (in private, he had been abject).

"Is this an apology?" Seth is asked.

"No," he says, but he is sorry that the whole thing happened.

As for the business about Richie being a puppet and Norman being a cheapskate and Randall being a Judas Iscariot punished by God Almighty . . . well, Seth falls back on the old standby.

He scowls into the cameras and invokes the mantra: "That's in the past."

And who's gonna argue with him?

15

THE EMPIRE

Giant, weary Reggie White's brown biceps and forearms are etched with nicks, scrapes, cuts, and scars. There are fresh red gouges, pink turf burns, scabs from burgundy to ashy gray, and random knots of shiny black scars, especially around the elbows, where the accumulated ravages of nearly two full decades of football have left a mottled collage of tormented dermis.

Reggie doesn't need the 92 on his back to be recognized on the football field anymore. His frame alone is famous, the shoulders, arms, hands, and barrel chest start thick and broaden down to sloping abdomen, horselike haunches and hams. He is knock-kneed and splay-footed enough to look almosy clumsy, until he moves. His face seems small outlined by all this size: a straight nose with widely flared nostrils; small, wide-set, searching brown eyes; thickly protuberant brow, low hairline. The mouth is his most prominent feature. It's wide and full lipped, with an underbite accentuated by a goatee. From behind the bars of his face mask, a smile emerges so broad, big toothed, and beatific it's like the chrome grill at the front end of a custom-styled eighteen-wheel interstate cruiser.

Reverend Reggie turns thirty-one this week, in December, the week of the '92 season's biggest game. On his birthday, Saturday, he shows up for the final walk-throughs and meetings, lingers to give the usual taped interviews to the CBS sports staff that will televise tomorrow's game, and then politely cuts out early to be home for a celebration with his wife, Sara, and his children, Jeremy, six, and Jecolia, four. Jeremy and Jecolia are excited because they have baked Daddy a cake—a *big* cake.

He is such a big man, six-five and about 300 pounds, and so amazingly muscular and athletic, that Reggie inspires heroic and biblical comparison. He is surely descended from the race of Philistines that produced Goliath—*And the staff of his spear was like a weaver's beam;*

and his spear's head weighed six hundred shekels of iron—and it isn't hard
to imagine, standing alongside Reggie, how deadly he might have been
as a warrior on some ancient battlefield, leveling whole ranks of men
with one swing of a broadsword too heavy for many men to lift. And
in his modern arena, Reggie is as formidable as any Goliath or Achilles.
He looks born to play the game. He believes he was born to play it.
Those who can match his build are smaller and those who can match
his size are pudgy or wooden by comparison. Ron Heller, the onetime
wrestling champ, comes the closest on the team to matching Reggie's
size and physique at six-six, 280 pounds, but as athletic as Ron is, his
moves on the football field are robotic by comparison. Reggie runs
the forty-yard dash in 4.6 seconds. He deftly hurdles blockers who
dive low, spins and dances away from those who try to knock him off
balance, and for those who try to meet him head up . . . well, the
mighty minister has a whole assortment of methods for handling that,
his favorite being just to run right through the poor soul. Reggie
preaches loving New Testament values, but on the football field, his
God is Jehovah, the God of vengeance, power, and might.

He goes about his business untroubled by the petty travails of
his teammates and tiny tempests of public interest. Reggie had kept
mostly silent during the Week of the Great Benching, uttering his
usual pieties, and has kept his thoughts to himself through the self-
inflicted trials of his troubled friend Seth. Not everybody is happy with
the way Reggie responds to these things. Richie is heard to sometimes
lament that the team's six-time all-pro defensive end is not a more
"verbal leader." But those who think Reggie isn't leading aren't paying
attention. He's leading all right. Whether the others choose to follow
is their decision. He's learned that.

Reggie's dimensions spill out of the ordinary frame of star athlete
and celebrity. He is larger than life. Even to call him the greatest
defensive lineman who has ever played the game is nothing particularly new or remarkable for him. He has been an athlete of legendary
stature now most of his life, ever since he first stepped on a gridiron
and basketball court back at Howard High School in Chattanooga,
Tennessee. He became the first high-school athlete ever to be named
all-state in both sports, and at the University of Tennessee, they had
already voted him a member of their all-time team. There's such a
thing as being so good at what you do, so naturally gifted (Reggie
would say "blessed"), that it becomes hard to lead. His nearly $2-
million-per-year salary, not counting endorsements and other in-
comes, is second on the team only to Randall's, and next year, when
he becomes a free agent, everybody knows Reggie's going to redefine
the upper limit of earnings for the sport. He's the only player in the

room who is definitely going to the Hall of Fame, Super Bowl ring or no Super Bowl ring.

But Reggie's stature separates him from others on the team, even its coaches and other stars. How can you coach the greatest defensive end ever to play the game? How can you expect to play up to his level?

Reggie works to bridge that gap. He goofs around with the best of them in the locker room, battling to dunk a wad of masking tape over the top of a teammate's locker, or launching into his spirited impressions of Elvis, Muhammad Ali, John Wayne, and barking dog—his nickname is "Big Dawg." He is humble and kind to a fault. There is hardly a person who knows Reggie to whom he has not, more than once, offered a sincere apology, sometimes for things barely worth mentioning, like momentarily losing his temper with an offensive line-man for hanging on to his shirt for dear life. More than one shame-lessly holding offensive tackle has felt a quiver of panic as the Minister of Defense came striding straight for him after a game, only to have Reggie offer a pained expression and one giant hand and say, "I had no business criticizing you out there, you're just doing your job." Like a giant who must always worry about breaking chairs or banging his head on the chandelier, Reggie is cautious with people. He treats those around him (except on the football field) like pieces of fine china.

In the same way, he's cautious about taking the lead. Despite his size and other heroic proportions, Reggie is not a born leader. He works at it. He studies the preachers he admires and the natural leaders he encounters. Take Jerome, for example. In some ways, Jerome stood for exactly those things Reggie preached against—living only for the moment, lusty and reckless pursuit of sinful pleasures—but Reggie not only loved Jerome, he *admired* him. He loved him for the natural virtues Jerome possessed in rich measure, his devotion to his parents and community, his joy in living, his natural affection for others. Reggie admired Jerome for his leadership. In some ways it was a mystery: How could Jerome, who seemed so careless about so many things, be such an effective motivator of men? Why were Jerome's teammates (including Reggie) so devoted to him? The answer, at least part of it, was that Jerome *didn't preach*. He made no effort to hide his faults or advertise his virtues. He lived large and drew others along in his wake. He was thoroughly and always himself. That was the key. Basically, Jerome was so damn good at being himself he made other people want to be like him. Reggie, on the other hand, had spent most of his young life preaching aggressively to people, whether they wanted to hear his message or not. He made a public show of his virtues.

But Reggie has changed—and Jerome is no small part of it. Not

that his beliefs have wavered. Not one bit. But Reggie's learned that
thrusting a well-worn Bible in someone's face sets them looking around
quickly for an exit. Whether leading people to Christ, or leading a
football team to a championship, Reggie has learned that speeches,
accusations, boasts, bluffs, insults, urgings, and clever quips will not
get the job done. He is, frankly, weary of it all. Sometimes he's even
weary of football itself. He might have stopped playing years ago were
it not for his religious beliefs and his wider personal ambitions. After
all, how important can a game be in a modern world beset by Satan?
In a godless city where young black men are murdering one another
nightly, selling drugs, living out doomed lives in a perpetual cycle of
poverty, crime, and prison, egged on by an evil culture glorifying
racial hatred and violence in rap music, TV, and graphic movies, and
where young black women, enslaved by social stereotypes, poverty,
ignorance, and a welfare system that destroys families, line up for the
privilege of allowing white doctors to kill their unborn babies? No,
Reggie's mind is wrestling with things far bigger than Seth's philosoph-
ical differences with Randall, the quarterback's moody persona and
quasi-heretical Cult of Self, or even Richie's blindered obsession with
the Game. There are times when Reggie feels like telling the whole
lot of them to grow up. But he checks himself. He mustn't put himself
above them, or anyone. He can understand all the tugs on his teammates, the pressures, jealousies, and temptations. He, too, loves the
game. Richie should be grateful for Reggie's nonverbal posture, because, truth is, he agrees with most of what Seth has to say—Norman
is a money-grubber, Richie *is* a puppet, Harry *is* an amateur—although
he cringes at his teammate's methods. Reggie leads by example. His
devotion is not to the Philadelphia Eagles, it's to Team, this fraternal
family, and to his own aspirations. The message conveyed by his calm
silence in the locker room and ferocity on the field is *Let's get this done.*

Actually, Reggie's own motives are more complex.

Jesus Christ is his first motivation. Fame and fortune offer Reggie
a platform to broadcast his fundamentalist faith, a solemn responsibility to spread the Word and save souls. Family is Reggie's second motivation. Born the bastard son of an itinerant semipro baseball player,
raised in a well-kept Chattanooga housing project by his grandmother
(and, when they were around, by a mother and an alcoholic stepfather),
mindful of the crisis in black families and in family values in general,
Reggie is devoted to his own wife and two children and determined
to provide not only for them, but for "my children's children's children." Pride is a third motivation—not blind Luciferian ego, but a
determination to live up to his personal goals, to that God-given potential. With all the gifts he has been given, Reggie, in all the years he

has been playing football, has yet to play on a championship team. He sees it as his one piece of unfinished business as an athlete and feels time running out for him. Love is the final motivation. Reggie has come to love his teammates, particularly Buddy's Boys on defense. He has been around long enough to realize how unique is the bond that Buddy gave them, and how unlikely it is that any of them will find it again. Buddy's firing, Jerome's death, and the coming whirlwind of free agency will destroy all that. Beyond this season, '92 (the number on his jersey—a coincidence or a sign?), Reggie knows that for this group, *his* Team, there will not be another chance.

And he knows he bears some responsibility for its dissolution. Reggie doesn't doubt that he has done the right thing, but in being the first to really challenge Norman, he helped stir the enmity most Eagles players feel toward the owner and management. In pursuing personal freedom in the football marketplace, he had played a key role in breaking down the gates. So this season, all of Reggie's dreams are centered foursquare: Christian empire, family dynasty, career goal, and his love for Team. To all this, Jerome's death has added a painful urgency, a reminder that chances run out. Reggie doesn't just want to go to the Super Bowl this year; he needs to go; he *intends* to go.

How can he express all these things? Reggie doesn't really try. To the never-ending parade of newshounds looking for a quote or sound bite he nearly always utters the expected thing. "The only important thing is to win," he'll say, or "We just have to make it work some kind of way," or "We all are just going to have to stay focused and play harder." To his teammates he'll invoke the name of Jerome, point out that they won't be getting another chance to go all the way together, and he has even spoken once or twice this season about his personal ambition to get a championship ring. Once a week he leads a Bible study group, practicing his ministry, trying to educate his teammates to the larger issues and responsibilities that absorb him, and lead them down the path of righteousness. But few of those who play with Reggie or write about him or comment on him nearly every day in the local media fully grasp the broader outline of the man. Reggie works on keeping first things first. He knows the foundation of his own success and goals is football, and each week during the season, that's where he keeps his focus. He knows that on the football field all that matters is hard work and divine favor. He delivers the former, week in and week out, and, for the latter . . . well, his whole life is a prayer.

Reggie concedes his physical gifts are not his doing. "I did not make myself six-five and three hundred pounds," he says. As a baby he was the size of a toddler, and as a grade-schooler, he looked like a teen. His mother, Thelma Collier, says she had to produce a birth certificate whenever she went to sign her second son up for sports, otherwise coaches wouldn't believe his age. He was also clumsy. Other children made fun of his splayfooted gait. They called him Big Foot and Goofy, and Reggie responded with Goliathan fits of anger.

With his mother and stepfather, Leonard Collier, with whom Reggie did not get along, he lived in the predominantly white, middle-class Chattanooga neighborhood of St. Elmo, but Reggie also lived much of the time with his grandmother Mildred Dodds (including an entire year when his mother moved with Leonard to Kansas and left her children behind). Asked to describe his childhood influences, Reggie will first name his grandmother. It was with Mildred that Reggie was exposed to Christianity. Mildred had two uncles of whom she was exceedingly proud who were Presbyterian ministers, and she faithfully attended a local Presbyterian church. The congregation was virtually all black, but the pastor was white. He ran programs for children, including hiking trips into the Appalachians. Reggie remembers the hikes, and talks with the minister, and his grandmother's strong faith, but recalls no blinding moment of revelation and Christian conversion, just an early and growing conviction that God was close by, calling him to a Christian life. It was like a tune he started hearing faintly as a child, and the volume grew slowly and steadily as the years went by. Coming up to bat in a baseball game at about age ten, Reggie remembers "testing" God by praying for a home run, and then hitting one . . . and feeling the warm breath of the divine down his neck as he rounded the bases. He was thirteen when a group of young evangelists knocked on his door, and he began studying the Bible with them. It was 1974, a time when there was a surge in youthful Pentecostal fervor all over America, and young Reggie got saved.

That's when he realized his life was set apart. He began carrying a Bible with him everywhere and confronting his classmates with the Word. He would preach his first sermon at age seventeen, before a congregation of ministers at St. John Baptist Church, and his family. His mother, who had never especially encouraged her son's evangelical calling, had to wonder at the young giant behind the lectern, wonder where he came from, and what had shaped him. It was hard not to see the hand of God in it. Indeed, Thelma believes she saw him at that moment bathed in an unearthly light. At school, he was regarded as a square and a freak, Bible-thumping Big Foot trying to save souls on the playground. He tried marijuana once, he says, and claims (not the first by any means) to have heard the voice of God. Only Reggie's voice warned him that if he continued to use drugs, he would die. His lapse into vice merely redoubled his fervor . . . and the ridicule by his classmates.

Sports became not just an outlet for Reggie's exuberant athleticism, but an avenue toward acceptance. His size and strength made him intimidating, but his conversion had mellowed him. Reggie prided himself on his self-control, on his ability to keep his once-furious temper in check. To his coaches, he seemed like a big ol' nice Sunday-school boy, more interested in making a good impression on his opponents than leaving his cleat prints on their backs. Robert Pulliam, the high-school football coach and a former high-school all-American football player himself, set about trying to toughen up his potential superstar.

Playing pickup basketball with Reggie and some other boys after school, the coach says, he went out of his way to rough the kid up: "I elbowed him, pushed him around, abused him." At first, his tactics did nothing but alienate Reggie. The school's athletic director complained to Pulliam about it, afraid it might accomplish nothing but chase the kid away from sports. Pulliam kept throwing elbows—"I was going to rile that kid up if it was the last thing I ever did." During a break in one session, the coach recalls, "Reggie looked over at me with big teary eyes, a real pitiful look."

"If you expect me to apologize to you, you had better get ready for your next whipping."

Reggie remembers rising to the occasion in a student-faculty basketball game, a different sort of conversion experience.

"I was determined I was going to rough him up more than he roughed me up," Reggie later told an interviewer. "I remember I knocked him on the floor a few times."

"From that day on," says Pulliam, "he was a holy terror."

Reggie had arrived at his own muscular brand of Christianity. "Christ is no wimp," he says. Reggie found that the respect he earned from his peers on the football field and basketball court carried over to the classroom and campus. People didn't necessarily line up to follow him, he still had a lot to learn about preaching, but the ridicule stopped. Reggie was like some mammoth, unstoppable force of nature. His convictions enhanced his stature. Years later, Reggie would perfect this synthesis of sports stardom and religious faith when he learned how much strength it took for someone rich and famous to lead a godly life. In his preaching now, at age thirty-one, he would exhort his listeners, "It takes a *man* to be a Christian and it takes a *woman* to be a Christian." He would shout it out like a challenge.

It was the PR department at the University of Tennessee who

dubbed him "the Minister of Defense," and where he laid the foundation for his future wealth and stardom. But Reggie remembers his
college years as a time when he was led astray. In violation of NCAA
rules, he accepted gifts from sports-program boosters and sold his
allotments of season tickets to raise spending money, and then later
lied about it in an affidavit when the association investigated. He neglected his studies, failed to get his degree, and failed to make the
most of his considerable intellect. Reggie says he got caught up in a
syndrome he calls the Self-Proclaimed Athlete, by which he means
he misplaced his Pentecostal perspective; he lost his humility, giving
himself credit for his amazing feats on the football field instead of
using his God-given stature to shout the name of the Lord. He began
to doubt his own calling, recognizing in his youthful fervor a desire
to draw attention to himself, to earn praise and recognition *for himself*.
Now he had more praise and recognition than he could have ever
dreamed. He didn't have to work at it especially. He was Reggie White,
the football star.

It was during this period when he met Sara, at church. She was
a student at East Tennessee State and filled with the evangelical spirit
that had long been Reggie's spur. She was a slight woman of uncom-
mon beauty and poise, and to Reggie, who had grown up seeing
himself as an oversized oaf, she was such a prize that for nearly two
years he couldn't bring himself to mention his feelings. Instead, he
volunteered to help with her Christian work. During that time they
exchanged letters and saw each other as coworkers in the Campus
Crusade for Christ. It wasn't until Reggie's senior year, when he was
one of the most sought-after college players in the country, that they
acknowledged romance. When the USFL offered Reggie a $3 million
contract to play five years for their Memphis Showboats, Sara transferred to Memphis State to be with him. They were married in January
of '85.

Reggie played two seasons for the Showboats, including eighteen
games in '85 before he jumped the sinking USFL ship and signed with
the Eagles. He played thirteen more games that year with the NFL.
His arrival in the higher-profile league, along with his new $1.6 million,
four-year contract with the Eagles (who had paid an additional $1
million to the Showboats to buy out the remainder of Reggie's contract), immediately placed him with Wes Hopkins and other Eagles
stars at the top of the pro game. But at the same time Reggie reached
this peak in his career, he was embroiled in crisis in his personal life
and faith. Part of the Self-Proclaimed Athlete syndrome involved, of
course, the Sis-Boom-Bimbos, to whose attractions even the Minister

of Defense was not immune. He refers to the experience now only as "a dark time, a hard time."

"In the same way I had to learn about marijuana, I had to learn that if I wasn't careful about women, they would destroy me," he says. "I didn't know nothin' about AIDS then, but I knew that if I wasn't careful about women, I was going to die. If I wasn't a born-again Christian, I'd probably right now be divorced, I'd have left my children . . . I'd have gotten involved in all kind of mess."

At roughly the same time, there were revelations about his role in NCAA rules violations back at Tennessee. Reggie came clean publicly. His revelations, along with others, landed his alma mater's football program on probation.

He grew through these ordeals. He salvaged his marriage and felt he had rediscovered the deeper source and purpose of his success. It made his coming battle with the Philadelphia Eagles, and eventually the whole NFL, something akin to a personal crusade.

"Everything with Reggie is personal," says his agent, Jim Sexton. "It's not just business. It's personal."

Reggie's feud with Norman started two years after the defensive end joined the team, during the strike. Reggie was in the front ranks of the strikers, a veritable symbol of what a joke the scab games were—reminding the fans that what they were paying to see in the NFL was, after all, not just football, but the best. And just as Norman, the relatively novice owner, took the players' strike and fans' support (along with the tacit endorsement of city police) as a personal affront, Reggie saw the matter through his own rigid religious and moral prism. What the owners were trying to do, in Reggie's eyes, was akin to perpetuating slavery. What you had was an all-white, wealthy club of owners exploiting the God-given talents of their players, who were mostly black. The League as slave plantation was a hard sell publicly, given the $600,000 or so Reggie himself would make that year, but it made sense to the players, who could see in the escalating salaries of unrestricted baseball players something like their true worth. They were, after all, the attraction. Reggie lent a moral righteousness to the picket line that rubbed Norman the wrong way. What the owner saw was a rabble of overpaid, egomaniacal young athletes who owed their wealth and fame to the marketing genius and capital of men like himself. In any showdown of who needed each other more, the League had the clear upper hand. The strike was a failure, but it crystallized Reggie's understanding of his own value and ambition. What he and the other players had failed to accomplish collectively, Reggie set out to accomplish for himself.

He established himself quickly as the premier defensive player in the league. He had twenty-one quarterback sacks in the strike season, the second-highest total in league history, and he'd done it in just twelve games. He started in the Pro Bowl for the second time (he'd been the game's MVP in '86). And yet Reggie's contract, to which he was bound for another full season, didn't even place his salary among the top-thirty defensive linemen in the game. The Eagles, to their credit, recognized the disparity and sat down in January of '88 to renegotiate. But when Reggie reviewed the old contract with his agent, he was shocked to discover how little of it he had properly understood. He learned that the $1 million insurance policy the team had taken out on him at the signing didn't name Sara and his son as beneficiaries, it named the team! And he discovered that the four-year contract gave the Eagles an option (Norman was always good with options on the back end) for a fifth year at just 10 percent salary increase.

Of course, Reggie had signed the thing. He bore ultimate responsibility for what he had failed to recognize or understand. But on this count, Reggie had another beef. Back in '85, he had been represented by a stylish former corporate public relations man named Patrick Forté, who, just months after the deal was done, was hired by Norman as an assistant to club president Harry Gamble. Put together the insurance policy, the fifth-year option, and the hire, and Reggie smelled conspiracy. He remembered, he said, a point in the negotiations at which the owner had told Forté, "When this is over, there's a job for you here."

Harry was mortified at the suggestion that he and the club had misled Reggie. He had been completely candid about the $1 million insurance policy, he argued. The Eagles had coughed up $1 million to buy out the Memphis Showboats' contract, a rare and unusual expenditure. None of the Eagles' player contracts was guaranteed, so if Reggie was seriously hurt, killed, or otherwise incapacitated in something other than a football-related event, the contract was over. Reggie's $1.6 million was something he would earn over four seasons, game by game. Not so the $1 million buyout. Reggie could die in a plane crash the next day, and the Eagles would be out a cool mil. So Harry had done the prudent thing; he'd insured the club's investment in the athlete. Was it his fault that Reggie hadn't understood? As for hiring Forté, he was a talented and experienced black executive, and everybody in corporate America knew how sought after a man like that was. Norman, to his credit, was conscious of the disgraceful lack of minority representation in the corporate ranks of the League and had done something about it, for God's sake! Was he now going to be taken to task for it?

So instead of a friendly contract extension acknowledging Reggie's remarkable contribution, the club found itself mired in a rancorous dispute with its star player that dragged on through the '88 season and on into the summer of '89. Reggie began publicly calling Norman a liar, portraying him as nothing more than a shrewd merchant bent on milking the franchise, not winning championships—a Pharisee in the temple of the Game. From the lips of the fundamentalist minister, few could miss the anti-Semitic flavor of his characterization—Norman sure as hell didn't miss it. The irony of it was that Reggie began questioning Norman's commitment to fielding a winning football team at precisely the moment when Norman began fielding a winning football team. But coupled with Buddy's contempt for the dilettante car dealer, the Guy in France, Norman found himself stereotyped, vilified, and effectively ostracized from *his own goddamn football team!*

Norman underestimated Reggie. He thought the defensive end was a dumb athlete and a hypocrite. If he'd gotten to know Reggie personally, he would have had a harder time dismissing the Reverend's very public evangelical role as a pose (it clearly was not), and he most certainly would not have found Reggie stupid. The truth is that Norman and Reggie had much in common. They were both driven, highly successful family men with broad interests and ambitions that spilled way outside the original dimensions of their success. Just as young Norman had seen the millions he made with Bargaintown USA, PP&C, and eventually the Florida car dealerships as a means of building a personal financial empire and even a political career, Reggie saw the millions he could make playing football, and the fame, as a means of fulfilling his larger religious and social agenda. Out there in Life after Football, Reggie hadn't ruled out the idea of entering politics. And, in keeping with his stern fundamentalist convictions, Reggie was politically conservative. A Republican even. The modern politician he most admired happened to be Norman's very own good friend and political grantee, Jack Kemp, President Bush's secretary of Housing and Urban Development.

But Norman and Reggie never really got acquainted. Face-to-face, on the relatively few occasions they met, both men observed a fitting mutual show of respect. But word got back to Reggie about Norman's real opinion of him, which fed his distrust. By the summer of '89 (Reggie had led the NFL again in sacks and started in his third Pro Bowl), they were headed for an ugly showdown in court. The Pack was salivating at the prospect. Norman and Harry and Patrick Forté would all have had to testify under oath; the inner workings of the organization would be laid bare; there would have been weeks of juicy revelations and discord. But Norman spoiled the fun. He backed

down. Rather than enter the '89 season locked in legal battle with his
star defensive performer, coming off a year when the Eagles had won
their division and made it to the play-offs for the first time in seven
seasons, when fan interest was going through the roof, Norman settled.
He and Reggie agreed on a new contract in the chambers of U.S.
District Court Judge Charles Weiner the morning the matter was
scheduled to be heard. Reggie became the highest-paid defensive
player in NFL history, with a fully guaranteed, three-year $6.1 million
contract.

Norman promptly forfeited any opportunity to build some goodwill on this solid ground by fining Reggie $29,000 for missing training
camp.

Reggie's teammates were all watching and taking notes through
his contract ordeal. They figured, if it took *Reggie White* a year and a
half of ill will and a trip to the federal courthouse to get paid what
he was worth, what could they expect?

The millions in that contract enabled Reggie to get started in
earnest on his ministry to the black urban underclass. On weekends,
he and Sara and some of his teammates would set up loudspeakers
on the asphalt parking lots outside Philadelphia or Camden housing
projects, and he would preach:

> I'm tired of drugs infiltrating the community! I'm tired
> of seeing young people die! . . . Especially in the inner-city
> communities. How Satan is destroying the inner-city com-
> munities! The reason we're here today is, we're *tired* of sitting
> back watching! . . . It's time for some *men* to stand up and
> start being accountable! We're going to run the devil out of
> here! . . . And we're going to *impact* people's lives!

His efforts were universally praised, but there was more than an
inoffensive call to prayer and goodness in Reggie's message. His beliefs
and ambitions were politically charged, and they had a dark side. They
were rooted as much on racial anger and suspicion as "turn the other
cheek." He believed, for instance, that birth control and abortion were
white supremacist plots, based on "Nazi racist ideas," designed to gradually eliminate "the unfit" from the earth. If you sat Reggie down and
probed, it was clear these were not just passing notions. He'd done
some research. Birth-control pioneer and feminist Margaret Sanger,
founder of Planned Parenthood, was, in Reggie's view, motivated not
by the deaths and mutilations of young women forced to seek out
illegal abortionists, but by eugenics—"If you read some of the strong
statements she made, she was concerned with promoting 'strong

genes,' which to her meant white Northern European genes, and weeding out 'weak genes,' by which she meant blacks, Catholics, Hispanics, Asians, and the disabled and retarded." Reggie believed that there was little benevolent in the motivations of those who established the social welfare programs in America during the New Deal; instead he saw a racist conspiracy to destroy black families, undermine black manhood. And these weren't just the doings of evil men, they were the handiwork of Satan himself, who for Reggie was not just a metaphor, but a living, lurking, lying demon, busily harvesting unwary souls. Reggie was intrigued by the "repressed memory" trials going on all over America, in which otherwise ordinary folk were testifying to bizarre sexual practices, Satanic rituals involving the slaughter of babies and animals, blood drinking. What many suspected was a form of mass hysteria, a modern outbreak of the emotions and superstitions that produced the Salem witch trials, Reggie saw as proof positive that Satan walks among us. Living as a Christian wasn't just a matter of leading a virtuous, loving life. Reggie had an agenda for combating Satan. He talked of turning the United States into a fundamentalist Christian theocracy, of using the power of government to "return this country to a godly path." He believed the U.S. government ought to pay reparations to black Americans. Reggie knew that many of his beliefs and goals outside football would force him into politics, either as a candidate or kingmaker. There's no doubt he would be a formidable contender, with his fame, his charisma, and his growing bounty.

Reggie was also untroubled by Christ's caution: *It is easier for a camel to go through the eye of a needle, than for a rich man to enter the kingdom of God.* His announced ambition in life was to become "a billionaire."

"Why?" he asks. "Because I'll probably give most of it away to good causes." Then he adds, with a meaty chuckle, "I can live off five hundred million dollars."

Indeed, Reggie's Baptist faith was a thoroughly Americanized Christianity, one that had absorbed the license of Calvinism without its stern face—one's wealth and public stature were reflections of God's grace, not worldly temptations leading away from the path of righteousness. Get Rich Quick was an earthly parallel to Get Saved Quick— *Just raise your hands, brothers and sisters, and step up front if you hear the call!* Reggie pursued with equal fervor his causes and his appetite for living well. He drove a Mercedes to his preaching engagements. Alongside the house he and Sara built outside Knoxsville to house unwed pregnant women, offering them an alternative to abortion, they had built a palatial home for themselves in the shadow of the Great

Smoky Mountains. He was working with a coalition of businessmen to set up organizations in Philadelphia and Knoxsville that would provide low-income mortgage loans and job counseling for the inner-city poor, but at the same time he was using his football fame to earn millions more endorsing products. Reggie drew the line at some things. He would not endorse beer or tobacco products and withdrew himself annually from competition for NFL Defensive Lineman of the Year because the award is sponsored by a brewery. He had his face taken off the Eagles' annual calendar because of sponsorship from a beer manufacturer. He refused to participate in any promotion that played on the theme of Halloween, because Reggie felt the tradition was grounded in Satanism. There was never a moment when Reggie's face appeared on screen, or when a microphone was thrust in his face, when he did not praise Jesus and publicly thank God.

His life was, in a sense, a heartfelt performance, and it was an act that all his teammates admired and respected, but that few could actually follow. Norman's feelings about Reggie's agenda ranged between uncomfortable and appalled. Norman had a lifelong distaste for displays of public piety, and, as a Jewish man, he was understandably uncomfortable with the whole Christian fundamentalist agenda of promoting a more "godly" life—whose God? He felt sure that Reggie was driven not by religious fervor but by good old-fashioned pre-Christian greed. To Reggie's face, Norman was always polite and friendly, and the owner had the same respect any football fan had for Reggie's accomplishments on the field, but as for the rest, he believed that no matter what Reggie preached, the Big Dawg's bottom line was money, and nothing else. When, after the season, the Reverend talked about wanting to sign with a team that would best enable him to further his ministry, and told the Pack he was "waiting for a sign from God" to tell him where next to play, Norman said, "He'll sign with whoever offers him the most money. Watch."

This dynamic had set the tone for the relationship of owner to Team every bit as much as the feud between Norman and Buddy. Reggie had his own reasons for playing his heart out, and for feeling affection for the silver-winged green uniforms, but he did and felt those things *despite* the organization that paid him millions. At the press conference where his new contract was announced in '89, seated alongside Harry, Reggie was asked if he thought the protracted contract haggle and legal maneuvering he had been through would have happened with any other NFL team.

"No" was his crisp response.

No. Reggie knew his days with the Eagles were done when this '92 season was over. The lawsuit on which he was lead plaintiff had opened the door to free agency for himself and 298 other NFL veterans. He knew Norman wouldn't bid for him. And he knew that even if he landed next year on some Super Bowl contender, and finally got his ring wearing some other team's colors, it would never feel the same as it would winning with these guys he had come to love, winning for Buddy, and for Jerome. Reggie had felt a part of this team like no other in his long career. His primary motivations—Christian empire, family dynasty, personal pride—would demand he go elsewhere when this season was done, but the last of them, the Team, that would be gone forever.

So this is it. Now or never, do or die. They beat the Washington Redskins, and they make the play-offs. Reggie is going to play this game like a man, quite literally, on a mission from God.

OUTWARDLY, at least, all is calm in the Eagles' locker room in advance of the big Redskins game. Richie hasn't breathed a public word of his fury over Seth's insulting and divisive remarks, and after Seth's public nonapology the issue subsides. Randall has had a new collection of snazzy $1,500 suits delivered to the locker room and amuses himself between practices and team meetings by trying them on.

This same week, Richie stops Randall to tell him that the thousand-dollar check he wrote to pay his fine for skipping out of the hotel is insufficient.

"It's two thousand dollars," the coach says.

"Sure," says Randall, with a shrug, as if to say *All the same to me.*

"It'll be double if you do it again," Richie says.

"Don't fine me next time," Randall suggests conspiratorially. "If you catch me again, just tell me, and I'll give *you* the two thousand dollars."

Richie is insulted. "I don't want your money," the coach says.

Jolly Mike Golic has a smile back on his face; he's been penciled in once more as a starter. Sad-eyed Antone Davis is quietly marking the days till his rematch with Charles Mann, the Redskins' all-pro defensive end who had so humiliated him on national TV the year before. Keith Jackson, down in his new Miami locker room, notes to reporters that both the Dolphins and the Eagles have 9–5 records and says he's looking forward to meeting his old teammates in the Super Bowl.

Wes Hopkins wants to play—badly. He's been sitting out since midway through the Niners game, and the left knee feels better. He's parked before his locker at midweek, pulling on socks and absently rubbing the crooked, scarred joint.

"Are you going to heal in time to play Sunday?" a hound asks him.

"I don't know," he says, looking up from underneath his thick black eyebrows. "I have no idea."

"Will you need an operation when the season is over?"

"Yeah, he's [Dr. Vince] gonna scope me."

"So, the reason you wouldn't get the scope now is it will definitely sit you down for the rest of the year, and you're still waiting to see if it'll get better enough for you to play?"

"Yeah, that's it," says Wes. "Only it's a little more complicated than that."

"Really? What am I missing?"

"Naw, I can't talk about it," says the veteran free safety.

What Wes can't discuss is a little negotiation taking place this week between his agent, Harry, and (of course) Norman. Whether or not Wes plays on Sunday has less to do with how his knee will feel after today's jog—Wes knows by now exactly how it will feel—than with what kind of answer he gets from the club.

Wes is in the final year of his contract, and his future, with the Eagles or anywhere in football, is far from certain. Life after Football is staring Wes in the eyes. He'll make $815,000 this season, and it's safe to say that without his college degree or any working experience outside football, his days of big earnings are numbered.

The knee joint just won't heal. It hurts when he runs and pivots on it, and it swells up painfully after any exertion. The joint is basically stable. He has reasonably good flexion and extension. Dr. Vince says he can play on it without aggravating the injury. But back in '86, when the joint felt like this, Wes had pressed on and played, with disastrous consequences. Mindful of how skeptical coaches had been after his earlier surgery and rehab, he knows now, at thirty-one, a setback like that would end his career. This isn't just Wes's hunch either. He's been to see another knee specialist, who disagrees with Dr. Vince. Wes's independent doctor tells him the knee is far more likely to blow now than if it were scoped and fully healed. Still, with the season coming down to this one big game, Wes feels the tug of his teammates and hears the unspoken urging of his coaches and trainers—*You can play*. The team has been hurting badly up the middle since both he and Andre stopped playing this season. They've got John Booty, a cornerback, trying to play Wes's spot, and Rich Miano, a backup free safety, playing Andre's spot at strong safety. Both are probably better in pass coverage than Wes and Andre, but neither carries the same weight or wallop, which is why opponents have been running the ball on the Eagles with more ease. Facing a well-rounded running and passing attack like the Redskins', the club strongly feels the need of Wes on the field.

But the risk is just too great. Wes feels he can play another two or even three seasons if the knee gets scoped before any more serious damage is done. But he's already made up his mind that if the Eagles make it to the Super Bowl, he's going to have Dr. Vince shoot it up with painkillers and play. "That's the last big goal in my career," he says. "Even if I never get to play another football game."

For any of these games on the road to the Super Bowl, however, Wes isn't going to take the risk. Instead, he comes up with a plan. He tells his agent, Harry Himes, to make the Eagles an offer: Wes will shoot up his knee and play on it *if* they'll offer him, right now, a guaranteed contract for the '93 season. The way Wes sees it, it's a fair trade. If he plays on the knee with no contract, he's risking the rest of his career; the Eagles risk nothing.

Himes thinks it's a bad idea and tells Wes.

"You shouldn't be playing on that knee, period," he says. But Wes is adamant, and Himes reluctantly approaches Harry Gamble with the proposal.

Norman doesn't see it the way Wes does. The club politely refuses to renegotiate, and that's that as far as Harry Himes and Wes are concerned—he won't be playing. What they don't know is that Norman is furious. Here's how the owner sizes up the situation: (1) the Eagles' season is on the line, it's now or never; (2) the single biggest setbacks to his team this year, apart from Jerome's death, have been the injuries to Andre and Wes; (3) Dr. Vince and the trainers say Wes could be playing, the knee is not that bad; (4) he's paying Wes $815,000 to play; (5) Wes says he'll only play if Norman gives him a guaranteed contract for next season? *Wait just an all-pro minute!*

Norman tells Harry, "If the doctor says he can play on the knee, he should be playing; that's what we're paying him for. If the doctors say he can't play, then he shouldn't be playing on the knee no matter what we're paying him!"

Wes's proposal, coming at this critical hour, smacks to Norman of an ultimatum. Wes and his agent don't know it yet, but Norman has resolved that Wes Hopkins, previously one of his favorites, will never play another down in an Eagles' uniform after this season.

SIXTY-SIX TIMES Reggie hurls himself into the Redskins' backfield on Sunday afternoon, a wet, cold, gray winter outing on the unforgiving plastic turf. Sixty-six times he crouches low in his three-point stance and charges into two, sometimes three, enormous Washington blockers. Again and again and again he comes up short, gets knocked down, held, chop-blocked, spun in circles, hit high and low and from both sides. On the stat sheet when the game is over, it will record Reggie's contribution as just one tackle, one sack. Some football pundit five states away will look at those tallies and conclude that Reverend Reggie is slipping, that he hadn't had that good a game.

Right.

Never mind that both Seth and Clyde also sack Redskins' quarterback Mark Rypien, in large part because of all the manpower the Skins are using to stave off Reggie. Or that Rypien throws two interceptions because all hell is breaking loose around him and he has to hurry his throw. Or that when it's over, even though Reggie hasn't figured obviously in any of the major plays of the game, the three words that keep coming up in both locker rooms are *that Reggie White.*

Like when the Skins finally get down into scoring range early in the second quarter. The game is scoreless, and Washington is stuck at third down on the Eagles' sixteen-yard line. Clearly Rypien is going to pass, so to help hold back the Eagles' charge, Washington has two tight ends in the game and a running back to stay in and help block. Fighting off two blockers, Reggie chases Rypien out of the pocket and then crushes into him at the same time defensive end Mike Flores arrives from the other direction. The weak throw Rypien manages to flip away before getting nailed goes for just five yards, and the Skins have to settle for a twenty-nine-yard field goal.

Washington threatens another touchdown late in the first half, up 10–3, but has to settle for a field goal—again in large part because of Reggie. All through the first half the Reverend has been double-teamed by tackle Ed Simmons and tight end Ron Middleton. So Bud Carson decides to toy with the Skins' blocking scheme. He sends Seth on a blitz inside, and with both big men preoccupied with Reggie, the linebacker sacks Rypien for an eleven-yard loss. Six plays later, Seth lines up in the same spot, and this time Simmons squares off to block the linebacker's charge, thereby violating one of the basic rules of playing the Eagles—never block Reggie White with one man, but if you must, *absolutely never* try to do it with a tight end.

After thirtysome fruitless charges at the quarterback, Reggie spots the opportunity instantly. Middleton is big for a tight end, and a good blocker, but Reggie's got him by three inches and thirty pounds— *Make ready, Jesus is coming!* The Reverend charges straight upfield about five yards at the snap, plants his big left foot, and clubs Middleton, whose momentum is backward, with his right arm. The tight end goes flying in the direction of the mothballed fleet of navy warships downriver from the Vet. Reggie folds Rypien in a hardy Christian embrace and escorts him to the turf. It's another four-yard loss, and, more important, it reasserts the imperative of blocking Reggie with more than one man. Washington kicks a forty-one-yard field goal and leads at halftime 13–7.

But this is looking more and more like the Eagles' day. Randall comes out after halftime and leads a seven-play, eighty-yard touch-down drive that gives Philadelphia a one-point lead. They improve on that in the fourth quarter when Vai Sikahema returns a punt forty-seven yards, all the way down to the Skins' twenty-five-yard line, which sets up a field goal.

So with three and a half minutes left in the game, Washington now needs a touchdown. If they fail, the Eagles make the play-offs. The Skins will still have a backdoor shot at postseason, but it will depend on their winning next week and the right teams' losing—their destiny will no longer be in their own hands.

Forced into a cautious deep-zone defense to prevent a big-play disaster, Bud leaves open the middle of the field, and Rypien chips away expertly, notching gains of ten yards, eight yards, twelve yards, eight yards, and then a nineteen-yard catch and run by Ricky Ervins that puts the Skins on the Eagles' thirty-one-yard line with just over a minute remaining.

Richie's offense is standing on the bench waving white towels at the crowd, trying to notch up the noise level a decibel or two, which doesn't seem possible. Reggie is still setting up and charging into his blockers, driving one backward and off balance, only to spin into the bulk of another. It's a study in frustration and heart.

The Skins get another first down, and with thirty-five seconds on the play clock and no more time-outs, the game has come down to two or three final shots at the end zone. All of the hope, energy, and excitement of an entire season in this football-crazed city is focused now on these final plays. The noise has achieved the level of a constant horrific roar.

The Skins have to throw, because a running play would eat up the remainder of the clock. So Bud has his linebackers dropping, and his pass defenders in five zones, Eric, Booty, and Miano inside, and Mark McMillian and Otis guarding the outside:

First and ten on the Eagles' twenty (thirty-five seconds): Byron Evans takes a lunging slap at a Rypien pass to Ervins, and the ball skitters on the wet turf.

Second and ten on the Eagles' twenty (thirty-two seconds): Near disaster. Otis is supposed to line up on the ten-yard line and protect against a pass route to the left corner of the end zone. He has Booty sliding over deep, so if Clark turns and heads for the corner, he'll be sandwiched—Otis in front of him and Booty behind him—with almost no chance of catching the ball. Only, Otis screws up. Instead of staying with Clark as the veteran receiver begins his cut toward the corner, Otis hesitates, watching the quarterback. By the time he pivots and chases Clark, Rypien has an open receiver in the end zone. He lays the pass out in front of Clark, who dives, his body parallel to the turf, and for a brief instant he has the winning catch in both hands. But he drops it. Otis leaps for joy (as well he should), and Clark sits cursing his hands in the end zone.

Third and ten on the Eagles' twenty (twenty-six seconds): The Skins try the same pattern on the other side of the field, only McMillian, the rookie, plays the coverage to perfection. Rypien sees his receiver sandwiched and throws the ball out of the end zone.

Fourth and ten on the Eagles' twenty (twenty-one seconds): This is it, or so it seems. The roaring continues like a bottled hurricane. Settled back in their zones, the Eagles' defenders figure Rypien has to throw for the end zone. With no time-outs, any running play will eat up the clock. Reggie mounts his charge one last time, bull-rushing back into the wide frames of Simmons and Middleton—and this time breaking through. Rypien quickly flips the ball to Ervins, who crashes upfield five yards, ten yards, fifteen yards . . . until he runs into Seth, who flattens him five yards shy of the goal line!

Victory!

The bottled hurricane comes uncorked, and an army of hearts leap for joy along with the Eagles' players and coaches. Booty, in the heat of the moment, scoops the game ball off the turf and runs upfield with the trophy, only . . . the refs are waving their arms wildly. They want the ball back! Players look up to see the clock stopped at seven seconds.

The rules say that with the first down the clock stops just long enough for the officials to spot the ball. There wouldn't have been enough time for Rypien to reassemble his offense fifteen yards downfield and run another play, except for Booty's exuberant gesture. By picking up the ball, he's forced the refs to stop the clock for five, ten, fifteen seconds, long enough for the Redskins to line up and snap the ball.

First and goal on the Eagles' five (seven seconds): Rypien flings it at the turf and stops the clock with just two seconds remaining.

Second and goal on the Eagles' five (two seconds): There's no time to be disheartened, to chew out Booty or curse fate. Washington is going to get one more shot. Right now. There is a sinking feeling in the Vet. The Redskins are *so close*. The Eagles' season has come down to this one play—keep Rypien from completing a pass into the end zone.

Reggie assumes his three-point stance one last time, again summoning every ounce of energy for the charge. Bud calls for complex man/zone coverage. Seth has the tight end. Eric has Art Monk, the NFL's all-time leading receiver. Miano has the deep end of the right side of the end zone; McMillian has the right side flat, so any receiver heading for the right corner will be sandwiched between them, and McMillian will have anyone in the flat in front of him. On the left side, Otis has Gary Clark, who dropped the game winner just a few plays back. Rypien is right-handed, and he's got most of his receivers to the right, so Reggie knows the ball is most likely coming to his side.

What happens next takes all of three or four seconds to unfold. At the snap, Monk runs to the right corner, which frees up Eric (he knows Miano and McMillian will pick him up in the corner). Sanders goes to the right flat, in front of McMillian. On the left side, Clark heads upfield, and then slices to his right across the end zone—meanwhile, Reggie has hurdled the attempted cut block by Middleton and swooped down on Rypien, who had wanted to roll out to his right. Instead, the quarterback has to duck Reggie and step forward, abandoning the original design of the play, and is now looking frantically for someplace to throw the ball. Rypien knows he's got just a split second before Reggie clobbers him, and in that instant he sees his favorite receiver, Clark, squatting in the end zone, toward the front, in line with the goalpost.

Clark has gotten open. Otis is a step too far behind him, and Booty is two steps too deep. The smart receiver drops to his knees in front of Booty, giving Rypien a clear low target. Rypien hurriedly releases the ball, which wobbles slightly in its trajectory—Clyde leaps and brushes it with one finger (not enough to deflect it)—and it is at this precise moment that the entire six months of hard work by forty-seven pro players, twelve coaches, all the confident orchestrations of multimillionaire Norman Braman and the club's management staff, the emotional urgency of Jerome's sudden death (the Eagles had invited Jerome's dad to say a few words in the locker room before this game), not to mention the cheerful dreams of millions of Eagles fans all over Philadelphia and the nation, come to turn on the well-oiled, highly paid synapses of twenty-seven-year-old Eric Allen.

In that same split second, having been freed by Monk's corner route, Eric makes a instant, all-pro calculation. Years of experience and hours of film study have taught him that, in a pinch, Rypien will always look for Clark. When he sees Rypien thrown off balance by

Reggie's rush, Eric breaks toward Clark. There's no thought process involved here; it's all reflex. The fact that Rypien is going to throw the ball to Clark is simply hardwired someplace deep in the cornerback's motor cortex. And in the precise millisecond that the fluttery pass arrives at the fingertips of Clark's eager reach, Eric's right hand arrives to smack the ball straight to the turf.

"Wow!" shouts CBS announcer Pat Summerall.

Eric races downfield with both arms held high, soaking up the deserved loud approval of the home fans.

In slow motion it's a thing of beauty, as if choreographed by some benevolent angel (Jerome?). From the camera behind the end zone you can see it unfold all at once, Reggie throwing Rypien off pace, the hurried pass, Clyde's outstretched hand, and, in the foreground, Eric streaking (you can actually see him break back toward Clark before Rypien lets go of the ball) right out of the frame. A side angle completes the view, the ball descending toward the kneeling Clark's outstretched hands, Eric's body hurtling toward the camera, his reaching, then slapping down the ball just as it arrives.

Bud Carson breathes into his headset, speaking to his assistant Peter Guinta upstairs, "Did you see that?"

All their planning, teaching, diagramming, and cunning—and it comes down to one great player making an instinctive play. Booty and Otis had both allowed Clark to slip in between them. If Rypien has time to throw the ball crisply, it's a touchdown. Credit Reggie's sixty-sixth bull-rush of the afternoon with disrupting that. But the pass was still on target. Eric had to guess where Rypien would throw the ball and move towards it in the same instant—a split second later would have been too late. The photo on the front page of the next day's newspaper will show Clark kneeling in the end zone, staring at his hands, the ball bouncing off the turf underneath his grasp, and Eric still airborne, hand outstretched.

"And they say baseball is a game of inches!" shouts color man John Madden. "Rypien wanted to roll out, get outside, but Reggie forced him to stop there, and when he stopped he saw Clark . . . and Eric Allen comes up with one of the biggest plays of his life!"

Winning cures all ills on a contentious football team. Today's win can't be credited to any one facet of the squad alone; all contributed, offense, defense, and special teams. Randall played well. Antone didn't allow Charles Mann a single shot at the quarterback. "I had my experience that one Monday night," he says, "and I'll never let that happen to me again." Vai Sikahema's heroic punt return set up the winning points, Roger Ruzek's field goals provided the margin of victory, and Reggie and Eric saved the game in the final seconds.

"Lord, we thank you for the competition," prays the Reverend immediately after the game, down on one knee on the field, hands joined with players from both teams. "We thank you for allowing us to do what we do. We thank you for the love you have given us."

Captured on camera coming off the field, Randall delivers his own postscript to the national TV audience.

"This is what it's all about, man," he says. "Before the game I said, 'Lord, when we win the game, I will praise your name.' We got out of this one. God is always with us. Always remember that. God is with us."

As opposed, presumably, to the Redskins.

THERE IS SAD NEWS waiting for Reverend Reggie when he comes home that night. His stepfather, Leonard Collier, has been found dead, beaten to death with a hammer in the front seat of his Ford Fairlane, outside the rec center in Chattanooga where Reggie got his start.

"They don't know who did it," he says, talking to a hound the night after the game. "He wasn't doin' nothin' wrong. They think he was robbed."

Reggie had never gotten along with his stepfather, a slender man with aviator glasses who married his mother when Reggie was just seven. Collier had battled the bottle all of his life.

On the flight to Chattanooga the next morning, Reggie struggles with this new tragedy. It doesn't touch him the way Jerome's death did, but it stirs up old feelings of guilt, anger, and now remorse. The events in Reggie's life, from the trivial to the profound, are perceived as lessons from above. Reading his feelings now, Reggie is at first surprised by the remorse, then saddened. He realizes that he has spent most of his life condemning his stepfather, looking down at him— how could he not? Reggie has become a success in life beyond even his own wildest imaginings, and here was this troubled, inadequate man who stepped between Reggie and his mother, who was supposed to assume the role of father. For most of his life, Reggie has been embarrassed by his stepfather, and because of that embarrassment and even contempt, he now realizes he's never been able to connect with him. He's never been able to show him the way.

Reggie has learned not to condemn his teammates for their failings. He has been deeply concerned all this season, for instance, with what Wes and Seth have done to their wives and children. Erika and Sara have grown closer through the ordeal. Erika attends the weekly Bible study classes. They have reached out to Jennifer. But Wes and

Seth aren't interested in Reggie's views on their personal lives. He can't reach them, and he knows getting in their face and saying "Man, you need to get your life right and stop doing this!" won't work. And his two defensive teammates aren't the only ones. His Bible study classes are now littered with jilted wives and girlfriends. Randall's ex-girlfriend Rose still comes. Reggie feels surrounded by the wreckage of the Self-Proclaimed Athlete lifestyle. It is something he has wrestled with all season, and he has finally come to accept there is only so much he can do.

Yet this wisdom had arrived too late for his relationship with Collier, his stepfather, now brutally slain. Reggie sees a divine hand in the coincidental events. At the very moment he is riding high with victory, being credited with a big part in saving the day, the Lord finds a way to bring him low, reminding him of a serious personal failing.

In his days in Chattanooga for the funeral, Reggie resolves he will never again miss a chance to connect with a fellow human being. He will no longer judge people's failings. He will accept even the lowest of characters with a full Christian heart, embrace the alcoholic, befriend the adulterer, accept the addict, the homosexual (Reggie considers homosexuality a grievous sin). . . .

This is all weighing on the Reverend as he flies home later in the week to play what will almost certainly be his last game as an Eagle in the Vet. His stepfather, his personal failure, pending free agency, all this is on his mind. At a team meeting before the regular season's final game, a now-meaningless contest against the Giants, Reggie starts talking about all these things, until he's cut short by Eric.

"Where's your head at, Reggie?" the cornerback asks.

Teammates don't usually challenge him. It's as if somebody has whacked him over the head.

In two weeks, in the New Orleans Superdome, this group of Eagles players will have their last chance to make it happen. It's no time to lose focus. The season, the JeromeQuest, the Christian empire, family dynasty, professional pride—all of it comes down now to a single-elimination tournament. Win three play-off games and you've made the Show. Win the Show, the Super Bowl, and you accomplish it all; you plant your flag on the top of the mountain.

Football, man. Reggie thanks his teammate and puts the rest of the universe, swirling in his head, to rest—at least for the next few weeks.

16

MARCHING IN . . .

No, Reverend Reggie decides against sharing the full range of his thoughts and emotions with his teammates now, down ten points at halftime in the New Orleans Superdome.

It's the same old story. All the emotion, all the energy, all the hours of preparation, the pain and frustration of five losses, the joy of eleven wins, all of it was expended just to get themselves here, at the starting line, and now they're playing poorly against the Saints, a team they can beat. The offense has made one big play, Randall's touchdown bomb to Fred, and that's it. They've earned just three first downs (the Saints have 14). And the defense . . . well, today, once again, they haven't done enough.

It could change, though. They had all seen it happen, seen their fortunes in a hapless contest suddenly turn. It didn't have to come on a touchdown or interception or even a big play. It might happen because of something one teammate said at precisely the right moment, or some gesture one of them made, or some inspiring extra burst of desire—the burners would ignite, and off they'd go. You couldn't make a moment like that happen, although you could see guys all around straining to do so. Right now, Reggie is listening to Andre, standing in his gray wool parka in the center of the room raising the roof in an effort to whip the bird into flight, begging for that chance to take a shot at Emmitt Smith and the Cowboys (Andre's broken leg will be healed enough to play next weekend, when the winner of this game will meet the Cowboys in Dallas for the NFC semi-finals). Reggie hears Richie pound through the usual exhortations, knowing these things are important but won't do the job, and then he falls back on what to him is the most reliable source of inspiration and inner strength—he quietly prays, "Lord, give us strength . . ."

· · ·

As THEY HEAD back out, Richie's not praying, he's thinking.

The problem on offense, aside from a few wrinkles in the blocking schemes that Dave Alexander had effectively diagnosed, is that they haven't been able to keep the ball long enough to develop any rhythm or confidence. They've barely scratched the surface of his game plan, and it's a good one.

Richie enters the game with a laminated sheet of plays broken down by situation—first down, second and short, second and long, third and short, third and long—and color coded, so that he knows which play to call first, second, third, et cetera, in sequence, according to down and distance. Based on the computer-aided study of his own team's tendencies (you have to stay unpredictable) and his opponents', the play list literally scripts the entire contest before it starts. Players, especially quarterbacks and receivers, are always eager to depart from it, based on their observations in action, and sometimes their ideas are good (you at least have to humor them), but compared with the in-depth reasoning behind every move on the game plan, spur-of-the-moment play calling is like feeling your way around with your eyes closed. Of course, there's a big measure of coaching pride on the line here, too. Dissecting opponents and discovering weak spots are what coaches do. If the players could just trot out every weekend and make it up as they went along—à la Randall—then what good is the whole lousy Pigskin Priesthood? Richie, the old special teams grunt, even more than most coaches, places his faith in the spadework done in the weeks preceding the game. There was a photo on the front page of the *Inquirer* sports section once, a stop-action shot that showed an Eagles ballcarrier frozen in the midst of an awkward tumble out-of-bounds before his own bench, and every face along the sidelines, all the players, coaches, linesmen, spectators, were watching with their mouths O'd and eyes wide—except Richie. There in the middle background, as the furious action unfolded, the coach's ample Levantine nose is bent to his laminated, color-coded play list, oblivious, already plotting the next call, like a man working a crossword puzzle in his living room. Richie isn't completely inflexible; he'll make changes on the sidelines to take advantage of opportunities as the game unfolds, scrapping plays that clearly aren't working and returning to ones that are, but the credo he lives by is Stick to the Game Plan.

Only in this opening play-off game, he's used only about one-tenth of the plays on his list. They haven't even gotten to exploit the crowning insight gleaned from their hours and hours of preparation. Reviewing New Orleans game tapes and studying the computer data, they noticed something about the Saints' all-pro right outside line-backer, Pat Swilling. Ordinarily the idea would be to stay as far away as possible from Swilling, one of the game's dominant players now for six seasons. But the computer data reveals a surprising nugget of information—lately, sweeps and screens run *at* Swilling, toward the right side of the Saints' defense, have been surprisingly successful. Studying the videotape of Saints games this season, they can see why. Few players in the league have a reputation as fearsome as Swilling's, but you don't game plan against players by their reputation. You plan according to what's current. (This, incidentally, is one of the common shortcomings of media pundits and the game's growing chorus of charlatan prognosticators, who judge teams and players on the basis of yesterday's news—it's like trading stocks with last year's listings.) The so-called best linebacker in the league may be playing only mediocre ball this week if he's got a sore knee or broken finger, or if he's at the tail end of his career and doesn't have the explosive strength he had, say, five seasons ago. Pro Bowl honors and lifetime sack and tackle totals are good enough for the Pack, the fans, and the archives people in Canton, but smart coaches scout each player anew every time out. Pat Swilling two seasons or even two weeks ago may not be the same Pat Swilling you'll face this week. Zeke prepares a brief abstract about every player on the defense, gleaned from close study of their play in recent games (for this game, the Eagles broke down and studied their season opener against New Orleans, and the Saints' games against the Dolphins, Rams, and Jets, the three most recent opponents who favor the Eagles' offensive style of two-back, one-back sets). Turns out that the very current Pat Swilling, ferocious reputation aside, is not particularly good at fighting off a block and moving laterally, he tends to dance away from cut blocks (he seems inordinately skittish about getting hit down around the knees), and he has a tendency to charge upfield so fast in his hurry to get at the quarterback that he leaves open his entire side of the field. Armed with these insights, Richie has a whole package of left-side screen passes and left-side sweeps behind pulling guards designed to attack Swilling. It's the Eagles' secret weapon in this contest, something Richie had planned to pull out as a surprise after lulling the Saints with more traditional modes of attack—only, half the game is gone and they have yet to spring the trap once.

When Richie tells his coaches and the offense *Let's get back to our game plan,* this is in part what he has in mind.

Back out in the reverberant indoor arena, draped with cheery homemade signs urging the Saints on—PROJECT PASADENA; THE SAINTS WILL MAKE THE EAGLES SORE; HERSCHEL WILL DROP, RANDALL WILL FLOP, SAINTS ARE THE TEAM THAT WILL COME OUT ON TOP—filled with raucous anticipation of a long-awaited postseason victory.

Rookie return man Jeff Sydner waits alone in the end zone, watching the second-half kickoff tumble down from the darkness of the upper Dome, catching the ball and then dropping to one knee.

And the contest resumes.

First and ten (Eagles' twenty): In the Eagles' self-analysis, a breakdown of all their offensive plays this season, the computer revealed that they infrequently throw on first down, and, beyond that, when they send a receiver in motion before the snap, they rarely, if ever, throw the ball to him. Richie knows, of course, that the Saints are looking at the same data, and predictably, the Saints have been playing off the Eagles' receivers on first down, giving them plenty of room, especially the motion receiver. So Richie signals in his tenth first-down play of the game, a pass play, sending Calvin Williams in motion from the left slot to the right and naming him as the primary receiver. It's a quick two-step drop for Randall, and he drills the pass cleanly to Calvin for an easy six-yard gain. Sometimes things work exactly as planned.

Second and four (Eagles' twenty-six): Here the Eagles can afford to waste a play by trying something fancy, or throwing deep. Saints coach Jim Mora plays it safe, dropping his pass defenders into a deep zone, so Richie plays it conservative, too; he sends Heath Sherman crashing into the middle of the line to pick up the first down. The Eagles' first goal here is to hang on to the ball for more than just three plays, find that rhythm with a first down or two, build some confidence, and plunge a little deeper into the game plan.

First and ten (Eagles' thirty): Richie sends Herschel Walker on a sweep to the right side (the way teams usually like to run against the Saints, away from Swilling and toward the left outside linebacker Rickey Jackson, the same Rickey Jackson who was a star at Andre's Pahokee High. Richie is still setting things up for a run at Swilling, like a boxer throwing lots of quick rights, holding back the surprise powerhouse left. This play almost works. Right tackle Antone Davis locks up Jackson for a moment, but then lets him slip off the block and flatten Herschel after just a two-yard gain—anything fewer than four yards on first down is a failure. Antone flings his huge arms in disgust. There was lots of open space if Herschel had gotten by Jackson.

Second and eight (Eagles' thirty-two): Randall hits Keith Byars over the middle for a four-yard gain. Keith had been so wide open so many times in the first half, and Randall had so consistently overlooked him, that the tight end and the coaches had harangued the quarterback at halftime to *get him the ball.* Voilà!

Third and four (Eagles' thirty-six): Richie sends in receiver Roy

Green, a cool old-timer with fourteen years of playing experience, with a nifty option route. Green is the primary receiver on this play, which is designed to employ his shrewd eye for getting open. Roy goes in motion before the snap, trotting from the right-side slot to the left side, which matches him in man-to-man coverage with right corner Reginald Jones. If Jones is lined up inside Roy, he'll break outside. If Jones is lined up outside, Roy will break in. Jones is inside, so Roy turns out. Randall's pass reaches him fourteen yards upfield. Academic.

First and ten (fifty-yard line): Now the Eagles finally have something moving on offense, two first downs in a row, matching their total for the entire first half. The crowd inside the Dome grows quiet.

Richie's ready to try one of his left-side plays, a counterscreen designed to fool the Saints (and Swilling) into thinking the play is sweeping right. Randall is supposed to roll to his right (the best way to avoid Swilling) and then, once the linebacker pursues, dump the ball over his head to Heath, who has slipped into the left flat. Only Antone misses his block on Rickey Jackson again. The big right outside linebacker charges straight at Randall, who instinctively abandons the play, sidesteps Jackson as neat as you please, and then fires the ball fourteen yards straight downfield to Calvin, who leaps between two defenders and somehow snares the ball with both hands. Nobody in the NFL makes this play except Randall, and it's all reflex. The move he puts on Jackson is so smooth and artful it could not have been thought out in advance. The pass is thrown like a bullet, high, so if Calvin can't reach it, the ball falls harmlessly about thirty yards downfield. But Calvin hangs on, and the Eagles have another first down. He hops up pointing back downfield at the quarterback, saluting the play.

First and ten (Saints' thirty-six): Now the Eagles' offensive motor is finally running. You can feel the hum in the huddle. Success breeds success. A touchdown and extra point here will put them only three points away.

Finally, Richie gets to spring his trap on Swilling. He sends Heath on a sweep to the left side, right at Swilling, a play on which Herschel's specific assignment (based on the tape review) is to launch himself low and hard at Swilling's knees—and it works like a charm. The linebacker leaps to avoid the hit, both arms fully extended to help fend off Herschel's lunge, and Heath scoots right around him for an eleven-yard gain before the Saints catch him. A third first down in three plays. Things are proceeding exactly according to plan. The Superdome has grown almost still.

First and ten (Saints' twenty-five): Switching things up again, Richie goes back to a simple running play, sending Heath into the right side of the line behind bigbodies Pink and Antone—only Antone executes what the coaches will later call a "Mark Spitz block," lunging forward into empty space, completely missing linebacker Vaughan Johnson. Johnson smothers Heath at the line of scrimmage.

Second and ten (Saints' twenty-five): Again Antone screws up, only this time with potentially disastrous consequences. On their opening drive of the second half, the Eagles have now controlled the ball for almost five minutes and advanced fifty-five yards—the most consistency they've shown offensively all day. They're already in field-goal range (they need a touchdown and a field goal to catch up), and they have real momentum.

But now Antone's Spitz block has left them at second and long, a situation in which New Orleans loves to blitz, because the highest-percentage plays are all passes. Richie sends in a pass play, but Randall hardly completes his drop back after the snap before linebacker Jackson runs right around Antone's right shoulder and smacks the quarterback unawares, dropping him and sending the ball skittering to the turf—where defensive end Wayne Martin falls on it.

The noise goes back on.

Antone comes off the field shaking his head and mumbling to himself. He's feeling humiliated again. He'd been feeling so good about himself and his game in recent weeks, after his fine outing against Charles Mann in particular, but now the old demons have returned.

"Rickey Jackson is just too quick for Antone Davis," comments CBS analyst Pat Summerall.

"Shake it off," line coach Bill Muir tells his huge second-year charge. But that's easier said than done. With expectations like those placed on Antone, there's no such thing as small failure.

So now Buddy's Boys trot out on the field, feeling more and more like they're the ones—once again—who have to make something happen if they've any chance left in this game. At halftime, Bud Carson stressed that there was nothing in their game plan that was wrong; they just needed to stay with their assignments, play more aggressively, and eliminate the big plays.

First and ten (Saints' thirty-one): Big plays like . . . this one. Saints quarterback Bobby Hebert drops a little screen to rookie running back Vaughn Dunbar, who races right around right-side linebacker William "Willie T." Thomas. Willie T. is just a second-year player and a bit overeager. He reads the screen perfectly, only instead of positioning himself to nail Dunbar for no gain or even a loss after the back catches the pass (he's in perfect position), Willie T. decides to try to *make something happen*. He angles slightly inside, trying to intercept the pass, misses, and then gets outrun by the fleet Saints running back. Eric Allen underestimates Dunbar's speed and, diving to reach him, winds up knocking the pursuing Willie T. off his feet instead.

Which frees Dunbar to sprint thirty-five more yards down the sidelines in front of his cheering teammates before safety John Booty can push him out-of-bounds. This is the last thing the Eagles need—another big play right out of the blocks. Suddenly, instead of the Eagles' threatening to narrow the margin, the Saints are in position to widen it. The Superdome is again ringing with gleeful noise.

First and ten (Eagles' thirty-four): Seth wraps up Dunbar trying to slip around the other side, only he gets his fingers caught up in the running back's face mask and is penalized. Seth storms around the field blowing off steam for a few moments, swinging his arms and shaking his head angrily from side to side. On TV the slo-mo replay clearly shows the infraction.

First and five (Eagles' twenty-nine): The Saints can afford to play cautiously here. They're up by ten, by one touchdown and a field goal. Even if they only get three here, the Eagles will need either two touchdowns or a touchdown and two field goals to catch up.

Mora sends his gigantic fullback Craig Heyward straight into the left side of the line. Bud has anticipated the play and has his linebackers charging up the gaps on the line—a run blitz—but they don't call the rotund Heyward "Ironhead" for nothing. He's met right at the line of scrimmage by both Seth and Clyde, a quarter ton of determined defense—and he still gains two yards.

"When you call a run blitz, that's the perfect call," says Madden up in the TV booth. "And when you blitz in the hole they run in, they shouldn't make any yardage. But when it's Ironhead Heyward, Bud Carson looks on saying, 'What the heck do I have to do?' "—shot of Bud looking annoyed and bewildered on the sidelines. The tone of the national CBS broadcast, which, of course, the players can't hear, is growing increasingly resigned to a New Orleans blowout. "Bud Carson is doing everything he can to stop this drive," says Madden, correctly sensing the desperation being felt on the Eagles' sidelines. "If they don't stop them on this one—they're already down 17–7— they know they can be put away right here."

Second and three (Eagles' twenty-seven): Bud decided at half-time that he had to put more pressure on Hebert, so he's running down his list of blitzes. It's all-or-nothing time—so what the hell. He sends everybody on this play. They're trying to drive the Saints backward, chase them out of even field-goal range. Hebert hands off to Dunbar again, and he manages to advance the ball two yards before Andy Harmon and Mike Golic drop him.

Third and one (Eagles' twenty-five): Another first down here would be almost as disastrous as another touchdown. It would enable the Saints to eat up most of the remainder of the third quarter, time the Eagles now desperately need to score points.

The Eagles line up in what they call their jumbo-even defensive front, virtually forsaking their pass defense in an all-out effort to stop the run. They stack five big men on the line (instead of the usual four), send in Ken Rose to supplement their usual three linebackers, and instead of lining the smaller Booty up with strong safety Rich Miano, Bud sends in the team's biggest healthy safety, William Frizzell. The Saints aren't trying anything fancy here; it's strength against strength. They pull guard Chris Port (290 pounds) to join Ironhead (270 pounds) in a right-side sweep behind tight end Hoby Brenner (245 pounds) and right tackle Stan Brock (280 pounds). It's like hitting the Eagles' line with a small truck to clear a path for Dunbar. The mistake they make is running it at Reverend Reggie.

The mighty Reverend rises to the occasion. He hits Brenner and Brock with so much force that he drives them backward. Brenner is thrown so far back that he knocks into Port, who falls into Heyward. The whole mass of bigbodies collapses in a heap in the New Orleans backfield, and as Dunbar tries to dance his way around them, he's flattened by Rose and Frizzell at the line of scrimmage.

Most fans can hardly make sense of the clutter of heaving bodies on the line—it looks like any other failed running play. But Madden, the crafty old coach, can sort it out. Apart from his genial gusty garrulity, Madden makes such an entertaining game analyst because although he sees and understands the game as a coach, he subscribes to the Great Man Theory of football—he's less interested than, say, Richie, in the artful complexity of systems than in the heroic accomplishments of individual athletes. He invests the game with personality and emotion, things fans can readily understand. Madden believes a single player can, in certain instances, change the whole course of a football game, inspiring tectonic shifts in momentum with sheer strength and will. He has just seen such a moment.

"You always hear people talk about a dominant defensive player . . . what is a dominant defensive player?" he asks, nearly breathless with excitement. "Watch Reggie White on this play." A slo-mo replay is shown. "He takes Hoby Brenner, knocks him backwards, and throws off the whole play. Brenner knocks into the pulling guard who falls into the lead blocker Heyward, and Dunbar gets stacked up behind the mess!"

It's a big play, and it's gone a long way toward keeping the Eagles in the game, but there's more excitement about it in the broadcast booth than there is on the field. Back on the bench, Reggie isn't even aware that his surge is what stopped the play. He knows he got a good push coming off the line, but that's nothing new for Reggie. As far as he's concerned, Ken and William made the stop. And it's not a particularly up moment at all. After all the speechifying and loud resolution of the halftime locker room, they've come out to turn over the ball and give up another big play to the Saints, and have dug themselves into an even deeper hole. New Orleans is denied the first down, but Morten Andersen kicks a forty-two-yard field goal to give New Orleans a 20–7 lead. None of the boys in white and green are ready to give up, but prospects are looking bleaker and bleaker. For the veterans, there's a familiar creepy feeling in the pit of their stomachs. The Superdome rocks with music and dance.

"Who dat say dey gonna beat dem Saints?" the crowd is singing, "Who dat? Who dat?"

The party goes on.

Andersen boots the kickoff out of the end zone, and the Eagles' offense manages to pick up only five yards on the next series and has to punt it away. With the third quarter almost two-thirds complete, Bud's defense takes the field once more. The Saints can seal victory here by making a few more first downs, hanging on to the ball right into the fourth quarter.

First and ten (Saints' twenty-five): You'd figure Mora would play conservatively here. But the theme of this game, announced on the failed opening bomb, is the opposite. Indeed, the Saints now try the same post pattern they tried to open the game, sending veteran receiver Quinn Early racing down the right sideline one step ahead of little Mark McMillian. The first time, Eric was playing a deep zone designed to help Mark out on a post route, but Eric hadn't moved over quickly enough. Only a badly thrown pass had prevented a touchdown.

This time, anticipating a return to just this play, Bud has switched up the zone assignments. He's got both Rich Miano and Mark sandwiching the post pattern, with Mark deep and Rich underneath. Eric is playing deep backfield again, and this time he recognizes the route and moves into position. Hebert sees the double coverage and decides to throw the ball away, but he doesn't see Eric waiting deep downfield. The ball floats high and far, and Eric waits underneath like Willie Mays fielding batting practice. He makes a basket catch.

And once more, the Eagles' defense gives Randall and Richie a chance to climb back into the game. If the offense doesn't do anything on this drive, they will have repeated the Eagles' standard formula for defeat—Buddy's Boys get the job done; the offense falls flat. The heat is on.

First and ten (Eagles' thirty-eight): Randall's first read on this pass play is Fred, who is wide open about fourteen yards upfield—New Orleans is now giving Fred lots of room, an opportunity Richie wants to exploit. But Randall has been hit too many times today by the rush from Antone's direction, and even though his big right tackle has linebacker Jackson squarely blocked this time, the quarterback just dumps the ball quickly to Heath, his secondary receiver, without even looking for Fred. The Saints have the play covered. By all rights, Heath should be dropped for a loss. But he shrugs off the tackle and runs eight yards down the right sideline before getting pushed out-of-bounds.

Second and two (Eagles' forty-six): In high school, they used to call Heath "Gopher," because of the way his squat, bowlegged body would disappear into a pileup of big grappling linemen, and then, moments later, emerge out the back end still churning forward. On this play he plunges straight into the roiling battle of bigbodies and squirts out the back end two-to-three yards upfield.

On the sidelines, Zeke wonders to himself, *How'd he do that?*

Heath is a big surprise. Despite all the Eagles' well-publicized efforts in the off-season to secure a first-rate ballcarrier, using two top draft picks to obtain Siran Stacy and Tony Brooks, and then humoring Norman by shelling out more than a million to sign Herschel, it turns out the team's premier running back for '92 was already on the roster. Sherman will finish the season averaging 5.2 yards per carry, more than a yard better than Herschel. Neither Stacy nor Brooks will carry the football even once (both proved to be strictly draft-day wonders, and would be gone within two seasons). When the season started, though, everybody figured that Heath was as good as gone, but the taciturn little Texan had thrived under the pressure. He had taken up a daily thirty-mile cycling regimen in the off-season that had built up his legs and stamina, and was impressive enough over the summer to win at least a fourth-string job. When Richie started throwing him in at midseason to spell Herschel, Heath ran so brilliantly it was hard to justify keeping him on the bench. With his distinctly canine, four-point running style, the man they called Wolf had been the offensive hero of that all-important Redskins game the week before, and here he's about to play the same role.

First and ten (Eagles' forty-nine): Fred was so wide open on the previous first-down play, Richie calls it again, this time out of a different formation. But Randall, again, doesn't even look for his primary receiver, even though Fred is moving once more into a wide-open zone. At halftime everybody was after Randall to throw the ball more to Keith, so—dammit!—throw the ball to Keith he will. This time the tight end hangs on somehow even though he's got two defenders draped all over him. A four-yard gain. The Eagles are moving the ball, but Richie and Zeke are growing more and more irritated with their superstar quarterback.

Second and six (Saints' forty-seven): Richie decides to attack Swilling head-on again, sending Heath around the left side behind pulling guard Daryle Smith and Keith Byars. Smith cuts Swilling down with another well-aimed low block, and Heath runs for nine more yards, once more vindicating the game plan—*Stick to the plan.*

First and ten (Saints' thirty-eight): Slot-ace-right-SLIP, a two-tight-end, two-wide-receiver, one-back formation (ace) with both a split and slot receiver to the right (slot-right), and the slot receiver in motion away from the formation's strength (SLIP). The play calls for a screen pass, right side. The motion of the slot receiver is designed to pull one potential tackler out of the zone to the left, leaving the Saints down one defender and the Eagles up one blocker (the second tight end). The play is also designed to exploit Rickey Jackson's tendency to chase too far upfield after the quarterback. It works well. Again, the ball goes to Heath—Richie is a believer in the "hot hand" theory, and Wolfie is hot. Heath catches the pass and races sixteen yards up the sideline, right in front of his teammates, and then, instead of stepping out-of-bounds when confronted by two tacklers—the way high-priced NFL talent does more and more these days—he lowers his head and refuses to yield, crashing into them full speed ahead, leading with helmet and pads, sending both of them flying. Heath has the breath knocked out of him—he winds up with his head down, gasping for air—but his grit has fired up his teammates. Jimmy Mac steps out on the field and just points in silent homage at the running back.

A chant goes up from the Eagles' bench, "Wolfie! Wolfie! Wolfie!"

"Way to play the game, Wolf!" shouts David Archer.

Heath has to sit down for a couple of plays. He doesn't know it, but he's done it. He's ignited the engine. Everybody on offense out on the field can feel it. Dave Alexander feels it as he summons his teammates back to the huddle—*Dammit, Heath at least is bringing the heat, he's going to do every little thing he can to win this football game!*

The bird is in flight.

First and ten (Saints' twenty-two): Guard Brian Baldinger executes an "oh, shit!" block, as in the exclamation that escapes his lips when he looks back to see the linebacker he was supposed to block (Vaughan Johnson), but completely missed, wrapping up Herschel for a one-yard loss. The exultant linebacker kneels over the runner pumping his fists.

Baldinger, looking back, cups his hands over the face mask of his helmet.

Second and eleven (Saints' twenty-three): Randall rolls a few steps to his right (a waggle) and fires a pass at Calvin, who just drops it.

Third and eleven (Saints' twenty-three): Richie steps out on the field to shout the play to Randall, "Red-flex-right-TIP," shotgun formation with a running back on either side of Randall (red), with the tight end widened out to the right (flex), and then coming in motion to the left before the snap (TIP). It's another screen, but Keith misses his block and Randall ends up ducking and dodging the rush. Instead of taking off on foot or throwing the ball away, the quarterback risks all by firing the ball upfield to Heath, who has three defenders grouped around him. It's a heedless and foolhardy roll of the dice—a Randall specialty—in a situation where the Eagles desperately need to capitalize on their field position for at least a field goal. The ball is nearly intercepted, but not.

Richie and Zeke resist the urge to throttle Randall on the sidelines as Roger Ruzek boots a forty-yard field goal. The score is now 20–10, and the third quarter is just about complete.

"You just sorta—at least I do, John—get the sensation that the Eagles' level of intensity is rising and the Saints are just leveling off," says Summerall.

"I think what you have here is intensity driven by urgency," says Madden.

As the fourth quarter begins, Bud's defense again stops the Saints in three plays, and New Orleans is forced to punt. Vai Sikahema makes a strong twelve-yard runback, giving the offense good field position for the crucial drive.

"The Eagles had better get something done," says Madden. There are fourteen minutes, forty-five seconds, remaining. The Eagles can't afford anymore to grind their way patiently upfield. They're going to need at least one touchdown and a field goal to tie the game. It's big-play time.

First and ten (Eagles' thirty-six): Richie decides to try to hit Fred long again down the right sideline, but the Saints, burned once by Fred's speed, are backing well off, giving the Eagles' star receiver lots of room. He's well covered, and the ball is nearly intercepted by diving safety Keith Taylor. Fred trips over the defender and goes sprawling into the end zone as the ball bounces away.

"They have to take that shot," says Madden, the unflagging Fred Barnett fan. "They have to keep taking that shot. They took it in the first half and it was a seven-point shot."

Second and ten (Eagles' thirty-six): Right back at Swilling, a screen pass to the left. Heath gets just five yards this time before the cornerback knocks him down.

Third and five (Eagles' forty-one): At this critical moment, Randall runs to escape the pass rush and fires an amazingly accurate, hard pass eight yards up the sidelines to Calvin, who snares it for the first down. It's the kind of pass that makes Zeke, the old quarterback, just shake his head with wonder. "It's like a missile," he says later, admiring it on videotape. "There's not another arm in the league that can throw the ball like that. And that's not a heavy ball. It's got so many revs [revolutions] on it, it's *easy* to catch, not a slow-moving rock."

One minute you could kill Randall; the next you could kiss him. So much skill, so little judgment. But the league is full of quarterbacks with great judgment and pedestrian skills.

First and ten (Eagles' forty-nine): Heath slips a tackle in the backfield, cuts back to his left, and scoots seven yards straight ahead.

Second and three (Saints' forty-four): Heath bangs out another two.

"Wolfie! Wolfie! Wolfie!" goes the chant from the Eagles' bench.

Third and one (Saints' forty-two): Keith runs a little option route from his tight-end spot. If the Saints are in zone coverage, he's supposed to trot out about four yards and squat. If they're in man coverage, he's supposed to slant across the middle of the field underneath his defender. Earlier in the game he'd blown it, misreading the coverage and squatting short of the first down. This time, Keith reads man coverage and runs the slant, and Randall throws him the ball for a seven-yard gain—just like the thing is drawn up in the playbook. Tank hops up and spins the football on the turf like a top, as if to say *As easy as that!*

When simple plays like this work, it reaffirms the Coach's-Eye View—if players can just execute the play as designed, they'd be unstoppable.

"How come we can do it now, and we couldn't do it before?" wonders Zeke.

First and ten (Saints' thirty-five): Randall rolls to his left on a naked bootleg, his favorite play, and tries to shovel the ball five yards upfield to Keith. But Swilling gets a hand on the ball, and it floats off in the wrong direction. The linebacker ends the play grabbing his gold helmet with both hands. He thinks he should have intercepted.

Second and ten (Saints' thirty-five): Antone Davis sends Rickey Jackson's helmet flying with an inadvertent right uppercut. "Shit happens," he says in the locker room later, by way of explanation. The infraction draws a personal foul and a ten-yard penalty, a potentially disastrous setback.

It's clear to Richie and Zeke on this play that Randall is now looking almost exclusively for Keith Byars when he drops back to pass. It's a pattern they recognize in the quarterback. Supersensitive to criticism and, hence, instruction (which he perceives as criticism) he frequently overcorrects, especially under pressure. They told him at halftime he wasn't looking to Keith enough, so now he's looking to Keith exclusively.

Second and twenty (Saints' forty-five): Randall hits Keith on a slant pass again, and, with the Saints' defenders now playing it safe in deep, soft zones, the tight end picks up ten more easy yards before getting hauled down by three tacklers. Tank lays the ball about a yard farther upfield and hops up clapping.

Third and ten (Saints' thirty-five): There are just over ten minutes left to play. Any likely scenario for the Eagles to come back and tie or win this game turns now on this play.

Richie wants to shake the Keith fixation, so he sends in a simple pass play to Fred, ace-right-900. "Ace-right" defines a two-tight-end, two-receiver, one-back formation with the strength to the right side, so it's a good bet that Atkins, the free safety, will be cheating a little to the right, leaving Fred one-on-one with cornerback Reginald Jones. With only thirty-five yards of field and ten yards of end zone to defend, and with defenders playing deep zones, the Saints figure Fred doesn't have enough room just to run away from Jones. And Atkins is playing centerfield, so he can react to anything thrown deep.

Fred hears the 900 call, and his eyes widen. It's a big moment, and the call is a vote of faith by his coaches—big moments call for big players. At the snap, Fred races toward the corner of the end zone, forcing Jones to stay outside of him, then, about twenty yards upfield, he angles back toward the post, effectively positioning himself like a basketball player angling for a rebound, between the cornerback and the ball. Randall, under pressure, has to get rid of the ball—he's flattened by Rickey Jackson as he releases it. Randall and Fred and Calvin spend a little extra time working on this pass after every practice. The quarterback knows that Fred, especially, can outjump just about anybody in the league (remember the six-foot, eleven-inch, high jump in high school?), so he works at laying the ball up just high enough so that only Fred can get it. The pass floats now toward the left corner of the end zone, a high lob that Fred sees the instant he makes his turn—every player on the field and every fan inside the Dome and watching at home has a second or two to anticipate its descent.

The ball is thrown so high that Atkins has enough time to break toward the end zone. It's going to be a jump ball. Jones is to Fred's right; Atkins arrives in time to go up on Fred's left. "I was gonna catch that ball," Fred will say a little later, in the locker room. "I just knew, as I went up, that nothing was going to stop me from catching that ball."

And Fred does. With both gloved hands a good foot higher than the straining reach of Jones and Atkins, Fred just rips the ball out of the air, fending off the cornerback and safety with his elbows, then falling to his rump in the end zone with Jones and Atkins crumpling to either side. The Superdome goes silent as Fred leaps to his feet between the vanquished defenders and, with his signature windmill windup, spikes the ball triumphantly.

"Fred Barnett! Diving catch. Spectacular catch," says Summerall to the TV audience. "Thirty-five yards away. They had him covered."

Madden explodes with excitement: "He's the kind of guy that can do that! I've always said that Fred Barnett is one of the best deep-pass receivers in football. He can do it against man; he can do it against zone. He can do it against double coverage. Here it is again." Slo-mo replay. "They had double coverage, and here he is. Fred Barnett just goes up and catches the ball. *That* will make all the highlights films. I think you just have to keep doing that. You do that six or seven times a game, you'll get two or three touchdowns."

The Eagles are back in the game, trailing by three points with just over ten minutes left to play. Now the Saints have to make something happen. There's no doubt the momentum has shifted in the Eagles' favor; the damp quiet that has descended in the Dome is ample testament to that. By now there's no doubt, the celebration—and nobody knows celebrating like N'Awlins—had gotten out ahead of the game. A gentlemen with his face painted black and gold, beard sparkling with gold dust, and his head enclosed in a gold-sequined helmet, leans over the wall behind the Eagles' bench and closes his black-and-gold gloved hands in prayer.

On the sidelines, watching Ruzek's kickoff returned to the Saints' twenty-five-yard line by Vaughn Dunbar, Seth turns to Reggie and growls, "I'm going to make a big play."

It's Seth's way of challenging himself. He believes there's a subtle difference between playing defense well and playing defense to win, a mental adjustment mostly, one that says *I'm not content with being in the right position and making the play that comes my way, I'm going to bring the heat . . . make something happen!*

First and ten (Saints' twenty-five): Throughout the first half, whenever the Saints lined up in trey, a three-wide-receiver formation, they'd been leaving the tight end, Brenner, in to block. Since Seth covers Brenner man to man in this formation, it had effectively been removing the Eagles' star linebacker from short-pass defense, where he had been so deadly all season. So at halftime Bud made a change, instructing Seth to drop back into pass coverage right at the snap.

At the snap, both Byron Evans and Seth drop back about ten yards. Byron's job is to pick up any receiver running a crossing pattern, but nobody breaks across the middle. So Byron charges Hebert, who is already being chased out of the pocket by Reggie and Clyde. Rolling to his left, Hebert can't find an open receiver, and Byron is closing in fast. So the quarterback makes a mistake. Instead of just throwing the ball deep, over the heads of everyone, avoiding the sack and lining up at second and ten, Hebert tries to *make something happen*. His favorite receiver in a pinch is Eric Martin, and he knows Martin, seeing his quarterback in trouble, will break across the center of the field. And, indeed, that's what Martin does. Only he's not just being shadowed by a cornerback and safety, there's a third unexpected presence lurking in the middle of the field.

Seth also knows Hebert in trouble will look for Martin, so he's alertly shifted his normal zone over to the right. With Mark chasing behind Martin, and Booty playing back, a well-thrown ball, lofted over Byron's reach, might reach the receiver in the center of the field. Martin is out there waving his hands in the air, begging for the ball. Hebert throws off balance, trying to propel the football to his right, out toward the center of the field, while he's moving to his left. He doesn't see Seth until the linebacker catches the ball.

Seth brings it back fourteen yards, all the way down to the Saints' twenty-six-yard line.

It's almost too good to be true. In two swift, spectacular plays, the Eagles have climbed back into the game, and now, thanks to Seth's interception, they're already in position to kick a field goal and tie it. The crowd in the Dome smells doom. Clyde and Eric drag a late tackler off Seth and pummel him as players come running from both sides of the field. As the officials try to break up the melee, Seth just trots off the field holding the ball, enchanging high fives with his defensive teammates, ignoring the offense as they jog back out.

In five simple plays, the Eagles chip down to within six yards of the goal line, picking up yardage in three- and four-yard bites, aided by a five-yard offside call on New Orleans. It's warm inside the Dome, and the long afternoon's work is starting to take its toll. Poor Pink is feeling the effects. After every play he lingers at the line of scrimmage, gasping for air, sweat pouring off his pudgy cheeks and brow, stinging his eyes.

Randall is peering over at the sideline, picking up signals for the next play, and Dave is circling the boys in the huddle—they have only forty-five seconds to get off the next play—and as he counts around the huddle he's missing his right guard.

"Pink! Pink!" he shouts. "Where the hell is my right guard at?"

And just as Randall leans in to call the play, Pink makes it back to the huddle.

"Pink, what the hell are you doing?" Dave asks as they break huddle and turn to set for the new play.

"I'm more tired than Phoenix," Pink complains.

Brian Baldinger, who is filling in at left guard for the injured Mike Schad, forms a hilarious contrast. Baldy is a pink-faced twelve-year veteran who is so wired for action that he sometimes seems a little off-kilter; his motor seems to idle in overdrive. He likes to wear his shirts buttoned all the way to the top, even without a tie, so his teammates have been heard to wonder if ol' Baldy's head is getting sufficient blood. Baldy loves everything about football; he loves practice; he loves meetings; he loves arriving at the stadium hours before game time—teammates have even heard him exclaim his enthusiasm for getting his ankles taped. Most of these guys like what they do for a living, but Baldy's gusto is often comical. And now, Baldy is starting *in a play-off game!* He seems to have found an even higher gear for his engine, sprinting on and off and on the field, chasing downfield after plays he couldn't hope to catch, then hustling back to the huddle, face growing pinker and pinker, lips stretched dry and white with excitement. After Heath plunges four more yards for a first down, Baldy comes hopping back gleefully. "This is great shit! Great shit!" he keeps shouting at Dave. To his right, Dave's worried about poor Pink passing out and suffering heart failure from sheer fatigue, and to his left he's worried ol' Baldy's heart is just going to explode with adrenaline.

Dave isn't feeling too much either way. His energy level is closer to Baldy's, but his eminently sane, jovial outlook on the game is more like Pink's. The two nudge each other and roll their eyes in the huddle at the newcomer's excesses.

A three-yard run by Heath, and a quick six-yard pass to Keith, and the Eagles face another important third-down play. They need one yard for first and goal. A touchdown gives them the lead; a field goal just ties the score.

Third and one (Saints' six): Time to attack Swilling again. Despite the success the Eagles have had running straight at the linebacker, Richie has used the plays sparingly enough that New Orleans is still anticipating that they will run away from him. To further that impression, on this one-yard play, Richie calls a strong right formation, which stacks players up on the right side. On the left side, Baldy is going to pull out and head to his left, but the rest of the line—left tackle Ron Heller, Dave at center, and behemoths Pink and Antone—is going to form a train banging down to the right. They call it an elephant block, because each lineman just places his helmet on the rump of the teammate to his right and crashes blindly ahead.

It's the counter OT play again, with Heath following Baldy, swooping straight down on the vaunted linebacker. With the rest of the Saints plunging in the wrong direction, fooled by a play fake and the elephant block into the right, Baldy lays a good hit on Swilling. Heath doesn't just get the one yard and first down, he doesn't stop running until he slams into a photographer behind the Girard Street end zone, right underneath the PROJECT PASADENA sign.

Untangling himself from the elephant heap back at the line of scrimmage, Dave can tell by the sudden sound vacuum that something very good has just happened. He sees Heath pop back up behind the end zone, sees the ref's hands held high—23–20, the Eagles take the lead!—and peers into the face mask of Saints defensive end Wayne Martin, who lies beside him on the turf. Martin looks at Dave angrily and shouts, "Why'd you do that?"

"What?" Dave answers. He figures Martin is going to accuse him of cut blocking him or doing something illegal.

"Why'd you guys score!" Martin says.

"Hell, man, we're trying to win the game!"

As they leave the field, the Eagles' players are now shouting at the fans, "Who dat? Who dat?" The point after puts them up by four—and the Saints suddenly need more than a field goal to catch up.

Baldy is so fired up after throwing the key block on this play that he comes off the field shouting at line coach Bill Muir, "We've got to keep running the ball. We can kick their ass. We can kick their ass!"

Muir goes down the line, asking each lineman for input. "Dave, what do you think we can do?"

Dave is Mr. Analysis. "Well, Bill, that trap block scheme seems to be working well if we . . ."

When Muir comes to Baldy, whose facial blood vessels are straining for deeper shades of red, the left guard blurts, "Who cares? Just do anything! We'll kick their ass!"

As bad as things are for New Orleans, they're about to get worse. Inside the windless and suddenly silenced Dome, Roger's kickoff sails out of the end zone, so the Saints take over on their own twenty-yard line. Over the last few years, the Eagles' fans have often seen what happens next. Smelling blood, with an opponent cornered, Buddy's Boys go into what local sportswriters have come to call a "feeding frenzy." They do more than shut down the enemy's offense; they actually begin driving the team backward, play after play, crashing in like waves on a swelling storm tide.

First and ten (Saints' twenty): With the pass rush swarming, Hebert tries to hit Eric Martin on a simple out pattern, but Martin is flagged for pushing Eric Allen.

First and twenty (Saints' ten): Hebert's pass is slapped out of the air and back at the end zone by Mike Golic, who jumps up triumphantly pumping one finger at the ceiling.

Second and twenty (Saints' ten): Noting that the Eagles' linebackers are dropping back into pass defense zones, Mora calls a play designed to exploit zone coverage, a quick screen to running back Vaughn Dunbar, who is a terrific open-field runner. Mora figures Byron Evans, who ordinarily would cover Dunbar man to man, will be playing off ten yards or so, giving the rookie back room to maneuver. But, instead, Bud has anticipated the play and signaled in a change in coverage. Instead of dropping back, Byron is hugged up on the smaller running back so close that he nearly wrests the ball away when Hebert flips it. Dunbar hangs on, but Byron just wraps his long arms around him and drops him for a three-yard loss. The Saints have now run four plays and have gone backward thirteen yards. Their backs are now against the end zone.

Third and twenty-three (Saints' seven): And here comes the next crushing wave.

Instead of dropping back into a prevent defense, Bud decides to gamble—send everybody. He feels the feeding frenzy, too. If the Saints anticipate the blitz, they have a remedy—they just send two receivers on quick slant patterns and Hebert dumps the ball fast. With just two men playing deep, the short pass can turn into a huge gain. If the receiver can dodge a tackle and outrun the pursuit, it could turn into a go-ahead touchdown, pull the plug on this late Eagles' surge. But Bud knows that on third down, with twenty-three yards to the stick, the Saints won't be anticipating a blitz. They'll be sending out at least four receivers. With Hebert dropping back to pass, that leaves just six guys to block. If he sends eight, somebody is going to get a free shot at the quarterback.

At the snap, all hell breaks loose. Hebert manages to drop back to the end zone, but before he has a chance to throw, Reverend Reggie runs right over tackle Stan Brock, whose co-blocker can't help him because he's picking up the charging Rich Miano. Reggie lunges, grabs Hebert's right leg, and pulls him down in the end zone.

The big man leaps up, joins his hands over his head (as if in prayer!), the signal for a safety. Two points! The Reverend comes dancing off the field excitedly before the humbled Dome crowd. The

Saints are still down only by six points, with more than five minutes left to play, but on the turf it smells like a blowout. The Eagles are just crushing them now.

"That's why they call them dominant players," enthuses Madden up in the booth. "Reggie White in the second half just took over this game. That's why Reggie White is the best defensive player in football. He can just take over and dominate a game, and that's what he did here today."

Reggie trots off the field into the embrace of Wes Hopkins, who slaps hard at his broad back.

And for these few blessed minutes, the team is soaring. They're in that zone of complete domination, offense, defense, and special teams playing at a level where no one can touch them, where all the petty rivalries and jealousies of the locker room, feuds with management, criticism of play calling, anger over contract talks, shabby accommodations, all of it is irrelevant now; all that exists is this moment on this field against this opponent, when everything they try works, when every player is better for being part of the family, the Team. It's bliss.

On the bench, Reggie sees the network camera pointed at him and seizes the moment. He points skyward with both hands, leans back, and shouts over and over, "Yes, Jesus! It's Jesus! Praise Jesus!"

Into the teeth of this surge, the Saints must now punt the ball back to the Eagles. Running behind Baldy, again right at Swilling, the Eagles sweep three times in a row around the left side, for eleven yards, then six more, then sixteen yards. Fred hauls Heath up from the last tackle shouting, "Stay in bounds! Stay in bounds!" The drive ends with a thirty-nine-yard field goal and just over two minutes left to play. If the Saints aren't completely finished, they will be shortly, when Eric Allen interrupts their next frantic possession with another interception. Pressured by the rush, Hebert tries to hit receiver Wesley Carroll, but the wily Eagles cornerback has it read the whole way. He just steps in front of the ball and practically walks the eighteen yards into the end zone. In their last five trips to the field, the Eagles' defense has intercepted three times and scored twice.

Buddy's Boys now break into a N'Awlins strut in the end zone, gloating before the stricken home crowd. Izel Jenkins points with both fingers at the crowd and shouts, "Go home! Go home!"

Byron taunts them with an impromptu mime. Helmet off, long arms extended, he gives an exaggerated shrug, and puts on a comically long face, wiping one eye sadly with the back of a white-gloved hand.

Exuberant and brazenly contemptuous, the Eagles welcome themselves to the Next Level.

"Dallas, here we come," shouts Keith Byars. "One more time, baby! Next week! New Orleans don't know it's a sixty-minute fight."

"Man, this is great shit," shouts Baldy. "This is what it's all about! This is the way it should be every Sunday!"

Forever and ever.

Epilogue

MARCHING OUT

Ernest Hemingway believed he had only a set number of orgasms allotted to him in his life. It's as good a way as any of understanding what happened the next weekend in Dallas to Richie and Randall and Buddy's Boys. They were plumb out of ammo.

There were lots of explanations: The younger and virtually injury-free Cowboys had been getting stronger as the season progressed, the Eagles weaker. The Eagles had left their hearts and souls on the Superdome turf in their comeback play-off win. Dallas (which would go on to win the Super Bowl handily in '93 and again in '94) was the Team of the Nineties, nobody could expect to beat them again this century. You heard a million theories. Reggie White was over the hill. Randall was on drugs. Troy Aikman was the second coming of Joe Namath, with healthy knees, and ol' helmet head, Jimmy Johnson, was the reincarnation of none other than St. Holy Vince. Take your pick.

"I wish I knew," offered a beleaguered Richie immediately after the slaughter. "I couldn't be prouder of this football team. It wasn't lack of effort out there today, it just didn't work for the Eagles today."

Two days later he was on a plane to Alabama to scout the Senior Bowl and begin preparing for the college draft and the '93 season.

The spirit comes and the spirit goes. Fresh from that heady triumph in N'Awlins—Reggie had entered the locker room shouting, "Finally! Finally! Finally!"—the Eagles emerged in Dallas woeful, dispirited, and sad. There would be little use in dissecting it play by play. Nothing the Eagles tried worked; everything the Cowboys tried did.

- The final score was 34–10, and that's misleading. It wasn't that close.

Rookie Mark McMillian had written on the front page of his playbook the warning "Harper likes to give stutter step, then break" and underlined it three times. In the second quarter, Cowboys receiver

Alvin Harper gave him a stutter step, blew by him, and caught a deep pass for a forty-one-yard gain, setting up a touchdown. The rookie was also beaten by Michael Irvin for a big gainer. Before the game ended, he was in tears on the sidelines.

Satisfying his months-long rehab quest, Andre got in the game in the second half, a desperate ploy to rev the Eagles' sagging spirits. Taped to the safety's forehead, a response to Emmitt Smith's "bad things" remark, was Andre's latest motivational slogan, Psalm 70, which reads, in part: *Let them be ashamed and confounded that seek after my soul: let them be turned backward, and put to confusion, that desire my hurt.* On his first play, unable to pivot on his left leg, and losing one of his contact lenses just before the snap, the Dré Master was burned for a twenty-yard completion by tight end Jay Novacek. Smith would gain 114 yards rushing and generally avoid taking any big hits from his nemesis. He'd later complain that Andre was running around shouting, "Hold him up! Hold him up! I want to break his leg!" Asked about it afterward, his playing gear in a heap at his feet, Andre looked confused, and said, "It never happened."

The most lasting memory of that game for Eagles players was of the seemingly endless slog of the fourth quarter—with the game already lost, the JeromeQuest dashed—and what seemed like hours of playing time left. It was like making a fighter finish all fifteen rounds after he's been KO'd in the ninth. One image stands out: Seth, Andre, Reggie, and Mike Golic waiting in the gray misting drizzle, seated in a row on the Eagles' bench. Behind them, sadistic Cowboys fans hurl barbs of invective into the open wound:

"Go home, you motherfuckers!"

"Philly sucks!"

"Whazzamatter, Reggie? Not paying you enough?"

Buddy's Boys were in shock. Reggie kept checking the scoreboard, then scanning the field, his expression frozen in a look of alarm and disbelief. Mike rested his chin in one taped, bloody hand, eyes up on the giant TV screen. Andre was talking to himself, and Seth just retreated into a black hole of gloom. They were all mystified at their ineffectiveness. They were angry, humiliated, and deeply disappointed.

When it was finally over, they trudged off the field and into the tunnel, passing through the exit where the Cowboys' fan dangled his effigy, the rubber chicken dressed up like an Eagle. Ron Heller paused after entering the tunnel, then reached one big taped hand to tear it from the startled fan, and threw it against the tunnel wall. It lay there in the corner soaking up the mud from their cleats, a pathetic, silly, trampled emblem of the dream.

The network TV cameras caught a hand-lettered sign held aloft in the stands by a Cowboys' fan with a good memory. It said: ANY QUESTIONS? This team, this family, had played together for the last time. Jerome was gone; Keith Jackson was gone; soon Reggie would be gone; Ron, Mike Golic, Keith Byars, Jim McMahon, . . . and eventually Wes, Andre, Clyde, and Seth. It was only a matter of time.

Every year, all but one of the twenty-eight NFL teams go home frustrated to varying degrees—that's 1,269 disappointed players, 47 happy ones. The degree of disappointment varies. For the dozen teams who make the play-offs, the end comes abruptly, when their spirits are soaring highest. Clearly the Bills, who lost their third Super Bowl in a row (and would lose their fourth in '93), felt worse than some rebuilding teams who ended with a losing, but improved, record. Every team in the league begins a season with its own special sources of inspiration, its own history, emotions, loyalties, dreams. But it's hard to imagine any team in any year wanting to reach the mountaintop, and believing it could, more than the Philadelphia Eagles did in '92. They just ran out of gas—or ran into the Dallas Cowboys.

"I'm disappointed," said Norman, back home in Miami the day after the defeat. Norman, ever the hard-eyed realist, favored the theory embraced by Dallas fans—the Cowboys were a new dynasty. "Dallas is a better team. It's that simple. It isn't just this one football game, it's a whole new level of competition. Anybody in the NFC East who wants to become champion is going to have to be able to beat Dallas, and right now they have a stronger football team that we have."

Norman hadn't decided exactly what he was going to do yet, but it was going to be drastic. He was heading into his third post-Buddy year as owner and was still fired up with visions of building a champion on his own, showing up the Id-people and cynics back in Philly.

"Reggie is gone," he said, months before the mighty Rev. signed with Green Bay. "But we still have the nucleus of a strong defense. It may be necessary to take a big step backwards now, maybe, but I don't want to wait five or six years. I don't think it's time to take that big step. It's at times like these, if you're not careful with things, that's when you go 8–8, then 6–10, then 4–12."

In '93 the Eagles would go 8–8.

Reggie is gone. Despite maintaining publicly that he had hoped to re-sign Reggie and thought the world of him as a football player, Norman had no intention of bidding for the Minister of Defense.

"My whole effort here has been to get the best compensation for him," said a bitter and emphatic Norman in late-March, up in the Miami high-rise offices of Braman Enterprises. He sat like a bony Ichabod behind his gleaming, blank desk, his neck still cocked at a slight angle with chronic stiffness. That same week, Reggie's big-toothed grin and massive arms and torso graced the cover of *Sports Illustrated*, which detailed the eager competition among the celebrated free agent's suitors, the Redskins, 49ers, Jets, Browns, and Packers.

"I look upon his departure as an opportunity for the Philadelphia Eagles," said Norman. "Period. We didn't make it with him. He's a declining football player. Everybody bitches about Randall Cunningham's performance against Dallas. Reggie's performance was putrid against Dallas. It wasn't against double-teaming or triple-teaming either; it was one-on-one. He didn't show up for that game. He didn't show up for a few other games in 1992 either. Reggie White is in decline. He has no finesse as a football player, he can be beaten. He cost us the second Dallas game because of a mental mistake that he made, giving Emmitt Smith a touchdown [actually, Smith's fifty-one-yard run, while resulting from Reggie's error, could not fairly be said to have cost the Eagles that game—it set up a forty-eight-yard field goal that gave Dallas a three-point lead on the first play of the fourth quarter, hardly a crushing blow]. . . . I think when this is all over, we'll wind up with two number-one picks for Reggie White. I think we're better off with that. We have to rebuild this club. With those two additional number ones, and some compensation for Keith Jackson, we could end up with four picks in the first two rounds [in 1994]. So I look upon Reggie White's departure as an opportunity to strengthen this football team."

Norman had glimpsed the future in Dallas, just as he had years before scouting out the self-shop department store up in Providence, Rhode Island, for his father-in-law. The Cowboys had obtained a rash of draft picks from the Vikings by unloading their superstar running back Herschel Walker. Well, Reggie and Keith were going to be Norman's Herschel.

"Of course, if we don't do a good job with the draft, then we'll all look like shit," he said with his impish grin.

Norman and Harry and Richie would wheel and deal their way through the off-season, acquiring Tim Harris, a former Pro Bowl defensive end, to replace Reggie. Harris had a history of alcohol-abuse problems and would be arrested again for drunk driving shortly before the season started. He would develop a nagging elbow infection early in the year and would hardly play. They would acquire Michael Carter, a former 49ers' star defensive lineman, but Carter would play miserably in training camp and opt to retire. They would sign former Jets safety Erik McMillan, another former all-pro, who would play so poorly that he would be cut midway through the year. Keith Millard, another former Pro Bowl player, would play intermittently, but hardly turn out to be the dominant force he once was. The two linemen Richie would select with his two first-round draft picks in '93, defensive tackle Leonard Renfro and offensive guard Lester Holmes, would play passably well in their rookie year. Holmes showed promise of developing into a good player; Renfro appeared to be yet another disappointment. Rookie receiver Victor Bailey, the only other draft pick who would play much, would look talented but not be much of a factor.

Two Eagles players would make the Pro Bowl in '93, the always excellent Eric Allen and Seth, who was picked as a last-minute alternate. The revamped Eagles would finish in the bottom half of the league in both offensive and defensive rankings, including an abysmal fourth from the bottom in stopping the run—a stat that would make poor Jerome turn over in his grave. Clyde Simmons, who led the NFL with 19 sacks in '92 playing on the opposite end of the line from Reverend Reggie, would finish the next season with only five. As a team, the Eagles would compile 36 sacks—Reggie, playing in Green Bay, made 13.5 all by himself.

SITTING BEFORE HIS LOCKER underneath Milwaukee County Stadium, after playing in his first game as a Packer (a win over the Rams), Reggie seemed uncomfortable. Since his much-publicized public courtship the previous spring, ending with a four-year, $17 million deal ($9 million for the '93 season alone), Reggie had become, if that was possible, an even more famous football player. One of the Milwaukee newspapers had a cartoon on the front of its annual Packers' season-preview tabloid of Reggie dressed up as Moses, parting the Red Sea of NFL opposition and leading the wandering tribe of St. Vince, Paul Hornung, Jim Taylor, Bart Starr, Boyd Dowler, Max McGee, and Herb Adderly back to the promised land of Super Bowl victory—they had won the first two ('67 and '68) and had not been back since. He was mobbed in the locker room.

"Are you worried that all this attention on you will be distracting to the team?" a hound asked.

"He's doing a pretty good job of ignoring it," piped up Packers linebacker Bryce Paup from two lockers over, trying to get dressed at the edge of the mob of questioners. "You guys are the ones who won't leave him alone."

"What was the final score in Philadelphia?" Reggie asked a familiar face, a member of the old Eagles' Pack who has flown out to witness his Packer debut.

"They won."

Reggie smiled. "That's good."

After growling his way through about a hundred postgame questions, trying to deflect attention away from himself and toward his new teammates, Reggie talked for a few minutes about the Eagles.

"It will never be the same here," he said. "We're working to capture some of that kind of spirit here, but it takes time. You know, we were so loose in Philly. We were always having fun. It's more serious here. There's a difference in style."

Reggie had been stung by the Eagles' refusal to even bid for his services and by some of the owner's comments, which reached him indirectly. In particular, he resented being criticized for accepting the sweetest contract offer, after declaring that he was equally interested in playing somewhere where he could work on problems of inner-city poverty and violence. Green Bay is hardly a major backwater of urban decay.

"I know I've been criticized for going for the money," he said. "But I know what I'm trying to do. I'm trying to finance some things. Mr. Braman don't know that. He don't know me. We went out to dinner one time four years ago, and me and Keith Byars one time sat down and talked to Norman and Harry [Gamble] about what we could do to bring us together, the management and the players. That's it. I'm confident that if I had a chance to explain what I'm doing to a roomful of a hundred people, and Norman Braman was the hundred-and-first person, and after we had that roomful of people vote on what Reggie White was all about, I'd have one hundred votes for me and one against. Mr. Braman makes comments about me, but he don't know me."

Reggie lead the Packers to the second round of the play-offs, right back to the same spot he had led the Eagles in '92. The Packers faced Dallas in Texas Stadium, and lost, another victim on the path to a second Super Bowl victory for the Cowboys. Reggie made the Pro Bowl for the eighth consecutive time. Green Bay's defense ended the season ranked second in the NFL, the Eagles, seventeenth.

The mighty Reverend also unveiled his first community development bank in Knoxsville during the '93 season.

Down in Brooksville, Florida, that spring for the Second Annual Jerome Brown Football Camp, Reggie was briefly reunited with a group of his former teammates. Seth teased him, "So, Reggie, did God say *exactly* seventeen million dollars?"

MIKE GOLIC, Ron Heller, Keith Byars, and Keith Jackson were all back in the Vet in mid-November wearing their new Miami Dolphins togs, helping Don Shula to his three hundredth win as a High Priest of the Pigskin. Shula was carried off the field triumphantly afterward, on a few former-Philly shoulder pads.

Tank finally made the Pro Bowl in '93. Starting all sixteen games at fullback for Miami, the long-suffering Eagle running back/receiver/tight end was the team's third-ranked rusher and pass catcher. He gained just over nine hundred combined yards and scored six touchdowns—which didn't equal his best years in Philadelphia. Keith Jackson had another strong, but not super, season. His six touchdown catches and 613 yards on thirty-nine catches were on a par with his stats during his last three seasons in green, but people (other than his agent, Mr. Upfront) weren't calling K-Jack the best tight end in football anymore. For the third straight season he was not invited to the Pro Bowl.

Ron Heller started all sixteen games for the Dolphins at right tackle.

Mike Golic decided to turn down a lot of the requests he got from radio and TV after signing with the Dolphins. His reputation as a media star preceded him to Miami. "It's incredible!" he said, midway through the season. "I could just pick right up down here where I left off in Philly, not even miss a step." But he didn't. He decided to earn his name on the field before taking to the airwaves.

Shula initially slated Mike as a backup defensive tackle, which bugged the big guy. "Hey, playing behind Jerome and Mike Pitts is one thing, I can handle that," he said. "Playing behind these guys down here, that's another thing." He started seven of the last eight games and toward the end of the year began doing little bits on the weekly Dolphins TV show.

He was an immediate hit.

KEN ROSE broke his left leg in the Eagles' fifth game, the first major injury of his long career. He spent the rest of the season watching, still mentoring Willie T.

RANDALL BROKE his right leg in the season's fourth game, against the Jets, after playing superbly and leading the team to a 4–0 start. The same quarterback who began the '92 season saying "Some guys get injured all the time; I'm just fortunate not to be one of those guys" will enter his ninth season having missed all or part of twenty-nine of the team's last fifty games.

He sobbed openly, wiping his eyes with a black handkerchief, as he exchanged marriage vows with dancer Felicity De Jager on May 8, 1993, in the Grand Ballroom of the Trump Taj Mahal casino-hotel in Atlantic City. Guarded by a detail of weight lifters outfitted in pink jackets, the couple starred in a $1 million nuptial song, dance, and dinner production that the Philadelphia *Daily News,* with admirable and uncharacteristic restraint, called "*borderline* excess." It featured an $18,000 fourteen-tier wedding cake that stood six feet tall; a sensational entrance by the bride from behind custom-made sliding French doors in a cloud of smoke, bathed in a pink spotlight; gospel music and modern dance; a five-course filet mignon supper for one thousand topped off with cake and washed down with Dom Perignon; a press conference with bride and groom; special appearances by the Donald and his pregnant Marla; small commemorative booklets featuring brief statistical abstracts of bride and groom (Felicity: five-eleven, and one hundred thirty-four pounds; hobbies include dancing and Randall; hero is Randall; ambition is twelve kids. Randall: six-four and two hundred and five pounds: hobbies include golf and Felicity; hero is director of the U.S. mint; ambition is thirteen kids). Reverend Reggie, Richie, Norman, Keith Jackson, Keith Byars, Fred Barnett, and Calvin Williams were among those from the football club present; Seth Joyner, Wes, Andre, Byron, Clyde, and most of the defense were among those not.

Randall's wedding invitation, which released a handful of sparkling confetti on opening, instructed guests to "dress fashionably," and the quarterback counseled one and all freely on what that meant— he designed his own beaded black silk tuxedo.

"Zeke, you've gotta scrap that watch; it's got to be gold," he instructed Zeke Bratkowski (whom Richie named offensive coordinator in the spring).

"How 'bout I wear my three championship rings?" countered the onetime Packer and Colts quarterback.

Randall presented his bride with not one, not two, but three diamond-encrusted gold rings. "One because we're married, one to keep us married, and one because God brought us together."

Which prompted some waggish comment along the lines of "three-ring circus." Lineman Mike Schad, the big Canadian, described the event this way: "Randall's wedding? There's only one word for it: *tasteful.*"

BEN SMITH made it back on the field wearing a knee brace early in the '93 season and played well, vying with Mark McMillian for the starting left cornerback job through most of the year. By the end of the season, however, McMillian had apparently won the job. When Richie said he planned to play Ben at safety in '94, Ben wanted out. It was just another instance of Coach wanting him to do something he didn't think was best for him. And true to the pattern he set back in high school, Ben was determined to go his own way. In April of '94, he was traded to Denver (the Eagles got just a third-round draft pick in '95). Broncos coach Wade Phillips promised to start Ben at cornerback.

ANDRE WATERS had surgery in the summer to remove part of the big toe of his left foot, a lingering consequence of the infection he suffered after breaking his leg. He would return to the lineup as starting strong safety midway through the season and play well. He still earned $300,000 less than Byron.

JENNIFER JOYNER offered Seth a $600,000 divorce settlement, promising to drop all future claims to alimony and child support. He quickly accepted it. The amount was about $600,000 less than what Seth made in '93. He played much of that season on a bad ankle, and while he led the team in tackles, he made only two sacks and just one interception. In the spring of '94, Seth signed a five-year $14.5 million contract with the renamed Arizona Cardinals.

Jennifer moved back to Holland with their daughter.

CENTER DAVE ALEXANDER signed a $1 million contract after the '93 season.

WES AND ERIKA HOPKINS seemed close to a reconciliation early in the spring of '93. After his knee surgery, Wes showed up at their New Jersey house with an apology and a promise.

"The relationship between me and Amy is over," he said, as Erika would remember it.

Erika said she was willing to work at it, and for several weeks Wes called daily. Erika thought, *this is it, maybe we've turned the corner.* But she still didn't trust him. So she decided to stop by his hotel room in Philadelphia early one morning to see if he was alone. In the off-season, Wes stayed out late and slept in late. Nine o'clock in the morning was like the middle of the night.

So Erika dropped their daughter off at school one morning in

April, skipped her aerobics class, and steered the Lexus over the bridge. As she pulled up to the hotel, she saw a car she knew belonged to Amy parked right behind Wes's van in the lot.

She was crushed. She had let herself hope.

She got in another brawl with Amy upstairs, with Wes trying to pull them apart hopping around on his one good leg, and Erika ended up going to the hospital in an ambulance with a separated shoulder after passing out in the hotel lobby.

In September, Erika got a phone call from Harry Himes, Wes's agent. The Eagles had decided after all to offer Wes a new contract, despite Norman's pique over the contract maneuver late in '92.

Only—Harry tried to explain this delicately—it seemed the club was a little concerned about Wes's personal life and the problems he'd been having "at home."

Erika told Harry that she and Wes were history.

"I'd still like for you to come in," the agent said. He said he just wanted Erika to show up at the contract signing, smile, make nice. Harry himself was still hoping to get the two back together, and he knew that Erika's presence might help allay the Eagles' concerns about *the marital situation*. All summer the Eagles had effectively been telling Wes to get lost. Knowing nothing about the contract-extension request that pissed Norman off, the public and the Pack, with whom the ten-year-veteran free safety had long been a favorite, were mystified. Wes had been an essential part of the Eagles' defense for a decade. When he was hurt late in '92, all Bud and Richie did was whine about how much they missed him in that spot. But now Richie was adamant. Wes was, at thirty-one, too old and slow for the position. It was time to turn a new page. The club had agreed to pay $1.2 million to Erik McMillan to play the position and had in Rich Miano a solid veteran backup with good legs, they explained. They didn't need Wes. It was your typical Eagles-style send-off.

When Himes and the Pack persisted, generating stories about how none of it made sense (Wes was calling in a few chits among the loyal scribes), the club put on a little show, inviting Wes to run several forty-yard dashes in front of their scouts—the usual free-agent tryout shtick. It was humiliating, but Wes could no longer afford to indulge his ego. When he was timed at 4.96 seconds, slug pace for an NFL defensive back, the team made public the results and figured it would get everybody off their backs. Himes challenged the times, and Wes, running on a track a few days later clocked by some New Jersey high-school coaches, bettered his performance by a few tenths of a second. It didn't matter.

In late August, Wes got a nibble from the Chiefs. He flew out to

Kansas City and played one exhibition game in a Chiefs' uniform. He was cut on the last day of training camp, but the club promised to re-sign him after he cleared waivers, which they figured (old and slow) he was certain to do.

Except . . . who should come calling but the Eagles?

With Andre's toe troubling him, and Erik McMillan playing far below expectations, and with rookie draft pick Mike Reid out indefi-nitely with a knee injury, the Eagles were suddenly desperate for a proven safety. And in twenty-four hours of hasty negotiations, Himes worked out a one-year contract loaded with incentives and contingen-cies, totaling $900,000 if Wes could make it through sixteen games and play reasonably well. The club was still bothered by that little episode with Erika at the Broncos game, but Himes told them things between husband and wife (Erika had always been a big favorite with Norman and Harry) might still work themselves out—in fact, Erika would probably attend the signing!

There were some hard feelings in K.C., but Wes flew back to Philly in early September to renew ties. As for Richie, who had been explaining for more than a month why the team didn't need Wes anymore—*All that stuff I said before? Never mind.*

"You have to be flexible and do the right thing and I think we're doing the right thing here," said the coach to his assembled, and slightly astonished, Pack. "I know we're happy to have him, he's happy to be back, and I know he's gonna bolster our run defense."

Erika, who knew that a no-good cheating husband with a contract was worth about $900,000 more than a no-good cheating husband without a contract, was all goodwill and cheer at the event.

Harry was just delighted to see Erika.

"Welcome back!" he said warmly. He and Norman, who called in his congrats from Miami (that episode last December forgotten), were under the impression that the Eagles' senior couple were together once more.

You could hardly blame the Pack for making the same assump-tion. One writer even assumed that Erika had been planning a move out to Kansas City.

"She began teaching her four-year-old daughter the tomahawk chop," he wrote.

"What a joke!" Erika said, when she saw the story. "Where did he ever get that idea?"

Wes played intermittently throughout the season, solid, but noth-ing spectacular. He earned $801,270. At thirty-two, he planned to reenter the free-agent market in '94.

. . .

ANTONE DAVIS played his best year in '93. He had become a steady, sturdy performer at right tackle and from time to time seemed to be almost enjoying himself.

FRED BARNETT was named to the Pro Bowl after the '92 season and was married in the spring, also to a dancer—the Barnetts were wed in an elegant, quiet church ceremony. Donald Trump did not attend.

Fred blew out his knee in the fourth game of the next season, in the same Jets game that claimed Randall, and spent the rest of '93 recovering from knee surgery. In his absence, Calvin Williams became the team's premier receiver, and after the season signed a new, one-year $1.2 million contract.

NORMAN FIRED JOE WOOLLEY early in the '93 season. The club accused its longtime personnel director of making derogatory comments to the Pack.

Truth is, Joe saw the dismantling in progress and thought he'd been damn polite about it. Not only had the team been hemorrhaging talent rapidly, it hadn't been replacing it. In contrast to his years with Buddy, Joe's experience with Richie and the draft had been disastrous. With Buddy's first three drafts, they had built the nucleus of a contender—Keith Byars, Seth Joyner, and Clyde Simmons ('86); Jerome Brown, Byron Evans, Dave Alexander, Cris Carter ('87); and Keith Jackson and Eric Allen ('88). With Richie, three drafts ('91–'93) had failed to reap a single star player. Only four of Richie's draft picks were even starters—Andy Harmon, "Willie T." Thomas, Mark McMillian, and Antone Davis. Joe thinks it's not because the Eagles' draft picks have lacked talent, it's because Richie lacks the patience to develop the players he picks. After he got over his initial anger, Joe's reaction to his firing was relief. He felt like he'd been ejected from a crashing plane.

MARVIN "ONE-FOR-ONE-FOR-ONE" Hargrove didn't get a phone call from the NFL in '93. He was unemployed, still waiting for that next big break.

"You don't want to get a serious job that you're going to have to leave if the phone rings," he said.

He was helping to host a radio jazz show at the University of Delaware and was thinking about pursuing a career as a jazz singer.

EVERYBODY FELT SORRY for Richie after the '93 season. First he lost all those starters to free agency. His free agents bombed, one after the other. He won the first four games anyway, then lost Randall and Fred for the season; Byron broke his arm and missed most of the year; he lost his starting right guard (Eric "Pink" Floyd) to a knee injury and then lost his left tackle, Broderick Thompson, the man he got to replace Ron Heller.

Behind the quarterbacking of former Steeler Bubby Brister, the Eagles went into a seemingly hopeless midseason skid, losing eight of their next nine games. At one point, Eric Allen lamented, "We may lose the rest of our games." When they salvaged a .500 record by winning their last three, Richie's stock rose a little.

He was seen less as a High Priest of the Pigskin, however, than as a kind of executive assistant with Eagles, Inc.

MEANWHILE, BUDDY RYAN was in the play-offs and back on the front pages. Buddy took over as defensive coordinator of the Houston Oilers in '93, and after a rocky start, the Oilers won eleven straight games. The new Buddy's Boys on defense fit the profile perfectly; they led the league at stopping the rush and were atrocious at stopping the pass. They had a reputation for bringing the heat, forcing turnovers, and hurting people. Buddy hadn't changed.

Even the ol' offense/defense locker-room rift took shape, with Buddy's thinly disguised contempt for the Oilers' chuck-and-duck offense erupting into a full-scale alphabet soup, national Pack event late in the season when Buddy took a swing at offensive coordinator Kevin Gilbride on the sidelines in front of national TV cameras.

"He's his own worst enemy," said Richie.

Buddy was brazenly unapologetic. He said Gilbride runs a "high-school" offense, and didn't belong in the Pigskin Priesthood. Lots of people figured Buddy, with this fracas, had blown his chances of ever getting another head coaching job in the NFL.

Not Buddy.

"If they want to win, they'll know where to find me," he said.

The Oilers lost the AFC championship game, and Buddy, two

weeks later, was hired as head coach *and* general manager of the desperate Cardinals.

"You've got a winner in town," Buddy said, beaming. He promptly signed Clyde Simmons and Seth Joyner. Season ticket sales soared.

ONLY THOSE who did not know Norman Braman well were surprised in the spring of '94 when he abruptly sold the Eagles to Hollywood producer Jeff Lurie. Norman's bitterness over the way he was treated by Philadelphia's press and the Id-people had long ago soured any sentimental attachments the Miami car dealer had with the city or the team. And despite his best efforts, the Eagles seemed bound for that long-term rebuilding mode he had hoped to avoid. It was harder to build a Super Bowl champion than he had imagined.

So when along came Lurie, a forty-two-year-old self-described football nut and heir to an enormous movie theater and publishing fortune, with an offer of $185 million, the largest sum ever paid for a sports franchise, Norman jumped. It was true to his life's pattern of shedding his skin every decade or so. After nine years of Eagles ownership, Norman said he was ready to become a full-time philanthropist and world traveler. As he had so often in the past, Norman left behind scores of disgruntled fans and a city that fell ill-used by his tenure as team owner, but he emerged from the deal much richer— the sale price was nearly triple what he paid for the club back in '85.

The rapid dissolution of Buddy's old team did, however, leave the Eagles with a rich bounty of '94 draft picks—seven picks in the first three rounds. The Pack embraced Lurie as a white knight, savior of a declining franchise. The new owner fairly shone with promise. So a new era was about to begin.

THAT SPRING in Brooksville, there were dead flowers and gray ribbons from old floral displays on the scruffy plot of earth that covered Jerome Brown, townsman now of a stiller town.

Tim Jinkens cleared off the mess, righting an upended three-legged wire stand for a plastic bouquet and repositioning a worn Styrofoam emblem of Jerome's old jersey. It wasn't a formal cemetery, just a weedy lot off Route 41 south of Brooksville.

It was not far from the corner of Hale and Garland, where the accident happened. There was still a gouge in the tree and telephone pole where the car had come to rest, and there were two small white crosses set in the weeds at the roadside. The two-lane blacktop road, lined with oak trees draped with silver-gray Spanish moss, was silent and empty at midday.

"Jerome used to fly down this road, just fly," said Tim. "When I was in the Bronco with him—you couldn't sit in back because of the speakers—I would just get quiet. Sometimes I would close my eyes. It scared me."

"Did you ever tell him that?"

"No way. Maybe I should have, but it wouldn't have done any good. There was no stopping him. That was just Jerome. You know, every once in a while, when I'm working behind the counter at the bar, the guy next door will turn on his stereo and this *whump-whump-whump* sound of the bass will start through the walls, and I get excited. I still want him to come through that door so bad."

Jerome was gone, but one of the many ways in which he lived on was in the courthouse, where his estate had turned into a wrestling match worthy of Dickens's *Jarndyce* vs. *Jarndyce*. In his will, Jerome left $10,000 for his sons, William IV and Dunell, but named as guardians of that money, and the rest of the estate, his parents, Willie and Annie Bell. Cynthia Sanders, Dunell's mother, who pursued Jerome in family court for five years before pinning down paternity and $800 in monthly child support, had sued Willie and Annie Bell for control of the money left to Dunell and some continuation of support from the estate. LaSonya Stewart Scrivens, mother of William Jerome Brown IV, who spent seven years chasing Jerome in family court before establishing paternity and winning a court-ordered $500 in monthly child support, had sued Willie and Annie Bell for control of the $10,000 and a continuation of support. Willie and Annie Bell had filed a petition asking that the Sun Bank and Trust Company be appointed legal guardians of the boys' inheritances. Consumers Credit had sued for $7,575.22 that was due on Jerome's account, First Fidelity Leasing Group, Inc., wanted $56,166.30 for the green Corvette destroyed in the accident, topping a long list of such claims connected to car loans, credit cards, unpaid legal fees, medical bills, unused airline tickets, leased jet-skis, back mortgage payments on condos and apartments, prepaid promotional appearances Jerome wouldn't be making. The horde of petitioners all awaited some ruling on what Jerome had left among his scattered assets, a thicket of bank accounts in Brooksville, Miami, and Cherry Hill, New Jersey, brokerage accounts, cars, and real estate in Florida and New Jersey.

Some answers were available by the spring of '94. Over his five-year playing career, Jerome was paid about $2.3 million by the Eagles, and he earned tens of thousands more through product endorsements and public appearances. Of those amounts, all that remained at his death was $216,023. Lawyer for the Brown family, Charlie Luckie, said he was so surprised at the final tally, he asked Jerome's agents to prepare a detailed accounting, which they did.

"The figure is apparently accurate," said Luckie. "Jerome went in style. He made a lot of money and he spent a lot of money."

Between NFL pension funds and social security, however, each of his sons was entitled to about $1,500 per month in benefits, money that the boys' mothers and the Browns were vying to control. "The Browns just want to make sure that at least some of that money gets set aside for the boys," said Luckie.

Meanwhile, lawyers for Jerome's estate sued General Motors, claiming that despite Jerome's reputation for fast living and fast driving (the official accident report cited Jerome's "careless" driving as the accident's cause, and enclosed a printout showing twelve separate speeding or reckless driving citations issued to Jerome in Florida alone from '86 through '92), the accident that killed him and his nephew was caused when the Corvette's airbag accidentally deployed, temporarily disorienting and blinding Jerome. If true, it would be the first known instance of an accidental airbag detonation causing a fatal accident, and would significantly enrich the various parties vying for the remnants of Jerome's estate.

A recent addition to the mess was a lawsuit by one Joseph Barnes, who joined with Jerome's older half sister Gloria, mother of Gus, in demanding some compensation from Jerome's estate for the death of the twelve-year-old. This last one hurt, because although Barnes was Gus's biological father, "He ain't never had one thing to do with that boy since the day he was born," said Gloria, who was named as co-plaintiff on the suit, as required by Florida law (parents must co-file). She said she wants nothing to do with it. For his part, Barnes claimed that he maintained a warm relationship with the boy despite Gloria's hostility and despite the fact that they did not live together.

Gloria's grief over her son, the lost victim in Jerome's tragedy, remained profound almost a year after the accident. She is a huge woman, bigger even than Jerome. She has an overbite, which makes her small face mildly concave. There is beauty, though, in her enormous sadness and the way she composes herself when asked to speak of it, resting two wide arms heavily on her knees and staring expressionlessly out the kitchen window of her tiny home in the projects. The deaths of her younger half brother and her oldest son make for a perplexing mix of pain and anger in Gloria, who had long felt—years before this happened—like someone left behind. She lives about three miles from Home Jerome, with its air-conditioning and swimming pool and ten acres and fine furnishings, crammed into a pink shoe box of a house with her remaining five children in the same neighborhood where she grew up (where Jerome grew up, too, and where her parents lived until the million-dollar payday and the DHM). Although Jerome was always kind to her (he bought her a car and from time to time gave her money), and she has no complaints about her father and stepmother, Gloria said she has always felt like an outcast. She has had her struggles with men, with alcohol, with drugs. She described herself as "unsophisticated," concentrating on getting the six syllables out correctly. She didn't intend to stay in this place. She had gone back to school to get her high-school equivalent and planned to earn a practical nursing degree, get a job, get off welfare. Despite the weight of bitterness and grief, Gloria is sturdy and determined.

Still, it hurts her that her own most grievous loss was overshadowed by her famous half brother's death.

"He was everything he could be," she said, speaking of Gus. "He was twelve years old. He was going to be thirteen in a couple of weeks. He sang in the church choir. He was an usher. He wanted to be a preacher. He wanted to be a pro football player. A couple of weeks before the accident, he said to me, 'Mama, I'm gonna get you some things that you need. You ain't gonna be beggin' no more. You ain't gonna be livin' on the welfare no more.' But Gus never got the chance. The Lord has his own plan."

If Gus had a father, Gloria said, it was her father, Willie. During a troubled time some years ago, when the boy was small, Willie had taken him in as his own. He raised him up through kindergarten and first grade, and then Gloria got herself settled again and wanted him back.

"It hurt," recalled Willie. "Gloria is my daughter, and I always tried to help her, so I took Gus when she needed me to. It hurt me when she said she wanted him back. He was seven or eight years old. He wanted to stay with Mother and me always. But he went on back. I told him, 'She's your mother and you have to do what she says.' But he was over here every chance he got. Not long before the accident we noticed he'd slipped his clothes back in over here. He still stayed with his mother during the week when he went to school, but on weekends and holidays he was always here."

The last time Gloria saw Gus, she had driven over to Home Jerome in the station wagon to bring him some clean shirts. He was mopping the kitchen floor.

"I'll see you later," she told him.

"If I'da known what was going to happen, I'd have snatched him up and carried him off out of there," she said.

Willie was leaving work on the day of the accident when he passed

Jerome's Corvette. Gus was in the passenger seat. Willie had gotten off work at 4:00 p.m. and was heading into town to stop at the bank.

"I passed 'em by, and Jerome, he throwed his hand up to me, so I throwed my hand back up to him," Willie recalled.

The accident happened at 4:15 p.m. Willie was on his way home from the bank when a policeman pulled up behind him and flashed his lights.

"Mr. Brown, there's been an accident," the cop said. "It's Jerome."

"No, that can't be," said Willie. "I just seen him, him and Gus."

Home Jerome hasn't changed in the year since the accident. It was still busy with grown kids and grandkids coming and going, the big TV on constantly in the family room just off the kitchen; the walls still crowded with photos and portraits of Jerome, the shelves lined with his trophies. Willie said they hadn't touched the wing of the house that was Jerome's. They know they've eventually got to go in and pack it up, but they were accustomed to leaving it be, to living in their side of the house, managing their own lives while Jerome was away— football season, vacations, weekend trips to his teammates' summer camps, golf tournaments. Somehow it still seems normal, just letting Jerome's things alone until he gets back.

"It's still hard for us to believe," said Willie.

He and Annie Bell don't want to talk about the legal tangle over Jerome's estate.

"We're just one big happy family," said Annie Bell.

Have the lawsuits caused any strain?

"No strain. Like I said, we're just one big happy family. Always have been."

Willie said there's no telling what will come of all the litigation. If he and Annie Bell wind up with any money, he said, "It'll just give me an opportunity to spend more time getting acquainted with the Word."

That night, a cool evening in early spring, Willie drove out to Kennedy Park at the edge of town, just a few blocks from the accident site. His grandsons, Dunell and Willie Jerome IV, were both playing baseball. Dunell was on the Dodgers and Little G was on the Giants. Under the park's bright lights, Willie positioned himself behind the steel fence backstop of the Little League baseball field. He was wearing a green Eagles windbreaker. This was the park where Willie once watched Jerome play his first games of baseball and football.

Overhead, the Spanish moss in the trees glowed silver against the night sky, lit from below by the lights over the diamond. There was a verdant moisture in the air, smell of fern and grass and old wood. Out on the illuminated field a boy in glasses strode from the wooden bench on the first baseside toward the plate, pulling on a batting glove with the bat pinched against his side. He was a broad-beamed kid, about ten, black as midnight, and as he passed the fence he turned toward Willie and waved.

"Hit one out," the grandfather said.

The boy flashed a suddenly familiar, wild, neon grin.

Author's Note

As the Philadelphia *Inquirer*'s Packman for three seasons ('90–'92), I reported almost daily on the doings described in this book. Thanks to everyone who helped me. I'd like to particularly thank Eagles assistant coaches Peter Guinta and Zeke Bratkowski, true monks in the temple, who spent hours reviewing game films with me and giving me the authentic Coach's-Eye View. I am also grateful to my agent, Rhoda Weyr, and to the fine crew at Knopf—Ashbel Green, Jennifer Bernstein, Dori Carlson, and Elise Solomon. Thanks to my brother, Drew, and my friend Don Kimelman for their careful reading and suggestions.

Events described that I did not witness, including dialogue, are based on the memories of those involved. In cases where scenes are based on the recollection of only one participant, it is so indicated. None of the names have been changed to protect the innocent because, as Kurt Vonnegut once so rightly pointed out, "God Almighty protects the innocent as a matter of heavenly routine."

PHOTOGRAPHIC CREDITS

Brown on sidelines: Andrea Mihalik/Philadelphia *Daily News*
Ryan and Braman: Jerry Lodriguss: Jerry Lodriguss/Philadelphia *Inquirer*
Gamble and Braman: Rick Bowmer/Philadelphia *Daily News*
Kotite: Andrea Mihalik/Philadelphia *Daily News*
Ryan with reporters: Michael Bryant/Philadelphia *Inquirer*
Carson on sidelines: George Reynolds/Philadelphia *Daily News*
Barnett: Andrea Mihalik/Philadelphia *Daily News*
Hargrove: Andrea Mihalik/Philadelphia *Daily News*
Waters smiling: Mark Psoras/Philadelphia *Daily News*
White moving into dormitory: Andrea Mihalik/Philadelphia *Daily News*
Davis before locker: Andrea Mihalik/Philadelphia *Daily News*
Heller, Alexander, and Golic: Andrea Mihalik/Philadelphia *Daily News*
McMahon: Andrea Mihalik/Philadelphia *Daily News*
Brown, Cunningham, and Byars dousing White: Andrea Mihalik/Philadelphia *Daily News*
Hopkins cooling off: Andrea Mihalik/Philadelphia *Daily News*
Joyner on sidelines: Charles Fox/Philadelphia *Inquirer*
Smith writhing: George Reynolds/Philadelphia *Daily News*
Cunningham at home: Andrea Mihalik/Philadelphia *Daily News*
Byars and Cunningham: Andrea Mihalik/Philadelphia *Daily News*
Cunningham crying: Andrea Mihalik/Philadelphia *Daily News*
White clowning: Andrea Mihalik/Philadelphia *Daily News*
Jackson at practice: Andrea Mihalik/Philadelphia *Daily News*
Waters with broken ankle: Andrea Mihalik/Philadelphia *Daily News*
White and Joyner on the bench: Andrea Mihalik/Philadelphia *Daily News*
Walker in the end zone: Michael Bryant/Philadelphia *Inquirer*
Rose, Feagles, et al.: Jerry Lodriguss/Philadelphia *Inquirer*
Joyner sprinting after interception: Rebecca Barger/Philadelphia *Inquirer*
Cunningham in classic form: Rebecca Barger/Philadelphia *Inquirer*
Joyner tackling Rypien: Jerry Lodriguss/Philadelphia *Inquirer*
Allen, Clark, et al.: Jerry Lodriguss/Philadelphia *Inquirer*
Brown's headstone: Mark Bowden

A NOTE ABOUT THE AUTHOR

Mark Bowden was raised in the suburbs of Chicago, New York, and Baltimore. He graduated from Loyola College of Maryland in 1973 and spent six years on the staff of the now-defunct Baltimore *News-American*. Over the last twenty years, Bowden has written extensively for newspapers and magazines, but primarily for the Philadelphia *Inquirer*, specializing in nonfiction storytelling. His book *Doctor Dealer* (1987) is about an Ivy League dentist who built the largest cocaine distribution business in Philadelphia history. His story "Finders Keepers" (1986) was made into the motion picture *Money for Nothing* (1993) by Disney Studios.

Bowden lives in rural southeastern Pennsylvania with his wife, Gail, and their five children.

A NOTE ON THE TYPE

The text of this book was set in a digitized version of a typeface called Baskerville. The face itself is a facsimile reproduction of types cast from molds made for John Baskerville (1706–1775) from his designs. Baskerville's original face was one of the forerunners of the type style known to printers as "modern face"—a "modern" of the period A.D. 1800.

Composed by Crane Typesetting Service, West Barnstable, Massachusetts
Printed and bound by Arcata Graphics/Martinsburg, Martinsburg, West Virginia
Designed by Robert C. Olsson